ACCLAIM FOR
CURSED IS THE PEACEMAKER

An engrossing account of Philip Habib's high-wire diplomatic inter
tion to stop the spread of chaos in Lebanon and prevent a wider war. Ha
angry jousts with General Sharon dramatize graphically the age-old
flict between diplomats and soldiers about how best to achieve peace.

Samuel Lewis, US ambassador to Israel, 197

Cursed is the Peacemaker is a unique account of diplomatic genius and
tenacity of one lone American. It is extremely well sourced. Boykin
caught the man, the maddeningly complex environment surrounding
work, and a string of setbacks that would have felled anyone but Phil.
portrayal of Ariel Sharon's and Menachem Begin's actions in this cris
riveting. This book provides background to be found nowhere else on v
is now happening in the Middle East.

Brandon Grove, US consul general in Jerusalem, 1980

A vitally important, hard hitting, and time-sensitive book. It provides v
able insights into Ariel Sharon and the Israeli Defense Forces. Every
Marine arrived in Lebanon with respect for them and departed sadly d
lusioned. Habib was a giant!

James Mead, Brigadier General of Marines [Retir
original commander of US Marines ashore in Be

An extraordinarily intimate story of an American diplomat and his worl
is a tragic story, with heroes and villains, brought to life by fast-paced n
rative. It yields insight into how diplomats and governments behave in
sis. A valuable addition.

Robert L. Gallucci, Dean, Walsh School of Foreign Servi
Georgetown Univers

Philip Habib was a unique American diplomat. Over and above his exp
tise and profound knowledge of the Middle East, he was a *mensch:* as go
as his word, decent, trustworthy, and humane. Before all else, Philip Habit
primary concern when addressing the challenges of war was to stop tl
loss of life and the suffering of the warring parties.

Ze'ev Schiff, defense editor of *Ha'are*
co-author of *Israel's Lebanon Wo*

Cursed Is the Peacemaker

The American Diplomat
Versus the Israeli General,
Beirut 1982

John Boykin

A selection of the
Association for Diplomatic Studies and Training
and
Diplomatic and Consular Officers, Retired
Diplomats and Diplomacy Series

Applegate Press

Applegate Press

2033 Ralston Ave., #68
Belmont, CA 94002-1737
info@applegatepress.com

www.applegatepress.com
www.diplomatbook.com

Manufactured in the United States of America

1 3 5 7 9 10 8 6 4 2

Boykin, John
Cursed is the Peacemaker: The American Diplomat
Versus the Israeli General, Beirut 1982/John Boykin
Includes bibliographic reference and index
1. Lebanon—History—Israeli intervention, 1981-83—Diplomatic
history. 2. Middle East—Politics and government—1981-83—
Diplomatic history. 3. Habib, Philip C. 4. Israel-Arab conflicts
5. United States—Foreign relations—Middle East

ISBN 0-9719432-0-6

For Laura

Association for Diplomatic Studies and Training
and
Diplomatic and Consular Officers, Retired

Diplomats and Diplomacy Series

For more than 220 years extraordinary men and women have represented the United States abroad under all kinds of circumstances. What they did and how and why they did it remain little known to their compatriots.

In 1995 the Association for Diplomatic Studies and Training (ADST) and Diplomatic and Consular Officers, Retired (DACOR), created a book series to increase public knowledge and appreciation of the involvement of American diplomats in world history. As exemplified by John Boykin's riveting book about legendary American diplomat Philip Habib, the series seeks to demystify diplomacy by telling the story of those who have conducted our foreign relations, as they saw them and lived them.

Kenneth L. Brown, President
Association for Diplomatic Studies and Training (ADST)
4000 Arlington Boulevard, Arlington, VA 22204-1586
703-302-6990
fax 703-302-6799
www.adst.org

Alan W. Lukens, President
Diplomatic and Consular Officers, Retired (DACOR, Inc.)
1801 F Street, NW
Washington, DC 20006
1-800-344-9127
fax 202-842-3295
dacor@ix.netcom.com

If you didn't know what to do, then you called for Phil Habib. But if you knew Habib, you knew in advance that you were probably not going to agree with what he would do. But he was the only conceivable piece of machinery that could be thrown into that situation and succeed.

Charlie Hill

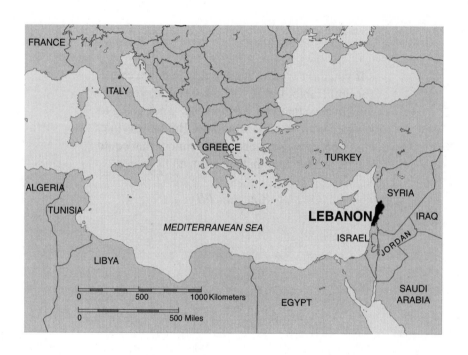

Contents

Foreword
by George Shultz

Phil Habib was a unique character. There will never be another Phil. But the world needs Phil Habibs, so anything that can be done to learn from his life and experiences that will help others try to emulate him is a real contribution. For me, that is the real point of this book about Phil.

I often tried to think of what made Phil so special. He was smart, he was realistic, he had a kind of quick savvy that enabled him to go from one situation to another and quickly grasp its essence. He was a keen judge of personalities.

Early in my teaching career, just after World War Two, I attended a faculty meeting and heard a newly appointed professor describe himself. He said that two of the old-timers in the little town in Maine where he grew up were commenting to each other after hearing on the radio the announcement of his appointment. One said, "I'm not surprised because that Bemis was always a smart kid, right from the first grade. Whatever went in one ear didn't come out the other, so he just got to know more and more." The other old friend said, "By this time, Bemis probably knows just about everything." His friend nodded and said, "Yep, that Bemis knows everything – but he don't realize nothin'."

Somehow, Phil Habib quickly seemed to know everything, but his real gift was in the realization.

I had many distinctive experiences in working with Phil, but two stand out in my mind. When I first became Secretary of State, the Israelis were besieging Beirut in their effort to remove Yasir Arafat and his Palestinians who had taken over that city as their headquarters for directing attacks on Israel. The Israelis didn't want the inevitable casualties of house-to-house fighting to capture the city. Arafat wanted to get out alive and move his entourage to another Arab capital. Whenever the Israelis eased their military pressure on the city, Arafat would cease negotiating. When the Israelis stepped up the pressure, the Lebanese government go-betweens would refuse to move because of the dangerous conditions. Phil went back and forth among the parties, cajoling, blustering, reassuring and always brilliantly attuned to the vastly different ways that the parties perceived the situation. After weeks and weeks of unparalleled diplomatic effort, Phil got an agreement that all could accept. It was not only a success in political, military, and diplomatic terms, it was also a work of psychological genius.

The PLO departure from Beirut bore out General Dwight D. Eisenhower's saying, "Plans are useless, but planning is essential." Every detail of the movement had been negotiated down to the nub before evacuation day, but what was planned was not what happened. As our embassy in Nicosia cabled to me, "Virtually nothing in the transit of PLO evacuees through Cyprus ... went according to plan, but everything went well." Indeed, everything went beautifully. Thousands of armed Palestinians moved out by sea and over the mountains to Syria without a hitch.

When Phil Habib returned to Washington, he received a hero's welcome. I went out to National Airport to greet him and proudly accompanied him to the White House, where President Reagan awarded him our country's highest civilian honor, the Presidential Medal of Freedom, saying that Phil's "successful negotiation of the cease-fire in Lebanon and the resolution of the West Beirut crisis stands out as one of the unique feats of diplomacy in modern times."

The *Washington Post* editorial, headed "One of the Best," said: "You can put aside the cracks about those effete cookie pushers, the ones in striped pants, over at the State Department. Yesterday, President Reagan awarded the Medal of Freedom to one of their best, Philip Habib, for his 'truly heroic work' in conducting the negotiations that halted a war in Lebanon and transformed the prospects for peace in the area as a whole....

"This man who is pleased to be called a rug merchant had something better going for him than magic, which is not reliably on tap to ordinary mortals. He had the imagination, toughness and perseverance to see the game through."

All this was true, but there was an extra dimension that made Phil unique. He was always himself—a tough-talking, explosive-tempered, arm-waving Brooklyn kid. Yet everyone knew that he was never really mad at anyone, that his purpose was clear and steady, that he could be trusted implicitly, and that he always sought the best for every party and the good for world peace and security overall.

I called upon Phil once again in the crisis following the election in the Philippines won by Corazon Aquino but threatened by Ferdinand Marcos's effort to seize the results and declare himself the winner. The president agreed that we needed to call Phil out of retirement. I remember the president thanking Phil for his willingness to come off the golf course to help. Phil replied, "Mr. President, this sure beats playing golf." Phil was like the old firehouse dog, always ready to respond when the fire bell started ringing.

I thought that Marcos had reached the point where he could no longer govern, no matter what maneuvering he tried to do. With characteristic energy, Phil talked to a wide array of people in all camps. He asked lots of questions, he said very little, but he, too, came to the conclusion that Marcos's days were over. He returned to the United States just in time to join me and other senior advisors to the president whom I had invited to an urgent meeting in the living room of my house in Bethesda just outside Washington. "I don't want recommendations about what to do; I want to see if we can reach a consensus on what the situation is," I said. Phil had just gotten off the airplane and he commanded everyone's attention with his realistic depiction of the scene in Manila. Later that afternoon, we met with the president with the unanimous view that Marcos could no longer govern. That led very shortly to the presidency of Corazon Aquino and the start of democratization in the Philippines. Once again, Phil's role had been critical in a crisis. Once again, he was quick to know everything and profound in his ability to realize what everything really meant.

The Great Seal of the Republic stands on display at the Department of State. The symbolism captures the spirit of Phil Habib. The center is the eagle holding arrows in one claw and olive branches in the other. The eagle is looking at the olive branches to show that the United States, as Phil Habib, always will seek peace. But the eagle always holds onto the arrows to show that the United States understands, as Phil understood, that to be effective in seeking peace, you must have strength and the will to employ it in just and honorable causes.

Preface

Philip Habib was the most interesting person I ever met. I wanted to write a book with him or about him as an pretext to hear his stories. We talked a couple of times about writing his memoirs together, but he couldn't be bothered to sit still long enough to work on a book.

Six months after he died in 1992, I decided to write a cradle-to-grave biography. But as the years of research rolled by, I concluded that there were just too many good stories. If I unearthed and told them all, the book would take too long and be too long. So I decided I had to focus it on the best story of all, his two-year mission as President Reagan's special envoy to the Middle East from 1981 to 1983, particularly his work negotiating an end to the 1982 siege of Beirut.

This book, then, is not about diplomacy, or warfare, or policy, or the Middle East, or US-Israel relations. While those certainly form the milieu, this is at heart the dramatic tale of a man and the ordeal he faced in trying to do a good thing. I therefore chose not to hang the tale on the military vicissitudes of the siege. It heated and cooled, heated and cooled, and heated and cooled. Besides, the story had too many strands going on simultaneously to be comprehensible if told chronologically. So chapters are thematic within an approximate chronology.

Nearly everything Phil Habib did that was interesting and important happened behind closed doors. And he rarely talked to the press. So when I began, I had only the vaguest idea of what the story might be. I knew only that he was a fascinating character who had been the central figure in one of the most dramatic episodes in the history of diplomacy. I gambled that, if I dug long enough and hard enough, I would discover what the long-hidden story really was.

It was several years before I realized that the theme of the story was conflict between allies. On the national scale, it is the conflict between the United States and Israel during some of the darkest days of their relations. On the personal scale, it is the conflict between Habib and his antagonist, Israeli defense minister Ariel Sharon. Frankly, this story of diplomacy versus violence makes Sharon and the administration he served come out looking pretty bad. I can say only that I neither knew nor cared anything about Sharon when I started, that I simply followed the most interesting vein of the story wherever it led, and that I do not generalize anything beyond the story at hand. The facts of history tend to show the exponent of diplomacy in this episode looking pretty good and the exponent of violence looking pretty bad. The journalism of the time reflects that. The literature published since then reflects that. And this book reflects that. I twice asked

General Sharon for an interview, and he twice declined. As the manuscript was nearing completion, I offered him an opportunity to review the manuscript for accuracy, and he declined.

Few tasks could be more futile than to try to write an objective account of anything significant and interesting that has happened in the Middle East. There is no such thing as objectivity when talking about events there. The very set of facts one chooses to adduce constitutes taking a position. So let me spell out my bias: My aim is to convey how the world looked through Philip Habib's eyes and tell the story from his perspective. I have tried to understand and represent what he experienced, what he thought about things, how he felt about them. And, as it turns out, his was probably the closest there was to an objective, well-informed perspective in the events of 1981-83. Even passages that sound like my opinions—such as describing helicopters as "those flimsy little deathtraps"—are meant to reflect the views of Habib or, occasionally, the other person who is being talked about at the moment, not my own. (I happen to enjoy helicopters.) The only opinion of my own that I hope to advance is that this is a remarkable story.

As used in this book, "the Israelis" almost invariably means Menachem Begin, Ariel Sharon, and/or their colleagues in the highest levels of Begin's administration; or the Israeli Defense Forces—not the citizens of Israel.

I have relied almost entirely on primary sources: declassified documents and interviews with participants in the episodes described. Since Habib was representing the United States, I have relied mostly on American sources. Nearly every sentence here is based on some source, and chapters have been reviewed by my principal sources. The Association for Diplomatic Studies and Training has also had the manuscript reviewed by Samuel Lewis and Brandon Grove, who were among my sources. The reviewers' feedback and corrections have been invaluable. For any inaccuracies that remain, I take sole responsibility and invite corrections for future editions in care of Applegate Press.

For the convenience of scholars and others who wish to tread the same ground, as this book goes to press I am arranging to place copies of my collection of declassified documents, other written sources, and most of my interviews on each coast: in the Hoover Institution archives at Stanford University and in Lauinger Library at Georgetown University in Washington, D.C. I am also arranging to make the declassified documents available through the National Security Archives in Washington.

Acknowledgments

The help and advice of the following people were crucial to getting this book done, and I thank each of them.

Above all, my wife Laura for her continual support, research help, bottomless patience and understanding while this was being written, and valuable Everyreader feedback on each chapter

Marjorie Habib for her many forms of helpfulness, letter of introduction, insights, and full access to Philip Habib's home office

George Shultz for his kind letters that opened so many doors

Tom Miller for his continual support and helpfulness, information, background, advice, perspective, reality checks, and letters of reference

My agents Laurie Harper, for her patience, enthusiasm, advice, and gratifying adjectives; and Margery Thompson for hanging in forever and for her efforts on behalf of the book

My editor, Susan Wels, for her graciousness, astute analysis, and perceptive advice; and Nancy Evans for her careful proofreading

Morrie Draper, Tom Miller, Charlie Hill, Jim Sehulster, Jim Mead, Bob Dillon, Brandon Grove, Sam Lewis, Bob Miller, Dan O'Donohue, and Jack Grazi for each reading one or more draft chapters and giving me their valuable corrections and feedback

The Jacobs Family Foundation for its early financial support

Richard Parker, Ed Mulcahy, Ghassan Tueni, Michel Dusclaud, and Stuart Eizenstat for sending me interviews they had done with Habib

Stephen and Susan Low for their hospitality during my research trip to Washington

Dianne Middlebrook, David Harris, and Gerald Gunther for sharing with me the benefit of their experiences

My editor friends Marty Lasden and Alan Venable for their helpful perspectives and advice after reading parts of the manuscript

Current and former staff members of the Association for Diplomatic Studies and Training Stephen Low, Charles Stuart Kennedy, Dennis Kux, Margery Thompson, Mary Ann Braycich, Jane Smith, and Da'ad Pierce for their interest and help and support and access to ADST oral histories

Helene Williams and Lori Goetsch of the Michigan State University library for their helpful orientation to the intricacies of researching a project this enormous

Anna Rivas, Lynn Takacs, Valerie Mollo, and Peggy Hernandez for transcribing interviews and photocopying

Nikolai Mikhailov, Tonka Cadoree, Brad LeVeck, and Paloma Young for research assistance

John D. Wilson of the LBJ Library; Rod Soubers and Steve Branch of the Ronald Reagan Library; Lone Beeson of the World Affairs Council of San Francisco Library; Brian Vandermark; Lisa Thompson and Peter Kornbluh at the National Security Archive; Byron Parham, Rodney Ross, and Bill Davis at the National Archives for their help in tracking down information

Jack Grazi and Finley McNaughton for special help in understanding Philip Habib's early years

Phyllis Habib, Lieutenant Colonel John Matthews of the Marine Corps University, Benis M. Frank and Joyce Hudson of the Marine Corps Historical Center; and Bill Collins of the Presidio of Monterey for leads, research help, and material

Gilda Duly for keeping a scrapbook of clippings about Habib for many years

Michel Dusclaud for conducting interviews in France on my behalf, and Alice Edde for translating them for me

Laura Rose, Susan Bree, Catherine Decroix, and Damon Kvamme for translating materials from French for me

Betty Alonso of the US Senate Committee on Foreign Relations and Frederick Monroe, Delois Ruffin, and Vernell Bellamy of the State Department's Freedom of Information office for helping me get materials

Miscellaneous thanks to Phyllis Habib, Christopher Ross, John Helble, Lori Bider, Daniel O'Donohue, Von Eshleman, Melinda Haden, my brother Mike Boykin, Dave King, Carol Jose, Sherry Symington, Lisa Weber, Detta Penna, Jamie Armistead, Tim Holl, Alfred Atherton, Julian Muñoz, Doug Waller; Bill Rorabaugh, professor of history at the University of Washington; Joel Beinin, professor of history at Stanford; and Brad DeLong, professor of economics at the University of California-Berkeley

Finally, my deepest thanks to each of the people who were kind enough to let me interview them. They are listed in the Sources and Bibliography section.

Key People and Places

Individuals

Amin Gemayel—Bashir's older brother, who became president of Lebanon when Bashir was assassinated in September 1982; usually referred to by first name only ("ah-MEEN juh-MY-el")

Arafat, Yasir—leader of the Palestinian Liberation Organization (PLO) and thus in many Israeli eyes the personification of terrorism

Assad, Hafaz al—president of Syria ("HOFF-ozz all OSS-odd")

Bashir Gemayel—scion of the most powerful Maronite clan in Lebanon, whose militia was the Phalange, Israel's ally who invited Israel to invade Lebanon to evict the Palestinians and Syrians, elected president of Lebanon in August 1982; usually referred to by first name to distinguish him from his brother and father ("bah-SHEER juh-MY-el")

Begin, Menachem—prime minister of Israel ("muh-NOCK-um BAY-gin")

Dillon, Robert—US ambassador to Lebanon, whose residence served as temporary embassy and Habib's headquarters in Lebanon

Draper, Morris—Habib's deputy, deputy assistant secretary of state for Near Eastern Affairs specializing in Lebanon

Eagleburger, Lawrence—undersecretary of state for political affairs, the number three position in the State Department, during Habib's Middle East mission

Gemayel, Amin or Bashir—*see* Amin Gemayel or Bashir Gemayel

Grove, Brandon—US consul general in Jerusalem, whose office/residence served as Habib's headquarters in Israel

Habib, Philip—American special presidential envoy to the Middle East ("hah-BEEB")

Haig, Alexander—secretary of state from January 1981 to July 1982

Hill, Charles—acting deputy assistant secretary of state for Near Eastern Affairs filling in for Draper while Draper was in the Middle East with Habib; the official who fielded most of Habib's daily calls to State

Lewis, Samuel—US ambassador to Israel from 1977 to 1985

Mead, Col. James—commander of US Marines on the ground in Beirut

Sehulster, Col. James—senior Marine adviser to Habib in planning MNF

Sharon, Ariel ("Arik")—Israeli defense minister, the driving force behind the 1982 invasion of Lebanon ("AIR-ee-el shuh-RONE")

Shultz, George—secretary of state from July 1982 to January 1989

Veliotes, Nicholas—assistant secretary of state for Near Eastern Affairs with overall responsibility for the entire Middle East

Wazzan, Shafik al—prime minister of Lebanon and Habib's main intermediary with the PLO ("shah-FEEK all wah-ZAHN")

Groups

Cabinet—the Israeli prime minister's council of senior advisors, which has a much stronger say in what happens than does an American president's Cabinet; made up of members of the Knesset

Druze—one of the stronger minority groups in Lebanon, an offshoot of Islam whose beliefs are secret ("drooz")

IDF—the Israeli Defense Forces, the Israeli army

Knesset—the Israeli parliament ("kuh-NESS-et")

LAF—the Lebanese Armed Forces, the official army of Lebanon (not to be confused with the Lebanese Forces)

Maronites—the Lebanese version of Roman Catholics, the dominant Christian group in Lebanon ("MER-o-nights")

MNF—the Multinational Force, composed of troops from the United States, France, and Italy, that oversaw the evacuation of Beirut and later maintained a peacekeeping presence in Lebanon

NEA—The State Department's Bureau of Near Eastern and South Asian Affairs, the office responsible for the Middle East

Phalange—the Maronite militia controlled by the Gemayel family, allies with Israel, more or less synonymous with the Lebanese Forces (not to be confused with the Lebanese Armed Forces) and the Kataeb ("fuh-LANJ" and "kuh-TEEB")

PLO—Palestine Liberation Organization, the largest organization devoted to regaining Palestine from Jews for Arabs; an umbrella group comprising many organizations, led by Yasir Arafat

Places

Baabda—a Maronite suburb of East Beirut, the seat of the Lebanese presidential palace, adjacent to Yarze ("BOB-dah")

Beirut-Damascus Highway—the single most strategic road in Lebanon, connecting the Lebanese and Syrian capitals, some 60 miles apart as the crow flies; the road runs right by Yarze, Baabda, and Zahle

East Beirut—the predominantly Christian half of town, dominated by the Maronites

Junieh—a small port city just north of Beirut, site of an LAF military base that Habib and Americans working with him often flew in and out of

West Beirut—the predominantly Muslim half of town, dominated by the PLO

Yarze—a Maronite suburb of East Beirut, site of the American ambassador's residence, which served as Habib's headquarters in Lebanon ("YAHR-zee")

Timeline

1981

Apr 28　Israel shoots down two Syrian helicopters in Lebanon

Apr 29　Syria places anti-aircraft missiles in Lebanon's Bekaa Valley; Israeli prime minister Menachem Begin threatens to destroy them

May 5　American special presidential envoy Philip Habib arrives in Middle East to avert war, soon works out informal understanding that neither side will shoot

July 24　Habib arranges ceasefire between Israel and PLO

Dec 5　Israeli defense minister Ariel Sharon sketches out to Habib his plan for invading Lebanon as far as Beirut, stronghold of the PLO; Habib opposes the plan

1982

late Jan　Sharon scouts out Beirut, coordinates invasion plans with his Lebanese ally Bashir Gemayel: Israeli army (IDF) will trap PLO in West Beirut; Bashir's militia, the Phalange, will go house to house killing trapped PLO fighters

May 25　Sharon in Washington describes his invasion plans to Secretary of State Alexander Haig, comes away believing that Haig's opposition is not strong enough to deter him

June 6　IDF invades Lebanon

June 9　While Habib is in Syria to convey Begin's assurances that Israel wants to avoid a fight, Israel destroys Syrian missiles and devastates the Syrian air force in dogfights in Lebanon

June 11　Under cover of a ceasefire, IDF keeps advancing on Syrians in Bekaa Valley; when Syrians respond by shooting, IDF trounces them; Syrian president Assad accuses Habib of setting him up for this humiliating defeat

June 12　IDF reaches outskirts of Beirut; city is now under siege, with thousands of PLO fighters and Syrian troops trapped; at Habib's and US ambassador Robert Dillon's urging, Bashir reneges on his end of bargain, refusing to massacre PLO; Sharon has no plan B except to keep bombing and blockading city until PLO surrenders

June 24　Reagan fires Haig, but lets him stay on as lame duck

July 3　PLO has agreed to leave Beirut; Habib feels deal is nearly set; Sharon launches waves of assaults that scuttle the deal and prevent Habib's intermediary to PLO from working; diplomacy freezes for most of July

July 16	George Shultz replaces Haig as secretary of state
July 22-26	Habib meets with Arab leaders to urge them to accept PLO evacuees; has first meeting with Marines to start planning Multinational Force's (MNF) work evacuating PLO and Syrians from Beirut
July 30	Habib tells Begin PLO has made unequivocal decision to leave; he is ready to start working out details
Aug 1-11	Sharon unleashes series of ever greater assaults on West Beirut, setting back Habib's progress; Habib begins regular, intensive planning meetings with MNF leaders
Aug 12	Despite Begin's acceptance of Habib's plan in principle, Sharon launches most massive assault ever on Beirut; Begin ties Sharon's hands; fighting basically stops
Aug 21	Evacuation of PLO and Syrians from Beirut begins
Aug 23	Bashir is elected president of Lebanon
Aug 30	Begin and Sharon demand Bashir sign a peace treaty that would give Israel immense power in Lebanon; he refuses
Sep 1	Evacuation is completed; Reagan announces regional peace proposal, which Israel passionately rejects
Sep 14	Bashir is assassinated
Sep 15	IDF enters West Beirut in violation of Habib agreement, surrounds Palestinian refugee camps Sabra and Shatila
Sep 16-18	Phalange massacres Palestinian civilians trapped in Sabra and Shatila
Sep 25-Oct 3	Habib tries to sell Israel and Syria a plan to get their troops out of Lebanon quickly; neither is willing
Dec 28	Despite Habib's efforts to promote informal understandings, Israel and Lebanon begin direct talks toward a formal peace treaty as Israel's price for withdrawing from Lebanon

1983

Jan 16-23	Israel rebuffs Habib's renewed urging of informal understandings
April 18	Car bomb kills 63 at US embassy in Beirut
May 17	Israel and Lebanon sign a formal peace agreement that will never be implemented; September 1 plan is dead by now
May 18	Syrian president Assad expresses his anger over the May 17 agreement by announcing he will no longer receive Habib
July 22	Habib resigns
Oct 23	Truck bombs kill 241 American and 58 French MNF soldiers in Beirut

1984

| Feb 7 | Reagan brings US Marines home from Beirut |

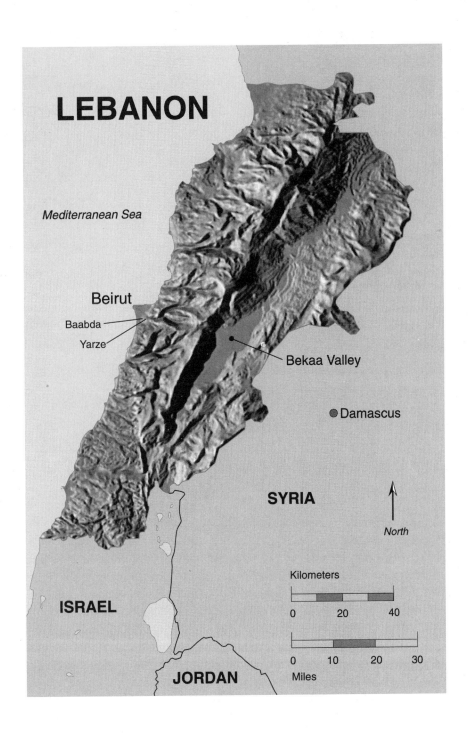

LEBANON

Mediterranean Sea

Beirut

Baabda

Yarze

Bekaa Valley

Damascus

SYRIA

North

Kilometers

0   20   40

ISRAEL

0   10   20   30

Miles

JORDAN

1
The Other Side of the Moon

For Phil, Brooklyn was not about being a street tough.
Brooklyn was about community, about family, about
values, about becoming an American. He felt that
Brooklyn, in *his* day, was the very epitome of the
American values that made America the great
beacon of hope for immigrants.
Richard Holbrooke

The East Room of the White House is a temple to high occasion, where all posture is perfect, all coughs are squelched, and all itches go unscratched. On this Tuesday afternoon in September 1982, the Cabinet, the generals, and the diplomats had all come early to be sure to get a seat. Ronald Reagan had cut short his vacation to be here.

When the President and the First Lady appeared at the far end of the long red-carpeted entryway, a ruffle of polite applause began. But when the audience caught sight of the portly, balding man taking up the rear, the applause quickened, thickened, and lofted into a clamor rare for the East Room. The standing-room-only crowd started cheering. Some stuck their fingers in their mouths and whistled. As the party entered the room and stepped onto the stage, the soprano of whistles, the alto of applause, and the tenor of cheers were joined by a rumbling bass of feet stomping. The man stared resolutely forward. But as the din rose ever louder and went on for an embarrassingly long time, he lowered his head, and his face muscles began to twitch. *Don't cry now, Philip,* thought one woman in the audience. *Don't cry now. Be happy.*

For most of the past three months, American diplomat Philip Habib had been the world's most conspicuous failure. The Israeli army, in an effort to destroy the Palestinian Liberation Organization once and for all, had been bombing the bloody hell out of the PLO's stronghold, the city of Beirut, Lebanon. The siege had degenerated into an aimless fiasco. Having gotten themselves into this unholy mess, neither the Israelis nor the PLO were willing to lose face to get themselves out of it. That was Philip Habib's lonely task. There were only two plausible outcomes: Either he would negotiate a peaceful end to the siege of Beirut, or Israeli soldiers would wade into the catacombs of the city and kill and kill and kill and kill and kill. As

1

the well-entrenched PLO fought back, countless thousands of Israelis, Palestinians, and Lebanese would die. Written off by many people as a Quixote and pitied by many others as a Sisyphus, Habib struck out at nearly every turn.

But in the end he had worked out an unprecedented solution to this unprecedented crisis. He was nominated for the Nobel Peace Prize, and now he was about to become the first career diplomat ever to receive America's highest civilian honor, the Presidential Medal of Freedom.

At the East Room podium, Reagan said, "His successful negotiation of the cease-fire in Lebanon and the resolution of the West Beirut crisis stands out as one of the unique feats of diplomacy in modern times. Ambassador Habib's efforts conducted in the most difficult and trying of circumstances . . . saved the city of Beirut and thousands of innocent lives." Reagan concluded by turning to Habib and saying, "In addition to the Medal of Freedom, Phil, you have earned a title beyond our power to bestow. You are a peacemaker."

Habib replied that it was "particularly fitting, considering that my mother and father came from Lebanon, that their son had something to do with bringing a bit of peace to that harried land." When the ceremony ended, he turned to his wife and said, "Not bad for a boy from Brooklyn."

The Lone Eagles

Technically, there was no such thing as Lebanon when Philip Habib was born. He entered the world on February 25, 1920; the modern state of Lebanon entered six months later.

The patch of land now called Lebanon had long been one corner of "the land of Syria" *(Bilad al-Sham),* which included today's Syria, Lebanon, Israel, Jordan, and parts of Iraq and Saudi Arabia. For four hundred years, it had been under the control of the Turks. Like most conquerors, the Turks were cruel masters and were warmly hated by their subjects. They forced subjugated peoples to serve in their army and singled out Syrian Christians for particular humiliation. So, driven both by a desire to escape the Turks and by hopes of seeing the gold-paved streets of New York, thousands of non-Muslims left Syria to start a new life in America.

One such was Iskander Habib Jamous, a young Maronite Christian of draftable age from around Sidon, a major port south of Beirut. He arrived in New York around 1900. Habib is one of the most common Arabic names, like Smith or Jones. It means *beloved.* Jamous means *buffalo.* Some immigration officer no doubt carelessly dropped the name Jamous from his papers, so Iskander dropped it too. He changed his first name to a nice Americanized Alexander, and his friends promptly changed that to Alex.

2

He married a lovely, educated woman named Miriam (Mary) Spiridon, who had immigrated from a coastal village a little north of Beirut. "I suppose it was one of those semi-arranged things," her son would later say, "in the sense that somebody decided this man would make a good husband, somebody decided they better get rid of their sister, and mutual arrangements were made."

Philip Charles, born in Brooklyn, was their fifth and last child. In 1927 or 1928, Alex managed to pull together enough money to buy a small row house in the Bensonhurst section of Brooklyn. This was not a district of tenements and squalor. It was a tree-lined neighborhood of single-family homes that no one ever thought to lock. None of the families in the neighborhood was especially poor or especially well off. "It turned out that we had moved into a 99.9 percent pure Jewish community," said Phil. "There were three non-Jewish families—two Italian families and us—out of what must have been at least fifty families on our one street."

Phil and seven Jewish neighbor boys soon formed a tight-knit group. "We were not a gang," one of them hastens to point out. "We were all good kids, and it was all good clean fun." It was also quite structured. They called themselves the Lone Eagles Social and Athletic Club. They held meetings and elected officers. There was no particular leader, but they took turns getting elected president and vice president. This grounding in orderly structure would stick with Phil for life and become a prime reason presidents would trust him.

The Lone Eagles paid little attention to the ethnic, religious, and other divisions that their elders took so seriously. In the abstract, Brooklyn in the 1930s represented a rich ethnic mix. At the street level, however, mixing was not encouraged, and venturing into another group's turf was often a good way to get a bloody nose. Even in the Habibs' neighborhood, Jews and non-Jews had little to do with one another; the Jews from eastern Europe (called Ashkenazi) had little to do with the Jews from Syria (called Sephardic); and the Jews from Aleppo, Syria, had little to do with the Jews from Damascus. Each group had its own church or synagogue, its own language or dialect, its own sense of community.

The Lone Eagles couldn't be bothered. Three of them were Ashkenazi, four Sephardic, and Phil was the only non-Jew of the lot, a matter of complete indifference to them all. He went to so many of their bar mitzvahs, "I was an expert. And I never dated anyone but a Jewish girl until I was 19." As a Lone Eagle, "I learned about things like anti-Semitism. Why? Because, being that I was with them all the time, everybody thought *I* was Jewish! Coming from Brooklyn, if you have a big nose, people automatically assume you're Jewish. And my nose was even bigger than theirs! So I experienced the same reactions among outsiders as Jewish boys. Everything they felt, I felt. By virtue of what these kids taught me when I was a young boy and by virtue of my own instincts, I can smell anti-Semitism."

Sanctity of Your Word

As orthodox Jews, most of Phil's neighbors observed the Sabbath scrupulously. Between sundown Friday and sundown Saturday, they would do no work: They would not feed the coal furnace, cook, or even turn a gas stove or electric light on or off. In eastern Europe, where many of them had come from, it was traditional to have a non-Jew (*goy* in Yiddish) do such tasks for them on the Sabbath, or *Shabbas*.

In this neighborhood, the *Shabbas goy* was Phil Habib. At sundown every Friday night, he had a route. At each house, he would shake up the grate on the coal furnace in the basement, bank the fire for the night, turn certain lights on, turn others off. On Saturday morning he would come back, shake up the grate on the furnaces, and throw a little coal on the fire. Then he'd turn on the gas for whatever they had left out on the stove, sweep any snow off the sidewalk, and do whatever other odd chores they needed. Each family paid him a nickel.

For their part, the Habibs were Roman Catholic, by convenience. Like most Syrian Christian immigrants—it would be over two decades before they would begin to call themselves "Lebanese-Americans"—Alex Habib was actually Maronite; Mary was Melchite. But the Melchite church and the Maronite church were both in downtown Brooklyn, and the Catholic church was nearby. Phil didn't know anything about Muslims. Between the three churches for the Habib family and the various synagogues for his friends, he concluded that "it didn't make any difference where you went to pray."

His family's religion did not stick with him for long, but his father's work ethic did. Alex worked for years as an accountant in an Arab bank in Manhattan. In 1932, the bank went under, a casualty of the Depression. Suddenly, for the first time in perhaps twenty years, Alex Habib was out of a job. He kept the family afloat by taking on odd jobs—doing a little bookkeeping, selling handkerchiefs, manufacturing cigarettes—but soon opened a Syrian grocery store on Atlantic Avenue in the heart of Brooklyn's Syrian community. He got up every morning at 7 A.M. and left for work before Phil was out of bed. "I didn't see him until I was gone to bed at night," Phil said, "and Sunday he was so tired from working all week that he'd go to sleep on the porch swing. I'd see him maybe for two hours, when we'd have a big Sunday meal."

The family and community in which Phil grew up were steeped in traditional Syrian ways. Syrian immigrants tended to be intensely conservative and very strict parents. They instilled a common set of values in their children. First among them was reverence for family and for upholding the dignity of the family name. "Their name meant more than anything else," says his cousin Isabelle Toomey. Joseph Jacobs, who grew up in the same community as Phil but became a friend only later in life, says, "Disgracing the family name was the most heinous crime. If you did something wrong, it was doubly reprehensible because you brought shame on the family."

Alex Habib did not consider himself an Arab. Instead, he proudly claimed to be able to trace his ancestry back thousands of years to the Phoenicians. Though his specific claim was dubious, his people were indeed descended from those ancient seafaring traders who traveled to the edges of the known world and invented the alphabet. His people taught their children that their Phoenician forebears' renowned success as traders had depended on upholding the sanctity of their word. Jacobs says that "the behavioral standards of the trader, as transmitted to us, placed great importance on pride, reputation, and integrity. . . . One simply did not *do* certain things. What would people say? No matter what sacrifices were needed, one's reputation for honesty and loyalty was paramount."

First-generation children of immigrants of many backgrounds shared a powerful sense of drive. "We were very conscious of the fact that we were immigrants," says Jacobs. "Our parents spoke with foreign accents, and we were ashamed of it. We were identified as Syrians, our parents thought like Syrians, and they spoke Arabic. But we wanted to belong in the worst way. We wanted to be accepted as indistinguishable from other Americans. The reverence for this country in the Lebanese community was something to behold. To this day, Phil and I and all of us in that generation are unabashed patriots. This country is loved fiercely by immigrants and immigrants' children. It's not taken for granted."

Baloney Sandwich

Phil was anxious to blend in both as an American and as a Lone Eagle. When he would come home from school or play, he wouldn't want to eat the *pietata* or *kusa* or other traditional Arab foods his mom fixed. He wanted a baloney sandwich. And when his parents would speak to him in Arabic or French, he would answer only in English.

As the youngest, he was more Americanized than the rest of his family. "Middle Eastern men also tend to be loud and domineering," says Marjorie Habib. "When the Lebanese have a conversation, they shout. One time when I was with Philip and his family, their voices kept getting louder and louder and louder, and pretty soon, Pop was going *whop!* on the table, so hard that the dishes were jumping. I thought, *Why are they angry?* But they weren't really angry. That's just how they talk. All the Lebanese I know are like that. Philip's sister was the same way, all of his brothers—they all shout! Philip shouted too, but not nearly as much as his family. He wasn't as Middle Eastern as his brothers."

There were only three ways in which Phil stood out from the other Lone Eagles. First, he knew more Arabic profanity than his Sephardic friends did, more Yiddish profanity than his Ashkenazi friends did, and more of either than he himself knew in English. "The Sephardic among us spoke Arabic," Lone Eagle Jack Grazi recalled, "but some of this we'd never heard before, and we'd laugh our guts out." His talent for Arabic profanity would later help earn him the respect of negotiating counterparts in the Middle East.

His second distinction was his delight in playing war games. "He loved to set out his toy soldiers and battle this side against the other side, knocking them down," Jack says. "He *loved* these war games. Nobody else in the group had any interest in them."

A third special interest of Phil's was travel. Brooklyn kids in the '30s rarely ventured far beyond their own neighborhood, and, as Joe Jacobs put it, "if you went to Manhattan, that was like a trip to a foreign country." But Phil had itchy feet his whole life. "I was always interested in geography, in the world, how to get places, how to travel. I used to dream about travelling all the time." He would send away for travel folders and talk with his sixth-grade teacher about different parts of the world.

So the Lone Eagles got around: to Coney Island, Fire Island, Ebbets Field, Yankee Stadium, occasionally even to Manhattan.

As an adult, Phil Habib would be known as a blunt, brusque, hard-nosed guy who didn't take crap from anybody and didn't hesitate to nail windbags to the wall. Friends and colleagues who knew him only as an adult often attribute these characteristics to his having grown up on the rough-and-tumble streets of Brooklyn. But that theory seems to miss the point of how Brooklyn shaped Phil. When Jack Grazi hears that theory, he laughs. "The Brooklyn aura! Every time you think of Brooklyn, you think of Murder, Inc., and all of the tough people out there. I didn't think Phil was all that tough as a kid. That's a side of Phil that we never knew. I think that developed later. There was nothing shy about him as a kid; he made himself heard. But I don't remember him being either bullying or very forceful as a kid."

Lone Eagles Jack Grazi and Joe Beyda both scoff at the notion that they and Phil grew up in a turbulent place. "Not at all," says Jack. "This was not a rough-and-tumble neighborhood. We were a very peaceful group in a peaceful neighborhood." Other parts of Brooklyn may have been bad news, but, Joe says, "Our neighborhood absolutely was not like Bedford-Stuyvesant. It was the other end of the totem pole. Narcotics, sex, crime, and all the rest of it—we didn't have that in those days."

Where then did Phil's tough-guy adult image come from? His oldest brother Fred. After getting fired from a garment factory job for going on strike, Fred became an organizer and business agent of the International Ladies Garment Workers Union, one of the strongest, flintiest unions in the '20s and '30s. Toomey says, "Fred was a very strong person. He didn't hurt anyone, but he didn't let anyone take advantage of him either."

Phil idolized Fred, who was ten years older. Everyone who speaks of Fred uses the same word to describe him: *brilliant.* He was "like a walking encyclopedia," a nephew recalls. "He had a photographic memory." Relatives would make a game of trying to ask a question on any subject that Fred couldn't answer or finding a word in a dictionary that he couldn't define. One relative says he spoke as many as seven languages and once won a bet by learning to speak Yiddish over the weekend.

It would be a decade or two before Fred's latent influence would manifest itself in Phil's persona. But one part of his influence was immediate. Before Phil had entered elementary school, Fred graduated from high school at age fourteen. He received a full scholarship to Rutgers University, but times were hard and his parents did not want him to be away from the family. So he passed it up. Fred's inability to get a college education made a deep impression on Phil.

By the time Phil graduated from high school in 1936, "my passion was the outdoors, and I was taken up with the idea of making my life the out of doors." He wanted to be a forest ranger. Fellow Lone Eagle Moishie Moroch had gone off to forestry school, and Phil decided to do the same.

Alex made him a deal: "If you want to go to school, you go to work. But you can save your money for college. You don't have to contribute to the house." His siblings Victor and Violet had never gone to college at all, and Fred had taken a few college classes locally but never finished. Phil was determined to be the exception.

Go West

Alex got him a job at a sheet metal factory that made medicine chests and other kinds of metal boxes. Phil was a shipping clerk. He made $10 a week for a fifty-two-hour, five-and-a-half-day week. "You could ride a subway to work for 5 cents each way, but I was interested in saving my money so I could go to *college*," Phil said, with a proud flourish on the word *college.* "So I used to ride my bicycle to work and back so I wouldn't have to pay a subway fare. It was about a forty-five-minute bike ride from our house. To save money, I used to take my lunch. Every Saturday when I would get paid, I would give my father my pay, and he would put it away for me."

After two years, in 1938, he applied for college. He was accepted to both Syracuse in New York and the University of Idaho. Both had excellent forestry programs, but Idaho was cheaper. Besides, "I wanted to get away, to go. I wanted to go west." So he chose Idaho. His family had known all along that he intended to go to college, but there had been no discussion of *where*. If venturing into Manhattan was like visiting another country, Idaho was like the dark side of the moon. And, what with tight money for travel during the Depression, when would they ever see him again? Mindful that family pressures had forced Fred to pass up his scholarship for Rutgers, Phil made all the arrangements in secret.

Finally, with the start of the 1938–39 school year approaching, he could wait no more. He went to his father and said, "I've been accepted to school, the course starts in September, and I want to go. I need my money now."

Alex looked him straight in the eye and said, "There's none left."

"What do you mean, there's none left?! There should be about $400! Two years I've been saving!"

"You've got to understand, times have been very difficult. I needed to use that money for the family."

"How could you do that?! I worked these two years! Pop, I want to go, and I want to go now."

"All right. We'll do it the best we can. We'll get enough money to get you started, and then I'll see what I can send you. When you get there, you can work."

Phil was furious about the situation, but he didn't really blame his father. "After all," he later said, "he wasn't putting the money into the ponies or anything. He was a very devout, very serious family man. He was supporting the family." Nonetheless, the loss of that $400—the equivalent of $6,000 in 2002 dollars—would haunt him for years.

Phil's mother was heartbroken at the thought that her last child was leaving home, and so far away from home. "She was right," he said. "I never saw her again."

Phil had stashed away about $90 on his own, and his father gave him enough for a bus ticket to Idaho. With a few belongings stuffed in a bag and $90 in his pocket, he kissed his family goodbye and boarded a Greyhound for the dark side of the moon.

Not Your Average Forestry Student

Moscow, Idaho, was just what the boy from Brooklyn hungered for: a world unlike any he had known before. Moscow had 8,000 souls, one narrow main street, one hotel, two movie theaters, and a couple of beer parlors. Phil could cross the Moscow city limits into vast expanses of beautiful, empty space. Though he didn't want anybody to notice, he positively luxuriated in the awesome beauty. The ethnic texture of Brooklyn faded into a dim memory. For the next forty years, he would be just another American guy.

It immediately became apparent that Phil Habib was not your average forestry student. Before classes had even started, a professor found him in the library browsing books by Adam Smith, Thomas Robert Malthus, John Stuart Mill, and Karl Marx. Those interested him; classwork did not. Despite his seriousness in anticipating college, once he got there he found the library much more interesting than the classroom. He skipped a lot of classes and slept through many of the rest. When he was present and awake, he was not taking lecture notes. He was more likely to be arguing with the professor.

At first, his roommate Roy Kuehner thought Phil was an "argumentative, communist-leaning New Yorker" because he would always argue in favor of the New Deal programs that Roy considered socialistic. "He would always argue for the good of the masses. Eventually I realized he was not a communist. He just delighted in stimulating thought and provoking discussion. Phil had an inquiring, analytical mind. He would always ask, 'Is it practical?' He challenged us to question facts that weren't substantiated."

Classmate Finley McNaughton says, "When Phil did anything, it was all-out." He'd spend countless hours in the library absorbed in whatever book on whatever subject had caught his fancy. He'd play poker or go carousing all night long. When he slept through a class, he'd be sprawled with his head flung back, snoring. Some nights he would work till dawn in the forest pathology lab; a few hours later students arriving for the first morning class would find him curled up and sound asleep on top of his small lab desk.

One habit of his made such a strong impression on his classmates that they all vividly recalled it fifty years later. Phil never bothered to study for exams. But the day before each exam he would borrow lecture notes from the best note taker in class, borrow somebody else's textbook, rip through them, give them back, and then ace the test. Several of his classmates chalked it up to a photographic memory. Ward Smith, the only student in his class to graduate with highest honors, wrote that "Phil's native intelligence was amazing. He had an uncanny ability to reason his way out of demanding situations. He could walk into a tough exam, apparently unprepared, and reason his way through to a good grade; no sweat."

He didn't make even that much effort to do well in ROTC. Every male student was required to take military training for two years, and Phil resented it. "He'd rather solve a fight than fight," says classmate Bob Kliewer. Besides, "He didn't like being given orders, and he would argue with anybody he thought was wrong." Each male student was required to wear a "monkey suit"—a military uniform—to class every Friday. Phil tended to skip class on Fridays. He had a B average in his other classes but got D's in ROTC.

Lumberjack

The twenty-eight forestry students in his University of Idaho class became very close because they took the same classes, went on the same field trips, and worked the same summer camp jobs. They also partied together. They were a bunch of fun-loving, rambunctious hell-raisers, and Phil thoroughly indulged in college excess. "The first two years," he said, "I was very good. The last two years I discovered booze, girls, and fun. We didn't smoke pot in those days. If we had've, I would've." Instead, "We took our nourishment in bottles." Phil relished slipping into the image of a rough, tough, hard-drinking, poker-playing lumberjack. He couldn't afford beer or dates nearly as often as he wanted, and he was never one to get falling-down drunk. But when one of his classmates, a teetotaler, got exasperated with him and demanded, "Do you even know what good, clean fun is?" Phil replied, "I'll bite. What good is it?"

One Sunday morning when Phil and his classmates were in McCall, Idaho, a hotel went up in flames. Phil and Bob Kliewer joined a crowd watching the building burn; then the two of them suddenly dashed inside— to rescue some booze from the liquor store on the ground floor. They tried to stack bottles in their arms like firewood, but kept dropping them. This was taking way too long. The crowd cheered as they emerged with one big bottle in each hand, just before the building collapsed and burned to the ground.

Among his forestry classmates he loved to sing and cut up. As a group of them would bounce along rough roads in the back of an old Dodge stakebed truck on a field trip, Phil would be in the back singing bawdy songs at the top of his lungs. His specialty was a dead-on imitation of Jimmy Durante singing "Minnie the Moocher" ("She was a low-down hoochie coocher . . . hidee hidee hidee ho"). One Saturday night he and some friends were singing at full volume on the steps of an old hotel; a guest upstairs opened a window, yelled "Scat!" and dumped a bucket of water on them.

At spring festivals, he was always very competitive in all the contests: climbing up a pole, cutting logs with a crosscut saw, and spitting chewing tobacco. He did a pantomime routine of a duck hunter, which climaxed with him stuffing toilet paper in his mouth. He almost got expelled for taking a dare and crowing like a rooster in Assembly Hall.

In recommending Phil to a friend for a summer job, the dean wrote that he was "quick on his feet, . . . has a good mind, in fact a keen intellect, and is widely read. I have asked him if he could keep his mouth shut and behave himself, and he has assured me that he will. Outside of a tendency to be a little wild at times, which I think he will control, he would deliver the goods. He has some foreign blood so that he is quite dark, but that need not interfere with his doing a good piece of work."

He was what one classmate calls a "vicious" poker player, because poker was to him not just a game. It was part of his income. Though the stakes were low—nobody had much money, so there was not much to win or lose—every dime mattered. He was a swaggering winner ("You don't know how to play this game. You think you can beat me?") and a very, very sore loser ("You rotten guy! How'd you ever do that?"). He could remember where every face-up card had gone, which several classmates attribute to a photographic memory, while keeping up a constant stream of chatter to distract the others. Given his talents, he had no interest in simple card games. The more complex, the better. "He really knew how to deal a tight deck," says one classmate. "He held the cards close to his chest and could bluff his way through damned near anything." His attitude: "When you get a good hand in poker that you feel has a good chance of winning, bet the hell out of 'em! Don't back off, even when you're playing with friends! You have no friends in a poker game."

The rest of his income he earned by more conventional means. He had various jobs during the school year: mopping floors, washing dishes in a greasy spoon, cleaning sacks in a seed-packing plant, bundling nursery trees for shipment, cataloging the school's pathology collection of dried fungus. A whole year of school, room and board, and clothes cost about $400—just the amount Phil had saved for college and lost. "Of course, you had one pair of pants you bought in the fall, you wore them all winter, got out and worked in the woods in them all summer and then you bought a new one the following fall." His clothes were sloppy, and he rarely bothered to wash them, prompting one classmate to write a poem that ended, "Nothing gives a stench that nox / Like Philip Habib's sweaty sox."

The manager of the forestry school's experimental nursery gave Phil a job for 35 cents an hour and let him sleep on a cot in the upstairs storage room. Once the weather got too cold to stay there, he moved and got a roommate with whom he shared "a little room that wasn't big enough to swing a cat in" and its one double bed. Out of the blue, his old Lone Eagles buddies scraped together $100 and sent it to him, enabling him to move into a co-op dorm officially called the Idaho Club and unofficially called Poverty Flats. Everyone there had to take their turn hashing in the dining hall. Most of the guys preferred to be out front waiting tables, but Phil preferred working in the back, washing and peeling potatoes.

His earnings were not enough to allow the one expenditure that would have meant the most to him: His mother died while he was in Idaho, but he couldn't afford the trip home for her funeral.

Poison

Despite his ample street smarts, this was forestry school, and the boy from Brooklyn was definitely the class tenderfoot. Forestry students were expected to spend their summers doing forestry work. Phil didn't like to get his hands dirty and never showed any interest in or talent for manual labor. At the end of one of his summer jobs, his performance rating sheet read in part:

Loyal worker:	Yes, but ineffectual
Energetic worker:	Must be—I never saw him do any, but his work was always in on time
Even tempered/loses temper:	Mixed about evenly
Neat personally and in tent:	Not too much
Trouble maker:	Could be easily
Originality:	High
Comment on potentialities:	Seems to have that Jewish trait of being interested in people and their problems to the extent of making a nuisance of himself

(Actually, most people at the university, not just this supervisor, mistakenly assumed he was Jewish. Being used to that, he never took the trouble to correct them.)

There was one striking exception to his aversion to manual labor. "His great hunger was to fight forest fire," says one of his classmates. The summer after his freshman year he and about sixty classmates worked at a remote camp in St. Joe National Forest in northern Idaho, accessible only by foot and pack mule. For the first few weeks of camp he kept saying, "Boy, I sure hope we get to fight fire," until the others were sick of hearing it. Finally, one night a lightning storm set three fires in the camp's Big Creek Basin territory. Around 3 A.M. somebody barged into the cabin and yelled, "Anybody want to go on fire?"

"We'll all go!" Phil said, to the irritation of everyone else. "That was probably the closest he ever came to being mobbed," one recalls. Phil and his sixty-odd colleagues collected their canned rations, filled their canteens, and headed off to fight some fires. The gameplan, as always, was to get ahead of the fire's path and clear a swath, even if only a few feet wide, where the fire would run out of fuel. For twelve straight hours they worked with axes and six-foot-long hand saws. When they got two fires out and had the third contained, they took a lunch break.

A few hours after lunch, one guy after another started falling violently ill with vomiting and diarrhea. Some were crawling on their hands and knees in agony. Some of their fire rations had been sitting around on shelves for years, and at least a dozen old cans of beef had gone bad. Their meat was poison.

By nightfall, the sick and the well had all straggled back to camp, improvising a route single-file through a thicket of ceanothus brush taller than their heads. Around 10 P.M., somebody noticed that one guy, Ralph Reid, was missing. Phil, who had not gotten sick, recalled having seen him fall out of line on the way back to camp. So he and camp boss Bob Kliewer led a search party out to find him. There was no moon, no flashlight, and no trail through the thicket. But, drawing on the uncanny memory that served him so well in poker games and exams, Phil led the party to Ralph within two hours. Ralph was still too sick to walk. The party carried him back on a stretcher made of a cot whose legs they had cut off. Bob says, "He would have perished if we had not found him." After five days, he was OK.

Another night, about 2 A.M., a truckload of forestry students was headed back to a different camp after an exhausting day fighting fires. Most of the guys were either sleeping or nodding on the four 2x10 boards that served as seats in the old truck. Bob was driving, with Phil beside him. On one downhill stretch of severe switchbacks along a steep cliff, Phil noticed Bob's head go down to his chest. He had fallen asleep at the wheel. Phil jabbed him awake just as the right front wheel went over the edge. Bob managed to swerve back onto the road in time to keep the truck from pitching over the cliff.

Though Phil was usually with his classmates, he spent one summer alone 10,000 feet up on a mountaintop in central Idaho watching for fires. Usually he just radioed in reports that others followed up on. But he once had to put out a lightning fire all by himself, working with just an ax and a shovel. At another point he developed a raging toothache. For three straight days and nights he stayed at his post because he felt it was his duty to finish out his assigned watch. Besides, he said, "generally the fellas had plans made."

Their four years together formed a lifelong bond among the forestry students. Phil would later say that his classmates "were my family" and that the University of Idaho gave him "the closest thing I've ever had to roots."

A Gorgeous Blonde

During his senior year, America entered World War Two, and Phil got drafted not long after his June 1942 graduation. The Army gave him two weeks to wind up his affairs after he got sworn in, so he promptly hopped a bus from Boise to Reno. This would be his second trip there: At Christmas 1939, he and his roommate Unc Henderson had driven to Reno to visit Unc's family for a week. There Phil had met "a gorgeous blonde" Unc knew named Marjorie Slightam. They went out five times, and then Phil and Unc went back to school. But Phil and Marge stayed in touch by letter. Now, as his bus pulled into Reno, he and Marge had not seen one another since those handful of dates two and a half years earlier.

The next day they eloped. "You know what struck me about him?" Marge says. "I had never met anybody who was as smart as he was. Not ever. I fell in love with his mind as much as anything else." He says, "Her mother, of course, was not very happy that her daughter was marrying this broken-down, strange-looking kid with no future who was going to be a private in the Army!" As for his own family, he didn't dare even tell them "because I knew my father would have a fit." Marrying outside of the Syrian/Lebanese community violated tradition. "It was several months before I got up enough nerve to write [Pop] a letter and tell him that I got married." When Alex got the letter, he was so shocked that he wouldn't speak to anyone for two weeks. It would be years before he would accept Marge.

Phil hated being in the Army—not least because he thought his officers knew less than he did, yet he was forbidden to argue with them—and he never forgave the Germans for robbing him of three years of his life. He got sent to England and France as part of an airborne engineer battalion that flew gliders in to damaged airfields to repair them so regular aircraft could then fly in and out. Sometimes fighting was still going on at one end of the airfield while repairs were going on at the other. But the glider program soon got cancelled. "Thank God," he said, "because those things were coffins." They tipped over on landing. After he had repaired a few damaged airfields, one day "they gave me a bunch of laborers and said, 'Go *build* an airfield.' I didn't know anything about airfields," but suddenly he had 1,500 guys working for him. Step one was to probe the ground—with bayonets!—for landmines. It's a wonder they survived to step two. But his most memorable moment in the Army was standing a few miles from Saint-Lô, France, in July 1944, feeling the ground shake as a thousand bombers flew overhead on the bombing run that began the battle of Saint-Lô, which helped clear the way for an Allied advance toward Paris.

When the war ended in 1945, he found himself stuck with the assignment he hated the worst of all: running a prisoner of war camp in Germany.

For reasons he never quite understood, the Army would not let him go home yet, but did offer him a chance to go to school in Paris for three months. "I said, 'Jeez, anything to get out of this POW camp!'" and headed off to the Sorbonne. His lecturer in philosophy there was Jean-Paul Sartre. There is no information about how much he argued with him.

By the time he got out of the Army, he had had his fill of manual labor and decided he would rather teach forestry than be a forest ranger. So he enrolled in the agricultural economics PhD program at the University of California, Berkeley. Marge worked as a legal secretary in San Francisco while he went to school and worked as a research assistant and taught Economics 1A. He published his first article: "The Spinach Situation in California."

One day in 1946 a leader of a Boy Scout troop in San Francisco noticed a poorly dressed, unshaven Phil Habib hanging around the church basement where the troop met, silently watching. After the third such visit, the leader, Henry Santé, asked him who he was. He told him he wanted to work with Boy Scouts. But not just any Scout troop would do. "He wanted a troop similar to the one he had been in in Brooklyn, where he could do some good," says Santé. The thirty or forty boys in this troop were 8 to 12 years old and too poor to afford uniforms or 50-cent handbooks. Marge recalls that "Philip said, 'I want kids from the worst district.' And he got 'em! From the Haight-Ashbury district. These grubby little kids brought knives to their meetings."

He helped lead them through the usual Boy Scout games and lessons and projects, but also took them up to the hills of rural Marin County, north of San Francisco, to camp and build a nature trail. When the other two leaders would go out for hamburgers after a meeting, Habib would make excuses and go home, embarrassed that he couldn't afford hamburgers. When the boys would get into fights—which was often—Habib or one of the other two leaders would have to jump in, maybe shove a kid up against the wall and threaten to "kick his ass" and throw him out of the troop.

Otherwise, Habib wasn't much of a disciplinarian. Santé recalls him as "almost meek, quietly introverted. He wasn't shy, but I had a little more money, and he may have felt a little inferior because of his dire economic straits." That was just one of several widely varying perceptions that different people had of his personality as a young man. The Lone Eagles had known him as just one more guy, nothing special. The forestry students in Idaho—all of whom were guys—had known him as a boisterous, rollicking extrovert. The girls in Idaho saw him as too shy to look up or speak when they walked by. Marge Habib says that when she married him, "he was not retiring, but he wasn't the personality kid either. He was introverted. God knows he grew out of that and became a terrific extrovert.

When I married him, he knew what he thought and why he thought it, but I don't think he had a tough streak ever."

The turning point in his life came in 1947 when a couple of recruiters for the Foreign Service visited the Berkeley campus. The Foreign Service at the time was the province of Ivy League blueblood WASPs, but the recruiters were looking for people who did not fit that mold. Phil Habib certainly did not. Nor had he ever given the Foreign Service a moment's thought or even taken a political science class, for that matter. He didn't even have any idea what diplomacy was. But the recruiters were particularly interested in students majoring in economics, and the idea of the Foreign Service suddenly appealed to him. He also enjoyed taking tests purely for the intellectual challenge, so he took the three-day Foreign Service exam on a whim, "not dreaming I would pass it."

Once he heard that he had scored in the top 10 percent nationally, though, he started thinking that maybe the Foreign Service might be more stimulating than forestry. He never got over his amazement that America might allow somebody from Brooklyn—and a son of immigrants, no less—to represent it to other nations. The State Department invited him to Washington, at his own expense, for the oral exam. He decided the expense of the trip would be worth the gamble, so he and Marge pulled together enough money for a new suit and a plane ticket. When he walked in the door, the four or five interviewers immediately started firing questions at him in French. They offered him a cigarette, but there was no ashtray. Both ploys were tests to see how well and how graciously he could think on his feet. The French he had picked up as his parents' second language and in France during the war suddenly served him well. He fielded the questions just fine, and he flicked the cigarette ashes into his pants cuff. He was in.

The boy from Brooklyn with the Arabic name, the big nose, and the background in forestry was going to be a United States diplomat.

2

Stop the Bombing and Negotiate

Phil had profile. He wasn't some obscure guy in a dark
gray suit. I mean, *he was Phil Habib!* He was banging
around and making noise in his unique way. What made
him so memorable was his exceptionalism against
the largely gray background of other
people doing the same thing.
Brandon Grove

"What kind of people are we taking into the Foreign Service these days?" sniffed the Deputy Chief of Mission when Phil Habib showed up at the US embassy in Ottawa, Canada, in October 1949 for his first assignment. That DCM may or may not have recalled his remark twenty-seven years later when he saw Habib step into the highest-ranking job in the Foreign Service, undersecretary of state for political affairs. But Habib never forgot it. Nor did he ever forget the other remarks like it that he heard early on, such as "Habib? That's such a funny sounding name!"

Like most young Foreign Service officers, he was competitive and ambitious. But he quickly realized that he couldn't compete with the Ivy League WASPs on their terms. So he decided to redefine the competition: He was never going to be the most patrician sipper of tea, but he could jolly well be the hardest-working, the best-informed, and the most blunt FSO in the business. He resolved to always become *the* authority on whatever issue or country he worked on.

That strategy paid off beyond his grandest ambitions. His eventual job as undersecretary, which capped his career, made him the number three official in the State Department. By then he would already be a legend in diplomatic circles. But it was *after* all of that, *after* he retired from a remarkable career, that he began the mission of a lifetime, negotiating an end to the 1982 siege of Beirut. In hindsight, he spent his entire career training for that mission.

Boundless Tenacity

He started at the bottom of the bottom: as assistant agricultural attaché writing hundreds of crop reports on wheat in Saskatchewan, hops in Brit-

17

ish Columbia, poultry in Ontario, and the like. Even in dealing with such mundane matters, he quickly evinced what would be a lifelong characteristic: throwing himself headlong into whatever work he was assigned. He often stayed up till 4 A.M. finishing reports.

Another characteristic that became apparent early on was a boundless tenacity. For example, in August 1951, Phil and Marge rented a cottage on the Gatineau River in Quebec for a few days. Two of the few Lebanese he knew, Fred and Pauline Salhany, came for a visit. While Phil and Fred rowed a boat around and Marge sat on the shore, Pauline waded out into the river. Suddenly she dropped neck-deep in the water, yelped, and started waving her arms. She had apparently stepped over a ledge on the river bottom. Marge started to go in after her, but then remembered she couldn't swim, so she tossed her cocker spaniel into the water toward her. While Phil and Fred scrambled over to the spot, Pauline grabbed the dog's leg and went under. The dog came back up. Pauline did not. Phil and Fred dove in and searched all around, but couldn't find her. By the time the police arrived, dragged the bottom, and pulled up her body, she had been under water for nearly an hour and a half. There was no chance she could still be alive. Nonetheless, "Philip worked and worked and worked on her," Marge says, giving her artificial respiration until the paramedics arrived and told him it was no use.

The Foreign Service is an itinerant life. FSOs generally get transferred every two years or so. After Canada, Habib was posted to New Zealand as junior economic officer, then to Washington as an intelligence researcher, to Trinidad as political counselor, back to Washington as an economic and intelligence analyst, then to South Korea as political counselor.

The first thing he did in each assignment was to get to know as many of the local players as possible: politicians, cabinet ministers, generals, bureaucrats, reporters, businesspeople. Whatever culture he was in, he had a feel for how to talk with people. "He had a lust for information and a way of pulling information out of people," says colleague Fred Ashley. "He made a point of talking to people who knew what was going on, and he had a good bullshit detector." With each assignment his reputation grew as a shrewd analyst and brutally hard worker. He became known, says a colleague, as an "extraordinarily competent career officer, forceful, intelligent, sophisticated in a hard-nosed way, with an extraordinarily adept feel for what's right and what's possible."

His South Korea assignment placed him at a focal point of the Cold War. This was his first taste of the big leagues. And he liked it.

He arrived in Seoul in 1962, ten years after the Korean War and one year after a military coup. With the Korean government run by generals and the capital crawling with American military officers still there to help the South face off communist North Korea, Habib got a constant and concentrated exposure to military thinking. He developed a deep skepticism about generals' penchant for seeing military solutions to political problems. "Some military men are very sophisticated," he said, "but you should use them for what they are competent to do. Political matters should not be left to the judgment of military men. They don't really have the background or the training to understand the relationship between political action and military." This view would later guide him in his Beirut mission.

He found the generals running South Korea to be a tough, brutal crew, but they were the people he had to work with. He stayed in touch with the beleaguered civilian politicians, but the best he and the ambassador, Samuel Berger, could do was persuade the junta to hold elections. He learned that, whatever situation you're in, "you take what you've got and do what you can." He instructed people beneath him, "You can't control everything, but you can make sure that what *you* do is right." But he also learned that even doing the right thing is not enough if Washington does not back you up. When the generals had taken over the government in 1961, the then-chargé d'affaires (acting ambassador) had opposed the coup, but Washington accepted it as a fait accompli. The chargé was, in effect, repudiated and was soon transferred out. The lesson, Habib said, was "don't get ahead of what Washington wants. Or if you do get ahead, convince Washington that what *you* want is the right thing to do. What the hell is the point of taking a position and having it cut out from under you?"

This kind of pragmatism would mark Habib's approach to every crisis he ever worked. He expressed his pragmatic views in plain, colloquial, and usually salty English. He was, after all, the diplomat from Brooklyn; and if you didn't know that before you met him, you never forgot it after. Whereas some diplomats would try to get ahead by saying nothing controversial, Habib got ahead by saying exactly what he thought. As Alexander Haig put it, "He was the exact opposite of what you expect of the typical State Department diplomat: a cold-blooded, steely-eyed bastard who you don't ever know what he's thinking. You knew what Phil was thinking. What you saw was what you got."

For example, in September 1964 William Bundy, the assistant secretary of state in charge of Asian affairs, came to Seoul to encourage the Koreans to normalize relations with Japan. As Bundy went over his brief with some senior people in the embassy, Habib sat listening. Eventually, Bundy writes, "Phil said in a polite but earthy way that the script was plain lousy" and told him how it should be rewritten. Bundy, five levels above Habib in the bureaucratic pecking order, was "tremendously impressed" and took his advice.

Six months later Bundy came back to town. The war in Vietnam was heating up, and Bundy felt that Henry Cabot Lodge, the ambassador in Saigon, was "impulsive in his political judgment and needed a solid political guy" to keep him out of trouble.

"We're looking for the best political officer in the business to send as chief of the political section in Saigon," Bundy said to Habib. "How would you like to go to Saigon? You don't have to answer immediately. Go talk it over with your wife and let me know."

"Bill," Habib said, "I don't have to go talk that over with my wife. That's a decision I make. The answer is yes."

More Than We Could Chew

Between the time Habib said yes and the time he was due to arrive in Saigon in August 1965, all Saigon embassy dependants were evacuated from Vietnam, and no new ones were allowed in. So for the first time, Habib would not be able to bring his family with him. When she got the news, Marge cried for a week.

By now she and Phil had two daughters: Phyllis, born in 1952, and Susan, born in 1955. His family was important to him, and he was disappointed that they couldn't come, but there was never a question about him going. He always just expected them to understand that his work came first. They quickly learned that it also came second and third. "Philip absolutely loved the Foreign Service," says Marge. "He was so interested in what he was doing that he just couldn't wait to get to work every morning. He always came home happy because he was doing something important that he loved." Appendix A is about his passion for the Foreign Service.

Taking care of diplomacy was what he did; taking care of the family was what Marge did. That was the arrangement, and exceptions were rare. One exception had come up in 1957 when Phyllis, then five, ran away from home. Her school was giving her too much homework. "Philip went driving around like a mad thing looking for her," says Marge. Within a half hour he found her near a major road and brought her home safely. "He was dark-complected," Marge says, "but this was the only time I ever saw him absolutely white."

When Phil headed off to Saigon, Marge moved the family to Belmont, California, on the San Francisco Peninsula so the girls could go to Notre Dame High School there. Being on the West Coast also made it a little easier to meet Phil somewhere in the Pacific now and then.

In Saigon, Phil was immediately swept up in the swirl of the escalating Vietnam war. When he arrived in Vietnam in August 1965, there were about 75,000 American troops there. When he left two years later, there were over half a million. South Vietnam had been through a series of coups in the past couple of years before he arrived. "We were getting new governments every ten days," says Saigon press officer Barry Zorthian. "It was absolute political chaos and military jeopardy." As political counselor, Habib's job was to stay on top of both political and military developments in Vietnam and the political dimensions of the US war effort, advise Ambassador Lodge, and keep Washington informed.

He had about two dozen young FSOs—"Phil's boys"—including Frank Wisner, Tony Lake, John Negroponte, Peter Tarnoff, and Richard Holbrooke—sniffing around the countryside to keep him informed. When one would return from a trip to the provinces, he would grill him: What is going on? What does so-and-so say about it? Is so-and-so right or wrong? What do *you* make of the situation? What do you recommend? Why? He demanded facts, details, precision.

"Phil was gruff, profane, candid to the point of insult, and smart—oh, so smart," says an FSO who worked with him in Saigon. "He had insights into insights, which constantly astounded us mere mortals in the political section." He had no time for blowhards, yes-men, or smilers. If any of his protégés ever gave him a vague "they say blah blah blah," he would throw a pencil at him. "He was unmerciful in zeroing in on people," Lodge's secretary Eva Kim says, "but they loved him for it." Generally, any FSO or secretary who worked with Habib in one job wanted to work with him in another.

One day in October 1965 Habib was in one of his "particularly irascible moods" when an American professor walked in whom Lodge had invited to come assess the situation in Vietnam. "Professor, I'm a busy man and you don't know a goddam thing about Vietnam," Habib told him. "I'll give you a couple of my boys, you go spend two weeks flying around the country, come back, and then *maybe* I'll talk to you. In the meantime, get the hell out of my office."

The professor's name was Henry Kissinger.

A couple of weeks later, Habib did talk to him. Among the topics were Habib's views of the war. He had started out believing fully in the war effort. He always accepted the basic premise of the war and always felt that the US had embarked on it with the best of motives: helping a weak ally, South Vietnam, stave off a takeover by a communist aggressor, North Vietnam, that was supported by the Soviet Union and China. But it didn't take long for him to pragmatically come to view the price in lives and resources as unacceptably high. "He was deeply affected by the slaughter, the terrible waste of human life," says Tarnoff. Whatever the merits of the effort in the abstract, two months into his tour in Saigon "Phil basically thought we had bitten off more than we could chew," says Kissinger. He was highly critical of the US military's "blunderbuss approach" to fighting the war: its dependence on massive firepower and saturation bombing. He felt a more selective rifle-shot approach would be more effective.

Habib later summarized his views as: "The war was undertaken for noble reasons and very consistent with our view of where our policy interests lay in the world. It just went sour."

But he also recognized that his own views of the war didn't matter. As a Foreign Service officer, he was in the business of implementing policy, not deciding policy. Throughout most of the 1960s and '70s, he was always the quintessential number-two guy. His superiors were the strategists; he was the tactician, the operator. He never hesitated to argue long and loud with them behind closed doors about what the strategy or the policy *ought* to be, but neither did he ever for one minute forget whose prerogative it was to *make* the policy decision. And once they made it, he accepted it and devoted himself to figuring out the best way to make it work. In later years Habib's colleagues would routinely describe him as "the consummate professional" because he epitomized the code of a diplomat: Follow orders. Follow procedure. Go through channels. Keep your superiors informed. Give them your best analysis and honest opinions, then shut up and implement the policy decisions they make. Let them do the talking in public. Keep private disagreements private. Keep secrets secret. Keep your personal biases, politics, and preferences out of the picture. If you don't like the policy, either get over it or get out.

This professionalism earned him the confidence and surprisingly passionate devotion of his superiors. "His attention to detail was so great, and his grasp and knowledge and wisdom and judgment were so good that the people he served loved him," says journalist George McArthur. "When I use the term *love,* I mean love! I never saw so many of those guys weeping in my entire life as at his memorial service."

Mr. Vietnam

Two years after sending him to Saigon, Bill Bundy brought Phil Habib back to Washington to be one of his deputies. Though his title would be deputy assistant secretary for East Asian and Pacific affairs, in his case it meant being "Mr. Vietnam." His job was to stay on top of everything that mattered about Vietnam—politically, militarily, economically, whatever. He formed and chaired a secret informal interagency Vietnam working group that met every day at 11 A.M. in his office. The core members were himself, CIA analyst George Carver, and Major General William DePuy. All had formidable real service in Vietnam.

"We were the peons," Habib said, "but we had a tremendous influence because we followed the war every single day. I lived, ate, drank, and slept that war. And we were trusted from above. Those of us at the working level had influence on the bosses, and the bosses then influenced the president." The dramatic case in point—which two *Time* and *Newsweek* journalists called "one of history's turning points"—occurred in early 1968.

Habib was talking on the phone to the duty officer in the Saigon embassy on January 31, 1968, when a ruckus at the embassy interrupted the call. A squad of commandos had forced its way into the embassy compound and was taking it over. This was an opening shot of what turned out to be a massive surprise attack on South Vietnam by North Vietnam and its Vietcong allies. Launched on the Vietnamese lunar new year's day, called Tet, this offensive would prove to be the turning point of the war.

The press portrayed the Tet offensive as a victory for the North, while the Johnson administration portrayed it as a defeat for the North. Whichever interpretation one preferred, it was certainly widely *perceived* as a victory for the North, and its psychological effects were devastating for President Lyndon Baines Johnson's war effort. The American public had repeatedly been assured that success was just around the corner. But "Tet turned the world upside-down," says one of Habib's colleagues, Bill Shepard. "It shattered our assumptions. Before Tet, everybody believed in what we were doing and that the good guys always won. Tet changed that belief." American public support for the war—and confidence in the Johnson administration—plummeted.

Washington didn't know what to make of Tet, but was clearly spooked by it. So as soon as the offensive let up, Bundy sent Habib back to Saigon on February 21 for three days to find out first-hand what was really going on.

What he saw and heard there disturbed him deeply. The war was going badly. It had reached Saigon, and he saw devastation he had not seen when he was working there a year earlier. Square miles of the capital were totally destroyed, the embassy had been hit by rockets, streets were barricaded, injured US soldiers were all around, curfews were in effect. Worse, everything he saw and heard disabused him of his last shred of hope that the corrupt, ineffectual South Vietnamese leaders—whom he had known for years—would ever be up to the job of building a government that the people could support. Nor did he see any better leaders on the horizon. Yes, the North Vietnamese attack had been repulsed militarily, but the South Vietnamese government showed no signs of getting its own house in order in the foreseeable future. If that government could not demonstrate, as historian Douglas Brinkley puts it, "a modicum of competence," then the US was wasting an enormous amount of lives and resources with no end in sight. If the people of South Vietnam couldn't support their own government, then it made no sense to Habib for America to continue carrying the burden of what should be their own cause.

Equally troubling to him was the growing anti-war movement in the US. Regardless of the rationale for the war and regardless of who had won the battle of Tet militarily, LBJ was badly losing the battle for public support at home. Habib took it as an article of faith that "the American people, *en masse,* will usually come down on the right side of an issue." When Americans came down *en masse* against the Vietnam War, Phil Habib took that as their verdict.

For several days after he got back, his usual Falstaffian joviality was gone. His demeanor was deadly serious. The Johnson administration was desperate for good news, something to justify its war effort and to silence its critics. But Habib's trip had convinced him that the US would have to either artificially prop up the South Vietnamese government indefinitely or find a way out of this deepening rat hole. That was a report his superiors would not want to hear.

One man who did want to hear what Habib had to say was elder statesman Dean Acheson. As secretary of state under Harry Truman, Acheson had established the policy of containment of communist expansion that provided Johnson his primary rationale for fighting in Vietnam. About the time Habib was getting back from Saigon, LBJ was asking Acheson for advice about the war. Acheson, who had begun to sour on the war in December, refused to give any advice, saying that he knew only what the Joint Chiefs of Staff had been saying and that "the Joint Chiefs of Staff don't know what they're talking about." He was tired of hearing their "drivel" and would give advice only after hearing the facts from "the engine-room people." So Acheson began meeting privately in his Georgetown home with Phil Habib and the other two core members of his Vietnam working group, Carver and DePuy.

After two weeks of pumping them for hard facts and details, Acheson finally had advice for LBJ. When the two met again on March 14, Acheson said, "Mr. President, you are being led down the garden path" about progress in Vietnam. He advised Johnson to stop listening to uninformed opinion and start listening to unvarnished facts.

The Wise Men

Acheson was the dean of a group of elder statesmen dubbed the Wise Men whom LBJ had convened to advise him about the war. The group gathered March 25 to prepare for a meeting the next day with the president. In addition to the Wise Men themselves at this gathering were the new Secretary of Defense Clark Clifford, National Security Adviser Walter Rostow, and Habib's chain of command: Assistant Secretary Bill Bundy, Undersecretary of State Nicholas Katzenbach, and Secretary of State Dean Rusk.

The group had dinner in Rusk's elegant private dining room on the seventh floor of the State Department. LBJ, who happened to be in the building for a speech, stopped in briefly to shake hands all around and then returned to the White House to pick bombing targets.

After dinner, Habib, Carver, and DePuy briefed the group. "The most important briefing came from Phil Habib," Clifford wrote. In his trademark blunt, earthy Brooklyn style, Habib gave what Clifford called "a bleak but balanced picture" of the South Vietnamese government and army. His message was that "there is a new ball game in Viet-Nam. We were winning; steadily if not spectacularly. Now the other side has put in a lot of new players and scored heavily against us. We did not win a 'victory' despite the losses inflicted on the enemy. The Tet offensive was a serious setback—but the situation is far from hopeless."

He pulled no punches about the corruption and ineptitude of the South Vietnamese leaders or their low odds of pulling themselves together within any reasonable amount of time. His estimate that it might take five to seven years to achieve any real progress in Vietnam dumbfounded the group.

"Phil was extremely candid in summarizing a lot of facts that some people refused to recognize," said the most dovish of the Wise Men, former undersecretary of state George Ball. "He was the most detached briefer and did not resort to the kind of ambiguities and deliberate confusion that the military briefers had done. He had a reputation for candor and straightforwardness, and he made a deep impression on my colleagues because we recognized that this was a man speaking the truth. Habib's briefing was an enormously important contributor to the Wise Men's conclusions and what they advised the president."

When Habib finished his briefing, Defense Secretary Clifford asked, "Phil, do you think a military victory can be won?"

Habib paused a moment, then replied, "Not under present circumstances."

"What would you do if the decision was yours to make?" Clifford asked.

Another pause. "Stop the bombing and negotiate."

Habib would say near the end of his life that this was the toughest moment of his entire career, because those words in front of his chain of command could have cost him his career. His recommendation was hardly novel, but "if the Wise Men had heard the exact same thing on Walter Cronkite the night before, they probably would have been able to turn it off and go on to a second dry martini," says Peter Tarnoff. "But to get the guy to come out of the trenches and dust off his uniform and tell this kind of crowd with the doors closed an authoritative insider's opinion that cuts across the policy—that had a very dramatic effect."

When the Wise Men had last met, five months earlier, they had almost unanimously advised Johnson to ignore the critics and press on to a military victory. But now, the consensus they reached after the briefings was that, in Acheson's words, "We can no longer do the job we set out to do in the time we have left, and we must take steps to disengage" from Vietnam. When the group met with LBJ the next day, they conveyed Habib's advice to the president, with their endorsement. McGeorge Bundy—the Wise Men's spokesman and the man who as national security adviser in 1965 had convinced Johnson to start bombing North Vietnam in the first place—told LBJ that the bombing was now doing more harm than good and that he now favored a complete halt.

Johnson was angry and demanded to know "who poisoned the well? What did those damn briefers say to you?" Only ten days earlier he had stormed, "Let's get one thing clear! I'm telling you now that I am not going to stop the bombing! Now I don't want to hear any more about it. . . . Is there anybody here who doesn't understand that?" But, as Wise Man Cyrus Vance puts it, the hard facts and recommendations that Habib had presented "needed to be told, and the president needed to hear them. He heard them, and they made a profound effect on him."

LBJ, whose re-election campaign was already in gear, was scheduled to give a major speech about the war a few days later. As of the moment he heard from the Wise Men on Tuesday, March 26, the speech was a belligerent defense of the war. Over the next few days it got fundamentally rewritten. The speech he finally delivered on Sunday, March 31, was perhaps the single most important speech of his presidency. In it he offered to stop the bombing of North Vietnam and begin negotiations. He concluded with a thunderbolt that shocked even his closest advisors: that he was dropping out of the campaign for re-election.

The decisions LBJ announced on March 31 "put a ceiling on the resources the United States was henceforth willing to allocate to Vietnam," wrote Undersecretary of the Air Force Townsend Hoopes. "They applied the brakes to the war, finally bringing to a halt the open-ended escalation which had been rising with gathering momentum and heedlessness since 1965." The number of American troops in Vietnam peaked and thereafter declined, never again to return to spring 1968 levels.

To be sure, there were many other factors beyond the Wise Men's advice involved in the decisions LBJ announced on March 31, and various proposals for bombing halts had been in the air for weeks. But there is also no question that the Wise Men's advice had seriously undermined his confidence that his Vietnam policy was on the right track.

One Bogomolov Wide

When North Vietnam accepted LBJ's March 31 offer to negotiate, peace talks began in Paris. LBJ appointed two of the Wise Men, former undersecretary of state Averell Harriman and former deputy secretary of defense Cyrus Vance, to be his lead negotiators there. They wanted Phil Habib as their chief of staff.

The Paris Peace Talks opened in mid-May amid a media circus and promptly fell flat on their face. Every Thursday the North Vietnamese and the Americans would read speeches at one another and then adjourn for the week. This was clearly a waste of time, so Habib arranged and joined Vance in conducting a series of secret talks with the North Vietnamese far away from the TV cameras.

Hanging over the secret talks was the upcoming American presidential election. With Johnson out of the race, his vice president, Hubert Humphrey, was the Democratic candidate running against Republican Richard Nixon. A breakthrough in the talks before the election would help Humphrey. So Harriman and Vance, both avid Democrats, were keen to produce a breakthrough. And indeed, in October 1968, the secret talks did produce a deal: The US would completely stop bombing the North in consideration of certain understandings of military restraint by the North and the North's consent to include the South in the talks. With the war thus cooled, all parties would finally get serious about negotiating the withdrawal of both the Americans and the North Vietnamese from South Vietnam.

So far, the South Vietnamese had not been a party to the talks. But clearly they would have to sign off on this or any other deal. At about the same time the October deal was coming together, a Nixon supporter named Anna Chennault convinced South Vietnamese President Nguyen Van Thieu that a Nixon administration would serve his country's interests better than a Humphrey administration. So Thieu worked to hold up the Paris deal until after the election. He rejected the agreement, announced he would boycott the talks, and, some believe, thereby helped elect Richard Nixon.

That deal would prove to be the only tangible progress the Paris Peace Talks ever made. "I'm convinced that if Humphrey had won the election," Habib said, "the war would have been over much sooner."

After the election, the Paris Peace Talks slid into a swamp and never came out. History remembers them mostly for a seemingly endless squabble about the shape of the table at which the parties would negotiate. Habib says, "People said it took us three months to decide on the shape of the table. That's a bunch of shit. We knew from the beginning that the table was going to be round." The argument, he said, was really just North Vietnam's way of stalling until Nixon got inaugurated and sent a new set of lead negotiators. The substance of the argument, such as it was, really boiled down to a question of who, in addition to the Americans and the North Vietnamese, were parties to the talks. The North Vietnamese were anxious to include their allies the Vietcong while excluding the South Vietnamese. The Americans were equally anxious to include their allies the South while excluding the Vietcong. The number of sides to the table (two, three, four, whatever) represented the number of parties to the talks.

Vance tells how the table issue was finally settled. He and Habib came up with the idea of having two small secretarial tables like ears at opposite sides of a round table, to symbolically divide "our side" from "your side." The North agreed, but the debate then became, How wide a gap should separate the secretarial tables from the main table? The deputy chief of mission in the Soviet embassy in Paris said, "we've got a very skinny guy here in the embassy named Sergei Bogomolov. Why don't we have the gap be one Bogomolov wide?" Vance and Habib took a look at Bogomolov and, Vance says, "he was absolutely perfect. He was tiny and skinny as a rail. We said, 'That's it!' The Russian said, 'OK, I'll go sell the North Vietnamese on that. Whatever his thickness is will be the thickness of the gap.' And that's the way we finally worked out the shape of the table!"

As the months of pointless talks droned on, Habib took consolation in the knowledge that he was doing what the president wanted him to do and in the gourmet restaurants of Paris. He got terribly fat on all the fine food, progressing quickly from what he called his thin suits to his medium suits to his fat suits.

With the change of administrations in January 1969, Vance and Harriman left to make way for Nixon's appointee, Henry Cabot Lodge. Habib also wanted to leave at the changing of the guard, but Lodge and Nixon both asked him to stay as the constant. Lodge wanted to rely on him in Paris as he had earlier in Saigon, and Nixon promised him any ambassadorship he wanted. Habib couldn't say no to either. When Lodge resigned in frustration within a year, Habib became acting head of the delegation for seven months.

There were many reasons why the Paris Peace Talks went nowhere. Within the US effort, there were severe restrictions from Washington on the negotiating team's latitude and severe divisions within the US administration about how much to support their efforts. Everything the delegation said in Paris had to be approved in advance by Washington. Then there was, of course, the South's opposition to the October 1968 agreement. But on a deeper and more enduring level, the talks went nowhere because the Americans were the only party really motivated to reach an agreement. The North Vietnamese knew they could outlast the US, so they had little reason to make concessions. The South Vietnamese were the turkey at

Thanksgiving: They had nothing to gain and everything to lose in any agreement whereby US troops would go home, so they did everything they could to keep any agreement from jelling.

The glacial pace of the negotiations were a "personal agony" for Habib, says one of his protégés. He later confided to another that "it broke my heart" that the US had not fought to win the war or pursued negotiations vigorously enough. The years wasted in Paris while soldiers continued to die in the rice paddies of Vietnam pained him. But, a colleague says, "he felt he owed it to the country to do his damnedest to bring the war to an end within the policy. He worked endless hours breaking his back to find ways to make the policy successful." It was all in vain.

He was right that negotiations were what would get America out of Vietnam. But they were not the negotiations *he* was involved in. What worked were a secret set of parallel negotiations that Henry Kissinger, now Nixon's national security adviser, was conducting in Paris with senior North Vietnamese official Le Duc Tho. Once the two of them reached an agreement in January 1973, Kissinger showed the text to Habib.

"I asked him if he thought this was a fair agreement and whether we could do better," Kissinger says. Describing Habib as "my conscience," he says, "If Phil had told me it was a lousy deal, I would have tried to modify it." But Habib told Kissinger "It's a shame it has taken so long to get it, but it is as good as you could get. You ought to stick with it and really jam it through." He went with Kissinger to Saigon to sell it to the South Vietnamese. He would later say, "You have to realize, we were not going to win the war! . . . There was nothing inherently wrong with the agreement. . . . Could you get any more and still stop the war? The answer was no."

The Paris Peace Talks accomplished little, but they did serve as something of a flight simulator for Habib's later negotiations in the Middle East. He got accustomed to working with people at the highest levels on a protracted, complex, enormous issue of global importance. He got accustomed to trying to mediate irreconcilable differences, exploring for nonexistent common ground, and dealing with intransigent counterparts who were willing to talk but unwilling to compromise. He learned that the closer negotiations are to the TV lights, the lower their likelihood of success. And he learned that, if you want to solve the problem, you've got to talk to the people with the clout.

The Family Curse

By the time of Kissinger's agreement, Habib had been "reprieved" from the peace talks in Paris. In July 1968 LBJ, having gotten over his anger for Habib's briefing to the Wise Men, had offered him any ambassadorship he wanted as reward for his service in Paris. Unprepared for such an offer, Habib replied, "Thank you, Mr. President, but I'm a Foreign Service officer. I go where I'm assigned." He instantly regretted that, telling friends later "I muffed it!" When Nixon made him the same offer six months later as a reward if he would stay at the Paris talks, he was ready: He wanted to be ambassador to South Korea. On October 11, 1971, he finally got his wish.

He was delighted at the prospect of finally having other problems to worry about besides the Vietnam War. But his first major problem was personal: Not long after arriving in Seoul, he got into a minor traffic accident and started getting chest pains two or three times a day. By February 1972 the chest pains had become so bad that he got airlifted back to Walter Reed Hospital in Washington. On March 14, while waiting for preventive heart surgery, he had a severe heart attack.

He was terrified. Both of his parents and one of his brothers had died of heart attacks in their fifties. Phil was now fifty-two. "In the hospital, he could hardly talk," says colleague Marshall Green. "It was questionable whether he would live." Green's wife, a nurse, went with him to visit Habib and felt "he was at death's door." Henry Cabot Lodge visited him in the hospital and told him, "If anything happens to you, I'll put your kids through college."

But if one is going to have a heart attack, Walter Reed is a great place to have it. Habib credited his cardiologist, Dr. Mel Cheitlin, with keeping him alive long after he should have died. Since leaving college and the Army, he had let his body go completely to pot: fattening up on rich foods, considering exercise and sleeping "a waste of time," working himself till he dropped, smoking four packs of cigarettes a day. He had always thought he was too tough to get sick. But this walloped him. He took two months off to recuperate, took up golf, stopped smoking, and went on a diet. He tried to become less of a workaholic, but was soon back putting in eighteen-hour days.

The most important event of his time as ambassador to Korea came in August 1973. Opposition leader Kim Dae Jung got kidnapped in Japan. It was not too hard to figure out who was probably behind it. Korean president Park Chung Hee had dissolved parliament, declared martial law, and arrested most of his political opponents. His most prominent and feared opponent was Kim, who had called Park "an Asian version of Hitler" and come within a few points of beating him in the 1971 election. When Park declared martial law, Kim went into exile in Japan, so he had been free to continue making speeches denouncing Park's regime.

As soon as word of the kidnapping came in, Habib said, "I know how things work around here. They're going to wait twenty-four hours, and if we don't say anything Kim will be killed." He ordered his embassy staff and the American military officers to get word to their Korean counterparts immediately that, if Kim did not turn up alive pronto, it would be a "terrible setback" to US-Korea relations "and we are not going to argue with you about it." He called Donald Gregg, CIA station chief in Seoul, who quickly ascertained that the Korean intelligence agency was indeed behind the kidnapping.

Habib chose not talk to President Park about the matter directly. Why? He judged that a direct message would give Park a powerful incentive to kill Kim: If Habib told Park to produce Kim or else, and Kim then reappeared, his reappearance would be proof that Park controlled the kidnappers. If, however, Kim did not reappear, then Park could claim that his inability to produce him proved that he did not control the kidnappers. To save Kim's life, then, Habib had to let Park save face.

Kim meanwhile was aboard a Korean freighter at sea, beaten, bound with concrete blocks tied to his ankles, his eyes taped shut, and tied to a traditional Korean funeral plank. While awaiting the OK to heave him overboard, his captors told him "Don't bother to ask for water. You are going to die." Instead, an airplane flew overhead and apparently communicated to the captors that Kim was to be spared. A few days later a limousine dropped him off on a deserted street in Seoul. Habib's discreet but forceful intervention had helped save his life.

Twenty-four years later, Kim was elected president of South Korea, and in 2000 he won the Nobel Peace Prize.

Habib and Kim respected each other because each was a man of principle and values. Habib's values, if articulated, might sound corny and quaint—things like decency, integrity, playing by the rules, doing your duty, arguing rather than shooting, saying what you mean, respecting authority, letting people live their lives in peace, respecting human life. But these were what this son of immigrants learned in Brooklyn to be essential American values. They were to him as a diplomat what the profit motive is to a businessperson: his driving force, his frame of reference, his raison d'être.

Henry Kissinger, who became secretary of state a month after Kim's kidnapping, thought political morality was all well and good, but that US foreign policy must be guided not by morality but by US interests. In the case of South Korea, he believed US interests were best served by staying out of their internal human rights matters. Habib disagreed and, for one of the few times in his career, skated over the line. In January 1974 Park decreed a fifteen-year jail sentence to anyone opposing or criticizing his rule. Habib recommended that the US urge moderation on Park; Kissinger ruled the US should not get involved. "My instructions were [that] I was not to raise these issues with President Park," Habib later said. "But when a government we support is pulling out people's fingernails, we can't keep silent. The US government has to stand for *something*." So he went ahead and spoke up to Korean officials—privately, discreetly. He got away with it because "I just didn't report what I was saying back to Washington." But within a few months word of his private complaints reached Kissinger, who sent him a cable telling him to get off their backs.

Not Living in the Real World

Kissinger did not hold Habib's rare breach against him. In fact, a few months later he promoted him to assistant secretary of state for East Asian and Pacific affairs. The State Department divides the planet up into a handful of large chunks—East Asia, Latin America, Africa, and so on—and assigns day-to-day responsibility for each chunk to various assistant secretaries of state. Though he had deputies responsible for smaller areas and specific countries, heading up this bureau meant Habib soon found himself immersed again in Vietnam.

Kissinger's January 1973 agreement had given the US its opportunity to bring its soldiers home from the war. But the only thing their departure really ended was America's interest in Vietnam. The war itself between North and South continued without us. The South Vietnamese were now on their own to fend off the still-aggressive North. So Habib spent the early months of 1975 trudging up to Capitol Hill time and again trying to persuade Congress to at least help the South Vietnamese financially. But the public and thus Congress had no stomach for spending another dime on the Vietnam War.

By March 1975, there was no doubt that the South was on the verge of collapse. The game was over, and the North Vietnamese had only to walk into Saigon to complete their victory. But there were still over a thousand Americans, mostly associated with the embassy, concentrated in Saigon. Habib, in constant consultation with Kissinger, was State's point man for the non-military decisions about getting those people out safely.

As the North tightened its noose around the city, Habib started working in mid-March to reduce the risk of US hostages and fatalities by pulling out a steady stream of those Americans, as well as Vietnamese who had worked for the US. What he aimed for was not a precipitous mass evacuation of Americans from Saigon, but a steady, moderate stream that started early enough to look like business as usual.

But the ambassador in Saigon, Graham Martin, was determined to impede any evacuation. Despite the relentless approach of Northern troops toward Saigon, Martin feared that a pullout of Americans would panic the South Vietnamese. So he fought Habib at every turn. To Habib, the merits of Martin's argument were beside the point: Regardless of the effect on morale in Saigon, "the stakes were just too high to horse around" and risk all those lives. While Habib and Kissinger repeatedly ordered the pace of the evacuation accelerated, Martin kept his foot on the brake.

"Martin was not living in the real world," says one of Habib's colleagues. Other sources say Martin considered himself a "Super-Ambassador" who reported to the president, not to "mattress mice" like Phil Habib. Phil Habib didn't trust him because Martin had his own agenda.

For all his idiosyncrasies, though, Martin was in a tough spot. He had responsibility for American lives under his charge and sincerely feared that even planning an evacuation would contribute to the collapse. He worried that Vietnamese, feeling betrayed, might shoot at the evacuation planes. Moreover, his own son had been killed in Vietnam, and he could not bear to think that his son had died in vain.

Nonetheless, the situation was lost and withdrawal inevitable, says Kissinger. "There was no question that the collapse would happen," he says. "The only question was, How many risks are you willing to run to save Vietnamese civilians?" March and April turned into a contest between Habib and Martin over how many people would get evacuated how fast. Habib's special assistant John Helble says, "Martin failed to produce at the desired rate, which was widely interpreted by those of us directly involved as deliberately recalcitrant and failing to obey orders. This wasn't the first time Graham Martin had pulled that. Phil felt very strongly that Martin was absolutely defying orders from headquarters and was determined to run his own show at his own pace regardless of who signed the orders." Vainly pressing Washington to demonstrate its commitment to Saigon, not abandon it, Martin repeatedly tried to go over Habib's head to Kissinger or the National Security Council. It did no good and only worsened matters. Kissinger's position was somewhere in between Habib's and Martin's, but ultimately he had greater confidence in Habib's judgment than in Martin's.

The ambassador even came back to Washington during March in hopes of persuading Congress to hang tough with South Vietnam. "Phil and Martin really had it out over that," says protégé Frank Wisner. Martin argued that American credibility in the world was at stake and that the US could yet stem the tide. "Where do you really think we are?" Habib countered, and explained that there was simply no support in Congress or in the public for pouring any more resources into Vietnam.

"Martin wanted to stay until the embassy burned," said Gerald Ford. And he nearly did. By dragging his feet for so long, Martin wound up presiding over precisely the kind of panic that he had hoped to avoid. Frantic Americans and South Vietnamese had to scramble aboard US helicopters on the roof of the American embassy a step ahead of the conquering

North Vietnamese. Crowds pounded on the embassy gates begging to be let in. Habib, like everyone else watching those images, was appalled.

Sometime in the wee hours of April 30 Saigon time, even while the choppers were shuttling one load of desperate evacuees after another away from the embassy roof, Martin phoned Habib.

"I'm going to stay," Martin said. He thought maybe he could negotiate some kind of relationship with the conquerors.

"You are *not* going to stay!" Habib yelled. The last thing the US needed was for its ambassador to be taken prisoner. He got Kissinger on the line.

"You will go," Kissinger told Martin. "We are finished. There is nothing left for you to do there. You will go."

An hour or two later, Martin finally stepped aboard one of the last helicopters and flew away. From his chopper he could see the North Vietnamese columns entering the outskirts of the city.

For most of the past ten years, Philip Habib had lived and breathed Vietnam. Now it was all over. Kissinger commanded him to take a week off.

Habib later said the Vietnam War was "a tragic episode. Millions of people lost their lives for nothing"—not because of what the US had done, but because of what others had done. "War is always more than battles," he said. And in Vietnam "we won all the battles. But we didn't win the war."

Quemo Sabe

For a Foreign Service officer, a job as assistant secretary would be the pinnacle of a career. The next level up, undersecretary of state for political affairs, is the number three job in the State Department and the top job to which a career FSO can aspire. In May 1976 Kissinger promoted Habib to undersecretary.

At his swearing-in ceremony, Kissinger, who had once famously described himself as the "Lone Ranger" of American foreign policy, joked, "from now on, Phil, you can address me with Quemo Sabe."

The two made a remarkable team. Kissinger was the grand strategist, Habib the nuts-and-bolts tactician. They agreed about most things, certainly about the broad strokes. But Habib was the master of the fine strokes: How should we present this? Who should we tell first? How will so-and-so react? "Phil was the great practitioner of the possible," says one of his protégés. "About 95 percent of decisions are 48-52: Phil lived within that narrow band."

The first Jewish secretary of state and the first Arab-American undersecretary liked and deeply respected one another: Kissinger would later describe Habib as "one of my heroes," and Habib would later describe

Kissinger as "the only authentic genius I ever worked with."

They also fought like brothers. Both were voluble personalities, and their frequent arguments would peel paint. Neither had any shortage of ego or confidence that he was right. Kissinger would sometimes begin a meeting by announcing his decision on the question at hand, and Habib would bellow, "The secretary has no right to act without first hearing me out!" In one instance, Habib was giving his reasons why the approach Kissinger wanted to take on some issue was wrongheaded. A colleague paraphrases their exchange:

"No, Phil, I want to do it this way."

"Mr. Secretary, that's not the way to do it," Habib said, and reiterated his reasons.

"Phil, I'm going to do it this way, and that's all there is to it."

"Mr. Secretary, I'm telling you that that's a mistake."

"Shut up, Phil."

"I'll shut up, Mr. Secretary, but you're still wrong."

Habib realized how extraordinary this was. He would sometimes return from a meeting shaking his head and saying, "Can you imagine I said that to the secretary of state?"

He got away with it because Kissinger respected his command of the facts, practical judgment, and absolute discretion. Kissinger knew he would never leak anything to the press or otherwise subvert a policy with which he disagreed. Once he had said his piece, he would keep his peace: loyally implementing whatever decision the secretary or the president made. "Phil was my conscience even if he brutalized me from time to time," Kissinger said. "I might not do what he said, but I wouldn't make a move without finding out what he thought."

Kissinger's tenure ended when Jimmy Carter replaced Gerald Ford in the White House in January 1977, and in the normal course of things, Habib's would have too. The undersecretary is nominally appointed by the president, so his head typically rolls when a new administration comes in. But Carter chose as his secretary of state Cyrus Vance, with whom Habib had worked closely in the Paris Peace Talks. Vance phoned him and said, "Don't think you're going anywhere. You're going to stay right there."

He never ceased to marvel at how far he had come. Every time he got promoted, he'd say to Marge, "Not bad for a boy from Brooklyn." Once, after a meeting at the White House, he ran into one of his protégés, Richard Holbrooke, on the street. "Look at these!" he said, holding one foot in the air and pointing at it. "They cost $100. Can you believe that I could ever spend $100 for a pair of shoes?"

Their Favorite Habib Stories

Philip Habib had long since become a legend in diplomatic circles. He was widely considered what Holbrooke called "the outstanding Foreign Service officer of our time." The impact of his briefing to the Wise Men had put him on the map as a heavy hitter in Washington. Kissinger and Vance each sent him around the world to negotiate in various hot spots, and he got a reputation as the best natural-born negotiator in the business. Within the State Department bureaucracy, he was both feared and loved. He had no time for foolishness, no patience for indecision, no room for mediocrity. "He wasn't one to hold a grudge," says one colleague: "He was one to deck you."

But he was at least as renowned as a boisterous, theatrical, funny, exuberant character. FSOs at embassies around the world traded their favorite Habib stories.

For example, there was the story of the memo he wrote after escorting Vice President Nixon around New Zealand in 1953. Among the highlights: "The dairy farm was thoroughly vetted before the [Vice] Presidential visit. I disclaim any responsibility for what occurred. Cows are notoriously undisciplined when in stall. I understand that it has a slight medicinal effect on the human skin, in any case. I hereby tender my resignation from the Foreign Service." It was all a joke. The trip went smoothly.

There was the one about the political counselor in Laos coming to see him in 1967. "They tell me you've got some strong views," Habib said. "I wanna hear 'em!" So the man explained why State's policy in Laos stunk. Habib then slammed his fist on the desk, sending papers and pens flying, and roared, *"Goddammit, I agree with you!"*

There was the time a deputy assistant secretary brought him some cables to review. As Habib read through them, says the deputy, "he started screaming and ranting and raving." Another aide came running in to find out what was happening. Habib then threw the cables at him and yelled, "This is the kind of work we should have in this department!"

There was the one about his special assistant, John Helble, who had been working seven days a week for a year and a half. One evening Helble finished writing a memo and took it in for Habib to sign.

"Is it all right?" Helble asked.

"I signed it, didn't I?"

"Phil, do you realize that in eighteen months, you've never said I was doing anything right?"

"Do you think you'd still be here if you weren't?"

There was the story about him collapsing from exhaustion during a trip to Saigon in 1969. FSO Thomas Dunlop loaded him into a Jeep and headed for the nearest Army field hospital. The Army medic there couldn't make up his mind whether he could admit a civilian. So Dunlop, who had worked with Habib in Saigon two years earlier, launched into his best Habib imitation: "This man has four-star rank and knows every general in Vietnam!" he shouted at the Army medic. "He's also very bad-tempered, eats majors for breakfast, and has a memory like an elephant!" By the time Habib got into an examination room, he was smiling faintly. "Well, Dunlop," he winked, "for once in your career you got one thing right."

And then there was the farewell party when Cyrus Vance left the Paris Peace Talks in 1969. The highlight of the party was a paunchy Phil Habib performing a belly dance in red silk shorts.

The Worst Day of His Life

Whether under Vance or Kissinger, Habib's job as undersecretary was to oversee State's handling of any crisis anywhere on earth that the secretary of state was not busy actively worrying about at the moment. He routinely worked fifteen- and eighteen-hour days seven days a week and never took a day off. He'd come home exhausted, the phone would ring at 3 A.M. to tell him about some crisis somewhere in the world, and he'd say "Get a task force together in a half hour. I'll be right down."

He loved it. In fact, the greatest mystery to Phil Habib was how anyone privileged to be a Foreign Service officer could want to do anything *but* work around the clock. He often said, "If you go home at 5 and your wife is happy, you're not doing your job." His own wife was glad he loved his work, but worried about his preoccupation with it. For example, one night he and Marge were driving to a party somewhere when he drove right through a stop sign.

"Philip! What are you doing?"

"What?"

"You just drove through a stop sign!"

"I did? Oh, I was thinking about something."

A few minutes later he drove through a second stop sign. At that moment, Marge decided to sell their house ten miles from the State Department and move closer to the office. "If he's driving that way now," she said, "he's doing it every day. He's going to kill himself or someone else."

His job as undersecretary gave him his first involvement with the Middle East. He traveled with both Kissinger and Vance to the region and got to know the players in the region well. On one visit to Damascus, the Syrian foreign minister used some Arabic profanity in the course of his remarks. When the interpreter gave a cleansed rendition, Habib interrupted. "You didn't interpret that right," he said. He didn't remember much Arabic from his boyhood in Brooklyn, but he certainly remembered the Arabic profanity Fred had taught him. That earned him the foreign minister's respect.

His first trip to the Middle East with Vance was the new secretary's get-acquainted swing through the region in February 1977. A civil war was going on in Lebanon, and the security officers received a threat against the Vance party before their plane landed in Beirut. On heightened alert, the security officers trundled the party into hardened limos and raced off to the ambassador's residence at top speed.

Somewhere along the way, Habib's limo broke down. The rest of the motorcade roared right on by, leaving him stranded at the side of the road. His colleagues feared that he had been ambushed, and he feared that he was about to be. But his Lebanese driver reassured him, "Aaah, don't worry. You're Lebanese. They won't kill you: They'll make you king of Lebanon."

The next day Vance's party got to Jordan. King Hussein had just ended the mourning period for his wife, who had died in a plane crash. As the group was chatting with him in his magnificent palace just before dinner, Habib recounted his experience at the roadside, concluding with "They'll make you king of Lebanon." He then turned to King Hussein, gestured to the surrounding splendors, and said, "And you know, King, it's not such a bad job, is it?"

The Americans froze, horrified.

But the king smiled, then laughed and laughed.

The others hadn't realized that Habib and the king were already friends. They both had the same cardiologist, through whom they had met in Walter Reed Hospital after Habib's 1972 heart attack. They hit it off immediately. Their friendship would later prove helpful in resolving the siege of Beirut.

He again accompanied Vance to the Middle East in December 1977. Egyptian president Anwar Sadat had just made his historic trip to Jerusalem, a breakthrough that would lead to the Camp David peace accords between Israel and Egypt. The Americans were trying to nurse the process along. Habib's role was far behind the scenes. For example, he flew to Moscow on December 2 to try to persuade the Soviets to back off from their opposition to Sadat's initiative. From Moscow he joined Vance in a swing through the Middle East, then flew home December 15. He had been working twenty- and twenty-two-hour days the whole trip.

The next day, December 16, 1977, was the worst day of his life. He was due to meet up with Vance and others at the State Department at 7 A.M. before driving over to the White House together for breakfast with President Carter and Israeli prime minister Menachem Begin. A chauffeur-driven car was assigned to him as undersecretary, but he wouldn't hear of having a chauffeur drive him to and from work. He was outside scraping the ice off the windshield of his own car, getting ready to head in to the office, when he started getting severe pains in his chest. He barely made it to the office—it apparently never occurred to him to go back into the house. As he lay down on his office sofa, one of his protégés, Tom Miller, came in, took one look at him, and said, "You look like crap."

"Aaaaa, I'm just tired."

"I'm calling an ambulance."

"I'm OK, dammit!"

Miller called an ambulance anyway while colleague Hal Saunders called Marge to bring his medical records. Embarrassed that this development might detract from business, Habib instructed Saunders to sit in for him at the White House breakfast.

Later that day, in the Walter Reed ICU, he had a massive heart attack. The doctors restarted his heart with shock paddles. A priest gave him last rites. A few days later, his heart again stopped, and again the doctors restarted it.

He pulled through and tried to go back to work. But he simply no longer had the stamina to do a fraction of his job. A State Department doctor sat him down, stared him in the eye, and said, "You either retire or you die."

For Philip Habib, there wasn't much difference. This was a man who loved life—every rich, juicy minute of life—with a passion that few people ever muster. And the Foreign Service *was* his life. Retire? What?

His first heart attack five years earlier had terrified him. But there was no escaping this one. At the peak of his career, he had to resign as undersecretary. No more adrenaline fielding crises. No more making decisions about major world events. No more advising presidents. He was devastated. As he glumly cleaned out his office, piling books and papers into boxes, he muttered over and over, "I just can't imagine sitting around in California at some fucking university." He was near tears.

He despised retirement. He taught at Stanford University as diplomat-in-residence, but felt like a caged lion. The State Department was dealing with crises around the world without him. That hurt. The inveterate workaholic could not endure the boredom of being out of the action. He did remain technically a Foreign Service officer, and as he regained his strength Vance gave him a few small assignments in the Caribbean, Japan, Central America, and the Middle East, largely so he'd have something to do.

Despite his radically slower pace, his health remained precarious. In spring or early summer 1978 he went to Israel, but he could barely walk up three steps without having to stop and gasp for breath. During a cardiac test on a treadmill, he collapsed and had to be resuscitated. A heart bypass operation in August 1978 went fine, but two days later a blood clot apparently reached his brain and he suffered a stroke. His left side was paralyzed. After two days, though, the paralysis cleared. His cardiologist, Dr. Cheitlin, said his recovery from the stroke was "absolutely miraculous. I've never seen anything like that before."

But two years after his second heart attack, the man who had made a career of mastering the brutal facts finally had to face up to the most personally brutal fact of all: that he was not coming back. He could no longer do the work. On February 29, 1980, he formally retired from the Foreign Service, thirty years after having joined it. At age sixty, Phil Habib was washed up.

3

The War That Got Away

> Let's face it, Sharon was just waiting for an incident to
> move across that border. He had already repositioned
> a lot of troops as part of his long-standing plan of
> how to solve the Palestinian question.
> *Philip Habib*

Phil Habib was in Florida to play golf in late April 1981 when he got a phone call from his old friend General Alexander Haig. They went back twenty years together to the time Haig, then a rising star in the Pentagon, visited South Korea during Habib's first tour there. When both were posted to Vietnam in 1966 or '67 they sometimes went out for greasy hamburgers together late at night in Saigon. They worked together some during the Paris Peace Talks when Haig was Kissinger's military adviser. And Haig had spent the night in Habib's residence during a swing through Asia while Habib was ambassador to Korea.

Now Habib was a has-been and Haig had just become secretary of state for the new president, Ronald Reagan. Haig was calling about the new administration's first foreign policy crisis: A war was brewing in the Middle East, and he wanted Habib to go try to avert it. Haig had always been impressed with "the agility and the ability of the guy. He's just as bright as hell, full of energy, and able to handle tough ones."

This would be a tough one. Few assignments would seem less appropriate for a man with Phil Habib's heart condition than trying to avert a looming war in the Middle East. But Habib leaped at the chance to get back in the big leagues. He did check first with his cardiologist. Dr. Cheitlin by now knew him well enough to know that pacing the cage of retirement would do a man like this at least as much harm as the mission, so he told him to go ahead.

This crisis would turn out to be only act one of a tragedy that would play out over the next two years and would echo loud over the next twenty. Making sense of it all requires a bit of background.

How the Arena Was Created

None of the national borders in the Middle East is over a hundred years old. Most of the region was part of the vast Turkish Ottoman Empire until the end of World War One. The Turks had made the fatal mistake of siding with Germany in that war, after which the victorious French and British carved up the Turks' empire into the countries we know today. They generally drew the border lines arbitrarily, with little regard for who identified with (or hated) whom locally. So there is ample room for disputing the legitimacy of any border that one dislikes.

The French took control of the area now known as Syria and Lebanon. Most people in that area were Muslim. France, a largely Roman Catholic country, had for four-hundred years been the designated protectors of Christians within the Ottoman Empire. Now that they controlled this part of it, they were in a position to give special protection to their protégés, the local equivalent of Roman Catholics, called Maronites. The Maronites and other Christians were concentrated in an enclave in Mount Lebanon, the mountain range east of Beirut. Rather than turn the land they possessed into a single overwhelmingly Muslim nation with a tiny Christian minority, the French in 1920 partitioned it to create two new nations: Syria (mostly Muslim) and Lebanon (mostly Christian). The Christian enclave was too small to be economically viable as an independent nation, though, so the French included just enough Muslim-filled surrounding lands to leave the Christians with a slight majority. Thus was created the modern state of Lebanon.

The land within those new borders had for centuries been a patchwork of turfs ruled by rival clans divided nominally along (and within) religious lines: Maronite, Greek Orthodox, Greek Catholic, Sunni Muslim, Shi'a Muslim, Druze, and others. Those clans were not about to join hands just because some Europeans had drawn lines on a map. Nor did the Syrians accept the idea that Lebanon was really a separate nation. So, while Lebanon worked at functioning as a putative nation, it did not really jell into a strong, cohesive whole. To a significant extent, having a national government just gave the clans something else to fight for control over. And Syria never came to view Lebanon as much more than its own front yard.

Around the same time that the French were creating Lebanon, the British were creating Palestine just to the south. Over the millennia, Jews, Arabs, Turks, Romans, Christians, and others had alternated controlling that land. In 1948 immigrant Jews declared the modern state of Israel on most of it as a homeland for Jews. In the War of Independence that followed, many of the Palestinian Arabs who had been living there became refugees; of those, many settled in Lebanon and Jordan.

The emergence of the modern state of Israel and displacement of the Palestinians who had been on that land set in motion the fundamental dispute that has roiled the Middle East ever since: Who is entitled to control the land on which the state of Israel sits? And if neither Israelis nor Palestinians can control all of it, how shall they go about sharing it?

After Israel humiliated the Arab states and took control of more land in the Six Day War of 1967, the Palestine Liberation Organization, or PLO, emerged as the leader of Palestinian efforts to win back that land—all of it. Israelis of course recognized the PLO's efforts as a mortal threat to their very existence. Being weak, the PLO resorted to the weapon of the weak, terrorism, to afflict Israelis at every opportunity. The PLO is an umbrella for a wide assortment of factions. Yasir Arafat headed the largest faction. He thus became chairman of the PLO as a whole and, in Israel's eyes, the personification of terrorism.

In the late 1960s the PLO struck at Israel from both Lebanon and Jordan, but its main base of operations was Jordan. Its rocket attacks and raids inevitably drew retaliation from Israel. Jordan's King Hussein did not need such problems, so in time he forbade the PLO to use Jordanian soil to launch any more attacks on Israel. The PLO responded by trying to assassinate him and take over his country. After a bloody struggle, culminating in "Black September" 1970, he finally managed to drive them out of Jordan. Those 20,000 or so PLO fighters therefore washed up in Lebanon, the only country in the region too weak to keep them out. The PLO already had a "state within a state" in Lebanon. The influx of comrades from Jordan intensified PLO control of southern Lebanon, concentrated the PLO leadership in Beirut, and increased their presence in the rest of the country.

The Old Antagonisms

By this time the Lebanese had had fifty years to develop a working modern government. The one they developed was hobbled by structural defects, but it limped along well enough to get by. Lebanon—thanks not to the strength of its government, but to ancient traditions and the exceptional talents of its entrepreneurial people—was the crossroads of East-West commerce. Their Phoenician forebears had, after all, invented bookkeeping and money in the modern sense. The story goes that, when asked by his teacher, "How much is two and two?" a Lebanese schoolboy supposedly replied, "Am I buying or selling?" No matter how much one clan might hate their next-door neighbors, they were not going to let that interfere with making money. So, while ancient antagonisms simmered beneath the surface, the Lebanon of the 1940s, '50s, and '60s seemed like an oasis of tolerance, a "Switzerland of the Middle East." Its glamorous, vibrant capital, Beirut, was considered "the Paris of the Middle East." In the mid-'60s *Sports Illustrated* and *Reader's Digest* respectively dubbed Beirut "the new star of Mediterranean tourism" and "the world's most exciting city." Besides having more restaurants per capita than Paris, it had more banks per capita than Berne, making Beirut the leading banker to the Arab world. The American University of Beirut was the premier seat of learning in the Arab world, and its renowned hospital trained the region's leading doctors. Sophisticates, investors, smugglers, spies, sheiks, and tourists crowded the city for the shopping, the gambling, the dancing, the horse racing, the water skiing, the fine dining. Champagne glasses clinked under crystal chandeliers. All seemed well.

Seemed. The new flood of PLO fighters—on top of the influx of at least 200,000 Palestinian refugees since 1948—shattered Lebanon's fragile equilibrium. On April 13, 1975, Palestinians tried to assassinate the patriarch of the strongest Maronite clan, Pierre Gemayel. His militia retaliated against a busload of Palestinians. The tit for tat quickly mushroomed into a free-for-all civil war of everybody against everybody. All of the old antagonisms quickly bubbled back up to the surface. Party A would ally with Party B to fight Party C—until A inevitably betrayed B, at which point B and C would ally to fight A. But the core fight remained Maronite versus PLO. As far as the Maronites were concerned, Lebanon was supposed to have been the land of the Maronites, and here the newcomer PLO was ruining everything.

Beirut was really two cities. West Beirut was the generally Muslim half, East Beirut the generally Christian half. The Maronites had long dominated East Beirut. By the mid-1970s, the PLO had turned West Beirut into its headquarters. The civil war formalized that division, with a booby-trapped no-man's land called the Green Line separating East from West. At only three points along the Green Line could anyone cross—if, that is, one were willing to risk getting shot for having set foot on the wrong side of town. Bullets and rocket-propelled grenades crossed the Green Line freely and routinely.

The government, meanwhile, could only wring its hands as the country exploded in street battles, car bombings, sniping, assassinations, and massacres. The wan power of the government evaporated as the army split along religious lines. So in 1976 the helpless Lebanese president invited the Syrian military to come try to quell the anarchy. The US facilitated the arrangement. Henry Kissinger brokered an informal understanding whereby Israel assented to this Syrian mission in Lebanon as long as the Syrians came no closer to Israel than a certain "red line." The Syrians did respect that line. And by the end of 1976 their brutal methods did succeed in putting a lid on the violence.

But then they stayed. The civil war had not entirely died down, and they considered Lebanon an estranged province of Syria anyway. So they never saw any reason to go home. Indeed, they started drawing up plans to install a puppet government in Beirut. By overstaying their welcome to the point of irritation and then anger and then rage, the Syrians inspired violent designs to drive them out.

Meanwhile the PLO continued harassing Israel with rockets and terror attacks launched from southern Lebanon. In the absence of an effective Lebanese government able to restrain the PLO, the Israelis felt entitled to do that job themselves in Lebanon on their side of the red line.

The Jews in Israel and the Maronites in Lebanon had at least three things in common: a determination to survive in the midst of enemies, a mutual enemy in the PLO, and a desire to dislodge the Syrians from Lebanon. The heart of Israeli prime minister Menachem Begin, a Holocaust survivor with a romance for the righteous quest, went out to the Maronites as a persecuted minority—never mind the history of atrocities they had committed against their rivals and against one another. Begin loved the idea of Jews protecting Christians. So in December 1980 Bashir Gemayel, Pierre's most ambitious son, cemented an alliance with Israel. There was no way his family's militia, called the Phalange, could whip the Syrian army. But the Israeli Defense Forces (IDF) certainly could. Emboldened by his alliance, Bashir promptly started picking fights with the Syrians in Lebanon's Bekaa Valley.

Bashir went too far, the Syrians felt, when he started building a road to connect the Maronite heartland in Mount Lebanon with the valley's main Christian town, Zahle. The Syrians considered Zahle a strategic part of their turf, and they considered that road a serious threat: a preparation for an Israeli-supported Phalange push into their turf. In April 1981 the Syrians started helicoptering troops into position to block the progress of that road and confront Bashir's militia. On April 28 Begin vowed not to allow Syria to "perpetrate genocide in Lebanon." The same day the Israeli Cabinet voted to authorize a limited attack on the helicopters—but then kept debating the issue. As soon as the vote was taken, though, the chief of staff left the Cabinet room to issue orders to the air force. The Cabinet ministers were still arguing about whether an attack was a good idea when the chief of staff returned to report that the mission was already accomplished: Israeli jets had just shot down two of those helicopters.

The next day Syria responded by moving surface-to-air missiles near Zahle, poised to shoot down Israeli jets. Begin responded by threatening to destroy the missiles.

Informal Understanding

This was the point at which Al Haig phoned Phil Habib.

News that Habib would be coming to try to work out a settlement reached Israel on April 30, soon after the Israeli Cabinet had authorized an attack to destroy the missiles. Bad weather had scrubbed the attack. When Begin heard that an American special envoy would be coming, he suspended the attack order indefinitely.

Back in the saddle, Habib positively vibrated with a new sense of purpose. He arrived in the Middle East May 5, 1981, and immediately started putting in twenty-two-hour days zipping back and forth between Jerusalem, Damascus, Beirut, and other capitals in the region.

Neither Begin nor Syrian president Hafaz al-Assad had really intended to get into a war with each other, so both welcomed the diplomatic out that Habib represented. "For several weeks, Habib played the role of an excuse for Begin not to bomb the missile sites," says US ambassador to Israel Samuel Lewis. Begin's initial aggressiveness soon gave way to a cooler realization that he did not need the war with Syria that bombing the missiles would likely spark. "Begin clutched Habib like a life-line," Lewis says, because "after having made such a public commitment to remove the missiles, it was very tough" for Begin to back down without losing face. While both Israel and Syria continued to huff and puff, both held fire to give Habib time to piece together a settlement.

The settlement he worked out was an informal understanding that the Syrians would not fire the missiles and the Israelis would not destroy the missiles. Israeli jets could continue to fly in Lebanon, and the Syrian missiles could continue to stand still in Lebanon. The would-be war between Israel and Syria was called off.

The would-be war between Israel and the PLO was not. The PLO had continued its sporadic rocket attacks on northern Israel. In late May and then again on July 10, Israel stepped up its bombing of PLO positions in southern Lebanon. The PLO held back but finally responded with an unprecedented two-week barrage. They had hit those northern towns many times before, but never to this extent, for this long, or to this effect. Israelis realized that they had no good defense against Katyusha rockets. A Katyusha launcher is small enough to mount in the back of a truck: You just shoot off a few rockets, cover it back up with a tarp, drive away, and by the time Israeli jets arrive it's miles away hidden in a garage ready for next time. Katyushas have a range of about eight miles. The rockets can be targeted precisely, but the PLO apparently didn't bother: Hitting here and there randomly around a general area seemed to instill more terror than precise hits at any particular target. Though few shells or rockets in this barrage did appreciable damage, the "War of the Katyushas" paralyzed northern Israel with fear, sent tens of thousands of Israelis into bomb shelters or fleeing south, and stunned the government. The Israeli Air Force pounded PLO positions in Lebanon, including Palestinian sections of Beirut, even harder. The body count reached five-hundred in Lebanon, five in Israel. But still the rockets came.

So when Habib met with him on July 24, Begin was ready for a truce.

And Habib had one in his pocket. The deal he had worked out in all his shuttling was another informal understanding, this time that the Israelis and PLO would each refrain from shooting and back away from the brink. As with the Syria-Israel deal, the terms of the PLO-Israel understanding were written down, but there was no common piece of paper bearing everyone's signatures. The PLO and the Israelis each just agreed separately with Philip Habib about what would and would not happen. The War of the Katyushas stopped. Everybody breathed a huge sigh of relief.

Ten Times What Must Be Done

Well, not everybody. One of Begin's Cabinet ministers, retired general Ariel Sharon, strenuously objected to Habib's ceasefire. He was extremely dissatisfied with the way Habib's deal had left matters hanging. It did not solve the underlying problem, Sharon argued: The PLO's whole raison d'être was still to harass and ultimately destroy Israel. Agreeing to this ceasefire would prevent Israel from bombing the PLO in Lebanon without preventing the PLO from striking Jews in ways not addressed by Habib's deal.

And he was right. The deal *did* have holes. It was a stop-gap ceasefire designed to let everyone save face and thus defuse an immediate crisis, not an elegantly crafted treaty designed to satisfy anyone long term. It left the Syrian missiles in place. It left the PLO's rocket launchers in place. It left the Israeli jets free to keep flying over parts of Lebanon. It left all three parties free to build up their arsenals. All the ceasefire did, really, was to coordinate agreement from the Syrians, the PLO, and the Israelis not to shoot. But Habib felt it would be absurd to let the bombs and rockets keep falling until the underlying problems got solved—which in this case would be never. The whole idea was just to stop the killing and let tempers cool so that the diplomats could then go to work devising more stable long-term arrangements.

Sharon was particularly galled that Begin had, for all practical purposes, made a bargain with the PLO. The Israelis had insisted that neither they nor the Americans must ever talk to or reach any kind of agreement with the PLO, since that would be rewarding terrorism. Indeed, in negotiating the deal, Habib had been forbidden by US policy to talk directly with the PLO and thus had to work through Saudi intermediaries. But a deal reached indirectly was still a deal, and Sharon was anxious to bury this one.

Ariel Sharon, nicknamed Arik, was a genuine hero in Israel. Many Israelis revered him as a "living symbol of unrelenting dedication to Israel's national survival." He had fought in each of Israel's wars since 1948 and had proven himself a brilliant soldier. He came of age as one of the "generation of giants," the soldier-politicians like Moshe Dayan and Yitzhak Rabin who were heroes of Israel's first fifty years. In the 1967 war he commanded the legendary armored division that captured the Sinai. In the 1973 war he led Israel's badly outgunned armored divisions to victory, again in the Sinai, with a brilliant crossing of the Suez Canal. He earned a reputation for initiative and fearlessness.

But he also earned a reputation among Israelis who worked with him as a loose cannon, reckless, duplicitous, untrustworthy, and prone to insubordination, inordinate zeal, excessive force, and indifference to life. Many Israelis viewed him as, in one writer's words, an "ultra-hawk with tendencies toward extreme action." In time he would make a powerful—and overwhelmingly negative—impression on American diplomats. Undersecretary Lawrence Eagleburger was among the more restrained in describing Sharon as a "bull in the china shop" and a "rogue elephant" who "would hear what he wanted to hear."

After trading in his soldier's uniform for a politician's suit, Sharon joined Begin's Cabinet as minister of agriculture. That post might seem like a backwater for a retired general. But having a seat in the Cabinet gave him a forum to argue for his hardline military views and, as one writer puts it, he "routinely invoked security to justify whatever he wanted to do." A master at creating facts on the ground that others could not easily undo, Sharon engineered an aggressive program of founding Jewish settlements in the West Bank, which Israel had captured in the 1967 war and occupied ever since. Those settlements were intended to colonize land that had been Palestinian with a permanent Israeli civilian and—not coincidentally—military presence.

When Ezer Weizman resigned as Begin's defense minister in April 1980, Sharon was the prime candidate to replace him. But Begin and his advisers mistrusted Sharon's political judgment and were, as Israeli journalists Ze'ev Schiff and Ehud Ya'ari put it, "appalled by the idea of concentrating such sensitive powers in Sharon's hands." An academic commented, "Begin will do what must be done; Sharon will do ten times what must be done." Former prime minister Golda Meir had reportedly once said, "If Arik gets near the ministry of defense, I picket that office myself." So, rather than entrust the army to Sharon, Begin chose to double as defense minister himself.

But Begin's Likud Party nearly lost the June 1981 elections. Polls in the final week showed Likud trailing the Labor Party. In the last two days before the election, though, Likud gained four parliament seats that polls had predicted would go to Labor. That gave Likud a majority of one seat. Ambassador Lewis says, "Arik controlled three Likud votes—his own and two others. He threatened Begin that if he did not become Defense Minister, he and his two friends would 'take a walk' and make the Likud a minority party. That forced Begin to give Sharon the Defense Ministry."

So a week or two after Habib's July 24 ceasefire was reached, Arik Sharon finally became Israel's defense minister.

Whereas Habib had been looking beyond the ceasefire to the more stable long-term diplomatic arrangements he recognized were needed, Sharon was finally in the position to look beyond the ceasefire to the war that he felt was needed.

Only in Force

Once he got the July 24 ceasefire wrapped up, Philip Habib came home, his mission complete. That mission had made him one of the most famous diplomats in the world, but the follow-up diplomacy would be a job for others. "I am retired," he said in August. "I play golf for a living."

By fall 1981, though, the situation in Lebanon had neither worsened nor improved significantly, and Begin was anxious to have him return. Begin "had a lot of confidence in Phil," says Lewis, "because he had skillfully helped Begin get out of the box he'd gotten into over the missiles."

So he returned to the region in early December, along with his deputy, Morris Draper. Whereas Habib had spent most of his Foreign Service career dealing with Asia, Draper had spent most of his dealing with the Middle East. He had narrowly escaped from Baghdad on the day of the 1958 Iraqi coup. He had learned Arabic in Beirut in 1959. As political officer in Jordan in 1970, he had been taken hostage for a few days by George Habash's Popular Front for the Liberation of Palestine. While Kissinger was secretary of state, Draper was his special assistant for certain Middle Eastern issues. His title now was deputy assistant secretary for Near Eastern Affairs—"Mr. Lebanon."

On this December trip, Habib and Draper's most important meeting was with Sharon. Unlike Begin, Sharon was not happy to see the American diplomats back.

Ariel Sharon did not believe in diplomacy. He believed in force, and only in force. Diplomacy had accomplished little for Israel, in his view. Israel's gains in the thirty-five years since its founding had come from its armed forces kicking ass. And he saw himself as the greatest ass kicker of all. Though he made suitable noises supporting Habib's efforts, he considered Habib's plan "hopeless."

Habib's agenda was to promote a formula to strengthen the July 24 ceasefire and arrange a staged withdrawal of PLO weaponry back out of range of the border, along with some concessions by Israel. "We made our presentation and Sharon shat all over it," says Draper. "In the most sarcastic way, he said, in effect, 'You dumb Americans. You've got this little pantywaist idea to separate the PLO and Israeli forces in stages. The realities are this.'"

He then had aides bring him some maps. Pointing to West Beirut, the Beirut-Damascus Highway, and other places deep within Lebanon, Sharon outlined his analysis of the problems there. The Lebanese were scheduled to elect a new president in August 1982, eight months hence. Lebanon needed free elections to bring about a legitimate government strong enough to influence the whole country, associate with the free world, and make peace with Israel. But, Sharon postulated, no such election or government was possible as long as the PLO was entrenched from Beirut south to the border, the Syrians were entrenched between Beirut east to Zahle, and Syrian missiles were in positions to deter Israeli spy flights.

Though Habib was proud of how carefully all three parties were adhering to the ceasefire, Sharon felt the PLO had violated it already. Though Habib insisted that the Israel-PLO dimension of the ceasefire applied only to actions across the Lebanese-Israeli border and that the border had generally been quiet, Sharon regarded any terrorist attack by anyone on any Jew anywhere in the world as a violation of the ceasefire. Such attacks had occurred within Israel, in Europe, and elsewhere since July 24. Sharon felt that if the PLO "continued to violate" the ceasefire, then Israel would be free to retaliate however it saw fit. He said, "What can be done [is] a swift, fast move . . . which will cause such heavy casualties to the terrorists that they will not stay there as a political or military factor. . . . It would solve it immediately, and 15,000 armed terrorists would not be there afterwards. . . . But that is if you really want to solve the problem."

The Audacity

There was no mistaking what Sharon meant. "It was quite clear that he would go out and destroy the PLO once and for all, as he put it," says Draper. "He said, 'We're not gonna repeat what we did in '78,'" referring to Operation Litani, an invasion of Lebanon that Israel aborted midway when President Carter intervened. Gesturing over his map, Sharon made it "quite clear that he would be marching up to the outskirts of Beirut at least and that he would bring all kinds of firepower to bear. He didn't say 'go right *into* Beirut,' but he made it very clear that that's where the Palestinians were, that's where the Israelis were going to attack."

Sharon emphasized that this was all just his own opinion of what should be done and that it did not yet enjoy Cabinet approval. But he also emphasized that he was not just brainstorming on a napkin, telling Habib that "he

50

had instructed his chief of staff to be able to respond at once, if something occurred and Israel was provoked."

Habib had listened skeptically to lots of generals in Korea and Vietnam spouting their ideas for military solutions to political problems. But he was stupefied by the audacity of the one he was now hearing from Arik Sharon. The two went at it hot and heavy. "General Sharon," he sputtered, "this is the twentieth century and times have changed. You can't go around invading countries just like that, spreading destruction and killing civilians. In the end, your invasion will grow into a war with Syria, and the entire region will be engulfed in flames!"

When Sam Lewis described this meeting to the press a few years later, some Israeli officials called for Sharon's head for having revealed to the United States secret plans for a military operation that Israel's own Cabinet had not even seen. Sharon angrily called Lewis' account "a blatant lie" and denied having revealed any operational details to Habib. But operational details were beside the point. The grand sweep told Habib all he needed to know: that while the PLO and Syrians were maintaining the terms of the ceasefire agreement, Sharon was seriously planning to invade Lebanon as far as Beirut to drive the Syrians back and utterly destroy the PLO. While Sharon may or may not have said explicitly, "We will invade as far as Beirut," he didn't have to. When a general rolls out a map, points at Beirut and other areas deep within Lebanon as the locus of problems, and vows to solve those problems, it requires little imagination to understand where he envisions his troops fighting. Indeed, Habib recalled Sharon describing "a plan for a move into Lebanon to trap Palestinian forces all the way up into the Beirut area."

Why did Sharon tip his hand? Draper believes it was largely because he was "so arrogant. He didn't come to this meeting with plans to lay this out. He lost his temper and decided he would tell us a thing or two. He had nothing but contempt for the United States as a power to be reckoned with. He never disguised that. He is a very cocky guy" who had grown so used to Washington's acquiescence to just about anything Israel did, that he had "absolute disdain" for the United States, to the point of being "anti-American." The US might make obligatory protests and even impose the occasional modest sanction on Israel. But rarely did it do anything to seriously deter the Israelis from whatever they wanted to do. Draper says, "Sharon and many of the people with him didn't think the Americans amounted to anything, that we were not going to oppose anything they wanted."

Schiff and Ya'ari believe Sharon was more calculating. Six months earlier, Israel had bombed a nuclear reactor in Iraq. That was one instance when Washington did protest, delaying a military sale and complaining that the US hadn't been consulted about the strike in advance. The journal-

51

ists say Sharon was deliberately using "the drip method" with Habib: giving the US a little information now, a little more later, so that when he finally did launch his invasion he couldn't be accused of surprising Washington. Besides, Draper says, if a foreign government tells you in advance of a planned military operation, "you almost become a party to it."

West Beirut Is Your Business

Habib wasted his breath arguing with Sharon about the folly of his invasion plan. Habib was only the travelling representative of Washington. To Sharon's ears, the only American voices that mattered were Haig's and Reagan's. Habib and Draper immediately sounded the alarm to Washington about Sharon's plans, taking care not to say that Begin was involved in the plan. But Washington, preoccupied with other matters, did nothing about the warning. The 1979 Israel-Egypt peace treaty called for Israel to withdraw from the Sinai Peninsula in April 1982—four months hence—and State did not want any flap with Israel to jeopardize that withdrawal happening on schedule. Besides, Draper says, "It's hard for Washington to go blasting back at Israel, especially about an idea proposed by one madcap Cabinet minister." So Washington's response to Sharon was, as Schiff put it, "feeble."

After reporting in to State, Habib returned to private life. Over the next several months, he was mostly out of the action, but would come in now and then as required.

Sharon meanwhile pressed ahead with his plans for Lebanon. In January 1982 he flew to Lebanon to scout out the lay of the land that he expected to invade. First stop: Beirut. His host was Bashir Gemayel, the Maronite ally who had sparked the missile crisis in April. This invasion would be a partnership of the Israeli Defense Forces (IDF) and Bashir's Phalange militia. The IDF would do the large-scale heavy lifting; the Phalange would handle up-close fighting that Begin didn't want Israeli troops exposed to. Bashir took him to Beit Meri, a suburb in the hills surrounding Beirut, to show him the panoramic view of the city. Sharon pointed to the Muslim side of town, which had become the PLO's stronghold, and told Bashir, "Israel will not enter West Beirut. . . . Our presence there would cause complex political problems for us. West Beirut is your business. . . ." Though Sharon spoke with Bashir in hypotheticals—"*If* there is a war, take that hill"—there was little ambiguity that they were coordinating plans for an invasion they both knew was just a pretext away.

That evening Bashir brought Sharon home to meet his father Pierre (whose attempted assassination had sparked the civil war in 1975), and former president Camille Chamoun, who had invited in the Syrians in 1976.

The men were all keen to have the Israeli army invade Lebanon to kick out the Syrians and Palestinians for them. Chamoun pressed Sharon, "Will you really come to Beirut, as you have said? Or is all this just talk?"

"We'll get there! Don't you worry."

Hostage to the Lunatic Fringe

Sharon's invasion plans were the worst-kept secret in the Middle East. The consul general in Jerusalem reiterated to Haig in February Habib's warning that it was coming. Bashir told the American ambassador to Lebanon in the spring that it was coming. The Lebanese ambassador to the UN announced in a speech that it was coming. Journals in February started publishing a stream of articles predicting it. The Israelis moved 25,000 troops near the border, their purpose easy to infer. The PLO laid in provisions in anticipation. American news commentator John Chancellor even broadcast an eerily accurate report of the plans on NBC April 8. The only questions were when and under what pretext Sharon would launch the invasion.

As the winter and spring of 1982 proceeded, Sharon kept waiting for the PLO to hand him his pretext. They didn't. They kept busy stockpiling all the weaponry they could get their hands on—a buildup Sharon repeatedly decried as intolerable—but refrained from shooting it across the border at Israel. "There hadn't been a single incident on the Israeli-Lebanese border" since July 24, Habib said. "Not a single rocket had been fired across that border, no attacks across the border from the day I had negotiated the ceasefire in 1981."

But there had been a number of horrible terrorist incidents against Jews elsewhere in the world. For example, Israeli offices in Athens and Paris were attacked, and an Israeli embassy official was shot in Paris. Begin took the violent death of any Jew personally. As long as he had guns at his disposal, he could not abide letting those deaths go unanswered. True, he had welcomed Habib's prevention of a war the previous summer. But as the months rolled by and the list of terrorist attacks against Jews lengthened, the July 24 ceasefire came to feel more and more to Begin like a straitjacket. It did not prevent terrorists from killing Jews in Europe, but it did prevent Israel from striking back at terrorist bases in Lebanon. Begin and Sharon thus insisted that terror attacks abroad frayed the thread by which the July 24 ceasefire was hanging.

Habib considered it unreasonable for them to try to extend that agreement around the globe. "I said, 'No, that was not the understanding.' I made it very clear that it was attacks *from Lebanon into Israel* that were forbidden." The Israelis had proposed back in the summer that the ceasefire should apply to any terrorist attack on any Jew anywhere in the world, and

Habib had batted down the idea. No one deal could possibly hope to solve every aspect of Israel's security problem or protect all Jews worldwide. "We cannot afford to make ourselves hostage to the actions of the . . . lunatic fringe" of the Palestinian movement, Habib told Begin. If all it takes to jeopardize the agreement is one hothead burning a synagogue a thousand miles away, then every hothead out there will be competing for bragging rights to having sunk the deal. Attacks on Jews in France or Brazil were certainly reprehensible, but, Habib argued, they were not covered by this deal.

Five months after showing Habib his maps of Lebanon, Sharon was losing patience. "With the situation between ourselves and the terrorists now just waiting for a spark," Sharon writes, he traveled to Washington in late May "to make sure the United States understood our intentions with total clarity." His fellow general-turned-politician Al Haig would be his most important audience.

Hunting License

Al Haig was the most fervent supporter of Israel ever to serve as America's secretary of state. He insists that "I'd kick the shit out of Israel tomorrow if that was in the interest of this country," but his colleagues perceived him as an enthusiast who, in the words of one, "did not feel inclined to be critical of [the Israelis] in virtually anything they did." The main reason was Haig's Cold War ideology: Israel was America's client, Syria and the PLO were the Soviets' clients. Supporting Israel and opposing its enemies, then, struck a blow against communism. Moreover, Haig had been briefly considered a candidate for president in 1979 and would indeed mount a campaign in 1988. "There's no question but that Al Haig's presidential ambitions heavily influenced the way he looked at a lot of issues, particularly on the Middle East," says his assistant secretary for the Middle East, Nicholas Veliotes. "We made major missteps . . . because he thought it would play [well politically]." His May 25 meeting with Sharon would prove to be perhaps Haig's greatest single misstep.

There were actually two meetings: nine Americans and twelve Israelis in the secretary's conference room, then Haig and Sharon privately in Haig's office. "I wanted all of the Indians to have exposure to Sharon and his thinking," Haig says. "I put the big meeting on as theater to be sure the dwarfs all knew what we were up against." The dwarfs included Habib, Undersecretary Eagleburger, Veliotes, Ambassador Lewis, and Director of Israel and Arab-Israeli Affairs Charles Hill.

Sharon outlined his by-now familiar grievances against the PLO and complained that Syrian flights in Lebanon were interfering with Israel's latitude to fly reconnaissance and photography missions there. He blamed 250 Jewish casualties, including 25 deaths, on 170 events he considered ceasefire violations since July 24. Though the acts may have occurred in Europe or elsewhere, he claimed that many terrorist organizations around the world were tied to the PLO and that "virtually all terrorist operations originate from Beirut," the PLO's headquarters. Despite such outrages, he said, Israel had shown great restraint. But now he saw no alternative to entering Lebanon to "clean out" terrorist bases, organizations, military structures, and political headquarters. A simple military operation would solve the problem, though "it would be very hard—almost impossible—not to 'touch the Syrians'" in Lebanon. Besides freeing Israel from danger for many years, such an invasion "could turn Lebanon toward the free world and help form a new, friendly government."

Haig prefaced his response by saying he understood Israel's dilemma. He said his earlier impression from Begin was that Israel "intended a substantial, deep, long-lasting attack into Lebanon." More recently, though, he had sensed Begin leaning toward a smaller operation. Now, Sharon seemed to be envisioning the substantial plan.

Sharon denied it. "Our intention is not a large operation," he replied. "We will try to be as small and efficient as possible."

"Like a lobotomy," Haig said.

The declassified record of the meeting gives little indication that Haig viewed an invasion as anything but inevitable. His concerns were how big it would be and what spark would pass muster in international opinion. "The U.S., as an ally, cannot tell Israel not to defend its interests," Haig said, "but the perception of the world is perhaps as important as the reality. There must be a recognizable provocation. . . . We hope you will be sensitive to the need for a provocation that will be understood internationally, and any reaction must be in proportion to the provocation. We must make every effort to avoid conflict."

In ministerial-level meetings like this, the principals generally do all the talking. But Habib could not keep quiet. He reminded Sharon that he would soon be back in the region to "improve the prospects for security" diplomatically. Sharon brushed him off: "If anyone is killed tomorrow, we are in Lebanon. Israel cannot live under these threats." Habib reminded him that Begin recognized the importance that any military response be proportional to the provocation. Sharon disdainfully mentioned Haig's "clear provocation" formula and said, "How many Jews will it take to make a clear provocation?"

Habib "firmly, loudly and unambiguously opposed Sharon's agenda," writes one participant. He particularly argued his own by-now familiar point that the ceasefire did not apply to terrorist attacks against Jews in Europe.

Sharon, of course, already knew what Habib thought and hadn't come to talk to him.

After two hours, Haig took Sharon into his office for what he considered the real meeting. He did not even invite Habib to this private session "so that there could be no question that I was playing to an audience." He says he gave Sharon the same message again privately.

Sharon's response was that "No one has the right to tell Israel what decision it should take in defense of its people." Having earlier volunteered that point himself, Haig conceded it. As legitimate as the right of self-defense may be, though, conceding it in this particular context had the effect of knocking the legs out from under everything cautionary Haig had said. His message became, in effect, *We don't think you should invade Lebanon, but it's really up to you to decide that for yourself.*

Much has been made of whether or not Haig gave Sharon a "green light" to proceed with his invasion. Habib thought he did. It wasn't that he thought Haig *meant* to: It was that he knew Sharon well enough to know what Sharon walked away believing. "The thing with the Israelis is that, if you don't make your opposition unalterably clear, they will take it for acquiescence," says Draper. "If you don't tell them No! they take it for Yes." Arik Sharon in particular—whom American diplomats routinely describe as a "bully" and worse—has to be bludgeoned, not cautioned. His course was set long before he described it to Al Haig. The only message with a prayer of getting his attention at this point would have been something along the lines of *Goddammit, the United States is utterly opposed to this reckless venture and will punish Israel severely if you go ahead with it in defiance of your greatest benefactor!*

And that he did not hear. Haig clearly agreed with his basic line of argument, even if not his planned remedy. Sharon went home confident that, while Washington might make noises once he invaded, he would get away with it. And he figured that, in the unlikely event Washington decided to impose some modest penalty in response, he could have the job done before Washington could act.

As soon as the meetings broke up, Habib told Haig, "He thinks he has an OK from us to run an operation into Lebanon." Several others told him the same. They all urged Haig to send a stern follow-up letter to Begin immediately to impress upon him the depths of America's opposition. A letter did go out, but it had no punch and had no effect.

Ultimately, Sharon had come to talk, not to listen. And he certainly had not come to seek approval. He came to inform Haig first-hand of what he had in mind so that when he did invade—as he fully intended to do, whether Washington liked it or not—he could say "Washington knew all about this." Haig's two stipulations, that the provocation be internationally recognized and the retaliation proportionate, had been given to the Israelis over and over for months. Repeating them now had no more effect than they had had before. Internationally recognized? Sharon was not going to poll world leaders on how bad a provocation was. Proportionate retaliation? *Dis*proportionate retaliation was explicit Israeli military policy.

Veliotes interprets the message Sharon heard as "'Don't do it unless you have an internationally recognized pretext.' Horrible thing to say. However Haig intended it, Sharon saw it as a hunting license. Listening to this, Sharon could only conclude that he'd been told, 'Find yourself a reason and then go at it.'"

Just Stupid

Al Haig was one of Habib's two bosses. The other was Ronald Reagan. As a Foreign Service officer, Habib considered it a matter of professionalism to report to the secretary of state. But his status as a special presidential envoy gave him the right and sometimes the responsibility to deal directly with the president.

It had taken Reagan no time at all to "fall wildly in love with Phil Habib," says Veliotes. Reagan related to people more than to policies, and here was a top pro who was not a product of Harvard or Yale, a guy with rough edges who spoke directly and with a strong Brooklyn accent. Every time Reagan saw him, says Veliotes, he "started breaking out in ethnic jokes and stories. Habib was a very, very important influence on Reagan. Reagan really respected him."

The president was a simple man who thought in simple terms. He and Habib shared a simple sense of right and wrong. Reagan thought in terms of general objectives more than strategies. The advantage of his style was that Habib always knew what Reagan wanted: for him to keep people from killing one another and to get them talking. That wasn't terribly sophisticated guidance, but it was clear. It suited Habib fine: Like any skilled diplomat, his attitude was, "Tell me generally what you want me to accomplish, but don't tell me *how* to do it. That's up to me. That's why I'm a diplomat." Reagan had complete confidence in Phil Habib because he liked him and because Habib came highly recommended and seemed to know what he was doing. That was good enough for Reagan.

The disadvantage to the president's style was that he had little understanding of the problems Habib was trying to solve. He was sadly misinformed—or simply uninformed—about the facts on the ground and the political realities of the Middle East. He thought Syria's missiles in Lebanon were aimed at the heart of Israel, that the troubles of Lebanon were stirred up by the Soviets, and that the PLO was an instrument of the Soviets. He read few papers on the subject, preferring instead to have his staff discuss problems with him and give him oversimplified digests. He entertained only a handful of recommendations, stripped of all details, from which to choose. His way of having a serious meeting about the Middle East was to read aloud the talking points prepared for him by his staff on a set of 3x5 cards. Habib found Reagan immensely likeable but a man "who couldn't remember one detail from one minute to the next."

So at their first encounter in 1981, Habib set about trying to educate him about the realities of the Middle East. "Starting point in Lebanon: No one wears a white hat," says Veliotes. "It wasn't good Christians against bad guys. And *Palestinian* is not synonymous with *terrorist.*"

Habib earned Reagan's trust also because he knew how to play the bureaucracy. Reagan always had James Baker, Edwin Meese, Michael Deaver, and/or a few of his other closest advisers—"the fellas"—with him. He had known and relied heavily on them for years, and no policy had a chance unless they bought into it. So Habib made sure to include them in his educating process right from the start. By winning their confidence early on, he sealed Reagan's.

Al Haig had not taken that approach. He felt foreign policy was his business, and he "didn't want that crowd mucking around in his business—a suicidal attitude," says Veliotes. Every US administration has some amount of tension and rivalry between the State Department and the White House's National Security Council. But rarely does it reach the degree of outright acrimony it reached during Al Haig's tenure as secretary of state. Reagan concluded that Haig "didn't even want me as president to be involved in setting foreign policy—he regarded it as his turf."

Whereas Habib had gone out of his way to cultivate "the fellas" around Reagan, Haig could barely conceal his contempt for them. He railed against Baker ("that son of a bitch is the worst influence I have ever seen in the federal government"), George Bush ("saw me as a threat because he wanted to be president, and he thought *I* wanted to be president"), and above all National Security Adviser William Clark ("didn't know his ass from third base. How could he?! He never read a book on foreign policy in his life!"). Haig bitterly despised them, and they had no enthusiasm for him. He felt that they were out to do him in, and he was probably right. He had tried early on to exclude them from his dealings with the president, but Reagan knew and trusted them far more than he ever did Haig. His ploy proved suicidal when they began blocking his access to Reagan.

The legitimate policy differences between the secretary of state and the White House were obscured by the personal rancor. Al Haig had little more regard for Ronald Reagan than he had for the fellas. He says, "Reagan was *totally* isolated from reality by the White House staff. He didn't have his hands on the tiller. In my experience, he usually didn't know the facts and was not engaged, no matter how serious the problem was. His staying power was zilch." Haig's bottom-line assessment of Reagan: "He wasn't a mean man. He was just stupid."

The Spark

Reagan and Haig wanted Habib to head back to the Middle East soon after Sharon did. His goal was to at least "sanitize the border" between Israel and Lebanon. To the north, he aimed to get the PLO to pull its heavy weapons back out of range of Israel. To the south, he aimed to get Sharon to pull back the tens of thousands of troops he had been mobilizing near the border. There was nothing he could do about terrorist attacks in Europe, but that border was his baby, and he wanted to keep it quiet. Habib felt that, if he could ease tensions along the border, maybe then he could make some progress on the broader issues.

He had two stops planned on his way back to the Middle East: a foreign policy conference in England and a short vacation in the Greek Islands with his eldest daughter, Phyllis. In the thirty years since she had been born, he had taken only four vacations. But now, for three days, father and daughter would have a little time together.

The conference, held at the Ditchley estate in Oxford every year, brought together Middle East experts, current and former officials from various countries, and a handful of journalists specializing in the Middle East to discuss issues of the region. Habib was the chairman.

As the first or second paper was being read Friday evening, June 4, Habib got word that the Israeli ambassador to England, Shlomo Argov, had been shot in London. Argov had survived, but Habib knew this was serious. He turned to the colleague beside him and said, "Oh, Christ, here it goes up again! The Israelis are going to use that to get after something." He told another he was going to have to leave and told Phyllis their vacation would have to wait a bit.

The Israelis' response to the Argov shooting was to bomb over twenty-five sites around Beirut and elsewhere in Lebanon, including Palestinian refugee camps, a PLO headquarters building, and an empty sports stadium where they suspected the PLO had an ammunition dump. The attacks killed more than sixty and wounded two-hundred. The Palestinians responded with a twenty-four-hour rocket barrage on southern Lebanon and northern Israel, killing one Israeli and wounding fifteen.

The minute that first PLO rocket whistled over the border, Arik Sharon finally had his *casus belli*. The July 24 ceasefire was off. The invasion of Lebanon was on.

4

Playing on Two Ropes

When all else fails and all appears lost, call in
Phil Habib, the master of lost causes.
Thomas Barron

As soon as he heard about the Argov shooting, Philip Habib started tapping
his foot, anxious to get going. But diplomats do not ordinarily initiate their
own missions, and State had not yet called to give him instructions. The
call he finally got came not from State, but from National Security Adviser
William Clark, telling him to fly to Paris. Reagan and his party were in
Versailles, outside Paris, for an annual economic summit of the Group of
Seven industrial nations. One of Habib's colleagues, Nathaniel Howell,
happened to be at Ditchley too, so he brought him and Phyllis along.

Apparently the only person surprised to see Habib show up at Versailles
was Al Haig. Relations between Haig and the White House had been deteriorating for months, and the stresses of the summit had only made matters
worse. So nobody had bothered to tell him Habib was coming. "Bill Clark
had ordered *my* subordinate to come over and see the president, and I didn't
even know it!" Haig shouted years later, bristling with indignation. This
would not be the last snub.

Habib was immediately ushered into a meeting with Reagan. Haig was
not invited. Reagan had enough confidence in Habib's judgment that he
offered no specific instructions. "My instructions were not really very precise," Habib later said. "They were basically, 'See whether you can put an
end to or defuse this crisis. Try to prevent it from going out into major
warfare.'" Habib then met separately with Haig. The secretary hadn't even
known that the earlier meeting was happening, much less what Reagan had
said, so Habib filled him in. Haig did give him instructions. While they
talked, Reagan came in and took Habib away for a photo op. Haig fumed.

The three did eventually all sit down together, at least briefly. But Habib
was troubled. He would later say that the differences and the anger between "the Reagan triumvirate" and Haig "were evident to me in the manner in which I was getting my instructions. I was getting different kinds of
instructions from different people." At the moment, though, he didn't tell
Howell much about the problem. "Phil only alluded to it," Howell says.
"He said it was very strange, like having two different mandates. My im-

pression was that the president said, 'Go over there and get this thing settled,' and Haig said, 'Go over there.' I didn't get a full read-out, but my impression from what Phil did say was that Haig wanted him to more or less go through some motions."

Going through motions was not in Philip Habib's nature. The conflict between what Reagan wanted, what Haig wanted, and what Habib himself believed had to be done would only intensify in the following weeks. But, as a professional, Habib saluted and marched off.

Forty-Three Kilometers

Sharon's long-awaited invasion of Lebanon began at 11 A.M. Sunday, June 6, about the time Habib was arriving in Versailles. Some people welcomed the invasion, dubbed Operation Peace for Galilee. In Lebanon, the Christians and Shi'a Muslims threw rice and rosewater on Israeli soldiers to welcome them as their saviors from the hated PLO. Some members of Haig's inner circle welcomed the prospect of the Israeli Defense Forces (IDF) finally destroying the PLO. Others in Washington "were just overjoyed," not that the IDF had invaded, but that this development gave the US a great opportunity.

Habib didn't buy that. Having warned Sharon six months earlier that an invasion would be a terrible blunder and an outrage, Habib was angry that Sharon had gone ahead and launched it anyway. He considered the invasion "a fundamental mistake," "stupid," badly conceived, badly realized, unnecessary, and counterproductive.

Habib arrived in Jerusalem on Monday, June 7. At his first meeting with Begin, the prime minister assured him that he had "no tantamount designs on Lebanon." Begin said he intended only to clean out the PLO up to the Alawi River 43 kilometers (just under 27 miles) north of the Israel/Lebanon border. Since the PLO's weaponry had a range of 42.8 kilometers, that certainly sounded reasonable. (Begin's original number 43 quickly got rounded down to 40 in general use.) But Habib "didn't believe it, because I remembered Sharon's original plan as he had shown me with the maps in 1981." On the third day of the invasion, with Begin's assurances about 43 kilometers fresh in his ears, Habib reported "I do not feel confident I have a clear picture of ultimate Israeli intentions." He wrote that he was suspicious "of an Israeli-Phalange decision to link up their forces and redraw the political map of Lebanon once and for all. This is not, repeat, not, the Israeli objective as Begin reaffirmed it again tonight to me. . . . Nonetheless, we need to take into account Sharon's more grandiose scheme of putting Israeli forces alongside of [Bashir's Phalange militia] east of Beirut to force Syrian withdrawal from the Beirut area." Even if Habib succeeded in arranging a ceasefire, it would only buy him a few days of quiet in which to try to get some kind of political underpinning in place to sustain a longer-term cessation of fighting.

The IDF had built its reputation on lightning strikes, and every indication was that Begin genuinely believed this would be another quick operation. He told Habib on June 7 that his major military objectives "could be attained by tomorrow" and told the Israeli parliament, the Knesset, that the war would take forty-eight hours, would be limited to 40 kilometers, and would bring Israel peace for the next forty years. For his part, Sharon told the Cabinet a mere twenty-four hours after the invasion began that "We have achieved almost all our objectives!"

Begin's and Sharon's assertions notwithstanding, there was little reason for anyone else to believe that this would be a quick, limited strike. In the first place, there was no element of surprise. Second, the sheer number of planes, tanks, and troops rumbling across the border was far too massive for the limited purposes Begin announced. Third, the Israelis fought best with jets and tanks, but Lebanon is largely a country of rugged mountains and narrow roads: terrible terrain for tank battles. Fourth, the PLO had no intention of going down without a fight.

"I don't think Phil had any illusions that this was just going to be a quick in-and-out once it started," says Lewis. Still, he apparently did not expect the crisis to be prolonged. He had brought Phyllis along with him to Jerusalem and booked her into the King David Hotel. Worried that someone might harm the daughter of Philip Habib, he told her, "I don't want you going around the streets. It's not safe. You stay here in the hotel until I come back."

He never did come back. After two weeks, Phyllis borrowed money from Consul General Brandon Grove for a ticket and flew home.

At the US embassy in Beirut, Ambassador Robert Dillon had no doubt on day one that this was a full-scale invasion with Beirut as the objective. Despite Begin's assurances, Dillon and his staff could see that Sharon's forces were already far beyond any 40 kilometers. His report to Washington was couched in polite diplomatic language, but he says his message was that Begin's claim "was clearly a lie." Though ambassadors are always slow to order evacuations of their embassies, hoping that the next day will be better, Dillon on day two ordered all non-essential personnel and dependents to leave the country.

A Race

Regardless of whether Sharon and/or Begin really intended to hit only the PLO, there was no way the operation could be that clean. The Palestinians and the Syrians were often physically intermingled, and some Palestinian fighters were under Syrian command. So it was often impossible to hit one without incidentally hitting the other. Hitting ragtag PLO fighters was one thing. Hitting troops of the Syrian army held far greater potential consequences. Habib's overriding immediate priority was to avoid a major Israeli-Syrian fight, because that could easily escalate into a massive conflagration whether either side intended it or not. Begin and Assad said they did not want such a fight, so he had reason for optimism.

But Sharon was throwing far more equipment and troops into the effort than he would ever need to deal with just the Palestinians. Indeed, on the second day of the invasion, Sharon was confronting the Syrians more than the PLO. He was "trying to provoke a little fight with the Syrians," says Morris Draper. But the Syrian troops had not been ordered to mobilize for war so they just played defense. They tried to withdraw, but Sharon threatened to outflank them and cut off their retreat. A day later, Sharon's forces attacked Syrian positions south of Beirut well within the Syrian zone that Israel had always respected under Kissinger's 1976 Red Line agreement.

Sharon and Habib were locked in a race. Sharon's war plan hinged on speed, achieving his objectives before Habib could intervene and force him to stop. But he underestimated his enemies: The Syrians and Palestinians both mounted a surprisingly tenacious defense that slowed Sharon's forces badly. He also overestimated the capacity of Lebanon's narrow roads and bridges to carry his swarms of troops and equipment. Instead of sprinting to a brilliant victory, his tanks and trucks were running out of gas while bogged down in skirmishes and traffic jams.

Meanwhile, Habib was furiously trying to bottle the crisis. Specifically, he was trying to get Israel to stop its attacks beyond the 40-kilometer line and pull its troops back to within that zone. Once they did that, he could work out a ceasefire in place and start designing a new security arrangement to keep southern Lebanon free of threats to Israel. The operating assumption was that the ineffectual UN force already in southern Lebanon, called UNIFIL, would be replaced by a bigger and stronger peacekeeping force, perhaps of American troops, perhaps of troops from multiple countries, perhaps a beefed-up and redefined UN force. With a new, strong peacekeeping force in place to keep PLO guns out of southern Lebanon, the Israeli army would go home.

Habib and Howell dashed from one meeting to another; then Habib would go catch a few hours of sleep while Howell wrote the reports for Washington. About the time Howell would finish the cables, Habib would be waking up and ready to head off to the next meeting.

Habib was thriving, but within days the burden of what was really going on began to get to him. "He got feisty," says Howell, "but not in the good sense that he usually got feisty. He was really worried about the kind of mandate he was operating under," that is, the conflict between what Reagan wanted him to do and what Haig wanted. "You see, Phil was really on delicate ice in that the secretary had in fact blessed this [invasion] without telling anybody," says Howell. "That put Phil in a very strange situation." It didn't help that Sharon kept saying, "Well, you all knew all about this." It was hard for Sharon to disguise his glee.

The First Ugly Shock

Habib was in for three ugly shocks in the next few days. The first two would destroy his credibility with Assad. All three would shatter his own assumption that the Israelis were playing straight with him.

The first shock came on June 9. Begin had met with the opposition leaders in the Knesset the day before and promised no wider war and no contact with the Syrians. He asked Habib to go to Syria and tell Assad that Israel would not attack Syrian troops, but that Assad must pull both Syrian and PLO units out of southern Lebanon and remove his missiles from the country entirely.

Habib went to Damascus June 9 to deliver Begin's message. In the car from the Damascus airport, a Syrian official shocked him by quoting Israeli press reports, leaked by the Israeli government, that Habib was "going to get the missiles out and warn Syria." Habib was furious: "These leaks are seriously undercutting my efforts. [Getting the missiles withdrawn] will become well nigh impossible if the Israelis choose to make a public issue of them, demanding their removal or linking them to my talks in Damascus. I realize in that case the Israelis will probably decide to take them out by force."

Habib conveyed Begin's message to Assad's foreign minister in the morning. Assad himself wouldn't see him until later. Assad was a night owl who frequently met with visitors in the wee hours of the morning, when he was at his sharpest. If that put the visitor at a disadvantage, so much the better. Even for daytime meetings, Assad "is not at anybody's disposal," says Robert Paganelli, the American ambassador to Syria. "You're at *his* disposal. That was the psychology." True to form, he kept Habib waiting—and waiting, and waiting.

Assad's little game backfired on him. While Habib sat in the Damascus embassy waiting to tell Assad personally that Israel had no desire to attack Syria, Israel attacked and destroyed the most prestigious symbol of Syria's presence in Lebanon: its missiles.

It's unclear why Sharon decided that this afternoon was the moment when those missiles had to be destroyed. Most of them had been in place in the Bekaa Valley for over a year. Only the day before, Israeli jets had flown within range of the missiles, yet the Syrians did not fire them and the Israelis were "careful not to strike" them. Whatever Sharon's reasons, Begin clearly did not want to take out the missiles until he heard from Habib. While Assad was keeping Habib waiting, Begin called Lewis over and over, "obviously extremely eager" for word of what had happened in Habib's meeting with Assad. Eventually, Begin apparently decided he could wait no longer and authorized the attack.

In any case, Syria's hopelessly outclassed air force bit Sharon's bait, rising to confront the Israeli jets. The Israelis shot them out of the sky one after another after another, like skeet. The afternoon's air battles among some two-hundred jets were the biggest of modern warfare.

Meanwhile, Habib, twiddling his thumbs in the Damascus embassy, knew nothing about these events going on 30 miles away. By the time he finally was ushered in to see Assad in the late afternoon, he had spent hours listening to the roar of Syrian jets taking off. But he didn't know where they were going or why. Assad started off the meeting, as he always did, with extended banter and pleasantries. If he knew about the day's military action yet, he gave no hint of it or of being upset. Habib presented Begin's message, as he always did, with the best spin he could muster to make it as palatable to Assad as possible. Messages from the Israelis with conditions were never welcome in Damascus, but Assad took this one no worse than any other.

Only when Habib returned to the US embassy after that meeting did he learn about the missiles and the dogfights. "He was really very upset" when he heard, says Paganelli. "He felt that he'd been deceived" by the Israelis. Washington too had heard about the fighting by now and wanted Habib to arrange a ceasefire to begin at 6 o'clock the next morning. He hurriedly called the Syrian foreign ministry to explain that he had known nothing about the attacks and arrange to see Assad again to explain that to him personally and to propose the ceasefire. He cabled Washington, "I am astounded and dismayed by what happened today. The prime minister of Israel in reality sent me off on a wild goose chase."

Sharon described the day's events as the turning point of the war. They were, in several ways. Israel's action crippled Syria's air defenses and put Syria's ground forces at the mercy of Israeli aircraft. But beyond that, it convinced Assad that, as Habib put it, "the Israelis are not only out to defeat him, but to humiliate him as well, and destroy his position in Lebanon." It also cut Habib off at the knees. His protests notwithstanding, the Syrians had every reason to believe that Israel had sent him to lull them into a false sense of security to facilitate this attack. As Assad's biographer reflects the Syrian view, "Habib's mission had itself been a feint." What surer way to discredit a diplomat? "His feet were just taken out from under him," Draper says. By now "Phil was beginning to recognize that there was more than one game going on at the same time," says Howell. "As the Arabs say, *Yilaeb ala hableen:* 'They were playing on two ropes.'"

Assad was not one to show anger, but his 11:35 P.M. follow-up meeting with Habib was noticeably more tense than the earlier one. The atmosphere reflected Habib's feeling that the Israelis had deceived him, and Assad's feeling that *Habib* had deceived *him.*

Habib urged Assad to accept the ceasefire proposed to start in six hours, even if he couldn't get all the details worked out by then. Assad agreed, provided the ceasefire was accompanied by a simultaneous IDF pullback. Habib must have been amazed: Despite the heavy losses Syria had suffered that day, Assad repeatedly spoke as though he were the victor, insisting that Israel withdraw immediately to the 40-kilometer line they had announced and then, as soon as possible, withdraw entirely from Lebanon. Habib knew the odds were nil that he could persuade the Israelis to do any such thing.

Someone interrupted the meeting by handing Habib two urgent cables from State. He excused himself to go read them. He came back to emphasize to Assad, as the cables directed, that he was speaking on behalf of Reagan, who was very serious about making sure this ceasefire worked. US policy, he said, was "that Israeli forces must be withdrawn from Lebanon."

Assad of course bore in on that point. He wanted the withdrawal now, but the cables instructed Habib to be vague about what might follow the ceasefire and when. Besides, instructions or no, the best Habib could hope for was a standard ceasefire *in place,* never mind a withdrawal. So he proposed that the Syrians and Israelis both issue orders that the troops not pull their triggers. Beyond that, Habib could only reiterate that the US agreed with Assad that Israel should withdraw entirely from Lebanon. He offered Assad no suggestions that they actually would or when they might. The only assurances Habib gave Assad were that he would "be moving on further measures" toward getting an Israeli withdrawal and that "in any case, [Assad's] position will not be jeopardized by the ceasefire."

Habib was determined not to let the fiasco about the missiles divert him from his purpose of defusing the crisis. So, despite their shared anger at the Israelis and despite Habib's embarrassment, he and Assad had managed to have a productive, professional meeting with tangible progress toward a ceasefire in place. At about the same time, Lewis met with Begin to read him a letter from Reagan calling on Israel to observe the same 6 A.M. ceasefire that Habib had more or less sold to Assad.

The Meat Grinder

Reagan's letter set the stage for Habib's second ugly shock.

The time Reagan had specified for a ceasefire to begin was 6 A.M. June 10, a few hours hence. But Sharon was not yet ready to stop. He still wanted to cut the strategic Beirut-Damascus Highway so "we would be in a very strong position for the coming negotiations" and completely flank the Syrian troops in the Bekaa Valley. So, despite Reagan's appeal, he fought on past 6 A.M. and throughout the day.

While this was going on, Habib met with Begin. Habib "was pretty pissed all right" about the previous day's events, Draper says. He made no secret that he felt double-crossed, but he stopped short of directly accusing Begin of that in so many words. They talked about the ceasefire that Reagan had proposed and that Sharon was busy ignoring.

But by the end of the day's fighting, Begin and Sharon were satisfied with the situation. Sharon told his commanders that they "had achieved the war's objectives in full." Begin was now willing to offer a ceasefire.

Habib flew up to Damascus to brief Assad at 11 P.M. To Assad, Habib's news was bleak. Habib reported that Israel was willing to stop shooting, but was not yet willing to withdraw. "Israel was proposing a ceasefire in place," Habib said, but would talk about withdrawal only in conjunction with negotiations about future arrangements in Lebanon—which, Assad knew, would take forever and go nowhere.

Habib asked Assad if he was expecting or prepared for a protracted fight with Israel. Assad said he did not want to fight at all, but that if Israel forced a fight upon him, Syria would rise to the occasion. He "made it very clear," Habib wrote, "that he would continue to fight despite military reverses."

That was Habib's worst fear: a major war between Israel and Syria. He wrote that "Syrian readiness to throw its air force into the meat grinder so far is a good illustration of their capacity to sacrifice." So he started probing Assad on ways to break the impasse. One suggestion was a ceasefire to begin at an appointed time "accompanied by a limited disengagement of forces but without a clear idea of the extent of withdrawal nor of the time frame for further withdrawals. This would begin the process of withdrawal but without any clear idea in advance of how fast and how far although the ultimate objective was clear." Assad said he could agree to that.

Assad asked if the US truly supported the principles of ceasefire and withdrawal. Habib said it did, "but I had to be frank. We had not been able to get Israel's agreement concerning a ceasefire and simultaneous withdrawal. The ideas that I had just raised were an attempt to break this deadlock and to look for flexibility so as to persuade Israel to move from its position of a pure standstill ceasefire to a position where it would deal with the principle of withdrawal in a practical way." Assad said he could be flexible on procedural matters, but that the two "fundamental principles on which Syria would not compromise were a ceasefire and complete Israeli withdrawal from Lebanon."

Improbably, Assad then suggested another idea: that Israel simply leave Lebanon all at once. Habib must surely have squelched his astonishment, saying only that "if I thought I could arrange a sudden and total Israeli departure from Lebanon I would try but that this simply was not a feasible idea." Assad did not press the point.

The two men had not formulated a concrete plan for a ceasefire, nor had they really even reached a firm understanding. But Assad's "preliminary positive attitude" toward a ceasefire in place was enough for Habib to work with. As he bade Assad farewell, the president said he would always be welcome to return.

The events of the next twenty-four hours would chill that welcome and come back to haunt Philip Habib eleven months later.

The Second Ugly Shock

Habib phoned in a report to Washington and got a couple of hours of sleep. He awoke to a cable informing him that in a few hours Begin would announce a unilateral ceasefire. Habib wasn't sure what to make of that, but he didn't like the sound of it. He cabled back to Washington, "I would have preferred to reach an agreed, negotiated ceasefire, with gradual Israeli withdrawal."

He left Damascus at 8 A.M. June 11 for the short flight to Israel, satisfied that he had Assad's tentative approval for a ceasefire and curious how he might marry that with the ceasefire Begin had in mind. Sure enough, at 10:45 A.M., the Israelis said they would cease fire at noon. Assad responded by announcing his formal acceptance of the ceasefire on the condition that all Israeli forces withdraw.

Assad was operating on the assumption that Habib had sold the Israelis on the tentative understanding that he and Habib had discussed in Damascus the night before. He was wrong. He missed the point that this would be a *unilateral* ceasefire. By declaring a *unilateral* ceasefire, the Israelis were not binding themselves to any conditions that Habib or Assad might have wanted. A unilateral ceasefire could mean whatever the Israelis wanted it to mean.

And "it soon became apparent," Habib said, "that Israel's ceasefire didn't mean a thing." Sharon's forces stopped shooting but kept advancing, flanking the Syrian forces in the Bekaa Valley. The Syrians naturally interpreted that as a prelude to an attack and responded by shooting at them. The Israelis shot back, and in no time "they got into a hell of a fight," Habib said. "The Israelis clobbered the Syrians. Holy Jesus!" This was serious: The Syrians considered these units, stationed as close as 15 to 20 miles from their border, their vital first line of defense of the homeland itself. By having sat still while the IDF improved its position, the Syrians had unwittingly yielded advantageous turf at no cost to the enemy. That made this both a "horrendous defeat for Syria and a humiliation for Assad," says one American official. "The Israelis had taken him to the cleaners."

After all of Habib's precision with Assad that the Israelis were offering not a withdrawal but "a pure standstill ceasefire," the Israelis had advanced on him. Assad interpreted their "ceasefire" as a Trojan horse, and he blamed Habib. First there was the Israeli attack on June 9 while Habib was in Damascus to say Israel would not attack. Now, two days later, this. Assad knew perfectly well who had actually wronged him. But there was no point blaming Sharon, so he took the position that Habib had deceived and betrayed him, breaking a promise to force Israel to withdraw and setting him up for this humiliating defeat. Assad would never forgive that.

The Confrontation

For his part, Habib was in a towering rage. "Goddammit, I gave my word!" he roared to Washington. Normally he treated Begin with the utmost courtesy, but when he confronted Begin and Sharon about this, "he really shouted at Begin."

"What the hell is going on?" he demanded. "We had a ceasefire. Why did you move?"

"Well, they fired on us," Begin said.

"Whaddya mean, they fired on you? You moved!"

"If there's any shooting at an Israeli soldier," Begin said, suddenly furious, "the Israeli shoots back! Jews are not going to turn the other cheek!"

Sharon jumped in and said, "When you've got a ceasefire, the smart thing to do, of course, is to occupy the high ground."

"What are you talking about?!" Habib said. "A ceasefire is a ceasefire *in place!* You can't just keep rolling up the hillsides and mountains in order to get some advantage for the next go-around."

"We agreed to a ceasefire," Begin said, "but we didn't agree to a ceasefire in place."

"You're dealing with the United States of America here. Your word has to be good. What the hell are you sending me off to do these kinds of things for if you're going to play these kinds of games?"

"Show us in the president's message where it says 'in place.'"

"Do you mean to tell me that your definition of a ceasefire is that you stop firing and he stops firing, you go where you want to, and if he fires he's broken the ceasefire?"

"Show us in the president's message where it says 'in place.'"

Habib was horrified. The term *ceasefire in place* is standard diplomatic parlance, and he had been using it routinely in his negotiations with both the Israelis and the Syrians. Reagan's message, however, did not contain the words *in place,* only *ceasefire.* So, in the most literal, legalistic sense, Begin was correct. Habib refrained from asking why he was not equally punctilious about the message's demand that Israel cease fire thirty hours earlier than they did. Instead, he just shook his head and said, "Well, I think I'll turn this one over to our military attaché so it can appear in the annals of the Naval War College as a new definition of *ceasefire.*"

Habib had thought that the June 11 ceasefire would bring an end to the crisis. The only end it brought was to his and Assad's illusions. Habib's credibility plummeted with Assad, who, Howell says, was now certain "that Phil was carrying water for the Israelis." Habib too now knew he was being used. "Phil felt he'd been snookered," and he began to view Begin and Sharon with a new wariness. He saw to it from then on that all communications about ceasefires specified "in place."

The Third Ugly Shock

Israel's rolling ceasefire was only the second of three shocks in five days that showed Habib that, as Howell puts it, the Israelis "were just barreling on ahead while we were chasing moonbeams." The third came two days later.

After blowing past the forty- or forty-three-kilometer limit that Begin had originally said they would not cross, the Israelis said they would not go past the Beirut-Damascus Highway. But on June 12, Sharon's forces crossed that highway to take control of the suburbs of Beirut. One suburb was Baabda, the site of the Lebanese presidential palace and defense ministry and a quarter mile from the American ambassador's residence—all some 60 kilometers from the nearest Israeli soil. There the IDF linked up with their ally Bashir Gemayel's Phalange forces. Together, they now had Beirut surrounded, with thousands of PLO fighters and several thousand elite Syrian soldiers trapped inside.

The next day, June 13, Sharon himself showed up in Baabda. As Sharon tells the story, he was just out looking for one of his generals in the mountains when, much to his surprise, he found himself in Baabda. As another writer tells it, "Sharon, in full battle-dress, rode triumphantly, like a latter day Tamerlane, on top of an armored personnel carrier into Baabda, the hillside seat of the Lebanese presidency".

Sharon's capture of Baabda changed everything. Beirut was now under siege. The focus now shifted from fighting the Syrians to crushing the PLO in Beirut. This was a turning point in the war—not just militarily, but politically and psychologically. Israeli journalists Ze'ev Schiff and Ehud Ya'ari wrote in *Israel's Lebanon War*:

> There is no getting around the fact that the Israeli Cabinet never ordered or sanctioned the IDF's entry into Beirut. When Israeli troops and vehicles began to sweep through the streets of the Lebanese capital, they did so in express contradiction not only to what their government wanted but to what their defense minister had promised. The events of Sunday, June 13, were among the most critical of the war in Lebanon, for they proved that Ariel Sharon had led Prime Minster Begin and his Cabinet down the garden path. Most important of all, perhaps, the IDF's arrival in Beirut marked the transformation of Operation Peace for Galilee from a limited military action to protect Israeli citizens into a runaway war to conquer an Arab capital, and eventually a kind of Frankenstein monster . . . .
>
> All of Israel's governments had lived by the axiom that the capture of an Arab capital—any Arab capital—was to be stringently avoided. Yet now, in what was supposed to be a relatively limited ground operation in South Lebanon, the inconceivable seemed to be happening. Only in retrospect did the ministers realize that the penetration of Beirut, the subsequent siege, and all that followed shattered the hallowed consensus on security, raised disturbing moral issues in Israel, offended international public opinion, and altered the attitudes of formerly sympathetic governments.

The Stakes

The quick, limited border sweep that Begin originally thought he was launching had become a quaint memory. Sharon's surge to the edge of Beirut suddenly raised the stakes dramatically. Unless Philip Habib could stop him, a disaster of epic proportions—a disaster for the Lebanese, for the Palestinians, for the Israelis, for the US, for the entire Middle East—was guaranteed.

Habib faced the very real prospect of Sharon's forces and/or the Phalange wading into West Beirut for unspeakably bloody hand-to-hand combat to dig out and kill every PLO fighter they could find. Sharon's forces were superbly suited to quick air and tank battles. But they were utterly unsuited to hand-to-hand fighting in the PLO's home turf, slogging through the streets and tenements of a city honeycombed with booby-trapped PLO hiding places. "Every bit of evidence I have," Habib wrote, "suggests that the cornered Palestinians will fight unless shown an alternative."

The IDF would surely prevail—eventually—but in the meantime untold thousands of Lebanese civilians, Palestinians, and Israeli soldiers would die. According to two of Habib's US military advisers, the standard estimation tables on which American Marines base their predictions of casualties suggest that the Israelis would have to throw about 40,000 ground troops at West Beirut to achieve the 4-to-1 ratio required to dig out such well-entrenched defenders. Quite apart from the number of Lebanese and Palestinian casualties or the number of Israelis who would be captured, Israel could expect about 2,000 of its attackers to die and 6,000 to be wounded.

Habib knew that Begin did not want that. Begin was extremely pained by each Israeli casualty, and a slow, ugly street fight would cost far more Israeli lives and captives than he was willing to lose. But Habib also felt that Sharon was a loose cannon with his own agenda in Lebanon that he was determined to achieve with or without his government's prior approval. He just might be obsessed enough to do this. He had, after all, pledged to exterminate the PLO, to wipe them out once and for all. His chance had finally arrived.

How likely was Sharon to plunge in? Habib always considered it an imminent threat. "In my opinion," he said, "Sharon would not have minded going into Beirut. He wanted to get the PLO. He just wanted to get them." George Shultz says, "I don't think there was any question in anybody's mind that if the PLO were not negotiated out, the Israelis—despite their misgivings—would storm into Beirut and try to kill them. They were heavily committed." Defense Secretary Caspar Weinberger also considered house-to-house combat "very likely. It was almost certain to happen. You would have had a major bloodletting."

Along with the PLO fighters, several thousand elite Syrian troops were trapped in Beirut. Those Syrians had been ordered to fight to the last man. If they did, that in turn might spark an all-out war between Syria and Israel on the order of the 1967 and 1973 wars. Syria had lost its battles with the Israelis so far, but Assad had so far been trying to avoid a fight. If he decided to really fight wholeheartedly, he would still lose eventually, but only after a nasty, bloody war.

The immediate prospects of a bloodbath and all-out war were obviously Habib's first concern. But his second concern was the broader political and diplomatic consequences that might reverberate for years to come if, for the first time in history, Israel conquered an Arab capital. He was also worried about the implications for American interests in the rest of the Middle East. The Israelis were dropping American-made bombs from

American-made aircraft to kill Arabs. The Arabs assumed that the US had given the Israelis the green light to do this and thus blamed the US as much as Israel. An Israeli conquest of Beirut would convince some Arabs that the US had no real influence with the Israelis, so why talk to them? It would convince other Arabs in this conspiracy-minded region that the Americans had planned precisely this with Israel all along.

It would convince all Arabs that Ambassador Philip Habib was at best an impotent, irrelevant Quixote and at worst the Israelis' shill.

Academic experts on the Middle East predicted that the whole Arab world could erupt in a firestorm of anti-American violence. Draper considered it "quite possible that fanatics might attack American embassies and businesses" around the world.

The invasion also raised the prospect of the Soviet Union intervening militarily on behalf of its ally Syria. That in turn might draw in the US militarily on behalf of its ally Israel. Already in this crisis Assad had secretly flown to Moscow with an urgent appeal for protection, and Soviet leader Leonid Brezhnev had used the hot-line for the first time in the Reagan administration to threaten to intervene if the US couldn't restrain Israel. Brezhnev also put a Soviet airborne regiment in Odessa on alert. "Although the information was still being evaluated," says a National Security Council (NSC) official involved in the crisis, "it certainly appeared that Moscow was signaling that it was . . . prepared to confront the United States and stand by its allies in the face of 'American-backed' Israeli aggression."

Any hope of averting all these disasters rested squarely on the shoulders of Philip Habib. His prospects were grim.

5

We Corner Them, You Kill Them

Bashir, when he wasn't murdering people, was a
likable man. He had great boyish charm.
Robert Dillon

As the invasion became a week old, its center of gravity shifted to Beirut. So that's where Philip Habib needed to be. The first problem was how to get there.

He was in Damascus June 14 with his deputy, Morris Draper, who had finally arrived to relieve Nat Howell. They couldn't take a plane to Beirut because the Israelis had closed the Beirut airport, so Draper suggested taking a helicopter. No helicopters, Habib said. We'll drive. *Drive?!* Draper couldn't believe it. Beirut is only 60 miles from Damascus by air: They could fly there in minutes. Drive? The road from Damascus to Beirut was notoriously bad, crossed two mountain ranges, climbed to 5,000 feet, and was at that moment the scene of tank, artillery, and air bombardment. A helicopter, Draper argued, would make much more sense.

But Habib hated helicopters. He loved airplanes, loved to be on the go, but could not abide those flimsy little death traps. However risky the roads might be, he felt, a helicopter would be the worst risk of all. If they couldn't take the Beirut-Damascus Highway, he said, they would take the back roads.

Bat Out of Hell

Now, Lebanon is a land of mountains and narrow, shabby roads. So a Lebanese "back road" is something better suited to a herd of goats than to a motorcade of armored limousines. Carved into the shoulders of mountains, these unforgiving roads look down over sharp drop-offs. The American ambassador in Damascus had once driven these roads under comparable circumstances and says "it was really one of the more harrowing experiences of my life. That's a hazardous trip in peacetime and really a foolhardy one any other time. Really a very *stupid* thing to do!"

But Habib had made up his mind, and his Lebanese driver knew the back roads, so off they went. "I must have had forty or fifty armed men taking care of me," Habib said. "Armored cars, escorts, guys out in front, guys out behind—going like a bat out of hell." They promptly drove smack into a battle zone, so they made a U-turn and cut north through the mountains ringing the Bekaa Valley. Those mountains were divided up among the various factions in the Lebanese civil war, so each stretch of road was controlled by a different faction. Habib never knew who might have a roadblock set up just around the next hairpin turn or how hostile they might be. His motorcade would race through a Druze area, stop for a Druze checkpoint; race through a Phalange area, stop for a Phalange checkpoint; then through a Syrian area, and so on. Any trigger-happy teenage guard at any checkpoint could have opted to shoot up the cars. The lead cars would go up ahead to pass through each checkpoint first and make sure it was safe before letting Habib's car proceed. The cars' diplomatic license plates somehow assured the checkpoint guards, so they each let the motorcade pass.

Habib also never knew whether a battle might be raging just around the next blind curve. There had been fighting in these mountains six hours earlier, and Israeli jets crisscrossed the skies the whole time Habib drove. He passed the carcass of a Syrian tank. But for the moment there was a lull. His motorcade managed to steer clear of any active combat, but the narrow mountain roads themselves—and the breakneck speeds at which his driver flew over them—were dangerous enough. Habib's driver was going so fast that when they started getting to the suburbs of Beirut he smashed a couple of slower cars. Even roaring along at high speeds, the trip took seven or eight hours.

Cat Fight

Habib's drive through the patchwork of mountain fiefdoms was a graphic reminder that Sharon's invasion had only interrupted the Lebanese civil war, not ended it. In six years that civil war had reduced the Lebanese government to irrelevance. "Lebanese government" was in fact widely ridiculed as an oxymoron. The government barely controlled the presidential palace, much less the capital or the country. But Habib respected President Elias Sarkis and Prime Minister Shafik al-Wazzan as decent, honorable men doing their best to hold together the last shreds of Lebanese integrity. When he arrived in Beirut, he found Sarkis deeply shaken by the siege. "My capital is in flames," he cried to Habib. "My fellow citizens are killed. It is almost no longer a question of politics; it is a question of life or death!"

The only Lebanese with any real clout were the squabbling warlords. So one of Habib's first goals in Beirut was to get them to stop fighting one another long enough to deal cooperatively with the Israeli invasion.

The Lebanese factions that he hoped to bring together set the standard by which political chaos is measured. While nominally divided along religious lines, they were just as much political, financial, military, territorial, and familial rivals. Their anarchy had created the vacuum that had sucked

75

in the PLO, the Syrians, and now the Israelis. To get those foreign forces out of Lebanon, Habib needed to do something about the anarchy that had let them in. He had no illusions about settling the warlords' stubborn and complex differences. But he did hope they could at least go back to coexisting as they had before the civil war began in 1975. Meantime, he would settle for persuading the main ones to cooperate in a temporary alliance of convenience to support his efforts to stop the war. He and Sarkis invited them to a meeting at the presidential palace.

The two most important factional leaders invited were Bashir Gemayel and Walid Jumblatt. Each had taken over leadership of their respective factions—Bashir the Maronites, and Walid the Druze—from their fathers. The two had not met face to face in six years, but Habib felt that, if the Lebanese were ever going to jell into a coherent nation, Bashir and Walid were the two men with the clout and the potential to lead them there. Habib was fond of both of them. Both were in their early thirties, and the sixty-two-year-old Habib looked on both of them almost like sons. The two despised one another.

More to the point, Walid was afraid that if he showed his face, Bashir's thugs would assassinate him. So Habib got assurances from Bashir not to kill Walid, at least not now. He then sent the embassy's political officer, Ryan Crocker, to fetch Walid from his castle in the mountains.

This was to be the first meeting of the "National Salvation Council." Habib had coached Bashir ahead of time—"Look, if we get these people together, I don't want you to insult them" and Bashir said "Oh, yes"—but it quickly dissolved into a shouting match between Bashir and Walid. "Bashir was at his most arrogant," says Draper. He was, after all, the Israelis' ally who had invited them to invade in the first place and had asked them a few days earlier to stay around Beirut until they could get him elected president of Lebanon. So he had no interest in helping get them out. He and Walid just shouted accusations back and forth and argued about changing the constitution and about whether Bashir should be the next president and about whatever else came to mind. They nearly went at each other with fists. "It was just murderous," says Draper. "Had there been any Palestinians in the room, I think Bashir would have cut their throats. It was just awful."

Habib jumped in and started yelling at the two to knock it off, throwing in all the theatrics he could muster. They paid no attention. He cursed them both with an extremely ugly, graphic insult in fractured French in an attempt to divert them from one another. It didn't help. "They were behaving like school children," Draper says. Finally Habib cursed them again and bellowed, "You're all a bunch of goddam, miserable Lebanese who can't get together even to save your country!" and stomped out. He hoped they would beg him to come back. They did not.

After the cat fight finally broke up, Habib had Crocker trundle Walid Jumblatt into his car to spirit him back home safely.

The Two Choices

Habib was not the only one cursing Bashir Gemayel. Sharon's Lebanon strategy had hinged on Bashir's pledge, "Leave Beirut to me," and Bashir was reneging on that pledge.

Sharon and Bashir's understanding was that, once Israeli troops reached Beirut, they would link up with Bashir's militia to surround it. Bashir's militia, the Phalange, would then do the dirty work of going door to door in Muslim West Beirut slaughtering Palestinians until the PLO fled Lebanon like rats from a burning house. This division of responsibility had been intrinsic to the plan all along: Begin, after all, did not want to risk his own boys in hand-to-hand combat. The link-up did happen, at Baabda June 12, and Sharon and Bashir did have the PLO and several thousand Syrian troops trapped in West Beirut.

But now Bashir refused to do his part. "Sharon knows he has the PLO on the ropes," Habib said, "but he prefers to have someone else finish them off. I doubt that he would want to risk the Israeli casualties involved in house-to-house fighting. But I cannot rule it out." Sharon was incredulous when he met with Bashir June 11, the day before their forces linked up. "We'll soon be here with tanks," he exploded at Bashir. "Do something!" Time and again Begin and Sharon cajoled and threatened Bashir to do their dirty work; time and again he danced away from them.

His refusal was in no small measure because Habib and Dillon had repeatedly warned him that, if he was going to remain allied with Israel, he must "be very, very careful. Remember, they are not interested in *your* welfare. They are only interested in their own welfare. There can't be a simply Christian Lebanon. That is not realistic. If you're going to be president of Lebanon, you've got to be president of *all* of Lebanon. You can't be president of just the Christian half. You've got to reach out to the Muslims."

Bashir's refusal to finish off the PLO left the Israelis with two choices, write Schiff and Ya'ari: "to let Philip Habib negotiate a withdrawal of the Palestinian forces or to force their way into West Beirut and clean it out themselves."

The Israelis did not want either. But Sharon, who "detest[ed] improvisation," had apparently not anticipated Bashir's nonperformance. So he tightened their siege of West Beirut, dug in for the long haul, and began bombing and shelling the bloody hell out of the city in hopes that the PLO would eventually give up. Some observers interpret the flailing siege as a manifestation of his not knowing what else to do.

The Grand Plan

In many people's view, this was not Israel's war. It was not the Jews' war. It was Ariel Sharon's war, his obsession, his blunder. Menachem Begin may have been the prime minister, but Sharon was the prime mover. "You can't really rely on anything Sharon says," said Habib. "He has his own agenda that doesn't necessarily coincide with the agenda of the Israeli government, but he seems to be able to pursue that without any problem."

As an Israeli court would later conclude, Sharon was a rogue who ran his war his way by misleading and withholding information from his own government. Sharon's war, the court held, vastly exceeded the modest operation that his government had authorized. His purpose was to reconfigure the politics of the Middle East to Israel's liking not by political or diplomatic suasion but by force. He would create military facts on the ground that no soft-palmed politician or diplomat—Israeli or American—would be able to undo.

Philip Habib's singular purpose was to stop him.

Sharon's plan was to drive the PLO and Syrians out of Lebanon, destroy the PLO as an organization, get a pliant Bashir Gemayel installed as president of Lebanon, and have Bashir sign a peace treaty with Israel. "The full Sharon scheme," Habib wrote, entailed Lebanon being "for all practical purposes, politically controlled by Israel."

The Lebanon problem thus solved, Israel would then annex the West Bank and Gaza, conquer Jordan, and transform Jordan into *the* Palestinian state to which all the Palestinians could move. The whole Middle East would then live in peace.

Sharon expected a spectacular victory that would realign the politics of the Middle East for years, maybe decades to come. He expected that he would then be swept into office as prime minister and into history as a legend. He made no secret of his ambitions. "Tell me," he would ask friends, "how can I become Prime Minister? How can I get rid of Begin?" His invasion of Lebanon was to be the masterstroke to set his grand plan into motion.

Any diplomatic settlement would rob him of his triumph.

Sharon's basic gameplan was thus to achieve his military objectives fast before the US, in the person of Philip Habib, could intervene and force him to stop. He wrote that he considered Habib's diplomacy "only a means of delay. Since there was no movement to be expected on that front, we had to take action."

Though Habib represented the United States, Sharon may have seen him as a greater obstacle than Washington itself. He had grown accustomed to American acquiescence. He knew Haig was too supportive of his efforts to stand in his way, and he knew Reagan wasn't paying enough attention to put his foot down.

But Phil Habib was different: He did object. And he made lots of noise. And Reagan listened to him. So, from the defense minister's very first meetings with Habib, *The Jerusalem Post* said, "Sharon appeared to have 'something against the man,' an attitude which fitted in with what seemed like Sharon's gut-distrust of the American role as a whole."

The feeling was mutual. "Philip hated Arik Sharon with a deep, dark passion," says Marjorie Habib. "It wasn't like him to hate anyone, but Sharon—oh, boy." He said that "what Sharon was doing in Beirut was absolutely brutal. He was doing it absolutely cold-bloodedly. He would fire the goddammed artillery and bomb West Beirut while I would be up on the hill [at Dillon's residence] watching it, horrified at what was going on."

Sharon's physical presence graphically reinforced his attitude of intimidation. "He had no concept of his own space," says one State Department official who was with Sharon often. "He'd bounce into you. He'd literally bowl you over. He'd get up six inches from your face to talk to you. He used that as a tactic to bull his way into getting what he wanted." And, as Bashir put it, "What Arik wants, Arik gets."

Not that Sharon was devoid of social graces. He owned the largest ranch in Israel and often showed visiting dignitaries around it "so that he could be seen in his country squire mode." says Sam Lewis. "He used to butter people up that way and exercise his quite formidable wiles. He could be very engaging."

On one such visit to his ranch, Sharon told Habib that, when he was a boy, his mother had taught him "never to trust the goddam Arabs." He absorbed the lesson deeply. Throughout the siege, Sharon's unshakable blanket refusal to believe anything the PLO said would undermine nearly every step of diplomatic progress Habib felt he had made. Describing Sharon as "the biggest liar this side of the Mediterranean" and a man whose "word was worth nothing," Habib could only shake his head at the irony.

A Pattern Emerges

Sharon's peculiar way of conducting his war—and his contempt for Phil Habib's efforts to moderate him—became apparent early on. One episode was emblematic of both. It began when Sharon's troops took over Baabda, the seat of the presidential palace on the outskirts of Beirut. On June 14 US ambassador Robert Dillon, whose residence was in the suburb Yarze, a stone's throw away from the palace, reported twenty Israeli tanks around his own garden and over a hundred ringing the area of the palace.

"Phil went ballistic," says Nat Howell. "He felt very strongly that, when you surround the president—even when he's only the symbol of a basket case of a country—and have your tanks pointed at him, you've really gone beyond the pale." Habib started scorching the phone lines. He called some key Israelis and shouted, "What the hell are you doing? You told me you weren't going to do this, and now you're all around the president's house! That's an independent country! In effect, you've taken the president of an independent country prisoner!"

Begin denied that Israeli tanks were near Baabda and said he didn't "understand its significance" anyway.

Even while many Israeli soldiers were openly driving through the streets of East Beirut, sightseeing and shopping, Begin continued to deny that the IDF was in Beirut at all. When Begin met with Habib on June 14, he insisted that the IDF was not going to Beirut. "Your tanks are *already* in Ba'abda!" Habib sputtered. "Our ambassador in Beirut has already reported the presence of Israeli tanks next to the presidential palace!"

Begin still didn't see what the fuss was about, but he got Sharon on the phone and handed it to Habib. For fifteen minutes Habib explained why Sharon must get the IDF away from Baabda: Its presence was a form of intimidation, it undermined the authority and independence of President Elias Sarkis as head of a sovereign nation, and it prevented Lebanese leaders from conducting the nation's business. Besides, Habib himself was on his way there and he didn't want the embarrassment of having to walk through a ring of Israeli tanks. The tanks and troops, he told Sharon, must get away from the seat of government. Sharon grudgingly allowed as how he would "send them further east."

Within a few hours he did move the tanks—to around Ambassador Dillon's residence, which is east of the palace. The Americans of course protested. *Well,* Sharon explained, *Habib wanted them moved away from the presidential palace.* In response to the protests he said he was giving orders immediately to have the tanks removed. But they stayed. On June 18 a tank left Lebanese army commander Victor Khouri's cabbage patch in Baabda—only to have four more come back to his house the same day. On June 24, thirty-five Israeli soldiers showed up at the palace and had the nerve to ask to establish an observation post there. On July 5—three weeks after Sharon said he'd have the equipment moved—there were still IDF emplacements and high visibility IDF patrols in the palace area that Habib had to drive through to reach the palace. Sharon again promised to "see what he could do." On July 8 there were still tanks and two self-propelled 155 mm guns at the edge of the palace boundary.

This way of doing business would prove to be Sharon's standard operating procedure throughout the siege.

Losing Sleep

Two things are certain: that Ariel Sharon and Menachem Begin were partners in this enterprise, and that Sharon was the leading partner. While Begin and his Cabinet occasionally tapped the brakes, it was Sharon's foot on the accelerator, his hands on the wheel.

Sharon and Begin made a fascinating team. However cynical Sharon may have been, Menachem Begin proceeded from an authentic idealism. One of his foremost characteristics was his deeply felt anguish over the suffering of Jews. One morning, for example, Begin arrived at a meeting with Habib visibly shaken. He told Habib about a Swiss film he had just seen about the Holocaust. One scene showed a young boy wearing a yellow Star of David on his chest. "I can't get that little boy out of my sight," Begin said. Suddenly his eyes brimmed over and he began to weep. For two or three entire minutes, tears streamed down the prime minister's face. Habib and the others at the table sat frozen. Nothing like this had ever happened before. Habib said nothing. In time, Begin recovered his composure, and he and Habib returned to the business at hand as though nothing had happened.

Begin's idealism took a beating in this war. The prospect of ending Jewish suffering at the hands of the hated PLO was his prime motivation for having launched it. But the number of IDF soldiers coming home in coffins was much higher than he had expected. Neither he nor Sharon greatly cared how many Arabs died, but each loss of an Israeli soldier pained Begin personally. "Begin couldn't stand Israelis dying," says Draper. "He lost sleep over every Israeli boy who died, over every Israeli who was wounded. It just preyed on him."

Begin's heartfelt aversion to Jewish casualties gave Habib something to work with. He would never be so clumsy as to wave it in Begin's face overtly. Rather, he led Begin to draw his own conclusions. Elliptically and tenderly, he might sometimes say, "I know the agony you're going through with all these young men dying" or "I know, Mr. Prime Minister, how every man who falls in battle causes you deep concern; you're not indifferent to those things." While such comments were calculated, they were also genuinely sympathetic. Habib shared Begin's heartbreak over the deaths and suffering of Jews. But, unlike Begin, Habib also felt the same heartbreak over the deaths and suffering of Arabs.

The Perfect Partner

In Menachem Begin, Sharon found the perfect partner. Begin liked to fancy himself a great military expert. But in fact, says a leading Israeli politician, Begin "didn't know *anything* about military affairs. He was a man of dreams and imagination, a believer, but never a pragmatist." He was more taken with the righteousness of the moral quest than with hard, inconvenient realities that might render his quest ill-advised. Lacking any military savvy of his own, Begin was enamored of those who had it. And Arik Sharon radiated it.

In Israel's earlier wars, Sharon was never the *top* military decision-maker. Now he was, and this time there were no Moshe Dayans around to point him in the right direction or overrule his more dubious ideas. One of his generals said, "Sharon was my battalion commander [in the 1950s]. I believe that at that time he was a military genius as a field commander. But not in the 1980s. . . . In the war in Lebanon, purely militarily, he was not good. I was the deputy commander of the northern command during this war, so I was very close to him. Every day I saw the way he reacted, and I made a note to myself that he was no longer first-class. He was ready to listen only to the people who thought the way he did." No one else in Begin's cabinet had a military background, and Sharon had forbidden his subordinates to advise Begin. Thus the prime minister's sole source of information and advice about military affairs was, by default, Arik Sharon.

He had sold Begin on the prospect of a quick, easy operation. As it turned out to be a slow, aimless quagmire, Sharon strung him and the Cabinet along one move at a time. "Sharon's preferred method of dealing with Begin," write Schiff and Ya'ari, "was to approach him at the veritable eleventh hour, convince him—almost breathlessly—that the men in the field were in mortal danger, and elicit his support for whatever move would presumably counteract the threat hovering over them." What else could Begin and the Cabinet do but bless his faits accomplis? The Israeli parliament never took a vote on the war. Even the Cabinet never held a proper discussion of the objectives of the campaign, being asked by Begin and Sharon to approve only a single chess move at a time.

Prodding the Alligator

Phil Habib and Sharon met their matches in each other. They were two pit bulls who had each gone toe-to-toe with the meanest SOBs in the business, and neither was about to let anybody push him around. Habib would sometimes tell stories about Sharon's attempts to intimidate him. The stories always ended with "But I can hold my own with that son of a bitch."

Sharon brought out "the submerged alley fighter" in Habib, and the two tangled almost every time they met. The first time they met after the invasion began, Sharon blamed the invasion in part on Habib. Sharon talked to him as if he were the enemy. After one particularly nasty shouting match with Sharon, Habib got overexcited and felt his heart acting up. A cardiologist had to be called in. Other times Sharon would behave in a reasonable, mild way and agree with what Habib wanted. He would then issue orders to do the opposite.

Sharon recognized that Habib carried Reagan's imprimatur, but he ridiculed Habib behind his back as someone who didn't understand the situation, didn't understand the Arabs, didn't understand the Lebanese. Sharon was nearly as blunt to his face. He was prone to blustering and lecturing him, usually implying American weakness and American inability to understand the Arabs. If Begin was in the room, Habib would pointedly address himself to the prime minister. Sharon might say something to Habib or ask him a question, and Habib would give his response to Begin. This was partly Habib's way of avoiding a fruitless direct argument with Sharon. It was partly his way of honoring Begin as the prime minister. And it was partly his way of tacitly encouraging Begin to take the control that Sharon so readily grabbed.

Playing to Begin instead of Sharon wasn't always possible. If Sharon was beating up on him, says Lewis, "Phil would sit and take it for a while, but then he would ultimately respond in pretty tough ways. He never let himself get out of control, but he didn't take a lot of crap either without reacting." Sharon never ceased prodding the alligator, but he did learn to use a long stick.

Whatever modicum of respect Sharon had for Habib did not extend to Morrie Draper. Whenever Draper came to see him alone, Sharon was "really nasty to Morrie and treated him as kind of a weak-kneed diplomatic bag carrier."

Draper tells of one particularly chilling moment. It was during a secret meeting with Sharon early in the war. Habib had brought Draper, and Sharon had brought along about twenty muddy, grimy IDF soldiers wearing combat gear. They had just come from a battle and were sprawled around the room, exhausted. Habib said to Sharon, "Arik, look around this place. You and I are the two oldest guys here, and all your men are falling asleep. You and I are the only ones really wide awake. And here, Morrie Draper, he's getting tired."

"Yeah, Mr. Draper," Sharon replied dryly. "We'd like to see him go to sleep for a long, *long* time." Draper knew that Sharon "really hated my guts," but this was the first time he came to believe that Sharon wished him dead.

6
The Other General

Phil disagreed with Haig almost every step of the way.
He never knew that he could trust Haig. They
could not have been more estranged.
Nicholas Veliotes

Arik Sharon was only one of the two generals who made Habib's mission particularly exasperating. The other was his own boss, retired general and now Secretary of State Al Haig, who wanted to let the war proceed. The two generals agreed more with each other than either did with Habib. The story of Habib and Haig during the siege of Beirut is a story of disagreement, mistrust, and barely bottled antagonism.

Haig was at once the man who gave Habib the mission of a lifetime and the man who made that mission impossible to carry out.

Their estrangement was due in part to basic differences in outlook. First, whereas Habib's approach to the Middle East was informed by the sensibilities of a diplomat, Haig's was informed by a general's fascination with the prowess of the region's premier military force. Having seen America's withering bombing in Vietnam, Haig couldn't understand why Habib and others made such a fuss about what Haig considered the minimal Israeli bombing in Lebanon. Having yawned through many generals' lectures in Korea and Vietnam about their notions of military solutions to political problems, Habib was unimpressed with Haig's political analysis.

Second, Haig was a vintage Cold Warrior. Whereas Habib had no time for grand geopolitical theories, Haig was an ideologue who saw the Middle East as just one more arena in the worldwide US-Soviet rivalry. Indeed, Haig's primary goal in the crisis was to gut Soviet influence there. Whereas Habib viewed conflicts in the region as homegrown, Haig believed the Soviets were really the ones "pulling the strings." Haig felt the US should thus wholeheartedly support its client Israel in whipping the Soviets' clients Syria and the PLO, regardless of the consequences in terms of the region's own logic. Haig saw Israel as the key bulwark opposing pervasive Soviet mischief in the Middle East. Habib considered all of that shallow thinking, an oversimplification by people who didn't really understand the complexities of the region. He had no use for the cornerstone of Haig's Middle East policy: trying to build a "strategic consensus" among Arabs and Israelis to resist Soviet influence in the region. "Nobody believed Al, that was the problem," Habib said in explaining why the Arabs had no confidence in a peace process while Haig was in office. "Al was so one-sided . . . and so caught up with this strategic consensus, that no one believed him. I am not so sure that he believed himself."

Third, Haig was content to let Israel call the shots in this crisis. Habib agreed in general with US support of Israel as an ally. But he felt that American foreign policy should be determined by American interests, and, when any ally's behavior conflicted with American interests—as he felt this war did in spades—America should not passively go along. Haig trusted whatever the Israelis told him, even if it contradicted what Habib told him, on the theory that they couldn't afford to mislead or lie to him. Habib felt they had already misled and lied to him plenty.

The Facts on the Ground

Habib and Haig also had sharply different perceptions of the basic facts on the ground and how to interpret them. Four cases in point stand out.

First, Habib would often stand on the veranda of Ambassador Dillon's residence in the hills overlooking Beirut, with the city spread out before him, and watch Israeli jets and artillery pound the city below. He would then call Washington to denounce the ferocity of the Israeli assaults he was witnessing and demand that Washington make it stop. Haig's view: "Bullshit! There wasn't any heavy Israeli bombing. It was fringe bombing. In the siege of Beirut, there was not a massive bombing *at all.*" Haig's standard was Nixon's bombing of Hanoi in 1972. By that standard, to Haig, "the Israeli bombings were more token than real. Phil wasn't there where the bombs were falling! He was recounting to me what he was hearing from the Lebanese officials. Believe me. I am saying that he overdramatized that, yes, absolutely."

Second, a prime reason Habib felt the invasion was unjustified was that the Israel-Lebanon border had been essentially quiet: "Not a single rocket, not a single Katyusha had been fired across that border from the day that I had negotiated the ceasefire on the border in 1981." Haig's view: "Oh, God, no. No, the border was really quite active. The Israelis *were* getting rocket attacks, right across the border into Galilee. Anybody who tells you they weren't absolutely doesn't know what he's doing."

Third, Habib and Haig disagreed over whether the recent facts on the ground violated that 1981 border ceasefire agreement that Habib had brokered. Habib always insisted that the deal applied only to attacks launched from Lebanese soil across the border into Israel. Sharon and Begin, however, eventually decided that any terrorist act against any Jew anywhere in the world constituted a violation of that agreement. As the author of that agreement, Habib maintained that terrorist attacks in Europe or South America were not addressed in the '81 deal and thus couldn't violate that deal. Haig's view: "That wasn't for Phil to decide. For Phil not to consider that part of the agreement is bullshit. It's a legalistic interpretation, which I don't think any Israeli would accept."

Fourth, Habib and Haig disagreed over priorities. Habib stated his top priority bluntly: "Keep one thing in mind: Beirut. Do not allow its destruction." Haig's view: "Phil is not on our marker. He is lawyering us. Destruction of West Beirut is not the issue."

The Most Basic Question

But the friction between Habib and Haig was mostly over the specific issue at hand: Should we or should we not pressure the Israelis to stop? On this, the most fundamental question of his mission, Habib and Haig profoundly disagreed. Every cell in Habib's body was utterly committed to stopping this war. Whatever it took, however long it took, he would either wrestle it to a halt or die trying. Haig, by contrast, wanted the Israelis to press on.

Habib would insist that the US bring down massive pressure to force Israeli troops to freeze in their tracks instantly. Haig's response, according to acting Deputy Assistant Secretary Charles Hill, who had the job of conveying Haig's guidance to Habib: " 'We don't want them to stop. We want them to go as far as they can.' Haig was in favor of going just about all the way, and then dictating terms. So he was exactly the opposite of Habib."

Haig approached the issue as a general. He insists he had not wanted the Israelis to invade and had made what he considered reasonable efforts to discourage them from doing so. But once they *did* invade, his military instincts told him that they should not stop until it made military sense to stop. Haig drew an analogy between the Israeli invasion and the 1961 Bay of Pigs operation: If the Israelis did not finish the job they began, a ragged inconclusiveness would cause agony for years thereafter. The US—in the person of Phil Habib—therefore should not intervene to stop them prematurely. So Haig was livid at the insistence by Habib and others that the US should force the Israelis to stop at this river or that imaginary line.

"But Haig was a renegade in this," Hill says. "This was not the view of the White House. It was Haig's view. He communicated it very openly, but to only a very few people, that he wanted the war to continue. He said, 'It's nuts to stop now.'" Habib's response to Haig was equally blunt: "You don't know what you're talking about. You're wrong. I'm here. I know what can and can't be done."

Reagan agreed with Habib, and Haig wanted Reagan to butt out. When Begin and his entourage came to Washington on June 21, Haig told the Israeli visitors "we have a problem with President Reagan." At the White House, Reagan lectured Begin about the brutality of the war and urged him to stop it. Afterward, says Assistant Secretary for Near Eastern Affairs Nick Veliotes, "Haig was fulminating that the president wasn't treating Begin right. He went on and on and said, 'By God, I'm going to tell Begin to go into Beirut and finish the job.'" And he did. He told Begin privately that once you start an operation like this, you have to finish it as fast as possible. When Begin heard that, he sent Sharon instructions "to prepare to go into Beirut itself."

The Israelis may or may not have picked up on the subtlety of what Haig meant by "finish the job." Like Habib and everyone else in Washington, Haig wanted all foreign forces—Palestinian, Syrian, and Israeli—to get out of Lebanon. But unlike Habib and most others, Haig felt that the only way to get all three foreign forces out was to have the PLO and the Syrians believe that "if the Israelis were forced to, they were going to do what they had to do militarily: Take Lebanon! Take West Beirut! And if necessary even go to Damascus." Haig says he did not want the Israelis to *actually do* those things. What he wanted was a *credible threat that they might.* That threat, Haig believed, would "accomplish it with mirrors": convince the PLO and the Syrians that their only hope was to leave Lebanon. He reasoned that, if the Israelis marched into Damascus—or even toward Damascus—"it might lead to an ultimate overthrow of the Syrian government. If the Syrians believed that was the outcome they faced, they were going to be strong advocates for a ceasefire and for a mutual withdrawal simultaneous."

Haig not only believed it was realistic to expect them all to leave at once, he was determined to settle for nothing less. "My guidance to Phil was to be damn sure we had an agreement in which there was simultaneous withdrawal of all the occupying forces in Lebanon. It was just that simple."

Habib, in contrast, thought simultaneous withdrawal was too tall an order and felt he would be lucky to get any of them out one at a time. From the earliest days of the war the Syrians told him in so many words that there was no way they would ever accept any linkage of Israeli and Syrian withdrawal from Lebanon, and they never wavered from that position. And Habib, unlike Haig, saw the problem of Lebanon as too much military presence and too much fighting. So he considered this invasion like compacting a keg of gunpowder.

The Art of the Impossible

Relations between Habib and Haig were abysmal. Even Defense Secretary Caspar Weinberger, from his distance in the Pentagon, sensed "a certain amount of hostility between Habib and Haig on policy matters." But there was more to it than that. Lewis says, "Habib didn't like Haig very much. Didn't respect him. Why? Disagreed with him! Thought he was kind of a megalomaniac and very pro-Israeli and not a very good diplomat."

But that was all for behind closed doors. And that's where Habib, as a professional Foreign Service Officer, wanted the tensions to remain. In the second week of the war, though, the *Middle East Policy Survey* newsletter reported that friction between Habib and Haig had reached a point where Habib considered resigning. "Habib believed that Haig changed US policy after he (Habib) had been dispatched to Jerusalem to obtain a cease-fire. 'Habib felt he was set-up,' one Administration insider declared. 'He thought he was sent to arrange a cease-fire after Israel had gotten its 25 mile zone. He then discovered when the Israelis didn't stop, neither did Haig.'"

Besides publicizing the friction, the *MEPS* article also publicized internal criticisms of Habib. It quoted an anonymous official saying that Habib was sending "hysterical" cables demanding US pressure to make Israel stop. One official was quoted saying "'Habib's advice was always too late. Events kept overtaking his recommendations'.... This official argued that there was a recognition that Habib's demand for Israeli withdrawal was not realistic . . . ." The article went on to say that "Habib was so distrustful of Haig that he was demanding that [one of his messages] 'be brought to the personal attention of the President.' . . . But it is also clear that Haig will brook no opposition from Habib on policy directions."

Habib was furious about the article and called in to Undersecretary Larry Eagleburger piping hot. Habib did not dispute the facts the article reported; indeed, he said it "quotes from my cables." What infuriated him was that these private matters had been leaked. A disruption in his diplomacy could cost lives, and the idea that somebody could die because of some game played in Washington revolted him to his soul. He also considered it "personally insulting. It sounds like I oppose Haig. If that's what he thinks of me, what am I doing here? It is intolerable that those guys are reading my cables!"

Eagleburger said he was sure the source of the leak was somewhere on the Seventh Floor—that is, the secretary's inner circle—but was not Haig himself. He tried to reassure Habib that Haig was just as outraged about the leak as he was.

"Yeah, but this is really a low blow," Habib said. Leaks leading to stories like this complicated his work, and that was the one unforgivable crime. "Set traps for those guys and cut their balls off," he bellowed. "I hope the Seventh Floor survives better than I am. After all the stuff I've gone through! In the Middle East, diplomacy is the art of the impossible."

Within two hours Haig shot Habib a cable: "Larry has told me of his conversation with you about the *Middle East Review [sic]* garbage. I want you to be in no doubt whatsoever about my respect for you, my admiration for all you have done under the worst possible circumstances, and my total commitment to supporting you in every way I can.

"I am only slightly less the target than you in the *Review* piece, so let us suffer together: The last thing either one of us can afford at a time like this is suspicion. Neither one of us is noted for his patience, but we will both need to take a deep breath once in a while—bad as that may be for the blood pressure.

"Stick in there, Phil: We can't get along without you."

Publicly, Haig supported Habib. On June 22 he sent a message out to all the ambassadors in the Middle East, saying in part, "Phil is doing a brilliant job and one which by its nature requires flexibility and freedom from stage management, either from here or from posts in the region." Privately, though, Haig told Reagan, "Phil has seen the dark side. He's panicky and tired. I'm worried about him when it gets to the shooting." Before long Haig was blocking Habib's reports from reaching the White House, says Veliotes, "because he didn't like what Habib was saying. Habib was determined that we were going to stop the killing. And Haig by that time had rather openly decided to side with the Israelis in capturing Beirut and finishing the job."

The Nightmare

The antagonism between Habib's two bosses put him in a delicate predicament. He took direction from both Haig and Reagan, and, theoretically, the secretary spoke to him on the president's behalf. But in this instance, Habib's two bosses profoundly disagreed about what he should be doing. They were in fact barely on speaking terms. While Habib was scrambling around trying to stop a war in Lebanon, Haig "had virtually declared war on the White House." For its part, the White House thought Haig was "serving Begin at a disadvantage to US interests."

In this atmosphere, foreign policy decision-making ground nearly to a halt. Habib dearly *wanted* instructions. After all, diplomats normally report to Washington on a situation, await precise instructions, and then obey. But this was no normal situation, and Habib was in no normal diplomatic role. The contradictions between what Reagan wanted him to do and what Haig wanted him to do put Habib in an impossible bind. Habib had made a career of following instructions—pointedly questioning and loudly arguing about them behind closed doors, but then, once the decision was made, faithfully carrying them out. He would never countenance disregarding instructions. But in this crisis, the instructions he got from Washington were variously conflicting, obsolete, useless, or nonexistent.

When they conflicted, it was up to Habib to choose which instructions to obey. He believed that, ultimately, the president makes the decisions and the State Department implements those decisions. The president's wishes obviously trump the secretary's. But which decisions was Ronald Reagan himself making, and which were being made on his behalf by National Security Council officials who, in Habib's mind, had no higher ranking than the secretary of state?

Sorting out the conflicting signals "must have been a nightmare" for Habib, Haig acknowledges. It was. Habib was angry because he thought he had been set up, sent out to do the impossible. The disarray in Washington undermined his credibility as a broker. But Haig's sympathy for Habib's plight went only so far: If he had ever believed that Habib was listening more to Clark than to him, "he'd have been gone in five minutes. Not even five."

Habib knew Haig's position; beyond that, Haig had little guidance to offer him. Essentially, says Hill, Haig felt Habib should devote his energies to "asking things of the Arab side while the Israelis were marching on them. And therefore he talked to Habib about his diplomacy but simply let the Israelis go forward with no comment by us." Habib sometimes felt that Haig simply wanted him to convey Israeli ultimatums to the Arabs. Habib, in turn, made it clear that he and Draper had no intention of being mere "messenger boys for the Israeli maximum position."

For example, on June 11 Haig sent Habib a cable saying "at no point will the opportunities be more favorable for extracting maximum concessions from Syria and you should attempt to do so." Habib thought that was uninformed wishful thinking and wrote back, "Everything Assad has said to me indicates that Syria will seek to continue the fight, rather than bow to [Israeli] demands. . . . The Syrians cannot be expected to stand by idly while Israelis try to restructure [the] Lebanese internal situation to suit themselves." Nor could he expect the PLO to be more receptive. They sent him a message that he summarized as "Don't come to us with the same conditions as the Israelis are giving us. . . . Because if you do we're going to give you the same answer—which is go to hell."

At the end of the day, Washington's policy guidance to Habib generally amounted to little more than "Do the best you can."

The Vacuum

The mess in Washington left Habib in the lonely position of working in a virtual policy vacuum. But, rather than let that situation paralyze him, the quintessential number two guy rose to the occasion. "He was not simply carrying out something that Washington had conjured up," says Brandon Grove. "He was telling Washington what to conjure up. Phil told Washington what to think, and Phil told Washington how to think about it."

For example, after hearing in Haig's cables a little too much acquiescence to Israel's designs for Lebanon, Habib wrote to Washington, "Frankly, this [Israeli] attempt at a short-cut to a solution to the problem of Lebanon . . . strikes me as badly conceived. It is an attempt to solve an extremely complicated political equation by the elementary use of force on a continued basis. Lebanon as it was before June 5 may not be the answer, but Lebanon before 1975 was. It may be that trying to put that together again, in the absence of a comprehensive peace, including the Palestinian question, is not in the cards. Something approximating it may be, and would be a reasonable objective."

Though Haig had thwarted Habib's efforts to halt Sharon's drive to Beirut, once Sharon *did* reach Beirut, that issue became moot. The whole complexion of the crisis changed. Diplomatic strategy and tactics now became the order of business. And the one who wound up calling those shots was Phil Habib. Reagan was inattentive to the crisis and understood it even less. But he did feel that the shooting ought to stop, and he had complete confidence that Habib would figure out what needed to be done. That was all the guidance Habib really needed. He could fill in the details.

"*Because* there were different views in Washington," says Sam Lewis, "Phil really was in control of the game. Habib was really in a situation where *he* could make the policy and then get the president to send the messages to back it up. That's basically the way he operated. He moved into a vacuum."

With events on the ground moving too fast for Washington to keep up, much less make decisions, Habib wrote his own instructions. As Draper puts it, "Washington didn't know what to do half the time, so they accepted Phil's views." Typically, he would call in to Charlie Hill in the Near Eastern Affairs bureau, roar about whatever the latest problem was, and say what he thought he ought to do about it. Hill would then typically say, "OK. Go ahead and do it." Hill had no such authority, but he was rarely overruled by his superiors Veliotes, Undersecretary Larry Eagleburger, or Haig.

Ideas that seemed perfectly sensible in Washington might make no sense whatsoever in Beirut. And Habib could always be counted on to shoot down such ideas. For example, the State Department sent him instructions to the effect that, if an individual PLO fighter did not want to leave Lebanon, it would be acceptable for him to lay down his weapon, give up participation in the organized struggle, and "fade into the local scenery." Sounded fine. But Habib said that policy would only give such people "a license to commit suicide," since any PLO fighter who gave up his weapon and tried to remain in Lebanon would be killed by Bashir's Phalange militia or some other armed group. The idea evaporated.

He knew how to shape his instructions. If the department sent instructions that he didn't like, he would never disregard or disobey them. Instead, he would ask for them to be "clarified," a euphemism for telling the department what the instructions *ought* to be. No matter how senior the person was on the other end of the line, he'd say, "That's stupid. We can't do that. That's just dumb." If he still didn't like what he heard, he would argue, he would rant, he would rave, he would say the instructions were wrong.

Sometimes he would be more subtle. For example, on June 29 Haig instructed him to meet with Sharon that day, period. Habib wrote back requesting instructions on several points, concluding, "Another reason [why I'm requesting] instructions is that I would be reluctant to see Sharon today or tonight to confront his simplistic, bulldozing tactics without guidance. In my view, talks with the Israelis on the political solution shaping up should be with Begin, not Sharon, since Begin would be a lot better equipped to foresee the advantages and better placed to put Israel's military objectives into perspective. Nevertheless, I am quite prepared to argue with Sharon if I know what we are prepared to accept."

Other times he would break the issues down into smaller and smaller parts to the point where it became difficult for his superiors to follow. "No one was better on the details than Phil," says one colleague. "Indeed, Phil knew this and was sure that Haig had neither the time nor the inclination to get into the daily details on a sustained basis. This left Phil a clear field." Occasionally, when he wasn't getting the instructions he wanted, he would ask for written instructions, then reply in writing questioning the parts he disagreed with. "This could drive people crazy," says a colleague, "particularly in a fast-moving, ever-changing environment like Lebanon." It was easier to just throw in the towel and let Habib have his way.

If he failed to get his instructions changed, he would salute and faithfully obey them as a disciplined pro. But he rarely lost these arguments. More typically, Washington would come around to giving him the instructions he felt were appropriate. He would then thank them very much and go carry out those fine instructions.

As Habib put it, "Remember, you're the guy on the ground. You're the guy who's dealing with the issues. You know more about what you face than anybody else does because you're there. The advantages are on your side. If you can't convince somebody when you're convinced yourself, then something's wrong with your argument. If you tell the president, 'Instead of saying it that way I think I ought to say it this way,' or, 'Instead of pursuing this objective, I ought to pursue that one,' chances are nine out of ten he's not going to argue with you. The day he starts arguing with you is the day he starts to lose confidence in you!"

Habib routinely got his way in terms of his own actions. But he routinely failed to get Washington to take the actions he wanted it to take. He repeatedly demanded massive US pressure to stop the Israeli advance. Haig would neither comply nor tell him to back off. He would just smile and do nothing.

No negotiator can succeed alone, any more than an astronaut can. The entire network of US embassy and consulate staff in the region and the resources of the State Department in Washington all mobilized to back up Habib's work. But nine-tenths of the analysis, creativity, and strategy of his mission originated in Habib himself. "He was the fount of what was going on," says Consul General to Jerusalem Brandon Grove. "He was immensely creative in terms of making it up every morning practically how to do something that was seemingly impossible—then pounding away on Washington to make his ideas happen." He understood how unique his situation and his degree of latitude were, and he dove headlong into the vacuum to fill it. He recognized that defusing this crisis was up to him, and he wasn't going to put up with anything that interfered with his work.

Reagan wanted Sharon's war stopped, and so did Habib. That was two out of three. Habib didn't want to have to overtly disobey Haig in order to obey Reagan. His solution—though he would never have expressed it this way himself—was to salute Haig as necessary while moving heaven and earth to do what he believed was right. He would not let General Haig stop him from stopping General Sharon.

A Gradual Sneaking Forward

One thing Habib and Haig did agree on was that this invasion could be turned into an opportunity to make progress on another front. The front that Haig focused on was pulling the rug out from under the Soviets and their clients. The front that Habib focused on was rebuilding a meaningful government in Lebanon.

A different special envoy might have tried to waltz into Lebanon as the great American savior and pay less attention to the government than to the humidity. But Habib spent much of his time trying to guide the Lebanese government to a bold reassertion of sovereign control over its entire territory, its entire population.

Odd. Habib had a reputation as a hard-nosed pragmatist. Yet one can think of few more quixotic ambitions than this. But he realized that one of the prime cripplers of the government, the PLO, would sooner or later be either slaughtered or relocated. Either way, their days in Lebanon were numbered. Violent anarchy had not prevailed in Lebanon forever and could not continue forever. The government had been viable up until seven years earlier and surely would be again someday. The tide had to turn at some point, and what better point than this nadir of its fortunes?

Besides, somebody had to be his intermediary with the PLO, since he was not allowed to talk with them directly, and the nominal government was the only semblance of structure he had to work with.

So he treated the feeble Lebanese government as a serious player to be respected. He met with, worked through, consulted, and involved Lebanese officials at every opportunity. He coached them, exhorted them, encouraged them. And if they wouldn't rise to the occasion, he was determined to raise them to it. "Phil believed in Lebanon more than the Lebanese themselves did," says one of his colleagues.

Habib's preference, therefore, was that the Lebanese pull up their socks and come up with a solution themselves. He rode them hard to "go get their act together and come up with a consensus." With his coaching, the Lebanese government on June 16 did produce a rudimentary but useful proposal: They asked for a guaranteed forty-eight-hour ceasefire, during which they would try to persuade the PLO to lay down their arms and agree not to conduct an armed struggle in the future. If that worked, the nation's army, the Lebanese Armed Forces (LAF), would then assert control over the PLO's stronghold, West Beirut.

That proposal was a good start, but Habib recognized the enormity of what Sharon was up to. Whatever Begin might have had in mind, Sharon clearly was not in Lebanon for a modest operation. He was out to destroy the PLO once and for all and to install Bashir as Lebanon's new president and, more to the point, as Israel's puppet. Given Sharon's ambitions, his trick ceasefire of June 11, and the fact that his troops were in Beirut, the proposal on the table was woefully inadequate. Habib wanted additional Washington muscle.

"The Israelis can't run Lebanon like a satrapy!" Habib shouted to Washington. Israeli actions, he wrote, "make it thoroughly clear that they have intended all along to ignore any real cease-fire. . . . As for comments out of Washington to the effect that the Israelis are not in Beirut and do not intend [to] occupy it, this is like saying that a foreign army on Chevy Chase Circle and the National Airport is not in Washington. It is imperative that Sharon

... be brought under control. ... I can see no alternative but for you [Haig] and President Reagan to make absolutely clear to Begin that we cannot accept what they are doing. It is time to be extremely firm with Israel. The Israelis should not only be brought to a standstill, they should draw back to reasonable positions in the Beirut area."

But Haig was not about to step in. The Israeli Cabinet agreed to a forty-eight-hour ceasefire, but did not specify a ceasefire *in place,* much less a withdrawal. Having been burned only a few days earlier by the Israeli notion of an advancing ceasefire, Habib had no intention of letting them slip that detail by again now. Indeed, Sharon was ordering what he called a "gradual sneaking forward" that same day. "I find it incomprehensible," Habib told Washington, "that [you] continue to accept—apparently without question—the Israeli contention that there is still a cease-fire. There is no repeat no cease-fire. We are all tired but please try to understand this fundamental point." He wanted Haig to immediately demand that the Cabinet decision be reworded to provide for a ceasefire *in place,* and he spelled out the wording he wanted. But Haig refused. Asking the Israeli Cabinet to revise its decision, Haig said, would hurt US-Israel relations, spelling an end to "all our hopes to make progress on Lebanon" and "an end to Habib in Israeli eyes."

Besides, the Israelis had assured Haig that they would not occupy West Beirut. That was good enough for him. But not for Habib, who knew Begin's and Sharon's way with words. "They only said they wouldn't *occupy* Beirut," he pointed out. "They didn't mention not destroying it."

Living in a Madhouse

Despite the fiasco of its first meeting, the National Salvation Council did eventually manage to get some actual work done. On Tuesday, June 22, they gave Habib an elaboration on the Lebanese government's week-old proposal:

1. An effective ceasefire in place should begin as soon as possible.
2. The IDF should pull back 5 kilometers so UN or US or the Lebanese Armed Forces could enter as a buffer separating combatants.
3. In this context, Lebanese officials would finalize details of a departure agreement with the PLO. The expectation was that this would take forty-eight hours.

Prime Minister Begin was in Washington at the time, so Haig and Veliotes had presented the proposal to him in person. Habib liked that situation very much, because it meant Begin could make his decision with Sharon 5,000 miles away. Begin accepted the proposal, including the 5-kilometer pullback. There were certainly details to work out, but Habib felt that the basic outline of a deal was set. "The PLO is frantic," he said. "They know what they face. The IDF have them by the throat. But we should avoid the IDF going in on the ground." As he spoke, Dillon was making arrangements for American civilians to evacuate Beirut by US Navy ship Thursday, two days hence; Habib felt that Thursday could be "breakthrough day. Our evacuation on Thursday could add to the PLO's panic and their willingness to deal."

Then Habib got word that Sharon was on his way up to see him. Damn. The last thing he wanted at this point was to have Sharon involved. But there was no way to avoid him.

They met secretly for an hour and a quarter June 23 at Bashir's headquarters in East Beirut. Begin's decision notwithstanding, Sharon started out saying he would not agree to any disengagement or pullback.

"Arik, give us something."

"No."

"I can't take that word."

Habib insisted he needed at least some symbolic withdrawal. In the end, Sharon grudgingly said he might pull back from the airport and would remove four posts from around Baabda. But forget about any overall 5-kilometer pullback. He demanded that all PLO fighters throughout Lebanon leave the country, a demand Habib knew there was zero chance of fulfilling.

Habib had been wrong about Arafat's readiness to give in. Though Begin had agreed to both this plan and the one a week earlier, Arafat had agreed to neither. Why? The same day as the earlier proposal, June 16, US Vice President George Bush and Defense Secretary Caspar Weinberger, attending the funeral of Saudi King Khalid, had told the Saudis that the US would pressure Israel not to enter Beirut. That news had the effect of telling the PLO that they were not about to be destroyed. So why should they budge?

The PLO's basic gameplan was shaping up to be: Stall. A joke began circulating in West Beirut: A PLO meeting is interrupted by a commotion outside. Someone tells Arafat, "There are 450,000 West Beirutis who have come here to bid you and the PLO farewell." "Why?" asks Arafat. "Where are they going?"

The PLO dearly wanted to stay in West Beirut. After all, they more or less ran the place. Besides, the longer they could string things out, the longer they could bask in the world's headlines as sympathetic underdogs. More substantively, they hoped to capitalize on the crisis to make a deal: some political bonus such as US recognition in exchange for their agreement to leave Lebanon. So their basic position was to cling to any scrap of hope that they could ride out this siege. On days when such scraps drifted by, they would grimly nurse them and stall. On days when their prospects looked especially bleak, they let Habib know they were desperate to leave. Habib never knew from day to day which way those winds might be blowing. And, forbidden by US policy and Israeli sensitivities from dealing directly with the PLO, Habib had no means of looking Arafat in the eye and impressing upon him personally that the time had come to get serious and end this.

So while the US and Israel were hammering out particulars of a ceasefire June 22 and 23, Arafat was conflicted. He had good reason to throw in the towel—Sharon did have the PLO checkmated—but he still clung to the hope that the US would prevent Sharon from finishing them off. So he didn't *reject* the proposal; he just floundered in indecision.

While Arafat diddled, events in Washington threw a bizarre kink in the string.

Cheering in the Halls

Al Haig was competing with Reagan's White House advisors for the president's confidence—and losing badly. The further his stock sank, the more he tried to press Reagan to bless him.

The only thread Haig hung by was Reagan's personal distaste for confrontations. That thread frayed perilously after Haig sent some instructions to Habib on June 13. The content of the instructions was not terribly noteworthy—Draper recalls their essence as "do what you can to work things out." The problem was that in the White House's eyes Haig could do no right and he had sent instructions to Habib without clearance from the White House. "This mustn't happen again," Reagan told Haig. "We just can't have a situation where you send messages on your own that are a matter for my decision."

On June 24, the thread finally snapped. Haig presented Reagan with his grievances about the White House's—particularly Bill Clark's—interference in foreign affairs. He accused Clark of undermining both his authority and Habib's mission by dealing with a Saudi official through a back channel. Reagan at last decided the time had come for Haig to go. The next day, he announced Haig's resignation.

As word of Haig's departure ricocheted around the State Department, says one diplomat, "they had to tell people to quit cheering in the halls." The American ambassador in Jordan uncorked a bottle of champagne and drank it all. Habib was at Dillon's residence when he got the news. Dillon and Draper dismiss a published report of him dancing in jubilation, but say he was very pleased, even elated. Habib was a savvy enough political animal to have seen since Versailles that Haig's days were numbered, so when the word finally came, he was more relieved than surprised. Characteristically, he spent no time celebrating, but instantly started speculating about who the successor might be. He guessed George Shultz. It was. Habib was delighted. He knew Shultz, had high regard for him, and, having discussed ideas for Middle East peace with him a few months earlier at Stanford, knew he would have a more balanced approach to Israel than Haig had had.

A Weird Limbo

Habib's initial joy at Haig's departure quickly vanished. Matters now entered a weird phase of limbo. Shultz couldn't pitch in until he was confirmed. And though Haig had been fired, he didn't quite leave. He rarely showed up at the office, but continued issuing directives by telephone. Veliotes refers to this period as "those sick few days when he would not let go and kept screwing things up." Haig's version is that Reagan "begged me to stay on" until Shultz could be confirmed. Whichever interpretation one prefers, while Habib was racing around trying to stanch the hemorrhaging in Lebanon, his masters at the State Department were "wandering around trying to figure out who the hell was running things," says Undersecretary Lawrence Eagleburger. "I guess the answer is 'not much of anybody.' But to the degree anybody was, I guess I was sort of the master of ceremonies, not much more than that. It was an enterprise in marking time."

Marking time was the last thing Habib could afford. While all of the intrigue was going on in Washington, Sharon was intensifying his siege of Beirut. Habib was frantically trying to keep his ten fingers plugging a hundred holes in a dozen dikes. The firing of Israel's staunchest American supporter in favor of a new secretary widely (and incorrectly) rumored to be pro-Arab wound up complicating Habib's problems. The PLO and the Israelis both expected a less pro-Israeli policy. That prospect encouraged the Israelis to hustle to crush the PLO before Shultz could stop them. At the same time, it encouraged the PLO to keep stalling until Shultz could save them. So for the time being, neither saw much reason to pay attention to Phil Habib.

Recognizing that, Habib promptly cranked up the volume on his demands that the president immediately apply massive pressure on Israel to stay out of Beirut. He had a strong aversion to making threats "unless you really mean to carry them out. . . . False threatening is bullshit. It just doesn't work." But the time had come to get Israel's attention. On June 27—the same day that Sharon first asked the Israeli Cabinet for authority to actually penetrate West Beirut—Habib called the State Department to dictate a recommendation he wanted taken to the White House:

. . . 3. In my view it is absolutely necessary that the United States assure that there be no repeat no further attacks on West Beirut and its immediate populated suburbs. The situation in Beirut has become a symbol of this war, and it is widely believed that the survival of a large part of the city and its people has become the responsibility of the United States. There is no way that official and public opinion in the Middle East and elsewhere will let us escape that responsibility. It will not devolve on to Israel, which is expected to behave ruthlessly, nor will PLO intransigence and lack of concern for their host nation be blamed.

4. I cannot believe that we will sacrifice our interest by standing by—as our failure to act will be viewed—and letting West Beirut suffer further. No matter that some Israelis believe that the PLO can and must be totally and visibly smashed into oblivion—we will pay a great price in terms of our broad interest and international image. Moreover, in my mind further pillaging of Beirut, by air, land or sea—with or without a ground attack—will be a monumental obscenity with which we must not be seen to be associated.

5. I understand that we have urged Prime Minister Begin not to attack West Beirut. I suggest that persuasion and a strong message need to be reinforced in a way which makes clear that we mean what we say and will brook no defiance. My specific recommendations are as follows:

[1] We should request of Prime Minister Begin today, following the cabinet meeting, a *flat and unequivocal pledge that there will be no attack on Beirut*. A ceasefire in place is to be maintained, with strength and proportionality will *[sic]* be the practice even under the kind of mild provocation that has led to massive retaliation hitherto. In place of violence Israel would now accept the continuation of the political-diplomatic effort without a deadline.

[2] We must *insist on a reply,* if we get the kind of equivocation that has frequently been the case in the past.

[3] If he is not prepared to give the assurances we seek, our answer should be brief but telling as follows: Israel is an independent country which has a right to make its own decisions and follow its own interests as it sees them. The United States has the same right. If Israel persists and attacks West Beirut despite our position, the United States wishes to inform Israel what will happen when the attack begins. At that point the president will *call a halt,* under US law, to *all military shipments* to Israel; we shall also be prepared to go immediately to the UN Security Council to seek

a binding resolution calling on Israel to *stop its military actions and withdraw from Lebanon;* we are prepared to vote for or at any rate *not veto Chapter VII Sanctions.* Mr. Begin must be left under no illusion that our action will be anything but immediate and un-relenting.

6. In sum, I believe we are at a crucial point where for the sake of our interests, and in the broadest consideration of the traditional American concern for what is decent, that we must bring an end to needless kill-ing. Otherwise we face an immense human tragedy in West Beirut.

In case there was any ambiguity, Habib told Veliotes, "Make sure Eagleburger and Haig understand that I will not withdraw my message and recommendation. I'm not opposed to Israel using psychological pressure; I'm talking about action itself."

When Eagleburger conveyed Habib's message to Haig, the lame-duck secretary's response was concise: "Tell Habib that I disagree with his analysis and his recommendation. There will be no presidential message to Begin. Israel must keep the pressure on. Take orders, or we will find someone who can."

When Eagleburger told Habib of Haig's response, Habib went ballis-tic. To calm him down, Eagleburger told him that if the US gave Israel the sanctions ultimatum he wanted, the Israelis would leak it to the press. The PLO would then take heart and never give in.

As a special presidential envoy, Habib had the right to bypass Haig and send his message directly to the president. But as a career Foreign Service Officer, he would never consider such a violation of protocol. Defeated, feeling like a handcuffed pianist, he sighed, "I accept your judgment."

Five Hundred in the Middle of Nowhere

The next day brought an even more exasperating episode to mark Haig's lame-duck period. On Monday, June 28, Habib's main intermediary to the PLO, Lebanese prime minister Wazzan, finally relayed to him what Habib considered the PLO's first good-faith offer to leave Lebanon. Their one firm condition was a face-saving measure: that they leave behind a sym-bolic Palestinian military presence under LAF control in some obscure part of Lebanon, such as the presences they had in Jordan and Egypt. Wazzan said he considered the residual symbolic force to be "the bottom line posi-tion for the PLO and that without it it would not be possible to deal with" the hundreds of particulars like where the PLO leaders would go.

Habib told Wazzan he wouldn't give him any kind of immediate response. This was far too serious a subject and had to be dealt with carefully. But he considered their offer promising and reasonable. "Clearly the PLO realizes the game is up," he wrote. "We can build on this situation." He said he saw "nothing wrong with putting five hundred of them in the middle of nowhere" as a means of giving the PLO "a face-saving way out of its corner. If they cannot find such a way out, . . . they will put up a last ditch fight."

Habib was sure this proposal gave him the opening he needed to weave a compromise solution. "What I will produce will not be seen as a PLO victory," he said, "but not as an Israeli ultimatum either." He set out trying to convince all the parties to sign on to the idea of a symbolic residual presence.

The State Department signed on. But the next day, in what Hill called "a major flip-flop," Haig reversed that position.

Haig issued nine points of instructions to Habib that called for the PLO to essentially surrender and leave Lebanon entirely with their tail between their legs. Point 4 read, "There will be no redeployment of any armed PLO fighters from Beirut to other locations in Lebanon."

Whatever the merits of the other eight points, point 4 reversed position on the pivotal idea of letting the PLO leave a symbolic armed presence in Lebanon. Habib was angry. He thought the instructions stunk. The more he thought about them, the angrier he got. Upon first hearing them from Eagleburger, he said, "This will not go. There's nothing symbolic left here. The previous position at least left a symbolic force. The Lebanese won't present this to the PLO except as an American ultimatum. My guess is this does not give the PLO any reason to go out. I don't believe the PLO will find it face saving, so they'll do what they think is necessary. The PLO does not think it is yet in a position to just lay down its arms and leave."

But Habib had made a career of arguing with his superiors behind closed doors, then, if he lost the argument, saluting and standing up for their decisions to the public and his negotiating counterparts. He wasn't about to change now. "It's a mistake to go this way," he told Eagleburger, "but I'll present it as best I can."

He did immediately present the nine points to the Lebanese government to pass on to the PLO. But he was not surprised that they viewed them as the equivalent of Israeli demands. "I'm trying to do something in this goddam thing," Habib yelled at Eagleburger over the radio. The Lebanese "are not stupid. I'll avoid getting a formal kick in the ass. They deeply feel we're being unreasonable, but I'll go do a little work."

Tap Dancing

The way the State Department handled these nine points caused Habib at least as much trouble as their content. On Monday, June 28, he had agreed with the Lebanese officials that the token presence idea was a reasonable, flexible proposal and begun advocating it. But on Tuesday, Haig forced him to reverse himself by presenting instead these "frightening and unreasonable" nine points that rejected a symbolic presence. Confused, the Lebanese asked Habib what was going on. Why was he rejecting or ignoring on Tuesday the very proposal he had welcomed on Monday? "We didn't ignore your proposal," Habib told them. "This is our response." That was the best tap dancing he could do, but it fooled no one.

As if that weren't bad enough, State quickly backed down on the nine points. In fact, its late Tuesday "clarification" suddenly gave so much flexibility that the US position looked remarkably like Monday's symbolic presence position. After a matter of hours, the idea of a symbolic presence was back in play.

Habib and Draper were mortified. They felt this whipsawing of instructions damaged their credibility as diplomats and made the United States look idiotic. "As a negotiating process, this is bad," Draper said. "These instructions are stupid. It looks like second-class negotiating. The Lebanese government doesn't understand negotiating. They believe I'm shrewd and devious. I have lost credibility with these people." For his part, Habib called Washington six and a half hours after receiving the nine points and said, "I'm sitting here brooding. We've made asses of ourselves! Who wrote these goddam instructions? Do you realize what you did? Tell Larry Eagleburger this is inconsistency. Also say I'm pissed off about these instructions!"

The problem wasn't just that the flip-flopping made Habib look bad. Worse, he feared this would be the last straw that would finally nudge the tottering Lebanese government to collapse: President Sarkis was too sick to even meet with Habib. Prime Minister Wazzan had resigned four days earlier, had only just come back, and was at his wits' end. Several members of the Cabinet had resigned four days earlier. And the National Salvation Committee had just disintegrated. The last thing the Lebanese government needed was for the mighty United States of America—the only government on earth that seemed to be taking them seriously, the one whose envoy had been coaching them on how to stand up and function like a world-class sovereign government—to start swerving all over the map on them. "Whereas we had looked to you for support," Wazzan told Habib, "you [are] burying us." Habib cabled Washington, "It is important to understand that I have kept the Government of Lebanon together for three weeks. I am not sure now how long I can continue to do that."

The next day, Wednesday, June 30, the Lebanese relieved Habib's problem ingeniously. They met with the PLO, talked and talked and talked, and never mentioned the nine points at all. Intentionally or not, that contained the damage. Habib had not wanted the Palestinians to hear the nine points, and they had not. He told Washington, "Despite the overly rigid and ill-conceived instructions we got yesterday, I have it back on track."

Time to Leave

Steaming over this latest mess, Habib was becoming as impatient for Al Haig to leave as he was for the PLO to leave. Reagan too was becoming increasingly uneasy with Haig's continuing role while waiting for the Senate to confirm Shultz. Finally, on July 5, eleven days after Haig had been fired, Shultz phoned to tell him his time was up.

Haig, who felt that "George Shultz, God bless his soul, didn't know shit from Shinola about the Middle East," still hesitated to release the reins. "Well, George, do you think you're ready?" he asked. He declined to bow out until he heard it from Reagan himself.

Only when Reagan called to confirm Shultz' message was Phil Habib, at long last, free of Al Haig.

7

Fight the Fire Anyway

"Tough, driven, dedicated, . . . Habib combined all the
old WASP diplomatic virtues of discretion and tact with
a Levantine gift for putting Arabs and Israelis at ease.
There was something about this short, balding man, his
health ruined by decades of compulsive overwork,
of a Le Carré veteran called back to untangle
yet another mess at the Circus."
Jonathan Randal

As the siege of Beirut dragged on, millions of people around the world
hoped that Philip Habib would succeed in stopping it. He was one of the
few who wholeheartedly believed he would. When it became apparent early
on that the only way to end the siege peacefully would be to evacuate the
PLO from Beirut, he was told flatly, "It's impossible. You'll never get them
out. No way! The city of Beirut is going to be destroyed. There's going to
be street-to-street fighting." But he had no interest in that kind of talk. So,
while others waited for him to fail, he went to work.

He never doubted that, if only he could keep tearing around the Middle
East twisting arms, if only Washington would let him have his way, he
could stop this war. He also never doubted that he was the only diplomat
who stood a chance of pulling off such a miracle.

Eyeball to Eyeball Diplomacy

What commended him to this crisis was a combination of characteristics,
skills, and style that made him a unique figure on the diplomatic landscape.
As *Time* magazine put it, Habib was one of a handful of diplomatic trouble-
shooters in recent decades "whose authority derives not from their titles
but from their willingness to operate in the highly volatile, here's-the-deal-
dammit world of eyeball-to-eyeball diplomacy. The formula is simple: earn
the trust of the principals, talk straight and cut the best deal you can; then
tell the boss what you have done."

Habib felt he was uniquely endowed for this mission in several ways.
He understood very well the stage he was playing on—to the extent that

anyone can understand the Middle East. He knew most of the players from having worked in the region off and on for six years. He knew their ambitions, their shortcomings, their problems, their quirks, and their relations to one another. Middle Easterners tend to care greatly who the negotiator is, and they knew Philip Habib well. He had long been renowned in diplomatic circles as a solid veteran pro, the best in the business.

This was a unique kind of crisis, and it called for an unconventional diplomat able to roll with its dizzying twists and wild assortment of players. "Phil was totally unconventional in the way he practiced the art of diplomacy," says a Lebanese diplomat. "Totally. Totally." He could sprint when he had to sprint and plod when he had to plod. He could charm, cajole, threaten, reason, bark—sometimes all within the space of twenty minutes. In a region teeming with intimidating personalities and absolute certainties, Habib was known as a guy who would not be bowled over. If they shouted at him, he could be counted on to shout back louder. But they also knew he was a guy they could do business with. He had a knack for getting along with just about anybody. No other diplomat has ever eased as fluidly back and forth between Israeli and Arab negotiating styles. When he lost—and he lost repeatedly—he had a remarkable resiliency to bounce back again and again and again and again.

He enjoyed Reagan's complete confidence, and Reagan's imprimatur was certainly a major asset in commanding people's attention. He also wielded a certain clout just because he represented the United States. But what clout Habib had lay less in whom he represented than in who he was. Sure, he represented Reagan, but everyone knew Reagan wasn't paying much attention. He represented Haig, but everyone knew Haig wanted Sharon's forces to keep going. Rather, Hill says, people dealt with Habib "because they knew that he was trying to solve the problem, that he was fair, and that he was a person of utter integrity. He had a kind of reverence from various parties because of his personality and his stature—*not* because of his influence with or because he was speaking for the president or the secretary of state."

Your Life in Your Hands

Above all, he was known as a straight shooter. He thought that one of the dumbest things ever said about diplomats is the old saw that they are people sent abroad to lie for their country. As he put it, "There are no flies on the people you're dealing with" in international diplomacy, and savvy leaders detect dishonesty very quickly. Once they do, the diplomat might as well go home. As Brandon Grove puts it,

If you're not trusted, you've lost the whole show. People believed Phil. He could be taken at his word. And that is the sine qua non for a negotiator. A mistake diplomats sometimes make is to sugar-coat the pill. Phil *never* did that. Even when he was telling people something they did not want to hear, they knew he was telling things the way they really were. He just laid it out. People had enormous respect for that.

He was always the same Phil, whether he was playing cards with my son Mark or talking to Begin and Sharon. There was a constancy with him. There weren't three or four Phil Habibs that you would turn on depending on the circumstances. He could be as candidly blunt with the prime minister as with anybody else. I would often hear him telling the same story to Israelis, then to Americans, and later to Jordanians— and he was telling it *exactly* the same way. People really respected that kind of bedrock integrity. That was perhaps his greatest single strength. And it is a stunning asset to have.

This was no mission for the faint of heart, and Habib had earned the reputation of a tough guy. He was there to get this war stopped, and woe to anyone who failed to help him advance toward that implacable purpose. He didn't hesitate to blast anyone who crossed or disappointed him.

In a region where arguing is everywhere the national pastime, Habib was right at home. A fellow diplomat says, "In Phil Habib's mind, ain't *no one* who could ever best him. And I think it's true. No one could push this Brooklyn street kid around. He'd go toe-to-toe with anyone. And he was so passionate in his views—and usually so right—that it was hard to argue against his logic."

It was hard to argue with him, period. Arguing was a skill he had mastered growing up in a Middle Eastern family in Brooklyn and perfected at the University of Idaho, and he thoroughly enjoyed it as sport. "The eyeballs would open wide, and the hands would begin gesticulating," says secretary Lori Bider. "He always took you by surprise by saying something shocking about you—which would stop you in mid-sentence—to throw you off. If you pursued it, he would then throw you off the track and digress, so that in the end you wound up defending yourself, your family, your feelings, what you had for breakfast, and the fact that you had disturbed him. That's what arguing with him was like! Futile! Take your life in your hands!"

He didn't really consider it arguing. To him it was just intense conversation and his way of continually learning. If you had something to say, he wanted to hear it. He might then challenge or ridicule your opinion or say something outrageous—"so-and-so sure screwed that up, and he's your friend! How could that happen?!"—just to see whether you could defend your view. However dismissive he may have seemed, he was listening to you carefully. If you made a good case for your point of view, he would accept it. But you'd better spit it out quick and you'd better know what you're talking about. He had no patience for rambling. If you weren't sure what your point or your opinion was, he was likely to start hectoring you to pin you down. If you didn't have a point or if you couldn't persuasively defend your opinion, God help you.

This style equipped him well to deal with some of the most intransigent people on earth. He was relentless. If his opposite numbers had an agenda that Habib didn't want to get sidetracked on, he would just overwhelm them: He would be the good cop one minute and the bad cop the next. He'd dig in his heels, then sympathize with their problem, then joke, then yell at them. He'd break the tension by making everybody laugh, then slam right back to the substance and push on. By constantly disrupting the other guy's attempts to gain momentum, Habib kept him off balance so he could keep driving progress forward.

His style was to use whatever method he needed to always appear on top of things, in control, moving forward—even when he wasn't. He did that two ways. First, as Ryan Crocker says, "Whenever some horror would erupt, he would react, 'We've gotta do this, we've gotta do that! Goddammit, Morrie, come on!'" A few hours later, as he had more time to think, he might dramatically change direction. But even that change was just another occasion for "his force of personality and generally very good judgment to create a sense of energy and motion and preparedness." His second way of appearing always in control was through silence. Crocker says, "Phil was remarkably good at being silent yet not appearing as though he didn't know what to say." Like George Shultz, Habib could just sit there pokerfaced and let the other person squirm imagining what he might be thinking. He knew that silence skillfully used would never betray him as indecisive or unsure, even when he was.

The Least Bad Solution

This was also no mission for the naive. Habib was a curious blend of idealism and pragmatism. As Menachem Begin once said, "Habib has a heart problem: He's got a good heart." In the case of the invasion of Lebanon and the way Sharon prosecuted this war, Habib simply felt it was wrong. He thought it was also politically stupid, diplomatically self-defeating, and militarily pointless—but above all wrong. The words he used most often to denounce it were *inhumane* and *indecent*.

Habib saw no conflict between idealism and pragmatism. He was relentlessly pragmatic in service to his ideals. It didn't matter to him how valid one party's point or demand might be if he knew that the other party would never buy it. "Look, you want this?" he would say to his negotiating counterparts. "I know that. I can't give you that. Don't waste your time." Nor was he interested in listening to demands that left no room for compromise, since he believed that "negotiation is compromise" and "negotiation without compromise is surrender" and that no party in this crisis was going to surrender. When someone raised an argument he thought led nowhere, he avoided bogging down arguing about what was wrong with it. Whenever possible, he'd just wave it off with "That's a joke; you can't mean that" and move on.

In a region obsessed with assigning blame for yesterday's wrongs, Habib considered blame a waste of time. "It is not up to us to blame," he once said. "It is up to us to further the process." When a problem arose–and his days were an incessant procession of problem after problem after problem–he would certainly thunder about "the goddam bastards" who were responsible. But his diatribe would mostly be about the problem itself. His attitude was always "That was an hour ago. Let's figure out where we go from here."

Habib had no use for the common diplomatic practice of laying the groundwork for an agreement by starting with generalities to which the parties can agree and then moving to specifics. Such statements of grand principles typically become the preamble of an agreement. But not a Habib agreement. "Forget laying groundwork," he would say. "That's a waste of time. Let's see if there isn't a little point of agreement we can reach." Once he got any little specific point of agreement, he would say, "OK, now let's see if we can enlarge on this." Working from the particular to the general was, for him, the only sensible approach. He and his counterparts used no particular method for reaching agreement on any point: They simply argued until they could agree.

He had nothing but scorn for academic theories, hindsight, second-guessing, and speculation. He would often yell at a Lebanese diplomat whose background was in academia, "Come on! Leave your books outside the room. Let's talk practical things."

The essence of his pragmatism was his definition of success: making the best of a bad situation. "Phil's great ability," says John Gunther Dean, "was to recognize that a diplomat must find the least bad solution. We believe sometimes that there are good solutions and bad solutions, but most solutions are somewhere in between. American foreign policy is about trying to find a solution you can live with, one that causes the least amount of damage. Phil was wonderful in working out compromises, at being able to look at any problem not only from our point of view, but from other people's points of view. He was not going to *win* this goddam thing like a football game! His approach was, 'How can I put an end to this mess in a way which is acceptable?' After all, a bad solution is terrific compared to a bloodbath." Had he held out for an ideal solution—ideal by any party's definition—he would have gotten nothing. By working toward the least bad solution, he stood a better chance of ending up with something.

But *solution* is probably the wrong word. His ambitions were even more modest. There are two kinds of conflicts, Habib once said: "conflicts that can be solved, and conflicts that cannot be solved. The Middle East is an instance of a conflict that cannot be solved. You do not have any hope of *solving* the problem: There is no solution to be found. It is intractable and it will go on. All you can hope to do is *manage* the conflict to keep it from getting out of hand and blowing up into a major conflagration." He thought it was "not always necessary to reach a conclusion: It is sometimes preferable to conserve the status quo. The nations continue to function as before, there is no breakdown, there is no war."

The closest thing to a theory he held was what he called Habib's Rule: *Who's got the guns? That's where you start.*

His point, says a colleague, was that "power is power, and you have to take that into account. Phil looked at the world in a very disciplined way anchored in *realpolitik*. He was a man of *deep* principle, but he wasn't peddling a moral story. He knew power, and he was dealing with elements of power and trying to maneuver people toward our objectives."

This is why he chafed so at being forbidden to talk to the PLO: They had guns, and thus had to be dealt with and should be dealt with directly.

The Signature Dichotomy

Philip Habib was a man of powerful emotions, but he was also a master poker player. He knew when to show more anger than he was really feeling, and when to show less. That dichotomy was his signature.

An outburst from him could mean he was genuinely furious. It could mean he wanted to get someone's attention. It could mean he wanted to redirect a negotiation onto a more productive path. Or it could mean nothing more than that he was frustrated and needed to blow off some steam. Those who knew him well and often saw him in action learned how to read his tirades. His secretary could tell his genuine anger from bluster by the tightness in his face and body. Others could tell by the seriousness of the situation he was ranting about. Charlie Hill, who talked with Habib by radio every day during the siege, could tell from the tone of Habib's voice, as a mother can tell whether her crying baby is really in trouble or just fussing. People who were not around Habib enough to interpret his tirades could be forgiven for being utterly confused by them.

"Every single Habib sentence had at least three parts to it," says Hill, with only some exaggeration. "There is the introductory part, which is 'Goddammit, how many times have I got to tell you?!' In the middle, there are words that are stuck in front of things, like 'What the hell...' or 'What kind of shit is this that you're giving me?' And at the end of it there's kind of a coda, which is 'I've had it with you assholes! I've told you this a thousand goddam times!'"

Habib had never been one to tolerate frustrations or disappointments quietly; in Beirut he got more frustrations and disappointments than ever. If he felt he had an important window of opportunity that someone was letting slip away, he'd storm. If he didn't feel he was getting the support he wanted from Washington or someone else, he'd storm.

His anger was not that of a hothead, but of a compassionate man pressing every ounce of his being into trying to stop a war that he considered pointless and being stymied at every turn. "Phil Habib was the master of the tirade," says Hill. "He let you have it, at the top of his lungs. It was stuff you didn't want to hear, but you knew he was right, and you never took offense, because underneath the shouting and the wild gesticulation was the constant, undeniable presence of a human being who was unwaveringly kind and good and honest."

A Few Histrionics Don't Hurt

In negotiating sessions, he was strictly straightforward on the substance. No diplomat can succeed otherwise. But tactics were a different matter. There he would throw in all the smoke and mirrors he could muster, stomping and ranting and raging. "This is a shitty way to deal," he'd bellow, and storm out of the room. Ten minutes later he would be back calmly negotiating.

It was largely an act, but one he took very seriously. For example, sometimes he would have Morrie Draper phone some Israeli official to say how upset Habib was about this or that and what he wanted them to do about it. As Draper would talk on the phone in his effective and forceful yet more diplomatic way, Habib would be yelling from the other room, "Goddam it, Morrie! That's not the way I said it. You tell them goddam well what I said!"

"Phil was a good actor," says Draper, and, when he needed to get someone's attention, "a few histrionics didn't necessarily hurt." Shultz says that Habib "didn't ever rant and rave in an uncontrollable way. It was an act to some extent, but he knew what he was doing. That's the real point. Sometimes people put on a similar act but they *don't* know what they're doing."

He once confided to one of his protégés that his storming and raging was "all an act." He advised his protégés not only that they could use theatrics, but that they should. He even acknowledged to an interviewer once that losing his temper and shouting were tools of the trade in negotiations. "Depends on whether I have a reason to. If they're being impossible or unreasonable, or they're getting nasty, then I don't let them let away with that. . . . Some people lose their temper deliberately. I've been known to do that at times to make them understand that I'm being serious. I raise my voice. Why not? They raise theirs sometimes. If somebody tries to bully me, he's going to get something back. You can't allow that to happen. You can't allow somebody to try to bully you or to run roughshod over you or to give you a bunch of crap and think that you're accepting it. If he gives you a bunch of crap, you've got to let him know that you know it's crap. Then he might not try it on you again."

Threats were guaranteed to set him off. He said, "Sometimes they threaten; sometimes *you* show a little steel fist so they realize it's not all hunky-dory. . . . If somebody threatens me, he's going to get something back to show him that I don't like to be threatened. Now, I may not threaten him, because I don't like the use of threats. . . . People call your bluff if you're bluffing."

While Habib's anger was sometimes an act and sometimes a tool of the trade, other times it was frighteningly real. Dishonesty, interference with his progress, and broken promises were the kinds of things that sent him into a genuine rage. When Sharon would break a ceasefire, shut off power and water to Beirut, or launch yet another overkill assault that prevented Habib from meeting with his intermediaries, Habib's anger was no act.

His anger tended to be over some transient event rather than over lasting matters, rarely overcame him, was never malicious, and always passed quickly. Ten minutes after a howling tantrum, the recipient might still be reeling, but Habib would seem to have forgotten all about it and have already moved on to the next thing.

Remarkably, people rarely took it personally. To one colleague, Habib epitomized the classic definition of a diplomat as a person who can tell you to go to hell in such a way that you actually look forward to the trip. Hill says, "Habib had the rare gift of yelling the worst criticism at someone, but without giving any sense of *real* anger or animosity. His tantrums all had a quality of play-acting, so they worked without offending."

For example, one day he read in the morning newspaper that the Syrians had made an important announcement that they should have first communicated to him directly. While he was talking to Charlie Hill about it, Hill mentioned that the story had been on the evening news in Washington the night before, "and we just brushed it aside."

"You mean you had this thing last night and you didn't tell anybody about it?!" Habib roared. "I mean, what the hell is the matter with you guys? Can't you read? Or did nobody bring it to your attention because they didn't think it was important?" He laughed. "It's not the sort of thing you brush aside, old boy." Tone of voice and a touch of friendliness softened the sting.

The person he beat up on the most was his long-suffering deputy, Morris Draper. "If you hadn't been told that Draper was his last name," says one colleague, "you'd think it was Goddammit, because what you heard so often was 'Morrie, Goddammit!'" He would dump on Draper for just about anything, from how he dressed to how long he took to write a cable to his choice in restaurants. Draper took it all with surprisingly good humor, recognizing it as play acting and Habib's way of letting off steam.

The second prime recipient of his fusillades was Charlie Hill, who took most of his calls into the State Department. "Ninety-nine percent of the time," Hill says, "he was just shooting off his mouth. He had to just scream and yell and rage at me at the end of the day. And it meant nothing." Habib might slam down the receiver, then call back ten minutes later as though his earlier tirade had never happened. Sometimes, while Habib was busy bellowing over the radio at him, Hill would be reading a magazine.

"The secret of Habib's success," Hill says, "was his ability to express screaming moral outrage—yell and scream and wave his arms at people—and yet no one felt it was directed at them personally as any kind of insult. In fact, they felt affection toward him. It's mock outrage in which you convey a point very, very effectively. That to me was the essence of the Habib personality."

Too Emotionally Involved?

There is no question that Habib was deeply emotionally involved in this mission. But his critics—and some of his colleagues—would later say that he was *too* emotionally involved. Shultz moderates his overwhelming praise for Habib by conceding that "he cared a great deal about Lebanon—to a certain extent, maybe he cared too much, but anyway he cared enough to pour himself into it wholeheartedly." Haig agrees, saying, "He was a Lebanese, and he was very emotional about it. That was both a strength and a weakness."

Sam Lewis is more blunt. "During the height of war, he was extraordinarily emotional vis-à-vis Washington and the shortcomings of US policy. When he was isolated and West Beirut was under artillery barrages, in the stress of the moment he got pretty carried away. By then he had been working this problem for over a year almost nonstop and, I think, had got very emotionally engaged in it beyond his professional responsibilities. He was so upset about the tragedies in Beirut that he became less and less able to see anything other than evil intentions on the Israelis' part, and over time his objectivity began to fray under the pressure."

Habib answered that kind of criticism directly: "I must say that the next time some Israeli tells Sam that I am panicking, I wish that Sam would tell them that I have been sitting here cool as a cucumber for weeks. But that doesn't necessarily mean that my anger is completely subdued. I'm not panicking about anything. But if you heard the stories the French Ambassador [told me this morning] about his visit to the French 'mini-camps' . . . where the nuns are crying because the kids are sick in front of them. They have no way to take care of them. They have no water. He says the stench is unbearable. Does anybody realize what that means?"

Others strongly agree with Habib. "I didn't feel that he was overly committed or swayed by emotion," says Nick Veliotes, whose ears Habib often blistered. "I thought that he was right on." Another colleague says, "I remember seeing Phil get pissed as shit often, but he never let his emotions override what he knew the policy was or what he knew the relationship with Israel was."

Of those who think Habib was too emotionally involved, none were actually in Beirut with him seeing what he saw. Colleagues who *were* in Beirut with him agree that he was emotionally involved, but dismiss the idea that he was too much so or that it affected his judgment. His top military liaison in Beirut, Colonel Jim Sehulster, says, "If you weren't there, you weren't exposed to all the various influences that were playing on him. Certainly he was very involved in this and had a very pointed opinion about it. But that opinion was based on the various elements he was exposed to. He put those stimuli through the prism of his training in the State Department. He reported *with* emotion, but not *out of* emotion."

Hill describes the background to criticisms of Habib's emotionality. "The tough guys in Washington—the generals and the FSOs—would say, 'If you're gonna be a real diplomat, you've gotta be willing to see some very ugly things take place. Like a surgeon: You can't let the sight of blood bother you. In fact, the spilling of some blood now will save more later, so you can't let yourself get emotionally involved in that.' They at times would indicate to each other that Phil was losing it, because he was so emotional in saying, 'We must not allow the human suffering to take place.'"

A case in point came on June 26. Habib believed the Israelis were preparing for a brutal assault on Beirut, and he was determined to prevent it. He called for Reagan to phone Begin to threaten sanctions if they assaulted the city. Undersecretary Eagleburger, one of the tough guys in Washington, suggested Habib was being too soft. Over the radio, Habib yelled at

Eagleburger, in effect, *The hell I am.* "You guys don't understand what this is all about," he shouted. "I was a lieutenant in World War Two. I saw the bombardment of Saint-Lô and the Ardennes."

Eagleburger shot back sarcastically, "Yeah, yeah, and I saw Sedan in 1870 and the Somme in 1916."

"You're like a young crow," said Habib: "all mouth and full of shit."

The question may boil down to Habib being, as Beirut political officer Ryan Crocker puts it, "quite a study in personal contrasts, if not contradiction. There couldn't have been a more marked contrast between his volatility of temper and his thoroughly steady, tenacious, persistent approach to the negotiations, no matter how grim it looked. I think all his thundering and roaring and crashing around was probably just his way of letting off steam. It could obscure, if you weren't watching the work closely, how absolutely methodical he was in his approach to what he was doing."

Foolhardy Tenacity

That persistence was partly emotional, partly intellectual, but completely indispensable. He was there to persuade intransigent people to make decisions they did not want to make. That would take time, and he was prepared to outlast them. Meanwhile, he endured bout after bout of posturing, recognizing that "posturing is a result of the unwillingness of the party to make the hard decisions. . . . When a man is ready to make a decision, he'll make it." He understood that the parties might buy the same agreement tomorrow that they rejected today: They would first have to be courted, pressured, sweet-talked, blistered, persuaded. That's what he was there to do.

Despite his repeated disappointments, despite Sharon's ingenuity for ever more ways to press the fight, and despite the disarray among the Washington decision-makers whom he represented, Habib showed an almost foolhardy tenacity. It was the same tenacity he had shown in trying to revive his drowned Lebanese friend in Canada in 1951. "He was like a firefighter who doesn't have the right equipment," says Hill. "He wouldn't say, 'I don't have the right equipment, therefore I'm not going to go fight the fire.' He'd go fight the fire anyway." He would call Washington and demand top-level pressure. Nothing would happen. He would call again and demand action. Nothing would happen. Again call. Again nothing. Call, nothing; call, nothing; call, nothing. "But Habib wouldn't stop," says Hill. "He'd just keep going."

To Habib's way of thinking, that was just doing his job as an FSO. "You have to keep on trying in this business," he once said. "You can't give up. You have to keep on trying." When his secretary would say there was no hope, he would insist "There's always hope." *"No hope!"* she would yell back. One time when he was meeting with Lebanese politicians who despaired about ever getting the PLO out, they said, "We can't do this. It's hopeless." Habib blasted them: "What do you mean telling me this can't be done after we've been working for a month trying to set this up?! What am I supposed to do, pick up and go home and leave this thing hanging?"

Habib certainly had his low points and sometimes seemed worried, "But I never saw a sense of despair, of loss of confidence," says Crocker. "There was always a sense of energy, dynamism, positivism throughout that period. Whatever the latest outrage was, he'd be ready to take it head-on and then move somewhere else."

Several beliefs sustained him through the dark days. One was a conviction that the Israelis—other than Sharon himself, perhaps—didn't really want to fight their way into West Beirut and that the Palestinians didn't really want to die to the last man. Second, he was acutely aware that he represented the sole hope of preventing those outcomes. "Of course you're conscious of the fact that you're dealing with this shockingly immediate question of the deaths of thousands of people and the destruction that goes with it!" he said. "That makes you realize you've got to get to work, get it done, get it over with, get it stopped."

Third, he knew that those two ultimate aversions meant the Israelis and the Palestinians had some common ground that he could build on. He said he "felt" he could pull off a settlement, but emphasized that the operative word was *felt*. "It was not," he said, "the result of a logical line of reasoning."

Some of what sustained him was more personal. Being retired, he had nothing to gain or lose professionally and no interest in how success or failure might make him look. But he relished the pure intellectual stimulation of dueling brains. "He *loved* challenges," says Bider. *"Loved* them. The more complicated the challenge, the more intrigued he became. Because then you need a solution, and finding the solution was part of his enjoyment of life." Many of the other reasons he hung in sound terribly corny: He did it to right what he considered a grave wrong. He did it because his president asked him to. He did it because taking on impossible, thankless assignments was his way of serving his country. He did it also because he was so delighted to have been called out of a boring retirement to do something interesting. He thrived at the center of high-level international negotiations, what he called "the jazzy part of diplomacy." As one of his best friends said, "Phil loved the drama of great political events and, with boyish delight, gloried in being an actor on the world stage. . . . He remained at heart a Lebanese boy from Brooklyn who marveled at having made it in the big time."

Ambassadors and Cooks

Habib was the point man and the negotiator with foreign officials, but half of his work was orchestrating American officials in the region and in Washington to do their part. And, as George Shultz was fond of saying, the hardest negotiations are within your own team.

No diplomat operates alone, and Habib devoted a lot of energy to tending the vast network of people he needed to get his job done. For example, at one point in July Habib concluded that the Syrians had not agreed to take in PLO evacuees because they had not yet received a request from the PLO. He needed for that request to get made. In a typical case of roundabout diplomacy, he coached Charlie Hill in Washington on how to coach the American ambassador in Saudi Arabia to suggest to the Saudis that they urge the PLO to ask the Syrians for asylum. The American ambassador "doesn't have to come right out and say, 'Ask the PLO,'" Habib said. "He might say to them: 'Have you been keeping the PLO informed? You noticed that [a Syrian statement] indicates that they haven't received the PLO request. Will the PLO be prepared to give a request?' You know, do it in the form of questions. Play like an Arab."

Some special envoys pride themselves in jetting into a hotspot, doing their very important business as solo performer, holding a press conference, and then leaving. Habib considered that the height of arrogance and took great pride in doing just the opposite: "I never went to a meeting without taking the ambassador with me," he said. "Before I'd go into a meeting I would go over everything with him and my staff: what I was going to do, how I was going to do it. And if anybody had any ideas, he would tell me. When we'd get out of the meetings we'd go back and have a skull session: 'What does it mean?'"

Habib considered it absolutely necessary to involve the local ambassadors this way. Having been an ambassador himself, he recognized that each local ambassador knew the personalities and local political pressures better than he did. It was also important for him to know, for example, if one of the wives of the Saudi king was ill. He counted on each local ambassador to fill him in on such things and to interject points and perspectives that would strengthen his hand. Being in the meetings, they could also chime in whenever he failed to appreciate a point that they recognized to be significant. This approach reinforced the ambassador's importance in the local leaders' eyes. The ambassadors in the region thus felt a strong personal stake in Habib's mission and worked overtime to help him succeed.

As he had done in every assignment from Canada to Korea, he sought out all the information he could get. He listened to the ambassadors and the prime ministers, but also to the cooks, the maids, the guards, and the drivers. In Lebanon, many of those staff lived in or had family in West Beirut where Israeli bombs were falling. So Habib made a point of sounding them out about what was really going on there and giving him a perspective he wouldn't hear from the politicians. He particularly listened to Jonny Abdu, the Lebanese intelligence chief, because Abdu's sources were good guys and bad guys high and low from all points on the spectrum.

Habib took in a numbing torrent of conflicting information from all quarters, but never let it paralyze him. Wherever he was on any given day, he would have the local embassy staff bring him the latest cables, intelligence reports, or other papers first thing every morning. A speed reader, he would plow through them, make his decisions without agonizing, write his replies or comments on the papers, and hand them back. He kept none of them. He would laugh at one staff member who always carried around copies of treaties and the like in a briefcase. "I don't carry any papers," he would say. "Anything I can't carry around in my head isn't worth remembering."

Tell Them I'm Not In

During the siege, the press made much of the fact that Habib's parents were Lebanese and that he had grown up in a Jewish neighborhood in Brooklyn. Who better to mediate disputes between Israelis and Arabs? But his Lebanese roots were both an asset and a liability.

Habib himself was ambivalent about them. He loved telling Irish friends that "when their ancestors were painting themselves blue, my ancestors were developing algebra." He once told Begin that his father was from Sidon and said, "Can I ask you not to bomb my parents' home?"

But Habib saw himself as a 100 percent red-white-and-blue American, end of story. He had spent sixty-two years ignoring his Arab roots, and his training as a Foreign Service officer only reinforced that habit. FSOs are trained to be acutely aware never to let their personal background get in the way of their professional judgments or responsibilities. In fact, the State Department had long had a practice (now discontinued) of not sending diplomats to the homelands of their forebears. It wasn't that State didn't trust its FSOs. It was that State didn't trust the local people. Local leaders might view the diplomat as being only quasi-American or less than even-handed and therefore susceptible to special influence or pressure. They might try to draw the diplomat in to taking sides on internal issues. They might try to use the FSO's local relatives as leverage to get some special treatment.

So Habib had always explicitly distanced himself from his Lebanese heritage. Whenever he sensed that an Arab diplomat was trying to cozy up to him as a brother, he would deflect him by saying that he was really a Far East specialist. When he first arrived in Lebanon to begin his mission as special envoy in 1981, he told the ambassador, "If anybody calls saying they're my first cousin or something, tell them I'm not in."

"Why?" the ambassador asked.

"They're just trying to get close to me. Tell them my name was Mafooz or something and that my father changed his name to Habib." He supposedly had an old uncle in the mountain town of Ein Arab, and he did have one conversation with someone claiming to be a relative. But he made no efforts to seek his family history or to look up his grandfather's grave. He couldn't afford the luxury of such distractions.

Persuading People You're Not God

Letting local people get too cozy with a diplomat is a touchy thing, especially in Lebanon. Many Lebanese, says Bob Dillon, are convinced that their destiny depends on foreigners, so they must influence foreigners, particularly Americans. Any senior American official in Lebanon, such as the ambassador, thus finds himself receiving an enormous amount of attention. "There will be a massive attempt to co-opt you," Dillon says. "People are terribly flattering. You have to keep reminding yourself that . . . the atmosphere is just make-believe. [This happens elsewhere too], but in Lebanon it went on to a degree that I had never seen any place else."

If the American ambassador in Lebanon is a target for fawning, an American special presidential envoy with Lebanese roots was a superstar. "Habib was sort of a Lebanese folk hero," says Hill, "the kid who went to the new world and made good. The ordinary Arab on the street—not just in Lebanon, but elsewhere in the Middle East—almost worshipped him. You'd go into a restaurant with him, and the Arab waiter would come to take orders, recognize that this was Philip Habib, and bow and say, 'Oh, yes, Effendi. Of course, Effendi. Whatever you like, Effendi.'" The waiter might then never bring a bill.

It was an extraordinary phenomenon. Dillon found that, as ambassador to Lebanon, "You spend quite a bit of time trying to persuade people that you're not God. You really do. Phil had become the symbol of the US in Lebanon. So the great Phil Habib was—well, to say this was God exaggerates it, but he was seen as a very, very important, influential person." The Lebanese would have just swept him away if they could.

Habib enjoyed the flattery up to a point, but it also troubled him. On this mission, says Hill, "he suddenly realized that the Lebanese people were looking to him, as the world's most famous [person with a Lebanese name], to protect them—and he was devastated to realize that he could not answer their cries. The greatest shock to him was to realize that ordinary Lebanese people actually saw him as someone who could bring peace to Lebanon and become their president—a kind of Lincoln of Lebanon."

He had always had an aversion to personal aggrandizement and would not let anything distract him from his mission. So he dealt with the attention by staying away from the Lebanese people. He didn't go to parties. Didn't tour sites. Didn't do press conferences. He made himself inaccessible—which only added to his mystique.

Can We Really Trust Him?

With Arab *leaders,* the situation was more complex. On the one hand, in Lebanon Habib's heritage made him "one of the boys," says their UN ambassador Ghassan Tueni. "We trusted him and would talk to him. We didn't have to explain to him all the things we would have to explain to some other diplomat. But it also made some people suspicious of him, because you can never be simply a Lebanese: You're always a Lebanese *plus something.* You're a Lebanese Christian, or a Lebanese Muslim, or a Lebanese Druze, or whatever." The fact that Habib was raised Maronite gave him credibility with the Lebanese Maronites.

Habib fell into the role of mentor—or, as Lewis puts it, high commissioner—to many Lebanese leaders. They tended to be young, inexperienced, and more comfortable as rival factional leaders than as national statesmen. Maronite leader Bashir Gemayel, age thirty-four, would often come to Habib for advice. In his unique avuncular way, Habib would often yell at him and tell him to go to hell.

Habib's Lebanese background was more important to his negotiating counterparts than it was to him—for better and for worse. To him, it was just one more arrow in his quiver, to be used only if, when, and how it served his purposes. But to Israelis, it was at best a handicap to be willfully overlooked. He had won their confidence in 1981 by negotiating an end to the Syrian missile crisis and the War of the Katyushas—but now, a year later, this guy with an Arab name was the most visible and noisy opponent of their invasion. Could they really trust him? Not surprisingly, many Arab leaders saw things just the opposite: They weren't sure they could trust him because he was an American and thus must surely be in cahoots with the Israelis. And some established major Arab leaders, such as Assad, didn't like him, didn't like his popularity with the Arab public, and saw him as an intruder they'd just as soon get rid of. The American ambassador to Syria says the Syrians saw Habib as "'another one of these goddam Lebanese rug merchants in diplomatic clothes coming out here to try to bamboozle us.' An undercurrent of that was detectable."

The Immorality of Balance

How did Habib's background affect his views? It is important for any diplomat to communicate to the Israelis that the diplomat understands the Israeli position and sympathizes with them. Habib was "basically, fundamentally, deep down sympathetic" to them as a people, says Draper, and he let them know that. He would often tell them about his experiences growing up in a Jewish neighborhood in Brooklyn and being mistaken for a Jew. He did not tell them about the day his sister disparaged a relative for having married a Jew. "Philip read her the riot act," says Marjorie Habib. "He climbed up one side of her and down the other."

But his sympathy for Jews was not synonymous with approval of the actions of the two Israeli officials named Ariel Sharon and Menachem Begin. And he regularly and vehemently denounced those actions—behind closed doors, of course; never in public.

Habib's colleagues differ over whether, and how, his views might have been affected by his Lebanese roots. Several perceived in him a certain pro-Arab bias. Haig feels his roots predisposed him to be sympathetic to the Lebanese and says, "Phil never liked the Israelis. You gotta know that." Lewis says he was much more sympathetic to the Palestinian position than were others in the government at the time. Eagleburger thinks Habib was pro-Arab, but much less so than most of his fellow FSOs.

Other colleagues, citing Habib's reputation as the consummate professional, dismiss out of hand any implication that his personal origins had anything to do with his professional views. *Any* American would feel sympathetic to the plight of the Lebanese, says his legal adviser, Alan Kreczko. "While Phil didn't have any great love for Israel," says another State official, "he *clearly* understood that our relationship with Israel was a very key part of US policy. When Haig says that 'Phil never liked the Israelis,' the 'Israelis' we're talking about was Menachem Begin, who was a hard guy to like." Indeed, as one writer put it, "Begin was clearly the most internationally disliked official in Israeli history." Even Barry Goldwater said that Begin's excesses made Arafat "look like a Boy Scout."

It is certainly true that, as the war dragged on, Habib became scathingly critical of the Israeli government's actions under Begin and Sharon—but then so did a large percentage of the Israeli public, who knew far less about what was really happening in Beirut than Habib did. Hill summarizes Habib's view as being "that the Arab side had a lot of right on its account, and that the Israelis were constantly stirring up trouble and being difficult." Over the course of his mission, Habib became increasingly sour on Begin's administration, eventually concluding that the Arabs and Israelis deserved each other, and a pox on both their houses.

The Israelis saw Habib as having "a balanced view" for the most part, says Eagleburger, but balance is not a welcome position in the Middle East. Both Arabs and Israelis "are just damned self-righteous," says Dillon. "That was one of the reasons that they were all exasperating to deal with. Each sees itself as the victim and the aggrieved. They each believe that their case is so self-evidently correct that if you do not accept it, there is something wrong with you, not with them. So a diplomat dealing with both Arabs and Israelis finds that both are distrustful and can be intensely hostile. The idea that an American can have a 'balanced' view is almost immoral in their eyes."

The Israelis did not view him as an enemy, but certainly not as a close friend either.

And a Good Bit of Whipped Cream

His colleagues also differ over whether any of his characteristics came from his Lebanese roots. Some who knew both the Lebanese and Habib well say no. He was a product of Brooklyn, not of Lebanon. Others feel he had several traits stereotypical of Arabs in general and of Lebanese in particular: Like many of them, he was happy, friendly, talkative, lively, emotional, short-tempered, prone to shouting and bullying people, and absolutely convinced he could handle any situation. When something went wrong that he obviously could do nothing about, he would tend to give the Arab shrug: shoulders up, palms up, as if to say *"Malesh.* Ah, well." All agree that his Lebaneseness came out most clearly in his love for Lebanese food.

One stereotype of Lebanese certainly did apply to Habib: He was a born negotiator with an instinct for compromise and a willingness to experiment. The essential truth of the Middle East, says Draper, is that "it is a bazaar. You have to know how to make a deal." And, as Brandon Grove says, "Phil had that kind of shrewd bargaining sense, that skill at reading human beings that many Middle Easterners have." He knew that in the Middle East you didn't ask the price of a rug, pay that price, and take home your purchase. The rug merchant whispers that he'll give you a special deal, a mere $2,000. You scoff at such a ridiculous price and offer $500. He comes down some, you come up some, you argue, you walk away, he lures you back, you drink some coffee together, and you wind up paying $1,000.

Habib enjoyed the dickering. He felt right at home with it. Menachem Begin reportedly used to say that Habib was like a Jewish haberdasher: You went in to buy a necktie, and if you didn't find one you liked, he'd sell you his old Buick.

To negotiate with both Arabs and Israelis, a diplomat must be able to both swim with the fish and fly with the birds. Phil Habib was one of those rare creatures. It was a prime reason he felt he was the only diplomat with any hope of settling this crisis.

His background gave him a Middle Eastern feel for things, Draper says. "He was really one of them. He had that kind of touch. He didn't have that typical austere American/European/Western approach to things." When he met Israelis or Arabs, he embraced them and kissed them on the cheek, as is the custom. Whereas other Western diplomats might grit their teeth going through such motions, Habib thought nothing of it. Many diplomats are uncomfortable with the Arab tendency to sit or stand very very close when talking. Not Habib. Lebanese tend to touch each other when talking more than Westerners do. There he patted people on the knee or the shoulder instinctively. When he would send a message to an Arab friend, he would address him as "brother," as is the Arab custom. When people came to visit him, he would serve them food.

Dealing with Begin's government required an inexhaustible patience for detail and precision. Dealing with the Arabs required an intuition for ambiguity. Habib was equally at home splitting hairs with Israelis in the morning and exchanging shrugs with Arabs in the afternoon. In Jerusalem, he would usually be all-business, with a strict agenda: cover the points at hand as expeditiously as possible, bid them adieu, and leave. In Beirut, he would have lunch or dinner with his counterparts like brothers in a very casual atmosphere. With Israelis he had to be quite direct. With Arabs he had to be more convoluted, to combine, as Eagleburger puts it, "some directness with a good bit of whipped cream." The Arabs might not tell him what they thought, or might tell him yes but mean no. The Israelis, says Eagleburger, "had a habit of saying yes and probably meaning it, but then changing their minds." Habib understood—and bore the scars from—both habits.

Begin and the people he surrounded himself with scrutinized every statement and every detail with minute legalistic precision. They insisted that all problems be negotiated through to agreement and expressed in a written document that the parties would sign. Begin personally decided what was and what was not permissible on every agreement. "Every provision," says Hill, "had to be negotiated down to thirty-five sub-paragraphs." Habib could keep up with Begin detail for detail: He could recall the finest print on any treaty dealing with the Middle East and quote it on cue.

He could, but he tried not to. For example, when he met with Begin to go over the hundredth draft of his plan, Begin started in on his list of quibbles. Habib broke in and said he hoped they could avoid a "lawyer's discussion" of the plan. *But of course we must have a lawyer's discussion,* said Begin: Since the plan was an "international document," the attorney general's lawyers would have to scrutinize it. *No, no, no, no, no,* Habib protested. This "is only a plan and not an international document, and we should accordingly avoid quibbling over each word and comma."

Begin was "a courtly nineteenth-century gentleman," and Habib rarely indulged in theatrics with him. Dour, serious, dignified, and formal, Begin wasn't given to small talk or jokes. Habib was the only person who would dare to tease him, and one of the few who could ever draw a laugh out of him. But it was rare for even Habib to succeed in lightening up Begin's mood. For example, one time, he wanted to draw an analogy to make some point, so he began by asking the prime minister, "Do you play poker?"

"No," Begin replied. "When I was a young man, I played cards with a group of friends. At the end of the evening, I went home and said I had wasted a whole evening playing cards instead of doing something serious, something that had some intellectual content and meaning. I've never played cards since then."

Habib, whose furniture at home was bought with his poker winnings, looked at Begin for a moment and said, "You must have lost!"

Everyone else in the room got the joke. Begin never did.

Taking the Eyebrow

In contrast to the stringent legalistic precision Begin and his administration required, the Arabs tended to operate more on the basis of informality, ambiguity, and trust in the person. Their typical style was to talk around the subject, testing the waters. Assad in particular was renowned for his habit of talking to foreign visitors for hours about every subject under the sun except the business at hand.

With the Arabs, Habib could deal in the traditional Middle Eastern way: They would trust him, he would trust them, and things would be carried out. They didn't need precise agreements: They were more comfortable with informal understandings. "If you tried to make things too specific and too clear," says Hill, "you would not be able to accomplish anything." So in Arab capitals, Hill says, "Habib could look at them, shrug his shoulders, throw his hands out to the side with his palms up, and they would know what he was saying. And he wouldn't say a word. Yet he would walk away knowing that he had a deal."

The lift of an eyebrow was not always enough, of course. Many issues did have to be pinned down, even when the Arabs didn't want to. Habib would make constant judgment calls whether or not to ask them questions. "If you don't want the answer they're likely to give," says Nat Howell, "you take the eyebrow."

Habib had the intuition to feel how ambiguous things needed to be and how specific they had to be. There was no formula, no way of explaining it or quantifying it, just a gut instinct that you either had or didn't have. When he thought it appropriate, he went to great pains to make sure the understandings were precise. And he always insisted that his messages back and forth with the PLO be in writing.

One way Habib dealt with all the differing negotiating styles was to sum up what he thought he had heard. When Begin would get wound up talking a blue streak, Habib would yank him back to the point by saying, "Prime Minister, what you're really saying is this. . . ." Howell says, "Whether it was exactly what they had said or not, if they nodded, you took it and ran. You've got to try to make the blocks fit the edifice you're trying to build, not necessarily take whatever they deliver!"

See the Naked Lady Dance

While Habib himself, his style, and what he brought to the table were strikingly unique, in many ways he simply typified a skilled diplomat at work. It is a diplomat's job to get people out of the jams they have gotten themselves into, by giving them a face-saving way out. It is a diplomat's job to fend off diversions, to keep the parties focused on central issues and on one another's interests.

Shultz felt that "Most of the State Department's top negotiators would say that, on the basis of innate negotiating ability and mastery of all the technique and so on, Phil was just outstanding." Habib used whatever technique he needed with a particular person in a particular situation. Many of them were standard arrows in the diplomat's quiver.

For example, he often used a classic mediating technique of *very slightly* exaggerating to one party another party's latest statement or ploy or admission. That technique requires a deft touch: Portray the other's guy's position as just a hair more positive than it really was, and maybe you can nudge this guy to be a little more positive himself. Do this deftly, and you can hasten progress; overdo it, and you lose your credibility.

A variation on that technique was to stretch his own situation a bit. For instance, if a counterpart in a negotiation was giving him nothing to work with, Habib might get their attention by saying, "OK, tell me what I can tell President Reagan when I call him tonight." As special presidential envoy, he had every right to phone the president anytime he wanted. What he didn't mention was that, as a career FSO trained to report to the secretary of state, he in fact talked directly to Reagan only infrequently.

He would also exploit his unique position as intermediary to sound out one party without revealing the other party's views. For instance, if Begin made some demand, Habib might not tell the PLO that Begin was demanding it. Instead, he might say, "In my opinion, I don't think Israel will settle for less. I'm not promising anything, but I strongly feel as if we can reach an agreement on this point. Can you concede on this point?" If the PLO sent back word that they would, Habib might then tell Begin, "The PLO hasn't made its position known on this point, but I have reason to believe they'll concede on it." This technique let him test one side's position without committing the other side. It gave him flexibility while letting both sides save face.

Like any good diplomat, Habib stayed focused on the ends and readily employed or discarded various means to those ends as necessary. "There's no one way of getting somewhere," he once told an interviewer in his living room at home on the San Francisco Peninsula. "There are usually all kinds of different alternatives. It's like, if I want to go to San Francisco from here, I don't have to go on Highway 101. I can take Highway 280. I can even take El Camino Real. I can drive, I can take a bus, I can have a friend drive me. I can walk. I could even run! I could swim if I wanted to. In a negotiation, it's the same thing: There are lots of ways of getting where you want to go."

Like many diplomats, he had a knack for articulating how the proposal he was trying to sell was in the other party's own interest. For example, one night in late July Bashir Gemayel came to Habib for advice.

"I'm coming under great pressure," Bashir said. "Sharon wants me to clean out the West Beirut [Palestinian] camps. He wants me to go in from the east while he comes up from the south. What should I do, *'Ammo?"*

"Well, what do you think you should do?"

"There'd be a lot of killing. It would be tough and I'd lose a lot of men. But how can I resist Sharon?"

"You know, Bashir, that I'm negotiating the withdrawal of the Palestinians. You also know you want to be president one day. If you do what Sharon asks it will damn you. It will make it hard for you to become president of all the Lebanese, Muslims as well as Christians. Don't do it, Bashir. Say no."

In another instance, he proposed a face-saving way for Assad to bring his troops home from Lebanon by suggesting that "practically speaking, they needed to return to Syria for re-equipping."

He was essentially the same person with anyone, but, like any good diplomat, he would adapt his manner to his audience. Profanity was his native language, but he always toned it down "around ladies." To fellow Americans, he would dismiss an idea by saying "That's a bunch of crap"; with a foreigner he was more likely to say "That's a joke." With American colleagues, he tended to shout, bully, push, argue, challenge, contradict. He rarely raised his voice with the courtly Begin, but often had shouting matches with Sharon. He considered the cool, calculating Assad "a wicked man," but would be reserved, polite, and outwardly respectful but also extremely firm with him. With Lebanese officials, Habib was comfortable acting "almost like a high commissioner." He had no such relationship with Israelis. Only the Lebanese would he usually curse.

Like any good diplomat, he had an instinct for what style was appropriate in a given meeting or a given moment. He wielded a baton or a bludgeon as needed. As he once told an interviewer, "Sometimes you want to hit [the other guy] with something bluntly, so you say it bluntly. Sometimes you want to open a crack in the door by showing him a way that might be useful, so you get a little subtle. Now you see it, now you don't. Pay another quarter and you get to see the naked lady dance in the back room. . . . Sometimes you don't want to commit yourself too openly until you see what the reaction will be, so you drop a hint. If the guy responds, he knows what the hell he's responding to."

In the end, though he used many of the same techniques as other diplomats, Phil Habib was unmistakably quite unlike any other diplomat. He was a character. He filled any room he entered. And it does make a difference in international discourse, Shultz says, to be dealing with an interesting person. His energy, sense of humor and force of personality made people enjoy being around him just out of curiosity: "What the hell is Habib going to say or do next?"

The characteristics, experiences, priorities, and values that Habib brought to the table combined to make him, as Brandon Grove puts it, "just serendipitously the right man doing the right job at the right time. I saw Phil at work both on the Lebanon problem and in 1980 on a rather mundane assignment. In '80 he was his genial self. But he was just gray in every aspect compared to what he was like when he had hold of this Lebanese problem. He *ran* this. He had it for breakfast, lunch, and supper. It consumed him. He was totally seized. He rejoiced in it, because it was what he felt he had been born to do. He realized that this was, in large historical terms, his moment."

8
The Plan

Glendower: I can call spirits from the vasty deep.
Hotspur: Why, so can I, or so can any man;
But will they come when you do call for them?
Shakespeare, Henry IV, Part 1

Armies have laid siege to cities since the days of battering rams and boiling oil. But earlier sieges were nearly always settled militarily: Attackers either conquered the city or gave up and went home. So Philip Habib knew of no precedent for negotiating a peaceful end to a siege. He had to make one up as he went.

He quickly realized that, since Ariel Sharon's quarry was not the city itself but a foreign element holed up inside it, the only way to end this siege peacefully would be to somehow extract the PLO from Beirut and keep them from coming back.

Like any good diplomat, Habib took his cues from the main parties. In the early days of the invasion, before it had settled into a siege at all, the Israelis proposed that a buffer force of 10,000 soldiers from several nations take over southern Lebanon to keep PLO rockets out of range of Israeli soil. Once such a force was in place and working, Begin told Habib June 13, "we will be out of Lebanon completely." The same day, the PLO was trying to organize its own evacuation from Beirut by sea. Neither idea went anywhere, but kernels of each evolved into pillars of Habib's plan.

Anathema

His plan would have to address a thousand issues large and small: How many PLO fighters would he need to evacuate? Three thousand? Ten thousand? Twenty? No one knew. Could fighters take their families? What security measures would suffice to assure the PLO that they could come out of hiding and depart Beirut safely? Whose soldiers would protect them? How many soldiers? Stationed where? Once the PLO fighters left Beirut, how would the Palestinian civilians left behind be protected? Where would the fighters go? Some other part of Lebanon? Some other country? Which country? Could some stay in Lebanon? Could a PLO political office remain to serve the administrative needs of the remaining 400,000 Palestin-

127

ian civilians? Should the PLO drive out in trucks? Fly out in airplanes? Helicopters? Sail away in ships? Whose ships? How could Habib schedule ships if he didn't know when the evacuation would happen or how many evacuees there would be? Should the PLO board ships at the port or somewhere else? What weapons, if any, could they take with them? What would become of the weapons they left behind? Would the Syrian troops trapped in Beirut leave too? Would they go to Syria or to some other part of Lebanon? How should Syrian-controlled (non-PLO) Palestinian guerrillas be handled differently than mainstream PLO-Fatah forces?

The answer to each question raised a dozen more questions.

The plan would be Habib's, but his own views of what should happen were less important than his judgments of what the various parties would accept. And there were lots of parties to satisfy: not only the Israelis and the PLO, but (at least as important, in Habib's eyes) the Lebanese government. Then there were the Syrians, the main Lebanese warlords, the broader Arab world, the French, and a gaggle of bureaucracies in Washington. The odds of agreement were slim: Any particular that was acceptable to one party would, almost by definition, be anathema to some other.

So he pushed the main parties to propose the elements of the plan themselves. He would then screen the various proposals and bat down the more outlandish ones. If he thought a proposal had some potential, he would refine it. If he thought it wouldn't fly, he'd tell them to come up with a better idea. And if they needed suggestions, he'd be happy to supply a dozen.

He thought most of the proposals he heard would never fly. The Israelis were a fount of ideas. But their ideas generally amounted to ever-escalating terms of surrender, and Habib was not particularly interested in listening to those. The PLO floated lots of vague proposals that left them vast wiggle room. He was not too interested in listening to those either. "I refuse to deal with stupidity," he said. "Every time the PLO comes up with a stupid idea, we'll jump all over it."

The party whose ideas Habib was the most interested in listening to, the government of Lebanon, was afraid to propose much of anything lest other Arabs accuse them of kicking the PLO out. While few other people cared what the government of Lebanon thought, Habib pressed them to take the lead, even if under his tutelage. This was their country, their capital, their sovereignty, and Habib was determined to use this crisis as a catalyst to restore them to relevance. He coached, nudged, and bullied the president and prime minister to come up with terms that were in *Lebanon's* interest. He dogged them to decide for themselves the fundamental question of what role if any the Palestinians and PLO should have on Lebanese soil. He stressed to them that "while the PLO could 'propose,' the Lebanese government should 'demand.'"

The basic plan jelled in the first few days of July, and Habib tried to cut off further haggling. Each time somebody tried to reopen some particular, he would stubbornly insist "I'm negotiating a package. I'm not negotiating pieces of a package." That was a good line, but he couldn't make it stick. The parties were too incorrigibly squirmy. Plus, as the facts on the ground changed, the plan had to change accordingly.

Though the specifics of his plan fluctuated and evolved from day to day, Habib never wavered from its essential elements: Everybody would stop shooting and back off enough for a neutral military buffer force to wedge itself in between the combatants. Under that force's protection, the PLO fighters would leave Beirut in an orderly manner and go directly or indirectly to some destination(s) where they would no longer be a problem. When the evacuation was over, the neutral force would stay on for a while to protect the Palestinian civilians left behind and help the Lebanese government reassert control of Beirut. Once the PLO was out, Habib's plan called for the Israelis and Syrians to leave Lebanon.

The operative word was *plan*. Habib knew that neither side would consider signing an agreement with the other. So he repeatedly stressed that this was a plan, not an "agreement." In his unorthodox approach, the parties would not have to agree with one another about anything. Each party would simply agree with him.

There was, of course, nothing simple about his plan. Moving thousands of edgy, undisciplined PLO fighters safely from their hideouts through the streets to waiting ships and then on to their destinations would be a mammoth operation of extraordinary complexity. And it could collapse over any detail.

Paralyzing Fears

The Israelis felt that, if the PLO were to leave Beirut alive at all, Habib's departure plan should consist simply of Israeli terms of surrender. No detail of his plan could give the PLO the slightest whiff of legitimacy. The PLO must leave not as survivors of the storm marching out under an international escort, but as broken, vanquished criminals crawling away to exile. Habib felt that, if those were the terms, he might as well go home now because such terms would give the PLO no incentive to leave at all.

His reason was that, while fear of annihilation may have motivated the PLO to leave, other powerful fears motivated them to stay. No way was he going to succeed unless his plan accommodated those paralyzing fears to some reasonable extent.

The PLO feared losing all the power and comforts they had enjoyed in the anarchy of Lebanon prior to the invasion. With a yearly budget of well over a billion dollars—drawn largely from subsidies from Arab states—the PLO was the second-largest employer after the government. High-ranking PLO leaders, each of whom had a nom de guerre starting with "Abu," lived in the luxury apartments of an area called the Neighborhood of the Big Abus. "The PLO really were in fat city in Beirut," says Charlie Hill. "I mean, they ran the place. They were the Mafia. They had the booze and the drugs and the girls and the funds. They really didn't want to give that up."

They feared losing face. Habib had learned in Korea and Vietnam the importance of enabling parties to save face, and he was convinced that if the PLO didn't find a face-saving way out, "they will put up a last ditch fight." Yasir Arafat emphasized that they would rather die in street-to-street fighting than walk out in disgrace. Libya's ruler Moamar Khadaffi urged the PLO leaders to commit suicide rather than submit. Egypt's president Hosni Mubarak believed they would never leave, preferring to become the stuff of legend by fighting to the last man. Some of this was surely just macho rhetoric, but Habib could not afford to dismiss it. Sharon did have the PLO in a genuinely desperate predicament, which leads to desperate measures. Besides, a last stand was not an unreasonable option in the PLO's calculus: Well-entrenched defenders, especially guerrillas on their home turf, always have an advantage over attackers. *Let the Israelis come get us in the catacombs of Beirut,* ran one strand of PLO thinking. *If we're going to die anyway, better to fight on to the last drop of blood, take with us more Jews than we could kill in decades of terrorist attacks, and go down in a blaze of glorious martyrdom.*

The matter of letting the PLO save face was a particularly tricky issue for Habib to deal with. For one thing, Begin and Sharon were determined not just to destroy the PLO, but to humiliate them in the process. For another, Arafat had personalized the issue, announcing that he would never "surrender to" Philip Habib, by name.

The PLO also feared that, even if Habib came up with acceptable terms for their departure, the minute they popped their heads above ground to leave Beirut, the Israelis would blow them off. If they got in trucks to drive to the port to leave, they feared that the Israelis would blow up the trucks. If they got to the port, the Israelis would massacre them there. If they got onto ships safely, the Israelis would sink the ships. And if by some miracle the fighting men sailed away safely, the women and children they left behind would be massacred by Sharon or his ally the Phalange. They were simply not going to budge without ironclad security guarantees *that they could trust.*

They feared that, even if an evacuation went smoothly, they wouldn't be able to strike Israel as easily from some more distant country, which might render them irrelevant. They feared that, if they left their weaponry behind, they'd be weak in a new place. They feared that a more stable host country somewhere else—say, Syria—would fence them in and wrest control of the Palestinian movement from them. They feared that, if they were scattered hither and yon, they would lose what little cohesion they had and their movement would irreparably splinter.

All in all, they had about as much reason to stay as they had to leave. So why cooperate with Philip Habib?

To the PLO, he represented little more than a chance to surrender and be paraded before the world in disgrace, with nothing to show for their struggle. So they stalled in hopes of wangling a better deal than he was offering. They kept hoping for a miracle: that Ronald Reagan, George Shultz, the French, the UN, the Arabs, somebody—anybody—would save them. They had good reason to stall, knowing that, as Henry Kissinger once said, "guerrillas win if they aren't defeated, whereas a regular army loses if it doesn't win."

Except for the brief interruption June 29 because of Haig's nine points, Habib had always argued that it was essential to let the PLO leave behind a token force and/or a political office so they would save face enough to leave.

On the question of a token force, Habib's view centered on timing. He did want all Palestinian combatants to leave Lebanon, but he saw no reason why they all had to leave at the same moment. There were thousands of PLO fighters scattered around the hinterlands of Lebanon: Why not just declare 300–500 of them to be the token force and put them under LAF control? Those few hundred could stay in Lebanon a little longer than the ones leaving Beirut—"two days later, three days later, that we can bargain on"—and then leave. But he insisted that the PLO and Lebanese government work up an explicit departure schedule of all PLO combatants. "This might be the minimum concession necessary to make the whole deal work," Habib told Sharon. He saw no reason why such an arrangement should threaten Israel's security.

On the question of a political office, Habib also saw no reason why "10 or 15 people left behind in an office to take care of the social, administrative, and certain other needs of 400,000 Palestinians in Lebanon was going to constitute a security threat to Israel." After all, he said, the PLO had small offices in countries all over the world—including one in Egypt, a fact that had not stood in the way of Israel's signing its 1979 peace treaty with Egypt. If this small representation was required to make the total package deal work, Habib said, Israel would just have to accept it.

But Israel would not accept either a political office or a token force.

The Israelis and Habib recognized that both measures were face-saving cosmetics. As such, both measures were consistent with Habib's goal of getting the PLO out—and inconsistent with Israel's goal of humiliating them. So on July 7 Begin told an American diplomat in Tel Aviv, "Habib keeps telling the PLO, and we know this, that they can have a PLO office and that there can be a residual military presence. We will never agree to this. This is absolutely unacceptable. If he continues to take this position, all his efforts will have been in vain."

The Cats Escorting the Mice

Habib certainly couldn't assuage all of the PLO's fears. But he was even more certainly not going to get them out of Beirut unless his plan addressed the main ones. With no assurance that he could persuade the PLO to leave at all, Habib went ahead with plans for *how* to get them out, should they agree.

To accommodate the PLO's fear of losing face, his plan called for "a ship to come in and take out the PLO leaders and their men, with their arms. They could be delivered to a country of their choice. Thus they would not need to lay down their arms in Beirut and could leave with their pride intact to go elsewhere." This general idea, which he first spelled out on June 26, formed the skeleton of the rest of his work to end the crisis. The PLO didn't want the terms of their departure in writing, for face-saving reasons, so Habib worked without a piece of paper that everyone might sign.

To accommodate their fear of the Israelis sinking the ships, he arranged to use Greek ships with five to ten Greek soldiers aboard each.

To accommodate the PLO's fear of the Israelis killing them once they emerged from hiding, Habib considered it a given that he had to insert a credible military force as a buffer between the PLO and the Israelis. "How else were you going to get the goddam withdrawal?" he said. "You had to have someone to separate the forces!" The timid, rickety Lebanese Armed Forces were always expected to play some role in this. But no one—most especially not the Lebanese government—imagined that the LAF was a serious enough military force to handle the task by itself. The LAF was, as one American Marine put it, "absolutely inept. All their officers had Gucci boots on, and they couldn't find their own platoons if they were given a map." The buffer force would have to be not only credible but also absolutely neutral, because the mistrust on both sides was so deep and unshakable that no one would accept the plan or budge otherwise.

But the Israelis didn't want any buffer force at all. First, they refused to accept that the PLO had any reason to worry about the security of evacuees or of their families left behind. Second, they saw a buffer force as a screen behind which the PLO would continue to stall. The Israelis proposed June 27 that the departing PLO's only protection should be the International Red Cross. That would of course be zero protection. Sharon at one point even proposed that, if there was going to be a military force, it should be the IDF. But that would be such a grotesquely unthinkable case of the cats escorting the mice that Habib wouldn't even discuss it. If the IDF couldn't *be* the force, Sharon parried, then it must at least be a *member* of the force. No way, Habib said. Then the Phalange. Nope. Then include the IDF in the liaison group of the multinational force that would plan the operation. Forget it.

Once resigned to a multinational force that he could not control, Sharon homed in on the timing of the MNF's entry onto the scene. The MNF, he insisted, could not enter Beirut until *after* the "last busful of terrorists leaves." No, Habib said, that would be the same as having no force at all. Well, then have them trickle in proportionately to the number of evacuees who have gone out. No.

Habib wanted the UN to make up the buffer force, mostly because he thought a UN force could be assembled quickly. The UN had, after all, invented peacekeeping and already had a force (albeit an ineffective one) of 7,000 called UNIFIL in place in southern Lebanon. But Begin absolutely refused to consent to a UN force. He wouldn't even allow it to be called an "international force," because he thought that word smacked of the UN. He insisted that it be called a multinational force. "The Israelis are pathological about the UN," says Draper. "They would not hear of it. They would not even agree to UN observers." Israelis had felt since at least 1956 that the UN was biased against them. The many UN votes critical of Israel over the years only reinforced that feeling. More fundamentally, half the member countries of the UN had no diplomatic relations with Israel, and many of them were its declared enemies. The UN, Begin said, was "absolutely hostile to Israel." So Habib scratched the UN.

If not the UN, then who? The Palestinians, the Lebanese government, and Begin (once he realized Sharon's objections could not prevail) all wanted a multinational force. Arafat and Begin both specifically insisted that this force include Americans. For his part, Arafat had two reasons. First, he felt that no force would have credibility unless it included Americans. Second, and more to the point, Arafat and the Lebanese felt that Americans were the only troops whom the Israelis could be counted on not to shoot. The IDF, they believed, might shoot Brazilians and they might shoot Dutch, but they would not deliberately kill Americans.

The idea of bringing American troops into Lebanon had been in play from the earliest hours of the war. Within eighteen hours of the first IDF tank crossing the border, the State Department was considering the prospect of US participation in a peacekeeping force there. As early as the third day Begin told Habib he favored withdrawing his troops from Lebanon if they were replaced there by a long-term American force. Even when the idea evolved from a buffer force in southern Lebanon to a buffer force in Beirut, American troops remained part of the equation. "My idea is very simple," Habib told Washington on July 2. "You pull the French battalion [800 men] out of UNIFIL, . . . you bring them up here and then you get whatever else you need immediately, but it has to be immediately. If you can get 600–700 Saudis, fine. If you can't, maybe you got to get 800 Americans off a ship and bring them in."

Habib had not originally wanted American troops involved, Draper says, because he thought he would then have to make room for the Soviets too. "We didn't want it. We didn't propose it. It just got to the point where there was no other possibility." But, since American participation was one of the few things the Israelis, Palestinians, and Lebanese all agreed on, he could hardly say no. And it would have its advantages. It would help restore US credibility with Arab states. And it would spare him the slow, probably futile task of trying to persuade other countries to do what his own country wouldn't do. Though the presence of Americans wouldn't guarantee success, the absence of Americans would guarantee failure. And that, Habib decided, was the clincher. He sent a message to Reagan July 2 asking him to commit US Marines. Reagan quickly agreed.

Playing Hard to Get

The French, with their long background of involvement in Lebanon, were an obvious choice as a second participant in the multinational force (MNF). In fact, they signed on in principle before the Americans did. The plan was to divide the "Franco-American" force fifty/fifty. In time the Italians joined too.

The French were invaluable, but they were also a headache. They not only volunteered to join, but "were very arrogant about it," says Draper. "They said, 'Forget about you Marines. We'll go in and take care of it all.'" Habib was happy to have the French aboard, since they would ease the process of working with the PLO. But he did not want them to be a solo act. "We have got to do our share," he said. "There is no way we can just dump the load on the French."

Coincidentally or not, as soon as American participation leaked to the press in early July, the French suddenly started playing hard to get. They now wouldn't join in unless the UN gave its blessing, and they might not join in at all. "They wanted to be begged," says a Marine. Habib and his colleagues had to recruit the Lebanese, the Saudis, and the PLO to goose them to commit. The State Department even started discreetly shopping for substitute countries in case the French dropped out.

After a week of the French holding out, Habib called Charlie Hill at State July 9 so frustrated that he ventured a "sacrilegious suggestion": that the US bow out of the MNF and just "tell the French to go ahead and get yourself an outfit blessed by the UN."

Hill replied, "Those of us who are the most cynical believe that the French are trying to do just that. That is, to edge us out while they appear to be responding to us . . . and ending up with themselves in charge of a non-U.S. operation."

Right around then, Yasir Arafat forgot his original insistence on American troops and suddenly declared that he would not accept American troops after all. Begin responded by declaring that the French couldn't join. Habib hit the ceiling. He told his intermediary to the PLO, *Oh, is that right? Well, Israel won't accept the French either. So there isn't going to be any MNF. The PLO asked for our guarantee, and we're giving them the best guarantee possible: the MNF. That's not negotiable. If they don't like it, they know what they can do!"* After some requisite posturing, Arafat and Begin both backed down.

Sticky Issues

One sticky issue that ate an infuriatingly large amount of Habib's time was whose troops would enter Beirut first. The French insisted that they come in first or not at all. Habib wanted the American Marines to come in first. But US Secretary of Defense Caspar Weinberger—who would really prefer that his troops not go in at all—would not hear of that, and neither would Sharon, the French, or half of Washington. It was mortifying to Habib for his own defense secretary to side with Sharon against him.

So Habib compromised. The French would come in first, and the Americans would come in only once the evacuation was well under way. It was a bitter disappointment to him, because "it made the Marines look as though they were a bunch of cowards," says Morrie Draper." The best Habib could arrange was for the Marines to float on their boats just over the horizon so they could come in on short notice.

Another sticky issue was how many soldiers it would take to supervise a PLO evacuation and to protect Palestinian civilians after the fighters left. Habib respected Jonny Abdu, the head of Lebanese intelligence, so he asked his opinion.

"Two hundred fifty thousand men," Abdu replied, pulling the number out of thin air.

"That's ridiculous!" Habib said. "Let's talk seriously."

But Abdu was not alone with such estimates. The American military command in Europe (EUCOM) estimated about the same number. Some officials in Washington "felt we should just militarily take over the country and run it for a while," says Draper. They were proposing putting in as many as five divisions—roughly 90,000 soldiers. Habib dismissed such notions as quickly as he dismissed Abdu's. When Lebanese president Sarkis asked for 16,000 men in the MNF to keep the borders safe, Habib told him to "knock it off."

It was crucial that he pick an optimum number. The Israelis and the Lebanese both believed that, if the force were too big, the PLO would feel safe and never leave. But the PLO also would not leave if the force were too small to protect them.

Habib wanted the force to be as small as possible and to stay as briefly as possible. He needed to bring in enough soldiers to do the job, but he did not want this to look like an invasion. Also, just as he prided himself in traveling with an entourage of one, he didn't want the logistical headaches of a large military force. In the end, he brought in 800 US Marines, 800 French Foreign Legionnaires, and 400 Italian Bersaglieri troops. There was no military significance to those numbers—none was the size of a company or a battalion or any other standard unit. Those numbers just felt about right to Habib.

A third sticky issue was what should become of the PLO's heavy weapons. The PLO and the Lebanese both wanted the heavy weapons to sail out with them. The PLO's reason was that they wanted to resume their struggle against Israel from their next home. This was an important symbolic issue for them. The Lebanese government's reason was that they didn't want those abandoned weapons to end up in the hands of Beirut's other crazies. The Israelis and Habib both wanted the heavy weapons left behind. The Israelis' reason was that a disarmed PLO was a crippled PLO. Habib's reason was that no recipient state would accept evacuees bearing Katyushas. His compromise advice: The weapons should stay behind, and the Lebanese government or the MNF should promptly dump them in the sea.

Every Kid Over 14

In planning the work of the multinational force, Habib's biggest problem after Sharon and Arafat was Caspar Weinberger. The defense secretary himself says only "I had not been particularly supportive of American presence" in the mission. Habib's top Marine liaison, Colonel Jim Sehulster, is more blunt: "Weinberger was deliberately dragging his feet, yes. He didn't want us committed, that's for sure."

Worse, from Habib's standpoint, was that Weinberger would not allow the Marines to do much of anything once they did land. While the French and the Italians would be out and about patrolling, Weinberger would allow his Marines only to huddle inside the Beirut port area.

Habib and his diplomatic colleagues were scathing in their denunciation of Weinberger's and the Pentagon's foot dragging. Habib called the Pentagon "a bunch of pussies." Hill says the Pentagon, still shattered by its fiasco in Vietnam, was now willing to take on "only missions where they could totally overwhelm a situation, where they would essentially mobilize for World War Three." Short of that, Hill continues, their attitude was that "diplomacy is supposed to solve the problem. And when diplomacy solves the problem, then the military can come in and stand around."

The result, says former Marine Shultz, was that the United States was "sending just the wrong message—a message of weakness—throughout the Middle East." That kind of signal, he says, "was an invitation in a place like the Middle East, which is always looking at these nuances."

The Pentagon and Congress were naturally nervous about the prospect of casualties. They insisted on assurances from all the parties—not just the Israelis and the PLO, but all the Lebanese militias as well—that the MNF would be warmly welcomed. Alarm bells went off July 6 when Israel's ally the Phalange said they didn't want the French—in fact, they didn't want any MNF at all. What they did want, Habib said, was "to go in and kill all those people." He told them, "I don't give a damn what you want. This is a package. I don't accept what you say." He assured Washington that neither the Phalange nor the Israelis would shoot at the MNF. But, he said, "There is always the risk that something is going to go wrong. Every kid over the age of 14 in this god damned country has got an automatic rifle." He recommended that the Marines wear bullet-proof vests.

Once the PLO had left Beirut, the feeble Lebanese government would need some time to reassert control over its own capital. Habib needed the MNF to stay on for a while to reinforce the government during this transition. The idea was that the MNF would gradually turn over their positions one at a time to a revitalized Lebanese Armed Forces.

This ongoing role was not an afterthought. It was intrinsic to Habib's basic concept and was at least as important to him as ensuring a smooth evacuation. He had not worked so hard for peace in Beirut only to turn the city back over to the factional thugs and bandits who had ravaged it for the preceding six years. He needed the MNF to remain as a deterrent to *all* the threats to the safety and security of the civilians of Beirut.

Habib said, "One thing that worries the hell out of the PLO, and it would worry me if I were them," was that, as soon as they left town, the now-defenseless Palestinian civilians they left behind would be slaughtered by the Phalange or some other group. Whatever other PLO fears Habib left dangling, he could not fail to assuage that one. He believed that the combination of the MNF and the Lebanese Armed Forces would be "a sufficient protection."

How long should the MNF stay in Beirut to complete this transition? Habib was wary of the Lebanese history of relying on outsiders to solve their problems for them. So he said privately on July 2, "I think we ought to make it clear that the multi-national force is there for a limited time. I would say set it up for thirty days or something like that." But he didn't want to specify a pull-out date in advance publicly. He knew that, if he did, the bad guys would just bide their time until that date and then go wild. There was also an element of bureaucratic minuet influencing his recommendation: Weinberger was not about to sign off on an open-ended mission. If Reagan was going to send the Marines against the Pentagon's wishes, Weinberger certainly insisted on yanking them back out at the earliest possible instant. So Habib reluctantly agreed to specifying publicly that they would be in Beirut for only thirty days.

But Where Would They Go?

Habib's plans for how to get the PLO out of Beirut safely were all well and good. But so far, getting them out was only half of the equation. The other half turned out to be even more daunting: Where would they go? As he put it, "Well, we can't dump the bastards into the sea."

Finding destinations was perhaps his single most intractable and perplexing problem. Unless and until this one was solved, nothing else mattered. Even if he got everybody to agree on everything and got the MNF landed and the PLO on ships, "if we don't have a place for them to go, we ain't going to do a God damned thing," he said. "We [are] just going to sit on our ass."

And no country would take them. To Sharon, the lack of destinations was proof that Habib's diplomacy was an irrelevancy and a failure. If the PLO wasn't leaving, Sharon felt, it was only because they were still too comfortable where they were. So he had to blast Beirut harder. To Habib, that reasoning was vacuous: Sharon could bomb the PLO to force them to leave, and Habib could argue to persuade them to leave, but if they had no place to go to, they *could not* leave. So what could further bombing accomplish?

Early in the war Habib's preference was to move all the Palestinians—fighters, families, everybody—from Beirut to an unpopulated area of northern Lebanon. But the Lebanese officials quickly vetoed that. The Palestinians had been nothing but trouble for them for over a decade, and they fervently hated them. They wanted them gone. Absolutely, entirely, irrevocably gone. They saw little to be gained by transferring their Palestinian problem from Beirut to the north. The Israelis also rejected Habib's idea, arguing that the PLO would just head back south as soon as the IDF left, and then they would be right back where they started.

If he couldn't send the PLO fighters to northern Lebanon, Habib thought, then maybe he could send them to some country with a strong government that could put them under strict control. The best candidate he could think of was Egypt. It had a strong army, good intelligence, and a solid police force. Disarmed and controlled by Egypt, the PLO would be less trouble to everybody. The idea seemed perfect: The PLO had itself proposed Egypt and Egyptian president Hosni Mubarak had once offered temporary asylum to PLO leaders. Habib speculated about getting Mubarak to "take them for 30 days and parcel them out after that. . . . Hell, it'll be Mubarak's ticket back into the Arab world for Christ sake, and he can control them. He can control them. These guys have been whipped."

But Mubarak said absolutely not. Although he had great sympathy for Arafat and the PLO, he was not about to jeopardize Egypt's recent peace treaty with Israel. Besides, Anwar Sadat had been assassinated only nine months earlier for having made peace with Israel. As Sadat's successor, Mubarak could not afford too many risks. He certainly could not receive Arafat, who had reviled Sadat and rejected Camp David.

So Habib suggested sending them to some initial destination, preferably Syria, then have them dispersed from there to several Arab nations.

Arafat's Great Shock

Habib was convinced by June 28 that the PLO "recognizes that the game is up in Lebanon. These guys want *out.*" Suddenly Habib could see the finish line. He sensed he was now within days of getting them a new home, getting them out of Lebanon, and getting this ugly war over with.

But he found no takers. Instead of doing their part to end the crisis, the Arab countries diddled and dithered. Some would take only certain PLO units. Some would take an allotment, but only for six months. Some gave Habib excuses. Some gave him no answer at all. Some could not make up their minds. Some kept changing their minds. At one point, Habib speculated that the PLO might have a deal with the Arab states *not* to take them, "just so they can stall and stay."

The Palestinian cause was genuinely popular among the Arab public, and Arab leaders had always found it expedient to show support for the cause. So why did they now refuse to take the evacuees? As the Saudis and Syrians explained it to Washington, they feared that if they took the fighters, they would soon wind up with all of the fighters' wives and kids and uncles and grandmas from Lebanon too. (And that was if those relatives in Lebanon didn't get massacred as soon as the fighters left.) Besides, they said, Israel wouldn't withdraw an inch after the PLO left anyway, so any Arab country naïve enough to accept the PLO in the interests of getting the Israelis out of Lebanon would be humiliated.

But the real reason, Draper says, is that "most of the Arab leaders hate the PLO." The various Arab regimes were quite happy to pay lip service and even subsidies to the Palestinian cause—as long as the Palestinians themselves resided somewhere else.

They had watched with alarm as the PLO had wreaked havoc everywhere it went. It had nearly ruined Jordan before moving to Lebanon and proceeding to ruin it. The PLO's activities there had, after all, sparked the civil war in 1975 that reduced Lebanon to anarchy. Its terrorist attacks on Israel had drawn Israeli air raids to Lebanese soil for years and had now drawn this massive Israeli invasion.

So the Arab countries had good reason to be afraid to take very many of them. Seeing the PLO as a band of subversives, some feared that importing a bunch of them would stimulate the country's own internal opposition groups to turn against the government. At best, Draper says, "Palestinians are like the Mafia. Put three thousand in a country, and before you know it they're running all the crooked business."

Once Arafat accepted that he and his people would have to leave Lebanon, Hill says, "the great shock was that his Arab brothers didn't want him. So the bizarre fact was that it was Europeans and Americans who were trying to save Arafat's skin, and it was Arabs who were saying, 'The hell with the guy.'"

While the Arabs were spurning the PLO, the PLO was spurning some of them. They didn't want to go just anywhere. They didn't want to go anyplace where they would not be able to carry on their struggle against Israel. Syrian president Assad, who hated Arafat, occasionally offered to take varying numbers of them. But they knew his motive was to split them so he could control the organization and "keep them under lock and key." So they declined his offer. Iraq said it would take all of the PLO, but the PLO knew the Iraqis would "just throw them into their war with Iran as cannon fodder," so they didn't want to go there either. Habib groused that "the problem is that the PLO will screw around saying they won't go here and won't go there."

Around and around it all went. Phil Habib had always enjoyed the intellectual stimulation of solving complex problems. But never had he encountered anything so fiendishly complex—and with so many lives at stake and so little prospect of success. Nonetheless, he said, "If you're a pessimist, you don't become a diplomat . . . . You've got to be optimistic about the most ridiculous and difficult of problems." This qualified.

9

The Darkest Days

The siege was terrible: water cut off, electricity cut off,
shells going in, bombing—getting ready to destroy the
goddam place. I was really fed up with this senseless
killing. There was no need. I had practically got an
agreement with the PLO and the Syrians to get
their troops out of Beirut. I was negotiating
the details and what follows.
Philip Habib

On July 3, Philip Habib's diplomatic settlement was at last coming together:
The PLO had agreed to leave, President Reagan had agreed to include
American Marines in the MNF, and Habib felt he had nearly everything
nailed down. This was to be a package deal. He told everyone "I can't go
on with this goddam bargaining. There are no further demands that I will
accept." Tonight would be an important night, he told Washington, because
Prime Minister Wazzan would meet with Yasir Arafat to have him sign an
official paper agreeing to a PLO departure. Wazzan would deliver the paper to Habib the next day. Despite his vexing lack of destinations, Habib
wanted the evacuation to begin "within the next few days."

As if on cue, Arik Sharon launched an assault. "There's a firefight going on!" Habib shouted on a call to Washington. "Flares are coming down.
The Israelis are moving forward northeast of the airport, across the railroad
track. They're putting the squeeze on the city. If they break the cease-fire,
it could screw it all up! This deal could be set in the next twenty-four to
seventy-two hours. Israeli pressure now won't help!"

When Menachem Begin heard about Habib's report, he got annoyed.
"Habib is hysterical," he said. "It is all highly exaggerated; we are just
returning fire."

But Sharon's assault marked the beginning of Habib's darkest days.

The Indignity

The IDF had Beirut surrounded, and the two halves of the city were physically blocked off from each other by barriers, land mines, and booby traps.

The only portals between Christian East Beirut and Muslim West Beirut were three main checkpoints. During the early hours of July 4, Sharon's forces took over those checkpoints. Wazzan was in West Beirut, carrying the paper that Arafat had just signed agreeing to leave. To bring it to Habib in East Beirut, though, he would have to pass through an Israeli checkpoint at a crossroads called Galerie Samaan. Wazzan and his fellow Lebanese officials were extremely sensitive about preserving the few remaining vestiges of their nation's sovereignty; for Lebanon's prime minister to submit to Israeli permission to travel across his own capital was an indignity he refused to suffer. He announced that he would not negotiate *at all* until the IDF got off of two checkpoints.

As a matter of security, Habib couldn't go into the war zone of West Beirut where Wazzan was. As a matter of principle, Wazzan couldn't leave West Beirut to come to where Habib was. So at what Habib considered the climactic moment, Sharon's assault and takeover of checkpoints brought diplomatic progress to a standstill.

Why did Habib and Wazzan have to meet in person? Why couldn't they just talk by phone? Habib sometimes did talk to his intermediaries by phone. But he couldn't *negotiate* that way because the Israelis, the PLO, the Lebanese Christians, and who knows who else might be tapping the line. For his part, Wazzan was using what little leverage he had to force Sharon's forces to pull back. Habib could easily have sent someone into West Beirut to get Arafat's signed paper, but Wazzan probably would not have turned it over, since he would then be surrendering his last modicum of leverage. Habib needed to see the actual paper Arafat had signed, because the PLO was notoriously unreliable. They had a history of seemingly agreeing to one thing, only to say later, "Oh, we didn't say that. You misunderstood us." Inexperienced diplomats often think they have a concession or agreement in hand, only to realize later that they had read into a statement what they wanted to hear. Habib was not about to make that mistake. But he needed to see more than the paper: He also needed to see Wazzan's eyes to understand all the subtleties of his account.

In short, Habib needed be sure Arafat really meant to go. Only the day before, in a meeting with former Prime Minister Sa'eb Salaam, Arafat had vowed not to leave in an undignified flight. He said that neither he

nor his men could be seen simply to abandon their strongholds under Israeli pressure. They would rather fight to the death and to hell with the consequences for everybody. Warming to his theme, the PLO leader summoned up the ghost of Yousef al-Azmah, the Syrian hero, who had, in spite of impossible odds, defied the French in the battle of Maysouloun near Damascus in 1920. "I reminded them," Arafat recalls today, "of when Yousef al-Azmah went out to fight the French; he knew he would lose, yet he went out to defend Damascus, so that it would not be said that an Arab city was subjected to an invasion, and no one defended it."

Within hours of making this ringing declaration, Arafat—a man prone to posturing and vacillating—wrote his letter agreeing to leave. So what was Habib supposed to believe?

I Cannot Negotiate

Whatever Arafat meant no longer greatly mattered. The momentum was lost. Overtaken by a rush of new developments, the critical moment had come and gone.

In an attempt to pick up the pieces, Habib met secretly with Sharon for over two hours near Beirut on the afternoon of July 5. Habib pressed him for a firm ceasefire to start within hours. Sharon agreed, and promptly ordered an aide to inform his forces and government. Habib pressed him to get his troops off the Galerie Samaan checkpoint that Wazzan had to pass through and the road that Wazzan had to travel to reach the presidential palace. "I cannot carry on negotiations if I can't see Wazzan frequently," Habib said, "and he won't pass that checkpoint if the IDF is still there." Sharon, who could have issued orders himself to clear the troops immediately, said he'd check with his government.

Habib then pressed him to restore water, power, food, and other essentials to West Beirut. After arguing the point, Sharon reluctantly said he'd check with his government, but that any restoration of utilities would be brief. Sharon threatened that, if Habib didn't get an evacuation process under way soon—which IDF action was preventing Habib from doing— he would resume shelling West Beirut and shut its water, power, and supplies back off again. Most alarming, Sharon said that, while he "would prefer a political solution, the IDF will go into West Beirut if necessary. As for the civilians, it would be better for them to become thirsty and leave, rather than stay and be killed later."

Sharon wanted to know where the negotiations stood. Habib said Arafat's declaration of intention to leave wasn't as precise as he would prefer, but "constituted an important commitment." Habib now had to "translate what I thought was general agreement in principle into a specific plan, with a schedule." Sharon pressed Habib to set a date now for the evacuation process to begin; if the deadline was not met, the IDF would clamp the pressure on once again. Habib refused to even discuss the idea.

The biggest remaining problem, Habib admitted, was the lack of Arab countries willing to take PLO evacuees. Sharon said he thought Jordan was the best solution. Sharon said, "Palestinians should be given political expression in that part of former Palestine where they already are a majority, namely in Jordan. Why keep the king there and let an entire nation suffer because of one selfish man?" Habib told him to forget it.

As the two men got up to leave, Sharon said that, although Israel would prefer a political solution, there was practically no time left for that. The Israeli Cabinet had already authorized the IDF to go into West Beirut if a political solution were not reached soon. Israeli patience would run out at the end of the week. "If necessary," Sharon said, "the IDF would go into West Beirut and kill or capture all the terrorists there. None of them will be allowed in Beirut."

Angry at Sharon's crude attempt to bully and threaten him, Habib threw it right back in his face. He argued that a political solution *could* be reached, that the package deal he was working on would meet most of Israel's concerns, and that he did not want to see the damage to Israel's reputation that a ground assault would ensure. "Under no circumstances would I go along with it. You have to understand that."

"Technical Difficulties"

The next day, as if to spite Habib, Sharon launched a new wave of fighting and shut off West Beirut's water and power. Despite Begin's instructions, IDF forces remained at all the checkpoints. They wouldn't let anyone through the Galerie Samaan crossing that Wazzan needed to pass to reach Habib. But not to worry, the Israelis said via Sam Lewis in Tel Aviv: There were just some technical difficulties.

Habib was furious. He called Washington over and over on July 6 and ranted and bellowed for hours. "I don't know what Sam Lewis thinks the situation is like here, but tell him the Israelis are refusing to allow the Lebanese army to take over the [Galerie Samaan crossroads] and the road to Baabda. . . . I cannot proceed with the negotiations, getting the PLO out, unless that goddam crossroad is cleared and turned over, as I told the Israelis it had to be yesterday. We've already lost time as a result of it! . . . Doesn't anybody understand that, if they're there [at the crossroads], the Prime Minister will not come out? Now, goddammit, I told it to Sharon six times. Why are people arguing with it? I don't want any explanations, I don't want any arguments, I just want them off the goddam crossroads! Now, can't anybody understand that? Simple English. And I want it turned over to the Lebanese army. I don't want [the Israelis] or the Phalangists to be on that crossroads. Period."

Two hours later Habib called back and shouted, "Begin says he issued the order last night" to have the power and water restored, but "his orders aren't carried out these days." The utilities were still off. "The 'technical difficulties' are that the Israeli guys down at the end of the line don't *want* to do it," Habib said. "There is no way, absolutely no way in which I can move the negotiations along under the present conditions."

While he was in full roar, the line went dead.

By the time he was able to get through again, he was only hotter. The Israelis "keep talking about I have to move in a hurry: They have lost two days by virtue of their refusing to do what I asked them to do! Two days of negotiation have been lost! . . . I want the president to understand it. I want everybody in the country to understand it. I'm getting sick and tired— . . . [If I can] get some contact with these people in the next 24 hours—which I have not had for four or five days—and I can get the negotiations moving quickly, I can close this thing out in the next three days."

Drastic Measures

With Sharon's pressure blasting Habib's diplomatic efforts into smoke, the State Department considered some drastic measures. On a call with Habib later in the day, Eagleburger raised two possibilities: "One, we pull you out with the proper public statement. Or two, we say that either the Israelis establish conditions suitable for diplomacy or you deal directly with the PLO."

"I prefer the second," Habib replied. "But don't bluff. If I get pulled out, I won't get back in, and Israel will claim that negotiations failed so they'd be justified in going into West Beirut."

At the same time, State briefly considered dispensing with negotiations, putting landing craft ashore three days hence, holding off the IDF long enough to load the PLO aboard, and spiriting them 115 miles north to the Syrian port of Latakia. The idea went nowhere, but it reflected the growing sense of futility and desperation.

At this point Reagan weighed in. The immediate impetus for his involvement was a peculiar ceasefire ordered by Begin, one that epitomized Israel's misunderstanding of or disdain for Habib's efforts.

On July 6, the PLO had killed six IDF soldiers in one vehicle. That loss prompted the Israeli Cabinet to demand retaliation, presumably air strikes. Begin said no. He ordered Sharon to "hold our fire for 24 hours so that Phil Habib can complete his mission." A fragile ceasefire began. When Habib heard of Begin's order, he said, "Twenty-four hours is a joke, because I can't negotiate with the [Galerie Samaan] checkpoint closed!" "We don't work under deadlines . . . especially when they have set it so that I can't even talk to people any more."

In consultation with Habib, State drafted a letter for Reagan to send to Begin. On July 7, Lewis met with Begin to read him the letter. Begin expected tough words, so he didn't want any witnesses. He and Lewis met alone. The letter said:

> . . . [I]t is impossible for me to ask Amb. Habib to negotiate under an arbitrary 24-hour deadline. Friends and allies should not deal with one another through ultimatums, and negotiations of course cannot be expected to succeed under such conditions. . . .
>
> [I]t is particularly difficult for me to understand Israel's purpose at this moment. Speaking frankly, the action of the IDF around Beirut over the past 72 or so hours has made it impossible for Amb. Habib to proceed with his negotiations. As you are aware, situations such as this are never simply stalemated. If there is no progress, deterioration sets in. . . .
>
> We [recognize that diplomacy] must be backed by strength and an awareness that strength may be employed. But the recent IDF moves around West Beirut have clearly been counterproductive. Rather than keeping the PLO focused on the need to negotiate their departure under reasonable terms, the situation now exists in which the UN and the press lament the inhuman conditions in Beirut. The Lebanese government leaders have been rendered incapable of conducting negotiations, and Habib himself is virtually incommunicado. . . .
>
> Unless [you turn over the Galerie Samaan checkpoint to the LAF so Wazzan can reach Habib], negotiations simply cannot proceed.
>
> Mr. Prime Minister, your message to me regarding the [PLO's desire to keep] a PLO office in Beirut and a token force temporarily remaining in Lebanon poses for me the troubling question of whether Israel continues to support this tremendous effort we are engaged in to achieve a negotiated solution. . . . The question has been raised whether Israeli forces may not now be seeking to undermine any hope of a negotiated solution while unilaterally pressuring the PLO to evacuate Beirut without a negotiated agreement. In this context, I want to state clearly that a military assault on Beirut is not acceptable and would have the most grievous bilateral consequences. . . .
>
> It should go without saying that the US does not welcome or encourage these points relating to a PLO office or token force. . . . It remains a fact, however, that we are engaged in negotiating an agreement to rid Beirut of the PLO leadership and armed fighters. If it transpires that such an agreement must encompass these two points or some variation of them, it will be well worth the overall achievement. . . . To deprive the negotiators of this small margin of flexibility, Mr.

Prime Minister, in effect would be to require unconditional surrender. We are not engaged in this, nor would it be in either of our interests. . . . We may be very close to a breakthrough in these talks if only they are enabled to proceed.

To this end, the Galerie Samaan crossing should be reopened and controlled by the LAF alone at the earliest possible moment. We expect Israel and its forces will not act in ways which make it impossible for Amb. Habib to continue his efforts to achieve a negotiated outcome to the West Beirut problem. If such cooperation is not possible, then we will have to consider other ways to preserve America's credibility while seeking to bring about a Beirut settlement. For example, if the Lebanese authorities cannot have unhindered access to Habib, then we will have to consider other ways to assure Habib's ability to deal with all the relevant parties.

Begin instantly—and correctly—understood that last sentence as a threat to have Habib talk directly with the PLO. He clearly disliked that point, but deferred comment on it until later. He seemed "chastened," Lewis said, and seemed to feel that he didn't really deserve this. He did argue that his twenty-four hours was not a deadline or an ultimatum, just a postponement of reaction to the six IDF deaths. He also said that Sharon had already ordered the Galerie Samaan checkpoint to be reopened.

Checkpoint Draper

But twenty-two hours later the checkpoint was still closed. Wazzan had still not got through to meet with Habib. "I've lost five days because of you!" Habib said to Sharon the evening of July 8. *The checkpoint must be cleared now.*

"We're prepared to do the right thing" at the checkpoint, Sharon said.

"I'm no longer prepared to take assurances," Habib replied. "I'm going to send Morrie down there with the Lebanese. When your guys have satisfied the Lebanese requirements, then I'll be satisfied. Until then I will not be satisfied."

So he dispatched Draper, who was a master at figuring out clever ways around obstacles, to work out an ingenious solution. Draper faked a checkpoint. He got Sharon's forces at the Galerie Samaan crossing to move their tanks back into the shadows of the surrounding buildings, take down their Israeli flags, and stand behind some palm trees. He then placed some Lebanese soldiers at "Checkpoint Draper" drinking coffee beneath a Lebanese flag long enough for Wazzan to drive through the next morning without seeing any Israeli flags. Wazzan did so without asking too many questions.

"It was a big thing," Draper says. "We laugh at things like this, but it was deadly serious to Wazzan. And we couldn't lose him. He was our critical channel to the Palestinians and the Syrians. If Wazzan had backed out at any time, we would have been screwed."

Get Yourself Another Intermediary

Actually, Wazzan *did* back out, more than once. For all of Habib's complaints about Sharon preventing Wazzan from working, it was also true that Wazzan was refusing to work. And even when he was working, he was a mixed blessing.

On the one hand, he was indispensable as the main intermediary because he was the prime minister, was a leading Sunni Muslim, was known as sympathetic to the Palestinians, and had the courage to take on the job.

But Habib couldn't rely on him 100 percent. "Wazzan is not the strongest reed" as an intermediary, Habib said. He sometimes had to confront Wazzan and say, "Look, you gotta tell Arafat the straight dope on this!" Wazzan had resigned for a few days in late June, and Habib often worried about losing him again. Wazzan sometimes protested Israeli bombing by refusing to negotiate. During one rain of shelling he told Habib, "Forget about me as your negotiator if this bombing is going to keep up. You're negotiating back to the Israelis; they're bombing us. You get yourself another intermediary with the PLO." Wazzan would sometimes call Habib in tears, saying that he could not stand being a party to the massacre of his people. Habib felt the same way about the suffering and destruction of Beirut, and only Habib could calm him down and reassure him in those phone calls.

But all of this disturbed Habib, whose own approach was to "get to work, get it done, get it over with, get it stopped." He had no patience with nonperformance. Any *American* involved who did any one of those things even once would have quickly found himself on the next flight home. But Habib couldn't very well fire the prime minister of Lebanon.

What he did, though, was to persuade Lebanese intelligence chief Jonny Abdu, in whom he had greater confidence, to meet with the PLO leaders "because I have been concerned that Wazzan has not been adequately forthright in his descriptions of the respective [Lebanese] and U.S. positions. I have sensed that [Abdu] would be more specific and, in the process, develop more insight into the PLO position. Fortunately, too, [Abdu] has been chronically skeptical of PLO intentions, and wary of Arafat's well-known negotiating style."

Proximity Talks

At any rate, by the time Wazzan finally drove through Checkpoint Draper to meet with Habib July 9, Wazzan's patience was thin. He had had it with Sharon's interference in his already cumbersome—not to mention danger-ous—process of picking his way across a war zone daily to carry messages between Habib and Arafat. Under the best of circumstances, it had been taking him twenty-four hours to get either side an answer from the other. Now Sharon had lost them five full days. So, to speed up the negotiations, Wazzan suggested putting Habib and Arafat in adjacent buildings or on separate floors of the same building. Wazzan would then walk back and forth between them.

This would hardly have been the first time such a thing had happened. In fact, this is precisely how UN Undersecretary Ralph Bunche had medi-ated armistice agreements between Arabs and Israelis in 1949. He had ar-ranged formal face-to-face meetings, but the real talks happened in corri-dors or in separate hotel rooms with Bunche going back and forth between the delegations.

Habib endorsed Wazzan's idea of proximity talks. He certainly rel-ished the prospect of efficient negotiating, especially after five days of zero negotiating.

But the risks were daunting. In the first place, there was no safe place to hold proximity talks. Sharon's forces had West Beirut impermeably sur-rounded, so Arafat would never be able to get out for talks in the suburbs. The talks would have to be somewhere within Beirut. But Habib couldn't go into Muslim West Beirut where Arafat was, because that was precisely the area that Sharon was blasting to rubble. And Arafat couldn't go into Christian East Beirut. Though that area was virtually unscathed by Sharon's assaults, it was "controlled by these Maronite fanatics," says Draper. "There's no way a PLO representative would have gone in there. The place was ruthless. Anybody that looked like a Muslim was dead."

Even if a safe place could be found for proximity talks, it would be easy for the IDF to track Habib to the site and attack Arafat there—perhaps killing Habib in the process. And even if Sharon's forces sat on their hands, the city was full of freelance crazies who would have been proud to blow up any building containing Philip Habib and Yasir Arafat.

Then there were the equally implacable political drawbacks. If prox-imity talks were held, Draper says, "we knew that the Israelis would go up the wall. It might even have sabotaged the chances for a ceasefire and with-drawal." As it turns out, the Israelis went up the wall at even the *suggestion* of proximity talks. At one point Sharon threatened that, if Habib got to-gether with the PLO, Israel would not wait one minute before attacking.

One Secret Exception

The prohibition against talking directly to the PLO—or even talking in the vicinity of the PLO—boxed in every move Habib made. The prohibition was particularly exasperating because of its flimsy basis and its recent history. It originated in an assurance then-Secretary of State Henry Kissinger had made to Israel seven years earlier. Kissinger has confirmed that he never told the Israelis that the US would not negotiate with the PLO; what he told them was that the US would not negotiate with the PLO *behind Israel's back.* But the Israelis took his words as an ironclad pledge never to talk to the PLO at all, period. Supporters of Israel put the State Department under tremendous pressure to have nothing to do with the PLO. So beginning with the Carter administration, government employees were forbidden to talk to any PLO representative, "and the Israelis watched it like hawks." The prohibition was virtually absolute, and Congress subsequently wrote it into legislation.

Virtually. There was one secret exception. American ambassadors in Lebanon had special authorization from both the secretary of state and the president to talk directly to the PLO—on matters of security only.

As a result, American diplomats in Lebanon had had plenty of direct, though secret, dealings with the PLO in recent years. John Gunther Dean, the US ambassador to Lebanon from 1978 to 1981, had thirty-five to forty-five meetings with a senior PLO official named Mahmud Labadi. Though the meetings were authorized, Dean kept them secret even from his deputy. When Habib came to Lebanon in 1981 to begin his Middle East mission, Dean tried to turn over to him his PLO contact, but Habib declined the offer. Dean's successor, Bob Dillon, accepted the offer and continued the clandestine contacts.

This was "a very rewarding relationship," says Dean. For example, after US ambassador Frank Meloy was assassinated in Beirut in 1976 by George Habash's group, the PLO helped recover Meloy's body. They protected American citizens in Lebanon and, when Americans were taken hostage, helped get them released. They "made possible the successful evacuation of the American staff" from Beirut in 1976, says Draper. After American diplomats were taken hostage in Iran in 1979, Draper himself used the PLO channel, and the PLO helped get the first group of American hostages released. They helped protect the American embassy in Beirut "and I can tell you," Nathaniel Howell says, "that embassy was damn glad to see them come."

Habib had no admiration or fondness for the PLO, but his position was pragmatic: "You don't like the PLO? Take a look at the alternatives."

Despite everything American diplomats and the PLO had recently been through together in Beirut, during the crisis when direct communication would have helped the most, Phil Habib was forbidden to speak to the PLO. He could have availed himself of Dillon's secret channel to them. And Washington would have given him permission to talk directly to the PLO had he asked to. But he chose to do neither. Though direct talks would have streamlined his work immensely, he knew that if the Israelis found out—and, with their sophisticated intelligence resources, they surely would have—he and the diplomatic alternative he represented would be finished.

Secret Meetings with Sharon

He faced no such obstacles in communicating with the Israelis. And they were up on the outskirts of Beirut all the time. During the war, Habib often met secretly with Sharon in a house behind the hills near Dillon's residence in Yarze. In fact, ready access to Sharon is one reason Habib spent most of his time in Beirut during the war. He never allowed Sharon to come to the ambassador's residence at Yarze, in deference to what little was left of Lebanese sovereignty. But practicality demanded that he talk with Sharon often, and the outskirts of Beirut was the most practical place to meet.

Hardly anyone except the participants knew about the secret meetings. The secretary of state was nearly the only one in Washington who knew. Habib was determined not to let anyone at the embassy except Dillon know—not even the Marines who were supposed to be protecting him. In the first place, he felt that, if word leaked out, publicity might lessen the odds of the talks being productive. Second, he found it distasteful enough to be meeting with Sharon on Lebanese soil; he certainly didn't want to do so with TV cameras out front. Third, he wanted to spare Lebanese officials the political embarrassment of having to admit that he was, in effect, talking to them in the morning and to Sharon just outside their capital in the afternoon.

For these secret talks with Sharon, Habib drew on his experience as the one who had arranged the logistics of the secret talks between the US and North Vietnamese delegations to the Paris Peace Talks in 1968. Normally, it was a major production for Habib to travel anywhere in Lebanon, requiring several speeding cars, lots of security guards, sirens, the whole production. For secret talks, that would never do. So about once a week, Habib and Draper would get into a jeep or a non-armored car with one American security guard to drive them. To avoid any checkpoints, they'd take back roads and alleys for about twenty minutes to a big house in a thinly populated vacation area for rich Lebanese in the hills above Beirut. Jonny Abdu owned the house, arranged the meetings, and ensured that nobody was around who shouldn't be. Habib would have the driver let him and Draper off and then wait in a garden house until the meeting was over. The driver never saw who else came to the house, and Habib didn't enlighten him.

The secret meetings usually lasted two or three hours. A servant would serve them coffee and sweets. Habib would fill Sharon in on the progress of his talks and then "try to negotiate his agreement to things that he didn't want to agree to." Sometimes they managed to keep the discussion civil; often they went at it hot and heavy. Sharon, characteristically, would try to push Habib around. Whereas in Jerusalem Habib could often deflect Sharon's aggressiveness by playing to Begin, he didn't have that option when it was just the two of them. He sometimes tried to use humor to deflate Sharon's bullying tactics, but Sharon had no sense of humor. Habib would thunder right back at Sharon when necessary as a deliberately selected tool of the trade, but he was disciplined enough not to let even Sharon goad him into losing his cool during a negotiation.

Several times, particularly in the first few meetings, Sharon apparently deliberately had his troops lob 155 mm shells directly over the house during the meetings, which Habib took to be Sharon's way of saying "I'm in charge here." At least once Habib called him on it, saying, "And stop the firing! It's strange that the firing started when our meeting began."

Locking Out the Chef

July 9 was the day Wazzan finally got through Checkpoint Draper. He had his first meeting with Habib in six days, then turned around and went back to West Beirut to carry Habib's latest information and questions to the PLO. Diplomacy seemed back on track.

Sharon picked that moment to intensify his assault. After preventing negotiations for six days, Sharon had opened a window for one day, and was now shutting it again.

"The shelling has become unreasonable!" Habib shouted to Washington. He was counting thirty to forty rounds of shells per minute and watching a huge fire blaze in the southwestern part of the city. "Wazzan just called and begged me to get it stopped. He was meeting with the PLO. He thinks the IDF is doing this deliberately, knowing he is there. This is the functional equivalent of the crossing problem. Stop the pressure, goddammit! Shells are blanketing populated areas of the city. It's overwhelming! I can't describe it! Goddammit, this is indecent! I might send a message scorching everybody. I have no credibility anymore."

Habib called the US embassy in Tel Aviv and demanded that Lewis tell Begin to get this stopped. Lewis talked to Sharon instead, telling him, "This is totally out of control. It is far beyond any conceivable reason." Sharon replied that he had already ordered his forces to calm down, adding "I don't want to disrupt the negotiations."

Perhaps he didn't. But, whatever Sharon's actual thoughts, he had a knack for professing hope for Habib's negotiations while preventing Habib from negotiating. On July 11, even as his forces were raining down shells, Sharon repeatedly and emotionally told Lewis that he wanted a political solution and wanted Habib to succeed. He said he had ordered his forces to reduce fire gradually "to eventually calm things down" so Wazzan could meet with Habib and with Arafat.

Habib was not much impressed with Sharon's gesture. "From fifteen shells per minute," he said, "it's now down to four. Go back to Sharon and say it's not good enough. He must stop this shit! Tell him, 'If a sniper fires, go after the sniper. Don't fire 2,000 shells into the city! Stop playing this game of 2,000 to one!' Wazzan can't leave West Beirut. They're shelling the road Wazzan rides along to see me. Negotiating is impossible under these circumstances! I've had two meetings in nine days. There's nothing left to negotiate but where and when the PLO will go, but it's slipping away every day."

Preventing a diplomat from talking with the necessary people is like locking a chef out of the kitchen. Israeli sensibilities prevented Habib from talking directly with the PLO, and Israeli actions cut him off from his intermediary to the PLO. Though his efforts had been continually stymied since the invasion began, at least he'd always been busy negotiating. Now, with Beirut getting pounded heavier than ever, he was just sitting high and dry.

Though the specifics varied from week to week, the pattern was clear: Nearly every time Phil Habib thought he was getting some diplomatic traction, Arik Sharon found a way to grease his shoes.

10

A Concise Formula for Hell

Modern war is a horrible thing, take it from me. People
are always worried about nuclear weapons: We were
sitting there watching modern *conventional* weaponry.
Conventional weaponry is pretty awful in concentrated
doses. It makes you understand the urgency of doing
something. Once you've seen a piece of shrapnel and
what it can do, it brings home the shock of war.
Philip Habib

One stubborn fact colors most other facts about the siege of Beirut: Sharon's
quarry, the PLO fighters, were largely riding out the storm safe in well-
stocked underground shelters. As Sharon ratcheted up his military pressure from tropical depression to tropical storm to hurricane, the fish beneath the waves remained largely cushioned from its rages.

And Sharon knew it.

West Beirut was extensively honeycombed with caves, and the PLO
used them as bomb shelters. By having long advertised his intention to
invade Lebanon, Sharon had given the PLO ample time to sensibly stock
up on supplies. Safe in their underground shelters, they had all the food,
water, electrical generators, fuel, and other provisions they needed. These
were not cushy dens that they would *enjoy* staying in for months on end,
but they could if necessary. Yasir Arafat's own bunker in the south-central
part of West Beirut *was* relatively plush: personal quarters, rooms for support staff, a meeting room, nice wall paneling, kitchen facilities, and even
an extensive library. It survived the entire siege unscathed.

"In urban warfare, Israel's firepower and mobility really meant nothing," says an American Marine who worked closely with Habib. "They
weren't going to starve them out. They weren't going to thirst them out.
And the fighters down there weren't ever going to run out of weapons or
ammunition. So I think the Israelis saw the futility of the siege."

That didn't stop Ariel Sharon, though. He wrote that "unless the PLO
was convinced they would be destroyed, they would never leave. Conse-
quently we had to bring the strongest pressure to bear, forcing them to
make the decision." The bitter irony that made Habib hopping mad was
that the ones doing the suffering and dying were those living above ground:

the civilians of Beirut. As he told Sharon over and over, "You're punishing the people, not the PLO."

The Second Prong

There were two prongs to Sharon's siege. The first was to shell and bomb the city. The second was to blockade the city. He repeatedly cut off water, electricity, and supplies.

For example, Israeli troops entered a power control station, ordered switches thrown to black out West Beirut, then settled in with sleeping bags and cooking stoves to keep anyone from restoring power. They shut off water at a water station, dismantled the control wheel, and took it away. They cut phone lines. They blocked shipments of flour. They even confiscated sandwiches that someone tried to take into West Beirut.

When Habib would protest a shutoff, the Israelis would first say, "Yes, we'll take care of it," then report that the water or power was indeed back on—then a few hours later they would shut it off again. Begin himself told Habib directly on July 30 that he would consider restoring supplies; the IDF then tightened the blockade. Three days later Begin ordered the water turned on; the IDF left it off. Habib yelled at Washington, "I wish somebody could get the Israelis to stop being assholes about things like turning off the water."

Without fresh running water, some people in West Beirut drank salt water. Children stood in line to fill gallon containers at burst water pipes. Eight children were blown to bits one day as they queued for water. Toilets couldn't flush. People couldn't bathe. There was no way to put out fires started by Israeli shelling. Cholera and typhoid broke out in the poorer areas. "There's disease in the city!" Habib yelled at Washington August 1. "The water from wells is impure. Water pipes get broken in the bombing. This is worse than an all-out attack on the city! Goddam it, it's not decent!"

Without electricity, pumps couldn't get water into buildings. Food spoiled in idle refrigerators. No air conditioners or even small room fans could relieve the sweltering summer heat. The phones wouldn't work. Hospitals could do little more than salve the wounded.

Without fuel, garbage trucks couldn't run, so garbage piled up, cultivating rats and disease. For fun, children threw stones at the rats scampering in the streets at midday. People were asked to burn their garbage in the streets to prevent cholera. The few bakeries that had flour were unable to bake it into bread in their diesel ovens.

Without normal supplies, people spent hours standing in lines for food or fuel—exposed to flying debris from incoming shells—only to find that meager supplies had run out. On July 12 the Lebanese prime minister told the UN that West Beirut was down to a one-day supply of food.

Sharon did relax his blockade to varying degrees now and then. He might restore water or power for a while—but not necessarily at the same time, so people still couldn't pump water into tanks. Israeli fruits and vegetables had no trouble getting into Beirut for sale. Israeli "banks on wheels" set up shop in the occupied areas of Lebanon. IDF soldiers at checkpoints "were running a black market selling water and food and other things," says Draper. "Don't forget, these people were corrupt!" They let one man bring in eight barrels of diesel for a bribe of a kilo of hashish. Resourceful Lebanese shopkeepers could bring vegetables from East Beirut into West by paying Israeli soldiers at checkpoints $20 bribes. Meat, which in some cases had to be smuggled in on the hoof, was prohibitively expensive. The price of a kilo of potatoes went from 2 Lebanese pounds to 25, lemons from 2 pounds to 60, a gallon of fuel from 32 pounds to 250.

The Visigoths

Though Sharon and Begin's overall justification of the war was to combat terrorism, Habib felt that Israel's actions in it were no less reprehensible than those of the terrorists they were fighting.

For example, Sharon said, "When you stop a Red Cross convoy to steal the milk powder for the children, and you laugh if you are begged not to do so, you are not a soldier. You are a terrorist, a murderer. . . . Arafat's killers do [that]. Always." Sharon neglected to mention that his own forces had done the same sorts of things. Though Begin had told Habib June 13 that Israel would take "a most positive approach" to international humanitarian programs for Lebanon, as early as June 20 the IDF was preventing UN agencies from bringing in food, medicines, and disaster experts. In early July relief agencies complained that the Israelis were obstructing deliveries of medicines, tents, clothes, food, and water to the displaced in southern Lebanon. The Israelis bombed and shelled hospitals. The IDF removed foreign doctors from local hospitals and shut down the Palestinian Red Crescent Hospital in Sidon. On July 30 Habib reported that Sharon's troops had stopped four trucks from bringing medical supplies to the American University of Beirut hospital. On August 6 Draper reported that they were keeping fuel and medicine from reaching the AUB hospital, even stopping and searching doctors' cars for medicines. "The problem is unbelievably serious," Draper said. "There's a threat of epidemics."

When IDF shells hit hospitals, schools, and other such civilian sites, Sharon and Begin justified the damage by saying that the PLO had, in typical terrorist fashion, placed their guns next to such places. Aiming for the PLO guns next door, the Israelis said, they had accidentally hit the schools and hospitals as regrettable collateral damage. But the IDF too placed its guns beside comparable civilian sites, including the presidential palace and the American ambassador's residence where Habib was headquartered.

Begin justified the blockade of Beirut to Washington as a necessary evil. Electric blowers ventilated the PLO's underground shelters, so electricity was cut off. PLO generators required fuel, so fuel was cut off. Most food was going to terrorists, Sharon argued, so food was cut off. Begin said the situation wasn't as bad as Habib made it sound: There was no shortage of food or drinking water, restaurants were open, and fresh fruit and milk were being smuggled in.

Habib was unimpressed. "Don't buy this horseshit!" he told Washington. "We are engaging in a phony game if we tolerate this." How could Begin and Sharon actually believe their blockade was hurting the PLO? Habib wondered. "The PLO's not short of anything!" he said. "They're distributing diesel fuel to people in West Beirut! They can last quite a while." Cutting off water, power, and food "is bloody *inhumane,*" he said. This "is not the Middle Ages. It is not the Duke of Burgundy's Castle under siege by the Visigoths."

He particularly rejected Begin and Sharon's strategic rationale. They reasoned, despite all evidence to the contrary, that if the people of West Beirut suffered enough, *they* would force the PLO to surrender. Habib believed that "only through negotiating can we get the PLO out, not through blockades." It was either negotiate them out or "blow them out. If you blow them out, you are going to have one hell of a mess on your hands." Far from forcing the civilians of West Beirut to expel the PLO, Israeli attacks actually had the opposite effect: The longer the siege dragged on, the more a sense of common destiny emerged among the besieged. As one Lebanese historian put it, "As much as [the civilians of Beirut] had wanted the guerrillas to be gone, they did not want to give the Israelis Arafat's head. It was as though West Beirutis recognized that in standing with the PLO against Israel they represented the last vestige of Arab dignity."

The PLO did not reciprocate the feelings, in Habib's view. "If the rest of the population in there gets cholera and dysentery and die, they don't care," he said. "They have their water, they got their food, they are nice and closed in, they got their guns and ammunition, and they will wait it out. . . . It isn't the PLO that are suffering."

Habib was both outraged at the inhumanity of the blockade and intensely irritated at the amount of time and energy he had to spend on it. The time he spent trying to persuade the Israelis to turn the power and water back on was time he couldn't spend on his main task: refining and selling his plan to end the war.

Sharon ridiculed Habib as "the mayor of Beirut" for worrying so much about the shutoff of water and power and medicine and garbage. Intercepted Israeli communications said that Habib was being used, diverted onto the blockade issue as just another means of PLO stalling. The Syrians too took snide potshots at Habib for his efforts to get electricity and water turned on, questioning how significant a presidential envoy's mission could be if he was bogged down in such mundane, trivial matters.

Habib agreed with them. "This discredits me!" he said. "How can I be credible in saying I can arrange adjustments in the IDF line if I can't arrange food deliveries?"

Looking impotent was bad enough, but the blockade also made America look complicit. "The Lebanese can't accept that we can't control the Israelis," he said, and thus "we look like a party to the whole thing." In fact, the Lebanese were more bitter against the US than against the PLO for it. On July 28 he considered telling the Israelis that, unless they restored electricity within twenty-four hours, he would stop working.

Unearthly

Sharon's siege of Beirut was overwhelmingly one-sided. While the press and even some top officials in Washington portrayed the fighting as "duels," it consisted mostly of crushing, thundering, massive Israeli artillery and aerial barrages that made the earth tremble, punctuated with game efforts by the PLO to nip at the IDF's heels. Though the PLO had had pretensions of making itself into a regular army prior to the invasion, it was so utterly outmuscled by Israel as to make any army-to-army comparison absurd.

With the glaring exception of the PLO's advantage of being well dug in defending their home turf, Sharon had nearly all the other advantages. He had an air force. He had a navy. He had the high ground. With 80,000 troops in Lebanon—more than Israel had sent into the Egyptian theater in the 1973 war—he had the PLO outmanned at least 4 to 1. By one estimate he had them outgunned probably 100 to 1. He had not only more weapons but also incomparably more sophisticated weapons.

The PLO had large caches of weapons and ammunition, but most of it was small arms, and much of it was obsolete and in dismal condition. Some of it dated back to World War One. They did own some reasonably sophisticated modern weapons, but lacked the expertise to use them correctly or at all. When the war was over, they left behind tons of weaponry—much of it brand new, unused, still in cases. They didn't use a fraction of the firepower they had, because shooting at the IDF rarely accomplished much more than revealing a shooter's location and bringing down torrents of retaliation. When they did shoot, as one of Habib's colleagues puts it, PLO firing consisted largely of "guys just closing their eyes and pulling the lanyard and hoping their shots went in the right direction."

The Israelis too usually struck indiscriminately, Habib said. Unlike the PLO, though, the IDF had the *ability* to strike with surgical precision when they chose to. But they usually did not choose to. "Aircraft strikes from 3,000 feet are not pinpoint!" Habib said. One of his colleagues who often stood with Habib on the veranda at Yarze overlooking Beirut said, "I will never be persuaded that most of what we saw was directed Israeli fire at specific targets. They were shooting to intimidate, particularly when they were shooting heavy: just laying down a tremendous amount of metal to demoralize and dispirit both the defending forces and the population at large."

Artillery shells, writes a British soldier, "can do things to the human body you never believed possible: turn it inside out like a steaming rose, bend it backward and through itself, chop it up, shred it, pulp it—mutilations so base and vile they never stopped revolting me. And there is no real cover from shellfire. Shells can drop out of the sky and . . . [slice] through ten-story buildings before exploding in the basement. . . . A bullet may or may not have your number on it, but I am sure shells are engraved with 'to whom it may concern.'"

Among the weapons the IDF used were cluster bombs—ordnance that Draper calls "weapons of terror." Cluster bombs spray up to 650 separate bomblets that each explode on impact, shooting out little pieces of shrapnel indiscriminately over an area several hundred feet in diameter. The IDF also used phosphorous bombs and shells, horrible weapons normally used only in open battlefields, not in civilian residential areas. Their effects were unearthly. For example, a doctor found two dead infants still on fire from phosphorous: "I had to take the babies and put them in buckets of water to put out the flames. When I took them out half an hour later they were still burning. Even in the mortuary they smouldered for hours."

Dresden it was not. But Sharon's bombs and artillery hit everything in West Beirut. Not a single house, not a single shop escaped damage. American military observers on some days counted 8,000 rounds of Israeli artillery pouring into limited areas of West Beirut. An engineering professor in Beirut conservatively estimated that during the siege the Israelis pumped an average of over 14,000 pounds of high explosives per square mile per day in an area of less than six square miles. He called this "a concise formula for hell."

An American ambassador in the region said he was "stunned by the blatancy of the whole thing. Israeli artillery units sat up on the hills overlooking Beirut and just lobbed shells and rockets into that city of totally unprotected people. The most modern technology of war [was] being used against defenseless populations. I was just horrified."

The Eerie Contrast

That was West Beirut. The siege was absurdly localized. While the Muslims of West Beirut were the Israelis' targets, the Christians of East Beirut were the Israelis' allies. From the veranda at Yarze, Habib could look down on the two cities of Beirut at night and marvel at the eerie contrast. Muslim West Beirut would be dark as a cave. Against the blackness he could see fires burning here and there from the bombings, or the occasional headlights of a car making a run for it. Just across the Green Line, he could see Christian East Beirut lit up like Manhattan.

West Beirut was a skeleton of a city. Everywhere you looked were blown-out buildings: facades with no sides, no back. Israeli Air Force (IAF) jets screamed overhead at night, sometimes shattering sleep with sonic booms, sometimes dropping cascades of flares that lit up the whole city in a fantasy of yellow light. The jets dropped aerial percussion bombs that sounded as if the whole city were collapsing. There were no more coffins for sale in West Beirut; people rented and returned them.

Meanwhile, East Beirut was a party town. People there still jogged, played tennis, ate in restaurants. By day women in bikinis water skied and sunbathed on the beach; by night they wore their finest jewels to cocktail parties and sampled the smoked salmon and caviar. People living in the Christian suburbs, says Bob Dillon, "could easily forget that the rest of the country was going to hell."

Despite their ordeal, the people of West Beirut insisted on living as nearly normal a life as they could manage. This was partly as an act of defiance and partly because they had already seen seven years of civil war, so they had learned to adapt to living in a war zone. "We get bombed every Wednesday and Sunday," observed one resident of West Beirut, Lina Mikdadi, "with a bonus on Thursdays and Fridays." The other days, they tried to visit friends, pick up whatever supplies they could find, and take their children out to play. The people of West Beirut got to where they could tell a Skyhawk from an F-15, a Kfir from a Mirage, just by the sound each made. They could jolt awake from an explosion and, in half-sleep, gauge whether it was near enough to worry about. The attacks were usually very intense for a very short time, followed by periods of tense quiet. "People are more controlled when the fierce battles are on," said Mikdadi; "it's only when there's quiet that reality hits them, and hits them hard. Then the suppressed anxiety, fear and despair surface."

The situation was unbearable, Mikdadi said, but "the more you beat a human being, the less he's liable to feel the pain."

The Israelis repeatedly dropped leaflets and beamed radio broadcasts into West Beirut warning people to clear out before the IDF launched the final assault. Thousands did flee in panic, choking the roads with cars and dropping the population of West Beirut from around 800,000 to around 500,000. But most—primarily the poor and lower middle class—stayed put. Some stayed because they were too old or weak to be moved. Some stayed to protect their homes from looters, armed gangs, and refugees seeking shelter. Some stayed because they had nowhere else to go. Some stayed because they mistrusted any message from Israel. And some stayed just to spite the Israelis.

Two Eight-Year-Olds Squabbling

In any given war, ceasefires are infrequent events. They generally are called for special occasions such as holidays, exchanges of wounded, or showing good faith as serious negotiations aimed at settling the conflict begin. But there were twelve ceasefires over the course of this war, an average of one every six days. Some would last a day, some an hour, some three days.

"Most of the things that have gone wrong," Habib said, "have gone wrong because of Israeli action, in my opinion." Dillon is more blunt: "Every time we had a ceasefire in place, the Israelis broke it." The Israelis insisted that the PLO or the Syrians were the ones who had broken each ceasefire, and that the IDF had simply responded. Habib considered that argument blatantly disingenuous. Yes, he recognized that "crazies" here and there on the Palestinian side often did take the first shot. But the problem, as he saw it, was "the now-famous military doctrine the Israelis have given the world—that is to say, that Israeli forces can *move forward* under a 'ceasefire in place' until they encounter resistance, at which point they can claim that the other side has violated the ceasefire and they therefore have freedom to fire at will."

It was like two eight-year-olds squabbling, says one American diplomat. "'He hit me first.' 'Well, I hit him because he called me a name.' Blah, blah, blah. It kind of becomes 'a pox on both your houses.'" Mikdadi describes one specific case:

At 4.45 in the afternoon the ceasefire is over. The Israelis say we breached it: Israeli gunboats were only trying to stage a landing, what was wrong with that? Did we have to shoot back at them for such a simple thing? We get the whole works for being so presumptuous as to try to stop them landing: air raids, gunboats, shelling from land artillery; neighbourhoods are on fire, cluster bombs explode everywhere.

. . . Where is Philip Habib? Isn't he going to do anything? This is genocide, pure and simple.

To his immense frustration, the only thing Philip Habib could do was to
howl about it to Washington and, like Sisyphus, start rolling his boulder
back up the hill.

Sharon's policy was so disingenuous and so systematic that Israeli soldiers joked that "each time we fire the army spokesman announces we're
being fired at." As if to concede the disingenuousness of it all, Sharon publicly admitted his policy of not necessarily returning fire at the source of
the fire. So, an Israeli journalist wrote, "A rifle bullet loosed off by a Syrian
soldier in the Bekaa could, theoretically, unleash a 16-hour bombardment
of West Beirut."

That was the other aspect of the broken ceasefires that infuriated Habib:
disproportionality. The Israeli policy of massive retaliation was in fact one
of the war's distinguishing features. Habib could not fathom how a few
Palestinian shots here and there warranted hours and hours of intense, indiscriminate Israeli bombing. He repeatedly yelled at Washington about it:

June 21: "The Palestinians fired 50 shells into Baabda, and the
 IDF replied for 14 hours."
July 11: "Two thousand shells is not the answer to two snipers.
 They have to stop playing the game of 2,000 to one!"
July 29: "This IDF threat that, if they get a few shots, they will
 open up is just impossible. If it's mild fire, the IDF has
 no right to shoot for seven days!"

Sharon said his responses were not a thousand to one, that Habib's reports
to that effect were all false, exaggerated, unprofessional, and hysterical.

Playing Games

Habib came to expect cynicism from Arik Sharon. For example, one morning Habib was at Yarze shouting over the radio to Washington for the thou-
sandth time, "Call them and tell them they've gotta stop! They've gotta
stop!" When he hung up, he said to the radio operator, Faith Lee, "We'll
have them stop at 10:30 tonight."

"Why 10:30?" she asked.

With a hint of gallows humor in his voice, he said, "That way they can
use up all the bullets they had laid out for today."

"You mean they have a certain amount of ammunition that they use for
a day?"

"Yeah, and they've got to use it all up."

A half hour later the noise started. Habib and Lee stepped out onto the veranda overlooking Beirut to watch the tracers flying and listen to the rumble of Israeli tanks and the boomboomboomboomboom of their cannon. All day long Sharon's assault raged. At 10:30, it stopped.

Habib may or may not have been joking. But he certainly felt that Sharon was playing games with him. Sharon would always "work one or another of his angles," said Charlie Hill. "If he has got to open a crossing point, he will take it out by shelling. If we tell him to stop the shelling, then he will turn the power and water off again. If we get the power and water back on, then he will close the crossing point. And we will go round and round like this."

A telling example of Sharon's approach to ceasefires was one that Habib had scheduled to start on June 28 at 9 P.M. The PLO had already agreed to it. While giving Washington instructions for arranging Israeli confirmation, he added, "And tell the Israelis 'Don't shoot from 8:30 to 9:02.'" Sharon said he couldn't have it arranged until 10:30. At 9, he started a mighty barrage. "They're bombing the crap out of West Beirut," Habib said at 9. "They have better communication than that. So we know now it has nothing to do with who fires first or with not firing unless fired upon. Pressure is not it. This is all after the PLO agreed to 9 P.M. at our urging. I feel like a damned fool." Habib called back to report "the biggest barrage ever" at 10:28. This was not a case of some uninformed gunner acting alone. "All this is done by order," he said. "Guns were firing a few hundred yards from the IDF headquarters. They could have *walked* down to tell them to stop."

Even while a ceasefire "held," people on the ground might not feel much relief. Mikdadi describes one ceasefire: "It had been such a quiet, peaceful day that Tuesday: the residential areas had just been bombarded a few times, and only 25 people had been killed and 75 wounded. That was our truce."

Radically Different Beliefs

Sharon kept up the pressure because he felt his chances of military success were greater than Habib's chances of diplomatic success. But there's no getting around the conclusion that he also did not *want* Habib to succeed. The Lebanese, the Americans, and even some Israelis noted the pattern that, as Habib put it, "every time we make progress, Israel restarts the fighting."

Sharon's cynicism about Habib's diplomacy was undeterred by facts. For example, Sharon writes that at the end of June "Habib for his own reasons was not pushing for any fast end to the situation. And the lack of any real American pressure encouraged [the PLO] in their determination to stay put." There was certainly a shortage of pressure from Washington, but none from Phil Habib. He repeatedly pushed his intermediaries to hurry it up: *When will you meet with Arafat next? How soon can you make up a timetable for their departure? Why can't you give me the decision I need here and now?* Sharon had it quite backwards about Habib dawdling at the end of June (or any other time): He met with Wazzan June 29 to pump him up for his crucial next session with the PLO, emphasizing that "time is vitally important. We cannot let this drag on. . . . You must complete the plan this afternoon so that we can discuss it before the day is over. There is no possibility of it being acceptable if the PLO strings us along or seeks to get out of this."

The underlying problem was that Sharon and Habib operated from radically different beliefs about whether the PLO was really willing to leave. Habib was of course forbidden to meet with Arafat, look him in the eye, and gauge his sincerity for himself. But the intermediaries talking with the PLO on Habib's behalf were all telling him that (at least at certain times) the PLO was sincerely, genuinely ready to go. Though he knew all too well of Arafat's vacillation and preference for stalling, Habib told Washington:

> June 28:   "The PLO recognizes the game is up in Lebanon. These guys want out."
>
> July 2:   "The PLO has agreed to get out."
>
> July 19:   "The PLO really want out."
>
> July 30:   "There no question but that there is an unequivocal and firm declaration on the part of the PLO to leave Beirut."
>
> August 9:   "Every indicator points to firm PLO decision to depart as soon as possible." "The PLO has caved in completely, and its members are without question desperately anxious to leave the city."

But departing would mean coming out of hiding, and he believed that they were never going to expose themselves while bombs were falling all around them. If only Sharon would give him a little breathing room, Habib reasoned, he could complete his negotiations of the particulars of their departure and get them out.

But Israeli intelligence in Lebanon was telling Sharon that the PLO was "defiant and almost euphoric because it was attracting so much worldwide attention. Furthermore, Israeli intelligence described the PLO as convinced that it could outlast the Israelis or that in the final analysis, the world would save them." Sharon thus concluded that his only option was to pound them into submission. Any relaxation in pressure, he believed, would only encourage the PLO to stay put. Habib believed that continued bombing could convince the PLO that Israel was not really interested in a peaceful settlement and thus that the PLO might as well stay and fight to the end.

The bottom line, Habib said, is that "Sharon was hell-bent on getting what he wanted, which was the wholesale destruction of the PLO in Lebanon; he was going to stop at nothing less."

The Spectre of Force

High-stakes crisis diplomacy is largely a matter of trying to persuade people to do what they do not want to do. What gives such diplomacy its leverage is the spectre of force. But during the siege of Beirut, Philip Habib found himself in a queasy position: The force that backed up his diplomacy was precisely the force that he was trying to stop.

There was no question that some degree of force was necessary to dislodge the PLO. The question was how much. Throughout the war, Habib repeatedly argued with Washington and Jerusalem about how much force was appropriate.

He recognized, pragmatically, that a degree of force had the advantage of motivating the PLO to leave. For example, after the IDF took out a joint Syrian-Palestinian checkpoint in Beirut, Habib said, "Such pressure is useful; massive attacks would not be." On another occasion he said, "I'm not opposed to psychological pressure. A degree of panic now in Beirut is good. But it must not lead to action." When George Shultz was just coming on board as secretary of state in mid-July, an Israeli newspaper erroneously reported that Shultz had told Israeli ambassador Moshe Arens that the IDF absolutely cannot go into Beirut. "Frankly I wish to hell they wouldn't publish that kind of stuff," Habib muttered. "We need a little bit of pressure on these bastards."

But he also recognized, equally pragmatically, that the disadvantages of Sharon's overkill vastly outweighed that one advantage. First, it inflicted egregiously gratuitous suffering on the civilians of West Beirut.

Second, it was obviously not working. The PLO had proven to be much tougher to dislodge than Sharon had expected. Arafat's ragtag band of guerrillas was holding out against Israel's army longer than had the armies of Egypt, Syria, and Jordan in any of the several regional wars of the past thirty-five years. Sharon reportedly once said to Habib as the PLO continued to refuse to budge, "I've thrown everything I've got at them, and still they are there! *Tell Arafat I've only got my atom bomb left!*"

Third, Habib thought it blindingly obvious that Sharon's campaign of massive force was defeating its own purposes and doing Israel much more harm than good. The PLO claimed that Sharon's pounding only increased their unwillingness to compromise. That claim could be dismissed as bravado—were it not for the fact that they did indeed hold out for weeks in the face of withering attacks. And the longer the PLO held out, the more legendary they stood to become in Arab eyes. Far from destroying the PLO, Sharon's assaults put the PLO and its cause center stage in the sympathetic spotlight of the world press. People tend to root for the underdog, and for thirty-five years the underdog had been "brave little Israel." Now, the world press was showing Israel as the cruel bully who had abandoned all pretensions to what had always been its trump card: the moral high ground.

Fourth, excessive force brought Habib's diplomacy to a standstill, delaying even longer the day when the PLO might leave. Sometimes it was by preventing his intermediaries from shuttling between him and the PLO. Other times it was by spooking the PLO. On July 1, for instance, Wazzan was meeting with Arafat and some other top PLO leaders when, as Habib put it, "the Israelis came over dropping flares and boom-boom stuff. The Palestinians said they weren't going to stand still while that was going on and took off like a bunch of birds." But beyond the specific cases, Habib feared that, if the violence reached a certain level, the PLO would break off the negotiations altogether either as an act of defiance, in a choice to go down in a blaze of glorious martyrdom, or by concluding that Habib was simply irrelevant.

The fifth reason Habib believed Sharon's force did more harm than good was that it ironically weakened Habib's leverage to persuade the PLO to leave. True, diplomacy must be backed up by the spectre of force. The *spectre* of force. The *threat of future force* was a useful diplomatic lever— "Get out of Beirut or else." But if the "or else" was already happening *and the PLO was weathering it,* then Habib's leverage melted. He could, and did, redefine the "or else" as the IDF wading into the streets for eyeball-to-eyeball combat, but that too proved to be a limp club. *He* certainly considered ground combat a profoundly imminent prospect all along. But after it didn't come and didn't come, the PLO started seeing that threat as just so much huffing and puffing. On July 6 Habib told the State Department that the Palestinians "think they have a new lease on life . . . in the sense that they don't think that the Israelis dare come in after them yet. Despite all the pressure." That belief persisted in most PLO circles inside Beirut until the end of the war.

Cutting Off the Stream

Habib felt that surrounding the city was all the force Sharon needed, no actual shooting required. Habib could then do his negotiating while the *threat* of an assault hung over the PLO's heads. "This will keep the pressure on the PLO to make a deal." All of his key colleagues except Haig agreed with him that Sharon was using too much force. But Shultz, Haig, Eagleburger, Hill, Lewis, and even Draper all believed that more force was necessary than Habib was willing to accept. This difference of opinion combined with political realities to dampen the effect of Habib's incessant calls for Washington to put "immense pressure" on Israel to stop.

The political realities were daunting. There was obviously zero spectre of American force that he could wave in front of the Israelis, and zero prospect of America cutting off diplomatic relations. But, short of that, he demanded that the US threaten to cut off all military aid to Israel. Most of the weaponry Sharon used was American. The US had sold those weapons to Israel on condition that they be used for defensive purposes only. This stipulation had given the US a decisive lever when the Israelis invaded Lebanon in their 1978 Operation Litani: President Carter insisted that they remove American-made weapons from Lebanon. Without the weapons, the troops of course could not stay. That strategy worked: It pulled the plug on Operation Litani. In this invasion, Habib repeatedly tried to pull that same lever by complaining to Washington that "there's no way in hell that what Israel is doing is a defensive use of our weapons. They're in violation of US law. We're in violation of our own law. We're being used! Protest this publicly." But Reagan, perhaps unwilling to run afoul of Congress or of domestic political interests, never did play the defensive-use-of-weapons card.

For all of Habib's banging and crashing that he needed immense US pressure—threatening sanctions, cutting off military and economic assistance, perhaps even going so far as to reassess relations with Israel—it is doubtful such measures would have worked.

In the first place, no US administration would ever be willing to take such measures. Even if an administration did decide to do something about non-defensive use of US weapons, all it could do in practice would be to send up a finding to Congress that says "a serious violation may have occurred." Congress then generally drops the matter. The US did take the modest steps of briefly suspending deliveries of aircraft in mid-June and of cluster bombs in late July. But neither had any effect on Israeli policy.

Which was the second problem: Even if Washington did impose serious sanctions, there was no way they would stop Sharon's juggernaut. Habib had no illusions about that. On the second day of the invasion he had written, "It is abundantly clear that the Israelis will adamantly resist any immediate withdrawal and return to the status quo ante, even if subjected to the most draconian sanctions by the UN or the U.S. . . . When I see Begin again [tomorrow . . . I] expect that he will restate again, with suitable bravado,

Israel's determination not to be pressured by sanctions into 'premature withdrawal' again, no matter what the cost to US-Israeli relations. While there will be hyperbole in that statement, Begin and indeed his countrymen become more obstinate rather than less under the threat of 'punishment.'"

Besides, Sharon's style had always been to create facts on the ground today that others could not undo tomorrow. He already had everything he needed to conduct this war. Cutting off his stream tomorrow would have no effect on his ability to make war today. Long before his war machine felt any practical effects of US sanctions, the battle could be won. Moreover, Carter's intervention had stopped Israel short in 1978, and Habib's diplomacy had forestalled a decisive war in 1981: Sharon and Begin did not want that to happen a third time. Habib wrote that the Israelis frequently reminded him "that they have not come this far, having taken casualties, suffered international criticism and expanded the material costs, only to find that they then could not accomplish all their objectives."

In short, Philip Habib knew sanctions wouldn't work. But he kept demanding them anyway. Why?

Principle. "I won't go along with it!" he said. "Tell Shultz it is indecent for the US to go along with this. Maybe nobody cares, but we can't go along!"

He faced the bleak prospect of carrying on his quixotic diplomatic battle virtually empty-handed. Though the Arabs never believed it, there was little Washington could do—and nothing it *would* do—to compel Israel to stop.

What Is the World Seeing You For?

Habib may have been empty-handed, but he was not alone. Revulsion with Arik Sharon's war grew in Israel, the United States, and around the world. People worldwide who had felt sympathy for Israeli victims of PLO terrorism now recoiled in disgust at the sight of Israeli bombs blasting innocent civilians' homes to rubble while killing and maiming their children. The prime minister of Greece likened the siege to the Nazi genocide of the Jews. From Bonn, survivors of Nazi concentration camps called on Begin to "stop the carnage." Israelis like to feel that they wear the white hats, but this war was instead making them look no better than the terrorists they denounced. On this, Habib pulled no punches. "What the hell is the world seeing you for, Arik?" he would shout at Sharon. "Here you're surrounding these Lebanese, there's 800,000 people cooped up in a hot summer week in Beirut with no water, no electricity. What the hell are you gonna say to people?"

What Begin said is that the IDF was "the most humane army in the world" and that "our boys got killed in order not to hurt civilians." But as an Israeli soldier put it, "We have an expression, 'tohar haneshek,' or purity of arms; it means you don't hurt civilians, but we did."

The American public, like Habib, was becoming increasingly critical of Begin and Sharon even while remaining committed to Israel generally. Official Washington's sympathy for Israel had begun to deteriorate six months before the invasion even began, soured markedly when Begin visited the US on June 21, shifted to the PLO and the Lebanese by mid-July, and by the first of August had turned anti-Israeli. US-Israel relations sank to, if not an all-time low, certainly one their lowest points ever.

Begin had bragged to Habib on the second day of the war that "we now have national unity" in support of the war. At that moment the Israeli public did generally support the war. But it quickly became apparent that the war was going badly. The Israeli press was critical. As more and more Israeli soldiers came home in body bags, a national sense of disappointment—then despair, anger, and horror—set in. The longer the war dragged on, the more Israelis themselves turned against it. This was unprecedented. For all their fractiousness on other topics, the one thing Israelis had always agreed about was support for their revered army. Most Israelis did support the war, and Begin's and Sharon's poll ratings went up. But the critics added up to an extraordinarily large minority for Israel. Never before had any appreciable number of Israelis opposed an action by their military. But opposition to this war was already forming by the second week. On June 12 a group of Israeli academics accused the government of launching an unjust war, of deception, and of "slaughtering the Palestinians en masse." In late June 20,000 Israelis demonstrated against the war. A week later, July 3, a hundred thousand Israelis turned out in Tel Aviv to demand an end to the war.

But the first to express disenchantment with the war were the Israeli soldiers fighting it. Soldiers in elite combat units berated an Israeli journalist for "mindlessly repeating official explanations [for the war] that we all knew to be false." A significant number of pilots refused to drop their bombs as assigned. Two thousand soldiers from elite paratroop units signed a petition opposing the war and demanding Sharon's resignation. Officers formed an ad-hoc group called Soldiers Against Silence and joined with the Peace Now movement to organize the July 3 anti-war demonstration in Tel Aviv. Thirty-five veterans of Israel's brilliant Entebbe raid signed a letter to Begin complaining that "I have been deceived and that I have been called to the first war in Israel's history which was not a war of defence but a dangerous gamble to achieve political goals." The Israeli press quoted an IDF tank soldier saying "Sharon is putting us into the family of nations that includes the Nazis." In mid-July Colonel Eli Geva, the IDF hero who had led the dash up the Lebanese coast, created a sensation by taking the unprecedented step of asking to be relieved of his command rather than lead an assault into Beirut.

Israeli elder statesman Abba Eban summed up the mood when he wrote that the weeks since the invasion began had been "a dark age in the moral history of the Jewish people."

Despite the opposition of their own people, despite international condemnation of their attacks on innocent civilians, despite the PLO's cushion from their blockade and assaults, and despite Phil Habib's efforts to halt it all, the siege rumbled on. As one of Habib's colleagues puts it, Sharon and Begin "seemed to be calling all the shots and not susceptible to any kind of diplomatic suasion."

11

Suspicions and Lies

Are there moments in the history of diplomacy and international relations when courage simply does not pay?
Somehow Philip Habib could neither believe this nor
accept it. Hence he never understood how, when calling on
some to invest more courage than they really had, what
you earn is fear, not love, and distrust rather than respect.
Ghassan Tueni

The strongest asset Phil Habib had in June 1982, his credibility, eroded
badly in July. He had not yet delivered peace; there had to be a sinister
explanation. In this land of a thousand conspiracy theories, Arabs became
increasingly sure that he was conniving with the Israelis, while the Israelis
became increasingly sure that he was conniving with the Arabs.

And they weren't the only ones doubting or undermining him. July
was marked by various major players' growing mistrust of Habib—and his
growing mistrust of them.

To many Arabs, it was a given all along that the US controlled or at
least cooperated in Israel's actions. A Jordanian journalist dismissed Habib
as "a postman, a parrot" who "supervised the massacre and executed American-Israeli policy." The Arabs tended to portray Israel as the lead partner in
the alliance. When Washington—particularly Alexander Haig—spoke, Arabs heard Israel's voice. Syrian President Hafaz al-Assad put it this way:
"The United States carry out Israeli decisions. . . . Not one [American en-
voy] has voiced the slightest idea different from Israeli ideas." A Palestinian official was more blunt, describing Habib as "a representative of one of
the sides involved—Israel."

As Washington's mouthpiece on the ground, Philip Habib was therefore seen as *Israel's* mouthpiece and as the symbol of US complicity in this
war. For example, on June 15 an Israeli commander gave the Syrians an
ultimatum to get their troops out of Baabda by noon or else he would destroy them. The Syrian foreign minister said "it was difficult for Syria to
believe that Israel could make a move such as this without American agree-

ment. It was also suspicious that a warning such as this came at a time when Habib was in Beirut."

Yasir Arafat put so little stock in Habib's efforts that on July 11 he sent his own eleven-point proposal for ending the crisis to France, the USSR, and the UN—but not to Habib. The PLO and some Lebanese were convinced that Habib often used Israeli military pressure as a lever to extract concessions from the Palestinians. While he raged privately over his inability to wring any cooperation from the Israelis, the Arabs simply could not believe that the US could not force Israel to stop. In their eyes, the mighty United States—in the person of Philip Habib—could force Israel to stop anytime. If Habib could stop the war and didn't, they reasoned, then it was obviously because he and his puppet masters in Washington wanted the war to continue. In some eyes, therefore, Habib appeared to be "presiding over the pulverizing destruction of Beirut."

"Colluding With the PLO"

For their part, many Israelis became convinced that Habib was biased in favor of the Arabs. The longer he repeated his insistence that the Israelis back off in Beirut, the louder they complained about him and the harder they tried to undermine him.

For example, on the same day that Habib first told Al Haig that "these guys [PLO] want out; we're moving in the right direction," Israeli intelligence was telling Haig that "Habib is getting bullshitted. There is no progress. There's nothing but stalling." Haig worried that Israeli mistrust of Habib might trigger an assault of West Beirut.

By July 6 Sharon, who had never had much use for Habib's efforts, decided that Habib's mission either would not work or would produce results that Sharon could not accept. As a result, Sharon decided the time had come to finish the problem militarily. The next day the Israeli Cabinet effectively endorsed Sharon's position that Habib "negotiate"—that is, impose—an unconditional surrender or else. On July 9 Lewis reported that Sharon had asked for a meeting because "clearly he wants to think about what happens when Habib fails."

Sharon's scorn for Habib infected Menachem Begin, who a year earlier had said Habib's "mind is brilliant. I think he is one of the most able diplomats of our time. I am so impressed by him, by his wisdom, by his energy and by his efforts—physical, moral, intellectual." But Begin was, in Morris Draper's words, "well known for his suspicious—almost paranoid—nature." For example, on July 11 Habib and Wazzan decided to call for a ceasefire to begin at 9 o'clock that night. Wazzan would convey the message to Arafat; Habib would convey it to the Israelis. Each did. But by the time the message worked its way around to Israel's ambassador to the US, Moshe Arens, it had become garbled: "Habib told the PLO that Israel asked for this ceasefire!" Arens complained. "The Prime Minister is losing faith in Habib. He misleads others, and he misleads us. This is very serious." A few days later Begin himself said that Habib "is the worst negotiator I've ever seen." Begin complained that American—that is, Habib's—treatment of the IDF in Lebanon was characteristic of enemies rather than allies and that the US—that is, Habib—had colluded with the PLO.

Campaign to Discredit Diplomacy

By July 21 Israeli complaints about Habib had reached the point that Begin and Sharon took up the matter with US ambassador to Israel Sam Lewis. Habib, Begin said, was engaging in "endless palaver without results while Israel is asked to restrain itself." Habib was "perhaps too nervous," Begin suggested. When Lewis tried to defend Habib, Begin cut him off, insisting, "Yes, he is too nervous: We know it very well."

What Begin knew was that "a friend in Washington" had leaked to him Habib's June 27 recommendation that Reagan threaten Israel with sanctions. "How could Habib even make such a recommendation," Begin demanded, "when Israel [has] rendered such a great service to the free world?" Lewis came away from the meeting understanding that

> Phil is suspected of holding back from the Israelis information about promises he is believed to be making to the PLO through Wazzan, et al., assurances that 'he will assure Israeli withdrawal from the Beirut area,' or assurances that he will 'produce Israeli agreement' on other issues where Begin or Sharon have repeatedly told us they will not agree. Phil is also well known to reject absolutely any further use of military force to eject the PLO, and is widely suspected of painting an unreal, over-optimistic picture of the PLO's commitment to leave and of other aspects of the negotiation—all in the interest of forestalling Israeli military moves.
>
> This unsavory suspicion contrasts totally with the high esteem Begin displayed publicly and privately for Phil throughout the past year, even when the [government of Israel] was disappointed with his lack of progress, as for example, on the [1981] Syrian missile issue. The current lack of confidence partly reflects, I believe, the lack of any personal contact between Phil and Begin since June 14. A frank tete-a-tete here soon can help a great deal to clear the air, at least with Begin. The despicable leak of Phil's recommendations to the president has, however, badly poisoned the well.

I cannot, however, dismiss the fear that some of what we are seeing reflects a deliberate campaign to discredit our diplomatic efforts, the Israelis having now concluded that they will not bear fruit. In short, the Israelis are building a case for the inevitability of some form of eventual military action; discrediting Habib may be part of that effort. If so, I see Sharon as the culprit, not Begin, but Begin listens all too much to Sharon these days.

Capacity to Lie

Habib came to trust Begin and Sharon even less than they trusted him. Though all of the parties Habib was dealing with were difficult in their own ways, he rarely complained about the PLO, the Lebanese, or the Syrians. But he griped constantly about the Israelis. The reason, says Draper, is that "the Israelis were in a class by themselves about posing problems." They were the actors, the initiators, the driving force; everyone else was just reacting to Israeli moves.

At first, he had had no reason to take the Israelis' words at anything other than face value. But time and again their actions failed to match their words. Over and over, the Israelis would assure the US that their troops were in some position when in fact they were 10 or 20 miles further. Over and over, they would agree to a ceasefire in place, and then creep forward under cover of the ceasefire. As time went on, Habib concluded that Sharon had "a pattern of false and inaccurate reporting" of what his forces were doing. By mid-July Lewis felt Habib had grown so suspicious of the Israelis that Lewis didn't even want Habib to come to Israel at the moment, saying, "It would be a disaster in his frame of mind." By early August Habib had concluded that "the capacity of Israel to lie is clear" and that "we can't trust Israel anymore." Appendix B is a sampling of the kinds of instances that led Habib to those conclusions.

There's no question that Habib considered Arik Sharon "the biggest liar this side of the Mediterranean." But what about Begin? That's more complex.

On the *general* question of Begin's truthfulness, there's a sharp difference of opinion among American diplomats. Some emphasize that, while Begin was stubborn and impossibly legalistic and sometimes misinformed, he was also scrupulously truthful. Habib could not budge him to say a word that he was unwilling to say; but if he did say something, he said it honestly and lived up to it.

Others strongly disagree. "We were being lied to consistently by Sharon, by Begin, and by the ambassador in Washington as to what their aim was," says Nick Veliotes. "It's hard for me to believe that Sharon misled Begin about his intentions. I believe Begin lied to us." Draper says, "Begin told flat-out lies to us, Israel's greatest ally and friend. One of the strict rules of diplomacy in intergovernmental relationships is that you should never tell a lie. But he sure did." Even Sam Lewis, the American ambassador in Israel who usually has very sympathetic things to say about the Israelis, writes that Sharon and Begin steadily lost credibility with Habib and with Washington "as their assurances about Israeli military actions and intentions deviate[d] repeatedly from actual military events in the Beirut area." Lewis blames Sharon for feeding Begin inaccurate battle information that Begin uncritically passed on to Habib.

One of the abiding *specific* questions about the war is this: Whatever Sharon's intentions, did Begin lie to Habib and the world in the early days of the invasion that his objective was only to push PLO artillery back 40 or 43 kilometers? Habib apparently didn't think so. But he wrote on the third day of the invasion that he was "filled with foreboding" that Israel's military successes were inspiring in Begin an "escalation of objectives," namely "that Sharon's more ambitious scheme is worth going for." In other words, Habib believed Begin meant what he said when he said it, but soon got more ambitious.

If that's correct, then the prime minister's intentions going in must have been grotesquely out of synch with his colleagues' intentions. As time went on, certain themes surfaced again and again in Habib's talks with other Israeli officials. One theme, he wrote July 14, was that "almost all of my Israeli interlocutors who come to Lebanon . . . make clear that their objectives were never confined to [pushing the PLO back to 43 kilometers]. They were out to do that incidentally to their larger purpose—which was to destroy the PLO as an effective mechanism for Palestinian ambitions."

Begin certainly protested his innocence. In a June 13 meeting with Habib, Begin became surprisingly emotional in complaining about "a tendency to blame Israel for everything." He described the casualties his troops had suffered, then added, with visible anger, that there had been an outcry that "I had misled people." He said it was "unfair to have been accused of deceiving people" and then abruptly left the room.

Years later, Sharon would claim that, when he had come to the Cabinet with plans for the war, it was understood that the war would entail Israeli troops going all the way to Beirut. But when Begin's son Ze'ev brought his father word of Sharon's claim, the long-since-retired Begin became agitated and said over and over, "These things aren't true. These things aren't true." Sharon, Begin said, had extended the goals of the war on his own. "So was I lying to everyone?" In 1997 an Israeli court ruled that Begin had indeed given Sharon a mandate for only a limited action, but that Sharon had proceeded with his own more ambitious plans.

Tar Baby

Habib was furious not only about how little he could rely on what the Israelis said to him, but also about how much they said to the press. His negotiations were extremely delicate. He was not about to risk letting his frail seedlings wilt in the glare of the TV lights. So he always tried to keep developments quiet until he could get them nailed down. Any small concession or small risk by any party could be read as a sign of weakness. If the press got wind of it, the party would deny having said any such thing. Habib would then be farther behind than he was before the concession.

For example, when the PLO had agreed in principle July 2 to leave, they sent word to Habib that if news of their agreement leaked, they would deny it. Sure enough, the Israelis leaked it. "These leaks have undermined our efforts . . . with the PLO, who now deny it all!" Habib shouted. "Unless the Israelis dramatically change their attitude and the atmosphere, there may be no way to achieve a negotiated outcome. If they leak each time, they can sabotage our whole effort." He then dictated to State a sentence he wanted included in an official statement: "Finally I must add that leaks out of Israel have materially damaged our negotiating effort, again raising questions about what course Israel is pursuing."

Habib's protest accomplished nothing. The leaks continued. His words were showing up in news stories. "This can't string out much longer, goddam it!" Habib yelled to Washington. "Each day there's a major problem. Kick diplomatic ass! Lewis has got to tell Begin to shut up!"

For all their mutual mistrust, Begin needed Habib. Begin had gambled enormous political capital on this quest to disarm the PLO and evict them from Beirut. He had to have something to show for it. By June 28 he was acutely aware that, if he backed down, the PLO would win a tremendous political victory while he himself would be ruined politically. The military effort had plateaued into a flailing, ineffectual fiasco. He couldn't stomach sending his boys into the streets of West Beirut for savage house-to-house combat; his only alternative was for Philip Habib to work out a deal.

By mid-July Sam Lewis was reporting from Tel Aviv that the Begin government found itself in "a cruel dilemma." They knew that, if they did launch a final assault of house-to-house combat in the streets of West Beirut, it would precipitate a major crisis with the US. Reagan himself would come down on them hard and might even force them to stop midway—which would humiliate them on the world stage. But as the Israeli public grew less and less supportive of a war that dragged on and on, Begin also feared that if he did *not* launch a final assault and get this blasted war over with, his Likud government could fall. In other words, Lewis reported, "An assault leads to disaster, but stringing out the war could lead to political defeat." The Begin administration did not like the way Habib was proceeding, sincerely believed he was being duped by the PLO, and was totally convinced that he would fail. But, with the notable exception of Ariel Sharon, they also realized that only a negotiated settlement could bail them out of this tar baby of a war they had gotten themselves into. So in an irony that made Begin morose, Lewis reported, "the success of the Likud depends on Habib."

This sour realization did not endear Habib to the Begin government. Nor did it soften their demands. For their definition of Habib's success did not entail any compromises on their own part, but only capitulation by the PLO to the terms of surrender they wanted Habib to convey. Indeed, the State Department alerted Reagan July 18 that "Begin's sense of frustration with the situation could result in an attack order before very long."

Baying at the Moon

The Israelis knew quite well what Habib had to say—*Stop shooting, back off, and let me work out a settlement*—and they were tired of hearing it. They got to where they'd rather see if they could hear something more to their liking from Washington. "Phil could talk to a certain extent," says George Shultz, "but the Israelis didn't pay much attention unless it came from Washington, and particularly in the end from the president himself." So a circuitous communication process evolved. Habib would tell Charlie Hill at State what he wanted the Israelis to hear, State would call Lewis in Tel Aviv, and Lewis would then go give Begin a message signed by the secretary or president that had originated with Habib.

And that's often how it worked. But as the siege dragged on, Washington got as tired of hearing from Phil Habib as the Israelis did. As far as Washington was concerned, Habib was over there to solve the problem. Solving the problem meant leaving them alone, not continually pestering them with demands to intervene.

Habib knew the system well enough to realize what he was up against bureaucratically. To get Begin and Sharon's attention, he needed the right noises to come from Ronald Reagan, and that wasn't going to happen often. Reagan, assured that the crisis was in Habib's capable hands, gave it little attention. And even if he were paying attention, presidents do not often insert themselves personally into foreign crises. Like cayenne, they must be used sparingly. Even secretaries of state don't personally get involved on a daily basis.

So as the novelty of the crisis wore off, Habib felt more and more like he was baying at the moon. But he was not one to let grim prospects deter him. "Habib wouldn't stop," says Charlie Hill. "He'd just keep going." That got old even for Hill—or perhaps especially for Hill, since he was the one literally hearing from Habib several times a day. For example, one day Habib was sawing away at his favorite theme to Hill over the radio: "Anything that keeps Israel from going into West Beirut is the answer. Make it clear that's my position. Sam Lewis should tell them they cannot go in. I don't accept it under any circumstances. Do you understand?!!"

Yeah, yeah, yeah, thought Hill. *Here he goes again.* But Habib was on a roll, and there was no stopping him.

"We will get the PLO out if it takes six months," Habib continued, "but the Israelis cannot go into West Beirut! That's my position. Everyone should know it. If it's not the position of the US government, then I should know."

"We're aware it's your clear position," Hill finally shot back. "I can't say whether it is the US position or not yet. Over and out!" He then slammed down the receiver.

More and more often, Habib would blister Hill's ears demanding that the secretary or president put pressure on Israel to back off, Hill would pass on the message, and nothing would happen.

Sniping from Washington

Worse, bureaucratic sniping set in. The Pentagon, the NSC, and other agencies all had their own opinions of what Habib ought to be doing. State had to pass on some of those ideas to Habib as instructions. When those instructions proved unworkable—as they usually did—Eagleburger would go back to the other agencies to tell them so. They'd reply, in effect, *It's not working because of that goddam Habib! Your guy, your State Department emissary, is not following instructions! He's supposed to be a hotshot, but he's failing. If he can't do the job, let's get rid of him and get somebody who can.*

That kind of sniping stayed behind closed doors. But in late July, Senator Larry Pressler started publicly calling for Habib's resignation. *The Washington Post* had revealed that Habib was a paid consultant to the Bechtel Corporation, a construction firm with projects all over the world, including the Arab world. Pressler, a member of the Senate Foreign Relations Committee, promptly charged Habib with conflict of interest and made the rounds of the Sunday morning talk shows demanding his resignation. Pressler called it a "very, very serious matter" because "Bechtel is viewed as being extremely pro-Arab." If Habib had such poor judgment as to accept a mission in the Middle East while Bechtel had projects in the Arab world, Pressler argued, "then I feel that he should resign because we placed our trust in him as negotiator and as ambassador." Some editorial writers picked up the theme that "the Bechtel connection can only undermine Habib's credibility with Israel" and called for him to resign not from his mission, but from Bechtel. One political candidate went so far as to say, "Bechtel is controlling our Middle East policy."

Habib apparently gave the stink little thought. He said nothing about it at the time. But later he explained that in 1981 George Shultz, then president of Bechtel, had asked him to advise the company about the facts of life in various countries. "I had an understanding with George that my job was not to lobby in Washington and not to go abroad and seek business." Between January and May 1982, he had attended three Bechtel meetings, including one that dealt with the Middle East. Bechtel paid him $7,500 per quarter.

Pressler was certainly right about the importance of Habib's credibility in Israel. But it had *been* an issue in Israel—for substantive reasons—for weeks before it occurred to Pressler that appearances might *make* it an issue in the future. Habib no doubt found a bit of grim comic relief in the notion that Bechtel's construction projects might impugn his evenhandedness more than having Lebanese blood in his veins.

He declined to resign from either his mission or Bechtel, the administration expressed full confidence in him, and the tempest quickly blew over.

But the press too was becoming restive. *Newsweek* columnist George Will wrote in late July that "The PLO sits in West Beirut, holding perhaps 300,000 civilians hostage, issuing demands from behind the screen of Habib's mission. . . . PLO intransigence has grown proportionally with U.S. involvement, and now the United States is protecting the PLO." Columnist Joseph Kraft wrote that Habib "is unaccustomed to closing a deal, so it may be necessary to pull him back from the present round of negotiations on Lebanon. . . . Precisely because he came up the ladder, . . . Habib is used to letting senior figures mount the pressures that foster a closing. When there is no pressure, he goes on talking for the sake of talking, without reaching a settlement."

Grubby Little Fingers

As if the decline of trust all around didn't cause enough problems, Habib also had some unwelcome competition for the role of diplomatic point man. France pointedly worked to scuttle his efforts in order "to prevent . . . a resolution mediated solely by the United States." France wanted to be the broker. Failing that, they wanted to be at least the intermediary between Habib and the PLO.

The government of François Mitterand saw itself as the PLO's advocate. The French felt that Habib was focusing solely on the immediate crisis of how to get the PLO evacuated from Beirut, while the French wanted the broader Palestinian political issues, such as Palestinian statehood, addressed. The French doggedly pressed Washington to give the PLO some kind of political bonus, such as US recognition, in return for the PLO's consent to quit Beirut.

The French were absolutely correct about Habib's focus on the immediate crisis rather than on the broader political issues. He felt it was frivolous to haggle about long-term Palestinian rights while bombs were raining down on Beirut. As he put it, "The French want to solve all world problems in this situation." He agreed that "we probably never will be able to produce a total solution until the Palestinians have a homeland." But he had worked in the Middle East long enough to know that that would take years—decades—to resolve. He was having enough trouble just getting the shooting stopped today. If he succeeded, then maybe everyone could talk tomorrow.

Eagleburger said Habib "resented the fact that the French were trying to stick their grubby little fingers into the middle of the thing." While Habib was busy trying to persuade the PLO to settle on what he considered reasonable terms, the French were busy advising the PLO to hold out. They accused him of misrepresenting his negotiations with the PLO in an "intoxication" campaign. They pushed a broad UN resolution intended to be "the only alternative approach to Habib's." And they warned the PLO that his evacuation plan was a "trap."

Habib did use the French to a limited extent as an intermediary to the PLO. But he said "the French are no good as a channel. They're just sucking up to the PLO." He wouldn't even tell the French what he knew. He scoffed at one French attempt to resolve the crisis via a UN resolution with a curt "You can't leave this to Liechtenstein in New York"—that is, the UN has no clout in this crisis.

Habib clearly wanted the French to butt out. One explanation might be that he was, as one Lebanese put it, just congenitally "sceptical about any process in which he is not the central figure." He certainly was brimming with self-confidence. But his own explanation was more pragmatic: Like it or not, the Israelis were running the show, and they were in town to destroy the PLO, not to improve its lot. This was not the time for political posturing about broader issues. That might well prompt Sharon to render the question moot by finishing off the PLO in house-to-house combat.

The Israelis thought *Habib* was too sympathetic to the PLO; no way would they ever accept the overtly pro-PLO French as lead players. And, as far as Phil Habib was concerned, that ended the discussion.

This Piece of Trickery

Habib's dilemma of trust was epitomized in an article published August 8 in *The Jerusalem Post*.

The day before, the Israeli Cabinet had gone over his plan for evacuating the PLO from Beirut. The ministers were divided on whether it was a good idea. Prime Minister Menachem Begin complimented Habib's efforts but emphasized that his prospects were not bright. Sharon blamed Habib and Dillon for what he called "mendacious" reports to Washington condemning the IDF's actions while commending the PLO's sincerity. Sharon told the Cabinet that Habib's plan was "a fraud and a deception."

After the Cabinet meeting, anonymous sources "close to" Sharon denounced Habib's plan to *The Jerusalem Post* as a "fraud" and accused Habib of deceiving both the American and the Israeli governments with it. "This is a piece of trickery," the anonymous source or sources said, "because the PLO does not intend to leave. The PLO has nowhere to go—despite Habib's sanguine statements about various countries that are ostensibly willing to take them in." While allowing that Habib might be "honestly deluded," the anonymous source(s) said his real purpose was to "save the PLO's skin." His plan, they said, would evacuate only a few hundred PLO while the bulk of them remained in Beirut, sheltered by an "international force of deceit" spearheaded by the French. The anonymous source(s) said that Habib had earlier agreed with Begin not to bring the MNF into Beirut until after all the PLO had left, and that Habib was now reneging on that agreement.

Along with the story, *The Jerusalem Post* ran an editorial criticizing this "unbridled attack" on Habib. "Apart from the uncouth tone of the attack," the editorial said, "its purpose seemed obvious: it was meant to nip in the bud any prospect of bringing about the evacuation of the PLO from West Beirut by diplomatic means." The editorial called on Begin to allay "the suspicions of some senior U.S. officials that Israel might actually be opposed to a peaceful resolution of the crisis, preferring that the PLO does not leave Beirut alive."

It had been less than two weeks since the French had warned the PLO that Habib's plan was a trap. Now the Israelis were calling his plan trickery to save the PLO's skin.

When Habib read the article, he seethed at the way things were turning out. "The PLO are desperate to leave," he bellowed at Hill, "but the IDF won't believe it. The attitude of Israel is incomprehensible! Is Israel interested in a political settlement or not? They are attacking me personally, and you guys in Washington have got to say, 'The Israelis are a bunch of goddam liars!'"

If Only . . .

Phil Habib had a simple way of dealing with the decline of trust he had in others and that they had in him: grit his teeth and persevere. His tenacity was legendary, says one colleague. He would not allow even the "piece of trickery" outrage to distract him from his task of stopping this war. When he met with Sharon two hours after reading the article, he said nothing about it.

Though major players were losing confidence in him, he never lost an ounce of confidence in himself. He knew—he just *knew*, in his bones—that success was just around the next bend. He knew he had a plan that would work. If only he could get this next concession, if only he could have a few more days of quiet to negotiate, if only an Arab country would agree to take the PLO, if only . . . if only . . . .

For weeks, Habib had been saying over and over that he was within days or hours of having a deal nailed down. Over and over, the deals had fallen through. On July 12 Eagleburger said, "If it is obviously not going anywhere, we will bring Habib home." A few days later State discussed pulling Habib out on a health pretext. Algeria suggested that Habib might have to come out. So did Sam Lewis, who reported that the Israelis were "totally convinced" that Habib was going to fail.

In discussions throughout July, the same prospective act, bringing Habib home, took on all sorts of conflicting meanings. Recall Habib as an admission that he was getting nowhere. Threaten to recall him to pressure the Arabs to get serious about taking in PLO evacuees. Threaten to recall him to pressure Israel to get serious about diplomacy. Recall him as a protest against Israel's refusal to get serious about diplomacy. Threaten to recall him to wash America's hands of the whole sorry mess.

On July 18, two days after Shultz was sworn in as secretary of state, the press carried a rumor that Shultz was going to send Henry Kissinger out to replace Habib. From Beirut Habib asked Eagleburger whether their former boss would be the special negotiator for the overall peace process "or is he just going to come and show us how to handle the Lebanese problem?"

"This press story is pure unadulterated bullshit," Eagleburger said. Shultz had just brought Kissinger and others in for a brainstorming session. There was no thought of sending him to the Middle East to do anything.

Habib did threaten to resign several times. On July 6 he threatened to resign over Sharon's preventing him from negotiating. On July 28, he considered telling Israel he would stop working unless they turned West Beirut's electricity back on within twenty-four hours. But resigning was the last thing he really wanted: "My staying is the only thing that we have going that is keeping the Israelis in check."

Eagleburger raised the inevitable question during a July 13 radio call: "What happens if you, A. succeed, or B. fail? When you decide it's not doable, you've said you would pack up and leave."

Habib's response was characteristic: "I don't like to contemplate failure."

12

Life in the Pressure Cooker

> Phil had a terrible heart condition and shouldn't have
> been working at all. Sometimes I didn't know if he'd be
> able to make it out the door. You could just see the color
> go right out of his face. But when it came time to do
> business, the adrenaline and the will and the force of
> personality overcame all his physical problems, and he
> would just reignite. It was an amazing thing to watch. I
> said, "Someday he's not going to be able to do that.
> We're going to go in there and he's going to be dead."
> *Robert Paganelli*

All during the siege of Beirut, the world press was transfixed with the drama of this mysterious diplomat trying to stop a war. Though Philip Habib did not speak to reporters, leaks from his opposite numbers gave the press a fairly good sense of the substance of what he was up to. But none had any idea what his daily life was like in the pressure cooker or in his one oasis.

Habib loved to be on the go. He delighted in jetting here and there and having people scramble to keep track of him. "Nobody knew where I was," he said. "Many days *I* didn't know where I was going to be. When I'd get through at one place I'd decide where to go next. Sometimes I would decide at two o'clock in the morning that I'm leaving, and I'd leave at three o'clock in the morning. That's the advantage of having your own airplane."

Airplanes were fine. He loved them. But the Beirut airport was closed during the siege, so, to get in or out of Lebanon, he had to take helicopters. And he fervently hated helicopters.

He knew them all too well from his days in the Saigon embassy during the Vietnam War. The aerodynamics of taking off from that famous embassy roof forced the helicopters to take a sickening plunge toward the ground before they could gain altitude. That terrified Habib, and he never forgot it. He vividly remembered the armor-plated bellies of those helicopters in Vietnam, the flak shot up at them, how often they broke down, and how a damaged or malfunctioning helicopter just drops from the sky like a stone. He remembered climbing up ladders to crawl into hovering helicopters, with the hydraulic fluid bursting out of the overhead valves and sliming all over the floor. He also knew about Morris Draper's recent flight in an Israeli helicopter when a door fell off in mid-air and the pilot just laughed.

Altogether, they did not inspire much confidence.

The American Marines in the Mediterranean routinely flew visiting senators, admirals, and other assorted VIPs around, but Habib got top treatment. His dignitary ranking was four star, one notch below the five-star rating reserved for the president. The Marines considered flying him a plum assignment.

That did not, however, translate into cushy equipment. Habib flew mostly in Hueys. These are very reliable, as helicopters go, but are also very spartan affairs, noisy and painful to ride. The incessant throbbing boomp-boomp-boomp-boomp-boomp-boomp-boomp prevents you from ever relaxing. You're always bouncing. It's a skeleton of an aircraft that seats six, with little padding for wimps. You may be sitting sideways on a narrow bench leaning against a big bladder of fuel. You're strapped in like a sea captain lashed to the mast in a storm. Since a Huey flies with all the doors and windows open for breeze in the scorching Mediterranean summer heat, you pray that the pilot doesn't bank too steeply. He usually does: A Huey is like a flying jeep. A pilot can zoom in at 120 miles an hour, reverse it in five seconds, thread it between high-tension wires, and plop it down onto a patio. A thrill for the pilots; hell for Habib.

Crew chief Graydon Geske hesitates to use the word *fear*, but says Habib made no effort to conceal his discomfort on board, especially over water. He would sit rigidly in the back, lost in his billowy Mae West life jacket and flight helmet. He'd look out the windows uneasily, attentive to all that was going on and listening through his helmet's intercom as the flight crews pointed out to him a town over here, an Israeli gunboat over there, what kind of jet was visible in the distance. He rarely conferred with Draper, never read papers, never jotted notes, and never ever made chitchat with anybody. When he did speak, his voice was tense.

The Marines tried to make him feel safe and comfortable. They always had a backup helicopter fly within a hundred feet or so of his. If his ever had to make an emergency landing—which it never did—the backup would follow it down, and he could just jump into it and keep going.

The Marines' good intentions could backfire, though. Before Habib's first flight with them, the flight crew was told that he was uneasy in helicopters and that he had a bad heart. So on their first flight, they brought along flight surgeon Dr. John Brady just in case any problems arose with his heart. During the flight, Habib asked him who he was. When he explained he was the flight surgeon, Habib apparently assumed he was there in case the helicopter crashed. The pilot says, with military understatement, "The ambassador became somewhat uncomfortable." The doctor never flew with him again.

Life in the Pressure Cooker

Hardly Considered Nasty

Habib was much more comfortable in cars. But they were hardly safer, particularly for diplomats in Beirut.

Diplomats in Beirut were in fact special targets. Only six years earlier Habib had given the eulogy for the American ambassador and embassy counselor assassinated in Beirut. In 1981, just before Habib arrived in town, a rocket-propelled grenade (RPG) barely missed the American ambassador's car. Soon after Habib arrived, assassins stopped the French ambassador's unarmored car: Instead of taking evasive action when the shooting started, his poorly trained driver dove onto the floor, leaving the assassins free to simply walk over to the stopped car and shoot the ambassador point blank. The US army attaché barely escaped with his life when Palestinian gunmen stopped him at a checkpoint on his way to the ambassador's residence and sprayed his jeep with bullets.

Whenever Ambassador Robert Dillon went out, he carried a .357 Magnum pistol in a plastic envelope in his briefcase. He had full confidence in his security people, but felt that, if his car ever got trapped, he wasn't going to sit there passively and let others do all the fighting. Habib apparently did not carry any weapon. Dillon's car took some long-distance sniping now and then, and once or twice his bodyguards even returned fire.

Nearly every career Foreign Service officer faces gunfire, an evacuation, or other such crisis at some point in his or her career. But Beirut was an exceptional case. Driving in or around Beirut was, under the best of circumstances, always the ride of your life. Maniac drivers in a city synonymous with anarchy were the most benign threat. Booby traps could be planted anywhere, and any pothole might be filled with a mine. Sniper fire, says Dillon, was so common as to be "hardly considered nasty or a real attack." Even if no one was aiming at you, stray rounds and falling shrapnel were a constant danger. Any parked car might be wired to explode when you drove by. Any gang who had guns and the ability to block off the road would stop anyone who wanted to pass through and arbitrarily demand money or liquor, drag them out of their car, harass them for no particular reason, or blow their heads off. A diplomatic passport offered little protection when handed to a twelve-year-old boy with an AK-47 who examined it upside down.

Wailing Sirens and Screeching Tires

It was thus an extraordinary production for Habib to drive anywhere, because that was when he faced the greatest danger. The road to and from his headquarters outside Beirut was under constant fire. Wherever he went, he would ride in the middle of a convoy of three to five cars, each crammed with American and Lebanese security guards bristling with Uzi machine guns. The lead or scout car, usually a hardened Chevy or GMC Carry-All, rode up ahead to alert the motorcade to any dangers. The last car in the line was called the chase or bumping car. If a strange car came out of a side street as Habib's motorcade was about to pass, the security men didn't pause to ask whether it was innocent or menacing; the lead car would just ram it out of the way. Habib's car would then speed up, the chase car would race ahead to take over the lead position, and the lead car would take up the rear. If a strange car ever tried to penetrate the convoy, the chase car would speed up and plow it out of the line.

Habib's American bodyguards included three members of the elite Delta Force. "They are just deadly accurate marksmen who are allowed to use the weapon of their choice," says one Marine. "Their mandate is 'Shoot them dead, and we'll sort them out on the ground.'" Habib didn't go anywhere without his Delta Force guards in the lead car and the chase car.

His Lebanese guards were carefully assembled to represent a mixture of religions so he would not be accused of being captive to any one group. The Shi'a and Druze security guards particularly reveled in their reputations as tough guys. When people shot at them, they readily shot back. Lebanese bodyguards generally tended to enjoy speed, shooting in the air to clear traffic, and shouting at any unfortunate soul in their path. They had even been known to contrive a conflict just so they could emerge as saviors.

The leader of Habib's security detail was almost always a flamboyant macho type named Muhamed Kurdi, who enjoyed being seen as tough and fearless. With Kurdi leading the advance car, Dillon says, "we would scream down streets, scattering people and other cars, honking and shouting, sometimes with sirens blaring." Kurdi wore black leather gloves, which he would stick out the window to signal other cars to stop. It wasn't clear whether he preferred the sense of power when other drivers complied, or the adventure of confronting those who didn't.

Roaring around at breakneck speed in a motorcade with sirens wailing and tires screeching might seem like the surest way to attract the attention of potential assassins, but the security experts considered it safer than trying to sneak around. Assuming that Habib's car was being watched and tracked anyway, the less time it spent in any given spot, the better. To Habib, whatever "the boys"—the security experts—decided was final: He accepted it with uncharacteristic docility and wouldn't hear of any dissent from his colleagues.

At the center of all this hustle and turbulence, Habib would spend his drive time reading the latest cables, talking with colleagues, or looking at the scenery he was passing. One colleague "can't think of any time we were ever out—either driving or standing on the patio of the ambassador's residence looking down on the city—that he didn't express concern about how the city was being raped."

The CIA reportedly got wind that George Habash's Palestinian extremist group was out to kill Habib. Draper acknowledges various "amorphous" death threats that he and Habib just let the security experts worry about. "The PLO could've gotten us many times," he says, "because we were very exposed in travel. But we had some intelligence that the word went out to the Palestinians that we were to remain immune. We weren't sure about the Syrians. And of course the Iranians, who had brought in their special people, were out to get all Americans."

In any case, Habib wasn't taking any chances. He rarely went down into Beirut proper except to see his intermediary to the PLO, Prime Minister Wazzan. He tried to stay out of areas where firefights were blazing, although he'd never know when one might break out around him. For example, two shells landed in the courtyard of the presidential palace July 5 soon after he had left. On one of his trips to Cairo, his host, Ambassador Alfred Atherton, took him out on the veranda of his residence to show off his garden: Habib ignored the garden, took one look up at the ring of tall apartment buildings surrounding the veranda, and said, "Anybody up there with a .22 rifle could shoot you! They could shoot me!" With that, he spun on his heel and went back inside.

Do Not Leave Tonight

Dillon had evacuated all dependents and non-essential staff from Lebanon as soon as the invasion began. Two weeks later, he closed the embassy in West Beirut and turned his own residence into the center of operations. It thus became Habib's headquarters in Lebanon.

The residence was high in the hills southeast of Beirut in a swank Maronite suburb called Yarze. It was a strategic location. President Sarkis' palace was a quarter-mile away in the adjacent suburb of Baabda. The Beirut-Damascus Highway, an artery as important to the Lebanese as the airport, was about two miles away. Habib could stand on the veranda at Yarze and take in a commanding, sweeping view of the entire city sprawled out below.

The house was large, but it was built for entertaining, not for around-the-clock crisis management by a live-in team of thirty-two. The place was a three-ring circus. As one Marine who met with Habib there puts it, "There were always a bazillion people in there with their combat boots and mud all over Mrs. Dillon's beautiful rugs." By day the bedrooms were bustling makeshift offices, the house crawling with twenty to thirty diplomats, support staff, servants, and visitors plus thirty to forty Marine and other security guards. By night, each of the ten-or-so bedrooms held two or three exhausted workers. Only Dillon had a bedroom all to himself. With his wife evacuated for the duration of the war, this was the one little privilege he as the ambassador reserved for himself.

Habib shared the choice quarters: the elegant guest suite of two bedrooms and a sitting room at the opposite end of the house from the work area. The suite gave him quiet whenever he wanted it. While he surely got the suite as a gesture of respect, its remote location may have also have been a factor: Habib snored to wake the dead. Dillon says, "You could hear him snoring through the door. Miles away! And anybody who had to share that suite with him would complain about it." Two people shared the other bedroom in the suite, and Habib's own roommate was usually the hapless Morrie Draper.

Habib often went to bed while many of the staff stayed up working, but his brain was still going. For example, one night, after communication specialist Dorothy Pascoe had worked until the wee hours yet again and then dropped off to sleep, a loud knock at her bedroom door jolted her awake.

"Dottie! Dottie!"

"What?"

"Gotta send a telegram."

She stumbled to the door, and there stood Habib in his bathrobe. "My God, it's three o'clock in the morning! I just went to bed!"

"Get up. Gotta send this telegram." Within minutes, the two sat in their bathrobes at the teletype, with Habib dictating while she dutifully typed.

Official business wasn't the only concern weighing on him in bed. Political counselor Ryan Crocker and his wife Chris, a secretary, chose to come in to work at Yarze by day and sleep in an apartment or hotel elsewhere. On two occasions during periods of shelling, Habib shuffled out in his pajamas and robe to tell the Crockers that they should definitely *not* try to leave that night. Ryan Crocker says, "He had been lying there, couldn't get to sleep, extremely worried that one of these nights we'd have a shell land on us. There weren't any great firestorms those two nights. But every now and then the explosions would just seem to activate his thinking that something was going to happen to the people who were supporting him. He obviously felt very responsible in a kind of moral way. It was very touching, and it was obviously genuine—all the more so because it was not based on anything objective. I think he just felt a general angst that people were at risk and, as the senior person, it weighed on him."

Shrapnel after Breakfast

Any belligerent who wanted to hit the residence easily could have. But for the time being, the belligerents had more urgent concerns. Habib and his colleagues thus never felt that the residence was necessarily a target. It did, however, lie in between shooters and targets. So the greatest danger was all the stray rounds that landed there. Shrapnel and small-caliber shells sometimes came in through the windows.

The difference between being the actual target and catching incidental fire was sometimes academic. In what Dillon wryly calls "the Israeli sense of humor," Sharon's forces made a practice of positioning tanks and artillery right up around Dillon's Yarze residence and proceeding to shell West Beirut from there all day long. That practice had several effects, in Dillon's view. First, shooting from beside Habib's headquarters was a way of spitting in his eye. Second, it forced Habib and the others inside the residence to try to live and work with the incessant thunder of outgoing fire from a hundred feet away ringing in their ears. Finally, it ensured that, when the Palestinians inevitably shot back, the residence would take a lot of the fire.

The Palestinians and others in West Beirut shot up at the Israelis surrounding Yarze, at Israelis anywhere else they might be, at the palace down the road from Yarze, and at nothing in particular. Mortars are not very precise weapons in the first place, and the shooters in West Beirut lacked the required means of targeting them. Their fire tended to be more for show than for effect. If they had ever happened to hit the American ambassador's residence and taken out Habib, it would have been just pure dumb luck.

That never happened, but shrapnel did frequently come down on the Yarze compound. One day Habib was talking to Washington when he interrupted his report: "Jesus, somebody just brought in a piece of shrapnel that would cut your goddam head off. It fell on the [communications] shack, which is about twenty feet from where I'm sitting right now." It was six or seven wicked inches of jagged metal with English writing on it, which meant it had to be Israeli. "We'd go out in the morning," he said, "and pick up the spent ammunition that had fallen outside the dining room where we were sitting for breakfast. That happened very frequently. . . . It makes you understand the urgency of doing something. Once you've seen a piece of shrapnel and what it can do, it brings home the shock of war."

Diving into the Laundry Room

Habib and his colleagues in Yarze were unbelievably lucky. RPGs sometimes hit alarmingly close. Occasionally he could go outside and see the gun that was shooting. An RPG once hit the roof of the garage, but bounced off without exploding. The only thing incoming artillery ever hit squarely was the air conditioner. But Beirut in the summertime is brutally hot and humid—a natural sauna. With so many people crowded so densely together during a sweltering Beirut summer, the air conditioner was perhaps the worst object they could have hit.

The acoustics of the hill on which Yarze sat amplified the noise of shells falling in West Beirut. Habib and colleagues quickly learned how to interpret the sounds of shooting and how to deal with it. If it was a long string of fire, that was just somebody aimlessly blowing ammunition into the air, perhaps just to enjoy the pretty tracers it made in the night sky. If the fire came in short, irregular bursts, that was serious fighting aimed at a particular person or building. By Beirut standards, a quiet night was one when only a few people got killed.

The residence was surrounded by a solid wall, but had no special windows. Habib and the others in Yarze learned that, if something alarming happened, the stupidest thing you could do would be to go look out the window: Whatever caused the noise might well shatter the window in your face.

The residence also had no bomb shelter. The next best thing was the cement laundry room in the center of the house. When shrapnel started hitting the roof and earsplitting incoming mortar rounds started hitting within twenty yards of the main building, everybody inside instantly leapt into the laundry room. There they would grit their teeth and tell strained jokes for the twenty minutes or so until the barrage was over. Habib viewed the hits at Yarze as just a light dose of what West Beirut was experiencing.

One Sunday right after the air conditioner got hit, Habib and the others were sitting around the dining room having lunch when they heard ominous fire. The cook had gone out into the yard behind the building, and a sniper opened up on him. In a flash, the Marine guards scattered and started shooting back while Habib and the others rushed to the laundry room. Jammed together in a small, airless room in the stifling heat, they cursed both today's sniper and the lucky stiff who had knocked out their air conditioner. Habib's only comment was the Arab shrug: silently raising his palms and shoulders, as if to say *Malesh. Never mind. Nothing we can do about it.* For forty minutes they huddled and sweltered in the claustrophobic little room before the Marines gave the all-clear to come out. The cook had only been hit in the heel.

A Bad Day in Hell

Shelling tended to be the worst at night. Even when waked from a sound sleep, Habib and his colleagues at Yarze got pretty good at telling whether fire was outgoing *from* nearby Israeli guns or incoming aimed *at* those guns, and whether it was close enough to worry about. If it was outgoing, they'd just put their pillows over their heads. If it was incoming, they'd try to gauge how close it was and then put their pillows over their heads. "I sleep well no matter where I am," Habib said. "Even with the bombs outside my door. They wake you up; you go back to sleep. Many a night we woke up. Bombardment—then we went back to sleep. What else was there to do? You couldn't get up and start running down the road!"

To those inexperienced with artillery fire, says Ryan Crocker, "it's all just a bad day in hell." Close fire, whether incoming or outgoing, "has the kind of crack to it that really does shake you down to your soul." It makes you feel completely helpless. It is "very loud. Very loud! *Very, very loud.*" But over time, repetition and exhaustion dull your senses to it. You never get used to it, but you do begin to tune it out. You note it, like you'd note the chiming of a clock, but seconds later you've forgotten it. In fact, weeks of constant noise are less unsettling than a resumption of artillery fire after a respite.

One day, while Habib was meeting with Marines to plan their role in the evacuation, they heard a sudden barrage of nearby fire aimed in a new direction. They ran outside to see what was happening. A Syrian MiG was flying directly overhead, and Israeli guns were pumping shells into the sky at it. As Habib watched, an Israeli jet shot a missile, and the MiG exploded in a flash like a firework. A second later, as the bang reached his ears, the main remnant hulk of the MiG dropped like a stone. The Marines immediately rushed him and the others into the laundry room as fragments of the plane, of the ordnance it was carrying, of the missile, and of the anti-aircraft rockets rained down. "There was shit flying all over the place that day," recalls one of the Marines. Warfare usually consists of long stretches of quiet punctuated by short flurries of combat; this whole episode took about three minutes. It convinced the Pentagon that the Marines meeting with Habib qualified for hostile fire pay.

Collapsing on Us

Falling shrapnel, exploding cars, and crashing helicopters were only the most obvious dangers Habib faced. Less obvious was his bad heart. His instinct was to push and push twenty-three hours a day, and he frequently did. "Twenty hours a day was sometimes low," says Draper. The mental challenge was stimulating, but the sheer physical grind was exhausting. Habib and Draper might spend twelve or thirteen hours at a stretch in meetings, then clamber aboard a wretched helicopter and fly three hours to their next meeting.

He ran on pure, wild, pumping adrenaline. "He had the stamina that even young men don't possess," says one colleague. He knew perfectly well that if he kept up that pace, he would probably provoke another heart attack. He had not yet reached the fifth anniversary of his second heart attack, the one that nearly killed him and forced him to retire. When asked why a man with his heart history didn't have any more sense than to take on the most stressful mission on earth, he shrugged and said, "Well, you know, that's something you don't want to miss out on. If you've got to go, what better way to do it?"

But it was more important to him to finish the job. So he forced himself to rest at every opportunity. Rest for any other reason was alien to his way of thinking. Dillon laughs at the very thought of anyone saying, *Phil, I think I need to rest. I need to recharge my batteries.* "He would have said, 'What do you mean, "recharge"? What's the matter with you guys? It's your job! Jesus, what's the matter with you?'" Dillon had Habib as his house guest constantly during his Middle East work and never saw him really relaxed.

Forcing himself to rest required a major act of will, but he did it. When he could get by on mere sixteen-hour days, he did. He generally stayed put in Yarze and let Draper do the traveling. Everyone around him was quite worried about his health, so they were careful to give him as much rest as he would take. As one says, "We didn't want him collapsing on us."

One of the few other things he did for his health was to carve out time to see a cardiologist when he was in Israel. One evening after he arrived in Jerusalem from Beirut, Draper and his host, Consul General Brandon Grove, agreed that he looked sufficiently run down and haggard to warrant calling in a doctor. From then on, whenever he was coming to town after particularly stressful times, Grove would arrange in advance for the doctor to come by. Habib would grumble about it and swear everyone to strict secrecy, but the visits seemed reassuring to him. The doctor would check him over in his bedroom, then tell him to get a lot more rest. Only once was the doctor called specifically because Habib got overexcited and felt his heart acting up. The provocation: a particularly nasty meeting with Sharon.

The only exercise Habib ever got as an adult was playing golf, and that was out of the question in Beirut. Not only did he not have the time, but players on the nearby golf course had to pick up shrapnel off the greens to putt. If they hit a ball into the trees, it might explode one of the many butterfly bombs that had landed in the branches. So Habib just walked around the residence at Yarze once in a while. In Jerusalem, he would walk around Grove's large oval driveway a few times, then say, "This is boring!" and go inside.

An Inch a Day

He forced himself to rest to stay alive. But he made little or no attempt to moderate his voracious appetite, which was equally likely to kill him. His reaction to stress was to eat. Since his stress on this mission was immense and constant, so was his eating. The excellent chef at Yarze managed to keep the kitchen well stocked, and Habib indulged in his creations with reckless abandon.

He had come to love the traditional Lebanese food that he had rejected as a boy. The only thing he loved better than digging into Lebanese food was directing other people to dig into it. Even if you already knew the proper way to eat hummus and olive oil and pita bread, it was obvious that you were not supposed to start until he had explained what you were having, how it was prepared, and how you were supposed to eat it. Meanwhile, he would tell you more than you cared to know about the Lebanese and their lifestyle. "I took all of that as a relief valve for him," says a colleague. "This was a way he could relax and let go of his frustrations for a while."

He sometimes overdid it. "Every morning he'd try to push this stuff on me," says a Marine. The conversation typically began with Habib sliding bowls of yogurt and plates of cheese across the table toward him.

"Here, have some of this."

"No, I just want some cereal and fruit."

"Aaaa, I thought you were gutsy. You Marines ain't worth a damn!"

"I don't really like this stuff. And I don't want to get fat on it. I'll just have some coffee and bread."

"If you don't eat this, you're a pussy!"

Time after time, someone would set a plate of pistachios or cherries or cookies on the table for the whole group, and within a minute Habib would single-handedly reduce it to a plate of shells, pits, or crumbs. He would say, "Don't give me any dessert tonight," and then would devour the entire large dish of crème caramel without realizing it was the main dish for everyone. On one of his visits with King Hussein in Jordan, the servants brought out four desserts to choose from: Habib took each.

He would complain that he was getting fat from eating so much of such good, rich food. And he was. But he kept right on stuffing himself. "You could watch him add about an inch a day on his waistline," says Crocker. Occasionally—rarely—a colleague would worry enough about his health to speak up. One recalls him "working away at a bowl of cherries. He couldn't stop. He became very angry with me when I suggested that he'd had enough. He got very angry. Very, *very* angry."

Denying himself fine food would be like a musician denying himself sound. He did want to take care of himself to beat the family curse of early death from heart attacks. But he wanted even more to live life to the fullest—which entailed stuffing himself to the fullest—here and now.

Even during negotiating sessions, the food and drink would keep coming. Habib said, "If it's a big negotiation, you bring in the sandwiches and you keep right on going. There are cookies on the table, so you eat. You gain weight. I've sat six, seven hours straight without getting up from the chair. Maybe a cup of coffee, glass of tea, another cup of coffee, another glass of tea, a glass of lemonade, a glass of orange juice, another cup of coffee, another glass of tea. Sometimes it becomes a game to see who's going to go to the john first!"

A Day in the Life

Yarze is where Habib spent most of his time during the siege. There he was rarely up early unless all hell was breaking loose. During breakfast he would read the newspapers and go over a summary translation of the Lebanese press. He would always dragoon any fluent Arabic speaker nearby to go over some points from the Lebanese press in more detail. While they ate, Habib and Draper would review the latest cables that had come in overnight and decide how to revise their gameplan according to the latest developments.

His days in Beirut were a blur of meetings in the residence, at a nearby embassy, in relatively tranquil East Beirut, or several times a day down the road at the presidential palace. Even the quick quarter-mile trip from Yarze to the palace could be harrowing. Shells would be flying over the car. Habib might arrive at the palace a few minutes after it had been hit, and would meet with President Sarkis in a room whose windows were all shattered.

By mid-afternoon Beirut time, Washington was beginning to wake up. That was prime time for Habib to call the State Department's Bureau of Near Eastern Affairs (NEA). The traditional model of a diplomat reporting in to Washington and awaiting instructions was not going to work in this crisis. The situation was changing too fast, and conventional communications methods were too slow. So the military rigged up one field radio at Yarze and one in a small bedroom beside the State Department's Operations Center and linked them via satellite. This "tactical satellite hookup," or tacsat, became Habib's main means of communication with Washington. It was the first time anyone involved had ever heard of communication via satellite.

Most of his calls went to Charlie Hill, acting deputy assistant secretary in NEA. Habib would rarely ask what Washington wanted him to do. He would usually report the latest events, tell Hill what he planned to do next and what he wanted Washington to do, and, as Hill puts it, generally "scream and yell and curse and swear." Hill would sometimes listen, sometimes shout back, and sometimes just ignore him. Many calls ended with one or both receivers slammed down. Hill was, says Sam Lewis, "sort of the psychiatrist for Phil."

The Marines set up the tacsat's transmission equipment out by the swimming pool at Yarze. The garage was converted into a communication center, where the tacsat itself, teletypes, and other gear were set up. Communications specialist Faith Lee had to get the tacsat connected each time. Because of her sweet, high-pitched voice, Habib and Draper nicknamed her Tinkerbell.

"Go get Tinkerbell in here so she can get us through to Washington," Habib would say. She would get everything set up for him, then leave. That was partly because he was going to be talking about secret matters, and partly because he didn't want to have to tone down his profanity with a lady around.

Privacy was not easy, though. One day the communication specialists were crammed into their room banging away on their teletypes when Habib came in to call Washington from the tiny adjacent tacsat room.

"Close the door!" he called out. "I can't hear."

They didn't hear him.

"Close the damn door!"

"Ambassador Habib," Tinkerbell squeaked, "there *is* no door."

Pause.

"Well, dammit, put in a door!"

Silent Movie

A day in the life of Philip Habib did not include interviews or press conferences or background briefings. The world press tried to track his every move. But unlike most other shuttle diplomats and special envoys, Habib did not talk to the press during the siege, period. The cameras showed him walking in and out of doors, getting in and out of cars, shaking hands, waving—but rarely talking into microphones. Early on he walked out in front of a mob of reporters in Jerusalem, looked straight at the TV cameras, and said, "Ladies and gentlemen, this is going to be a silent movie." He then laughed and walked away. The press soon learned to expect nothing more.

There were several reasons why he wouldn't talk to the press. One was that he felt that was a job for the secretary of state or the president. But his main reason was that he felt a diplomat cannot negotiate in the press. One leak or one ill-chosen word could undo a week of progress. He was trusted in no small measure because his counterparts knew he would keep his mouth shut in public about their private discussions.

By late afternoon on a typical day in Yarze, he might have a second round of meetings with his intermediaries to the PLO or talk to local Israeli commanders. He didn't hang around the residence's work areas if he wasn't engaged in the work of the moment. He would tend to use such times to go gorge on pistachio nuts in his favorite haunt, the library. Occasionally he might go sit by the pool by himself to read a book, or wander off to his room. He often took a nap after lunch. If he had a particularly important meeting in the afternoon or evening, he would take a nap ahead of time so he could be at his best. For especially important meetings, he would wear his lucky tie, a blue-and-gold University of California-Berkeley number spangled with little golden bears.

He had to leave the residence for many of his meetings, but going out for dinner was optional. Going out was such a complicated security operation that he tended to just stay at the residence for dinner. But often, if things were quiet, he and his colleagues might go out for dinner to an elegant Chinese restaurant in Junieh, a Maronite suburb north of Beirut. Or they might go down the hill to a favorite restaurant of his in Baabda. Sometimes a group of Israeli soldiers would come in there too. Though Habib never said anything about their presence, tension sizzled whenever they came in. When they became regulars in the neighborhood and the restaurant, he stopped going there.

Dining at a restaurant was itself a major production. As soon as they arrived and a table was selected, the head of security would say, "OK, if anything hits, the table's going on its side this way. Ambassador Habib, you go that way; Ambassador Draper, you go right here." A guard stood behind Habib's table scrutinizing the movements of everyone in the place. The driver of Habib's car stayed with it for the entire two hours or so the Habib party was inside the restaurant, walking around the car constantly to make sure no one came near it. When Habib would finish dinner, a security officer would kneel by each wheel of his car and look underneath for any tiny explosives that a passerby might have planted when the driver wasn't looking. Only then could Habib get in.

Oasis

Whenever Habib was in Jerusalem to meet with Israeli officials, his headquarters was the residence of the American consul general, Brandon Grove. This was a whole other world from Yarze.

It wasn't just that in Jerusalem Habib didn't have to sleep through artillery or dive into the laundry room. It was that this residence and the people in it warmed and soothed his soul unlike any other.

198

The residence was a grand, graceful Ottoman structure rich with the aromas of the long-gone old Middle East. At least a hundred years old, the building stood tall inside a wall with old shade trees everywhere and a lovely oval garden out front. Its large stone block walls, polished rose and yellow stone floors, winding stone staircases, and vaulted ceilings imparted a sense of grounding, solidity, permanence. The residence embodied the courtly sensibilities of the *pashas* who valued books and gardens and cuisine. It was an abiding, working relic of the high moments of Islamic civilization. For Phil Habib to walk into this building was to step back into the Middle East of fable that his parents had told him about as a boy.

This spot was his oasis. He occasionally came here just to escape the stress of Beirut.

The house was run by a majordomo, or head butler, named Muhammad Latif. Muhammad was a gracious old Palestinian gentleman who had served as cook and head butler in this house for decades. Though he scrupulously observed the social distinction between majordomo and ambassador, no one could miss the special affection between him and Habib. Muhammad would serve the drinks, and Habib would give him a wink. Habib would say something funny, and Muhammad would give him a wink. Habib relished using his minimal Arabic and joking with him during dinner. Though their relationship was always one of master and servant and their conversation more banter than substance, it was clearly affectionate.

If Habib saw this residence as a return to his roots, Muhammad saw Habib as the Arab *pasha* of his boyhood, the statesman who cared for his people. Grove says, "Muhammad would have walked off of a cliff for Phil."

The World of His Fathers

To Habib, a visit to the consul general's residence was like coming home to family. Whenever his motorcade would pull up out front, Muhammad would be standing at the door grinning from ear to ear. Habib would give him a big hug, and they would kiss on both cheeks in the traditional Arab way. Grove too would meet Habib at the front door and take him upstairs to the guest room on the second floor. As he unpacked his suitcase, Habib would pointedly brag to Grove about how he kept his suits from wrinkling by packing them in plastic dry cleaner's bags. He'd hang up his suits, strip down to his boxer shorts and T-shirt, and stretch out on the bed for a nap.

As soon as he woke from his nap, he would start taking over the place. He'd head downstairs to the kitchen and snoop around to see what Ata the cook was fixing for dinner. If he didn't like it, he'd try to convince him to change it. He'd then wander out to the garden to see if Sayed, the old gardener, was keeping it up to his standards.

During his two and a half years as special envoy to the Middle East, Habib worked with Sayed in redesigning the garden from an oval into a horseshoe-shaped showcase of roses. He never had become the forester he originally set out to be, but nor had he ever lost his fascination with managing plants and watching them grow. He "loved, loved, loved flowers," especially roses, says his daughter Susan. He gave Sayed precise instructions of what to order to fill his garden with the most beautiful colors. Grove says, "Under Phil's supervision we had a dark purple rosebush that used to take people's *breath* because nobody had ever seen anything like it."

Habib had ample experience giving gardening instructions, to his wife back home. The operative word there is *instructions*. He was not one to dig in the dirt himself. But Sayed was delighted at his interest. The two of them would spend as much as forty-five minutes at a time walking here and there around the garden, pointing at this and that, making plans, discussing seeds and cuttings.

Sayed probably never realized how deeply this gardening refreshed Habib's spirit. The Jerusalem garden was not a place for him to brood after a bad day, but a place to forget about RPGs and F-14s for a while by concentrating instead on rose cuttings. It was not a place to decompress in solitude, but a refreshingly different set of problems he and Sayed could get absorbed in solving together.

Habib's dealings with someone like Sayed were quite different from his dealings with his State Department colleagues. He tended to treat people inversely to their station in life. He would pick on his superiors and beat up on his colleagues. But "he spoke to cleaning ladies more kindly than he spoke to me," says his secretary, Lori Bider. "He thought that anyone who did anything well or who did it for a living—whether it was sweeping the gutter, planting a garden, or whatever—deserved exquisite courtesy. He might *ask* the gardener, 'Wouldn't it be better to do it this way?' but he might *tell* me, '*Do it* this way!'"

In the quiet of the consul general's residence, says Hill, "Habib turned Lebanese. When he was thrown into the Middle East, he saw Lebanese being suppressed by other Arabs and by the PLO, as well as being strafed by Israelis. He really identified with them, and he began to see himself as Lebanese. He began to see that his natural instincts really were rooted in his cultural background." In that old Ottoman building filled with the ambiance of ancient Arab culture and the aromas of Arabic food being cooked just for him, "Habib was welcomed as an Arab by an Arab, Muhammad. He just re-entered the world of his fathers."

Habib had always compartmentalized his life: never telling his family about his work, rarely talking to colleagues who knew him in one phase of his career about any other phase. Likewise, he indulged his sense of roots only within the walls of the consul general's residence. He carried his love of Arab food wherever he went, but otherwise, once he left those walls, his attention to his ancestry vanished like last night's sleep.

Playing to Win

Brandon Grove, the consul general, was divorced. Two of his four children lived with him year-round in Jerusalem; the other two visited in the summer of '82. Habib became close to all of them, but he was particularly fond of Grove's youngest son, Mark, who was eleven during the siege. Mark would come down for breakfast before heading off for school, and Habib would always greet him, "Good morning, Smartass." Mark loved it. Habib would then urge him to eat lots of *zata,* assuring him that it would make him really sharp in math.

Unlike the live-in pressure cooker of Yarze, the Jerusalem consul general's residence slept only Grove, his children, and Habib. The diplomatic staff and domestic staff in Jerusalem went home every night.

Even in the quiet of the consul general's residence, Habib's mind was busy chewing on problems eighteen hours a day. *How can I do this? How can I approach that? What do I say if they say this? What will they say if I say that?* He might slow down long enough to chat with someone or read a novel, but, Grove says, "you could tell that the responsibility he felt never really left his consciousness. He was conscientious in the extreme. He gave this effort everything he had."

There was the obvious work: the negotiations, the skull sessions, the briefing books, the reporting back to Washington. But even just chatting with Grove about the events of the day was a way of settling his thoughts about his work.

But when he decided he wanted to, Habib would let himself relax in this oasis unlike any other place on his Middle East circuit. He would occasionally stroll around the garden alone or sit on one of its benches, maybe read a book out there. But not for long. He never much liked being alone. "The worst thing you could do to Philip would be to put him in a room by himself," says his wife. "He'd be in there talking to the walls—yelling at the walls." Relaxing to him meant being with someone—talking, playing a game, eating. It meant *doing* something, rechanneling his energies into something absorbing. "But all the while," says Grove, "you could see that a lot was turning around in the back of his mind."

Grove prizes a snapshot of the Three Monkeys: Grove with his hands over his eyes, Draper with his hands over his mouth, Habib with his over his ears. Habib was always ready to play charades or bridge or Scrabble with Grove's kids and staff, and he played to win. "These games were *competitive,"* Grove recalls, "and the fact that they were competitive *really* appealed to Phil, because he was a terribly competitive person. He would throw his heart and soul into Scrabble or bridge. He'd get as excited about a game as he would about a negotiation. He'd be shouting and laughing. When he won, he'd be absolutely beaming. If he lost, he'd growl.

"It was a way of letting off steam. You would think that would tire the man out even more, but you could see it visibly relax him. He just took all this energy and, like switching the dial on a TV, he would channel it into bridge or into Scrabble or into laughing. He was out to win, but he relished the way you *get to* a win. Watching him finesse the relationship with his partners and his opponents, you could see he was a born negotiator."

For example, one night after dinner, Habib was playing Scrabble with Mark and Grove's secretary, Martha Hayward. Someone had placed letter tiles in the middle of the board to form the word "SURF." Someone else had spelled "GIRL" up above it, with two blank spaces between the two words. Someone added ER to make "SURFER," then someone added an S to make "SURFERS." Habib now found that he had an I and an E, so he gleefully plunked them down between the two existing words to form "GIRLIESURFERS."

"Ambassador Habib!" Mark protested, "That's not a word. You can't use that!"

Habib looked him straight in the eye and deadpanned, "Mark, I'm from California. And anyone who lives in California knows that GIRLIESURFERS is a word!" Case closed. Mark knew he was beat.

One day when the negotiations were going nowhere and Habib was uncharacteristically down, Grove prevailed upon him to go with him to the Jerusalem Museum's exhibit of Roman glass. They stayed for less than an hour, but for Habib it was like a cool drink on a hot day.

One or two rooms were devoted to ancient perfume bottles, vases, and vials, perfectly lighted to accentuate their magnificent colors and wonderful shapes. "I knew Phil liked Roman glass," Grove says, "but he completely lost himself in this exhibit. I could see he was absolutely absorbed in going from case to case and admiring what these people had done over two thousand years ago. Seeing that exhibit was a *major* relaxation for him. It was marvelous to see him relax and enjoy those colors and shapes. When you saw him unwind like that, you realized how much tension he was really under."

Guiltily Concealed

Habib prided himself in traveling light. Unlike many other high-profile diplomats, Habib had no retinue of aides, no entourage of reporters, no

press conferences, no photo ops. He traveled with one deputy, and sometimes with a secretary and maybe one other staffer. He preferred to rely on
the local US embassy or consulate staff of whatever country he was in. If
today he was in Israel, somebody from the Tel Aviv embassy or the Jerusalem consulate would coordinate his schedule, type his outgoing cables,
compile his incoming cables, take notes in his meetings and write them up,
and organize the morning intelligence summaries (which he would more
often than not describe as "junk"). If tomorrow he was in Syria, he would
use staff from the Damascus embassy. Besides enabling him to travel light
and turn on a dime, this practice rooted his negotiations in the local expertise.

When he was in Jerusalem, he and his team took over Grove's office
on the third floor. Only Habib, Ambassador Lewis, and the embassy staff
in Tel Aviv were accredited to deal with the Israeli government. But the
Israeli government offices were mostly in Jerusalem, so that's where Habib
usually stayed. The Tel Aviv embassy provided the substantive support for
his mission, and the Jerusalem consulate provided a physical place to work
and sleep. Habib confined his team to Grove's one office to minimize his
impact on the consulate's normal business. From there he would call Washington over a secure telephone. After calling Washington, he would often
call Marge in California. "That meant a great deal to him," Grove says.
"All of us would clear out and leave him alone in my office, where he
could have a little family time."

In Israel, Ambassador Lewis and Consul General Grove assigned him
some of their most junior staff "so they would learn both how the Foreign
Service works and how a really first-class diplomat functions." He crystallized his thinking by talking things through at enormous length with them.
There was no doubt who was in charge, but he was quite open to their ideas
and reactions and suggestions. At strategy sessions, he listened to what
anyone—the ambassador, Draper, the lowliest newcomer—had to say.

But there was a catch: If you had a view, you had to be willing to say it
at least twice, because his first reaction would usually be to just blow it off
to see whether or not you really believed it. He'd say, "That's a lot of
bullshit," or more charitably, "That's a joke. Let's get serious." If he got
really worked up, he might shout, "We tried that before, and it didn't work!
Those bastards won't pay any attention. I'm sick and tired of hearing that
kind of shit!" But the people around the table realized that he was storming
for effect and that he wanted them to stand up to him. If they did, he respected them. They knew that, if they made a good case and if he liked the
idea, he would accept it. It didn't matter whose idea it was: If he thought it
was sound, he took it seriously.

But he took no votes: In the end, Habib made the decisions and then moved on to something else.

He rode his team hard. He scrutinized the cables they wrote, reporting to State on the day's events. He would frequently send a cable back to some poor soul at ten o'clock at night to rewrite it to reflect his view of what had happened in a meeting. He let them know what he wanted and how they could best help him. He did not insist on stellar performance so much as he assumed it. If the staff did well, they heard no compliments; as far as Habib was concerned, that was just doing their job. If, however, their work came up short, he would say, "This isn't worth the paper it's written on!"

If any of them resented his treatment, they kept it to themselves. In fact, Grove says, "everybody loved working for him. They were absolutely devoted to him. Every last one of them wanted to be the best possible professional," and they recognized that he was just enforcing high standards. The result was that the most junior officers who were putting together his briefing books and organizing the cable traffic felt that they too had a stake in his mission.

He could chew out a junior officer in the morning for a sub-par briefing or poorly organized cable, and then josh with him affectionately at dinner. He wasn't making up or manipulating. Grove, who describes him as a man of "almost guiltily concealed gentleness," saw this dichotomy day after day. "He wanted to conceal his tenderness toward people. When he was kind to people or thanking them, he would do so quite shyly. He was almost a little embarrassed when he was caught being a really nice guy, which is what he was. Because that doesn't fit very well into his image of pounding the table and barking 'Where the hell is this? Who are these dumb bastards? Can't you get your staff work right?' But underneath it there was a very caring man who somehow was just reluctant to show it."

13

The Marines

He needed us to do the damn thing right and not add to his
shots. We were around Habib enough to sense that, one, the
man knew what he was doing; and two, what he was trying
to do was extremely difficult. As long as it didn't jeopardize
our force, we were going to hang tough with him.
Colonel James Mead

Despite having spent much of July grousing that his negotiations were dead
in the water, in late July Phil Habib began the process of handing off his
plan to the people who would execute it. He did so partly because of his
inexplicable optimism and partly to drum up some momentum. The most
important of those people were the handful of American Marines chosen to
coordinate with him. On July 26 he helicoptered out to the carrier *USS
Guam* in the Mediterranean to discuss his concept of the military role with
some of them and with Colonel James Mead, who would command the
Marines ashore.

They did not like what they heard.

Habib started by laying out a map of Beirut and explaining the situation on the ground. He pointed out Muslim West Beirut, Christian East
Beirut, and the no-man's land called the Green Line that separated them.
He summarized the civil war that the Israeli invasion had only interrupted
and the reasons the Syrian army had been invited into Lebanon as peacekeepers and turned into hated occupiers. He showed how Sharon had the
PLO and several thousand Syrian troops trapped in West Beirut, surrounded
by Israeli troops, by his Maronite Christian allies, and by the sea. He explained why the Palestinians were nearly as afraid of the Christians as they
were of Sharon's forces, fearing that either enemy could move in for the
kill at any time.

His goal, he explained to the Marines, was to evacuate the PLO and
Syrians from West Beirut before the Israelis or the Christians went into its
streets and tenements to root them out. His fear was not simply that they
would kill PLO or Syrian fighters. His fear was that, as those guerrillas and
soldiers fought back, house-to-house combat would also indiscriminately

205

kill countless women and children, bystanders, Israelis, Christians—anybody within reach. "Unless we can defuse this crisis," he told the Marines, "there's going to be a bloodbath of enormous proportions."

The centerpiece of his concept was that the Marines would insert themselves as a buffer to separate the IDF and Christians in East Beirut from the PLO and Syrians in West Beirut. Without such a buffer, an evacuation was unthinkable. The Marines, he said, would be like the meat in a sandwich, separating the two slices of bread. He wanted to bring them into the port of Beirut, then have them extend about 3 kilometers along the Green Line.

The Marines gave Habib a soaking splash of cold water. Mead said, "Of course we can deploy along the Green Line. But what do you want us to do once we're there?"

"First, I want you to disarm all the Muslims."

"Then what?"

"Then I want you to corral all the arms together and burn the weapons."

"Uh-huh. And then?"

"Then you disarm the Christians."

The Marines had been listening poker faced. They realized that Habib was speaking conceptually, that he had not yet worked out the details. Still, one of them says, "my jaw was down around my ankles" at the audacity—or naïveté—of Habib's scenario. At this point Mead drew his Boston accent to full strength and said, "Let me see if I understand this properly, Ambassador. You want to put 1,000 United States Marines between some 15,000 Israelis, some 4,000 to 5,000 Christian forces, and some 20,000 to 25,000 Palestinians and Syrians and other forces. Is that what you want me to do?"

"Yeah."

"And then you want me to disarm them?"

"Yeah."

"I'm going to tell you right now, Ambassador, we're not going to do that. That is not possible to be done."

Habib looked at Mead as though the Marine had just spat in the punchbowl. For a long moment, the two men just stared at each other. Finally Habib asked, "And why *aren't* you going to do it? What do you think *is* possible?"

Sobering Realization

That moment set the tone for their whole relationship from then on. Habib's willingness to listen won the Marines over. In the weeks ahead Habib never shrank from telling them precisely what he wanted—loudly and bluntly—

but he always listened to their comeback. They respected that. They considered his attitude reasonable and conducive to coming up with workable solutions. The 6-foot 6-inch Mead, who describes himself as a street kid from Boston, felt right at home with the 5-foot 10-inch diplomat from Brooklyn. "Guys from Brooklyn don't hem and haw," he says. "They let you know what the hell they're thinking. A lot of times you're not going to like it, but you're going to get it straight in the chops the first time. That's the way he was."

Beyond the specifics, Habib was asking the military to take on a mission unlike anything for which they had been trained. Soldiers are trained to kill and destroy. In a peacekeeping mission, by contrast, they're trying to keep other people from killing and destroying. Warriors force their way into a situation; peacekeepers must be welcomed in, small in number and lightly armed lest they come across as conquerors and occupiers. So they are always outnumbered and outgunned by the belligerents. They thus have to keep the peace through tact, diplomacy, and voluntary cooperation.

As the Marines explained to Habib the logistical impossibilities of what he had in mind, he quickly saw that, unless he wanted to send in a massive force—and he did not—the vastly outnumbered MNF was not going to be in much position to compel anybody to do anything. If the PLO, the Syrians, the Israelis, and the Lebanese Christians were going to follow his program, it would have to be by their voluntary consent. This was a sobering realization. He had so far seen few glimmers of cooperation from anybody.

Four days later, on July 30, the PLO again offered to leave Beirut, an offer Habib considered firm and sincere. He decided the time was right for his Marine liaison team to come ashore to start nailing down the particulars of the MNF's job. The Marines chosen to coordinate with him were Colonel James Sehulster, who would be the highest ranking officer; Lieutenant Colonel Edmond Gaucher Jr., Lieutenant Colonel Robert B. Johnston, and Lieutenant Colonel Charles R. Smith Jr. But Sharon's massive assaults in the next few days made it impossible for them to come into Beirut. By August 5 Sharon had backed off, and Habib told them to come now. For Habib, this was the beginning of the endgame, like the start of rehearsals for a playwright. His negotiations with the Israelis and the PLO were continuing, and he felt that, once his liaison team came in, he could complete arrangements for the MNF's deployment and get the evacuation going in a matter of days.

The Marine liaisons finally met with Habib at Yarze for the first time at 9 A.M. August 7. He went over the general outline of his plan but emphasized that "this is not going to be a textbook exercise. Flexibility is going to be the key. We've gotta be realistic and recognize that we could be thwarted in what we're trying to do here." He briefed them on an ongoing obstacle: Sharon's demand that no MNF troops set foot on Lebanese soil until after the last PLO fighter had left. Habib thought that notion was ridiculous, since it would be pretty much the same as not having any force at all. He was certain that no PLO guerrillas would come out of hiding except under MNF protection, and he told the Marines that he had flatly rejected Sharon's demand.

The Marines raised the matter of command. Like the Israelis and the French and everyone else, the Marines thought the MNF should operate under a single commander. Habib disagreed. His plan was that the American, French, and Italian forces would each operate autonomously. They would have unity of effort without unity of command. That way, if any one country backed out at the last minute, as he feared Weinberger might, the evacuation could proceed with the other two countries' forces. The Marines tacitly understood that the closest thing to an overall commander would be Philip Habib.

They had several other issues to cover at this first meeting at Yarze. The French had insisted on coming in first, and Weinberger had insisted that no Americans come in until the operation was well under way. So Habib leapt to the front of the parade, telling the Marines, "Let the French do the dirty work, then we'll take positions when they're cleared by the French." He also said he was "worried about the dollies," that is, that once the Marines came ashore they would be distracted chasing the beautiful Lebanese women. The Marine officers smiled indulgently and assured him that discipline would not be a problem.

There were still hundreds of issues and details to go: How would the three countries' forces coordinate operations? Where would each be stationed? What would they be required, allowed, and forbidden to do? How should they coordinate with the Israelis? How could they respond if they got shot at? But those were questions for another day.

After this first meeting ashore, Johnston reported, "All going well. Amb Habib in good spirits. No question who is in charge." But Habib was not just in good spirits; he was buoyant. "I'm ready to close out," he told Washington in his own report. "We'll get going by the twelfth. That's only five days away."

The First Incident

The IDF chose this point to launch three extraordinary attacks on Habib's mission that physically threatened his team.

Habib had always been protective of the people working for him, his "boys." He wouldn't think twice about working them to an early grave or scorching their ears anytime their work dipped below his standards. But he wouldn't stand for anybody else giving them trouble. These Marines were not his boys, and they didn't especially require his protection, but they had become an essential part of his team. They now represented his mission.

When they finished their first meeting ashore with him late in the day August 7, they boarded two Huey helicopters at the little Lebanese naval base nearby at Junieh to fly back to their ship. They had barely taken off when two Israeli F-16 jets swooped down on them. One roared from left to right just over them, shaking the Hueys violently. Before the Marines could cuss, the other jet zipped just under them, shot up right in front of them, and kicked in its afterburner. One jet wheeled sideways between the two Hueys, which were only a hundred feet apart. The jets, flying at about 600 miles per hour, came close enough that the Marines could clearly see the Israeli pilots' faces.

"We'd been in helicopters before, and we knew what peril we were really in," says Sehulster. "It scared the hell out of the pilots," says Gaucher. Reports of the incident said the jets "buzzed" the helicopters, but "buzz" hardly describes it. A helicopter is not a very stable kind of aircraft to begin with. Its ability to stay aloft depends heavily on the condition of the air around it. What the Israeli jets were doing was creating wickedly curly air turbulence all around the Hueys and shock waves for them to fly into. Bouncing and reeling, the two Hueys were close enough together to collide.

"They damn near knocked the helicopters down!" says Sehulster. "It wasn't just a matter of being in the same airspace: They were within 20 or 30 feet of us, which is awfully goddam close. It was a deliberately provocative act. Absolutely. Fully intended." The jets did not wag their wings to indicate friendliness. Johnston and one of the Marine pilots thought this was just a case of a couple of pilots hot-dogging, but others on board decidedly did not. Sehulster points out that Israeli pilots are all officers, and no pair of officers would do such a rash act without orders. The Marines considered it "direct hostility toward us" and "blatant harassment."

The Marine Huey pilots dropped from 500 feet down to 100 feet to prevent the jets from flying under them. But then the jets circled back and roared all around them again. Then again and again, for the next fifteen or twenty minutes. The Huey pilots gritted their teeth and grimly tried to ride out the buffeting, boring forward rather than making any evasive maneuvers that might encourage or antagonize the Israeli pilots.

Habib's liaisons did get back to their ship, shaken but undamaged. A Navy captain who had been along for an inspection ride charged up to the admiral's office and angrily reported the incident. The admiral sent a strong message back to the Joint Chiefs of Staff saying that he intended to send an armed fighter escort with Habib's liaisons the next day and, should any

Israeli jets try such harassment again, "it was his intention to issue the orders to shoot them down." But the brass worried that any such retaliation might disturb Habib's delicate negotiations. They vetoed an armed escort but said, "Should a hostile act be committed use such force as is appropriate to respond."

Weinberger and Shultz furiously protested the incident, and Begin personally apologized for it.

The Second Incident

The IDF's second physical attack on Habib's mission came the next day, August 8, when his team of Marine liaisons flew back to shore for their second meeting with him. As their Hueys approached Junieh at 8 A.M., an Israeli patrol boat tracked them, with a manned and loaded machine gun trained on them. The Hueys landed at Junieh in a small bowl surrounded by a berm. As soon as the pilots put the rotors in neutral so the Marines could get out, five or ten IDF tanks rolled up over the berm, surrounding them, and aimed their cannons at them. Ground troops came up to the top of the berm, pointing their automatic weapons at the Americans. Israeli jeeps blocked off all the ground exits and aimed their 50-caliber guns at the US embassy vehicles that had come to pick the Marines up.

"We were captured," says Gaucher. The top Israeli officer on the scene, Colonel Yahya, gave them what Sehulster calls "a rash of trash" about who they were and what they were doing there. Though the Marines were in civilian clothes, Sehulster had no doubt that Yahya knew perfectly well who they were and why they were there. After all, Israeli jets had been flying within a few miles of their base ship and monitored all flights on and off of it. The Marines had just come from an American aircraft carrier in American-marked military helicopters and landed at an American-controlled landing spot with American embassy cars there to pick them up. "Who else would be coming in and out like that?" Sehulster says. Even if Yahya didn't know the identity of the individuals, he certainly knew what they represented, that is, Habib's liaison team. Sehulster was "madder than anything else at the arrogance of the SOBs." He thus refused to answer Yahya's questions, saying only "We are on our way to the American embassy, and you have no authority in Junieh."

When after twenty minutes it became obvious that the Israelis were not going to let them go, the embassy's defense attaché who had come to pick them up called Yarze for instructions. Dillon told them to give only their names, ranks, and Social Security numbers. "Being the obstinate son of a bitch that I am," Sehulster says, "I took the smallest piece of paper that would accommodate very, very small printing. I put the five names and

Social Security numbers on it, handed it to Yahya, and said, 'There. That's who the hell we are.'" He added only that they were there to provide support for Ambassador Habib. After another forty-five minutes or so, Yahya decided to have his troops escort the Marines to Yarze. Along the way, the Marines veered off onto a side street, sped away, and lost them.

When they got to Yarze and told Habib about the two incidents, he "just went goddam ballistic at the audacity of the Israelis harassing us," says Sehulster. "He just absolutely came unglued: 'Who the fuck do they think they are? Where do they get the goddam nerve to harass people?'" He picked up the phone and blasted the general in charge of Israeli forces in Lebanon. To Habib, the issue was not so much that the Israelis had seriously endangered American lives, though they had; it was that harassment of his team was an attack on his mission.

He had no doubt that the incidents were deliberate and sanctioned. This was a "clearly orchestrated power play," says Johnston. The IDF "didn't do *anything* without orders from above," says Sehulster. Habib considered the incidents IDF attempts to show that they were in control, that "we were playing in their sandbox, and they wanted us to damn sure know that."

Rather than give the Israelis more opportunities to harass his team, Habib decided to have his Marine liaisons stay ashore from then on.

Having dealt with the problem, he started the meeting they had come for as though nothing had happened.

The Third Incident

Two days later, August 10, it was Habib's turn to fly. He and Draper needed to go to Israel to resolve the last outstanding issues with Begin. Around 4:30 they arrived at Junieh to board their US Navy helicopter and were angered to find Israeli troops there. Habib's helicopter was hovering 300 feet above its landing pad with "Israeli machine guns, 20-millimeter cannon, and other things trained on it, ready to shoot it down," says Draper. "They were preventing it from landing so that it could pick us up."

Habib was hopping mad—the most fervently furious Draper ever saw him. Red-faced and quivering with rage, he seemed ready to wade in and start busting heads. It wasn't just that he was insulted at yet another incident of harassment. It wasn't even that one of America's closest allies was poised to shoot down an American helicopter and kill American pilots. It was that, in Draper's words, "the Israelis were trying to interfere with the mission." And that, to Phil Habib, was unconscionable.

He was so hot that he wouldn't trust himself to talk. "He would have blown up," says Draper. So he spun away, seething in silence, and let Draper do the talking.

For twenty minutes Draper and the Israelis argued. "It was a touch-and-go problem," Draper says, "because these guys were trigger happy half the time." Finally, the Israeli commander radioed back to headquarters, got the OK to back off, and let Habib's helicopter land.

Only once he and Draper were safely on board did Habib allow himself to erupt. "Phil was just beyond himself," Draper says. "He exploded in the biggest temper tantrum I ever saw him in. He kept cursing about this and what the Israelis were doing and the harassing and so forth. He was getting pretty sick of it. Phil and I had both been in the military, and we talked about whether it was just a standard military fuck-up or deliberate." Draper strongly suspects that it was deliberate and was "ordered by Sharon to show how much control they had."

Within an hour they landed in Israel. Habib had a productive meeting with Begin, dealt with the issues at hand, and never mentioned the incident.

It wasn't that he forgot. It wasn't that he forgave. It was that he would not allow anything—not his anger, not his righteous indignation, not any Israeli provocations—to distract him from stopping this war.

Sitting Ducks

Habib's plan was not really as fully developed as he let on. It was extensively developed in his own mind, but the Marines still had serious disagreements with him about key elements. Habib envisioned the PLO, in effect, surrendering to the Marines. The Marines saw no possibility of that happening. Habib wanted the Marines to then shelter and feed the disarmed PLO until they could be evacuated. The Marines said they simply lacked the resources to, in effect, run refugee camps. Habib wanted the Marines to clear the innumerable land mines and booby traps that littered the city. The Marines said absolutely not. That is extremely dangerous work, and they refused to have anything to do with it. Yes, they would provide ordnance experts to teach the Lebanese Armed Forces (LAF) to do it, but, no, they would not do it themselves.

Habib did not give up lightly. Despite the Marines' refusal, he clung to his insistence that a buffer along the Green Line was critical to success. The reason Habib wanted the Marines there was precisely the reason they refused to go there: They would be standing between the belligerents. He considered that they would be an essential trip wire, preventing anyone on either side from passing through their lines; they considered that they would be sitting ducks vulnerable to hair triggers on their left and right and to mines below their feet. He was adamant that he wanted them there, and the Marines were equally adamant that they were not going to go there. They countered that, if anybody was going to deploy along the Green Line as a buffer, it should be the LAF. But Habib wanted Americans in there: Positioning Americans in that strategic piece of territory, he felt, would send a clear signal that the United States meant business.

He talked about having them patrol around the Green Line too, but the Marines considered that idea so unworkable that they wouldn't even discuss it with him. "It was a real bone of contention," Sehulster says. "This was probably *the* most testing time of the whole relationship. This is one of the times he got mad and called me a pussy."

After two days of Habib and the Marines going around and around about whether they would deploy along the Green Line, the commander responsible for American operations in the Middle East finally weighed in with a definitive veto. Habib then let it drop. He would try to get someone else to do that.

As Habib had continually reworked his plan based on the input of the Lebanese, Israelis, and PLO, he now set about reworking it based on the input of the Marines. He kept the essentials, but revised the specifics. Maybe instead of actively disarming the PLO, he could just have them passively leave their arms behind. Maybe he could get the French, Italians, or Lebanese to do the jobs that the Marines rejected. And maybe some of the jobs, like holding the PLO in some staging area before they left town, didn't really have to be done at all.

Once they got past their rocky start, Habib and the Marines worked superbly together. The Marines actually came to appreciate his grasp over when and how to use the military. On a personal level, he made them feel that they were not just doing a job, but were saving lives. They gave him their enthusiastic support because he let each one know that what they were doing was important and that he appreciated it.

These Marines, not known for sentimentality, fairly gush about Phil Habib. They describe him with words like *charisma, personal magnetism, forceful, immensely talented,* and *steel-trap mind.* "We loved him," says Sehulster. "He just tickled the shit out of us," says Mead. "A brilliant man. He's one of my all-time heroes."

Habib kept them apprised of where his negotiations stood and never failed to keep them apprised of how furious he was at the Israelis, the PLO, the Syrians, the State Department, and the Defense Department for their latest sins. The result, intended or not, was that the Marines on the ground "knew just how incredibly difficult this whole thing was," Mead says. "We also knew that he didn't need any problems out of us."

That understanding did not extend back to the Pentagon, however. Habib would roar about the Pentagon's insistence on deciding unilaterally what the military should do instead of going along with what *he* thought they ought to do. When he didn't get his way, the Marines on the ground with him were displeased too.

Habib demanded quick decisions and commitments from his military liaisons. "It was a freewheeling, fast-moving situation," says Mead, "and he needed to operate like a gunfighter. But the other agencies involved just couldn't suit up as fast as he wanted them to. There were too many people involved in trying to cut the same piece of pie. The military superimposed a World War Two chain of command on an operation that needed a lot more direct communication between those doing it and the final decision-makers. We had to go back through six layers of chain of command to get a decision. It was ludicrous."

The one saving grace was that this evacuation operation was unprecedented. It was Philip Habib's unique solution to a unique problem. "So nobody knew the book on it," Mead says. "I wanted to work directly for Ambassador Habib, but the chain of command would not allow that. But they did give me very wide latitude, because *they* didn't know what the hell to do." The brass imposed general restrictions on where the Marines could and could not go, but left it to Mead to decide specifically where and how they would deploy within approved areas. That gave him a lot of wiggle room. Whenever Mead could give Habib what he wanted, he did so without hesitation.

The Holy Ghost

Though Habib viewed his American Marine liaisons as the most important part of the team that would implement his plan, they were only one part. He met daily at Yarze with his team of diplomatic and military representatives of the United States, France, Italy, and Lebanon. Each of the men at the table—and they were all men—was a strong personality in his own right, but Habib didn't chair the meetings; he ran them. As Smith put it, Habib functioned as "the officer in tactical command. There was absolutely no doubt who the leader of that pack was. Habib was a commander, running that operation on pure force of his personality. He was like a thousand-watt light bulb, burning bright the whole time. I never saw anyone argue with him!"

This was not a time for brainstorming or thrashing out basic issues. These were not really even planning meetings. Habib had learned quickly from his early arguments with the Marines and moved on. He knew what he wanted done, everyone at the table accepted his authority, and the meetings consisted mostly of him issuing directions. He would hold forth for hours, rarely asking anyone's counsel. When problems arose, he would turn to the person he thought should handle it, snap out a quick command,

and say, "Can you do that?" The answer he wanted to hear—and usually did hear—was "Yes." He would accept their answers as gospel. In requesting these liaisons originally, he had specified that he wanted only a few "responsible guys who can give an order and have it carried out, who know what the hell they are doing." Now that they were here, he expected everyone at the table to have ready answers and to speak with full authority to commit the party they represented. They understood that he wanted things instantly in order to exploit fleeting windows of opportunity.

Woe unto anyone who couldn't give him a definitive answer on the spot. He might know perfectly well that the Marine at the table was simply not authorized to make certain decisions or commitments that he wanted. Didn't matter. He'd still thunder, "Well, goddam it, why can't you tell me the answer? You're a goddam Marine and you can't answer my question?!" He had assigned the LAF to come up with a plan for their role and would ask the Marines for an update on the LAF's plans, only to hear that the Lebanese generals were still dithering. "What the hell are these goddam generals doing?" he would say. "Doesn't anybody make a decision up there?"

The people at the table didn't take his tirades personally or begrudge him his impatience. As Smith says, "I think he was driven to impatience by sensing that this thing could explode any minute."

In the meetings, Habib's approach was that they needed to get certain things accomplished, and everybody was going to stay until they did. His big meetings typically started around 4 or 5 each afternoon and ran till around 8 P.M., when the group would break and go somewhere for dinner. They would then often resume around 11 P.M. or midnight and run till the wee hours of the morning. The meeting wouldn't end until Habib was satisfied that things were lined up pretty well for the next twenty-four or forty-eight hours. Sometimes they went all night long.

The fifteen or twenty participants would sit around the great mahogany table in Dillon's dining room surrounded by beautiful Persian carpets on the floor. Habib would sit at the middle of the table and let everybody else sort themselves out however they liked. The French and Italian ambassadors usually staked out spots close to Habib.

One day, after his plan had crossed a major hurdle, Habib anxiously gathered the team to go over the latest version. This time he moved the group out of the dining room into the living room. He sat in an easy chair; everyone else pulled up chairs into a circle. As he got more and more intense ticking off the particulars of where each contingent of MNF troops would go, he said, "Get a map! Put a map down here so we can all see it!"

Sehulster fetched an enormous map, about 4 by 6 feet in size, and spread it out on the living room rug. As Habib named off the various positions for each military unit, Sehulster pointed out each one on the map. One by one, the ambassadors and military officers got down on their hands and knees to study the map as Habib talked and Sehulster pointed. Within a minute, everybody was down on the floor—except Habib, who "sat presiding in that great big chair waxing eloquent!" says Sehulster. "He was in his true element. Absolutely glowing: the master and his students. Unbelievable!"

The people in his coordinating committee meetings at any given time represented at least four languages. There was no translator. Habib spoke French well, and he certainly remembered all the Arabic profanity his brother Fred had taught him as boys in Brooklyn. Beyond that, there is an intriguing difference of opinion.

One of his Lebanese friends says Habib "didn't know three words of Arabic," and Draper and Howell agree. Yet the Marines at the table, none of whom spoke Arabic themselves, were convinced that he spoke Arabic fluently. In fact, they called him the Holy Ghost because he could switch back and forth between so many languages in the blink of an eye. They recall him routinely turning to the French ambassador and speaking French, turning to a Lebanese and speaking Arabic, then giving the Marines a summary in English of what had just been discussed. Some Marines even remember him speaking Italian.

Perhaps the most accurate report is that of the embassy's political officer, who says Habib spoke Arabic like an undereducated Lebanese, which "absolutely enchanted" whoever he was talking to.

Whatever his actual facility with languages, the Marines considered his use of language a deliberate tool of his diplomatic trade. "It had a very positive impact," says Sehulster. "You could just sense that the others in attendance truly appreciated and recognized his leadership by his deferring to their language at critical points to be sure they understood."

There is no disagreement that he was exceptionally fluent in what Mead calls Marine language: "He swore beautifully in five languages, and I swear it was simultaneous! You could always tell by his eyes whether it was profanity or not."

Eventually, the meetings lapsed into French, since that was the one language that just about everybody at the table could at least follow.

Mixed Blessing

After the American Marines, the second most important element of the MNF, in Habib's mind, was the French. But the French turned out to be a mixed blessing for him. On the one hand, they were indispensable. The MNF was simply not going to fly without them. And, whereas Habib had spent weeks dealing with some of the most infuriatingly intransigent people on earth, the French were refreshingly willing to do whatever was asked of them. Habib needed somebody to deploy along the Green Line. The French volunteered. Habib needed somebody to secure the port prior to the evacuation. The French volunteered. Habib needed somebody to clear out minefields. The French volunteered.

That's the other hand: They were *too* willing. "All they wanted to do was everything," says Sehulster. "It was so evident that the French wanted to lead this whole thing. We had to rein them in. I mean, they would have done it *all* on their own had they been given license to." Still, Habib seems to have used even this problem to his advantage. Weinberger was loathe to commit American troops to this risky mission, and Habib apparently played the French enthusiasm as a trump card with Washington, pressuring them to get with the program by saying, "We can't let the French do it by themselves."

Why were the French so anxious to play a major role? Part of their agenda was to be seen as protectors of the PLO. Another part was that, as Sehulster put it, "They were just green with envy at the prospect of getting their foot back in the door and re-establishing their predominant influence in Lebanon." They would then be in a good position to sell weapons in Lebanon and the rest of the region.

Habib didn't greatly care about France's long-range agenda, but he was determined to keep the MNF strictly neutral and to keep any one country from getting out too far ahead of the others. He recognized that, if the French handled everything, his whole plan would collapse. Officials in Washington and Rome were jittery enough about being part of this unprecedented mission: They might welcome such an excuse to back out altogether. Moreover, the Israelis frowned on the pro-PLO French being involved at all: Sharon might welcome an excuse to reject the French, leaving Habib with no troops to do anything and thereby scuttling his plan altogether.

The French official with whom Habib was working most closely was the ambassador to Lebanon, Paul Marc Henry. Habib had a love for all things French, and he clearly liked Henry. He appreciated his shared commitment to ending this siege. And the two just hit it off.

Habib never missed a chance to needle him. While virtually all the wives and other dependents of the diplomats in Beirut had gone home when the invasion began, Henry had kept his mistress with him. She was strikingly beautiful, witty, and charming. Everyone enjoyed being around her. At the team's many dinners together, Habib would pretend to flirt with her, just to rib Henry. At the group's meetings, Henry usually showed up late. "How many girls this time, Paul?" Habib would say. "Which woman is keeping you late this time?"

Late or early, Henry tended to chime in with "weird, bold, off-the-wall, cavalier recommendations" for where the troops should go and what they should do. He would blindside Habib with these ideas that were militarily unthinkable and totally at odds with Habib's plan. Having already been set straight by the Marines about his own naïve ideas, Habib had no time for new ones: "Paul Henry, you're not going to do it, and that's all. I say *fini*. That's it." He would then try to calm everybody down by saying, "No, we're not going to race off like that."

The French members of the team caused him headaches on less substantive issues too. Soon after Habib's Marine liaisons began meeting with him at Yarze, the French joined in, and then came the Italians. When it was just the Americans and the French, the two groups of military officers had sometimes socialized together. One day, after the Italian officers had arrived, the French officers invited the Marines to a formal dinner party at Henry's residence. Sehulster asked his French counterpart who all was invited.

"Just you."

"You mean, just the Americans?"

"Yes."

"Well, I'm sorry, but if the Italians aren't invited too, we're going to have to regret."

The French colonel then "flipped a hissy," says Sehulster, and went to Henry to complain. Sehulster got to Habib first. Habib was upset at the French attempt to divide the MNF team by leaving out the Italians. Had this been just a casual get-together, that would be one thing. But a formal dinner party at the ambassador's residence was too blatant a snub. When Henry called Habib to complain about this affront, Habib lit into him. "There's no goddam place for this not acting as one! We're here to work together. I just won't put up with any of this."

The Sign of the Pill Box

Though the Marines slept elsewhere, they were virtually living with Habib and the embassy workers crammed into Dillon's residence in Yarze. They saw him in meetings, at breakfast, in the car, during bombardments, and during lulls. They saw his humor, his compassion, his anger, and his unique blend of impatience and perseverance.

They also saw how he dealt with the continuous, throbbing, grinding stress. They never saw him looking nervous or disheartened, but often saw him looking worried. They could clearly see when he was particularly stressed. His face, already jowelly from too many rich meals, would look drawn and haggard. His usual ready smile wouldn't come. His cheeks sagged. He would pace the living room. He would run Arab worry beads through his fingers. He'd sit at the dining room table with papers scattered all in front of him, holding his head. He'd tap a pencil on the table or waggle it between his fingers. "You could read all kinds of things behind his eyes," one colleague recalls. "You could just see the torment, that he was having difficulty reaching some person or having him see his way."

The Marines could almost quantify Habib's stress by how often they saw his little pill box. Every hour, his alarm watch went off, and he would pause from whatever else he was doing, pull the box from his pocket, and take a heart pill. But he'd pull out the box also whenever he got especially agitated or stressed. Before taking the pill, though, he would look at his watch, realize that it was nowhere near time, and stuff the box back in his pocket.

When the stress did become too much, he would simply break off his meeting, excuse himself, and go to his bedroom to gather his wits, sort things out, and settle down.

"We always worried about him," says Mead, "because, one, we knew that no one was going to pull off this mission except him, and, two, we knew the man's health history. We had so damn much respect for the guy, because we knew he was 'in combat' and he probably wasn't going to survive it."

14

The Endgame

Sharon is winning the race against a political settlement.
Sa'eb Salaam, August 4, 1982

For Phil Habib to end the siege of Beirut peacefully, three things had to happen: the PLO must agree to leave Beirut, Begin must agree to stop shooting so they could leave, and one or more Arab states must agree to receive them.

That third issue was the linchpin. Up until mid-July, Habib's goal had been to get a single Arab country to take the entire batch of evacuees. As it became obvious that none would, he concluded that the only hope was to divide them among various countries. Morris Draper had already been shuttling around to Arab capitals, and Washington now joined in an intensive effort to persuade various Arab states to take Palestinians.

But inertia prevailed. The Arabs just stared at their shoes.

Like a rock climber clinging to a ledge with no way up, no way down, and no help in sight, Habib was stuck. In the grimmest depths of the darkest days, he wrote from Beirut July 17, "I am not now in an active negotiating situation. I cannot negotiate a final political solution as long as we have no agreed place to put the PLO combatants. . . . In a sense, I too am a hostage in the present impasse. People here depend on me to buck up their spirits and to intercede with the Israelis over all sorts of daily problems. If I left Lebanon—even briefly—it conceivably could be misread as my giving up or, worse, giving the Israelis a green light to proceed against Beirut."

Get on My Horse

But Habib was never one to sit still. He also refused to settle for two options: prolonged impasse or a final assault. There had to be a way to break the impasse. So the next day, July 18, he decided that, despite the risk of misperceptions, the time had come for him "to get on my horse and go around and start selling these bastards to these other countries." He figured he could avoid the misperceptions if he explained clearly to the Israelis in advance the purpose of his trip, "then they'll know they're not to do anything while I'm gone." He arranged to leave July 22 for a swing around the various Arab capitals to twist some arms in person. He was wrong about

220

the Israelis exercising restraint while he was gone. Coincidentally or not, Sharon launched a massive new wave of attacks on July 22. Habib went ahead with the trip anyway.

His first stop was Syria. He really didn't know what to expect. And he had long since learned not to assume that any development—positive or negative—would last. His experience in the preceding four weeks with Syria as a potential destination was a case in point:

June 28   PLO refuses to go to Syria

July 1   Habib does not want them to go to Syria

July 3   Syria has become the prime candidate recipient; Draper prefers Syria

July 5   Syria apparently agrees to take the PLO

July 7   PLO wants to stay in Lebanon under Syrian protection

July 10   Syria clarifies it will only take the leaders and the offices, not any fighters

July 12   One report reiterates that Syria will not take fighters; another report says Syria will take fighters as well as leaders, but not their families

July 13   Habib says the Syrian option is lost

July 15   Syria offers to take leaders only; Habib says Syria is out as a recipient

July 20   Syria suggests it would take the 5,000-6,000 fighters from West Beirut

Another reason he didn't know what to expect was that this would be his first meeting with Assad since the June 11 rolling ceasefire fiasco. Assad had taken Habib's words back then as assurances of Israeli withdrawal from Lebanon; the Israelis had instead advanced on Assad's troops and walloped them. *What went wrong?* he now asked Habib. Why had Habib's "assurances" not been honored?

"It was beyond my powers, Mr. President," Habib said, embarrassed.

"Is the word of the United States not to be trusted?" Assad asked. "What then is the meaning of any international agreement?"

There was no point blaming the Israelis for their actions. There was no point explaining that they had deceived Habib as much as Assad. The best Habib could think of to say was, "Mr. President, we are living in very bad times."

Assad was in no hurry to help Habib. As far as he was concerned, the sooner this crisis was over, the sooner an Israeli puppet in the Lebanese presidency would pressure him to pull all of his troops out of Lebanon— the last thing Assad wanted. He reiterated his standing offer to take the

PLO leaders and offices, said he would take fighting units that had originated in Syria and the Palestine Liberation Army (PLA), and said he might let Damascus airport be used as a staging area for fighters on their way elsewhere. This wasn't much, but it was in the right direction.

Holding Out for a Plum

Habib's next stop was Saudi Arabia to visit King Fahd. He knew the Saudis would never take any evacuees themselves, so he didn't bother asking. But they were the most influential Arabs, and he urged the king to prevail upon his brethren to sign on. Though they didn't discuss *how* that might be done, they both understood that Saudi money was a powerful incentive for other Arab states to cooperate with them. While Robert Barrett, deputy chief of mission in Beirut, believes the Saudis paid other countries to take evacuees, Draper will say only that in the end the Saudis "put pressure on their friends. It was done through the back door."

Habib then went to Egypt, which had always been his prime prospect. He planned to ask Mubarak to accept 5,000 in hopes that Mubarak would accept 2,000. But he was too late. Since after all these weeks the IDF had not launched a street-to-street assault on West Beirut, Mubarak no longer feared that they were going to. So he considered it unnecessary for the PLO to leave in order to forestall an Israeli attack.

Absent a sense of urgency, Mubarak hoped to capitalize on the situation to win some political points for the PLO. The PLO desperately wanted to be viewed not as a scruffy band of terrorists, but as the legitimate representatives of the Palestinian people. US recognition of them as such—most immediately in the form of Philip Habib sitting down to talk with Yasir Arafat face to face—would be a great political plum. It would also put pressure on the Israelis to deal with them. So Mubarak told Habib that Egypt would accept PLO evacuees only if the PLO got some political bonus—such as US recognition—in return for leaving Beirut.

Habib was happy to sweeten the pot for Mubarak with some gesture for the long-term peace process. But US recognition was too much. He believed that US recognition at this point would only prompt Israel to "jump the traces and just rub out the PLO." He argued that getting out of Beirut intact and with honor *was* a bonus. Besides, he said, the PLO wanted out without any quid pro quo. But Mubarak didn't buy that, and he never did change his mind.

Worse, Habib now started hearing Mubarak's same argument from the other Arab states. He despaired of finding even a temporary home for the PLO. He was seething in frustration.

So he was extremely gratified and relieved to meet with his old friend

King Hussein of Jordan, whom he had first gotten to know in Walter Reed Hospital right after his first heart attack. On July 26 the king happened to be at a residence he owned in London. So Habib flew to London to meet with him.

No Arab leader could have a better reason than King Hussein for refusing to even consider taking in anyone from the PLO. It had been less than twelve years since he had driven them out of Jordan. And now Philip Habib had come to ask him to take some back. Habib gave him a detailed review of the negotiations up to this stage, emphasizing points that underlined the need for the Arab states to meet their responsibilities for the Palestinians. He laid out the facts and candidly described his dilemma. His argument was simple: "Somebody has to go first. The United States has a very close relationship with Jordan: If you don't start the ball rolling, it will be very hard to sell the exodus to the other countries." He concluded his pitch by saying, "Your decision will strongly influence the Egyptians and other Arab leaders. Can we count on you to help us at this critical juncture?"

King Hussein replied in his dignified way, "I will take anyone who is my responsibility. Jordan will not deny accepting the return of its nationals." He estimated that might mean as many as 3,000 PLO fighters he was accepting.

He had conditions, of course. The Palestinians would all have to come disarmed. No Arab state would even consider accepting heavily armed PLO fighters. And any guerrilla with outstanding charges for crimes committed in Jordan would have to face those charges. But the king also surprised Habib by saying he would consider sending Jordanian officials to Beirut to screen evacuees in advance and that he had already contacted Iraq and obtained their agreement to accept some PLO fighters.

Habib was elated. Finally, finally, progress. He was deeply impressed and gratified by what he called the king's "decisive and statesmanlike attitude." On his way to the door, he thanked his old friend and urged him to help get other Arab leaders to follow suit. The king's sobering parting words explained much: Sharon's grand strategy for the whole region was no secret, and "We know we are the next target in Jordan."

Breaking the Weary Cycle

Habib completed his tour confident that he now had destinations lined up. Not everyone shared his confidence. "These were all *impossible* conditions for the PLO to accept," says Hill. "We knew it at State even if Phil thought he had made progress." The Arabs had to show some willingness to take the PLO—but in the process they set conditions that either the PLO would never accept or that would mean taking them as virtual prisoners.

When Habib returned to Beirut and crowed to President Sarkis that King Hussein had agreed to take a share of PLO evacuees, Sarkis was no more impressed than State. Sarkis pointed out that Jordan had agreed to receive only guerrillas who had not been condemned by its courts. "Yet all the Palestinian guerrillas from Lebanon are sought by the justice of Amman."

Unfazed, Habib said, "I am not as naïve as you think. I received amnesty from King Hussein . . . for all the Palestinian guerrillas from Lebanon."

Sarkis smiled indulgently. "You are still naïve and do not know the Arab soul. It is not sufficient that Hussein grant amnesty to the Palestinians. *They have to believe in it!* They are not dupes and will not give themselves up. They have not forgotten Black September. It will take you at least two more years to understand Lebanon and to presume to make recommendations to me."

Whether Habib's progress was real or imagined, it at least gave him a badly needed sense of momentum. On July 30 he sent a message to Begin that "there is no question but that there is an unequivocal and firm decision on the part of the PLO to leave Beirut." He would start detailed negotiations within the next twenty-four to forty-eight hours about the how and when of their withdrawal. "Therefore, it is extremely important that every effort be made to maintain the cease-fire on all sides" and to immediately lift the blockade of West Beirut. "I am convinced that we are now on the road to a political settlement although there remain many loose ends to be tied up."

But around 4 P.M. the same day, fighting broke out yet again. The IDF said yet again that the PLO started it, Begin sent word to Habib yet again that "we will hit back hard," and Wazzan threatened yet again to cut off negotiations.

Thoroughly fed up with this weary old cycle, Habib thought the time had come to break it by resurrecting a previously rejected idea: proximity talks. He and Arafat would sit geographically near one another, and Wazzan would walk back and forth between them. All of the old objections still applied, but at this point, it seemed worth the gamble. Jonny Abdu had safe houses on the fringe of the city near a crossing that might suffice. Another possibility was the Alexandria Hotel. Though Habib viewed proximity talks as a way of speeding up negotiations, Begin—listening to Israeli intelligence that the PLO was stalling for time—viewed them as a plot by the PLO to string things out. But Habib said, "I can't be stalled. I know how to kick ass. I can move fast."

Bill Brown, the deputy chief of mission in the Tel Aviv embassy, reported that Begin would "hit the ceiling" if Habib moved toward proximity talks. "It would be the end of the Habib mission. The whole world will see it as a move toward US recognition of the PLO. My advice is *don't ask me* to convey the word to the Prime Minister. Nobody in Israel will see it other than as a political victory for the PLO." Lewis worried that proximity talks "could push the Israelis over the edge to chop off a piece of south Beirut."

Habib tried to remind Begin that proximity talks were an arrangement the Lebanese government had asked for. He tried to emphasize that he would hold proximity talks only if necessary, that is, only if Israeli attacks left him no other means of communicating quickly and efficiently with the PLO. Besides, he said, he would not be meeting with the PLO: "They'd be on the first floor and I'd be up above. I will never even see them. There'd be no handshakes." But Begin wouldn't hear of it. He told Habib that it was totally unacceptable for him to sit in the same building as any PLO official, even if on different floors, or even to sit in nearby buildings. He specified they could be no closer together than 300 yards.

The same day that Begin protested Habib's recommendation of proximity talks, August 1, Sharon intensified his assault. At least 50,000 Israeli shells landed on West Beirut in a fourteen-hour attack. Habib believed the timing of this attack was no coincidence, but that the Israelis were using the proximity talks issue as a pretext for an attack they had planned anyway. It prompted one of Habib's few threats to resign. "This is such goddam overkill," he told Washington with as much weariness as anger. "It's so unnecessary. If the Israelis say this attack was started by a PLO ceasefire violation, that's bullshit. And it's *not* related to the proximity talks idea. This attack was well planned. They are doing this at this hour so that no one in Washington will be able to make a tough decision. We shouldn't be associated with this. If we let this go on and don't stop it here, we should get the hell out. It's a goddam charade! I don't see the usefulness in my being here. I've become a symbol of American ineffectiveness. People are calling me a cover for this. The IDF would be delighted to get rid of me. I'm a thorn."

Begin made yet another offer of a ceasefire, subject to his standard condition that it be mutual and absolute. "Don't take that shit," Habib told Washington. "I will not be a party to another phony ceasefire. If they want a ceasefire, tell them to go ahead and announce a unilateral one themselves. They'll just start up again anyway. It's inevitable that the ceasefire will be broken in a massive way around the camps, because the Israelis and Palestinians are now eyeball to eyeball there. I can't negotiate under these circumstances. I don't know whether I can resume negotiations even if a ceasefire does take. It became possible to get the PLO out several days ago. Now I can't do it. I don't believe there is a peaceful settlement of this."

Out the Window

Though he was exaggerating somewhat for effect, the facts on the ground certainly justified pessimism. What Habib had always feared most was that Sharon would fulfill his oft-repeated threat to launch a ground assault in West Beirut to "clean out" the PLO bunker by bunker. On August 4, the first Israeli ground troops actually entered West Beirut proper. They were a hundred meters inside each crossing point. The French ambassador had seen them at the Normandy Hotel. Tanks equipped with bulldozer blades led the way for armored personnel carriers, clearing out six-foot-high dirt and steel barricades. Their route suggested the aim was to isolate the largest Palestinian camps. An Israeli official said, "For eight weeks we are waiting for Habib to fulfill his mission. It's costing Israel in public relations, it's costing us in blood—just for the sake of an American request. We gave the PLO a chance to leave, but if they don't take that chance, they must know we will have to do it by other means."

At the same time this was happening, Habib received the PLO's latest letter to him. "I'm ashamed to get this paper," he said. "The IDF is encircling West Beirut, and here the PLO has sent me a very constructive paper, their most forthcoming ever." Written before Sharon's ground assault began, it made several important concessions, but had now been overtaken by the IDF's entry into West Beirut. Arafat was now urging his followers to defend their turf to the death, "because martyrdom is the key to victory." No longer could Habib "pursue the plan we have presented honestly to the PLO. We can't just ask the Israelis to stop: We have to get them to pull back. We can't have a ceasefire from where they are now. Reasonable positions we took before are stupid now."

A cloudburst of Israeli shells and rockets rained down on West Beirut that morning, the worst bombardment Habib had seen in the eight weeks of war. "I called Sharon on the phone," he says. "He said it wasn't true. That damned man said to me on the phone that what I saw happening wasn't happening."

Habib then raged about the onslaught to Charlie Hill over the tacsat. Hill had Habib on the tacsat in one hand and the Tel Aviv embassy's Bill Brown on the telephone in the other hand. Brown also was working two telephones: one to Hill, and the other to Begin. So word went from Habib to Hill to Brown to Begin and back again. As Habib angrily described the shelling all around him, Begin calmly denied there was any shelling at all; Sharon had just told him so. Israel was observing the ceasefire, Begin said. Moreover, "there is no intent today to occupy West Beirut. If we had such an intent, I would write to Ronald Reagan." Washington, Begin said, was being fed hysterical, inflated reporting.

When Hill relayed Begin's denials to him, Habib said "Oh, yeah?" and stuck his receiver out the window. As the familiar poomf of outgoing Israeli artillery just east of his window kept up its steady racket, Habib yelled, "Listen carefully to the ceasefire! The noise outside is war, my friends! What the hell is the matter with you? Do I have to place the phone on the roof for you to believe me that all hell has broken loose here? Tell Begin someone there is lying to him." He then slammed down the receiver. In the thirty seconds before he did, Hill had counted the unmistakable sound of eight 105-mm howitzer shells.

When Begin asked Sharon for an explanation, Sharon acknowledged that the IDF was indeed shooting, but minimized it as merely returning fire and denied that his troops were advancing.

Hitler

This war had always been more personal than most. Yes, the Israeli government was out to destroy an organization called the PLO, and the American government intervened. And yes, Begin, Sharon, and Habib all represented governments. But Begin's idiosyncratic motivations, Sharon's idiosyncratic conduct of the war, and Habib's unique role in trying to rein them in were all distinctly personal. Replace any one of those three individuals with someone else, and the course of events would have gone quite differently.

There was another decidedly personal aspect: Ariel Sharon and Menachem Begin were out to kill Yasir Arafat. One historian calls it "the world's first manhunt by air." Begin likened Beirut with Arafat and the PLO to "'Berlin,' where among innocent civilians Hitler and his henchmen hide." The Israelis had agents in the city; any sighting of Arafat or report of his whereabouts was almost instantly followed by some sort of attack, usually artillery. Habib's top Marine adviser, Colonel Sehulster, says, "Their obsession with trying to get Arafat was demonical."

The eeriest instance came during a ceasefire on August 6. People walking by the public gardens in the Sanaye district of West Beirut looked up to see two Israeli jets swoop down and then heard a sound like the cracking of a whip. There was no other sound, no explosion, no fire, no dust. Just the sudden disappearance of an eight-story building. The Israelis called it a PLO security building; others called it an apartment building. Perhaps it was both. In any case, Arafat had left it just moments earlier, but 250 other people were still inside. An American-made vacuum bomb obliterated it by implosion. This was one of the first uses of a "smart" bomb, one able to find its way precisely to its programmed target. Whereas destruction of an apartment building could always be called regrettable collateral damage when a regular dumb bomb was dropped near a military target, the use of a smart bomb allowed for no such excuses. "If that was a smart bomb," Habib said, "we are in big trouble. We are partners to murder." He confronted Sharon about it.

"You used a laser-guided bomb and violated the ceasefire," Habib said.

"It was a special target."

"Arik, you violated the goddam ceasefire! A cold-blooded violation!"

Sharon blamed the PLO for shooting first at IDF loudspeakers near a checkpoint. He did not deny using a smart bomb, but justified the attack because Arafat was supposed to be there.

"Where is Arafat now?" Sharon asked.

Incredulous, Habib sputtered, "I wouldn't tell you if I knew!"

Habib and Sharon each viewed the other's actions as needlessly prolonging the siege. Each felt that, if the other would just stop complicating matters, he could get this thing wrapped up in no time. Sharon's view got some high-profile articulation by *The New York Times'* columnist William Safire. While Habib raged about what he considered Israel's pointless escalation of the past week, Safire proclaimed August 6 that "This week, the Israelis have taken their own war back into their own hands." He decried Habib's "interminable negotiations with the terrorists" and complained that

> For eight weeks, Israeli forces at war with the PLO have been restrained from defeating their enemy by U.S. negotiator Philip Habib. . . . [He] has not been a closer of deals because he views a cease-fire as a success when terrorists view it as their victory. The reason Habib has so far failed, while always seeming to be on the brink of success, is that the Reagan administration is publicly stating that negotiation is the only way to get the PLO out. That is a self-defeating lie. . . . The sole impetus for the PLO to leave is the real alternative of its destruction. Incredibly, however, Habib's current alibi for the failure to close is the noise of Israeli guns—as if that is not his only bargaining tool. Israeli military pressure, not sweet State Department reason, is what can "give Habib a chance."

Safe Behind the Barrier

Safire was certainly right about Habib always seeming to be on the brink of success. For two months his diplomatic dance had been nine steps forward and eight steps back, time after time after time. But eventually those single-step net gains did add up. On August 5 he said "We're in the homestretch."

He hoped to have a final draft of an evacuation plan ready the next day to present to the Israelis, Lebanese, and Palestinians within days. The evacuation would begin August 12. The package plan, he said, would contain "elements that the Israelis have objected to, but which in my considered opinion are reasonable and acceptable." His plan would achieve their goal of getting the PLO out of Lebanon, and that's what mattered. The Israelis would surely not reject the whole package over one or two unpalatable elements.

But Sam Lewis urgently warned that they would do exactly that. The main sticking point was an issue that Habib and Sharon had been arguing about for weeks: the timing of the MNF's entry into Beirut. The PLO had all along wanted the entire MNF in place no later than D-Day, the day the evacuation would begin. The Israelis would never buy that, but Habib did recognize the validity of the PLO's fear that, without MNF protection, they would be slaughtered by the IDF on their way to the boats. So he proposed a compromise: Some of the French could come in on D-Day, with the rest of the French, the Americans, and Italians coming in some days later. That compromise then became a prominent feature of his package plan.

But the Israelis didn't want *any* MNF in Beirut at all until the evacuation was complete. As Eagleburger put it, "Israel has some insane paranoia that we're conspiring to save the PLO." The PLO, the Israelis believed, would change its mind once safely behind the barrier of French forces. Lewis said the Israelis were "convinced, perhaps unreasonably but no less unshakably" that once the French arrived "Arafat's apparent readiness to leave under Phil's plan will suddenly evaporate, to be replaced by a prolonged effort to renegotiate issues which now seem to have fallen away."

To Habib, that was a bogus issue. Intrinsic to his plan was what he called a "fail-safe mechanism": that, if the PLO failed to depart *on schedule* once the MNF arrived, the MNF's mandate would immediately terminate. They would then turn around and go home. As Shultz assured Begin, "no contingent of the Multinational Force—French, Italian, or American—would allow itself to be used by the PLO in the manner Israel has suggested."

Standing up to Sharon and Begin on this issue may well have been the single most important thing Phil Habib did on his entire mission. When he and Sharon met August 8 to argue about it yet again, Sharon not only repeated that he would not allow the MNF to enter Beirut until all the PLO were gone, but emphasized that this was a Cabinet decision. "We're too far along for that," Habib replied. "Besides, after all your artillery fire of the last few days, do you really think the PLO would expose themselves to an unsheltered withdrawal? If you have positive suggestions to improve the safeguarding of the withdrawal, I'll take them into account. But I can't accept that the MNF can't come in."

Sharon reiterated that Habib did not have destinations for the PLO and that the PLO really had no intention of leaving anyway. Habib replied,

"The plan won't *start* until the PLO are ready to withdraw. If there are no places for them to go, then D-Day won't be set. Don't forget the terms of the MNF's mandate: If they are deployed and the PLO fails to withdraw, their mandate terminates immediately. Arik, my objectives are the same as Israel's. I had been told that Israel wanted a political solution. That's true, isn't it?"

"Yes."

"I now have such a plan, and I can implement it in a short period of time. Egypt and Syria are the only loose ends. I've given you every possible detail. The Cabinet made its decision without full knowledge of the facts. You should now give them the facts."

But Sharon was not about to suddenly become Habib's advocate in the Cabinet. He and Begin continued to reject any MNF presence in Beirut on D-Day. The whole deal threatened to collapse over the issue. So on August 11 Habib went to Israel to give Begin the facts himself. He showed him on a map exactly where the French troops would go: in the port area. The port was in Christian East Beirut, which Sharon controlled, just across the Green Line from Muslim West Beirut. It was simply not possible, Habib said, for some 8,000 PLO in West Beirut to hide behind 350 French Foreign Legionnaires in East Beirut.

But Begin was not convinced. The French, he said, could not be trusted because they wanted to save the PLO. Nor would he allow Americans or Italians to do the job. Sharon insisted that, if any force was going to be on the ground when the evacuation began, it should be the Lebanese Armed Forces. Habib argued long and loud against that, since he and everyone else knew that the LAF was the military equivalent of a poodle. Sharon then made what he may have considered a concession: No member of the MNF, he said, should set foot in Beirut until an actual majority of the PLO and Syrians had left. Calculating a total of 13,000 PLO and Syrians, Sharon wanted the MNF to wait until 6,501 evacuees had left. "I'm not a mathematician," Habib replied. "We ought to work on a more practical basis."

He agreed only to try his best to sell Israel's demand to the Lebanese government and the PLO, knowing full well that there was zero chance of either buying it.

They didn't. While Habib met with the Lebanese government the next day, August 12, to brief them on his talks in Jerusalem, Israeli bombs thundered across Beirut for the fourth day in a row. Prime Minister Wazzan was in no mood to listen to any more Israeli demands. Regardless of what the PLO wanted, *he* wanted the French in on D-Day. No, he would not send in the LAF without the French, "and if the Israelis do not like this, let them come in and finish the job militarily!" *What's the difference,* he said, *since they are doing it anyway.*

We Accept

The combination of Ariel Sharon and Menachem Begin was the catalytic mix that fueled the siege. But in late July strains between the two started surfacing. The episode of Habib holding the tacsat out the window August 4 seemed to intensify those strains. The Israeli press had reported before that Sharon had deceived Begin, but the tacsat episode was the most dramatic demonstration of facts that contradicted what Sharon had told him. Their views began to visibly diverge. On the seventh of August Begin praised Habib's diligent mediation while Sharon denounced Habib's plan as "a fraud and a deception." Begin said "there is a basis for the assumption that [the PLO] will leave soon and we will not have to go into West Beirut," while Sharon threatened Habib about the "need to clean out" the Palestinian camps.

Late at night August 9, Lewis passed Habib's "final" package plan to Begin. Though Begin was in pain from a leg injury, he was determined to tend to this business. He stayed up much of the night studying the plan. When Lewis met with him and Sharon to go over the plan the next morning, Begin didn't look well. Throughout the meeting he showed animosity and annoyance toward Sharon. Lewis raised an issue he thought had not come up before: Habib felt that the Syrian troops who would also be leaving Beirut should not be treated as a humiliated army. Though the plan called for the PLO to leave with only their individual weapons, Habib felt the Syrians should be able to take their heavy weapons out with them. Sharon replied that Habib had indeed raised the point with him before, and that he had rejected it on the spot. While Sharon and Lewis argued the matter, Begin broke in. "Let them take their arms," he said, pointedly overruling Sharon.

Begin then went on to say that, subject to certain amendments and conditions including the timing of the French entry, "we accept the plan in general principle." The Cabinet would have to make the final decision, but this would be the prime minister's recommendation. Lewis observed that "Begin clearly wants to wrap up the package plan and implement a political solution quickly."

Sharon apparently did not. He launched the most savage assault so far that day. "Sharon has prepared for the military assault," Draper reported that day. "It's very worrisome. They want to go in and finish it." *The Washington Post* reported that Sharon was trying to sabotage Habib's plan.

By this time, Lewis reported, Begin was "highly sensitive to the growing charges that Ariel Sharon was leading him around by the nose and ordering military operations on his own." Begin was clearly frightened that Habib's diplomatic solution might be falling apart, so he invited Habib to

Jerusalem to talk about the plan. Habib saw the meeting as an opportunity to "argue Begin over the top while the momentum seems to be shifting." Lewis' assessment was that the prime minister was "pleading for help from us to get a political solution. Phil has to be here to back up Begin."

When Habib and Begin met the next day, August 11, Begin virtually apologized for Sharon's air attack on West Beirut earlier in the day, saying that the attack had been launched before he could tell Sharon not to strike. Sharon held forth on sharply limiting how long the MNF, particularly the French, could stay in Beirut; Begin curiously said nothing to back him up. As Sharon lectured Habib about what restraint Israel had shown so far in the face of recent provocations—the implication being that such restraint would soon end—Begin interrupted. "We do not want to go into West Beirut in light of the latest developments," he said. "We shall not go into West Beirut. We consider this matter finished since we are now in the phase of technical realization of the plan."

The Logjam Breaks

Those were the words Habib had waited and worked nine weeks to hear. Begin was now basically on board. The Arabs finally came on board about the same time.

Habib had thought the Arab leaders were on board two weeks earlier. He was wrong. The offers of asylum for the PLO that he thought he had received in late July failed to firm up as August wore on.

So Habib and the State Department decided to shift their emphasis. In early August the Americans put massive pressure on Tunisia to take both a substantial proportion of the fighters and, at least as important, the PLO leadership. The Tunisians *really* did not want any part of this. But the US argued that Tunisia—1,200 miles from Israel—had the advantage of distance from the region. The closer the relocated PLO were to Israel, Americans said, the more trouble they could cause Israel and the more likely the Israelis were to come after them in their new host country. But Tunisia was far enough away that there couldn't be any danger to them. Besides, there was something in it for Tunisia: Most of the Arab world had low regard for the Tunisians, says Draper, so taking the PLO headquarters would be a way to save the other Arab states a huge headache and thus "improve their Arab credentials."

After due hemming and hawing, the Tunisians gave in on August 10. They would take the headquarters and some fighters. After his own due hemming and hawing, Arafat consented to go there. Suddenly, it became much easier for the other Arab states to come through. Yemen and South Yemen would take some. So would Sudan. Syria and Jordan confirmed.

The logjam broke for several reasons. Despite their aversion to the PLO and to participation in an Arab Dunkirk, the Arab states could no longer be seen as standing idly by indefinitely while Israelis killed more and more and more Arabs in Beirut. Arab leaders could not be seen as the obstacles to a solution while an American diplomat did all the heavy lifting. If the United States had committed ground troops to supervise a PLO evacuation, Arab states looked bad preventing an evacuation from taking place. They realized that they might face uprisings from their own domestic PLO sympathizers if they let the PLO get slaughtered in Beirut. And they had a hard time resisting Saudi pressures and promises of economic assistance.

On a deeper level, they did not want to see Israeli soldiers occupying an Arab capital. Moreover, they saw that the passage of time only increased the prospect that the Lebanese Christians would make a real alliance with Israel, enabling the Israelis to stay in Lebanon as occupiers forever.

Egypt, however, never did come through. Editorials in the Egyptian press criticized both the US and Habib as not being genuine mediators. A Palestinian official in Cairo was quoted describing Habib as a representative of Israel.

With the PLO having agreed to leave, the Arab states having agreed to take them in, and Begin having accepted the plan in principle, Habib had his plan basically in place. But Ariel Sharon did not believe the PLO had really agreed to leave, and he had never believed in Habib's diplomacy. He still had other plans of his own.

The Climax

Sharon's pounding of Beirut had continued apace as though nothing at all were happening on the diplomatic front. The less necessary it seemed, the harder he hit West Beirut—August ninth, the tenth, the eleventh, the twelfth. Everything came to a head on the twelfth. While Habib was at Yarze briefing his Marine liaisons on his meeting the day before with Begin, Sharon outdid himself with the most awesome saturation bombing ever: 220 sorties, 44,000 shells, 800 homes destroyed, 200 people dead, 400 wounded in eleven hours of relentless, thundering destruction from land, sea, and sky. Two *Newsweek* reporters who witnessed it wrote that "Watching the Israeli Air Force smashing Beirut to pieces was like having to stand and watch a man slowly beat a sick dog to death." A Marine watching the *"blitzkrieg"* with Habib at Yarze says, "It really was like watching World War Two. I thought, 'My God, it's like they're bombing Berlin.' "

At the very moment of success, diplomacy evaporated. Wazzan again refused to mediate with the PLO. Why, he asked Habib, should he continue wasting his time trying to negotiate with the PLO when the Israelis were destroying his capital despite his and Habib's efforts? "We are in effect letting a wild beast do exactly as it pleases." Wazzan couldn't understand why the US couldn't prevent this; it must be collusion.

Habib got on the tacsat and yelled, "The President should tell Begin he should fire his Defense Minister! We can't take this!" He told Shultz, "The city is being progressively destroyed, and the Lebanese are asking me what there is to negotiate about." He had just met with Mother Teresa, whom the Pope had sent to evacuate children from West Beirut. She told Habib she would pray to the Virgin Mary for him. He then went outside and watched the Israeli air force drop sticks of bombs on Beirut from 10,000 feet.

"This has got to stop!" he told Shultz. "This just can't go on this way."

"What do you recommend?" Shultz asked.

"What do I recommend? That the President pick up the telephone and tell Menachem Begin to stop!"

Shultz charged over to the White House to brief Reagan. But by the time Reagan could finally get through to Begin on the phone, the prime minister and the Cabinet—"appalled by the mayhem being perpetrated in its name"—had already ordered the attack halted. Reagan blistered his ears anyway.

This wanton August 12 blitz "was the straw that broke the camel's back with Begin's view of Sharon," says Lewis. Begin was furious with Sharon about it and deeply embarrassed by it. Shultz says, "It was increasingly looking as if Begin had been something of a victim of Sharon's manipulation throughout the war." Begin said he had known nothing about the day's assault until it was well under way. He forbade Sharon to take any further military actions without his approval and sharply hinted that he might fire him. The Cabinet too had had it with Sharon. "What's the point in sabotaging the political settlement?" one minister asked him. "What's going on is contrary to the Cabinet's decision," said another. Sharon shouted, "Any decision not to advance is a bad one." Begin growled back, "Don't raise your voice! You should know who is conducting things here." The Cabinet divested Sharon of his authority to activate the air force, a profound humiliation and a damning vote of no confidence unprecedented in the history of the state.

Sharon's wild assault of August 12 made sense to hardly anyone but himself. Habib's deal was set. Arafat had signed off on it. Begin and the Cabinet had basically signed off on it. Destinations were basically in place. Sharon explained that he launched his assault "Because Arafat continued to play, to trick, to lie. Because he made a joke of us, that liar. You can never trust him, you can never trust them. They live on shrewdness and they always betray their word, their agreements. . . . The 11th of August they still demanded that we withdraw from Beirut to be replaced by the international forces. So I bombed them, yes . . . [and] it worked. The following night, that is the night between the 12th and the 13th, they bent to our conditions."

But even Sharon's own hard-nosed intelligence chief, Yehoshua Saguy, had concluded at least two days earlier that the PLO did indeed want to leave. Begin had said he was "satisfied" with Habib's plan, and Foreign Minister Yitzhak Shamir had described it as "very reasonable." Sharon's August 12 assault is difficult to interpret as anything other than a last-ditch, damn-the-torpedoes attempt to win his war his way—militarily—before Phil Habib could end it diplomatically. He had apparently been so fixed for so long on the means that he didn't recognize the end when it came.

Deliver

Once Begin tied Sharon's hands on August 12, Habib was able to get back to work. Two main snags remained. The first was the argument about when MNF troops could enter Beirut. After a flurry of back-and-forth about it, Begin finally dropped the matter on August 15 and agreed that the French could enter on D-Day.

The second snag was a demand for the PLO evacuees' names. Various estimates were floating around of the *number* of PLO evacuees, but no one really knew who those human beings were. The Israelis wanted a definitive list of all their names, and the Jordanians wanted the names of those who would go to Jordan. The Israelis wanted identities partly for intelligence purposes and partly because their intelligence analysts believed that the PLO was planning to leave 2,000 to 2,500 fighters behind and evacuate ringers in their place. The Jordanians wanted identities partly as an excuse to reject evacuees and partly because no country wants to admit immigrants without at least knowing who they are.

Jordan was perhaps even more punctilious than Israel about getting complete, detailed identity information. Habib said he'd try to get it, but the PLO could not or would not produce. The PLO, Habib explained, was simply too disorganized and the situation too chaotic for specifics like that. Begin finally gave up on getting names August 16, but King Hussein held out. One of Habib's protégés, Edward Djerejian, was the chargé d' affaires in Jordan, so he had the thankless role of middle man. The king blasted Djerejian: "The US is not living up to its word! How can we bring in people when we don't even know who they are?"

Caught in the middle, Djerejian went back to Habib to try yet again. "Ed, I can't get names!" Habib said. "The Jordanians are just going to have to take this on faith with us."

"Phil, I need the names," Djerejian protested. "The king wants the names."

"Goddam it, Djerejian, deliver!" Habib roared. "You figure out how you're going to convince him! You're not getting chargé pay for sitting on your ass!"

Djerejian went back to the king and said, "I deeply regret that we are not able to live up to our commitment to provide names. You must take it on faith that all the necessary checks will be done. We are looking to your Majesty as one of our closest friends to help us start this process. Ambassador Habib is depending on you, the Secretary is depending on you, and the President is depending on you." Dismayed, the king went to the phone and ordered his prime minister to proceed with the operation without names.

A Nice Little Two-Act Play

Both of the two major issues were now cleared away. By August 15 the Israelis were finally speaking of the plan as a foregone conclusion. They scrambled to wring out every last drop of advantage they could, though. On August 17 Sharon presented Habib with a list of eleven new demands—just a taste of the "twenty million suggestions for the plan" Habib said Israel was raising. Habib accommodated the points he could and batted down the rest.

On August 19, the Israeli Cabinet at last approved his plan. Some details remained, but the deal was now firmly set. Finally, finally, after ten grueling weeks of nonstop frustration, outrage, and setbacks, Phil Habib had succeeded. The Israelis had formally bought his plan. The evacuation would start in two days.

Washington, of course, was anxious to announce his success. Presidents love to announce successes, and their advisers always try to orchestrate such announcements to make maximum splash. This one was especially important, because it was really the first major foreign policy success that the Reagan administration could brag about. But even on the day that the Israelis finally signed off on the plan, Habib still felt an announcement by Reagan would be "premature and dangerous." Too many things could still go wrong.

And something promptly did. This problem came from out of nowhere. The Lebanese parliament was scheduled to elect a new president on August 23, four days hence. Maronite Christian militia leader Bashir Gemayel was the only candidate. But the Muslims rejected him because he was Israel's ally and stood to be Israel's puppet. The only way the Muslims could deny him the presidency was by boycotting the election in parliament and thus preventing a quorum.

So Bashir played some clever hardball: He used the evacuation as black-mail. Habib's plan called for the Israelis to turn over their positions at the port to the Lebanese army Friday night, August 20. The French would then move into the port Saturday morning so that the PLO could move out from the port Saturday afternoon. But now, on Thursday, Bashir had made a deal with the Israelis to turn over their positions at the port to *his militia.* Unless the Muslims allowed a quorum for the election, Bashir's militia would not allow the French to land at the port. No quorum, no MNF. No MNF, no evacuation. No evacuation, no end to the siege.

Habib was furious, not only at Bashir, but also at the Lebanese govern-ment. For weeks he had been coaching them to act like a sovereign govern-ment, to reassert control over at least their own capital. He was damned if he was going to let this evacuation come unglued now because they were too weak to stand up to Bashir. Habib met with President Sarkis and said, "I am only going to deal with one government at a time. If *you* don't want the multinational force to arrive, *you've* got to say so. The multinational force is arriving at *your* request. . . . If Bashir tries to interfere with this arrival after *you've* asked us to come, [then] we don't land. . . . But *you* [then] have to take the blame for the city remaining under siege. *You* have to take the blame if the Israelis become fed up and come in and take the place apart. *You* have to take the blame if the ceasefire is broken, because I am not going to take the blame. If it goes long enough, I am going to get on my horse and get out of here, if that's the way you are going to run your country."

He then had it out with Bashir. Habib's position was simple: While he did support Bashir's election, this thing was a lot bigger than that. It was not acceptable, Habib told him, to foul up the whole show by preventing the MNF's arrival. If he did that, he would at one fell swoop destroy his Israeli support, American support, and what little Lebanese support he had outside of his own faction. If the evacuation fell through, the siege could well re-ignite—leaving Bashir to preside over a smoking wasteland of a capital with no friends inside or out. Was that the kind of presidency he wanted?

Bashir couldn't back down without some way of saving face. "So Phil and Bashir dreamed up a nice little two-act play," says Draper. The next morning Draper got representatives of France and the LAF and "a whole lot of press together. On Phil's behalf I marched down to the headquarters of Bashir's outfit in the harbor and ostentatiously had a meeting with him and his lieutenants to talk about what was going to happen in the evacua-tion." Bashir's men being suitably impressed with this public American show of their leader's importance, he withdrew his threat.

"Now you know why I've told you not to let [Reagan] make any statements, don't you?" Habib said to Hill. "They should not have a statement until the first guy starts to move. . . . Don't do it until the French arrive and the boat is there and [the PLO is] on the way. That would be approximately the middle of the night your time, so they could wait till Saturday morning. I know you'll miss the Friday night specials, but I tell you, I'd be careful."

But Reagan did not wait. At 9:30 A.M. Washington time Friday, August 20—three hours after Draper notified Hill that "Bashir may be neutralized"—the President walked to the Rose Garden and announced the deal. "The negotiations to develop this plan," Reagan said, "have been extremely complex and have been conducted in the most arduous circumstances. At times, it was difficult to imagine how agreement could be reached, and yet it has been reached. The statesmanship and courage of President Sarkis and his colleagues in the Lebanese government deserve special recognition, as does the magnificent work of Ambassador Habib. Phil never lost hope, and in the end his spirit and determination carried the day. We all owe him a deep debt of gratitude."

Congress passed a resolution commending Habib, and Senator Charles Percy promptly nominated him for the Nobel Peace Prize, writing that "seldom in the annals of history has one man demonstrated as much ingenuity, persistence and perseverance in resolving an intractable international problem as Ambassador Habib."

Last-Minute Tangles

Habib had no time for congratulations or celebrations. There were still brush fires to put out.

Through all the PLO's vacillating over the past ten weeks, at least one thing had remained constant: their fear that, if their fighters left Beirut, the families they left behind would be slaughtered by the IDF or its ally the Phalange. As the siege and the negotiations dragged on, the PLO had scaled back its demands and conditions farther and farther. In the end, Arafat drew the line at one last either-you-accept-or-we-remain-and-fight-till-the-death demand: an American/international guarantee for the safety of the Palestinian civilians left behind.

To accommodate the Palestinian fear, Habib had built into his plan all the safeguards he could (i.e., that the Israelis and the Pentagon would allow) to assure the civilians' safety. He had got from the Israelis their assurances that, after the PLO left, the IDF would not enter West Beirut and would not take any reprisals against the Palestinians left behind. He got confirmation of Bashir's like assurances August 5 on behalf of the Phalange. And he had repeatedly given, both verbally and in writing, American assurances of the civilians' safety.

238

He had complete confidence in the integrity of the United States to back up his guarantees. He had minimal confidence in the Israelis or the Phalange. But, as he was painfully aware, it was *their* behavior he was guaranteeing. His assurances could be only as good as the Israeli and Phalange assurances on which they were based. How could he believe their assurances after the experience of the past ten weeks? He certainly felt that Sharon had deceived and lied to him repeatedly in the course of pursuing the military objective of evicting the PLO from Beirut. But once that military objective was accomplished, such duplicity should no longer be in Israel's own interest. Having now signed off on rules burnished with their own fingerprints, the Israelis should now find it in their interest to play by those rules. Besides, the Israeli assurance was not the word of Arik Sharon. It was the formal word of the prime minister and the Cabinet.

So, formally, Habib carefully specified that "The United States will provide its guarantees [for the safety of the Palestinian civilians] on the basis of assurances received from the Government of Israel and from the leadership of certain Lebanese groups with which it has been in touch," that is, the Phalange. Informally, he said on more than one occasion, "*I'm your protection!*"

In accepting Habib's plan, Arafat had formally accepted all of those assurances. But now, as the moment drew near when the PLO would actually step aboard ships, his emotional foreboding intensified. Habib needed to give him one last push.

Habib got a reiteration of the Israeli assurances, then he and Dillon met with Bashir in the library of Dillon's home at Yarze. The boyish thirty-four-year-old Bashir, who had never really taken this odd little man named Arafat seriously, made several little jokes, each quickly followed by "OK, I know this is serious." Diplomats cannot choose their counterparts, but must work with the ones there are. Habib bore in to impress upon Bashir the gravity of the situation. Both expected that Bashir was within days of being elected president. However much he might despise the Palestinians and however much dried blood was on his hands, Lebanon's next president could ill afford fresh blood on his hands. Bashir wore a wry smile that Dillon interpreted to mean *I guess I've got no choice but to cooperate, huh?* He again gave Habib his personal guarantee that the Phalange would not take any action against the Palestinians remaining.

He then left, Wazzan arrived, and Habib told him what Bashir had said. Satisfied, Wazzan got Arafat on the phone.

Arafat was frantic. Listening on the library speakerphone, Habib and Dillon were riveted to the anguish in Arafat's voice and on Wazzan's face. Arafat said he couldn't go because the people left behind were going to be murdered. Habib coached Wazzan in French, Wazzan talked to Arafat in

Arabic, and a little English got thrown in here and there. Wazzan tried every argument and angle he and Habib could think of to convince Arafat that the assurances were sincere: Safeguards were built into the plan. The MNF would stay on to protect the civilians. That was intrinsic to the MNF's mission. Permanent security arrangements could be made by the time the MNF left. The United States government was putting its own name on the line as guarantor of Israeli and Phalange assurances.

After listening to and questioning all of the arguments for fifteen wrenching minutes, Arafat finally accepted them. He and his men would sail.

Though Habib never got proximity talks, he had now used the electronic equivalent—without Israeli permission. Though Begin and Sharon would have been horrified, these fifteen minutes of efficient communication had enabled Habib to pick loose one of the last tangles in the knot and save the evacuation.

Another last-minute tangle was Begin's insistence that the evacuation could not begin until he got back two captured soldiers and the remains of nine dead soldiers, including at least four killed in Israel's 1978 invasion. The PLO, naturally, tried to make a trade for the Palestinian prisoners of war that the Israelis held. But Habib told the PLO that it was too late for that; they would have to turn over the remains unconditionally. When the impasse threatened to sink the whole deal, Habib broke through it by writing a letter stating that the US was concerned about the fate and the treatment of the POWs held by Israel, that they should be treated well in accordance with international conventions, and that the US would continue talking with Israel about them. That seemed to suffice: The PLO dropped their insistence on a trade.

But now the Israelis announced that, for religious reasons, they could not accept the bodies on Shabbat, the Sabbath (between sundown Friday and sundown Saturday). Habib had the evacuation scheduled to begin Saturday, August 21. The PLO had handed over the bodies recovered by 4:30 Friday, an hour before Shabbat was to begin. But that did not leave enough time for the various Jewish rituals for the dead to be completed before 5:30, at which point everything would have to stop for twenty-four hours.

Rather than let the evacuation be delayed by a day, Habib encouraged some key Israelis to figuratively unplug the clock. The army's chief rabbi did just that. The rituals were completed "before sundown," the snag was removed, and the evacuation was back on schedule.

The Endgame

Breakthrough

What was the breakthrough and when did it happen? There is no consensus among participants or observers. A good case could be made that it was Begin's August 10 acceptance in principle of Habib's plan. Sharon says it was his August 12 bombing and a subsequent supposed ultimatum by Habib that finally convinced Arafat to go. Many Americans at the time pinpointed the breakthrough as Reagan's phone call to Begin August 12 demanding that Israel *stop* that same bombing. Some people point to the bombing of August 4, or of August 11 and 12. Others point to Tunisia's decision August 10 to accept the PLO headquarters and fighters or to Assad's decision the same day to accept most of the fighters. One observer points to Habib's letters of August 18 and 19 giving the PLO assurances it needed.

Pinpointing the breakthrough makes for pat journalism and tidy historiography. But perhaps the reason there is no consensus is that this crisis was too fiendishly complex for there to have been any one breakthrough. There were three main fronts on which breakthroughs were required: Arafat's willingness to leave, Begin's willingness to stop, and the Arabs' willingness to receive evacuees. No breakthrough on any one front was sufficient without the other two. And no breakthrough on any front was final: Some had to be repeated several times before they finally stuck.

What is certain, though, is that when the various parties were finally ready to make their sour decisions, the one to whom they all resorted was Philip Habib. None of them wanted to. None. All of them tried every squirm and dodge they could think of to avoid going along with his plan. Each principal decision-maker in turn came on board only when he realized that what Habib offered was the least bad solution.

By sheer cussed persistence, the bellowing diplomat simply outlasted them all.

This being the Middle East, though, the story wasn't over quite yet. It was miracle enough that everyone had finally bought the plan. But no one had yet performed.

15
Sail Away

With its heavy superstructure of Israeli "ifs" and Pales-
tinian "yeah buts," Ambassador Philip C. Habib's Beirut
peace mechanism always looked rickety and accident-
prone. But yesterday, with the last of many preconditions
bolted in, the contraption rattled into gear.
The New York Times

As dawn broke Saturday, August 21, the French ship *Dives* threaded its way past the carcasses of sunken freighters that littered the entrance to Beirut harbor like rusting icebergs. Before the 350 French Foreign Legion-naires aboard could even step ashore, they saw that something was amiss. They were supposed to be joining Lebanese Armed Forces soldiers who were supposed to have taken control of the port from the IDF the night before. But there was no sign of the LAF, just Israelis.

"What are you doing here?" a surprised French colonel asked an Is-raeli officer. "When are you leaving?"

"We are ready to leave when your soldiers land."

The French then proceeded to land and, as the press put it, "traded harsh words" with the Israelis as they displaced them directly. When an LAF officer drove up, a French colonel shouted at him and asked where his troops were. His wan reply: "They would not let us in."

Phil Habib had been saying all along that "this is a very tenuous plan. There will be surprises." This was just the first.

He and French ambassador Paul Marc Henry were there at the port to greet the arriving Legionnaires, the first contingent of Habib's long-awaited multinational force. He was thrilled to see them. *By God, they're really here. After all the talking, all the arm-twisting, all the preparations, they're actually standing here.* At last, it looked like this evacuation was really going to happen.

But Habib was quickly distracted by a second problem. The port was like an amphitheater surrounded by tall buildings—ideal for snipers. Is-raeli soldiers were still in some of those buildings observing. If they were in positions where they could observe, then they were in positions where they could snipe. Habib wanted them gone before the PLO arrived to board ships. He barged up to an Israeli general and demanded an explanation. The general insisted that he could not move his troops and, Habib said, "he had maps telling me *why* he could not move them. We had a hell of an argument. I did not win the argument." Habib also objected to the presence of some IDF tanks by the port entrance. He was worried they might fire on the evacuation ship once the PLO boarded. The general refused to move them either, but he did promise not to fire on the boat. Rather than hold up the process, Habib gave in and just crossed his fingers that the tanks wouldn't spook the PLO.

If they did, the PLO didn't let on. As hard as Begin and Sharon had worked to humiliate them, the PLO now worked just as hard to pass off their departure as a victory parade. The world press was out in force to cover this unprecedented operation, and the Palestinians had spiffed up for their turn before the cameras. They got shaves, haircuts, fresh uniforms. Some arrived at the port wearing garlands of white flowers around their necks and in their hair. An American diplomat observed that "the PLO looks like a regular army; the IDF looks like the guerrillas." As they rode in LAF trucks from a staging area in West Beirut to the port, they waved Palestinian flags and portraits of Arafat and chanted "Revolution until victory!" Some people along the route bade them a fond farewell; others, good riddance. The Palestinians grinned, flashed "V" for victory signs, danced around a bagpiper, and sprayed celebratory bursts of Kalashnikov gunfire into the air. The noise of all the gunfire was at times so loud that one couldn't hear a conversation. On this first day at least three people were killed and at least forty hospitalized when the rain of bullets that went up inevitably came down.

Today 397 Palestinians would board the Greek Cypriot civilian car ferry *Sol Georgius* to sail to Cyprus. From there they would catch planes for Jordan and Iraq. As the truckloads of Palestinians arrived, IDF soldiers were "generally getting in the way and obstructing efforts to clear the port area and maintain order," says George Shultz. "Phil Habib insisted on being on the spot in the port; his presence was calming, preventing what could have been violent flare-ups in the tense atmosphere." At 3 P.M. the *Sol Georgius* pulled away from the dock and maneuvered out past the sunken freighters to the open sea.

The reporters naturally wanted comments from Habib and Sharon. Habib, as always, said nothing to them. Sharon said the PLO had suffered a crushing defeat. "The P.L.O. has lost its kingdom of terrorism, which it used as a base for the cruelest, most atrocious terrorist actions against Israel and throughout the world." He told an interviewer later, "I made those murderers a gift: the gift of life. I gave them the chance to live. They are alive because I chose to leave them alive." Sharon's spokesman announced that the invasion had now achieved its primary objective.

Watching the *Sol Georgius* chug out to sea was a fine moment for both Habib and Sharon—though for very different reasons.

"Mr. Habib," said Sharon, "don't you think that in light of this great accomplishment, our brave soldiers deserve a special decoration: the Expulsion Medal?"

"A yellow ribbon perhaps?" said Habib.

"Why yellow?"

"Why, for cowardice. Not *yours,* of course."

For all his satisfaction about Day 1 of his expected two-week operation, Habib's only celebration was to turn to Draper around midnight and say, "Well, that was pretty good."

The First Showdown

Day 2 was pretty awful. Palestinians showed up at the port with a number of British Range Rovers and other jeeps. They told one of Habib's Marine liaisons, Lieutenant Colonel Ed Gaucher, that they wanted to load them onto the ferry, the *Sol Phryne.* He radioed Habib.

"Mr. Bumstead, this is Bismark," Gaucher said, using their call signs. "They want to bring these vehicles aboard. This is not according to our memorandum of understanding. What do you want me to do?"

"Goddam it, Gaucher, you get those vehicles aboard and don't worry about it," said Habib, paying no attention to call signs. "Never mind about what's good and what's not. You just get those goddam vehicles on."

"OK, roger that."

The French inspected the jeeps for weapons, then cleared them to load. As the jeeps were getting loaded aboard, though, an Israeli officer came by and said, "No more vehicles. The ship can't leave unless those vehicles are off." The Israelis then blocked in the *Sol Phryne* with two gunboats.

A flap suddenly became a full-blown crisis. Begin was furious at what he considered a PLO attempt to cheat on the plan. Sharon, by contrast, made a point of stressing that he really would like to be helpful in this case to demonstrate a "new era" of close cooperation with Habib, but he just could not allow the jeeps to go. Whether with a smile or a glower, though, the bottom line was that the Israelis would not allow the ship to sail with the jeeps aboard. The evacuation, barely twenty-four hours along, stalled.

Habib decided the United States had to win this one. "We cannot allow the Israelis to dictate every little dot and comma on what we do," he said. "Any interruption in these arrangements could hurt the confidence the PLO has in us, all unnecessarily." Though the plan was silent about vehicles,

Habib decided it was "perfectly acceptable" for the PLO to take any vehicles that carried no weaponry. Sharon and Begin insisted that jeeps were military equipment not permitted in the plan. Habib objected strongly to any disruption in the orderly evacuation; Sharon and Begin objected just as strongly to allowing anything they considered exceptions to the plan. Habib felt the simple solution was just to let the jeeps go; Sharon and Begin felt the simple solution was just to drive them off the ferry.

In Jerusalem, Sam Lewis did his professional best to argue Habib's case to the Israelis, but his heart wasn't in it. "It's all a matter of face," he told Washington. "Habib should not have made this a big deal. Now it's so far along that it's hard to back down. This is just like children fighting over a tricycle."

Habib sent word to Shultz: "Tell Israel to let the ship go now. We'll talk about our differences later. Bring our destroyers in close, put our helicopters over the ship, and say it's under United States Navy protection." Shultz agreed to that. Weinberger agreed to that. Lewis informed Sharon that the United States would tell the Beirut harbormaster to clear the *Sol Phryne* to sail forthwith. The jeeps would be impounded at one of the ship's ports of call and held until the matter was resolved. Habib called Shultz and said, "There's no way we can back down if we go this far. If we decide to do this, we must be prepared to go all the way to back up our decision." The Pentagon instructed its Navy ships to prepare to defend the ferry and themselves against Israeli attack.

Sharon responded by ordering the jeeps seized and unloaded. The crisis reached the point of showdown. The PLO backed down and offered to unload the jeeps, but the Americans ignored the offer. Those goddam jeeps were going to sail. Frantically, Lewis got to Begin. The message he conveyed from Washington was simple: This was not a matter of the PLO cheating, but a decision by Phil Habib that shipping these jeeps was permissible under his plan. A few jeeps did not compromise Israel's security. The *Sol Phryne* was going to sail on schedule, United States Navy destroyers would be escorting it, and Washington hoped that Israel would not stage a confrontation with the United States Navy.

Begin decided to let the ferry go. "We thought that the whole arrangement might come apart over these jeeps," says Lewis. But about 9 P.M., six hours after the standoff began, the two Israeli gunboats moved away from the port, a tugboat pulled the ferry away from the dock, and the ferry sailed off surrounded by American ships. At the *Sol Phryne*'s first stop, Cyprus, the jeeps were offloaded.

A year later Washington got a message from the government of Cyprus asking, "What are we supposed to do with that warehouse full of jeeps gathering dust?"

The Second Showdown

It was no coincidence—but was something of a miracle—that those Navy ships were available to escort the ferry. The day before the evacuation began, Habib had turned to MarineBob Johnston and said, as though the idea had just occurred to him, "I want escorts." Johnston gulped. How was he, a mere lieutenant colonel, supposed to tell the United States Navy to commandeer enough ships to escort sixteen voyages over the next eleven days, starting immediately? "I owned a battalion, and I had a bunk in one of the ships," says Johnston, "but I sure as hell didn't have a very long string on the United States Navy! But it was reflective of Ambassador Habib's belief that nothing was too hard: 'Just do it. Make it happen.'" Johnston took a deep breath, translated Habib's demand into a request, and passed it up the chain. To Johnston's amazement, the Pentagon delivered.

This meant that American Navy ships and Israeli Navy ships were now plying the same waters off Beirut. More to the point, Johnston says, the Israeli gunboats were "within eyeball distance" of the civilian, commercial evacuation ferries in the port. They were thus "clearly in a position, by their very presence as gunboats, to prevent the ferries from leaving port with the threat of 'Don't move or we'll blow you out of the water.'" Sharon had earlier instructed his forces to prepare for the possibility of stopping the MNF from ever landing, and the PLO had feared all along that the Israelis would sink their ships once they left port. So Habib took the threat posed by these gunboats very seriously. He hollered at Colonel Jim Sehulster, "I want two destroyers in here *immediately* to stay between these ships and the Israeli patrol boats. Get destroyers in here and move those things. I don't want you to fire on them; you just shoulder them out of the way. Make a hole for these ships to get out of here."

It was one thing to give Israel a stern warning in the jeeps episode. It was something far graver that ships at sea were now about to tangle. As the American destroyers started moving into position to do what Habib had requested, Lewis asked Begin to withdraw his navy from the area. Begin was outraged and indignant. He refused, insisting that it was essential for his forces to observe the evacuation process to ensure that it was meeting all the conditions of Habib's plan.

The American Navy then threatened to sink the Israeli boats. Lewis told Begin. More furious and offended than before, Begin reiterated his refusal to order his navy to withdraw. An ugly standoff set in. "Everybody took a very macho position," says Lewis. "Our Navy appeared almost anxious to demonstrate its fighting capabilities."

A swarm of phone calls zipped between Jerusalem, Tel Aviv, Beirut, the State Department, the Pentagon, the White House, and the American fleet commander. Lewis got off the phone long enough to draw up a brief statement of understanding between Israel and the US, using language artfully drafted to save face for both. Begin agreed to it and issued a brief statement of confidence in the MNF. The Israeli gunboats moved back slightly, and the American Navy withdrew its threats. The second showdown ended the same day it began.

The episode received little notice in the press. "Everyone played it down," says Lewis; "it served no one's interest to highlight it." But the fact was, as he put it, that the crisis "almost caused an exchange of fire between the Israeli Navy and the American Navy."

Kabuki

The third day was somewhat less arduous than the second. One contentious issue all along had been what weapons the PLO would be allowed to take out with them. The resolution was that they could not take out "heavy weapons," which, Dillon says, primarily meant crew-served weapons, that is, machine guns, mortars, or rockets. Habib's plan specified that each individual could take out "one individual side weapon (pistol, rifle, or submachine gun) and ammunition." Even that scared the captains of the commercial ships. The captains were alarmed at the sight of these hardened and angry Palestinian fighters, whom they were supposed to cart off to places they did not want to go, approaching the ships draped with AK-47s and bandoleers. The captains insisted they put all the weapons in big crates that could be safely stowed away—far away—from the passengers.

The PLO interpreted "one individual side weapon" to include RPGs: rocket-propelled grenade launchers. An RPG is in fact carried and fired by a single individual, as opposed to a crew. But it also can destroy a tank and was not specified in Habib's plan, so the Israelis objected. Habib took the PLO's point, but said it was too late to add RPGs to the agreed-upon list. If the number were small, however, "I might consider looking at the issue again." On August 20, Habib authorized twelve RPGs per 100 men.

On August 23, the ship *Alkyon* was ready to sail for South Yemen with 479 people aboard. Suddenly the Israelis declared that they would not allow it to sail because the PLO had carried two RPGs aboard. Israeli troops with telescopes and sensitive listening devices were watching from observation posts in some of the high-rise buildings surrounding the port. But Lieutenant Colonel Johnston had been on the spot watching the PLO board that ship. "So I knew damn well that nobody had carried on RPGs," he says. "I viewed this as absolutely being a power play, another way of the Israelis demonstrating, 'If we don't want you to leave, you're not going to leave.'"

But to placate them, Johnston boarded the ship himself and dutifully walked through the well decks and the troop spaces looking for RPGs. There is no way one person can search an entire ship, he says, "but I knew it was a kabuki I was playing with the Israelis. So for about thirty or forty minutes I looked around, then came back off and formally declared, 'I have inspected the entire ship. There are no RPGs on this ship.' Then they let the damn ship go."

Abu Jackass

The Israeli military was just as anxious about what the PLO was leaving behind as it was with what they took out. They viewed the evacuation as "a Trojan horse," says Lewis. Israeli intelligence had been reporting for weeks that the PLO was scheming to leave behind thousands of fighters and evacuate ringers in their place. As the evacuation proceeded, Israeli worries deepened that the PLO was indeed doing so.

If they were evacuating ringers, there was no way of knowing. The processing of evacuees really did turn out to be every bit as dubious as the Israelis feared. Habib had not succeeded in getting the PLO to turn over lists of names and identification numbers of evacuees in advance, as the Israelis and Jordanians wanted. Nor did the MNF want long lingering shipside queues for bureaucratic processing, because they did not want responsibility for PLO fighters in the port for one minute longer than necessary. They wanted the fighters to drive right to shipside, get aboard, and get gone. So the best Habib could arrange was to station some LAF and MNF officers at eight tables in the port to take names as evacuees boarded the ships. The Israelis complained about the poor verification procedures, but Habib said it was the best that could be done. "That was a madhouse," he later muttered. "Who knows what names they give you: Abu This, Abu That, Abu Jackass. It was a stupid thing. Quite clearly, you couldn't move 14,000 men so quickly and get exactly who, what, and everything."

The MNF and the Lebanese had a pretty good count of noses, but definitions were purely seat-of-the-pants. "Combatant" came to mean any male over age seventeen who, by showing up at the port for evacuation, declared himself to be a combatant. Some women were classified as combatants simply by virtue of showing up in a uniform. Nearly all "non-combatants" were children. Some of the "Palestinians" leaving Beirut were in fact Pakistanis, Sri Lankans, and other Arab mercenaries. (And, to round out the definitional elasticity, most of the French Foreign Legionnaires were in fact Eastern Europeans, Balkans, and Germans.)

248

George Shultz, Philip Habib, Morris Draper, Ronald Reagan.

"We'd go out in the morning and pick up the spent ammunition
that had fallen outside the dining room where we were
sitting for breakfast. . . . Once you've seen a piece of
shrapnel and what it can do, it brings home
the shock of war. . . . That makes you
realize you've got to get to work,
get it done, get it over
with, get it stopped."
Philip Habib

Top: Courtesy of Morris Draper. Bottom: John Boykin.

Top left: Courtesy of Jack Grazi. Top right and middle: Terry Payne.
All others: Courtesy of Marjorie Habib. Paris delegation photo by Y.R. Okamoto.

This page, top: Habib spent most of a decade as State's main expert on Vietnam. LBJ (center) sees off his delegation to the Paris Peace Talks in 1968 (left to right): Habib, Cyrus Vance, Andrew Goodpaster, Averell Harriman, and William Jorden. Bottom: Henry Kissinger insisted that anything pertaining to China go through Habib or two other top aides. Here Habib meets Mao Zedong in 1975 as Gerald Ford looks on.

Opposite page, top left: Habib as a teen in Brooklyn. Top right: As a forestry student in Idaho, he slept through many classes but pored over whatever library books interested him. Middle: Forestry class field trip. Habib is, characteristically, front and center, with lettering on his sweatshirt. Bottom left: With Marge in their first post, Canada, early 1950s. Bottom right: Showing off with a Hula-Hoop in Trinidad, late 1950s.

Above: Despite Henry Kissinger's shock at their first meeting, he promoted Habib to the top job for a career diplomat. They argued often and loudly. "Phil was my conscience," Kissinger said, "even if he brutalized me from time to time."

Below: Habib almost couldn't talk without his hands, here with Jimmy Carter and in a rare moment of leisure while ambassador to South Korea. His workaholic ways contributed to the heart attack that nearly killed him in 1977 and forced him to retire.

All courtesy of Marjorie Habib except Sharon and Haig: Courtesy of Ronald Reagan Library.

Above: Habib came out of retirement in May 1981 to avert war between Israel and two of its enemies, Syria and the PLO, both of whom had a large armed presence in Lebanon. Here Habib and his deputy, Morris Draper (to his right), meet with Israeli prime minister Menachem Begin (foreground).

Below: Israeli defense minister Ariel Sharon, in light jacket, and Habib's boss US secretary of state Al Haig, right, agreed more with each other than either did with Habib about how the US should respond to Israel's 1982 invasion of Lebanon. Both are greeted here by Begin and Reagan.

Above: Political Officer in Israel Paul Hare, Habib, Draper, Ambassador Samuel Lewis, Consul General Brandon Grove, and Deputy Chief of Mission William Brown confer in the garden of Grove's office/residence in Jerusalem. This was Habib's headquarters in Israel.

Below: Israeli foreign minister Yitzhak Shamir, Sharon, Begin, Habib. The Israelis and Habib came to trust each other less and less over time. In 1981 he worked out informal understandings that held for nearly a year. To evacuate the PLO from Beirut in 1982, he again relied on informal understandings. But then Begin and Sharon insisted on a formal treaty with Lebanon, which proved disastrous all around.

All courtesy of Marjorie Habib except Haig and Reagan: Courtesy of Ronald Reagan Library.

Above: As the Israeli invasion of Lebanon was beginning on June 6, 1982, Habib met with Reagan and Haig to get instructions. Reagan wanted him to get the violence stopped; Haig thought it was foolish to interfere with the invasion once it had started. At this point Haig and the White House were barely on speaking terms. Reagan fired him eighteen days later and replaced him with George Shultz.

Below: Though their animosity didn't show when cameras were around, Habib-Sharon meetings tended to become shouting matches. While trying to focus on the business at hand—stopping the siege—Habib also had to fend off Sharon's repeated efforts to undercut, discredit, and bully him.

Above: US Ambassador Robert Dillon and Bashir Gemayel. Bashir, scion of the dominant Maronite Christian clan and Sharon's ally, was the linchpin of Sharon's plans for Lebanon. Their arrangement was that Israeli troops would surround the PLO in West Beirut but keep a safe distance; Bashir's militia would then go house to house slaughtering the trapped PLO. Influenced by Habib and Dillon, Bashir reneged on his part.

Below: After Bashir Gemayel was elected president of Lebanon in August 1982 and assassinated three weeks later, his older brother, Amin, was hurriedly elected president in his place. Amin's yielding to Sharon's bullying doomed Habib's plan for getting Israeli and Syrian troops out of Lebanon.

Above: The captain of the USS Independence escorts Habib to a Huey. Habib feared helicopters, but they were the only way to fly in or out of Beirut during the siege. Israeli troops once threatened to shoot down his helicopter, and Israel jet pilots once deliberately endangered the helicopters of US Marines on his team.

Below: Habib hated the one-on-one aspects of being the world's most famous diplomat, but loved collecting newspaper clippings—and particularly cartoons—about himself. This one was his favorite.

Above: A portion of the Green Line, the booby-trapped no man's land separating Christian East Beirut from Muslim West Beirut. Israel's Maronite allies dominated the eastern side of town; the PLO dominated the western.

Below and opposite page: While Israel pounded West Beirut and shut off its utilities and supplies, the PLO fighters were generally safe in well-stocked underground shelters. The people doing most of the suffering were the civilians of Beirut living above ground. Sharon ridiculed Habib as the "mayor of Beirut" for making so much noise about the civilians' suffering.

Above: Sharon and Haig often criticized Habib's reports of Israeli military action in Beirut, saying he was not in Beirut per se and thus didn't know what was really going on. This is approximately the view of the city he had from his headquarters at Dillon's residence in Yarze, a suburb overlooking the city.

Below, left: With Washington in disarray, Habib had to make up policy and his own instructions as he went. He would radio Charlie Hill at State several times a day to storm about the latest outrages, demand action by Washington, and say what he planned to do. "OK, go ahead," was usually all Hill could say. Below, right: Lebanon became the PLO's stronghold after King Hussein expelled them from Jordan in 1970.

Opposite page and top: Courtesy of Jim Sehulster.
Hill: Courtesy of Charlie Hill. Hussein: Courtesy of Ronald Reagan Library.

Above: The essence of Habib's plan for ending the siege of Beirut was simple: Insert a multinational buffer force between the Israelis and the PLO to shield the PLO's departure to other Arab countries. But the evacuation could collapse over any detail. Habib's team of American, French, Italian, and Lebanese military leaders and diplomats worked through the details daily at Dillon's residence. Sharon placed guns next to the residence, drowning out their meetings and drawing return fire that often hit the residence and forced them to dive into the laundry room for shelter.

Below: Only the members of Habib's team mentioned in the text are identified here.

Morris Draper | Jock Covey | Italian ambassador Franco Olitteri | Col. Jim Sehulster | Habib | French ambassador Paul Marc Henry | Lt. Col. Ed Gaucher | Lt. Col. Charlie Smith

Above: Reagan couldn't wait to showcase a major foreign policy success by giving Habib the Presidential Medal of Freedom on September 7, 1982, for his work in Beirut. On stage with them are Marjorie Habib and Nancy Reagan.

Below: A cartoon Habib mounted on his wall at home.

By Meyer for the San Francisco Chronicle

Above: The area of the Sabra and Shatila refugee camps in West Beirut. The September 16-18, 1982, massacre there was a microcosm of the bloodbath Habib had worked all summer to prevent.

Below: When the Israeli invasion of Lebanon began in June 1982, US Ambassador Robert Dillon closed the Beirut embassy building and moved its operations to his suburban residence, which thus became Habib's headquarters in Lebanon. Here Dillon talks to the press after a truck bomb hit the re-opened embassy on April 18, 1983. He was in his eighth-floor office at the time; Habib was a few miles away.

"I GAVE UP... HERE'S PHILIP HABIB'S PHONE NUMBER."

Above: "Habib can do anything" was his image going into his final mission, as special envoy to Central America in early 1986. But he was working for a diplomatic solution on behalf of an administration that was committed to a military solution. He resigned in disgust over Reagan's rejection of the peace plan he had helped Costa Rican president Oscar Arias with.

Left: The consul general's residence in Jerusalem was Habib's oasis during his Middle East mission. The rose garden he designed there, a portion of which is visible here, was dedicated in his memory by Secretary of State Warren Christopher in 1993.

The Hatfields and McCoys

The third day of the evacuation coincided with the date appointed for the Lebanese parliament to elect a new president. Habib had an extraordinary role for a foreigner in the election. As Druze leader Walid Jumblatt reportedly told him, "You have become part of the system." Habib had directed much of his energy over the summer toward preparing the Lebanese government to start reasserting its sovereignty, and he viewed the evacuation and election as the twin opening bells of that new era.

Habib and Dillon believed that, if anyone stood any chance of uniting Lebanon now, it was Bashir Gemayel. They both felt that, despite his bloody track record, he was the best hope Lebanon had. They felt he had matured greatly in the past year and had genuinely taken to heart their advice that he had to distance himself from the Israelis and to work with (not against) the Muslims so he could be president of *all* of Lebanon.

The Muslims and Druze, however, believed that, if anyone could *worsen* Lebanon's divisions, it was Bashir. As one Lebanese official put it, "Bashir was anathema to all the Muslims and to all the Arabs. He was Israel's puppet." When Muslim children misbehaved, their mothers would sometimes tell them, "Don't do that. Bashir will come and get you." Walid tried to persuade Habib that the election of Bashir would be the ruin of the country and asked Habib to use his influence to see to it that the next president would be anybody *but* Bashir. Habib made an effort to seem impartial, replying that he was not in the business of electing Lebanese presidents, but that Bashir was clearly going to win.

That was a safe prediction. A Lebanese election bears little resemblance to the Western democratic ideal. Regardless of what anyone thought of Bashir, there was literally no other candidate. By the unique Lebanese formula of government, the president must be a Maronite, and no other Maronite was suicidal enough to challenge Bashir. And if he were not elected, at least one anti-Bashir Lebanese official believed, he "would have taken power by force and maybe caused a partition of the country."

Lebanese elections were notable also for foreign involvement, threats, violence, and suitcases of money. On July 27 there had been discussion within the State Department's Near Eastern Affairs bureau of drawing on a contingency fund to give money to Bashir "in case he needs it to buy votes." One official involved noted that "If he becomes president, we will be a valued adviser. Habib has influence." But the CIA opposed "paying off Bashir," and Habib recommended waiting. As it turned out, Bashir neither needed nor got American money to bribe deputies. He had plenty of his own.

While Bashir and his Phalange militia were bribing and terrorizing parliamentary deputies to come vote for him, the Syrians were threatening deputies to stay home and thus prevent a quorum. The election had already been postponed for four days, and there was serious doubt whether it would be held at all. In the end, says Draper, Bashir was elected "only because Bob Dillon swung a couple of Lebanese into Bashir's camp at the last minute, and we told everybody we knew that the United States was supporting him. Even then it took huge bribes [by Bashir] to get across the last few votes. But Bashir didn't get the money from the United States." Habib told Washington that Bashir "has got most of the Shi'a paid off. He's got some Sunni. This is not Cook County, though: This is the Hatfields and McCoys with automatic weapons." Indeed, the day before the election, one deputy was shot in the back and another kidnapped. On election morning, August 23, Bashir's Phalange thugs escorted deputies to the election in an army barracks surrounded by Phalange gunmen with Israeli soldiers in the background. Some deputies brought their own armed bodyguards, and at least one asked his Phalange escort to hold a gun to his back so others would think he was being brought there by force. Seventeen homes or offices of deputies who participated in the election were blown up.

Bashir of course won, and Habib was delighted. In Christian East Beirut, Bashir's stronghold, celebrations swirled all afternoon and all night with the standard Lebanese celebration of shooting in the air. Two of Habib's Marine liaisons were sitting in a villa in Baabda that night, when the room suddenly filled with bullets whistling and flying everywhere. One Marine looked over the edge of the balcony and saw "this little girl about nine years old standing there holding a 9 mm pistol just wanging away!"

The Absolute Low Point

While East Beirut celebrated Bashir's victory, West Beirut continued the evacuation. As it proceeded, Habib saw that the basic concept of his plan was working fine, but several of the particulars were not. There were far more people to evacuate than anyone had anticipated. The PLO wanted to speed up its departure schedule. The LAF was not rising to its responsibilities. The Syrians and at least one major Palestinian unit refused to turn over their positions to the LAF. And the LAF was afraid to do much of anything without MNF troops alongside them.

All of this meant that Habib did not have nearly enough MNF bodies in place to do the job. He had always wanted *all* 2,000 of them on the ground in time for the first boatload of evacuees, but Sharon had always insisted that *none* of them land until after the last evacuee had left. The compromise was to bring in 350 French troops on Day 1 and the rest on Days 6 to 8 of the expected two-week operation. Now, on Day 3, Habib realized he had drawn the compromise too close to Sharon's position, jeopardizing the operation.

All of the departures so far had been by sea, so the 350 French troops at the port had sufficed. But the first overland convoy was due to start rolling on August 25, and the rest of the MNF weren't due in until August 26. Somebody had to serve as a buffer protecting the overland convoy along its route through Beirut, including along the treacherous Green Line that divided West Beirut from East Beirut. So on August 23 Habib decided that he needed more MNF soldiers on the ground pronto.

Even though the Pentagon had long since vetoed the idea of sending the Marines along the Green Line or into West Beirut, Sehulster decided on the morning of August 23 to go see for himself just how dangerous those areas really were. He spent the morning driving all around West Beirut with no problems at all. Though he still couldn't recommend sending Marines in there, he did report that doing so would not be nearly as dangerous as Washington feared.

That was good enough for Habib: Maybe this on-the-ground report would persuade the Pentagon to give him his American buffer force after all. He promptly dragged Sehulster into the tacsat room and called Shultz. He wanted Shultz to lean on the Pentagon to allow at least *some* Marines to join French, Italian, and Lebanese troops along the Green Line. Sehulster says, "Habib was wailing away, getting red and screaming, 'George, goddam it, we've gotta do this!'"

He got so excited that he forgot that the tacsat was a radio, not a telephone. He forgot to press the transmit button. He was shouting into a dead microphone.

Sehulster tried to interrupt him to say, "Mr. Ambassador, he can't hear you," but Habib was in no mood to be interrupted. On and on he roared, until the calm voice of George Shultz broke through, saying, "Phil, when are you going to start? You've got to push the button to transmit."

Deflated like a stuck balloon, Habib drooped down into a chair. He took a deep breath, shook his head, cursed the fates, and started again, quieter.

Weinberger and Sharon both forbade putting Marines along the Green Line. "The US Marines can't just sit on their ass all the time!" Habib howled. He sent Weinberger a blistering cable arguing why the Marines should be out and about with the other MNF partners. But Weinberger wouldn't budge. Habib was particularly galled that his own secretary of defense was agreeing with Sharon against him.

Though Weinberger refused to put Marines along the Green Line, he did say they could arrive at the port early. Sharon said no, they couldn't. "I won't accept [Sharon's veto]," Habib told Shultz on the 24th. "We can't get the PLO out if we don't take over the checkpoints. We must move our force *tomorrow!* I need the goddam forces *tomorrow.* Any slowdown raises the risk of something going wrong. I don't understand Weinberger's policy about the Green Line. There's no rule that says the plan can't be changed. I have the French and the Italians all ready to do it. We give in on every issue. At some point we have to take a stand. If we pull out of this operation, the French will do it alone, and IDF can go to war with the French. I hope they will. It will be done my way or it won't be done at all—or it'll be done by the French alone. This is the absolute low point in these ten weeks of hell. The United States will be laughed at; it's an international disgrace."

The French were livid at Weinberger's and Sharon's refusal to give the MNF the scope to do its job. The Lebanese were sure it was a plot to let the IDF or the Phalange attack the remaining civilians. The PLO was hesitant to continue withdrawing without more MNF cover. Habib told Shultz, "I have a furor on my hands."

After seething a while longer about Sharon's veto of the Marines' early arrival, Habib decided he could live without Marines on the Green Line but could not wait another day for them to come into the port. He called Washington back and said, "Get the president to call Begin and say we do it our way or we cut off the tap. Tell the president and the secretary. It's a new program: We *have* to come in tomorrow and the Italians tomorrow night." He insisted on a definitive answer by 7 P.M. "I can't run without them. If I can't bring them in, it'll be total confusion here. It all comes to a halt."

He got the answer he wanted: The Marines would definitely come ashore a day early, Wednesday, August 25, whether Arik Sharon liked it or not.

Speeding up the arrival of the Marines meant the Italians and the rest of the French would come in early too. Though the Marines would be bottled up in the port, Habib set about preparing for the French, Italian, and Lebanese troops to take up positions around town. Those preparations included one particularly tricky task.

The soldiers would have to travel down certain streets to take up their positions along the Green Line and near the airport. Everybody knew that the Green Line and some surrounding streets were mined and booby trapped. But nobody knew *which* streets or where the mines and booby traps were. Habib's plan required the PLO and Syrians to disclose the locations, but people who plant mines in city streets are not known for careful record keeping. Besides, the PLO and Syrians were not the only ones who had planted mines. They might not know—much less remember or disclose—all of them.

"We just gotta find out if these roads are open," Habib said to one of his Marine liaisons, Lieutenant Colonel Charlie Smith.

"I'll call my guys to get a Huey in here," Smith said. "We'll do an aerial reconnaissance, and I'll give you a report tomorrow."

"Naaaa, a chopper doesn't do any good," said Habib, who in World War Two had probed for mines with a bayonet. "I thought Marines took and held ground. I want you to take an embassy car and drive the route. Then I want a personal report."

Smith wasn't quite sure what to make of that. *Drive a car down streets to see if they are mined? Are you insane?* Smith took it as an instance of Habib's humor—but he also took an armored embassy car the next morning and drove the route. To his immense relief, he didn't get blown up or shot at.

And that was that. Assured that the roads were safe for the non-American forces to move into position, Habib got ready to greet the Americans.

The Marines Have Landed

Habib leapt out of bed well before dawn Wednesday morning, dressed, and headed for the door. The Marines were due to arrive at the Beirut port at 5 A.M., and he was dying to greet them as they stepped ashore. Sure, he had greeted the French when they had arrived and was happy that the evacuation had been proceeding for several days. But today was special. Today the United States Marines were coming ashore as the crescendo of his mammoth symphony. Like a prisoner minutes away from release, his adrenaline was pounding so hard he could have run all the way to the port. He would have gladly swum out to the first landing craft and opened the bow doors himself.

But he couldn't leave. For reasons that seemed compelling at the time but that no one could later remember, he would have to wait. This was like telling a playwright to stay in the parking lot during opening night. Habib crashed around Dillon's house, pacing and cursing, demanding of anyone within earshot why he had to wait. He would take two steps toward the door, Draper or someone else would tell him "Not yet, Phil," he'd turn back, swear, pace some more, then make another move toward the door.

Finally the signal came that it was OK to go, and Habib dove into his big armored Chrysler. He got to the port about half an hour after the first Marine stepped ashore. As the Marines set up, Sehulster says, "Habib was there in all his glory. He was effervescent, just elated, with this great big smile all over his face."

The port was crawling with reporters. Habib paid them no mind, walked over to the Marines' commander, Colonel Mead, gave him a wink, and said, "The Marines have landed. The situation is well in hand, right?" Mead took a long skeptical look around at the swarms of reporters and drawled, "Yeah, right." Habib had no intention of talking to the press, so, Mead

253

says, "he just got out of the way and threw me to the wolves and let me do all the tap dancing."

Mead had expected Habib to be as tense as everybody else, but "he seemed greatly relaxed. He was having a good time, all full of sightseeing." He pumped the hand of every Marine he could get to and had Mead introduce him to each commander. Mead told him about a decision he had made before the landing craft had even reached the dock. The Marines were taking over the port from the French, and as they sailed in Mead noticed the French flag flying over the port. The Lebanese had a long sorry tradition of foreigners coming in and trying to take over. Mead immediately ordered a corporal to take down the French flag and put up the Lebanese flag. Habib was pleased: "These guys have got the sensitivity that we need."

How the Hog Eats the Cabbage

They also had the toughness he needed. For example, the Israelis had placed two or three tanks behind a building just a hair beyond the Marines' perimeter. Habib had argued with an Israeli general a few days earlier about removing them, but failed. Soon after the Marines landed, one of the tanks rolled around the building into a menacing position where it could shoot point blank at the line of evacuees and the evacuation ship. A Marine corporal promptly picked up a shoulder-fired anti-tank weapon, walked over to the tank, and told the Israelis inside, "If that tread moves half an inch, I'm going to blow you away." A Marine officer then joined him and added, "You are going to remain here with your tanks until you are told when and where to go. Do you fully understand that? If you move it, you will be destroyed."

Radios started buzzing. Between the Marines' judgments on the spot and Habib's hurried negotiations with the Israelis, the decision was to allow the tanks to stay as long as they remained back behind the building out of sight and outside of the Marines' perimeter.

The Marines neutralized these few tanks by surrounding them, but then there was the rest of the IDF to worry about. "The IDF kept breaking into our positions throughout the entire time we were ashore," says Mead. "What they were doing was symbolically showing us how the hog ate the cabbage in that part of the world." The IDF gagged at the sight of American Marines, their supposed ally, protecting the mortal enemy they had originally set out to crush. "In their incandescent anger, they had gone in to smash the PLO once and for all," says one diplomat. "I don't think that anger was over. I think they felt thwarted by the peace that Phil was arranging in Beirut."

The PLO also tested the Marines' mettle, at least once. Early on, a few

Palestinians rolled some hand grenades toward a group of them. The Marines, who prided themselves in being able to handle anything and everything, could see the pins in place in the grenades, so they stayed nonchalant. The Palestinians quickly learned that they were not going to intimidate them, so they stopped trying.

American, French, Italian, Israeli, Palestinian, Syrian, Lebanese—it was extraordinary to have so many armed groups in such close proximity, all under separate command yet ostensibly cooperating in the same effort. The communication between them was equally extraordinary. Habib had instructed the Marines not to deal directly with the IDF. All communication was to go through him, Draper, or his group of liaison officers. Yet Lieutenant Colonel Johnston coordinated military matters directly with a PLO lieutenant colonel. So, though Habib had been prohibited from dealing directly with the PLO diplomatically to reach this point, once they were at this point the US military easily dealt with them directly. Though word of the Johnston-PLO meetings would have set off a political firestorm had the Israelis realized they were happening, the meetings themselves were utterly mundane. For example, Johnston told his PLO counterpart that evacuees would have to stop their celebratory shooting once they reached the port, he agreed, and they complied.

Within twenty-four hours of the Marines' arrival, the balance of the MNF came ashore. The Italians, concerned about what Johnston calls "the showmanship of the French," didn't want to look like stragglers. So they had wanted to come in second. But they arrived with a fleet of ships loaded with an enormous number of armored personnel carriers, Fiat trucks, and other Fiat vehicles—all painted white. The logistics of all that equipment slowed them down so much that they wound up coming in last after all. As they unloaded more and more and more vehicles, Habib ribbed Italian ambassador Olitteri, "Franco, you're coming down here to do more then sell your Fiats!"

The Daily Juggle

This grand clunking pageant of ferry boats and destroyers, trucks and tanks, soldiers and guerrillas, heroes and bunglers was Philip Habib's Olympics. His feelings were mounting exhilaration that his plan was working, tempered with a grim determination to keep it from falling apart. He drove to the port nearly every day to soak up the Marines' company and exult in seeing his plan being implemented. Otherwise, he generally stayed at Yarze fielding problems. He had Draper, his Marine liaisons, and embassy staff members fanned out to various key locations to monitor what was happening and report back to him over walkie-talkies. He would then get on the telephone or tacsat to deal with problems as they came up.

Hundreds of problems large and small came up. Any one of them had the potential to jeopardize the operation.

For example, an Israeli taxi driver took two journalists into West Beirut, let them off, took a wrong turn, and suddenly found himself captured by a Shi'a group. Since he was carrying a gun, his captors thought he was a spy. The Israelis told Habib that the evacuation could not proceed until the taxi driver was released. Habib called Nabih Berri, who, as leader of the Shi'a militia Amal, was influential in the neighborhood where the driver had been taken. After twelve hours, Berri had the driver turned over to Habib and Draper. No voyages were affected.

Habib called Berri again late in the game. This time Amal itself had captured two Israeli journalists or sightseers. As they talked on the phone, Habib ascertained that Berri's biggest concern at the moment was knowing the fate of eighteen of his men who had been missing since a battle two months earlier. So Habib tapped his contacts and called Berri back with authoritative word that all eighteen were dead. Grateful for the information that he could now pass on to those men's families, Berri returned the favor by releasing the two captured Israelis.

Most of the problems Habib had to deal with involved the intricate logistics of transportation. He had good help handling the details. Tom Miller, a Foreign Service officer on the Israel desk at State, and colleagues in Washington had scrounged around for the few commercial ships in the eastern Mediterranean whose owners were "brave, stupid, and/or greedy enough" to charter them for such a risky operation. Jock Covey, the deputy principal officer in the Jerusalem consulate, came up to Beirut to handle the logistics. But Habib had never been very good at delegating. This was his symphony, and he was jolly well going to orchestrate it and conduct it. "Phil was not given to anxiety," says one participant. "He was just damn insistent that it would come off the way he said it would." So he constantly looked over their shoulders at where things stood, which ship was due in when, which group of Palestinians would be on it, how many of them would be aboard, where it was going, which US Navy ship would escort it and for how far, what objections the Israelis had raised, and so on.

Juggling his ad hoc assortment of commercial ships, passengers, and destinations was a nightmare. Even two-thirds of the way through the evacuation, no one knew how many people needed to be transported. Some of the nine ships were nice liners with fine appointments, some were car ferries with none. The car ferries didn't have enough beds, so Habib and Covey had to rustle up a mountain of air mattresses and blankets. (Covey snagged one air mattress for himself to sleep on the floor at Yarze.) One ferry was a reliable workhorse with a willing captain, but it sailed at a glacial pace, so it couldn't be scheduled for frequent voyages. The owner of one ship bound for Sudan decided in mid-voyage that he didn't want it to go to Sudan after all; he wanted to unload his 500 passengers at Suez, Egypt—even though the Egyptians had refused to accept any evacuees. Never knowing whether some other jittery owner might bail out altogether, Habib had to keep some ships on standby for days on end. Two of the ships were not certified to carry the numbers of people that Habib needed to put on them, so the US embassies in Athens and London scrambled to arrange upgraded capacity certificates.

None of the ships was really equipped to care properly for wounded evacuees. So the Americans arranged for the Red Cross hospital ship *Flora* to evacuate wounded Palestinian civilians to Greece for medical treatment. But the Israelis objected, worrying that the press would see mutilated kids and circulate pictures of them around the world. Draper countered by emphasizing "the public relations risk that the IDF would run by stopping a child with burns on her body." Habib told Sharon that "we would not prevent wounded women and children from departing on [a Red Cross] hospital ship, just because of his concern that the PLO would make propaganda with them." The *Flora* sailed despite Israeli concerns, but Habib and Draper worked out a compromise for the second boatload: The Red Cross would take another seventy wounded Palestinians out two days *after* the last boatload of fighters—and therefore the last camera crew—had left.

Idiot Lecture

As he and his colleagues batted down one problem after another to keep the evacuation on track, Habib radiated a sense of accomplishment and profound satisfaction. But he had been through too many setbacks in the past twelve weeks to relax until the last fighter on the last boat on the last day was soundly gone. No champagne. No whoops. He did take time out to phone Marge on August 27, their fortieth wedding anniversary.

His tacsat calls to Charlie Hill remained all business. Hill never detected in his voice or words any sense of joy or relief. But the people with him in Yarze did. Mostly he felt vindicated. He had been insisting all along that he could negotiate an end to this ugly siege, and he had. Despite all the critics, all the skeptics, all the stalling, all the duplicity, all the aggravation, he had done what he set out to do.

This was the twenty-sixth mile of his marathon. He was exhausted. Everybody around him had been worried all along that he was on the verge of another heart attack. He had seemed fine earlier, but during the evacuation he was clearly a sick man. "He looked awful," says one colleague at Yarze. "Just ashen. Those of us who had seen him in full song before were struck that this enormously robust, vigorous character suddenly looked frail and gray and ill." On August 28 he fell asleep talking. He even did something the Phil Habib of old would never do: He *admitted* being tired. He simply could not work what that colleague calls "the usual Phil Habib twenty-two-hour day. But he insisted on going ahead with things. Even an exhausted Habib had twice the energy of most people and three times the force." He would make himself rest as long as he could stand it, then "get up and stomp around, hollering at everybody—Did they get this thing done? Did they get the other thing done?—and taking off pieces of people's hides." But his stomp and holler no longer shook the rafters.

Once the comings and goings of ships settled into the Beirut equivalent of a routine, Habib could turn more attention to a different dimension of the evacuation that would go on simultaneously with the ship voyages. Though he had always poured most of his energy into getting the PLO out of Beirut, they were not the only combatants he had to evacuate. He also had to get out 3,600 elite Syrian soldiers and 2,600 Syrian-controlled Palestinian Liberation Army (PLA) guerrillas.

Since the Syrians had originally been invited into Lebanon by the Lebanese government and authorized by the Arab League, they claimed to deserve special treatment. Though Begin was determined to disarm and humiliate the PLO, Habib persuaded him to let the Syrians leave with their heavy weapons, their trucks, and their dignity. There was also the touchy subject of their Arab League mandate to be in Lebanon. Habib therefore arranged what he called "a redeployment. Their mandate is not ended. This will all be untidy, but it will happen. It's an Arab solution." In other words, while the Palestinian fighters would have to leave Lebanon entirely, the Syrian troops would only "redeploy" east to the Bekaa Valley. This was purely a face-saving measure: Habib fully expected that, once the spotlight darkened, they would drift home to Syria for "re-equipping."

For all of these reasons, they could not go out on ships like the PLO. They would have to drive out in truck convoys along the Beirut-Damascus Highway. Unfortunately, neither Habib nor any of his colleagues had any idea how to organize something as "burdensome, tricky, and inherently very dangerous" as a truck convoy. The Israelis, whose own convoys had bogged down on the bad roads of Lebanon during the initial invasion in June, kept telling him, "you will never, *ever* get a convoy to work over those hills." But Tom Miller at State found a US Army logistician in Washington who had extensive experience running convoys through difficult terrain. "Give us an idiot lecture," an FSO in Yarze told him over the tacsat. "You've got to train us now, in the next couple of hours, how to build a convoy that won't come apart." And he did, starting with basics like "put your slowest vehicles first."

The first convoy set out from Beirut on August 27, with the Italian MNF soldiers escorting them and spectators lining the route. As a face-saving measure, the evacuees rode out manning their weapons, as though this were a military parade. Toward the rear of the convoy sat a gunner in the back of a jeep or pickup truck mounted with a powerful double-barrel 50-caliber anti-aircraft gun. All of a sudden, "Goddammed if that gunner didn't grab the trigger and rip off some shots!" says an observer. Spectators started diving for cover. So much for an orderly convoy. "But when people saw the look of absolute horror on the gunner's face and how he threw his hands up," says the observer, "it was clear that it was an accident. It was a credit, I must say, to Israeli discipline that nobody started firing. It was a total accident, but it scared the shit out of everybody."

Heckling the Parade

Accidents like that were one of the risks of Habib's having structured his plan to let the evacuees save face. But without such face-saving measures, he would never have gotten any of them to agree to leave in the first place. He therefore did not want any evacuees to have to run a gauntlet. He had told Sharon in early July that he wanted IDF soldiers far enough away from the road "that your guys aren't standing by the side of the road thumbing their noses at them as they go by." David Kimche, director general of Israel's Foreign Ministry, had given Habib a guarantee as early as July 7 that the Israeli troops would be far enough away from the road that no evacuees would see them. This guarantee became part of the final text of the plan.

But Sharon was much less punctilious about this aspect of the plan than he had been about the RPGs and the jeeps. As that first convoy of 201 vehicles rolled out toward Syria, an IDF squad stood along the roadside hooting and giving them all the finger. An IDF squad car broke into the two-mile-long convoy and wove in and out between the trucks. When the second convoy was ready to drive out two days later, the IDF mounted a procession of Israeli flags on ten-foot poles every fifty yards or so as far as the eye could see along the route. IDF troops were also posted along the way. "They could not resist showing they had won," Habib said. "They hoisted Israeli flags along the road and lined it with triumphant Israeli generals." At Hazmiye Circle, where the convoy was supposed to form, they had posted a tank battalion as well as flags. "It was clearly provocative," says Smith. "It was a way of saying, 'We're going to rub your face in it. We're still in control.'"

Habib interpreted these kinds of violations of the plan not as misbehavior by an ill-disciplined force, but as deliberate IDF policy. He first got word of the flags from Faith Lee, the embassy communication specialist whom he called Tinkerbell. She was going to a store in a suburb of Beirut. As she approached the road where the evacuees would be going, she saw about twenty huge Israeli flags lining the route. She immediately had her embassy driver turn around and take her back to Yarze. "Habib!" she said, "the whole road is lined with Israeli flags!" He would never curse in the presence of a lady, but he was clearly very angry. He started burning up the phone lines, barking, "You had better get those flags out of there, or we don't move at all." When he got hold of Sharon, he says, Sharon "insisted that I had never said any such thing about their not being on the highway, and he was absolutely refusing to put his troops out of sight."

Meanwhile Smith and Sehulster were confronting IDF commanders face to face with the same message: Back off, or the convoy won't move. One general was embarrassed and said he'd do his best about the flags and the fingers. Faced with the choice between heckling the parade or having no parade at all, the Israelis eventually took down most of the flags and lightened their presence along the route.

But they only lightened it. For example, once the convoy did get moving, four Israeli generals with four Israeli flags were sitting on the curb at the Galerie Samaan crossing to watch it go by. Lieutenant Colonel Gaucher went up to one of them and said, "General, you told me during the meeting yesterday we wouldn't have any problem with this. You're being an obstruction. To begin with, you're going to get shot. I suggest you all leave." They did.

Habib was angry about the flags incident, but not surprised. "At this stage," says Sehulster, "nothing that the Israelis were doing to embarrass anybody was a surprise to us. It was all part of their pushing on any soft spot they perceived to gain their advantage. Unless challenged, they would persist. If challenged that they were going against the protocol, they would usually back down. It was a contest about who was going to get their way."

The next round in that contest came as the next convoy started heading out overland on August 30. Sehulster was on the street along with an Israeli officer, "the Mossad guy who was my shadow," to watch it pass. A call came on the Israeli's radio.

"We're stopping the convoy," he told Sehulster. "There is a PLO vehicle in there, and it has got to be removed. We are not letting anybody move."

"You go to hell," Sehulster said. He then dashed up the stairs of a nearby building to the top floor, where the IDF's northern commander, Gen. Amir Drori, was watching the convoy. He got in Drori's face and said, "You are *not* stopping this goddam convoy! This is ridiculous. It doesn't matter if one goddam vehicle gets through. We'll gladly pull it out and discuss who it belongs to later. But the rest of this convoy has *got* to continue."

Generals are not accustomed to being addressed this way, especially not by colonels and particularly not by foreign ones. Drori at first professed not to understand English, so Sehulster argued with him through a translator. After a while Drori decided to speak English after all. He then turned to his radio operator and said in English, "Let the convoy continue."

When Sehulster later told Habib about the incident, Habib said, "I owe you one." It was the closest Sehulster ever saw him come to thanking anybody.

Arafat's Imponderables

The trickiest event of this whole evacuation would be the departure of Yasir Arafat. Whatever else might happen, Habib had to get him out safe and sound.

Arafat sent word to Habib August 23 that he was anxious to go. The French and the Greeks offered to handle all the arrangements. A jumble of scenarios, dates, destinations, and ships were proposed; there was even some discussion of sneaking him out secretly and rumors that he had snuck out already. But Habib was worried that the PLO fighters would lose discipline after Arafat left, so he wanted him to be one of the last people out. Besides, Arafat's departure would require extraordinary security arrangements—including obtaining an ironclad Israeli guarantee not to kill him at the port—and all of that would take time. Arafat's departure was also not the kind of thing Habib wanted to spring on the Israelis as a surprise. So he stuck with his planned target date of Monday, August 30, for Arafat's departure. Habib flew to Israel August 25 to discuss that and other issues with Sharon.

"How is the expulsion going?" Sharon asked.

"The evacuation is proceeding according to plan," Habib replied.

Habib emphasized that the United States was responsible for Arafat's safety. Supplementing the US Navy escort, five Greek military officers would be aboard Arafat's ship as a disincentive for the Israelis to sink it, and a Greek frigate would also accompany it. Jets attached to the US Sixth Fleet routinely patrolled the Mediterranean, and Habib wanted them to "watch over without flying over" Arafat's boat. Sharon objected that Habib's scenario, especially the air cover part, was too much like a triumphal departure. But Habib said, "I won't change one thing. We are in charge of this. It's a Greek, French, and American operation. We have informed the Israelis of our plans, and that's all."

Arafat had two special jeeps equipped with communication gear that he wanted to take out with him. Habib had no problem with his taking out the radios, since he thought it reasonable for a political leader to have communication capability. But he said the jeeps were out of the question, since he had offered during the jeep crisis of August 22 to bar future shipments of jeeps. The radios could be removed from the jeeps and stuffed into a suitcase. Habib knew the Israelis would object to even that. As Hill puts it, "the Israelis started playing games: 'He can't take this, he can't take that, we have to count the bullets, blah, blah, blah, blah,' on and on and on and on. It was clear they were just playing games with us to stop this, just trying to annoy everybody and cause the maximum amount of trouble."

Habib was prepared to take on the Israelis over the issue, or to ask Begin to let the radios go as a favor, or to look the other way if Arafat tried to walk onto the ship with the radios. But Shultz disagreed with Habib on all three ideas. In the end, they decided to let French Ambassador Henry take responsibility for Arafat's various "imponderables" and ship them to him later.

Confrontation at the Port

Arafat's departure on August 30 would be the climax of the evacuation. Habib's instructions to the Marines were simple: "Don't fuck it up."

Prime Minister Wazzan rode with Arafat to the port in Wazzan's own black bullet-proof Mercedes, perhaps to help ensure that he really would leave. The car worked its way to the port amid a raucous mob of supporters, reporters, bodyguards, dignitaries, and onlookers. The press and the Palestinian show of support were to be expected, but the Marines waiting at the port were surprised to see French Ambassador Henry and a convoy of armored French vehicles with the tricolor waving leading the parade.

Habib resented Henry's display. "That goddam son of a bitch!" he said when Henry kissed Arafat on both cheeks. "Who the hell does he think he is?" Later Habib wrote, more temperately, "Obviously under instructions from Paris, the French ambassador tried his best to mount a French 'spectacular' of sorts to show French support for Arafat and the PLO. He insisted on parking his car in the center of the narrow road leading to the port entry-way controlled by the Marines. He and his officers made clear their intentions to carry out departure arrangements according to their own plan."

But the Marines stuck to Habib's plan. According to his plan, the port was their sole responsibility, conducting Arafat safely from its entrance to the ship was their sole responsibility, and no French or Palestinian guards— much less any unauthorized gunmen or stray hangers-on—had any business being inside their lines. The Marines prided themselves on being able to handle any kind of security task and considered it a professional affront for the French Foreign Legion to presume to escort anybody through their sector.

At the narrow port entry Checkpoint 54, the loud, aggressive, heavily armed mob of 300 or so encountered a dozen Marines. Those dozen Marines' weapons were unloaded, but Lieutenant Colonel Johnston's best sharpshooters had loaded rifles and M-60 machine guns trained on the crowd from the windows of the nearby tall buildings. The sharpshooters could spot any troublemaker and take him out more quickly and accurately from above than could anyone on the ground. In addition, a platoon stood by just out of sight, poised to step in and help if needed. As the crowd surged into the Marines' turf, intent on escorting Arafat all the way to the ship, the dozen Marines formed a line and physically pushed the crowd back ten yards to the checkpoint. Some French vehicles nudged forward aggressively, and some Palestinians slapped their rifles, made threatening gestures at the Marines, and tried to push through the checkpoint. The Marines blocked them all. The sharpshooters held their fire.

Lost somewhere in the middle of the crowd was the short man with the famous stubble and headdress, Yasir Arafat. He stepped out of Wazzan's Mercedes to review a PLO honor guard that awaited him. The mob made that impossible. French camera crews nearly knocked him off his feet. He inched forward for ten minutes into a sea of humanity, then was summarily shoved inside a limousine. As the Marine in charge, Johnston confronted Henry and demanded to know why he thought French troops were necessary in the Marines' sector. He let Henry and the Italian ambassador come and let four of Arafat's bodyguards sit on the bumpers of the limo with their AK-47s, but he told the Legionnaires, Arafat's elite bodyguards, and everyone else to stay back. As the dozen Marines kept the rest of the crowd behind, Johnston got in his own jeep and led Arafat's limo the three-quarters of a mile directly to the ship.

Habib had impressed upon Sharon that he would brook no stunts from the IDF during Arafat's departure, and the Israelis were notable for their absence during this whole episode. An IDF sharpshooter had Arafat in his crosshairs at the port, but Habib had obtained Israeli guarantees not to kill him, and the sharpshooter obeyed his orders. Arafat boarded his ship safely and sailed away uneventfully. Philip Habib could again breathe.

Two days later, Wednesday, September 1, the ship *Mediterranean Sun* pulled out into the channel of Beirut harbor at 12:40 P.M. and headed off to Tartus, Syria, carrying 682 Palestinian fighters and 33 others. This was the last of sixteen shiploads. Four overland truck convoys. Nine countries. Eleven days. Altogether, 15,116 people evacuated Beirut, including 8,494 PLO fighters, 2,631 PLA fighters, and 3,613 Syrian troops. Habib had evacuated half-again more people than Sharon had thought there were.

The evacuation was over. The siege of Beirut was over. The mission of a lifetime was over.

The Annals

Did Philip Habib stop the siege? No. Menachem Begin and Yasir Arafat did that. What Habib did was to provide the *means* for them both to call off their mutual blunder without losing face. By painstakingly designing a mechanism that gave everybody what they most needed and by doggedly pushing and adapting and selling and finally enforcing his mechanism, he gave them all an out. When they had run out of other options, Phil Habib was still there to give them the diplomatic cover they desperately needed.

Though Habib's personal style and the circumstances of his negotiations were unique, what he accomplished was what any diplomat aspires to: He kept a bad situation from getting worse. That saved countless lives—Habib himself estimated "tens of thousands"—and pulled both sides back from the brink of catastrophe.

Lancing the boil of West Beirut ended the immediate crisis, but daunting problems remained: how to get Israeli and Syrian and the remaining Palestinian forces out of the rest of Lebanon, how to get the Lebanese government back in control of at least its own capital, how to help Bashir stand up to Begin and Sharon, how to get Israelis and Palestinians to be good neighbors.

But those were problems for another day and another diplomat. Habib had, after all, been called out of retirement to take on this mission. "Phase two," he said, "is not my baby." His pay for the mission of a lifetime: zero.

It had been three months since the invasion had scuttled his plans for a vacation in the Greek Islands with his daughter Phyllis. Now the inveterate workaholic was ready for a vacation at home.

After the last ship sailed, he went down to the port to thank, congratulate, and say goodbye to the Marines.

"Where you heading now?" Smith asked him. "Will you take a rest?"

"Yeah, Franco's offered me use of his villa outside of Rome," referring to Italian ambassador Franco Olitteri.

"You going there by yourself, sir?"

"Well, that's none of your goddam business, Colonel!" Habib said with a puckish wink. "At my age, who would you *expect* me to be going with?"

When he got back to Yarze, says Draper, "all kinds of people came swarming up to talk to Phil. Olitteri was very emotional in telling Phil that this was the greatest diplomatic accomplishment in his lifetime. Other people were saying the same thing. Phil, of course, was characteristically very modest about it: 'No, no, no.' But after working night and day for so long, he was just exhausted too." That night, Draper gathered a lot of embassy staff, French and Italian colleagues, and others to go out for a big celebratory dinner and dancing. Habib was too tired to go.

But he was also the happiest his colleagues had ever seen him. "The man walked lighter," says one. "His eyes lit up. He was exuberant. Something big had worked. He would almost—I was about to say 'dance around the room,' but that's not accurate. He just walked around happy as he could be, telling everybody how well everything worked, taking the telephone calls of congratulations. He was just plain beaming. I think it was particularly impressive because we knew the other side of Phil so well too: how he could really turn on the grumpiness. But you could just see that he felt *'We did it!'*"

He and Dillon went over to President Sarkis' house for a meeting and for him to say goodbye. At the end of the meeting, Sarkis suddenly whipped out an Order of the Cedars medal and put it around Habib's neck. Sarkis felt that Habib's plan "will remain forever in the annals of world diplomacy." There was no ceremony, no audience. Only about half a dozen people were in the room. Habib had received many medals and many awards over his career, and the Lebanese give out the Order of the Cedars medal rather freely. But he mistakenly thought he was the first foreigner who was not a head of state ever to receive it. He was deeply moved. It was the only time Dillon ever saw Habib's feelings about his parents' homeland come out.

Fighting back tears, Habib said in an uncharacteristically soft voice, "You know, Lebanon means a lot to me. During my career I had avoided serving in this part of the world. It's only been in recent years that I have been involved here. This is the most important thing that I've ever done."

His throat choked. He cleared it.

He paused.

"If I've been able to contribute, I'm—"

16
Foreigners in Combat Boots

Phil pulled off a miracle in Beirut.
George Shultz

Miracles in the Middle East blink out pretty fast.
Morris Draper

And then everything went to hell. The bad guys who had laid low during the siege of Beirut soon crawled back out from under their rocks. Philip Habib's work would soon become forever overshadowed by theirs.

The train of events began with American defense secretary Caspar Weinberger's decision to bring the Marines home early. He had never wanted them there in the first place, and he wanted them out at the earliest possible moment. Weinberger felt that they had done their job, that job was finished, and they should now come home.

Habib passionately disagreed. Intrinsic to his plan all along had been the idea that the MNF would be on the ground for about thirty days. Their presence for three weeks or so beyond the evacuation was to serve two purposes: to help smooth the transition from anarchy to Lebanese rule, and to protect the remaining Palestinian civilians. Once the PLO fighters were gone, the families they left behind would have no other protection from their enemies, the Israelis and the Phalange. The PLO fighters would not have left without Habib's guarantee of the civilians' safety. Without the MNF there to protect the Palestinian civilians, Habib's guarantee would be empty words.

But Washington suddenly got nervous about taking casualties. So they "did not complete what Habib wanted," says Colonel Jim Mead. "Habib was absolutely furious when there was any discussion of not going the full thirty days. We told our chain of command, 'Hey, we need to hang tough here a little bit longer to get done what the ambassador wants done.' But no, boom, we got the order." Mead even took it up with Weinberger when the secretary came to Beirut to visit the troops in early September. "We think if we come out early it could possibly jeopardize what Habib's going to do," Mead told Weinberger. But this was a colonel talking to the secretary of defense, and Weinberger ignored his advice.

Habib's arguments were no more successful. Weinberger controlled those Marines, Weinberger had made up his mind, and Habib recognized that this was one fight he was just not going to win. So he backed off and bowed to the inevitable. The final text of his evacuation plan had specified that the MNF would depart between September 21 and 26. But even before the evacuation was complete, Shultz and the French foreign minister agreed on a departure date of September 10. Habib resigned himself to that date.

By the time the soldiers left town, Habib had received the Presidential Medal of Freedom from Ronald Reagan and headed back home to California to play golf. The summer had brutalized him and left him deeply weary. He had used up most of his goodwill with the Israelis and Syrians. In August he had said, "Phase two is not my baby," and, as an inveterate mentor to younger Foreign Service officers, he wanted Morrie Draper to have his time in the sun. He checked in with the State Department now and then, but Draper was the point man now. Habib's only certain plan was to return for Bashir's inauguration in a few weeks.

Bashir never saw his inauguration day. On Tuesday, September 14, two days after the last MNF soldier left town, a twenty-six-year-old Greek-Orthodox Lebanese named Habib Tanious Sartouni hid a bomb in his sister's apartment in the same building as Bashir's headquarters. Around 4 P.M. Bashir arrived to give a speech. At 4:10 Sartouni, sitting on a nearby roof, pressed the button of his remote control and watched the building explode. As the rafters and the rubble hurtled down onto Bashir's head, the linchpin of Habib's and Ariel Sharon's separate and very different hopes and plans for the future of Lebanon crumbled with them.

"Terrorists"

What happened next would be a microcosm of the bloodbath Habib had worked all summer to prevent.

With the MNF gone, Beirut had no functioning civil authority. And with Bashir dead, it had no prospects of strong leadership anytime soon. So in the wee hours the day after Bashir's assassination, Wednesday, September 15, Begin told Draper in response to his pointed inquiries that the IDF was moving into checkpoints in West Beirut "with the object of keeping things quiet and insuring that there were no incidents to mar the peace." Begin made the move sound modest and innocuous, but Draper warned him to move cautiously and to avoid undercutting the Lebanese Armed Forces' emerging authority there.

Three hours later, Draper arrived in Beirut for Bashir's funeral and saw that "the city was in flames." Despite Begin's assurances that the IDF was taking only "strictly limited precautionary measures," Draper saw the IDF going at it hot and heavy with tank and artillery fire. The funeral could wait. He ordered his car turned around and headed off to the IDF headquarters outside Beirut "where I essentially could get only incomplete information and pap to the effect that 'Everything is fine.'" Draper felt he'd been had. "Begin told me as a representative of the United States goverment that the Israelis were not going to move into the heart of Beirut," says Draper. "And within hours they were inside the heart of Beirut. He told a straightout, 100 percent, baldfaced lie to the United States government, his great friend. I mean, a solemn undertaking by the prime minister of a friendly state? Unheard of!"

One of the few things Philip Habib had known for certain during his negotiations was that Menachem Begin did not want to risk his boys' lives by sending them into the dangerous streets of West Beirut. Firm in that knowledge and in Begin's assurances—not just Sharon's, but Begin's—Habib had assured the Lebanese and everyone else that the IDF would stay out of the city.

And now here they were.

In a nasty meeting the next day, Thursday, September 16, Draper and Sam Lewis confronted Sharon about his violation of the Habib agreement and the damage it had done to Habib's, America's, and Israel's credibility. Sharon's icy reply: "Circumstances changed, sir."

It was all the PLO's fault, Sharon argued. They had violated the agreement. They had left behind vast stores of weapons and 2,500 terrorists to use them. Those terrorists, Sharon said, were hiding in the Palestinian refugee camps of West Beirut, including Sabra and Shatila. Sharon now had the camps surrounded.

Habib had never imagined that he would get 100 percent of the PLO fighters out of Beirut. Though the Americans considered Sharon's number highly inflated, there was undoubtedly some unknown number of fighters still in town. To Sharon, it was obvious that he had to go after them. To the Americans, it was equally obvious that the Israelis had no right to invade the city for any purpose after the whole evacuation had been predicated on their promise not to do so.

Draper kept asking the Israelis for the source of their belief in thousands of stay-behind terrorists, but he never got a good answer. "At most there were a handful of guerrillas" left behind, he says. "There were a few armed men in the camps . . . but they were all men sixty or seventy years old. They may have had old shotguns, but they were not a threat. Essentially, the camps were disarmed."

Though in life Bashir had reneged on his end of the bargain that he and Sharon had struck eight months earlier, it was not too late for his militia to make good on it. The essence of the Sharon-Bashir alliance had always been a division of responsibility: The IDF would corner the "terrorists" in

West Beirut, and the Phalange would go room to room doing the actual wholesale killing. Bashir's nonperformance had in fact been why the siege of Beirut ended with PLO fighters leaving in ships after ten weeks instead of leaving in coffins after one.

But now Bashir was dead, and now the IDF was finally surrounding the camps in West Beirut. Now was the time for somebody to go in and deal with those stay-behind PLO fighters, Sharon felt. Habib and Draper had always argued that any fighters in West Beirut were the Lebanese Armed Forces' problem, not the IDF's. So, though Sharon and his chief of staff had little confidence in the LAF's ability to do much of anything, the IDF's top general in Lebanon went through the motions of inviting the LAF to "clean out" the camps for them. When they predictably refused, Sharon decided to send in the Phalange. This time, with no Bashir under Habib's moderating influence to restrain them and seething over Bashir's death, the Phalangists were more than willing.

The nearest American equivalent to sending the Phalange into the camps would be sending heavily armed Ku Klux Klansmen into an African-American neighborhood with a license to kill. Chosen to lead the operation was the head of Phalange intelligence, Elie Hobeika. Dillon knew him from his service as Bashir's personal bodyguard and describes him as "a pathological killer." Hobeika had led various massacres of Druze and Palestinians, most notoriously a 1976 massacre of 3,000 Palestinians at Tel Za'atar.

Most of his squad belonged to an intelligence unit that the Israelis "considered specially trained in discovering terrorists." His squad apparently had little training in discovering anyone other than terrorists, given their view that "Pregnant women will give birth to terrorists; the children when they grow up will be terrorists," and both were thus fair game. The Phalangists' reputation prompted the IDF to repeatedly instruct them to kill only terrorists, not civilians. Since both considered *terrorist* and *Palestinian* more or less synonymous, this was sort of like giving the Klan a license to kill only African-Americans they considered troublemakers.

The Coyote and the Chickens

Begin would later say his "pure and genuine intention" in taking control of West Beirut was "to protect the Muslims from the vengeance of the Phalangists" in the wake of Bashir's assassination. Sharon professed no such idealism, justifying the move as a necessity to take out those stay-behind terrorists before they could get back on their feet. To the Americans, the IDF's forceful entry into West Beirut was a flagrant violation of the Habib agreement and a case of the coyote moving in to protect the chickens. In a meeting with Draper and Sharon at 5 P.M. Thursday, September 16, IDF General Raful Eitan said that "the Phalange . . . are obsessed with the idea of revenge. . . . I'm telling you that some of their commanders visited me, and I could see in their eyes that it's going to be a relentless slaughter."

It was. At about the same moment Eitan was speaking, Hobeika's squad of Phalangists began their messy business of cleaning out Sabra and Shatila. All Thursday night, all the next day, and all the next night they worked their way through the camps, systematically killing everywhere they went. The IDF quite openly sponsored their business, keeping the camps surrounded and the Palestinians trapped inside, allowing in Phalange reinforcements, hosting Hobeika in their forward command post near the camps while he stayed in radio contact with his men inside, and providing maps and aerial photos of the camps, a bulldozer, and illumination flares through the night.

There is no question that the Israelis knew the Phalangists were killing a lot of people. That was the whole idea. The only question was *who* was to be killed. Sharon no doubt really did believe that he had sent the Phalange in to kill the 2,000-plus stay-behind terrorists he believed he had surrounded in the camps.

But what Sharon apparently did not anticipate was that his intelligence reports were wrong: The Phalangists found rather few people in the camps who fit any but the most all-inclusive definition of *terrorist.* Indeed, the IDF intelligence officer on the spot monitoring events reported within four hours of the Phalangists' entry, "there are evidently no terrorists in the camp." So the Phalangists slaughtered pretty much whoever they did find: defenseless women, children, old men, even cats, dogs, and horses. Whereas actual PLO fighters had fought rabidly earlier in the invasion, the Phalangists encountered hardly any resistance in the camps.

From the earliest hours, the IDF had clear indications that the Phalangists were killing civilians, lots of civilians. To stanch that hemorrhaging, they again approached the LAF to take the Phalangists' place. "Let the LAF go into the camps," Sharon said to Draper on Friday, apparently neglecting to mention that the Phalange was already in the camps. "They can kill the terrorists. But if they don't, we will." The LAF again refused, saying they could not cross the IDF ring around the camps to do anything without looking like a tool of the IDF.

By Friday evening, General Drori, the Israeli commander in Lebanon, had heard enough and halted the operation—sort of. He ordered the Phalangists out, but gave them about 12 hours to get around to leaving. No one knows how many Palestinians had been slaughtered by the time the last Phalangists straggled out after 38 hours in the camps. Estimates ranged from 700 to 3,500.

As Sharon tells the story, the problem was not that hundreds of people got killed. It was that too many of the *wrong* people got killed. The Phalangists just "went too far," he says, killing too many civilians when they were supposed to be killing only terrorists.

To Phil Habib and most of the rest of the world, the problem was that no such operation should have happened at all. In the first place, the Israelis had no right to take over West Beirut at all. As Dillon puts it, "The Israelis, who had promised to stay out of Beirut, immediately invaded to 'restore order.' That was just a pretext; there was no disorder." In the second place, neither they nor any surrogates had any right to be in the camps killing anybody at all. Draper put it this way to Sharon on Saturday morning: "You must stop the acts of slaughter. They are horrifying. I have a representative in the camp counting the bodies. You should be ashamed. The situation is absolutely apalling. They're killing children! You have the field completely under your control and are therefore responsible for that area."

Phil Habib was sitting on the terrace of his home overlooking the San Francisco Bay when someone phoned to tell him the news. He was devastated. Like the rest of the world, he was appalled and outraged about the atrocity. But he felt it more sharply than most others. It wasn't just that everything he had worked for all summer had now gone down the toilet. It was that he was the one who had promised the civilians' safety. "I had signed this paper which guaranteed that these people [the Palestinians] in west Beirut would not be harmed. I got specific guarantees on this from Bashir and from the Israelis—from Sharon." He said he "had been given assurances by Bashir that no action would be taken against the Palestinians remaining in the camps and by the Israelis that they would not enter West Beirut. On the basis of those assurances we had given our word. We had been deceived." Their guarantees had been the basis of Habib's. But the MNF was no longer in Beirut to back up Habib's, Bashir was no longer alive to back up his, and Sharon had a poor record of backing up anything he told Habib.

"Sharon was a killer, obsessed by hatred of the Palestinians," Habib said. "I had given Arafat an undertaking that his people would not be harmed, but this was totally disregarded by Sharon whose word was worth nothing."

The Tail-Chasing Question

As soon as Habib got the phone call about Sabra and Shatila, he headed back to Washington. By the time he strode unexpectedly into Shultz' office, Shultz and Reagan had already decided what to do about the massacre: send the MNF back. Habib agreed it was the right thing to do. The MNF would be "a presence behind which the [government of Lebanon] could assert authority over West Beirut."

Habib was on his way back to Lebanon too. Bashir's older brother Amin Gemayel had been hastily elected president in Bashir's stead, and Habib went out for the September 23 inauguration. As long as he was in the region anyway, Shultz asked him to visit all the capitals to see if he could explode the inertia that was setting in.

Inertia was the opposite of what the Reagan administration had hoped for. They had tried to capitalize on the momentum of one dramatic diplomatic success by pushing through another. Hours after the last evacuation ship had sailed out of Beirut harbor on September 1, Reagan announced a bold regional peace plan. Shultz had formulated the plan based on conversations he and Habib had had at Stanford University a year earlier. The plan's essential idea was the creation of a Palestinian state on the West Bank in association with Jordan.

Though the plan was well received in some quarters, Menachem Begin fervently denounced it. He was particularly indignant that the US had consulted with King Hussein of Jordan—but not with Begin—in formulating it. The first he heard of it was in a briefing by Sam Lewis just hours before Reagan announced it to the world. Getting back at the US for this affront would factor strongly in many of Israel's actions in the next eight months.

More disturbing to Habib was the inertia in Lebanon. The country was still overrun with foreigners wearing combat boots: Syrian, Palestinian, and Israeli. He had done well to get thousands of them out of Beirut a month earlier; getting the remaining thousands out of the rest of the country had been too big a bite to even attempt during the crisis of the summer. But now that that crisis was past, the agenda was to pry out the rest of them. There was no way Lebanon could ever get back on its feet as an independent nation with sovereignty over its own territory until all of those armed foreigners left. And there was no way to get a regional peace process going—along the lines of the September 1 plan or any other—until Lebanon ceased to be a flashpoint. So those foreign forces had to go—all of them. The question was, What's it going to take to persuade them to go?

Timing would be crucial. One trap Habib was determined to avoid was the tail-chasing question of who would leave first. So in his swing around the region from September 25 to October 3, he proposed that all of the foreign forces withdraw at the same time. The Israelis and Syrians were each too mistrustful to risk moving until they were sure the other was moving too. After all, if one moved in good faith while the other sat still, the one who moved would be humiliated. So Habib envisioned a "self-enforcing plan" by which each party would take certain visible steps at specific times. With international observers monitoring the withdrawal, everybody could know that everybody else was on board. Specifically, he proposed a two-stage withdrawal: The Syrians and Israelis would each pull back to some negotiated lines on October 15, everybody would see that the plan was working, then the last soldier from each army would cross the border home on November 1. He picked those dates not because he imagined they would hold, but "for negotiating purposes," so everyone would know what he meant by "as soon as possible."

Informal Understandings

He knew he had a very brief window of opportunity within which to sell and implement his plan. The MNF was back in Lebanon for a sixty-day mission, by the end of which he wanted the Syrians and Israelis gone. That would only give him until late November.

So to every president and prime minister he talked to, he tried to drive home the urgency of getting a plan nailed down right now, this week. *I didn't come just to talk,* he told each, *but to get specific answers and decisions.* What he was racing was not a looming cataclysm, but the likelihood that "a constant series of incidents without real purpose" would distract the parties from the business at hand. While they then fell back into their safe, familiar inertia of aimless squabbling, he feared, their forces would sink ever-deeper roots into Lebanon's soil. Bashir's assassination and the Sabra and Shatila massacres had already knocked the wind out of diplomacy's sails. In a region notorious for its endless cycles of offense and retaliation, Habib could not afford to let the next disruptive outrage—and the next and the next—shred those sails.

The best way to move fast, he felt, was for him to play the honeybee. Rather than seat national delegations around negotiating tables to plod their way toward formal agreements, Habib would shuttle between the parties and piece together informal understandings based on his own plan. Not only would formal agreements take too long, but the Arabs and Israelis would not talk to one another in the first place. And even if they did, and even if one Arab country did reach a formal agreement with Israel, the other Arab countries would punish it. There was no time to waste on such pointless exercises. So, Habib said, "I was going to negotiate the kind of understandings I had negotiated previously" in both the summer of 1981 and the summer of 1982.

There might have to be some meetings of national delegations, but if each country bought into his basic concept right now, he argued, then the meetings could be quick coordination on the technicalities of transportation. Figure a week.

273

But the Syrians and Israelis were in no hurry at all.

Syrian president Assad was not even sure he wanted to interrupt his vacation to talk to Habib. If the United States had so little influence over Israel as the IDF's entry into West Beirut and the massacre indicated, then why should he bother talking to the American envoy?

By the time Habib finally got to see Assad on October 3, he had a pretty good idea of what to expect. "Assad's position," he said, "was always that he didn't have any intention of staying in Lebanon forever, blah, blah, blah, blah." He had told Habib earlier that he did not need to keep troops in Lebanon in order to assert influence there and would gladly withdraw if the Lebanese government asked him to. But there was a catch. He would "listen to the opinion of the [Lebanese government] when it was truly free," but argued that "the Lebanese are not now in a position to exercise their free political will . . . with Israeli bayonets pointed at their heads." So only after the Israelis had left Lebanon would he entertain a request that his troops do the same.

Assad's bottom line was that the Syrian military presence in Lebanon could not be equated with the Israeli military presence there. He never tired of pointing out that, whereas the Israelis had invaded, his troops had entered Lebanon legally in 1976 at the request of the Lebanese government and with the blessing of the Arab League. Since the two armies had entered under very different terms, Assad felt, they should depart under very different terms. That meant, in Assad's view, that Syrian departure and Israeli departure could not even be negotiated as part of the same package.

Moreover, Syria must not be seen as buckling to Israeli pressure. Assad would not allow Israel to gain any rewards from its invasion: no peace treaty with Lebanon, no residual military presence there, not even bragging rights as having driven the Syrians out. The only thing Israel could leave behind was guarantees that no more Muslims would be massacred. Assad would "be prepared in principle to leave Lebanon one day after final and complete IDF withdrawal." But he would not even formally discuss doing so until the minute the last Israeli crossed the border home.

Habib, of course, considered Assad's position utterly unworkable. "We have to be practical and pragmatic and deal with the situation as it is," he replied. It was "inconceivable that the IDF would withdraw from Lebanon without some understanding that the Syrians also would withdraw more or less simultaneously." He offered to work out an informal understanding whereby both armies would just happen to withdraw "within the same time frame." The Syrians rejected the idea.

Habib argued that simultaneous withdrawal was in Syria's own interest. As long as Syria insisted that the Israelis leave first, he said, the Israelis would not leave at all. That would defeat Syria's own main objective of getting them out. The Syrian position thus "means no chance of progress in the immediate or foreseeable future." They could cite legalities all they wanted, he said, but "the main objective is not to stand on form but to get results." Simultaneous withdrawal will work; *them first* will not. The Syrians, he said, "should drop their demand for a political spectacle glorifying their role and agree to a mechanical plan for simultaneous departure. It should be a transport problem."

All in all, the meetings in Damascus were a disheartening signal that Habib should expect no more cooperation in the fall than he had gotten in the summer.

Full Justification

Begin and Sharon were just as clear—and just as unrealistic—as Assad about the terms under which they would bring their soldiers home from Lebanon. They had zero interest in Philip Habib, shuttle diplomat, arranging a quick departure of all foreign forces from Lebanon. What they wanted, Habib said, was "full justification for this stupid invasion of Lebanon. How do you get full justification? You get a peace agreement. And they wanted one on terms which they dictated." Forget any informal understandings. As Habib saw it, Begin and Sharon had staked their political futures on getting a peace treaty with Lebanon and were prepared to drag things out as long as it took to get every detail they wanted. Only then would they bring their troops home.

For decades many Israelis had believed Lebanon would be the second Arab country to sign a peace treaty with them, even though they did not know until 1979 who would be the first. That was the year Egyptian president Anwar Sadat broke ranks with the Arab world to sign a treaty with Israel. For his trouble, Sadat had been assassinated and his country ostracized from the Arab world. Now Israel was demanding that Lebanese officials follow in Sadat's footsteps. Egypt was powerful enough to withstand concerted shunning; Lebanon was not. Israel's many enemies within Lebanon would surely topple any Lebanese government that signed a formal treaty with Israel. Moreover, as one Lebanese leader put it, "Lebanon could not afford to lose its historical ties to 20 Arab states to establish ties with one state—Israel; it could not lose its export market to Arab countries, representing over 90 per cent of the total, to gain an export market of about 5 per cent of its total." In the case of Egypt, a peace treaty had meant that two peer states agreed to stop fighting each other; in this case, however, the peace treaty Begin and Sharon had in mind would mean turning Lebanon into what Habib called a satrapy: little more than an Israeli province.

Begin may have had the treaty he wanted written in August. Even before the last boatload of PLO fighters had sailed out of Beirut on September 1, he flew Bashir to Israel and told him the time had come to sign it. But by then Habib and other influences had persuaded Bashir to keep a distance from Israel. So Bashir balked. Annoyed, Begin demanded a signature within a couple of months. He lectured Bashir, write Schiff and Ya'ari, "like a schoolmaster scolding a delinquent pupil. Bashir was insulted to the depths of his being." Begin and Bashir yelled at each other, then Sharon stepped in to remind Bashir who ran the show. At that point Bashir thrust out his wrists and shouted, "Put the handcuffs on! I am not your vassal!"

The treaty was only one of Begin and Sharon's preconditions for withdrawal from Lebanon. They would be quite happy to withdraw at the same time as the Syrians. In fact, they insisted on it. But they would not withdraw at all until the 6,000 or so PLO fighters still in northern Lebanon and the Bekaa Valley left. And all captured and killed and missing IDF soldiers would have to be returned or accounted for. Over time, their list of preconditions would grow—and grow, and grow.

While Israel and Syria would each have been delighted to see the other pack up and go home, that was not either's priority. Each was far more interested in preserving its own prerogatives in Lebanon. Rhetoric aside, each would rather see Lebanon partitioned into a Syrian sphere and an Israeli sphere than give up their own prerogatives there.

Here, then, is the situation Habib faced: The Syrians would leave only after the Israelis did, the Israelis would leave only after the PLO did, and the PLO would leave only with the Syrians. Habib concluded that the linchpin to getting them all out was to get the Israelis to agree to leave. Without that, nothing else was possible. So that is where he and his colleagues focused their efforts.

Butt Out

The evacuation of Beirut would turn out to be not a springboard for even greater diplomatic achievements, as Habib and Washington hoped, but the high-water mark for American diplomacy in the region for the entire decade. The Middle East was becoming less and less hospitable to American involvement, diplomatic or otherwise.

Morrie Draper got the first taste of that in mid-September. The world press, led by the American press, had been showing ugly photographs of the bombed city of Beirut and its maimed children ever since the siege began. Americans were disgusted, and Israel's moral standing in their eyes had plummeted. By the time the press began showing pictures of the heaps of bodies in Sabra and Shatila, some Israelis felt they were victims of a propaganda war. Around the time of the massacre, Draper drove out to an IDF installation outside Beirut. One of the IDF soldiers he saw there was an old friend of his, a senior foreign ministry official called up for reserve duty as a lieutenant colonel. As Draper walked up to greet him, the friend "just blew up. He cursed me and was aiming his carbine at me and threatening to kill every American he could find. He started screaming about me and Phil, 'You Americans are nothing much but Arab lovers! You're aiding and abetting this propaganda against us!' The Israeli dislike of the Americans at that point was intense. Individuals would spit at you. As far as they were concerned, we were the enemy. Both before this incident and after, my friend was a perfectly normal kind of character. But in the middle of this tension, I thought he was going bonkers."

The Marines found out how unwelcome they were by the Israelis a week and a half later when they arrived to take over Beirut airport from the IDF. The Americans couldn't believe what the Israelis had left behind for them. "When I first went in," says Charlie Smith, "I was overwhelmed with the smell of human feces." The Israeli troops had left the terminal and offices littered with their feces: at the base of walls, in the elevators, in desk drawers, on chairs, everywhere. "It was like coyotes," says Ed Gaucher. Jim Sehulster interpreted it as a stiff-fingered housewarming present for the Americans.

The Israelis had also left the airport littered with more serious debris. Smith says they had sown countless golfball-sized bomblets, "like mines and booby traps, almost like a terrorist type of thing." He describes the airport buildings as "just coated with" bomblets and considered them not the residue of battle but a deliberately laid minefield.

On the diplomatic front, the Israelis left little doubt that Phil Habib, whose swing around the region had been extended into a full-blown return to active duty, was no more welcome. They had tried several times before to cut him out, and Washington had rebuffed them every time. On October 6 Israeli ambassador to the US Moshe Arens tried again to bypass Habib, by proposing a "U.S-Israeli working-level consultative group in Washington to deal with problems in Lebanon on a day-to-day basis." The State Department gave him the same answer it had before: *Habib and Draper and the American embassies in the region handle that job, thank you.*

With their failure to impose a treaty on Bashir, Begin and Sharon resigned themselves to the need to negotiate one with Amin. In time they dropped the word *treaty* but not the concept. They just replaced the word with *normalization* and *mutual relations*. Habib called their goal "a treaty in all but name." Their equation for negotiations did not include any meaningful role for the likes of Philip Habib. Though they made the minimal requisite nods to the value of American involvement, what they really wanted was for the US to butt out. They felt they were more likely to get what they wanted from Amin if Phil Habib were not there telling them to back off and urging Amin to resist their pressure. They also felt that, if Habib did succeed in mediating an agreement, that success would strengthen his hand in selling Reagan's September 1 regional peace plan, which they despised.

The Israelis and Lebanese frittered away the fall bickering over where the negotiations would be held, who would and would not sit at the table, what role if any the Americans would have, what the agenda would be, and so on. As far as the Americans were concerned, Begin and Sharon were just stalling until the floundering September 1 plan fell off the table.

Habib had about had it with the stalling. Reagan had on October 11 appointed him chief salesman for that plan. The longer the weeks and months dragged on, the dimmer the plan's bleak remaining prospects would get, the longer the MNF might stay in Lebanon, and the greater the likelihood that some lightning bolt would derail diplomacy entirely. "I do not believe," he wrote, "that we can allow the situation in Lebanon to fester any longer and to jeopardize our broad policy interests. . . . I do not believe we can let the problem trail off in the indecisive way which now threatens. Nor do I believe we can accept the leisurely schedule which the Israelis seem willing to contemplate."

The time had come, Habib decided, for him to get back in the saddle, analyze what each party wanted, formulate the least bad solution that everybody could live with, and then sell it to them.

On December 9, Habib and Draper had lunch with Reagan in the president's study. Habib was gloomy. He told Reagan that, while the Israelis and Lebanese had been squandering weeks and months, the situation on the ground had been deteriorating. Israel was worried that the PLO might return to Lebanon, so the IDF refused to pull out. Their refusal to pull out was convincing the Arabs that Israel really did not want peace, and thus the Arabs saw no reason to waste their time talking to Philip Habib. Palestinian extremists were gaining more influence, increasing resistance to any compromise with Israel. At the same time, the Soviet Union had begun resupplying Syria to more than make up for what it had lost to Israel in the summer fighting.

All in all, Habib felt Lebanon's prospects were getting worse each day. Time was of the essence. He had to get all foreign forces out of Lebanon now or lose the chance to get them out at all. Reagan agreed and authorized him "to tell Begin that Israel's intransigence might cost it its special relationship with America." On December 14 Habib flew to Israel, carrying a letter from Reagan to Begin emphasizing that Israel bore primary responsibility for the mess in Lebanon.

The Big Surprise

Habib felt that Lebanon's new president, Amin Gemayel, was in no position to stand up to Begin and Sharon alone. It wasn't just that his country had no clout. Lebanon's political weakness gained nothing from Amin's personal characteristics. Contemptuously nicknamed "Travolta" and "the Hairdresser," Amin was not the stuff of which leaders are made, says Ryan Crocker, the political officer in the American embassy. "That was certainly the view of his own family. It was never intended, even in the Gemayel clan, that he should be president." But with Bashir's death on September 14, Amin had suddenly found himself in that seat. Amin sincerely wanted to be a good president, says Dillon, but didn't know how. He was jealous of Bashir's success, afraid of criticism, mistrustful of anyone who had been on good terms with Bashir, and secretive. Some unqualified people, when thrust into power, recognize their limitations and surround themselves with the best advisers they can find, Crocker says. That was not Amin's approach. He "did have his little trusted entourage," says Crocker, "who were people even worse than he was."

Both Phil Habib and the Lebanese believed it was up to the US to protect Lebanon's interests. This meant, in Habib's mind, formulating a plan that would accommodate Israel's essential objectives by means that enhanced, rather than diminished, Lebanese sovereignty. For example, Begin and Sharon wanted a peace treaty in all but name as the price, payable in advance, for IDF departure. Habib envisioned no peace treaty, just a mutual declaration that the two countries were not at war and, only once the IDF was already gone, low-level talks between the two about what their future relations might be. Begin and Sharon wanted residual listening posts and patrols and surveillance pretty much wherever and however they wanted in Lebanon. Habib envisioned a complete absence of the IDF from Lebanese soil, conceding only high-altitude surveillance flights, naval patrols in international waters, and a 40-kilometer security zone along Lebanon's southern border under Lebanese government sovereignty and patrolled only by the Lebanese Armed Forces, the MNF, and some United Nations troops (UNIFIL) who were already there. Begin and Sharon wanted completely normalized relations—that is, trade relations—between the two countries. Habib envisioned letting the Lebanese decide for themselves which people and goods could enter their country from Israel.

What Habib had in mind was a departure program comparable to the Beirut evacuation, but scaled up to cover the entire country. PLO, Syrian, and Israeli forces would leave Lebanon over a period of about thirty days.

He met with the Israelis to go over his plan on the evening of Thursday, December 16. The Cabinet room in Jerusalem was packed with Begin,

Sharon, the Cabinet, and the whole Israeli foreign policy and national security establishment. On the American side were Habib, Draper, Lewis, legal adviser Alan Kreczko, and some staff. The Israelis seemed to be in a good mood. Habib started his presentation with a detailed overview of his idea of what a draft agreement might look like. Since the Israelis and Lebanese had wasted the past few months squabbling, he was proposing to step in and mediate between them. His dramatic reentry into the ring would shatter the impasse and bulldoze through an agreement for Israeli, Syrian, and PLO withdrawal quickly. Implicit or explicit in everything he said was his theme of urgency: The time had come for action, the US would not accept any more footdragging, and he expected to get everything wrapped up in a week or two.

On and on he went. The Israelis all sat listening patiently. They had few questions as he ticked off the American position on each point that the Cabinet had raised in an earlier proposal. This seemed to be going pretty well.

Two things were a little odd, though. Ordinarily the Israelis would be furiously taking notes to get down every word. Not this time. No notes. And one Israeli giggled while Habib talked.

When he finished his overview, he said that, before starting in on the specifics, he would like Begin's reaction to what he had heard so far. Begin got what Kreczko calls a big cat-who-swallowed-the-canary grin on his face and said, "Phil, I think now I'd like you to hear from Defense Minister Sharon."

Fairly bursting with delight, Sharon said, "That's all very interesting, Mr. Ambassador. But while you've been back in Washington, we have already reached an agreement with the Lebanese on how to proceed." He then pulled out three sheets of paper and said, "We're way ahead of you. We've got this working paper with the Lebanese. These are the terms of the settlement."

Forfeiting the Match

Habib was stunned. His number one rule of diplomacy was to always have the facts, and here Sharon had blindsided him.

The fact was that for the two months that the Israelis and Lebanese had been busy publicly arguing about the prospect of official talks, Sharon had been conducting authorized secret talks with a close friend of Amin's, a wealthy Lebanese businessman named Sami Marun. Habib had always had contempt for amateurs—he always pronounced the word *amateurs* with an inflection of pure scorn—trying to play diplomat in the big leagues. This epitomized why. "In the first place," Habib would later say, "Sami Marun didn't know anything and didn't speak for anybody. In the second place, the Israelis knew they had a pigeon and they obviously took advantage of him."

Habib sat in shocked silence as Sharon gleefully began reading the paper aloud. God, how he hated that man! By the time Sharon reached the end, Habib was boiling. But he was also checkmated: How could the United States oppose an agreement that Israel and an Arab state had reached? Summoning up all the self-control he could muster, he mumbled something about the United States only trying to help facilitate the process. In some of the most forlorn words he ever spoke, he asked Sharon what the next steps were. Sharon, the master of creating irreversible facts on the ground, was only too happy to tell him. Habib asked a few more questions, said he would have to hear what Amin Gemayel had to say, and ended the meeting as quickly as he could.

"The Israelis were laughing their heads off," Draper says. Sharon wouldn't even give Habib a copy of what Habib called "this goddammed piece of paper that they wormed out of Amin."

The problem was not the public humiliation. Habib was professional enough to get past that. The problem was not even the substance. In fact, much of the secret Sharon-Amin deal resembled the plan that Habib had in his pocket. The problem was that, *because of the way the deal had been reached,* none of the other parties with a stake would ever buy it. Amin Gemayel could sign whatever agreement he wanted, but an agreement is only as good as its prospects for getting accepted and implemented. In the anarchy of Lebanon, Amin's was only one of many voices that mattered. And he had no clout with anybody. Worse, Syrian president Assad and any of the Lebanese warlords were quite capable of torpedoing any deal that they felt had been dictated by Israel at gunpoint, which this one pretty much had been. Habib would have a hard enough time selling any Lebanese-Israeli agreement to them. There was zero chance they would buy a secret deal sprung on them as a fait accompli. Diplomacy is a process, a courtship, during which parties have to be wooed and persuaded and maybe even backed into a corner and bludgeoned before they'll go along. Amin had, for all practical purposes, forfeited the match before the opening whistle. Assad and the Lebanese warlords would certainly reject this deal—and thus any deal that resembled it, including the one Habib had come to push.

Screaming at the President

Once he got out of earshot of the Israelis, Habib grabbed the first phone he could find and barked, "I'm choppering up to Beirut, and I want an immediate meeting with Gemayel—alone!" Despite his fear of helicopters, he was in no mood to delay, and they were the fastest way to get to Beirut. A night's sleep and a one-hour flight did nothing to improve his mood. Once he got to the palace, he left Dillon and Kreczko out in the waiting room and strode into Amin's office with only Draper to have it out with him in private.

Through the walls Kreczko could hear Habib "screaming" at the president. "What the hell is this?!" he yelled. "You signed an agreement! You didn't tell me anything about this. What have you done?"

"This is not an agreement," Amin said, mortified that he'd been found out. "It's nothing. It's just some guidelines for the negotiations. Besides, they were supposed to remain secret!"

"Well, they were made public by Mr. Sharon."

"I didn't sign it. They wanted me to sign it, but I didn't sign it."

"What in God's name were you doing? You didn't tell us anything about it! Do you realize the position you've put me in? The way you've undercut the United States' ability to broker this?"

Amin soon asked several advisers to join him in the office. Soon Dillon and Kreczko joined them too. After a while the foreign minister, Elie Salem, arrived fresh off the plane from Washington. He came bounding in and boisterously started shaking hands all around and howdying everybody—until he suddenly noticed the somber air in the room and how hurt and withdrawn Amin looked.

"What in the name of Christ is going on?" he asked. "Who has died and was left unburied?"

Habib recounted the story, building up to "[Sharon] allowed me to talk and talk, and then you know what he said? You won't believe it! Elie, he said, 'Habib, you are not needed any more. Your mission has just ended.'" Habib, who had gotten a copy of the paper from someone since his meeting with the Israelis, then handed Salem his copy, turned to Amin, and said, "Mr. President, it seems you do not need me, good luck to you and to Sharon, I am going home."

"Calm down!" Salem shouted at Habib. "Let me read this!"

As foreign minister, Salem had known nothing about this agreement or the secret talks that had led to it. When he finished reading, he said the agreement was unacceptable in every way: Lebanon would not normalize relations with Israel, would not sign a peace treaty, and would not allow a continued IDF presence on its territory. This paper was a grave mistake, he said, and Lebanon should return to having Habib mediate with the Israelis for them.

Habib seemed relieved to hear that. Amin tried to paper over his mess by backpedalling further, which only made Salem angrier. When the president said that this was just a list of talking points, Salem said, "What talking points? We have nothing to talk about under such headings. . . . Who interjected such irresponsible thoughts into a delicate diplomatic process?" As Salem considered resigning on the spot, Amin asked him to say and do whatever he thought was necessary to bury the Sharon paper and rescue the Habib mission.

"OK," Habib said, "you boys must issue a communiqué" to counteract the story Sharon had just leaked to the press. It should emphasize that Amin had not in fact signed Sharon's paper because it was full of unacceptable provisions. They got to work on it.

Sharon had popped up to Beirut hot on Habib's heels, gotten wind of a communiqué in the works, and threatened to move his tanks to stop it. Habib stepped back and let the Lebanese deal with Sharon's threats themselves. Whereas the Israelis had made it very clear to Amin that they did not want the United States involved, the communqué that they issued— despite Sharon—said that the Lebanese would not engage in any negotiations without the Americans.

After his confrontation with Amin, Habib went back to Jerusalem to see Begin and Sharon twice on December 19. They were surprised to hear from him that Amin considered the paper only a basis for negotiations and not, as they did, a "fully agreed document." Sharon suggested that one way to overcome the difference in their interpretations of the paper's significance was to have both sides just go ahead and sign it before starting the negotiations. Habib dryly suggested that Sharon not add to the problems at this point.

Habib flew home dreading the prospect of a formal written agreement. Despite his drubbing in Jerusalem, he felt he had one last chance to head off what he considered a sure fiasco. He and Assistant Secretary Nick Veliotes met with George Shultz in California to urge the secretary to put his clout decisively behind the informal understandings approach rather than Begin and Sharon's formal written agreement approach. As Veliotes tells the story, Habib made an impassioned plea not to go along with Israel's strategy for normalizing relations because it would lead to disaster. The Arabs would punish Lebanon severely if it normalized relations with Israel. "Look," Habib said, "the only way to get the foreign forces out is in the context of these informal agreements. Let's put muscle behind this. We've got a chance something will stick." But Shultz felt that the opportunity for informal understandings had come and gone. So, Veliotes says, Shultz heard him out, made no substantive comment, and chose not to follow his advice. The three finished their discussion over lunch at a country club, then Veliotes dropped Habib off at his home in Belmont. Habib's last words to Veliotes were, "Don't let him get off the plane to Washington unless he agrees."

But, Veliotes says, "there wasn't the ghost of a chance Shultz would agree." Sharon's secret deal with Amin had changed everything: "We were boxed by the Sharon-Gemayel back channel," says Kreczko. "Phil did not favor direct talks, but there's no way an American can stand in the way of an Israeli meeting with an Arab. Once that process of Israeli-Lebanese talks started, we were stuck with it."

Sharon's secret paper thus became the basis for the official talks that, with the outlines of the formal outcome now in place, the Israelis were happy to begin.

17

Baking Stones

No force in the world can change our minds.
Israeli negotiator Avraham Tamir

As 1982 turned to 1983, Philip Habib had spent three months trying in vain to get the parties, particularly the Israelis, to hurry up. His goal was to get all foreign forces out of Lebanon as quickly as possible so Lebanon could start healing, so the MNF could go home, and so Reagan's September 1 regional peace plan could get some traction. But there was a broader, more ominous reason to hurry, which was only just starting to become apparent: The American welcome in the Middle East was wearing out fast.

Lebanese officials were certainly happy to have Habib and Morris Draper helping them cope with their occupiers. And most parties were happy to have the Marines and their MNF colleagues back on the ground in Beirut. But the two parties who had the most clout, the Israelis and the Syrians, viewed American involvement as at best a necessary evil and at worst an unnecessary evil.

The long-awaited Lebanese-Israeli direct negotiations finally began on December 28. At that first meeting, Sharon demanded that the agenda omit any mention of an American role in the talks. He wanted the Americans out because they were likely to influence the Lebanese to resist making concessions. The Lebanese insisted on having the Americans involved because, Habib wrote, they knew "they could not stand up to the Israelis and needed a shield."

Habib did not attend that opening session—or very many of the subsequent ones. Draper was the lead American in these talks. Habib avoided them.

He regarded those formal talks as an exercise in futility, the Arab expression for which is "baking stones." And indeed, after two weeks the talks had gotten precisely nowhere. So Habib went back to Begin on January 13 to say—politely but strongly—in effect, *OK, you've tried it your way, and it hasn't worked.* He then proposed to speed progress by leapfrogging over the stalled formal talks. Using his own draft plan—essentially the one he had had in his pocket the night Sharon sprang the secret paper on him—as the new starting point, he would spend a week or so intensively working out agreed wording with the Israelis. He would then take that agreed draft to Beirut and sell it to the Lebanese. The negotiators in the overt talks would be welcome to keep squabbling while he did the real work. Once he had a plan everyone agreed to, the overt talks would endorse it.

Begin and Amin both approved his approach. He wanted finality in a matter of days, not weeks, so he asked Begin to appoint a small, nimble team that could move fast and authoritatively. What he got was Arik Sharon, foreign minister Yitzhak Shamir, and a battery of aides. At their first session, January 16, Sharon demonstrated his disdain for Habib's efforts: He did most of the talking for the Israelis, and much of what he had to say consisted of reading from his formerly secret paper. He was dead set against any expanded American role like this and tried to keep the focus on the overt talks. After that first session, he headed off to Zaire for four days. So much for getting finality in a matter of days.

The Kitchen Sink

In Sharon's absence, Habib presented his draft agreement to Shamir, and Shamir presented Israel's. Habib's was bare bones. It drew heavily on earlier Israeli statements of what they required. He welcomed the Israelis to suggest "improvement or embroidery" on his draft, keeping in mind that its substance was "as much as the traffic will bear at this time."

Shamir then presented the Israeli draft as likewise representing their minimal requirements. Habib was shocked at its effrontery. It envisioned relations, as Shamir put it, like those between America and Canada. It dealt with high-level issues like security and terminating the nominal state of war. But it also specified early warning stations in southern Lebanon manned by patrolling IDF troops. Further, it went into surprising detail about trade relations, including veterinary regulations, bus services, banking, advertising, bonded warehousing, postal services, and motor vehicle licensing. As a Shamir aide read through all the provisions, Habib asked what had happened to the kitchen sink.

"This proposal is a non-starter," Habib said. It was "totally, completely and impossibly unworkable." He told the Israelis it was so "unsuitable as a basis for discussion" that he could not and would not even take it to the Lebanese.

The Israelis replied that they had to go for everything now because they would lose their leverage once they withdrew. Habib argued that, if Amin ever did agree to this, it would have "disastrous consequences" for Lebanon by shattering the fragile internal consensus on which Amin's government rested and by sparking a near-certain "total ostracism and boycott from Arab states which would destroy the Lebanese economy."

Around and around they went. The Israelis wouldn't budge. The longer they argued, the more futile Habib came to see this whole exercise. He said bluntly that if they clung to this approach, failure was certain. By reaching too far, the Israelis would end up with nothing. And Washington was not prepared for several months of negotiations just "so that Israel could get possibly one percent more than what we can produce immediately."

In hopes that "wiser heads can still prevail," he and Sam Lewis made a final appeal to Begin. "Your draft agreement is just overkill," Habib said. But Begin had not even read Habib's draft. The Israeli position was, as Habib paraphrased Sharon's words, "that I should either take the Israeli draft or leave it, that there was no alternative, that I should take it to President Gemayel and sell it."

So Habib pulled out his biggest stick. He quoted what Reagan had said in their December 9 lunch meeting, "'I am in no mood to accept delays. I have had it.' The fact is, the basic relationship between our governments is now coming to be at stake in this process."

Begin asked, "What in the world is wrong from a moral point of view in Israel asking for the essence of a peace with Lebanon?"

"There is nothing wrong from a moral point of view," Habib replied. The problem was "from a political point of view of what is possible at this moment. We cannot deal with your draft which is almost a peace treaty in all but name."

Bristling, Begin sarcastically asked him to "quit referring to the Israeli draft as if it were some kind of evil document."

There was nothing more to talk about. Habib and Lewis ended the meeting with a somber reiteration that unless Israel adopted more reasonable positions, "the fundamental relationship between our countries is headed straight for a terrible crisis."

Two days later Begin thanked Habib for his efforts, sadly unsuccessful. "Your mission is complete," he said. Israel would now return its focus to the formal negotiations with Lebanon.

Ill Will

In any given arena, any given diplomat has only so many bullets. A seasoned diplomat knows when he has shot the last one and the time has come to bow out. The successor may or may not do any better, but at least has the advantage of starting with a clean slate. Habib knew he was depleting his stock of good will back in August, which is why he did not plan to come back after the evacuation. But George Shultz felt that no one else had the gravitas to drive progress in the Middle East. "Phil was our best guy," Shultz says, so he wanted him out there as much as his health allowed and exigencies required. Habib couldn't say no.

He had returned to action in the fall with little enthusiasm for further dealings with Menachem Begin and Ariel Sharon. After what he considered a summer full of duplicity and broken promises, getting "double-crossed" about entering West Beirut, the Sabra and Shatila massacres, and then Sharon's secret deal with Amin, Habib was not at all sure he could trust them on much of anything.

They sensed that mistrust and returned it in spades. By early 1983, Lewis says, Habib had spoken his mind to the Israelis often enough that they "had come to see him as a biased, non-objective mediator. They didn't take him as seriously as they had in the earlier months."

Likewise, the Syrians for their part had denounced Habib to his face as one who "is not only not [an impartial] mediator between Syria and Israel, but is giving an advantage to Israel" through his proposals.

Attacking the mediator was, of course, nothing new in the Middle East. But Habib realized that Israeli and Syrian suspicions had begun to seriously interfere with the work. One day in Washington, he seemed unusually pensive. His secretary, Lori Bider, walked into his office and closed the door.

"You're terribly quiet today, Philip. Are you well?"

"Yes."

"What's wrong?"

"Aaaaa, I don't know."

Bider was not going to settle for a nonanswer. She stood waiting for more.

"I don't know. . . . The Arabs hate me. The Israelis hate me. I don't know. . . . I don't know. . . ."

He was not one to wallow in self-pity. This was a clear-eyed assessment of the facts. It was the facts that saddened him.

"A lot of the Israelis felt that Phil was nothing more than an Arab in disguise," says Draper. And the Syrians, says the American ambassador to Syria, "viewed Phil as 'another one of these goddam Lebanese rug merchants in diplomatic clothes coming out here to try to bamboozle us.'"

Lewis wrote that "Habib had by [early 1983], after two years of draining frustration, lost some of his professional rudder as a skilled negotiator. . . . He had lost some credibility in Israel as a mediator and was by now too openly suspicious of every Israeli move to be fully effective." Lewis says much the same about him during the summer of '82, and the people who had actually been in Beirut then with Habib strongly disagree. But even Draper and Shultz agree it was true in '83.

Only Game in Town

But Reagan and Shultz still considered him their biggest gun, and he was still determined to get all foreign forces out of Lebanon.

So despite his declining credibility, despite his belief that direct formal negotiations leading to an explicit written agreement were the wrong approach in this case, despite his disgust at the way the Israelis had handled everything, and despite his concern that Assad would scuttle any deal, Habib worked as hard as he could to produce an Israeli-Lebanese agreement. What he—and Shultz and Reagan—cared about was seeing the Israelis leave Lebanon now. Whatever would bring that about, he favored. If the Israelis agreed to leave under whatever terms, there was at least a chance Syria would leave too. If they did not agree to leave, there was zero chance Syria would. The Israelis had decided that the only thing that would pry them out of Lebanon was this agreement, so Habib worked to midwife the agreement.

Did he have profound misgivings about it? Yes. Was he deeply skeptical that it would work? Yes. Was there the slightest prospect of getting the Israelis and Syrians out by any other means? No.

These negotiations were, in short, the only game in town. Though Habib never actively opposed this venture, neither did he ever come to genuinely believe in it. He was trying to do the best he could in what he considered a disastrous situation. The one who warmly believed in it was George Shultz. Habib had tried to dissuade Shultz from this path, but Shultz was the boss, he wanted an agreement, and these negotiations were the only way to get one.

So Habib shifted his tack. He would continue with one half of his equation (his process of shuttling), even though the other half (his draft agreement) had fallen off the table. And now, rather than count on his shuttling to be the real action, he would shuttle in service to the formal negotiations. He would take on the most contentious issues and probe for the least the Israelis could settle for and the most the Lebanese could give. Beyond listening, he would read between the lines to form his own sense of what each side might bend on, urge each to yield further, and craft language to bridge the gaps.

And in February the effort did begin to pay off. The timing was apparently no coincidence. On February 8, an Israeli panel appointed to investigate the Sabra and Shatila massacre, the Kahan Commission, released its report. It concluded that Ariel Sharon "bears personal responsibility" for "these blunders," for having "disregard of the danger of a massacre," and for failing to take any meaningful measures to prevent one. "In the circumstances that prevailed after Bashir's assassination," the commission said, "no prophetic powers were required to know that concrete danger of acts of slaughter existed." It recommended that Begin fire him. Within a week, he resigned as defense minister.

With Sharon off of the negotiation's steering committee, the Israelis started showing their first glimmers of moderation and of genuine compromise. But he remained in the Cabinet as a very vocal and influential minister without portfolio. So those glimmers never brightened enough to warm the negotiations significantly.

The Next Patrol

Sharon's departure from the defense ministry also did little to improve relations between Israeli soldiers and the American Marines in Beirut. As bad as American-Israeli tensions were on the diplomatic and political fronts, they were even worse on the military front.

As the months had rolled by and the MNF's second-round stay had been extended from sixty days to indefinite, the Lebanese civil war had resumed with a vengeance all around them. Operating as a calming force in the context of a civil war, the Marines relied heavily on the only weapon they really had, their neutrality. And the Marines did not want the perception of their neutrality compromised by appearing too chummy with the Israelis. As Habib put it, "We did not wish to bless the IDF presence by mingling MNF and IDF troops." So the less the Marines had to do with the IDF, the better they liked it.

But the territory that the Marines were responsible for was adjacent to territory that the Israelis occupied. The Marines insisted that the Israelis stay out of their areas of operations. But in January 1983 the IDF began a practice of wandering into American sectors. "It was absolutely continuous," says Colonel Jim Mead, commander of the American Marines on the ground. "On a daily basis the Israelis went wherever the hell they wanted to go." Dillon calls the practice "the Israelis' sense of humor. They liked nothing better than to take a tank column into American lines and then later say that it was all a mistake. . . . They had a great contempt for the Americans."

It wasn't just that the trespassing offended the Marines' sense of territoriality and threatened their image of neutrality. It was also that the intruding Israeli patrols practiced "reconnaissance by fire": driving tanks and jeeps and armored personnel carriers around shooting for no apparent reason at groves of trees, open fields, vacant buildings, whatever. Stray IDF rounds would land on Marine positions. That was a danger the Marines could not countenance.

The tensions took a dramatic turn on February 2. Six IDF tanks tried to break through a joint US-Lebanese checkpoint. Fearing that the intrusion might spark a firefight between the IDF and the Lebanese, Marine Captain Chuck Johnson planted himself in the center of the road. The lead tank stopped six inches away. "You will not pass through this position," said Johnson. The tank officer got out, talked with him, then climbed back aboard and said he was going through. "You'll have to kill me first," Johnson said, aiming his pistol at the officer. While the astonished officer labored to comprehend a pistol challenging a tank, two other IDF tanks revved their engines and sprinted around him. Johnson then jumped up onto the lead tank, grabbed the officer, and demanded that he order the other tanks to stop.

They did. So did the practice of tank intrusions after that episode. But patrol intrusions continued unabated.

In mid-March, Habib heard from the Israelis that Colonel Mead was threatening to shoot their soldiers. For months Habib had paid little attention to the military issues on the ground. But as soon as he got wind of Mead's threat, he stormed out to the Marines' command post at the airport to head off a US-Israeli clash.

Through his second-floor window, Mead and some other officers watched Habib's motorcade screech to a halt and Habib pop out and come charging up the circular staircase. "Here comes the Holy Ghost," Mead said.

He burst in the door fuming. "Hey, Colonel, what the hell is going on here?"

Mead let out a big belly laugh and said, "You're gonna have a goddam heart attack on me here, Ambassador. Would you please sit down and let me brief, and *then* chew my ass?"

"Deal."

Once he got Habib calmed down, Mead said, "Mr. Ambassador, what you've heard is bullshit. I'm now going to tell you the facts."

Mead described in detail half a dozen recent encounters between Marine and IDF patrols. He said there was one detail about the most recent incidents that, on top of everything else, had really iced it for him: Israeli patrols had started spitting on American patrols. This had happened several times within a week or two. When a staff sergeant had first told him about this, Mead had snapped, "Fine! I will personally lead the next patrol, and the first Israeli who does that, I'm taking him out!" He told Habib he had sent word of his intention to the Israelis, and that was the report Habib had heard about.

Habib was stunned. Spitting? At United States Marines?

"Goddam it, Colonel," Habib said, "you're not going to lead the next patrol. *I'm* going to lead it, and the first Israeli who does that, *I'll* take the son of a bitch out!"

Once he cooled off, Habib arranged a secret meeting in the mountains outside of Beirut between Mead and the senior Israeli officer in the area, Brigadier General Amnon Lifkin.

"The next time one of your troops comes into any one of my areas," Mead told Lifkin, "we will engage them with fire. And we will destroy them. You do understand what that means, don't you?"

"Yes. Oh, that will never happen again."

"That's bullshit, General. You've been doing it now for months and months and months. I'm just telling you what the consequence will be next time. We will not tolerate any longer the freewheeling nature of the IDF, and I'll hold *you* culpable."

The IDF had some accusations of their own against the Marines. One was raised to Washington by Israel's new defense minister, Moshe Arens: "rumors" that terrorists were obtaining American Marine uniforms in exchange for goods. Mead rolled his eyes and shook his head when he heard that one. All he could guess was that the Israelis had seen American Special Forces personnel who operated elsewhere and wore clothing similar to the Marines'.

Mead and his colleagues thought the Israelis were fine ones to impugn the Marines' discipline. From their fecal souvenirs and what the Marines considered the IDF's ill discipline and juvenile recklessness to their mendacity and the way they fought, the Israeli Defense Forces had made a consistently sour impression on the Marines. Mead says, "Before we went over there, the average Marine had a tremendous respect for what they had read about the Israeli Defense Forces as being a hard-hitting, decisive combat outfit. What we found out was that the enemy the Israelis were fighting was so bad that it wasn't difficult to be hard-hitting and decisive against them. But in basic military tactical procedures, the Israelis were incredibly lacking. Also, they would give us their word that things would go down in a certain way, but they would not honor their word. We wound up absolutely disgusted with the IDF, especially with those who had given their word. We left with no respect for them whatsoever."

Mack Sennett Comedy

Habib's life in 1983 was quite different than during the siege. Whereas during the summer of '82 he mostly stayed at Yarze, in '83 he was constantly bouncing between the various Middle Eastern capitals and even came home sometimes.

But he was still all business. He drove himself brutally to make the most of every hour. For example, after one late night marathon with the Syrians, Habib and Paganelli got back to the ambassador's residence in

Damascus around 2:30 or 3 A.M. "Wake me up at 6," Habib said, going into his room. "I have to get back to work and get the reports done." When Paganelli knocked on his door at 6, Habib was still dressed. He had never even gone to bed. His reports were all done.

He expected that same 100 percent devotion to the work from everyone around him. He had no patience for any interruptions, delays, or distractions from the business at hand. This made life exasperating for the people working with him.

For example, while the secretaries of other high-level officials would come home from trips abroad with jewelry and clothing, Habib wouldn't let Bider go shopping, even when things were quiet. He would look her in the eye and say, "You are not on a cruise. You are here on taxpayer's money." Never mind that she was working ten, twelve, even twenty-four hours a day. He let her go shopping only once. "Be back in forty-five minutes," he grumbled. That included travel time.

One day Habib and his team, which had by now expanded to three or four, were going to fly from Beirut to somewhere. "Wheels up 8 A.M." he told everyone the day before. When the security people arrived at the ambassador's residence early in the morning to pick them up, one of the team members, a Foreign Service officer named Chris Ross, was missing. Without waiting, Habib, Bider, Draper, and a security guard climbed into the armored limo and went screeching off to the airport. There they boarded Habib's military executive jet. The copilot came into the cabin and gave him an inquiring look.

"Wheels up," Habib said, as coolly as reminding a waiter that, yes, he had indeed ordered a glass of chablis.

As the plane taxied down the runway toward a takeoff, a dusty black jalopy suddenly appeared racing up alongside the sleek, shiny jet. Inside were Chris Ross and a Lebanese driver, both looking frantic. Through the small jet windows, everyone could see sweat running down the driver's face and Ross yelling "Faster, faster!" Everyone, that is, except Habib, who had seen the car but was resolutely staring straight ahead, expressionless.

"It looks like a Mack Sennett comedy," says Bider. "This vintage car is chugging its little heart out beside the plane! The door is shut. We are taxiing. Chris is looking stricken. I turn to look at Philip, and he is still looking straight ahead. I am ready to explode, 'Enough already! We've been taxiing for at least a minute with this car beside us. Either stop the goddam plane or say "take off!" ' "

By now there was not much runway left. The worried copilot popped his head back into the cabin and said, "Ambassador, there is a car alongside us. What should we do?"

Habib said nothing. "It is the longest goddammedest minute!" says Bider. "I am ready to scream, and Philip is cool and calm. Everybody else in the cabin is ready to explode."

Finally, Habib said, "Let him on."

The pilot stopped and swung the jet back around to the terminal. A rattled Chris Ross skulked aboard and tried to disappear into his seat.

"My friend," said Habib, caustically but with a twinkle in his eye, "I hope this teaches you not to keep people waiting. Next time we're taking off without you."

Dinner that evening was Bider's first chance alone with Habib to demand, "Why did you do that to Chris?"

Habib kept chewing and slicing his fish, then said, "Because this has happened more than once, and I did say takeoff was at 8 o'clock. And when I say 8 o'clock, I mean 8 o'clock."

Put You in a B Movie

Ross' reaction to the incident was typical among colleagues who ever ran afoul of Phil Habib: "This, to Phil, was the best way to teach me a badly needed lesson! He was a man I respected and loved."

Respected, yes; loved, yes. But few of his colleagues would describe him as a gracious man. "He had people working their *asses* off for him," says Dillon, "but I never saw him say thank you to any of them."

Nor did he reciprocate. For example, one night Bob and Sue Dillon were hosting a dinner party at Yarze. When the guests heard that Philip Habib was their houseguest elsewhere in the residence, they begged to meet him. Sue asked him to come out and just say hello. He declined. His heart condition was so bad—not especially on that night, but generally—that he did not want to make any unnecessary exertions. She says, "He felt that if he started meeting people and doing that sort of thing, he was going to kill himself and he wouldn't be able to do his job. I admired him because he was sick and was risking his life. Still, he was the rudest man I ever met."

Her concerns about his health were well founded. He was in terrible health throughout this mission. Sue worried about how ill he always looked and how often he would say "I'm not feeling well; I gotta go take a rest." She worried he was going to pass out. At one meal at Yarze before Christmas '82, he stopped eating, muttered that he wasn't feeling well, and slumped. A couple of men helped him walk back to his room to rest. A few months later, at a working dinner, he was holding forth in his usual gregarious way when his head suddenly jerked once and then dropped splat into his food. For a moment, everyone froze, then they all sprang up to grab him. Before anyone could reach him to help, he snapped back up. "I think he went down in English and came back up in Arabic," says Mead, "where-upon he just wiped his face off and continued the conversation. It was bizarre. We knew he was working these incredible hours and travelling all the time, and we thought, 'Aw, shit, he ain't gonna make it.'"

His cardiologist suspects those two blackouts were from a form of the heart episode that would eventually kill him.

Even though his health was much worse than in the summer, so was his gluttony. Lori Bider, who describes herself as a control freak about the vast amounts of rich food he was inhaling, tried nagging him. She tried snatching food out of his hands. She tried telling him, "Philip, you look like a bourgeois mayor in some small French village. All you need is a watch fob and chain and we could put you in a B movie!" She arranged for one of his golfing buddies back home to mention on the golf course how fat he was getting. Once, after he had boarded a plane for home, she even phoned his cardiologist's office in San Francisco and arranged for the doctor to raise his voice in advising him to diet. The next time she saw him, Habib said quietly, "Dr. Cheitlin says I weigh too much. He raised his voice at me." It didn't help.

On his airplane, he occupied four seats: The Marines turned two seats around for him to put his feet up on so the blood would not pool in his legs and clot. When his circulation was particularly poor, his face would get bluish. Sometimes Bider could get him to lie down to dictate his cables. Other times she would simply demand that he lie down to rest and stare him down until he complied. When he would get up fifteen or twenty minutes later, she would say, "You see, Philip, the world continued revolving on its axis. It doesn't need you to hold it up."

While in the region he typically got about four hours of sleep a night. Quite apart from his workaholic ways, his heart medication made sleep elusive and his back maddeningly itchy. Nobody but his younger daughter Susan had the right touch to scratch it for him. Since she was five thousand miles away, people would often walk into a room to find him rubbing up against a doorjamb to scratch between his shoulder blades.

When Habib is Scared

On this mission, says Bider, "his life was the most miserable life. Because of the security instructions, he was virtually a prisoner. I almost cried inside." In Jerusalem, he was not allowed to walk on any street or go outside the consul general's grounds. In Tel Aviv, he and his team would stay at a beach resort outside of town, but he was not allowed to go out onto the beach. He was always surrounded by security guards. He was now on the hit list of many terrorist organizations. So even when he stopped off in

Rome, his hotel would be conspicuously surrounded by the military police. It was a grim, lonely life.

Lebanese foreign minister Salem tells of a time he gave Habib a ride in his car in April '83. "My driver moved leisurely through streets in the suburbs of Beirut which Habib knew were dangerous. When he looked back and found no security car behind us, he screamed: 'Elie, do you mean to tell me that you ride in this god-damned town without a security car behind you? Do you know who is with you in this car? Do you know how many people want my head? I sure hope you are not one of them!'

"I calmed Habib down and urged the driver to speed up, which he enjoyed doing anyway. Soon Habib was uncertain which was the greater danger, a bullet in his back or a car crash. He was uncharacteristically silent until we reached the presidential palace. I learned, to my amazement, that when Habib is scared he goes silent and blank."

Even his own normal security measures could offer only so much protection. For example, one day Habib and Draper were leaving the Beirut airport to go back to Yarze. Their full-regalia motorcade headed north up the highway that separated the Marines from the Israelis. An enormous Israeli armored personnel carrier "came roaring at high speed right down the middle of the road toward us," Draper says. At the meeting point, the APC swerved toward the limousine, missing it by inches. "They seemed to be deliberately going out of their way to challenge us." He doesn't think the APC driver knew or cared that Philip Habib was in this limousine: He was just forcing a game of chicken on whoever happened to be on the road.

Travelling was less dangerous outside the Middle East, but that raised a different kind of problem: fame. Despite having been the most famous diplomat in the world for nearly two years, he wore fame uncomfortably. He loved some aspects of being famous, like mailing home newspaper articles and cartoons about himself for his scrapbooks and silently waving to the reporters and photographers tracking his every move. But he hated the one-on-one aspects of fame. When he was outside of the Middle East, he did not have his own plane—and he was instantly recognizable in airports in the US and Europe, travelling usually with one security guard and a colleague or two. The moment he noticed people nudging one another and pointing at him, he would start staring resolutely at a wall. People were forever coming up to shake his hand. He hated that. It embarrassed him terribly. He would reply politely but offer no encouragement to chat.

He had an ample ego, loved the dueling brains of negotiating, took great pride in how well he did it, and relished being a hero among Foreign Service officers. But that was all behind closed doors and within professional circles. Public recognition was distasteful. "He did not like being fawned upon," says Bider. "If you're going to go into 'I think you're terrific, I think you're marvelous,' you've lost him." Once, when a stranger came up to him and said, "Are you Philip Habib?" he replied, "No. My name is Shultz."

Another time he heard that a reporter's father had had a heart attack. Though he would rarely answer reporters' questions, he phoned the father in the hospital, told him about his own heart history, and (ironically) gave the man some advice about taking care of himself. The reporter was so appreciative that he organized a testimonial dinner to honor Habib. The only one who did not know it was a testimonial was the guest of honor. He thought he was just going to dinner. As the first speaker proceeded through his remarks about how wonderful Habib was, his expression slid from joviality to alarm. By the second speech, he was beginning to realize what was up, and his face was getting red with anger. By the third speech, Habib took the microphone and said, "The party is all over."

Pickles

Meanwhile the negotiations plodded on. And on. "There was this goddammed quibbling over the agreement," Habib said. "And I can assure you, the quibbling was unbelievable. Sharon came up with the goddammedest demands. The Israelis wanted everything. They weren't going to get it, and they knew it. Even the Lebanese couldn't give them what they wanted in this agreement." The only leverage the Lebanese had was the word *No,* and they used it constantly. The Americans believed the Israeli contentiousness was deliberate, that Sharon wanted the talks to drag on and on until the September 1 plan withered and died.

The two trickiest issues in the negotiations were mutual relations and finding a way to ensure Israel's security from attacks launched from Lebanese soil.

Mutual relations—the euphemism for *peace treaty*—largely boiled down to buying and selling one another's goods. For the Lebanese, this was "the make-or-break, life-and-death issue": Putting up with foreign troops in their midst was one thing; economic suicide for this business-savvy country was another.

Arab nations as a bloc had long boycotted trade with Israel. Habib argued incessantly with the Israelis that having a formal agreement detail the terms of normal trade relations would bring down on Lebanon's head "disastrous retaliation by Arab nations, upon whom Lebanon is totally dependent economically." Instead, he urged them to be practical, to settle for informal, de facto understandings that the other Arab states could acquiesce to. He advocated a Lebanese idea that the Lebanese just turn a blind eye to the "smuggling" of Israeli goods into the country. Then, six months after the Israelis left, they and the Lebanese would start talks on more formal economic relations.

The Israelis went along with the six-month delay idea to a surprising extent. But they were severely wary of informal understandings. Menachem Begin was, as Charlie Hill puts it, "the quintessential international legal scholar and admirer of all things legal." So the Israeli negotiators relentlessly pursued each topic in excrutiating detail. One of the lowest points in the talks came on April 21 when one Israeli negotiator strode in "with storm clouds on his face and insisted that [lead negotiator David] Kimche and the Israeli delegation pack up and leave instantly." The problem, he said, was that the Lebanese were backpedaling on four issues, including changing the name of the "Military Committee" to the "Security Arrangements Supervisory Committee."

But the absolute nadir in the months of talks, says one participant, was arguing over the pricing of Israeli pickles.

Ragamuffins

The security issue was no less thorny. There was no question that Israel had to be protected from future attacks via south Lebanon. The question was who would patrol the area to ensure that. A basic Israeli defense doctrine was that Israel should never be beholden to anyone else for their security. They certainly weren't going to entrust it to any outfit as bumbling as the Lebanese Armed Forces. They therefore insisted that the IDF have pretty much free run of south Lebanon to patrol and otherwise detect and deter would-be terrorists.

They demanded further that their Lebanese ally Major Sa'd Haddad, who ran a militia in south Lebanon, be their security partner there. They viewed Haddad as a loyal and reliable friend. The Lebanese and Syrians both viewed him as an Israeli puppet and traitor who had to go.

Habib respected Israel's legitimate security needs, but felt that their demands were "unreasonable" and "overkill." Their "obvious desire," he wrote, was to "dominate and more or less control southern Lebanon." He was particularly skeptical of their unwavering demands about Haddad. "What the Israelis really want is to do the job themselves," he said. "When they say 'Haddad,' they don't mean Haddad or even Haddad and his 1,500 ragamuffins. They mean Israeli leadership and Israeli patrols on top of that."

Habib and the Lebanese accepted the idea of a security zone in south Lebanon. But they argued that neither the IDF nor Haddad could be the ones patrolling it. They felt that was a job for international troops accompanied by the LAF. Any residual IDF or Haddad presence, they argued, was a deal breaker. First, it would eviscerate the very idea of the Lebanese government starting to exercise sovereignty over its whole territory—which was the ultimate goal everyone paid lip service to. Second, the various Lebanese factions by whose sufferance Amin held office would topple the government (such as it was) if it signed a deal leaving Israeli soldiers or Haddad patrolling Lebanon. Third, the Syrians would rightly say that the Israelis had not in fact departed, so they wouldn't either.

Begin wouldn't hear of Haddad being humiliated or neutralized. So Habib and his colleagues came up with all sorts of proposals to get rid of Haddad honorably, such as giving him some cushy civilian job in south Lebanon, just giving him an impressive title with no responsibilities, or making him Lebanon's ambassador to, oh, say, Australia.

But the Israelis and Lebanese both rejected all such compromises. Neither side would budge. By late March, the negotiations threatened to collapse over Haddad. Facing the prospect of "civil disobedience on a national scale" if Amin compromised on Haddad, the Lebanese parliament considered breaking off the negotiations entirely, going to the UN or the Soviets for help, even joining with the Syrians and PLO to fight the IDF.

In a private conversation with Draper on April 1, David Kimche, the lead Israeli negotiator, "let his hair down and ruefully acknowledged that Israel had painted itself into a corner not only on Haddad but on various security arrangements," Draper wrote. But "even if Israel had made a mistake," Kimche confided, it was a fact of life and somebody would now have to come up with "a face-saving formula" to get them out of it.

On April 14, Habib began reviewing with Amin Gemayel the various formulas about Haddad to save face all around. Amin had had enough. "You ask me to accept [Haddad]?" Amin shouted, his face reddening. "I would prefer to resign." The president whom Habib had blasted in the fall for giving away the store now blasted Habib for favoring Israel. "America has applied more pressure on Lebanon than on Israel, and we have already conceded in this agreement all that we could concede. We cannot do more. We either have the agreement in accordance with the Lebanese text, or let us not have an agreement. . . . The Israeli conditions are becoming preposterous! There must be an end to their appetite and you Americans must put your weight behind your word. We are wasting our time on silly arguments. Your method in negotiating leads us to make one concession after the other. . . . We did not expect you to be so lukewarm. . . . For the tenth time you bring up the question of Sa'd Haddad. I am tired of this issue. Haddad is our problem. He is Lebanese. I am telling you this is the last time I will permit you or anyone else to raise the Haddad issue with me. The subject is closed."

For one of the few times in his life, Habib was at a loss for words. He was visibly angry, but kept his composure. After all the Israelis' lectures at him for favoring the Lebanese, he did not need a lecture from Amin about favoring the Israelis. He had sometimes deliberately provoked the Lebanese to anger about Israeli demands so that, when he conveyed their rejection to the Israelis, he could flavor it with the appropriate drama. But this was not one of those times. He said he understood Amin's position about Haddad and would not bring it up again.

The Spectre

The Lebanese-Israeli negotiations trudged on through January, through February, through March, through April—never mind the October, November, and December preliminary arguing about even having talks. While Draper represented the US in the day-to-day working-level sessions, Habib kept up his negotiations with Begin and Amin. He also made occasional trips to brief Saudi King Fahd, Jordanian King Hussein, and Egyptian president Hosni Mubarak.

That list did not include Syrian president Hafaz al-Assad. The reasons were painful.

Though Assad was not a party to the negotiations, he was the spectre hanging over them. His troops still occupied 60 percent of Lebanon. He alone would decide whether they would leave, and he could easily crush any Lebanese government that displeased him. Since 90 percent of Lebanon's exports went out through Syria, he could also easily cripple the Lebanese economy by closing the border. So nothing that the Lebanese and Israelis might agree to would matter unless it satisfied Assad.

And Assad made it clear from the beginning that he would never swallow anything resembling the deal that they were busy negotiating. While Begin and Sharon had made it clear from the beginning that they were out for maximum payoff for their invasion, the only kind of deal Assad was willing to accept was one in which the Israelis agreed to go home now, period, in return for nothing.

Assad's absolutist position was a nonstarter. Israel's absolutist position was a nonstarter. So what do you do? Just say there's no hope and turn out the lights?

Habib and Shultz had decided at the beginning that the only sensible approach was to try. After all, it is standard procedure for parties to begin a negotiating process with unreasonable demands so they have room to back down over time and still get a reasonable agreement. Habib had argued that, since Syria's priority was to see the Israelis leave Lebanon, a reasonable deal that resulted in their departure was in Syria's best interest. If the Americans could midwife such a deal, that might be what Habib called "enough of a lever that the Syrians would accept it." Besides, there was precedent. During the siege of Beirut, Assad had refused for weeks to even consider taking PLO fighters. Draper remarks on "how astonished we had been when Assad agreed *instantly* to our final request that Syria accept PLO fighters. . . . This tended to make us hope for a similar turn-around when Israeli withdrawal became a potential reality."

Satisfying three parties is exponentially harder than satisfying two. So the American strategy was to concentrate on getting the Israelis and Lebanese to agree on a formula for Israeli withdrawal. The Americans believed that, once the Israelis agreed to go, the Syrians too would go without appreciable fuss. Most indications during the winter of '83—including Arafat's assurances that he would pull out the remaining PLO forces along with the Syrians—validated that strategy.

But it was hard to know what approach to take to satisfy Assad in the meantime. On the one hand, the Syrians kept warning the American ambassador, Bob Paganelli, "Unless we're involved, this will not work." On the other hand, Assad was certainly not going to be a party to any negotiating effort involving Israel. He wanted Habib to butt out of negotiations about Syrian withdrawal because he considered that "a matter for Syria and Lebanon to discuss directly." He had "deep distrust and suspicion" of the US as mediators and felt the US "should not try to arrogate to itself the role of intermediary" between Syria and Lebanon. As far as Assad was concerned, there really wasn't much to talk about. Over the months he and his foreign minister did little but restate the position he had articulated to Habib on October 3, that he would pull his troops out of Lebanon when his conditions had been met, and not a minute sooner.

Habib and his colleagues believed that Assad would reject anything the Americans proposed. "There was no dealing with Assad," says Charlie Hill, "because Assad understood the horrible truth that the US had no staying power and no muscle." So Habib and the State Department agreed that there was little point in trying to engage him substantively.

He could not be ignored and was not ignored. But when Habib would remind the Israelis that any terms would have to pass muster with the Syrians, they would reply, "We're not negotiating with the Syrians. Why do you keep bringing them into it?"

So the Americans decided to let the Lebanese—albeit coached, supported, and encouraged by the Americans and Saudis—handle dealings with Syria. At American urging, the Lebanese did get started on separate negotiations with Assad—and stopped, and started, and stopped. They were hesitant to tell the Syrians much about the status of the talks with Israel, because they didn't trust them. Habib said, "They feared Syria was 'lying in the weeds' in preparation to ambush the agreement."

Habib agreed with them that "the only argument which may possibly convince [the] Syrians not to sabotage [the] agreement will be assurance of total Israeli withdrawal." Until such an assurance was in sight, Habib and the Lebanese each felt Assad could be counted on only to raise objections and interfere. Assad should only be informed, not engaged, and Habib left it to them to do that.

Assad's disingenuousness was epitomized in a discussion on March 19. A month earlier he had sent a letter to Lebanon confirming that he would withdraw within the framework of an Israeli withdrawal—a major concession. On March 19, his foreign minister, Abd al-Halim Khaddam, told Lebanese foreign minister Salem "unambiguously and emphatically" that Syria had indeed dropped its earlier insistence that Israel leave first; Syria would withdraw simultaneously with Israel. Just to be sure, Salem pressed him to repeat that. "The Americans keep asking about withdrawal," Khaddam replied. "They are forcing us to play a tape for them—fine, we play it. We will withdraw, we will withdraw, we will withdraw!"

So far so good. But the kicker was Khaddam's encouragement of the Lebanese to use Syria as an excuse for not making any concessions: "Use us as a means to pressure Israel. When you reach an agreement free of concessions with Israel, come to Damascus, and in half an hour we will agree on the withdrawal of our forces from Lebanon."

An agreement free of concessions? Conquerors imposing the terms of surrender get agreements free of concessions. Weak governments like Lebanon's do not. Assad was far too shrewd a politician to imagine that there was the slightest chance Lebanon could emerge from their negotiations with anything but a long, long list of concessions.

As it turns out, he was stringing them along, for reasons that would become clear later.

Yankee, Go Home

So far, the main expressions of the fraying of America's welcome had come from the Syrian government, the Israeli government, and the Israeli army. A little after 1 P.M. on Monday, April 18, 1983, a new voice weighed in.

Habib and Draper were at the Lebanese palace going over the latest changes in the draft text of the evolving Lebanese-Israeli agreement with Amin when they heard an explosion—not an unusual event around Beirut. A Lebanese officer came into the room and said that there was a fire at the American embassy down in the city. One of Habib's first thoughts was that rumors might spread that he had died: "That would please people," he said sardonically as he dialed a phone, "and I have no intention of doing so." He called Shultz to let him know he was OK, then grumbled, "I hope he takes this as good news."

There was no point in Habib going to the embassy. His presence there would only complicate the situation, whatever it was. So he drove the half mile from the palace back to Dillon's residence at Yarze.

Draper, meanwhile, had sped off to the embassy, where his wife had been scheduled to meet him at 1. What awaited him was no mere fire. The most massive car bomb ever detonated to date had blasted away the front half of the V-shaped building. Bodies lay here and there on the ground. One hung over a balcony. Some passersby had been blown across the street into the sea. Fires shot out of holes in the building. Tear gas punched the air, as cannisters in the embassy's stock of mob control supplies exploded. Amid the jangle of rubble and smoke and tear gas, survivors coated in white dust staggered out of the hulk coughing and retching while firefighters, police, reporters, and spontaneous rescuers ran around like ants. Most of the Lebanese relief workers helped selflessly; some looted the dead. Draper's wife had been at a beauty shop a few blocks away, so she was safe. The two met and hugged in front of the shambles.

With 63 people killed, the embassy bombing was the bloodiest terrorist attack ever against an American diplomatic mission. The Iran-backed Hezbollah was apparently behind it, although it could not have been pulled off without at least acquiescence from Syria. The friendly little Palestinian porter who worked out in front of the embassy had been the lookout man. The PLO and the Druze militia had previously protected the embassy, but they were now gone and the MNF was deployed elsewhere, leaving the embassy to its own meager resources for protection.

Habib did visit the embassy the next day. The rescue efforts were still going on, and embassy political officer Ryan Crocker was helping in the round-the-clock search for bodies. Crocker had been the first American inside Sabra and Shatila as the massacres were winding down, walking around with a walkie-talkie reporting everything he saw. That had been horrible enough. But this time, the bodies being carried out were those of his colleagues and friends. The emotional trauma and exhaustion were getting to him. His team had just uncovered another body, badly mangled, and was carrying it over to a Red Cross tent when Habib walked up to him.

"Ryan, I need to talk with you about the political situation and what we need to do," Habib said.

Crocker just stared at him in disbelief. *The political situation?!* With all the self-control he could muster, he replied, "I'm pretty busy right now. We've just uncovered someone else. Maybe you'd like to see what high explosives do to the human body."

Habib just nodded, and the two of them walked over to the Red Cross tent. The corpse, its arms and legs blown off, was ravaged beyond recognition.

"Well, pretty clear from the style of underwear that this was Lebanese, not American," Crocker said numbly. "That's what we make our identifications on these days." He then walked out.

Habib followed out after him. When he caught up with him, he said in a calm, level way, "Ryan, you're the senior political officer here, and we've got some urgent things to do. I need to know what Walid Jumblatt is thinking, how the various factions are reacting, how the Lebanese leaders are positioning themselves in the aftermath of this, whether they see us as politically wounded. You're the guy who's got to get out there and do that."

Crocker couldn't argue with that. It was his job to help Habib deal with the complexities of Lebanese politics. He later said, "Phil was exactly right. The situation obviously had me pretty well at the limits of my endurance, and I probably needed somebody just to give me a shake and get me to hand over the rescue work to other people. Phil, for all his renowned temper, was so carefully controlled at a time when I was ready, just waiting. One flash of temper from him and I probably would have taken his head off."

The Cliff

By the time of the embassy bombing, Habib had long since lost any illusions of driving the negotations to a desirable outcome. Six months had passed since he started pushing to get a quick deal in a week. Thousands of hairs had been split since he had started urging informal understandings. By now he had become like a man clinging to a runaway horse and struggling just to wrestle it away from the cliff.

He was struggling also just to get the blasted thing finished. If it succeeded, it succeeded; if it failed, it failed. But nothing else of any consequence was going to happen in the greater peace process—namely Reagan's September 1 plan—until this eleven-month pregnancy bore whatever fruit it was going to bear.

But finality always seemed just around the next corner. The essential problem was that the Israelis kept their price too high and never ran out of additions and changes, while the Lebanese resisted signing what they increasingly came to regard as their death warrant.

The time had come, Habib decided, for the United States to stop simply mediating between the two and start forcing reasonable decisions. So he wrote a new draft agreement "which I believe is reasonable." It would slice the remaining issues the Lebanese way. The Israelis would not like it. In fact, he said it would inevitably spark a public confrontation between the US and Israel. But he proposed to Washington that the Lebanese present it, then the United States powerfully "escalate the level of persuasion" on the Israelis by sending Secretary of State George Shultz out to press them to accept it.

And for one of the few times since the days of Al Haig, Habib did not get the State Department's blessing. Shultz was indeed already planning to come join him, but did "not wish to be injected into a situation where there is an already structured and highly visible confrontation with Israel." Even if a confrontation later developed, Shultz wanted to at least walk in the door "as a mediator." So State instructed Habib to hold off on his plans.

A visit by Shultz had been in the wind for well over a month. Shultz had written to Reagan in early March that "always a key question in negotiating with Israel is whether they will give the last concession to the negotiator or hold it in order to give it to a more senior official, such as the Secretary of State or even the President." By early April, it was clear to ambassador to Israel Sam Lewis that "the Israelis are only going to give the final agreement to the Secretary."

So on April 25, Shultz arrived in the Middle East to help conclude the agreement. Within the US government, he had long been the venture's strongest advocate. He considered this agreement a priority and was anxious to get a diplomatic success nailed down. He had put off a visit as long as he could "as a deliberate effort to give Phil as much centrality in it all as possible." But, knowing that the Israelis paid any on-the-scene negotiator a fraction of the attention they paid the secretary of state or the president, and with Habib's stock in Israel sinking lower and lower, Shultz finally concluded that Habib and Draper "needed an extra oar."

With Habib by his side, Shultz took over his role of shuttling back and forth between the Israelis and the Lebanese, probing for give, and trying to bridge gaps. After a week and a half of revisions and counter-revisions, Shultz told the Israelis, "The cabinet should accept or reject the agreement *as it now stands.* The negotiations should not, and cannot, go on without end."

After all the months of haggling, hearing that from the secretary of state made the difference. The next day, May 6, the Israeli Cabinet accepted the agreement in principle. The Lebanese, by now strung out far beyond the red lines they had repeatedly redrawn, held their noses and joined the Israelis in signing it on May 17, 1983. Draper signed for the United States as a witness. Habib did not attend the ceremonies.

Run Out My String

Habib had no illusions about the deal's prospects. "By the time the negotiations were finished," he said, "they weren't worth the paper they were written on, because they obviously couldn't be implemented." As if there weren't

305

enough aspects of the agreement itself for Syria to object to, at the last minute the Israelis added a side letter that said Israel would not be obliged to withdraw its troops until Syria and the PLO withdrew first. That gave Assad a veto over the whole agreement. When Shultz and Habib briefed him on the agreement, Assad said nothing until Shultz reached the point about Israeli withdrawal being contingent on prior Syrian and PLO withdrawal. "Would you repeat that?" Assad said. Shultz repeated it. Assad slapped the arms of his chair and said, "This agreement will never be implemented!" His veto rang with resounding finality. The logic was devastatingly simple: The Syrians refused to leave, so the Israelis wouldn't leave, so the Lebanese had nothing to show for their trouble except the thick coating of dust settling on their two now-permanent occupiers. Everyone had wasted seven months baking stones.

Shultz had believed all along that Saudi pressure was the key to getting Syria to withdraw. And he and Habib hoped Assad's posture was tactical and that he would change his mind. But neither Saudi nor American efforts to influence him were any match for Assad's implacable opposition.

The day after the signing, May 18, Assad announced that Philip Habib was no longer welcome in Syria "because we have nothing to discuss with him, and especially because he is one of the most hostile American officials to the Arabs and their causes." In declaring him persona non grata, Assad cited not only the May 17 agreement but also the June 11, 1982, ceasefire—the one in the first week of the invasion that Sharon had used as cover while continuing to advance on the Syrians and then clobber them—which he had always blamed on Habib. "I don't think it was that he didn't want to deal with *me,*" Habib said; "I think he was just unhappy with what we were doing and this was his way of demonstrating his unhappiness. I came home and said to the president and secretary of state, 'You've got to get a new boy. I've lasted longer than most in those circumstances, but I've run out my string."

But Shultz was not ready to lose him quite yet. So Habib dutifully made the rounds trying to drum up support for the agreement. But between meetings, he sadly confided to Ryan Crocker that "it simply wasn't going to fly." It was too one-sided for the Muslim Lebanese, the Syrians, or anyone else with a direct stake to swallow. Without access to the player who now mattered most, Syria, Habib had little productive business to do.

The last straw, apparently, came in mid-July. National Security Adviser Bill Clark sent his deputy, Robert McFarlane, on a secret three-day trip to the Middle East to determine whether Assad, having rejected Habib, would do business with McFarlane. Assad of course welcomed the prospect of replacing Habib with a newcomer who knew next to nothing about the swamp he would be stepping into. On his trip McFarlane met with

Assad, the Lebanese, and Saudi King Fahd. Neither Shultz, Habib, nor the American ambassadors in those countries had known anything about McFarlane's trip. When they did learn about it after the fact, Shultz and Habib were outraged that the NSC staff was usurping their functions.

Habib saw no further point in going on and resigned. Reagan announced his departure—and McFarlane's appointment as his successor—on July 22.

Three days later, Shultz says, "I went to the White House and resigned. I said to the president, 'You can't do this to me and you can't do this to Phil Habib. You have totally undermined him by sending McFarlane out there this way. It's one thing to send him with all of us agreeing and with the parties he's visiting all knowing. But to do this behind our backs is an impossibility. You don't need me for secretary of state if this is the way things are going to be conducted. And I don't want to be secretary of state.'" Reagan was visibly shaken. He apparently had known nothing about the back channel, declined Shultz' resignation, and said this would not happen again.

Shultz stayed. McFarlane stayed. Habib went home.

Charade

Few diplomatic efforts of recent decades have attracted as much uniform scorn as the stillborn May 17 agreement. The consensus of the critics is that it was a losing proposition from the get-go and that it's a wonder any-one could have been naïve enough to believe it would ever work.

Which is pretty much what Habib had been saying all along. He took no comfort in having been proven right. Assistant Secretary of State for Near Eastern Affairs Nick Veliotes says, "The May 17 agreement was a charade that we were put through by the Israelis. Phil Habib knew very well that the only kind of agreement that had any hope of lasting was a series of informal but real agreements acquiesced in by the Syrians. That was the policy he had tried to implement. The Arabs were never going to support the equivalent of a treaty with Israel. So Phil knew this wasn't going to work. But he was a pro, so he made the best of a bad situation. The utter failure of the May 17 agreement was a tribute to Phil Habib's fore-sight."

Habib's own assessment was less charitable. "I did my best to help, but I failed."

Assad's rejection could hardly have surprised anyone. Other than the temporary softening of his condition that withdrawal could not be simulta-neous, all of his other conditions—unworkable as they were—held consis-tently from beginning to end. Habib and Shultz had always *hoped* Assad would see reason and play ball, but they never had solid assurances he would. They had proceeded anyway because they felt their only alternative to likely failure was certain failure.

In the end, it probably didn't matter how engaged Assad was or what the terms of the agreement were. Habib had suspected that "Syria could be opposed to any agreement whatsoever."

With the benefit of hindsight, something he rarely indulged, Habib would say, "The Syrians, in my opinion, led the Lebanese down the garden trail. And, I suppose, to a certain extent, therefore led us down the garden trail. But why? Because meanwhile they're buying time, rebuilding their forces. Before February, that same agreement might have held. But by March or April of '83, the Syrian forces had basically been rebuilt. Different circumstances. It was like night and day."

That would account for Syria's lethal obstinance. What would account for Israel's? It may have been a genuine belief that they could get their way in a vacuum. But Menachem Begin and Ariel Sharon were not naïve men. It may have been they too were buying time, in their case until the September 1 plan died of neglect. That was certainly the effect. But perhaps the surest explanation is that Israel, like Syria, never cared as much about seeing the other guy leave Lebanon as they did about preserving their own prerogatives there. Begin and Sharon felt they had little to lose by trying and—who knew?—maybe they'd get lucky. A prospective gain is easier to lose than what you already have.

"One of the problems in the Middle East," says Alan Kreczko, "is that whoever gets the upper hand tends to try to overplay it. And the Israelis definitely tried to overplay their hand in Lebanon. Had they been willing to settle for a quick, simple agreement, they might've walked away from Lebanon with something."

Speculation

Characteristically, Habib left without a word to the press. In later years, he remained certain that he could have gotten a better agreement had Sharon's secret deal with Amin not set the baseline for everything that followed. He was proud of having kept it from becoming a peace treaty and of having kept "some really silly things out" of it. "We put a lot of pressure on the Israelis to get an agreement which the Lebanese said they could accept. Could we have put more pressure? Yes, I suppose we could have. *Would* we have? I doubt it."

He summarized his two years of Middle East work generally this way: "We had minor successes and major failures. The minor successes were that we stopped the mass killing in the summer of '82. The city of Beirut would have been totally destroyed. I got the Medal of Freedom because I saved the city of Beirut from destruction. Of course, a year later the Lebanese were out destroying it themselves!

"But at least we did some useful and helpful things. We had good intentions. We had the right policy. I have no doubt that our policy direction and concepts—restoring a Lebanese entity and getting the foreign forces out—were fundamentals that were correct and will stand up to any kind of scrutiny.

"Now, whether we could have done more to bring them about, that's a matter of debate. What we could have done, how it would have worked, under what circumstances—that's all a kind of speculation that a lot of people love to go into who've not had any responsibility. The journalists love that kind of bullshit. It doesn't impress me. And writers, academics, people who love to speculate—if we'd done this, or we'd done that, or 'Did you recognize the signs?'—it's all a lot of bullshit."

18
Denouement

Pessimists are merely onlookers: It is the
optimists who change the world.
François Guizot

Any vestigial hope of the May 17 agreement ever taking hold evaporated in late August 1983. While the Israelis had been stringing out the negotiations for months, the Lebanese civil war had been heating back up to full boil. In fact, it got worse than it had been before the Israeli invasion. This was due in part to Assad's determination to punish Amin's government by stirring up trouble through his allies and proxies in Lebanon. Not coincidentally, the IDF troops occupying much of Lebanon were smack in the middle of the hottest spots. With IDF casualties mounting, the Israelis suddenly pulled out of the dangerous areas down into southern Lebanon.

With that unilateral partial withdrawal, there was suddenly no longer any bargaining chip to persuade the Syrians to leave. The Israelis and Syrians were now permanent occupiers, having effectively partitioned Lebanon into an Israeli zone in the south and a Syrian zone most everywhere else.

The IDF's departure from one particular area, the Shouf mountains overlooking the Beirut airport, left a vacuum quickly filled by a Druze militia allied with Syria. Right below the Druze guns were the American Marines stationed at the airport. The Marines had been training the LAF for over six months. The idea was that, the more capable the LAF became, the less need there would be for either the MNF or the IDF to stay in Lebanon. But, though the LAF was the country's official army and was officially non-partisan, it was in fact made up mostly of Maronite Christians. So the Druze regarded the LAF as just a partisan prop for the government's dominant faction, the Maronite Christians. Since the Marines were supporting the LAF, the Druze reasoned, then they too were enemies. As that perception increased, so did fire at the Marines from the Druze and other factions.

Robert McFarlane, Habib's successor and a former Marine, was alarmed at the deteriorating situation. He was particularly horrified by a September 10 Druze attack on the LAF in the town of Suq-al-Gharb, in which the LAF

310

commander was hacked to pieces with an axe. In what would come to be called "the sky-is-falling" cable, McFarlane persuaded the White House on September 11 to order naval artillery fire and air strikes to support the LAF. With the Americans now shelling Druze positions in the Shouf in support of the LAF, the Marines lost their only real asset, their neutrality. They were now seen as full partisan participants in the civil war, and the attacks on them by various factions increased even more.

Then at 6:22 A.M. Sunday, October 23, the driver of a yellow Mercedes Benz stakebed truck crammed full of explosives barreled through the Marines' perimeter defenses at the airport, crashed into the central lobby of their headquarters building, and set off the largest non-nuclear explosion on record to that point. The blast killed 241 Marines and wounded another 100. At nearly the same moment, a similar truck bomb exploded at the French MNF headquarters, killing 58.

Reagan came under increasing pressure to pull the Marines out of Lebanon. For over three months he refused, but on February 7, 1984, he finally agreed to bring them home.

Years later, Phil Habib was still angry at how McFarlane had handled things as his successor. All Habib would say about the bombing of the Marines was "It did not happen on my watch, baby!"

Here is what became of Habib, Arafat, Begin, Sharon, Lebanon, and the Israeli role in Lebanon in the eighteen years following Habib's resignation.

The Invasion's Legacy

Israel's 1982 invasion of Lebanon was one of Israel's most thoroughly planned military campaigns ever. It was also the most ambitious, the most personal, the longest, the most one-sided, the least popular, and the least successful—against the weakest of its enemies. It was, in short, as Morrie Draper put it, "one of the most colossal blunders in Israel's history." Three years later, even Menachem Begin said, "I cannot stand it anymore—the consequences of this tragedy." It is often referred to as Israel's Vietnam. Whereas Israelis have always celebrated their many military successes, they have generally tried to forget this fiasco like a bad former marriage.

Nonetheless, the end of the siege of Beirut in August 1982 did mark a turning point, on several fronts. The siege did succeed in ending the PLO's career as a serious violent threat to Israel. But as Phil Habib said, "If you don't like the PLO, take a look at the alternatives." Virtually unnoticed during the summer of '82 was the arrival in Lebanon of 300-500 Iranian revolutionaries sent to resist the Israeli invasion. This group formed the nucleus of what came to be called Hezbollah. Before long Hezbollah would take the PLO's place as the ones shooting rockets from southern Lebanon into northern Israel. In the seventeen years following the invasion, an average of 25 Israeli soldiers a year would be killed fighting Hezbollah in southern Lebanon (not to mention the unknown number of Lebanese, Palestinians, and others who died in the fighting). Israel would even launch a mini-invasion of Lebanon in 1996—an eerie microcosm of its 1982 invasion—in a vain effort to halt shelling by Hezbollah.

Thus the 1982 invasion, in effect, replaced one terrorist threat with another.

Sharon also accomplished the opposite of his own equally important goal of destroying the PLO as a political factor. He had expected that, by destroying an organization called the PLO, he would destroy an idea called the Palestinian movement. He did neither. By neutralizing the PLO as a violent force, he left them no option but to transform themselves into a political force. Eleven years later, with Hezbollah and another terrorist group called Hamas having picked up where the PLO left off, Israel would officially recognize the PLO as the representative of the Palestinian people and cede territory to it.

Not only did the invasion fail to force the Syrians out of Lebanon, but Syria was by all accounts the long-term winner of the war. Whereas Sharon and Begin had hoped that Bashir Gemayel would be Israel's puppet in Lebanon, one of Sharon's successors as Israeli defense minister described Lebanon in 1999 as a "puppet state" controlled by Syria.

The siege changed Israel's reputation by undermining its claim to the moral high ground. No longer could a simplistic good-guys-versus-bad-guys analysis hold. Whereas for years the Israelis had condemned the reprehensible tactics of PLO terrorists, the nightly news in the summer of 1982 had shown Israeli tactics that millions considered at least equally reprehensible. No longer would "brave little Israel" be thought of as David confronting Goliath. Israel now *was* Goliath. As one Israeli scholar wrote, "the epitaph to be placed upon the war in Lebanon will read: Here lies the international stature and moral integrity of a wonderful people."

The south Lebanon "security zone" that Sharon and Begin had demanded did become a reality, though it offered Israel little that could be called security. IDF troops patrolled it for eighteen years until Israeli prime minister Ehud Barak unilaterally pulled the plug on their occupation in May 2000. It was hard to say what they had accomplished in that time, other than skirmishing endlessly with Hezbollah. Israelis had long since come to view the whole exercise as a pointless waste of lives. By the time Barak undid the security zone, as many as 1,550 Israeli soldiers had died there. In bringing the troops home, Barak declared "This 18-year tragedy is over."

Denouement

Lebanon

No one knows how many people died in the Israeli invasion of Lebanon. Estimates range from 12,000 to 30,000 dead and from 30,000 to 40,000 wounded, including more than 650 Israeli soldiers.

Lebanon plunged further into chaos and civil war. Amin Gemayel's main accomplishment as president was managing to stay in office until his term ended in 1988. After two more chaotic years, in 1990, the government enacted political reforms recommended by the Arab League that gave Muslims more representation in the government. The civil war ended a few months later. Lebanon remained a launching point for terrorist attacks on Israel, despite the presence of IDF troops in a security zone in southern Lebanon. Syria remains the dominant player in Lebanese affairs.

Menachem Begin

Menachem Begin left office a broken man, devastated by the death of his wife and by how badly his Lebanon effort had turned out. He announced his resignation—"I cannot go on any longer"—on August 29, 1983, five weeks after Habib's resignation and simultaneous with Israel's decision to withdraw down into southern Lebanon. He was seen in public only once after he left office. He died in 1992.

Yasir Arafat

Yasir Arafat, his fighting capability devastated by the siege of Beirut, transformed himself from a guerrilla leader into a political leader—and, in Israel's view, back again. In 1993 he and representatives of Israeli prime minister Yitzhak Rabin secretly negotiated mutual recognition in Oslo, Norway. Arafat and Rabin shook hands on the White House lawn in 1993 and signed the Oslo Peace Accords, for which they shared the 1994 Nobel Peace Prize. Under those accords, Arafat became president of the Palestinian Authority in charge of the Gaza Strip and portions of the West Bank. At Camp David in 2000 he rejected the most generous peace offer Israel ever made. When a cycle of violence sparked by Ariel Sharon began a few months later, Arafat was accused of encouraging it or at least failing to rein it in. His rejection and the violence all but killed the Oslo peace process.

Ariel Sharon

Though a political outcast in the eyes of many Israelis for his debacle in Lebanon, Ariel Sharon remained in the Israeli Cabinet. In the 1980s and

'90s he was minister of industry and trade, minister of housing and construction, and minister of national infrastructures.

In 1991 an Israeli newspaper published an article that said, in part, "Menachem Begin knew very well that Sharon had deceived him" about "this disastrous and unnecessary war" in Lebanon. Sharon sued for libel. Begin's son Benny testified for the defense that his father had explicitly told him that Sharon had misled him. An Israeli judge agreed in November 1997, finding the evidence conclusive that Sharon had indeed done so. The judge wrote that "Menachem Begin knew . . . that Sharon had not dealt with him honestly, and had taken advantage of his trust." The judge rejected Sharon's contention that he had done nothing without Begin's and the Cabinet's blessing. He concluded that, while Begin and the Cabinet had approved the limited 40-kilometer operation that Begin declared originally, they had not granted Sharon permission to wage an all-out war in Lebanon. Sharon, the judge found, had deceitfully gone ahead with his own unapproved and far more ambitious plan. Sharon denied doing any such thing and vowed to appeal to Israel's supreme court.

At the time of the ruling, Sharon was minister of national infrastructures in the government of Prime Minister Benjamin Netanyahu, whom he had helped win election. Despite the ruling, Netanyahu made Sharon his foreign minister a year after the verdict. In a surreal denouement unimaginable during the siege, Foreign Minister Sharon and Palestinian Authority President Arafat met with American president Bill Clinton at Wye River Plantation, Maryland, in October 1998 to negotiate the Wye Peace Accord. Sharon refused to shake Arafat's hand.

In May 1999, Netanyahu lost to Labor Party leader Ehud Barak and returned to private life. Leadership of the Likud Party fell to Sharon. On September 28, 2000, Sharon made a well-publicized and highly provocative visit to Jerusalem's Temple Mount, venerated by Jews as the site of the second temple and by Muslims as the spot from which Muhammad ascended into heaven. The site is dominated by the al-Aqsa mosque, administered by Muslims, and off-limits to Jews because of rabbinical rulings. Palestinians immediately began rioting to protest Sharon's visit. The riots continued and grew until they took on a life of their own. In the next four months, this second *intifada* resulted in some 400 deaths, stopped the Israeli-Palestinian peace process dead in its tracks, and convinced many Israelis that the Palestinians did not really want peace, only blood. They thus lost confidence in Barak, who had staked his career on making peace with the Palestinians. In a desperate gambit to resuscitate his administration, Barak resigned to force early elections that would pit him against Likud leader Sharon, who was considered unelectable.

But Barak underestimated how disillusioned Israelis were with him

314

and his failed peace efforts. On February 7, 2001, Ariel Sharon was elected prime minister of Israel.

His first year in office was dominated by an ever-spiraling cycle of violence between Israelis and Palestinians. Sharon declared Arafat "irrelevant" to peace efforts and had him under virtual house arrest in the West Bank city of Ramallah. Harking back to the evacuation from Beirut in 1982, Sharon said just before the one-year anniversary of his election, "There was an agreement in Lebanon not to liquidate Yasir Arafat. Actually, I am sorry that we did not liquidate him."

Philip Habib

Habib ended his Middle East mission as one of the best-known names in diplomacy. After resigning in July 1983, he made a living serving on the boards of various companies and giving speeches. After having earned only modest government salaries his whole life and nothing for his Middle East work, he enjoyed finally making some good money. He had no secretary and didn't answer his mail. "If somebody's serious about wanting me, they can call me. I'm here. I'm in the book."

He relished his fame—Johnny Carson joked to an unruly audience, "If you don't calm down, I will have to send Philip Habib up there"—but was extremely selective about giving interviews. He gave a few oral histories and interviews with a handful of academics, journalists, and authors. On the day one journalist visited him at his home in December 1983, a major news story that had been brewing in the Middle East came to a head. "I've had fifty requests for interviews in the past month," he said. *"New York Times,* the newsweeklies, the networks, everybody. I won't talk to them. They'd just ask what's my reaction to whatever the hell is going on in the Middle East at the moment. All they want to do is run ten seconds of it on the evening news. That's not serious. I'm a serious man. That's not serious." When that journalist asked whether he was enjoying the rest or missed the action, he said how busy he was but added, "Sure, you miss the big leagues." Showing the visitor his garden, he pointed to a seven-foot tall rose bush and said, "I've spent the past two days pruning roses," then added dryly, "that's pretty meaningful work, isn't it?"

He showed off the tokens of his long career on his walls and shelves: photos of himself with every president and secretary of state and key diplomat of the prior twenty years, newspaper editorial cartoons of himself, awards, certificates, medals. His Medal of Freedom was too ostentatious to put out in view, so he kept it in its fine wooden box on a closet shelf. His only souvenirs of Beirut were a few sets of worry beads on the coffee tables and a wicked-looking four-inch-long piece of shrapnel on a bookshelf.

He was plenty proud of these tokens of his past, but that was the problem: They were all about his past. There was no prospect of new missions, new assignments, new problems to solve. He was wanted by all sorts of people but was no longer needed. When he wasn't on the road doing something to stay busy, he would get bored and depressed.

He kept an office in the State Department and showed up from time to time. Shultz liked having him around to bounce ideas off of, particularly in 1985, when Shultz got a "feeling that the world was shifting gears" and that the US needed to make sense of it all.

In 1986 Shultz sent him to Manila to prepare to persuade Reagan to drop his support of Ferdinand Marcos after the latter tried to steal the February 1986 election from Corazon Aquino. Immediately following that brief mission, Shultz made Habib the US special envoy to Central America. For a year and a half he worked to produce a diplomatic solution to the region's conflicts, but the White House was committed to a military solution via its clients, the Nicaraguan Contras. Though he was instrumental in the development of Oscar Arias' peace plan, he eventually resigned in disgust over the White House's resistance to a diplomatic solution. Appendix C tells the story of his Manila and Central American missions.

Back in the exile of retirement, Habib's spirits and health spiraled down. He loved life as lustily as ever, but he had less to live for. He went with Shultz to the Middle East in 1988, but the trip accomplished little. George Bush, who took over the White House in January 1989, considered Habib "a mentor" from the days when he reported to Habib in the mid-'70s. "I loved the guy. . . . [He was] one of my friends and heroes." But the new president's State Department had no need of him. He felt discarded. "Things in the Dept. are no longer concerning me as in the past," he wrote to an old friend in 1989. "Not that I couldn't give them some good advice, mind you—but they seldom ask." His cardiologist and friend Dr. Mel Cheitlin said, "He always did well when he was running around, but he moped around a lot when he was not getting called."

Phil Habib moping would be considered hyperactivity in most other people. He was constantly traveling to give speeches, receive awards, visit friends, play golf, and attend conferences and meetings of the various business and charitable boards on which he served. But he considered all of that "nothing that is truly socially redeeming. But it makes me feel as if I'm doing something." His Foreign Service career was over, and that was what he cared the most about.

During his Central America mission his heart had started acting up again. Chest pains—angina—had returned in October 1986. He had gotten up to 205 pounds. In January 1987 he was walking back to his room after giving a speech in Paris when he suddenly broke out in a drenching sweat, became lightheaded, and nearly fainted. He had to be hospitalized overnight. By August 1988 his heart was failing badly, and before the year was out he had his second open heart operation. He never again felt really healthy. Angina returned in 1989. He was hospitalized for gallstones, slept badly, looked depressed, and felt he was running out of steam. After another heart attack in 1990, he felt terrible. He lost his appetite—but would binge on pistachio nuts and then have trouble breathing.

In April 1992 he and Marge attended his fifty-year reunion of the University of Idaho class of 1942. He had loved those reunions, in part because he was always the star attraction. In May he seemed to have gout in his ankle and was walking with a cane. He wrote to a friend on May 18 that he was about to go give a talk at the Bilderberg conference in Evian, France. "I still can get around. Not too well, but good enough to keep going. My condition does not improve but it doesn't worsen significantly. . . . I have a number of trips to various places scheduled over the next few months and then I think I will hang up my travelling shoes. I find it harder and harder to live at hotels and spend my time with strangers instead of staying at home and watching the flowers grow. On the other hand, I still have itchy feet."

A week later he gave his talk at the Bilderberg conference and visited with Henry Kissinger, David Rockefeller, and other old friends and colleagues. He then connected up with an old French friend, Yves LeGouar. In the forty years they had known each other, Habib and LeGouar each had always suspected the other of being an intelligence agent, so all they had ever talked about was food and wine. On this visit, LeGouar drove him to Pouligny Montrachet in Burgundy, 150 miles southeast of Paris, for a few days of winetasting and visiting vineyards. They dined that evening on one of Habib's favorite meals: escargots, coq au vin, and a bottle of light Burgundy.

At breakfast with LeGouar in his hotel the next morning, May 25, Habib was in good spirits. He even ordered eggs, despite their being bad for his heart. Another friend was due to join them for their outing, but was late. At 9 o'clock Habib said he'd wait in his room. When the friend arrived at 9:15, LeGouar phoned Habib's room. There was no answer. He went up to the room and knocked on the door. Still no answer. Worried, LeGouar summoned the hotel manager, who forced the door open. Inside they found Habib motionless. They carried him to the bed and tried CPR while the latecoming friend called an ambulance, but it was no use. He had had a cardiac arrhythmia, similar to what had made him pass out in Yarze in '83, but too prolonged this time to snap out of. The electrical impulses in his heart had gone haywire, making it beat faster and faster until it could no longer do its job. At seventy-two, almost thirty years after his first heart attack, Philip Habib was dead.

Flags flew at half-mast at American embassies around the world. *The New York Times* noted his death on the front page. The *Times* and *The Washington Post* both ran op-ed pieces honoring him. Marjorie Habib got cards and letters from hundreds of his friends, colleagues, strangers, prime ministers, presidents, and kings. George Shultz, Henry Kissinger, and Cyrus Vance gave eulogies. In time the ambassador's residence in South Korea was named Habib House. The East Asian Bureau at State dedicated its conference room in his name. And at the consul general's residence in Jerusalem, Secretary of State Warren Christopher dedicated the garden that Habib had designed during the siege as the Philip Habib Memorial Rose Garden.

Not bad for a boy from Brooklyn.

Habib had wanted to be buried in the military cemetery in Colma, California, half an hour north of his Belmont home. But it was full. The next closest military cemetery with space was in Oregon. Marjorie Habib mentioned that to Tom Miller, one of Phil's protégés. Next thing she knew, a space inexplicably became available. "How did you do that?" she asked. "You learn a lot when you work for Phil Habib," Miller said. He had called the head of military cemeteries in the United States and said, "Philip Habib wanted to be buried there. What can you do?" The director called Colma and told them to find a spot. They did.

It is odd that Habib chose to lie in a military cemetery. His military service had been the one portion of his life that he utterly hated, yet "Capt US Army World War II" is the only particular of his life etched into his white marble marker. But he considered service to the United States government the highest calling, and only military cemeteries honor government service. It also placed him a mile from San Francisco Airport, beneath the flight path of the jets that he had seemed to spend half his life on.

It was an odd choice also because he had always been the standout: the Gentile growing up in a neighborhood of Jews. The Brooklynite at forestry school in Idaho. The big-nosed guy with the Arabic name entering a Foreign Service full of blueblood WASPs. The specialist in thankless, impossible assignments. Yet here he was beneath one of thousands of identical white marble markers in perfectly straight rows. Only one thing stood out. No grass had ever grown under his peripatetic feet, and, while it typically takes two or three weeks for the grass over a grave to grow back to normal, it took more than two years to grow back over the bellowing diplomat's. He would have liked that.

The Foreign Service had been Philip Habib's art, his mistress, his religion, his life. So this was, in a sense, the second time his life had ended. The first was the day in 1980 that he officially retired from the Foreign Service. What he said that day would suit this one: "Some lifetimes are worth living. My only regret is I can't start it all over again."

318

Appendices

Appendix A
The Greatest Career

When one of his many protégés, Richard Holbrooke, decided to leave the Foreign Service to work in the Peace Corps, Philip Habib strongly disapproved. On December 23, 1970, while working in the Paris Peace Talks, Habib wrote him a letter that crystalizes his passion for the Foreign Service.

1970
Dec 23

Dear Dick,

As you can see from the color of the paper, I am taking away precious time from pressing duties to write to you. I keep putting it off because I want to do it right this time. Once and for all I am going to advise you—and then you can go on and make your own mistakes. If I did not think you were worth it, I would not even try. But somehow, some way you must be reachable on the subject of the Foreign Service and your future in it.

First of all, the Foreign Service isn't merely the *next* assignment. It isn't only whether it can offer younger FSOs a challenging assignment. It's all the assignments and all the frustrations, and all the excitement of a lifelong *career*. It's also the cumulation of experiences and associations—not just one. The other foreign affairs agencies can't hold a candle to the role of the State Dept.—and their personnel can't compare to the true FSO—and you know it. That doesn't mean that I object to FSOs working for another agency—I don't. I do believe in an integrated FS of the U.S. But I do believe that the basic training in Foreign Affairs that you get in the regular service—as against training only in Foreign Operations—makes our career development at the lower levels all the more important.

For the young FSO, the problem is not how many lousy assignments he may get. For the bright ones—and you know you are one of the brightest—it's a question of picking the spot and going for it. By picking the spot I don't necessarily mean where but what.

The curse of the F.S. is not really bigness. As you recognize, it is an elite group. We are not going to lose out to the other agencies—because part of that small elite group is made up of people like you, and Peter [Tarnoff] & Frank [Wisner].

There are enough good jobs for the FSOs. And you can get one of them. Just decide what you want—and be sensible. Then tell me, and tell a few others who can do something about it—or at least try. Just what kind of a next assignment do you really want—and in what general area? If I go to a post before next summer, you know that you can come along if you want to. But you won't be DCM [deputy chief of mission, the number two job in an embassy]. And you won't be special assistant. But you will get a chance to really work and you will be listened to. It may only be a piece of the world but it will be your piece. And if it isn't all that you want it to be, then just wait a couple of years and change—but meanwhile get everything out of it that you can. One thing is for sure, being DCM in a post that is a shambles, with 6 agencies working at cross purposes (which you recognize can happen) isn't the same as being number 3 in the political section of a properly unified US mission, with the right leadership, where people down below do know what is going on.

Now, that [names of two colleagues] comparison is really not up to your standards. I meant to shock you and obviously did. What I meant was, Don't try to be the perennial special assistant—and I was afraid you were susceptible to that. If not, o.k. I accept your concern about the usefulness and challenges of a career. But I do not accept your desire that career services must be so prescient as to provide for perfect sequences of assignment. We have to help it do that. I am willing to help if you will give me the chance. So what do you want—maybe even a couple of alternatives. Then let us see what can be done. Don't walk out on us. It's still the greatest career around. . . .

Best,
Phil

Appendix B
Basis for Mistrust

During the siege of Beirut, Philip Habib found that the Israelis' actions repeatedly failed to match their words. Here is a sampling of the kinds of instances that led him to that conclusion.

Date	Israeli statements	Facts on the ground
June 6-8	Begin assures Habib that invasion is a limited action meant to go only 40 km and to take only about 48 hours, that actions beyond 40 km are only temporary	Sharon's troops already beyond 40 km, that limit soon forgotten; Gen. Eitan later says he was never instructed to conduct a war limited to anything like 40 km or 48 hours
June 13	Begin promises Habib "a most positive approach" to humanitarian programs for Lebanon	IDF repeatedly obstructs relief efforts in June and July
June 14	Begin says Israel has no intention of going to Beirut or Baabda (site of palace)	IDF troops are already in Beirut, IDF tanks are already ringing palace in Baabda
June 14-July 5	Sharon repeatedly says he'll remove equipment and troops from Baabda and Yarze	IDF equipment and troops remain in Baabda and Yarze
June 15	Israeli Cabinet this morning is unanimously determined to maintain calm and a ceasefire with Syria; no hint at meeting that any moves against Syrians are even being considered.	IDF commander gives ultimatum to Syrians to clear out of Baabda area by noon or he'll follow orders to clear them out
June 22	Begin accepts ceasefire and 5-km pullback	Sharon tells Habib no pullback

Appendix B: Basis for Mistrust

Date	Israeli statements	Facts on the ground
July 5	Begin orders power and water turned on and IDF off of checkpoints	Next day power and water still off, IDF still blocking checkpoints
July 30	Begin tells Habib he'll consider restoring supplies to West Beirut	IDF tightens blockade
July 31	Begin agrees to ceasefire in place	Next day Sharon launches most massive attack so far
August 1	Begin agrees to ceasefire in place	IDF advances next day beyond ceasefire lines, takes over airport
August 2	Begin orders water turned back on	IDF leaves water off
August 2	Sharon says IDF not moving at all	Habib reports tanks "moving all over the place" to improve positions in vicinity of airport
August 11	Israel says it would let one of Habib's intermediaries travel to Damascus	IDF refuses to let the intermediary pass

Appendix C
Habib's Last Two Missions

Anyone who knows Phil should know that if you name
him special negotiator, he is going to try his darnedest
to negotiate an agreement. Unfortunately, there were
many around who did not know him well.
Friend of Habib's

Philippines

On February 9, 1986, George Shultz interrupted Philip Habib's golf game
in Florida with a phone call: Might he be willing to take on a special assignment? An election in the Philippines two days earlier had gone quite
sour, and the country was being torn apart. Philippine president Ferdinand
Marcos—whose regime had grown increasingly corrupt, dictatorial, and
brutal—had called a snap election to bolster his plummeting credibility.
His opponent was Corazon "Cory" Aquino, the charismatic widow of an
opposition leader whose assassination Marcos' top general was widely suspected of having ordered. Every indication was that Aquino had trounced
Marcos at the polls—every indication, that is, except the official count,
which Marcos controlled. He was clearly trying to steal the election. Only
Ronald Reagan had the clout to convince him that his time was up. Would
Habib go to Manila as Reagan's special envoy?

You betcha.

Habib knew Marcos well from his two years as assistant secretary of
state for East Asian affairs in the 1970s and considered him a phony and a
crook. "He's doomed by his own faults," Habib told Shultz, "but he won't
go easily. There are no flies on Marcos: he's a smart guy."

Shultz and most other key figures in the administration had already
concluded that Marcos had to go. The problem was that, despite their advice and despite the overwhelming evidence of election fraud by Marcos,
Reagan was loathe to cut him loose. The US had supported the staunchly
anti-communist Marcos for over twenty years, and Reagan viewed him as
America's strongest ally anywhere. Reagan was haunted by the disastrous
consequences flowing from America's botched handling of the departure

of another longtime ally, the shah of Iran, eight years earlier. So, though Reagan was the only one who *could* give Marcos the push out, he did not want to be the one to give that push. While he recognized that the election was messy, he thought Aquino should be a good sport and give in. His refusal to recognize Aquino as the real winner convinced her followers that the great champion of democracy didn't really care about clean elections after all.

Marcos and Aquino both claimed victory, and neither was about to back down. Her supporters poured into the streets to protest his theft of the election and demand his resignation. A violent showdown loomed. Aquino's supporters protested peacefully, but communist insurgents were poised to inject violence, which the government would surely use as a pretext for a brutal crackdown. If Marcos did not admit defeat and leave peacefully, the chances were high for a bloody revolution.

Habib, characteristically, said nothing to the press, even as the press and other observers widely misinterpreted his mission. Viewed as Reagan's initiative, his mission appeared to some as a cynical effort to buy time, a dunderheaded effort to find out what the Filipino people really wanted (as though they had not already made that clear), or a naïve effort to arrange some sort of Marcos-Aquino coalition government. To one Filipino columnist, Habib was a "deodorant" for Reagan's "stink[ing]" policy of supporting Marcos. But his mission was really Shultz' initiative, intended to change Reagan's mind. Shultz believed the best prospect of changing Reagan's mind—and thus of changing Marcos' mind, and thus of lancing the boil in Manila—was to have Phil Habib go assess the situation there personally so he could come back and tell Reagan personally that Marcos was finished.

While the bogus vote count dragged on, Habib headed off to Manila on February 13. Marcos hurriedly arranged to get himself declared the winner before Habib arrived. Habib spent six days talking with Marcos and Aquino themselves, their running mates, poll watchers, and various leaders of the Catholic church, the business community, the expatriate American community, and the military. Despite speculation in the press that he had come to pressure one side or the other to do this or that, he explained to each that his purpose was not to second-guess the election, but to understand what lay ahead. Specifically, he wanted to know whether Marcos could continue to govern and whether Aquino could sustain her movement long enough to prevail. He asked a lot of questions and said rather little.

One of his interviewees, a sugar magnate, was a close friend of Marcos. The president had personally phoned him to ask him to go tell Habib some negative things about the opposition and what fine reforms Marcos was initiating. The businessman dutifully read Habib the report he was supposed to give, then candidly told him what he really thought: "Marcos can't govern, can't change, won't leave. . . . Marcos will attempt to ride out the storm peacefully. He views the U.S. as troublesome children easily bluffed—handled with a minor concession when the heat gets too much."

That assessment closely matched Habib's own observations. In their two meetings, Marcos made every effort to appear presidential, to talk about the economy and national security, and to brush aside the revolution howling outside his window with vague assurances of reforms he would soon put in motion.

Habib was unimpressed. He thought Marcos was isolated, looked "horrible," and refused "to realize that he faces a widespread movement to dump him." He respectfully but firmly reiterated questions Marcos had ducked, parried his dubious assertions, and steered him back to the issues at hand. For example, Marcos had told him in their first meeting that he was remaking his Cabinet: In their final meeting, Habib asked what progress he had made. When Marcos said he hoped Reagan had no doubts that he could handle the crisis, Habib replied that the question was whether Filipinos believed he could. When Marcos mentioned his reform idea of selling off some state-owned corporations, Habib said it sounded like "trying to persuade someone to buy all the losers." When Marcos mentioned that some business people had come around to supporting him late in the campaign, Habib asked if others were still holding back because they did not consider the election credible. When Marcos mentioned a problem with the nation's money supply lately, Habib asked if that was not a result of how much government money he had spent on the election. When Marcos accused the opposition of fraud and blamed the press for victimizing him, Habib pointed out that the press reports were reinforced by those of American, Filipino, and international poll watchers.

Habib phoned Shultz on February 19 to give his mid-point assessment: "The dominant view here is that Marcos is finished, but it will have to be the U.S. that gives him the boot. Marcos doesn't have the strength, will, or ability to do what's needed to govern effectively." Shultz was anxious for Reagan to hear that from Habib directly.

By the time Habib got back to Washington to meet with Shultz and Reagan on February 23, Manila was poised for an explosion. Marcos' defense minister and acting chief of staff had joined the opposition, called on Marcos to resign, and holed up in the defense ministry. Troops loyal to Marcos were advancing on them in tanks. Crowds were fighting the troops back with sticks. Marcos was expected to send in gunships and artillery within hours.

As he sat down with Shultz and Habib in the White House Situation Room, Reagan was troubled. Habib told him what he had observed and heard and concluded. The upshot was unmistakable, but Reagan's chief of staff, Don Regan, objected. *We must not abandon Marcos like we abandoned the shah,* he maintained. The meeting quickly became "a verbal brawl" between Habib and Don Regan. In the end, Habib repeated his case against Marcos and then said bluntly, "The Marcos era has ended."

Silence.

After one last nudge from Shultz, the president gave in. He authorized a message to Marcos that it was time to make a peaceful transition from power.

The American ambassador in Manila, Stephen Bosworth, gave Marcos that message. Marcos had said earlier he would not give up unless Reagan directly urged him to accept a dignified transition from power. But, while he cared deeply what Ronald Reagan thought, he had little confidence in the authenticity of what anyone else—Stephen Bosworth, Philip Habib, George Shultz—said on Reagan's behalf. The only American he did trust to speak for the president was Senator Paul Laxalt. A close personal friend of Reagan's, Laxalt had represented him to Marcos before. He was in fact the one who had persuaded Marcos on Reagan's behalf to call the election in the first place.

The next day, February 24, Shultz and Habib were in a secret room at the Capitol briefing thirty key members of Congress, including Laxalt, when the phone rang. It was Ferdinand Marcos, calling for Laxalt. *Was that message from the White House calling for a peaceful transition genuinely from the president?* Marcos asked. *Yes, it was,* the senator assured him. After conferring with Reagan, Laxalt talked with Marcos again later. *Does Reagan want me to resign?* Marcos asked. Laxalt said that wasn't for him to say. *What do you think I should do?* Marcos asked. "Cut and cut cleanly," Laxalt replied. "The time has come."

After an excruciatingly long pause, Marcos said, "I am so very, very disappointed," and hung up. Within the next sixteen hours he staged a face-saving inauguration for himself and then boarded an American Air Force plane for exile in Hawaii.

Marcos was out. Aquino was in. The crisis was over.

Central America

As soon as Habib completed his Manila mission, Shultz and Reagan had another assignment for him: special envoy to Central America. This assignment would put him on a collision course with Reagan and the hardliners in Washington who advised and influenced Reagan.

The whole region was in an uproar. The linchpin was Nicaragua. Revolutionaries called the Sandinistas had taken over Nicaragua in 1979 and set up a Marxist regime. Now the US was sponsoring a new wave of rebels called the Contras trying to oust the Sandinistas. The fighting directly hurt the neighboring democracies—El Salvador, Honduras, Guatemala, and Costa Rica, which the US called "the Core Four"—in several ways. First, the Contras operated in part from bases in the surrounding countries. Second, hundreds of thousands of Nicaraguans had fled the fighting, usually to the surrounding countries. Third, the Sandinistas tried to export their revolution to their neighbors. Moreover, El Salvador and Guatemala had their own nasty guerrilla wars going on. Altogether, over 100,000 Central Americans had been killed and 4 million made refugees in seven years of aimless fighting.

Habib was parachuting into the middle of not just the crisis of the hour, but the administration's longest running forest fire. Indeed, *The New York Times* called the 1980s Washington's "Nicaragua Decade." As the National Security Archives puts it, "During the Reagan era, Nicaragua became the subject of more Executive Branch deliberations, more covert plots, more presidential speeches, more newspaper coverage, more congressional debate and more citizens' protest than any other foreign policy issue."

Whereas in 1982 nobody in Washington had any idea what to do about Lebanon, everybody in Washington knew what to do about Nicaragua. At least everybody had an opinion, often with a fervor bordering on the religious. And whereas during the siege of Beirut disarray in Washington had left it up to Habib to make most of the key decisions, disarray in Washington now made him just one more voice—and not the loudest. The loudest and most fervent voices were those of the hardline Cold Warriors, including ideologues to the right of Ronald Reagan.

The president and the hardliners viewed Nicaragua under the Sandinistas as a Soviet beachhead in America's own back yard. They considered it "a mortal threat to the entire New World" that had "launched a campaign to subvert and topple its democratic neighbors." Unless the US could roll back the Sandinista revolution, Reagan said, "the malignancy in Managua" would become "a second Cuba . . . right on the doorstep of the United States." His dedication to ousting the Sandinistas was variously called "a moral crusade" and "an eschatological issue." He was therefore passionately devoted to the Nicaraguan Contras. He called them "the moral equivalent of our founding fathers."

Certain that nothing would ever convince the Sandinistas to negotiate in good faith or stand for fair elections, the hardliners saw the Contras as the only means of getting rid of the Sandinistas and thus as the solution to the region's problems. They also saw to it that the Contras were well funded by the US treasury. The Contras could not carry on the fight—indeed, could not exist, in many people's view—without US funding. Though the Contras did keep up pressure on the Sandinistas, by the time of Habib's appointment they had little else to show for their five years of struggle and the hundreds of millions of US dollars. They had more ammunition than room to store it all, yet they could not fight effectively. Even staunch supporter Robert McFarlane called the Contra leaders "well-meaning, patriotic but inept Coca-Cola bottlers. . . . They just cannot hack it on the battlefield." Though hardliners were sure the Contras would ultimately prevail if given enough money, Congress was losing patience with the Contras' high bills and modest results.

So the timing of Habib's March 1986 appointment was no coincidence. Reagan had a request on the table for another $100 million in Contra aid, but no real diplomatic effort going. He needed one—not because he had much interest in diplomacy going anywhere, but for show, to lend an appearance of balance to his military effort. Having just played a high-profile role in ending the Philippines crisis, Philip Habib was again on top of the world. "'Habib can do anything,' was the aura around him," says Shultz. "He had the confidence of the president and me and of the Congress." Who better to represent a diplomatic track to supplement Reagan's military track?

But as far as the hardliners were concerned, says Peter Kornbluh of the National Security Archives, "the whole point of the diplomatic track was to elicit support from Congress for Contra aid." Reagan made no secret of his gameplan of using Habib's appointment as leverage to persuade a skeptical Congress to approve his $100 million Contra aid request: "Ambassador Habib's efforts to achieve a diplomatic solution must be accompanied by an increasing level of pressure on the Nicaraguan communists," he said. "What we are asking Congress for is the tools so that Amb. Habib can do his job."

The question was what his job was. George Shultz genuinely wanted Habib to make serious diplomatic headway. Ronald Reagan and the hardliners did not. They wanted him to just string out visible diplomatic busywork while the Contras did the real work. Habib later told a friend that Reagan "was totally uninterested" in his diplomatic efforts. At least once he went to the White House to get instructions on what he was to do on a trip to Central America, but Reagan spent most of their time telling stories about the old days. When Habib returned to report on what he had done, Reagan spent their time rehearsing how they would stand at the press conference that would follow their meeting.

Reagan's wan support notwithstanding, Phil Habib was no more capable of busywork now for Reagan than he had been for Al Haig when the Israelis invaded Lebanon. He promptly set about throwing himself into the effort with his characteristic gusto, studying the issues and conferring with State's country experts and with all the key players in Latin America. Two typical days:

April 18	6:30	A.M.	Picked up by State Dept. car & driver
	8	A.M.	Depart Andrews Air Force Base
	11:25	A.M.	Arrive Guatemala
	12:30	P.M.	Meeting with President Cerezo
	3:30	P.M.	Depart Guatemala
	4	P.M.	Arrive El Salvador
	7	P.M.	Dinner with President Duarte
April 19	8:30	A.M.	Depart El Salvador
	9:05	A.M.	Arrive Tegucigalpa, Honduras
	10	A.M.	Meeting with President Azcona
	12	P.M.	Depart Tegucigalpa
	1	P.M.	Arrive San José, Costa Rica

The last day of that particular trip was far from typical. On April 28 he and three colleagues were flying home in his fourteen-seat Gulfstream executive jet. It would fly so high that the sky was black, because it was at the threshold of space. They were cruising 43,000 feet above the Gulf of Mexico when the plane suddenly started shaking violently and dropping from the sky like a stone. A nervous steward phoned the pilot to find out what was going on. No answer. The plane kept shaking as it zipped down through layer after layer of clouds. Out the large windows Habib and the others could see the sun setting as they hurtled closer and closer to the water. The steward tried the phone again. "Don't bother us!" a pilot snapped. "We're busy!"

After a harrowing eternity, the shaking finally stopped. At around 14,000 feet the plane leveled out. It seemed to be flying normally again. A few minutes later, a pilot came back and said a bird had shattered the outer windshield. Habib and his colleagues wobbled into the cabin for a look. The inner windshield was fine, but the outer one looked smashed and splattered with blood and feathers. But they had been miles higher than birds fly. As it turned out, a short circuit in the heating element of an anti-fogging device had melted the outer windshield. Fearing an imminent loss of cabin pressure, the pilots had made a textbook emergency dive to a safe altitude, plunging about five miles in about five minutes. The combination of melting glass and freezing winds produced the illusion of blood and feathers. The inner windshield held, and the plane landed safely.

The ordeal on the plane was over in a few minutes. But the ordeal Habib was returning to in Washington was just warming up.

While his agenda was diplomacy, Washington hardliners' agenda was to keep the Contras fighting. As one of them put it, "We needed a plausible negotiating track. We did not realize he would view it as his role to achieve

330

a treaty this spring or summer." So while Habib was busy working toward a negotiated outcome, says Shultz, "the hard right in Washington deeply distrusted such negotiations, resented Habib's appointment, and sabotaged his efforts."

Prominent among the hardliners was the official to whom Habib ostensibly reported, Assistant Secretary of State for Inter-American Affairs Elliott Abrams. Abrams' views were harsher than Shultz', but congruent with Reagan's. Habib and Abrams were in conflict from day one. "Phil abhorred Elliott Abrams and everything he stood for," said one colleague. At one meeting early on, they had what one participant calls "an almost theological discussion" about the nature of the problems in Central America and what the US should do about them. Though the two took great pains to be civil—they were meeting with Shultz—each would disagree with whatever the other one said. It was as though conceding any premise the other stated would lead to some conclusion that the first could not accept.

Not long after that meeting, Habib began grousing that Abrams was opposing him at every turn. For example, in the first month of his mission, Habib met with a few members of Congress to brief them on US policy. One of his points was that, if the Central Americans reached a peace agreement that forbade outside aid to guerrillas, the political reality was that the US would have to cut off aid to the Contras at that point. The congressmen asked him to put that in writing. So Habib asked John Hamilton of State's Bureau of Inter-American Affairs to draft a letter summarizing the US position. Sent over Habib's signature, the letter said US aid to the Contras would end "from the date of signature" of a verifiable agreement by all five Central American nations.

Habib and Hamilton both said the letter was just a restatement of existing policy, not a shift in policy. But aspiring presidential candidate Representative Jack Kemp jumped on the word *signature*. He accused Habib of planning to "sell out" the Contras and demanded that Reagan fire him. Kemp wrote that Habib, "with misplaced faith in the omnipotence of diplomacy, would have us walk away from the democratic resistance for the false promises of an unenforceable treaty." *The National Review* agreed that "Habib's blunder" warranted his removal. The conservative *Washington Times* newspaper dismissed Habib as "an agreement machine" and quoted Representative Robert Dornan saying "Habib knows nothing about the 'contras.' He thinks everything can be solved by a piece of paper."

Habib could easily ignore criticism from sources like that. Kemp, after all, was positioning himself as the preeminent anti-communist for the 1988 campaign. But Habib was livid that Abrams had said the letter "was in error. . . . I'd just change the word 'signature' to 'implementation.'" Habib felt Abrams was taking potshots at his reputation by criticizing him for a letter that both Abrams and the NSC had approved in advance. Hardly any document of any consequence ever leaves the State Department without several approvals. "We got the letter cleared around the department and interagency-wise," Hamilton says. "Everybody who probably [agreed with calls for Habib's sacking] cleared the letter. Some of them later didn't *remember* clearing it, but they did." Habib said Abrams had "played a nasty, dirty game. I didn't speak to him for a while."

Habib agreed with the hardliners that the US should fund the Contras. But he valued the military pressure that the Contras put on the Sandinistas as "an indispensable element . . . *at the service of* an active diplomacy." In other words, he felt the purpose of the Contras was to drive the Sandinistas to the negotiating table, where he could work out a settlement that everybody could live with. Therein lay the difference between him and the hardliners. While he viewed the Contras' military pressure as a means to a diplomatic end, the hardliners saw his diplomacy as a means to a military end. The Contras could not fight without US funding, and Congress would not approve more funding unless the administration had a parallel diplomatic track. It served the hardliners' purposes for the famous Philip Habib to go through a diplomatic charade to placate Congress so Congress would keep funding the Contras. But the last thing they wanted was for him to do any real diplomacy. The problem with Habib, Abrams said, was that he failed to "realize that he was just a symbol" and had the temerity to act "as a negotiator" who "wanted to get something negotiated." The hardliners believed the Sandinistas had to be defeated militarily, period. Any negotiated settlement, they felt, would be a mirage. Just as Ariel Sharon had been certain in 1982 that this supposedly naïve bleeding-heart diplomat would get duped by the PLO, so were the Washington hardliners now certain he would get duped by the Sandinistas. Both were certain that their enemies would either never negotiate in good faith or never honor any agreements they made.

Almost as quickly as he found opponents in Washington, Habib found an ally in Central America. A month before Habib's appointment, an earnest and soft-spoken young legislator named Oscar Arias Sánchez had been elected president of Costa Rica. He had campaigned on a promise of regional peace. Regardless of what Habib's appointment meant to Washington, it signaled to Arias that the time was ripe for a diplomatic breakthrough. Yes, Washington had sent other special envoys to Central America before, "but not with his status," says Arias, "not with his prestige. He was Philip Habib! He was almost of the same rank with George Shultz."

When Habib and Arias each came on the scene in early '86, the only diplomatic effort of any consequence was an international initiative led by Mexico. Called the Contadora Plan, it had been on the table for three years.

Habib spent much of his time trying to give it some oomph, but it attracted far more argument than agreement. By mid-1986 it barely had a pulse.

Once Arias decided that Contadora had run out of gas, he started thinking about a regional peace plan of his own. Whereas the Contadora plan had been mostly about detailed military issues, Arias' plan would be mostly about democratization. And, whereas Contadora had been the initiative of outsiders, Arias' plan would be home brewed. He went off to the beach alone for a few days in early January 1987 to write it.

In addition to being earnest and soft-spoken, Oscar Arias was strong willed and fiercely committed to his plan. He declined to attend any summit of Central American presidents unless his plan was the only one on the table. And when he met with the Pope to elicit his support, Arias said, "Excuse me, but we have only thirty minutes, and you need to listen to me." He then held the floor for the next twenty-five minutes.

His plan called for immediate ceasefires throughout the region, talks between the various opposing forces, a prohibition on the use of one country's soil as a base for rebel attacks on another, amnesty for the Contras, an end to external military aid to rebels, and free elections.

The Arias peace plan drew immediate opposition. Among the Core Four, Honduras and El Salvador had deep reservations about it. The first time the Salvadoran president and generals discussed the plan with Arias, they agreed to only one line in the prologue and had what Arias calls "an encyclopedia of doubts" about the rest. In Washington, the hardliners felt the plan boiled down to pulling the plug on the Contras in exchange for an empty promise of elections in Nicaragua. They variously ignored, scorned, and opposed Arias' plan. Reagan tepidly said he "welcomed" it, but treated it as a distraction. He and Abrams were willing only to humor Arias, certain that once his plan failed, they could use its failure as leverage for more Contra aid.

But Philip Habib did something remarkable: He took the Arias plan seriously. He treated it as the new agenda, the starting point for discussions. While the hardliners set about trying to scuttle the plan by obstructing and discrediting Arias, Habib set about helping him strengthen the plan so it would work. Arias says, "The members of the Reagan administration were very critical of me, of my ideas, ideals, goals. They were all obsessed with a military solution for the conflict in Nicaragua. They always thought that I was very naive, utopian, foolish. The exception was Philip Habib. He supported me from the very beginning. The difference between him and [the hardliners] is that he got to know me and he trusted me. He knew about my democratic convictions and that I really did want to get rid of the Sandinistas. He was my best ally at the highest levels. But he was trying to accomplish a diplomatic solution on behalf of an administration that was counting on a military solution."

That is not to say Habib was enamored of the Arias plan. He was not, at least not at first. He thought it was riddled with holes. He wanted it to succeed, but feared that its weaknesses would doom it. Having seen how easily Ariel Sharon could skirt stronger deals than this one, Habib worried that the Sandinistas would "take minimal cosmetic steps to appease Arias and Congressional and international opinion until contra aid is halted" and then revert to their old ways. So time and again he told Arias, "This plan of yours has no teeth." In fact, Habib had *more* arguments with the plan than anyone else, Arias says, "because he really dealt with it *in depth*. He slept with the plan under his pillow. The others had never studied it. No one else was really interested in trying to improve it and to look at the loopholes."

Habib's main contribution to the content of the plan proved crucial: specifying that almost all of the plan's main provisions would happen at the same time, within ninety days of signing. Without that simultaneity, Arias says, the process would take forever with everybody insisting that the other guy move first.

Arias says that once he accepted Habib's advice about making events simultaneous, "Philip Habib became *my* ambassador to the rest of the Central American presidents, because he believed in the peace plan. It was *our* peace plan. He always claimed it did not have enough teeth, but in the end he defended it." His support made the critical difference, Arias says. "Philip Habib sold the peace plan to my colleagues. He helped me more than anyone else."

Habib's selling of the Arias plan consisted less of commending it to the presidents of El Salvador, Honduras, and Guatemala than of showing them that he took it seriously and was looking for a way to make it work. That message came through loud and clear to them. For a century, the United States had, as one historian puts it, "dominated the area at will." Now the special envoy of the United States—and a special envoy with the stature of Philip Habib, no less—treated a home-brewed peace plan as the basis of discussions. That made a deep impression on the region's presidents.

It made an equally deep impression on the hardliners in Washington. They urged Reagan to fire him for all the attention he was giving the Arias plan.

The five Central American presidents—including Nicaragua's Daniel Ortega—planned to hold a summit meeting in the summer of '87 to discuss and vote on the Arias plan. Their vote could well set the tone around the region for years to come. Would the five presidents all endorse the plan? Would Nicaragua be the sole hold-out? Habib could accept either of those outcomes. His worry was that Honduras and El Salvador would refuse to sign the plan because of its defects while Nicaragua cynically signed it with no intention of honoring it. The Core Four would then be split and negotiations might drag on for months or years. He expected that that was precisely Nicaragua's objective.

So he spent the winter and spring pressing the Core Four presidents to consult closely, resolve their differences about the plan, and coordinate tactics in advance of their summit. He urged Arias to make the changes necessary to satisfy the US, El Salvador, Honduras, and Guatemala. But Arias jealously guarded his plan against any changes he considered unwise. He feared the presidents would end up debating security issues interminably instead of focusing on democratization. He also felt that, if he accepted changes from the other Core Four presidents, he would have to accept changes from Nicaragua too. So all through the spring, he refused to make many of the changes that Habib and the other Core Four presidents urged.

Habib understood Arias' reasoning, but felt strongly that the wiser course was to make the revisions. "[Arias] doesn't want to change a thing in his plan," he told Shultz. "The Democrats in Congress tell him it's perfect. It isn't. Some of it is crazy. Parts of it don't make sense, like how you get a ceasefire." Scarred by his own experience with ceasefires in Lebanon, Habib knew all too well how complicated, subjective, and ephemeral they could be. And having been scarred by the May 17 agreement, he had little appetite for a plan that could not be implemented. "No agreement is better than a weak agreement," he said.

By mid-June, Habib had made six trips to Central America since Arias announced his plan in January. His message on each trip had been the same: Resolve your differences, and revise the plan. Arias had revised it to the extent he considered appropriate, but, in Habib's view, not nearly enough. By the end of his sixth trip, Habib was frustrated. He saw no point in further travel, feeling that "there is little else I can do in the region at this time." He could now only wait and see whether the Central American presidents would pay more heed to his advice.

They did. In late July, Arias personally visited each of the other Central American presidents, including Ortega, to confer about the plan and to make sure each was still committed to attending the summit. He revised the draft much more on the basis of these face-to-face conversations than he had before.

While all of this had been going on, Washington had been bathing in scandal. Hardliners in Reagan's National Security Council had been caught carrying support for the Contras to astonishing lengths. Congress had forbidden further funding of the Contras. Undeterred, renegades in the NSC had arranged various forms of illegal covert funding. Most notably, they had violated US restrictions by secretly selling weapons to Iran and then shunting the proceeds to the Contras. Congressional hearings into the Iran-Contra scandal, as the episode had come to be known, made household names of the people involved, such as Oliver North, John Poindexter, Robert McFarlane, and Elliott Abrams.

"What a bunch of cowboys!" Habib muttered when he learned of their work. Their illegalities, bungling, and lying earned them his most withering insult: "Goddam amateurs." This had all happened during his time as special envoy to Central America, and he "would rail against this stuff," says one colleague. "He'd just absolutely go crazy. He'd say these things were done outside of channels, that Ollie North and his crowd ignored the experts who really knew Central America, and that people who could have raised red flags were cut out. Elliott, Ollie North and his crowd—don't get Phil started about them. You'd cause a heart attack."

Habib remained devoted to George Shultz, but his respect for Ronald Reagan and the rest of the administration had plummeted. He had previously said "the president is determined . . . to get a satisfactory diplomatic solution," but the Arias peace plan had had the effect of calling Reagan's bluff. Habib could no longer escape the conclusion that, regardless of what he and Shultz might hope to accomplish, "Reagan didn't want to make peace." The administration had used his prestige for their own ends and repaid him with grief. With Reagan uninterested in anything but the Contras and opposed to the Arias peace plan, hardliners sniping at him and Arias constantly, and the NSC running amok, Phil Habib had had about all he could stomach. "He always blamed that football player, what's-his-name [Jack Kemp], for convincing Reagan that what Philip was doing was wrong," says Marjorie Habib. Since at least mid-June he had been feeling that his position had become untenable. On June 16 he confided to the Senate Foreign Relations Committee that "my job at the moment is to convince you that the Administration is not altogether stupid about this [Arias plan] negotiation."

Shultz had also about had it with the hijacking of foreign policy by the NSC. On July 23 and 24, Shultz testified in Congress' Iran-Contra hearings that, as *Time* put it, "he and his department had been humiliated, betrayed and ignored, cut out of some of the Reagan Administration's most crucial foreign policy decisions. . . . His blunt description of 'guerrilla warfare' within the Administration, his public denunciation of the way things were run and his refusal to tone down his criticism . . . were unprecedented. . . . [He described] the 'systematic way in which the National Security staff deliberately deceived me.'"

As Shultz was wrapping up his testimony on July 24, Habib was typing up his resignation. He commended Shultz for his testimony, which "settled the hash of those who have worked against good government." He said he would go home to California until just before the Central American summit about the Arias plan, scheduled for two weeks hence. "I would then give you my views and recommendations [about the summit's outcome] and quietly leave."

But on August 7, the presidents of Nicaragua, Costa Rica, El Salvador, Honduras, and Guatemala shocked the world—and Philip Habib—by agreeing to the Arias peace plan. Habib and Shultz were delighted. "We're home free!" Habib said. Diplomacy had just got a tremendous boost. Never mind that resignation business: He said he was anxious to fly down to Central America to start "improving, filling the gaps, strengthening the [plan's] security aspects which were non-existent, and making sure the Central American democracies got it together. I considered it an opportunity to end the war on terms acceptable to us. . . . I wanted to take advantage of it, really make it work." In all his fifteen months on this mission he had never gone to Nicaragua or talked with the Sandinistas. Now, he told Shultz, "It's time to go to Managua." Shultz, he said, "agreed with me 150 percent."

But Elliott Abrams disagreed with him 150 percent. Abrams and the other hardliners considered the agreement a catastrophe. In their view, it sold out the Contras for a cynical Sandinista promise of fair elections that they would either never hold or never honor. Travel to Central America now? To Managua? The hardliners felt Habib, having taken his diplomatic track too seriously, had done quite enough damage already, thank you. No way did they want to bless this agreement by having him go to the region now. What they wanted was his head.

Shultz made the case to Reagan on August 10 that "Phil should leave now and go down there and meet not the four but the five." But Abrams had marshaled Defense Secretary Weinberger and new National Security Adviser Frank Carlucci to present a united front to Reagan in opposing any trip by Habib. The issue was not really whether Habib should travel; it was whether the US accepted or opposed the Arias plan. But Carlucci couched the question to Reagan this way: The US had just suffered the consequences of its long reputation as the "colossus of the North," so "do we send someone now and get accused of trying to tell them what to do, or do we wait and let them try to work it out and try to assist them?"

Expressed that way, it was an easy decision for Reagan to make. "I don't want Phil traveling," he said.

"If he can't travel, Mr. President, you've lost confidence in him," Shultz said. "and if you have lost confidence in him, I should tell him to leave. He should quit."

"No, I don't want him to quit," Reagan said. "I just don't want him to travel right now." He said he was afraid that he and Shultz and Habib would get "skinned" by the right-wingers in Congress who didn't trust them or anyone else to negotiate effectively with communists.

Shultz told Habib about the meeting. "They didn't buy it."

"Fine. I won't stay," Habib said and headed off to his office to write his second letter of resignation. This one stuck. By the time the press learned of it, he had cleaned out his desk and headed home for California.

Philip Habib thus became the fourth of Reagan's special envoys to Central America "forced out for trying to seek a two-track policy in Central America involving diplomacy as well as military strength," says Shultz.

Two months after Habib resigned, Oscar Arias received the Nobel Peace Prize for his plan. It was a huge embarrassment for the hardliners and sweet vindication for Arias and Habib. But their sweetest vindication was that the plan worked: The civil wars did wind down as a result, and in February 1990 the Sandinistas did hold elections—free, fair, and on schedule—and lost. President Daniel Ortega lost to opposition candidate Violeta Chamorro by a wide margin and, to Washington's amazement, stepped down. Though the country's and the region's problems were far from over, this stunning outcome effectively ended the Nicaraguan revolution and Washington's obsession with it.

Notes

Each note begins with the page number(s) and a few
key words to link it to the passage to which it refers

1 The Other Side of the Moon

1 Brooklyn was about: Holbrooke 8-2-93

1-2 Medal of Freedom ceremony: Bider 4-26-93 --and 5-23-93; Marjorie Habib 9-28-93 and 7-18-93; Phyllis Habib 7-7-97; "Reagan Presents A Medal to Habib," *Washington Post,* 9-8-82; "Phil Habib Wins Presidential Medal of Freedom," *State,* October 1982. Habib's friend and one-time boss Walter Orebaugh received the Medal of Freedom in 1946 ("A Hero's Words," *Naples [Florida] Daily News,* date illegible, probably May 14, 1972), but Habib was the first career diplomat ever to receive the re-named *Presidential* Medal of Freedom (Carol Jose email to author 1-2-02).

2-8 Brooklyn, Lebanon, Syria: Habib interviews with Mulcahy and Tueni; Habib speech to Jewish Federation of San Francisco at Silverado resort 1-84; Meir Zamir, *The Formation of Modern Lebanon,* p. 1; Willensky, p. 103-04; "Making Sense of the Middle East," *The Stanford Magazine,* Spring 1986; Jacobs p. 9-10, 14, 17, 21, 26; letter from Joseph Jacobs 3-18-94; author interviews with Philip Habib's wife Marjorie Habib on many dates 1993-95, daughter Susan Habib Michaels 3-14-93, cousin Elaine Habib Moore 8-16-93, sister-in-law Alice Habib 5-23-93 and 8-16-93, cousin Isabelle Spiridon Toomey 8-20-93, nephew Bob Owen 7-22-93; author interviews with Jack Grazi on many dates in 1993, Joseph Beyda on many dates in 1993, Richard Holbrooke 8-2-93, Joseph Jacobs 7-11-93, Raymond and Evelyn Jabara 8-4-93, Monsignor Hector Doueihi of Our Lady of Lebanon Cathedral (Maronite) in Brooklyn. Brad DeLong calculated the 2002 value of $400 of 1938 dollars (email to author 10-15-01). One of Habib's siblings died in infancy.

Immigrants from what is now called Lebanon did not begin using the terms *Lebanon* or *Lebanese* until the 1940s. When Philip Habib applied for admission to the University of Idaho in 1938, he listed his nationality as "Syrian-

American" (Admission for Application, 8-5-38). Since Jews from Syria thought of themselves as Jews first and Syrians second, the unqualified term *Syrian* is used here to apply specifically to non-Jews.

Playwright Arthur Miller described Brooklyn as "a lot of villages" (quoted in Greace Glueck and Paul Gardner, *Brooklyn: People and Places, Past and Present,* p. 35).

Maronites and Melchites are both sects of Roman Catholicism. Maronites celebrate Mass in Aramaic, the language Jesus spoke; Melchite priests celebrate it with their backs to the congregation and the altar hidden from view. Maronites are the largest single Christian group in Lebanon.

Phil Silvers, who would become a famous TV comedian in the 1950s, lived right across the street from the Habibs.

8-13 Idaho: Habib interviews with Tueni and Mulcahy; "Philip Habib—A Distinguished Alumnus," article in an unidentified 1983 University of Idaho publication in Habib's study; "Habib always held his cards close to chest," *The Spokesman-Review,* 8-9-82; "U.S. Expert at Peace Talks Idaho Forestry Graduate," University of Idaho Press Service release 5-16-68; Frank M. Seiden letter to Habib 2-26-82; Ernest Wohletz memo to President Hartung, "Personal Report Concerning Philip Charles Habib," 1-29-74; "Silver & Gold Day," *Idaho Update,* April 1983; *Swiss Boy Adopts America,* by Hans Wetter; "Looking back," *Idahonian,* 4-6-83; "Habib recalls poor and happy UI days," in unidentified newspaper; "Habib, UI friends remember college fun," *Lewiston Morning Tribune,* 4-7-83; "Cards and College," *Idahonian* (undated); Habib's University of Idaho Application for Admission, received 8-5-38; Kliewer letter to George [apparently Lafferty] 1992; Roger Guernsey letter to Habib 9-8-76; Robert Patton letter to Elizabeth A. Zinser 6-13-92; letters to Finley McNaughton from Charles Simmons 4-11-94, signature illegible 4-25-94; letters to the author from George Lafferty 12-6-93, Roger Guernsey 3-22-93, Terry Payne 10-15-93,

Duane Town 10-10-93, Ward Smith 6-4-92, Charles Simmons 5-6-94, Bob Kliewer undated, Paul Easterbrook 12-2-93; Jeffers letter to D. Nelson Jeffers 4-30-42; Jeffers "Report on Candidate," 3-3-42; Summer Rating Sheet 1940; Bider 4-24-93; William Price letter to Habib 2-4-82; "Philip Habib: UI alumnus returns to high accolades," *Argonaut,* 4-8-83; interviews with McNaughton 11-13-93, Kuehner 11-15-93, Bob and Betty Kliewer 11-11-93 and 12-6-93, Hendee 1-5-94, Marjorie Habib 3-26-94. Bob Kliewer, who was Habib's boss in some jobs, and Easterbrook both disagree with the work review quoted in the text.

14-15 Married, Army: Marjorie Habib 2-27-93, 8-22-96, 10-28-01; Habib interviews with Tueni and Mulcahy; Draper 9-19-97 and 4-13-93; "U.S. Expert at Peace Talks Idaho Forestry Graduate," University of Idaho Press Service release 5-16-82; "Genealogy Class 42 Reunion" by Finley McNaughton 4-27-92; interviews with Gaucher 5-15-94, Marjorie Habib 5-22-96, Howell 9-6-93

15-16 Berkeley, Boy Scouts, Personality, Foreign Service test: Marjorie Habib 3-26-94, 2-27-93, and 8-14-93; Santé 5-30-93; Habib interviews with Tueni, Mulcahy, and Kreisler; Bob and Betty Kliewer 11-11-93; "World Affairs Council salutes Philip Habib," *San Mateo Times,* 3-7-83

2 Stop the Bombing and Negotiate

17 Phil had profile: Grove 6-12-94.

17 What kind: Habib interview with Tueni

17 Funny: Bider 4-26-93

17 Hardest-working: Habib interview with Tueni

17-18 Canada: Habib in Staar, p. 23; Habib interview with Mulcahy; Marjorie Habib 11-28-93 and 2-27-93; Dean Brown ADST oral history; "Wife Of Lawyer Is Drowned" and "Swimmer Goes Under 20 Feet From Shore," 8-14-51, both in unidentified newspapers in Habib's scrapbook and both of which were full of inaccuracies, says Marjorie Habib 11-28-93. While in Canada, Habib worked nights and weekends to finish his agricultural economics dissertation. He got his PhD in 1952.

18 Lust: Ashley 3-27-93

18 Extraordinarily: Helble 2-21-94

19 Some military: Habib interview with Tueni

19 1960s Korea: O'Donohue 3-20-93, 3-28-93, 4-7-94, and 4-12-94

19 Right thing, chargé: Habib interview with Tueni

19 Colloquial, what he thought: Krezcko 10-6-93; Howell 10-11-93

19 Exact opposite: Haig 5-11-94

19-20 Bundy in Seoul: Habib interview with Mulcahy; Bundy 5-29-93; Bundy letter to Marjorie Habib 6-5-92; Bundy letter to the author 4-27-93; Zorthian 7-26-93. In September 1965 Habib wrote a friend that "When I asked them why they chose me [for Saigon], the answer was that they wanted a tough S.O.B. All these years of work and that's my reputation!" (Habib letter to Guilda Duly 9-20-65).

20 Dependants evacuated: The reason was to reduce US risk in preparation for US bombing of North Vietnam (Robert Miller letter to the author 2-15-02).

20 Couldn't wait: Marjorie Habib 2-27-93

20 Ran away from home: Marjorie Habib 6-20-95

20 Belmont: Marjorie Habib 2-27-93

20 72,000, half a million: Gibbons, p. 317; Habib interview with Tueni

21 New governments: Zorthian oral history, LBJ Library 5-26-82, tape 1; also Zorthian 7-26-93

21 Young FSOs: Zorthian 7-26-93

21 Smart: Thomas Dunlop letter to author 5-7-93

21 Unmerciful: Kim 9-21-93

21 Wanted to work: Marjorie Habib 2-15-93

21 Professor: Habib interview with Mulcahy; Kissinger eulogy at Habib's memorial service, June 10, 1992, in "Philip Habib: A Remembrance," *Foreign Service Journal,* July 1992; Kissinger remarks at Habib's swearing-in as undersecretary 7-1-76. Habib and Kissinger each told the story of their first encounter many times, and told it somewhat differently each time. This account is a compilation.

21-22 Habib's views of Vietnam War: Habib

interview with Mulcahy; Tarnoff 7-22-93; McArthur 10-3-93; Negroponte 9-20-93; Kissinger 5-16-94; Zorthian 7-26-93

22 Strategists, operator: Kissinger 5-16-94

22 Consummate professional: Such principles, and Habib's embodiment of them, come up over and over in the interviews conducted for this book, such as Paganelli 11-2-96; Bider 4-24-93; Hill 7-12-95; Grove 6-12-94; Draper ADST oral history; Dillon 11-5-96 and 11-16-96

22 Love: McArthur 10-3-93

22 Mr. Vietnam: Bundy 5-29-93

22 Vietnam working group: William Bundy, LBJ Library oral history 6-2-29, tape 4, p. 36-37; tape 5, p. 14; Habib interview with Mulcahy. Some reliable sources spell the general's name DePuy, while other equally reliable sources spell it DuPuy.

22-23 Peons: Habib interview with Mulcahy

23 Turning points: Isaacson & Thomas, p. 699

23 Tet: Habib interview with Mulcahy; Shepard 9-13-93; Oberdorfer, p. ix, x, 2-3; Brinkley, p. 256; Rusk, p. 475-76; Cronkite, p. 254. Habib said, "The Tet offensive was being played up as the great disaster, even though it was not militarily a disaster [for the US and South Vietnam]. Psychologically it was a disaster."

23 Spooked: Rosenthal 3-24-93

23 Devastation: Kim 9-21-93; Weyand 6-26-94

23-24 Support: Katzenbach 5-30-93. It wasn't that he thought the two leaders of South Vietnam, Nguyen Van Thieu and Nguyen Cao Ky, were especially bad people. "I don't bad mouth Ky or Thieu," Habib later said. He recognized that they were ineffective, but said Thieu "wasn't totally corrupt," was intelligent, hardworking, astute, and not as bad as the media portrayed him. He also said he considered Ky better than his image: "tops, fine, a very courageous guy." Both were "victims of circumstances beyond their control" ("Peace Envoy's Postscript," Habib as told to Larry Engelmann, *Vietnam* magazine, April 1993).

24 Anti-war: Weyand 6-26-01

24 *En masse:* Habib interview with the author, *The Stanford Magazine,* Spring 1984, for example. This did not mean he sympathized with

protesters. As a red-white-and-blue patriot, he particularly scorned actress Jane Fonda, who had gone to North Vietnam to demonstrate her solidarity with them and opposition to the American war effort. "She didn't know a goddamned thing about the goddamned war!" he said. His view was that, if you don't like what the government is doing, you change it; you don't support an enemy that was torturing American prisoners of war. For the rest of his life he would not watch a movie she was in or even allow her name to be spoken in his presence (Bider 4-26-93).

24 Several days, artificially prop: Ashley 3-27-93; Rosenthal 3-24-93; Weyand 6-26-01

24 Acheson advice, privately, garden path: Brinkley, p. 255-57; Isaacson & Thomas, p. 686-87. *Drivel* is Brinkley's word, not necessarily Acheson's. In July 1965 Acheson had advised Johnson that "he was wholly right on Vietnam, that he had no choice except to press on" (Isaacson & Thomas, p. 651-52). Acheson greatly respected plain-spoken, down-to-earth people (James Chace on Charlie Rose 11-12-98), so he took instantly to Habib. In Joseph Alsop's words, Acheson considered him one of "the wisest young men in town . . . a rare bird who spoke from factual certainty about situations not glib cocktail party whim" (Douglas Brinkley letter to the author 3-22-94). Brinkley adds that "Acheson thought Habib was the model of State Department thoroughness and competence."

24-25 Elder statesmen: The group included Acheson, former undersecretaries of state Averell Harriman and George Ball, former national security adviser McGeorge Bundy, former ambassador to Vietnam Henry Cabot Lodge, World War II hero General Omar Bradley, Supreme Court Justice Abe Fortas, negotiator of the Korean War settlement Arthur Dean, former treasury secretary Douglas Dillon, and former deputy secretary of defense Cyrus Vance. Habib already knew several of the Wise Men. Besides having served under Lodge in Saigon and having briefed Acheson recently, he had worked under Dillon and Ball in 1962 (Habib interviews with Tueni and Mulcahy), gotten to know Harriman when the latter came to Korea in 1964 (Harriman Papers, box 573; Habib interview with Tueni), and had dealings with Vance during Vance's time as secretary of the Army (Vance 2-14-95; Habib interview with Mulcahy). McGeorge Bundy and William Bundy were brothers. Acheson was William Bundy's father-in-law.

25 Bombing targets: Isaacson & Thomas, p. 699

25 Bleak: Clifford, p. 513

25 New ball game: Habib memo "Observations on the Situation in Viet-Nam," 2-26-68, par. 30 (LBJ Library 72D207, Box 7611); Isaacson & Thomas, p. 693. There is no record available of what Habib actually said in his briefing. This quote is from the report he had written following his trip, which was surely the basis of his briefing. Fifteen years later he said, "I don't remember what I said to them. I remember I spoke from my heart. Usually I had an outline on yellow paper, but I never kept any papers, so I don't know what the hell I said" (Habib interview with Mulcahy). In contrast to Habib's briefing, Carver outlined a promising, optimistic picture. Habib interrupted him several times. "That's not true," he would say, and question Carver sharply (Katzenbach 5-30-93).

25 Dumbfounded: Karnow, Vietnam, p. 562.

25 Extremely candid: Ball 8-11-93

25 Clifford's questions, toughest: Clifford, p. 513-14; Holbrooke 4-1-93. Holbrooke, who was Clifford's co-author, is the one Habib told that was his toughest moment. Habib's boss, William Bundy (6-13-93), disagrees that Habib was putting his career on the line. The difference may have to do with the perception in Habib's mind as the subordinate and the perception in Bundy's mind as the boss.

25 Dramatic effect: Tarnoff 7-22-93

26 Ignore the critics: Brinkley, p. 254. Carver and General Earle Wheeler had given them upbeat briefings in November, saying victory was within reach (Brinkley, p. 254; Isaacson & Thomas, p. 678).

26 No longer do: Isaacson & Thomas, p. 702, also p. 700. This was McGeorge Bundy's quote of Acheson's view, which crystallized the group's consensus. Some in the group dissented. Several of the Wise Men had been growing disenchanted with the war since their prior meeting but, like Acheson prior to his private sessions, had had little solid information on which to base their unease. As the group gathered March 25, Vance sensed "a feeling among the Wise Men that there hadn't been enough of a facing of the facts and telling them as they were" (Vance 2-14-95).

26 McGeorge Bundy: Oberdorfer, p. 311. McGeorge Bundy had been LBJ's National Se-

curity Adviser until February 1966. In May 1967 he had written LBJ to say that bombing of the North, particularly of power plants, was "both unproductive and unwise," but at that time he stopped short of proposing stopping the bombing altogether (Pentagon Papers, p. 527).

26 Poisoned: After hearing from the Wise Men, LBJ demanded that Habib, Carver, and DePuy give him the same briefings that had so moved the Wise Men. Habib was scheduled to give a speech about the war in Dayton, Ohio; canceling the speech at the last minute could be interpreted as the administration having something to hide. Clifford's account (p. 518) says "Habib deliberately went ahead with a previously scheduled speech in Dayton, Ohio, thus avoiding the meeting with the President." Isaacson & Thomas (p. 703) suggest that presidential adviser Walt Rostow made the decision to "let him go, figuring he had done enough damage." In fact, the decision to let him go to Dayton was LBJ's, who wrote on an action memo about bringing in Habib, "Don't need him" (Rostow Action Memorandum "4:00 P.M. briefing," 3-27-68, NSF Vietnam country file 7E(4)a 2/68 - 4/68, Public Relations Activities, Box 100, LBJ Library handwriting file). Carver and DePuy did give LBJ an encore, after which he shook his head and said, "I don't know why they've [the Wise Men] drawn that conclusion" (Isaacson & Thomas, p. 703).

Here is Habib's account: "I'm sitting in my office, and a phone call comes from Walt Rostow: 'The president wants to see you. He heard about the briefing, and he wants to be briefed.' I said, 'Walt, I'm just walking out the door. I'm leaving for Dayton, Ohio, making a speech to 1,000 students on the Vietnam war, explaining the policy and all that. But of course, if you insist, I'll cancel it and I'll be over there.' He said, 'Well, just a minute and I'll call you back.' Five minutes later he calls back and says, 'You go ahead and make the speech'" (Habib interview with Mulcahy).

26 Let's get one: Isaacson & Thomas, p. 695; "The Fight for the President's Mind," by Townsend Hoopes, The Atlantic Monthly, January 1969. In late February, Secretary of State Rusk had said that suggestions of a bombing halt were "almost obscene" (Abramson, p. 656).

26 Profound effect: Vance 2-14-95. Karnow (Vietnam, p. 562) writes that their advice "had swayed [LBJ] profoundly." Katzenbach 5-30-93 adds that Habib's remarks unquestionably

had a major impact "because this respected professional with a reputation for integrity was now so skeptical" about the war effort. "The Wise Men were surprised to hear that things were not going as well as they had suspected."

In his memoirs, Johnson (p. 416) said he felt that the Wise Men had heard "a fairly gloomy assessment" from the briefers, but suspected that the briefings had been based on "outdated information. In any case, I decided that the briefings had been much less important in shaping the views of these outside advisers than was the general mood of depression and frustration that had swept over so many people as a result of the Tet offensive." That was not the feeling of the Wise Men themselves. While many of them had been growing skeptical of the war effort already, they made it clear that the briefings had been very influential. One of them, Arthur Dean, said "Maybe I am just speaking for myself, but I think all of us here very reluctantly came to the judgment that we've got to [start looking for a way to disengage] and we only came to it after we listened to the briefing last night" (in Thomas Johnson's collection of excerpts from 3-26-68 meeting, 3-27-68, 3:15 P.M., Diary Backup 3/26/68, Box 93, LBJ Library). Douglas Dillon too said, "The briefing last night led me to conclude we cannot achieve a military victory" (Thomas Johnson notes "Continuation of Meeting with Foreign Policy Advisers in the Cabinet Room [Summary]," March 26, 1968, 3:15 P.M., LBJ Library).

26 LBJ's speech: Clifford, p. 484, 519; Oberdorfer, p. 317-23. Habib and Bill Bundy were among the many people who had a hand in the rewriting of LBJ's March 31 speech (Habib interview with Mulcahy). LBJ did authorize one last troop increase—of 13,500, a fraction of the 206,000 he had been considering sending prior to the Wise Men's meeting. It was the last major US troop increment ever authorized. LBJ had talked to Rusk in 1967 about withdrawing from the presidential campaign because of health (Rusk, p. 483). LBJ had announced six months earlier his "San Antonio formula," an offer to stop bombing if Hanoi would start productive discussions (Karnow *Vietnam*, p. 683), but nothing had come of it.

Johnson wrote in his memoirs that he had been mulling over the possibility of not running for re-election ever since his January 1965 inauguration. In his speech, he wrote, "I went forward with the decisions that had taken shape in my mind years, months, and days earlier. I repeat: No President, at least not this President,

makes a decision until he publicly announces that decision and acts upon it. When did I make the decisions that I announced on the evening of March 31, 1968? The answer is: 9:01 P.M. on March 31, 1968" (Johnson, p. 419, 424-25).

26 Put a ceiling: "The Fight for the President's Mind," by Townsend Hoopes, *The Atlantic Monthly,* January 1969

26 Number peaked: "LBJ Claims Lead Role in De-escalating War," *The Washington Post,* 2-7-70; Brinkley, p. 262

26 Wise men misc.: Brinkley, p. 254-62; Clifford, p. 507-19; Isaacson & Thomas, p. 676-706; Oberdorfer, p. 308-323; Karnow *Vietnam,* p. 561-66; Johnson, p. 416-24; Habib interview with Mulcahy; "LBJ Claims Lead Role in De-escalating War," *The Washington Post,* 2-7-70; Thomas Johnson notes "Continuation of Meeting with Foreign Policy Advisers in the Cabinet Room (Summary)," March 26, 1968, 3:15 p.m., LBJ Library; Bundy 6-13-93 and 1-29-94; Zorthian oral history, LBJ Library, 4-24-81, II, 19

27 Secret talks: Vance 2-14-95; Habib interview with Mulcahy. In the secret talks, ground rule number one that the North Vietnamese insisted on was that everyone check their weapons at the door. "What the devil are you talking about?" Vance sputtered. "We're not going to have any weapons in here!"

27 October 1968 deal: "Far From Vietnam, the Words Drag On," *The Washington Post,* 5-9-71

27 Chennault, I'm convinced: Habib interview with Mulcahy; R. Miller 3-30-93 and 2-19-94; Negroponte 9-20-93; Bundy ms., ch. 5; Diem, p. 238-44; Abramson, p. 669-71; Rusk, p. 487-89. In conducting the ADST oral history with Habib, Ed Mulcahy offered Habib a chance to retract from the tape recording what he had said about Chennault persuading Thieu to drag his feet, but Habib said, "No, let it stand. It's true" (Mulcahy 10-11-93). Habib, Harriman, Vance, and Johnson all believed that Chennault's advice to Thieu had swayed him to hold out lest a peace agreement help Humphrey win the election. LBJ did not think Richard Nixon himself had anything to do with the episode (Harriman oral history, LBJ Library; Negroponte 9-20-93), but he certainly believed Chennault had scuttled the agreement.

27-28 Shape of the table: Habib interview with

Mulcahy; Vance 2-14-95; Abramson, p. 670-73; Isaacson & Thomas, p. 713. The Soviets were North Vietnam's allies. Vance says they were very helpful in trying to get the negotiations off the ground.

28 Fat suits: Whitehouse 9-6-93

28 Lodge: Habib interview with Mulcahy. Nixon did appoint a number two negotiator, Lawrence Walsh, to keep an eye on Lodge, but Walsh contributed little to the effort. In later interviews Habib and his colleagues almost always had a hard time even remembering Walsh's name. In the 1980s Walsh became special prosecutor in the Iran-Contra scandal.

28-29 Reasons talks go nowhere: Holbrooke, p. 82-83; Katzenbach 5-30-93; Whitehouse 9-6-93; Rosenthal 3-24-93; Abramson, p. 666-67; William Bundy manuscript, ch. 5; Weyand 6-26-94; R. Miller 3-30-93. Rosenthal adds that the only concession the North made was that South Vietnamese president Thieu could stay in office.

29 Agony, broke my heart, damnedest: R. Miller 3-30-93; Negroponte 9-20-93

29 Kissinger's secret negotiations: Kissinger had told Habib about his secret negotiations (Kissinger 5-16-94), but Habib never revealed that he knew. The most he would say, even to his colleagues, was "I have a feeling that something else is going on somewhere else. I'm just over here holding the horse while the real race is somewhere else" (Sullivan 4-21-94).

29 Fair agreement, conscience: Kissinger 5-16-94; Kissinger eulogy at Habib's memorial service, in "Philip Habib: A Remembrance," *Foreign Service Journal,* July 1992

29 Good agreement: Habib letter to William H. Sullivan from Seoul, 1-26-73; Kissinger 5-16-94. Habib wrote to Kissinger, "It's a good agreement, a conclusion for which not many are better judges than I. My heartiest congratulations and deep admiration" (letter from Seoul, 1-26-73). Kissinger wrote to Habib that "I take your praise [for the agreement] more seriously than that of anyone else. You are in a position to know where we have been, and what we have been through" (Kissinger letter to Habib 2-20-73 in Habib's study, also in National Archives' Kissinger file).

29 Have to realize: "Peace Envoy's Postscript," Habib as told to Larry Engelmann, *Vietnam* magazine, April 1993

29 Reprieved: Habib letter to Wyn Hall, 2-24-71

30 1972 heart: Habib interview with Mulcahy; Marjorie Habib 2-27-93, 3-5-93, 3-13-93, and 9-24-95; Green 7-9-93; Marjorie Habib letter to Wyn Hall 3-3-72; Sullivan 4-21-94. "All my family die young," he once said. His sister too would later die of a heart attack. His other brother, Fred, died young of brain cancer. He had had some chest pains in Paris, but these were worse. Before he went to Korea, State's Office of Medical Services had examined him and cleared him not "for full Foreign Service duty," but only "for Foreign Service duty at a post with adequate medical facilities" (Medical Clearance form 10-1-71).

30-31 Kim Dae Jung: O'Donohue 4-7-94 and 3-28-93; Kim Dae Jung letter to Habib 8-20-83; Dan Oberdorfer interviewed on NPR's "All Things Considered," 12-19-97; "Cloak-and-dagger games: Saving the life of a leader," *Time,* 3-2-98; "Angry Koreans Elect Longtime Dissident," *The New York Times,* 12-19-97; "Wild Plot," *Time,* 8-20-73; "Bizarre Homecoming," *Time,* 8-27-73; "Kidnapping Debate in Japan" and "Slip-up by Clerical Worker Releases Confidential Files," *Washington Post,* 6-6-79; Boettcher, p. 225-27; Buss, p. 132. The Japanese also pressured Park not to have Kim killed. The role of the airplane is unclear: Kim himself is the only person on the boat who has talked about what happened, and he was of course not privy to how the boat received the message. He knows only that, right after the plane appeared, he was taken away from the brink. Japan took his kidnapping as a grave violation of its sovereignty. Three months after the kidnapping, the prime minister of South Korea apologized to the Japanese for the kidnapping. He blamed it on a former Korean official and suspected agent of South Korea's CIA whom he insisted had acted as a private citizen ("Honorable Settlement," *Time,* 11-12-73).

31-32 Human rights: "S. Korean Abuses Tolerated," *Washington Post,* 5-17-76; O'Donohue 4-7-94; Frank Underhill ADST oral history; letter to the editor of *The New York Times,* by Abraham M. Sirkin, in response to a 5-29-92 article. The letter was not published, but was sent to the author by Sirkin.

32 Persuade Congress: Habib interview with Mulcahy

32 Not precipitous: Wisner 6-12-94. Wisner says that, if zero were doing nothing and 100

were a full evacuation, Habib's position was about a 55. "Phil did not want to bug out," Wisner says, "but there was no way of rolling back the final North Vietnamese offensive."

32-34 Fall of Saigon: Kissinger 5-16-94; Helble 2-21-94; O'Donohue 4-12-94; McArthur 10-3-93; R. Miller 2-19-94; Wisner 6-8-94; Habib memo to Sisco 8-12-75; "Peace Envoy's Postscript," Habib as told to Larry Engelmann, *Vietnam* magazine, April 1993 (italics added and punctuation altered for clarity); "Fall of Saigon: A Discovery Channel Special," Discovery Channel 4-28-95; Snepp, *Decent Interval;* Boettcher, p. 221; Lehmann ADST oral history; Kissinger, *Years of Renewal;* "A Bloody Rite of Passage," *Time,* 4-15-85. After Saigon fell, Martin became a tragic figure. When he returned to Washington, nobody wanted anything to do with him. He wandered the halls of the State Department like a ghost, hoping to find someone—anyone—to whom he could prove he had been right. Despite their lack of respect for one another before and during the crisis, subsequently "Phil was the only person now who treated Martin with dignity," says O'Donohue (4-12-94). "Phil would invite him into his office and let him talk." Kissinger 5-16-94 agrees this is a fair characterization.

Years later, without mentioning Martin by name, Habib said, "Does it give you an ego to say, 'I deal only with the president'? I know guys who've talked that way, but they're wrong! That's all, just wrong" (Habib interview with the author, *The Stanford Magazine,* Spring 1984). One of the few recorded things he ever said about Martin by name was, "Graham—strange man. He was wrong about a lot of things. And he was very stubborn. It destroyed him. It destroyed him physically and somewhat mentally too. He and I had a real falling out. We later made up" (Habib interview with Mulcahy).

34 Assistant secretary: Nick Veliotes, who served at that level, says, "Any career officer who becomes assistant secretary should . . . conclude this is the last assignment" (Veliotes ADST oral history).

34 Quemo Sabe: "Remarks at the Swearing In of Philip C. Habib," 7-1-76. In the 1950s TV show, the Lone Ranger's sidekick Tonto called him Quemo Sabe (pronounced KEE-moe SOBB-ee).

34 Team, agreed: Kissinger 5-16-94

34 Practitioner: Wisner 6-12-94

34 Heroes: Kissinger letter to Marjorie Habib 5-27-92

35 Genius: Habib interview with the author 12-20-83

35 No right to act: Eagleburger eulogy at Habib's memorial service, June 10, 1992, in "Philip Habib: A Remembrance," *Foreign Service Journal,* July 1992

35 Shut up: R. Miller 2-19-94

35 Can you imagine: Helble 2-21-94

35 His peace, conscience: Kissinger and Eagleburger eulogies at Habib's memorial service, June 10, 1992, in "Philip Habib: A Remembrance," *Foreign Service Journal,* July 1992; Leslie Gelb column, "The Ultimate Pro," *The New York Times,* 5-29-92

35 Head rolls, don't think: Habib interview with Mulcahy. As Alexander Haig puts it (5-11-94), "The terrible reality is a dialectic in the career of a Foreign Service officer: The better he is, the higher up the flagpole he goes; and the higher up the flagpole he goes, the more dangerous his position from the standpoint of a change of administration."

35 Shoes: Holbrooke, "Philip Habib: Brave Bureaucrat," *Washington Post,* 5-31-92

36 Outstanding: Holbrooke, "A 25-year-old letter from Phil Habib, and its relevance today," *State,* August 1994, p. 16. This was the consensus of his colleagues (e.g., William Bundy letter to Marjorie Habib 6-5-92).

36 Grudge: An FSO who asked not to be identified by name

36 Nixon visit: Office Memorandum to the Ambassador, from P.C. Habib, "Visit of Vice President," October 16, 1953, from Habib's scrapbook

36 Laos: Veliotes 4-29-93

36 Screaming: Veliotes 4-29-93

36 Eighteen months: Helble 2-21-94

36-37 Saigon hospital: Thomas Dunlop letter to author 5-7-93

37 Belly dance: Weyand 6-26-94

37 Eighteen-hour days: Marjorie Habib 2-27-93

37 Stop sign: Marjorie Habib 10-28-01

37-38 Foreign minister's profanity: Saunders 6-14-93

38 King of Lebanon: According to a colleague who asked not to be identified by name; Elva Murphy 4-8-94; Marjorie Habib 9-24-95. King Hussein had long come to the United States for medical treatment.

38 Sadat, Moscow: Habib interview with Mulcahy; "Moscow Caustic to U.S. on Mideast," New York Times, 12-6-77; "Soviets Attack Sadat; Habib Holds Moscow Talks," Washington Post, 12-6-77. The Soviets accused Sadat of selling out the PLO in collusion with the Israelis and the Americans.

38-39 Heart attack 1977: Habib interview with Mulcahy; AFSA Journal April 1978; Cheitlin report 3-29-78; Marjorie Habib 6-5-97; T. Miller 2-28-93 and email 1-23-02; Saunders 6-14-93. Saunders' and Miller's recollections of that morning differ, but they may not always have been in the room with Habib at the same time; each may thus not have heard what he said to the other. Saunders recalls Habib looking perfectly normal, saying "I think I'm having a heart problem," and asking him to call an ambulance. What Habib said to Miller is quoted here since it is so similar to what he said to Thomas Dunlop in Saigon in 1969 under comparable circumstances.

39 Retire or die: Marjorie Habib 10-28-01

39 Can't imagine: "Habib the Peacemaker," Newsweek, 8-30-82. The article bowdlerizes his profanity as "F——."

39 Small assignments: Habib interview with Mulcahy; Vance 2-14-95

39-40 Heart during retirement: Habib interview with Mulcahy; Hill 7-19-95 and 3-27-93; Cheitlin report "Followup—September 11, 1978, RE: Mr. Philip Habib"; University of California, San Francisco, "Record of Operation," by Daniel Ullyot, MD, 8-25-78; Cheitlin 3-26-93

3 The War That Got Away

41 Let's face it: Habib interview with Mulcahy

41 They went back: Haig 5-11-94; Kim 9-21-93; "Gen. Haig Arrives Here To Brief Park on

Viet," Korea Times, 1-21-73

41 Avert it: The US' top priority in the Middle East at the time was to ensure that the 1979 Egyptian-Israeli treaty be implemented on schedule by the end of April 1982. That treaty called for the Israelis to give back the Sinai Peninsula, which they had captured from Egypt in the 1967 war. The deadline was now a year away, and none of the preliminary steps had been taken that might convince the Israelis to go through with their promised withdrawal. So State's policy priority was to keep Lebanon quiet, "at least keep it quiet long enough so it doesn't screw up our top priority, which was to make sure that the treaty was actually implemented" (Veliotes 4-20-93; Veliotes ADST oral history).

41 Agility: Haig 5-11-94

41 Cardiologist: Cheitlin 3-26-93. Habib assured Haig he was "in tip-top shape." Haig himself had had a heart bypass operation the previous year and felt fine now, so he readily took Habib's word for it (Haig 5-11-94).

41-45 Historical background on Lebanon, Israel, PLO: Massoulié, p. 22-29, 135-47; "Making Sense of the Middle East," parts 1 and 2, The Stanford Magazine, Spring 1986 and Summer 1986; "Beirut—Up From the Rubble," National Geographic, February 1983; Dunnigan, p. 29-40; Kissinger Upheaval, p. 787-89; Friedman, p. 8, 11-18; Gabriel, p. 33-34; Zamir, preface and p. 1-3; Schiff & Ya'ari, p. 19, 31-32; "War or Compromise on Security," Washington Post, 5-14-81; Habib cable from Beirut 08674, 010735Z Dec 81, par. 3; "Beirut: City of Money and Mystery," Reader's Digest, 11-64; "Sport on the Far Shores of Eden," Sports Illustrated, 3-29-65; Dillon 2-28-02; "Superpowers and Small States: an Overview of American-Lebanese Relations," by Paul E. Salem, The Beirut Review, Spring 1993, www.lcps-lebanon.org/pub/breview/br5/psalembr5pt2.html.

In France's original conception, the Christians enjoyed a slight majority in the new Lebanon. That slight majority became the basis of power allocations within the government. But as demographics shifted over the decades, Christians became a smaller and smaller minority. Yet no new census was ever conducted, and power allocations were not recalculated to reflect changing realities. Much of the contention within Lebanon can be viewed as attempts by Muslims and Druze to win the proportional share of power that they feel they have been denied. Druze are a sect that splintered off from Islam in the eleventh century. Their religious beliefs are a closely guarded secret, and they do not allow converts. Lebanon became independent of France in 1943. Technically, the Syrian army entered Lebanon under the auspices of the Arab League. Syrian president Hafaz al-Assad said on July 20, 1976, "Historically, Syria and Lebanon are one country and one people" (Israeli, p. 260).

Some years after Pierre Gemayel's militia attacked the bus full of Palestinians, his son Bashir laughed about it to the American ambassador to Lebanon, saying, "We showed them. We killed everybody who had a Muslim name!" (Dillon 2-28-02).

45 Bashir, alliance, Zahle: Parker, p. 174-75; Zamir, p. 2-3; Seale, p. 369-70; Schiff & Ya'ari, p. 11-34; Petran, p. 259; Gabriel, p. 60; Sharon, p. 428-29; Lewis in Quandt, p. 230; Randal, p. 231; Cobban, p. 35; Friedman, p. 137-40; Hill 7-17-93. Since Pierre Gemayel and his sons Bashir and Amin were all well-known players in the story, they are generally referred to by only their first names for clarity. Notions of a Jewish-Maronite alliance went back to the nineteenth century, and discussions about an alliance to fight the PLO began in March 1976 (Schiff & Ya'ari, p. 11-13). Bashir's alliance with Israel was no secret (e.g., Beirut 08673, 010730Z Dec 81, par. 3). Zahle stands by the highway that runs between Beirut and Damascus. Both the Israelis' downing of the helicopters and the Syrians' introduction of missiles violated the Red Line Agreement.

The missiles, Soviet-made SAM-6s, were placed 30–50 miles from Israeli territory and had a range of about 5 miles. They thus posed no offensive threat to the people of Israel in the way the PLO's Katyusha rockets did. The missiles were only a defensive threat to Israeli aircraft flying in that part of Lebanon (Dillon 5-9-94 and 11-16-96; Dillon ADST oral history; Howell 9-6-93). The danger those missiles posed, says Haig 5-11-94, was "with respect to Israeli air superiority" and the need "to keep Israel's qualitative edge in military terms in place inviolable."

45-46 April 30: Schiff & Ya'ari, p. 35; Sharon, p. 429. Whereas conventional ambassadors are accredited to deal with only the single country to which they are assigned, a special envoy is authorized to deal with any countries that are relevant to the issue at hand.

46 Excuse, cooler, life-line: Lewis ADST oral history

46-47 Really intended, informal understanding, Katyushas, ready for truce: Schiff & Ya'ari, p. 35-37; Schoenbaum, p. 278; Davis, p. 64; Seale, p. 371; Randal, p. 236-39; Evron, p. 99; Gowers, p. 186; Petran, p. 261-62; Sharon, p. 430-32; Lewis ADST oral history; Lewis 2-17-02; Sehulster 1-5-02

47 Informal understanding: Habib interview with the author 12-20-83; Parker, p. 181; Lewis ADST oral history; Lewis 2-17-02; Dillon ADST oral history; Beinin 10-30-93

47 Sharon objected: Sharon, p. 432-33

47 Long-term arrangements: For example, Amman 08896, 051454Z Dec 81, par. 11, 13

47 Bargain with the PLO: Draper 4-13-93, 4-25-93, and 2-24-02; Draper ADST oral history; Beinin 10-30-93

47-48 Sharon hero, symbol, military achievements: "Ariel Sharon: Feisty Politician Is Not a Natural Diplomat," *The New York Times,* 10-10-98; "Sharon's Muscle Evokes Hopes and Some Fears," *The New York Times,* 10-20-98; Sachar, p. 170

48 Also earned a reputation: Sachar, p. 170; "Desert Hawk," *Vanity Fair,* January 2002

48 Ultra-hawk: Davis, p. 65

48 Eagleburger: Lewis cable from Tel Aviv 11097, 221519Z Jul 82, par. 2; Eagleburger 7-3-93. Begin objected to these "zoological" references to Sharon by Eagleburger.

48 Invoked security: Davis, p. 66, based on Ezer Weizman, *The Battle for Peace,* p. 141, 222

48 Judgment: Lewis ADST oral history

48 Appalled: Schiff & Ya'ari, p. 37-38. The context of the quote is Sharon's earlier lobbying to be special coordinator of the various security services. Being defense minister would entail even more sensitive powers than coordinator.

48 Ten times: Davis, p. 65, citing Prof. Nadav Safran

48 Golda Meir: quoted by Oriana Fallaci in "Sharon: 'I Wanted Them Out of Beirut; I Got What I Wanted,'" *Washington Post,* 8-29-82

48 Entrust: Schiff & Ya'ari, p. 38

48-49 1981 election, take a walk: Lewis ADST oral history. As Lewis tells the story, what turned things around at the last minute was a night club entertainer telling jokes as a warm-up act at a Labor rally, during which he referred to Sephardic Jews as "bums." Begin seized upon the crack, saying that that's what Labor thinks of Sephardic Jews. Lewis adds, "Had [that entertainer] not made that crack, Sharon would not have become Defense Minister; Begin would not have been Prime Minister; there would not have been a Lebanon War; there would have been no Sabra and Shatila; and the whole course of the next five or ten years would have been different."

49 Mission complete, golf: Dillon 11-16-96; Habib interview with Mulcahy; "Ex-envoy urges change in Latin America policy," *San Jose Mercury News* 8-30-81

49 Confidence: Lewis 4-10-94. Early in his mission, *Newsweek* wrote, "If the Arabs and Israelis agree on anything about the Lebanese missile crisis, it is that Philip Habib is a superb diplomat. In Beirut, Damascus, Jerusalem and Riyadh—the capitals he visited during two weeks of shuttle diplomacy—the special U.S. envoy won high marks for diligence, discretion and a deft personal touch. 'His mind is brilliant,' Israeli Prime Minister Menachem Begin told a television interviewer last week. 'I think he is one of the most able diplomats of our time. I am so impressed by him, by his wisdom, by his energy and by his efforts—physical, moral, intellectual.' After a pause, Begin added: 'But he did not yet achieve results'" ("Habib Still Plays For Time," *Newsweek,* 6-1-81).

A few months after the July 24 ceasefire, Begin and Sharon started putting the Americans on notice that, while the deal was fine as far as it went, it did not go nearly far enough. The PLO was still causing trouble in ways unaddressed by the ceasefire, Begin and Sharon said, and if the PLO didn't stop, the ceasefire would be off and the Israelis would have to take matters into their own hands in Lebanon. The first warning came from Begin to Haig at Anwar Sadat's funeral in October 1981 (Haig 5-11-94; Cannon, p. 393).

49 Returned to the region: Haig's objective in sending Habib back was, Haig wrote, "to defuse Israeli interests in exercising the military option in Lebanon" while advancing the political and security situation (Haig memo to The President, "The Next Habib Mission,"11-11-81; State Department press briefing, 10-13-81, in State 273438, 140016Z Oct 81; State 278253, 192147Z Oct 81). The Egyptians too were anx-

ious to have him come back. The Syrians were not. Just before he arrived in the region, the US signed a military agreement with Israel. On December 2, leaders of Syrian president Assad's ruling Baath Party led some 300,000 Syrian demonstrators on a march through Damascus, ostensibly to protest a bombing there but chanting "Habib, Habib go away" ("300,000 Syrians protest visit of U.S. envoy Habib to Damascus," *Los Angeles Times* story in *St. Petersburg Times* 12-3-81). Habib encouraged the Syrians to withdraw their missiles gradually while things were quiet. They replied that they would not do so as long as Begin demanded their withdrawal (Amman 08896, 051454Z Dec 81, par. 11).

On the eve of his arrival, Lebanese security forces said they had uncovered a plot by a group of Libyans in Lebanon to assassinate Habib when he came to Beirut. If there was a plot, exposure and tighter security measures foiled it (Beirut 08799, 041620Z Dec 81; Tel Aviv 18674, 041808Z Dec 81; UPI report of 12-4-81 quoted in Tel Aviv 18675, 041809Z Dec 81).

49 Draper's background: Draper ADST oral history; Dillon 2-28-02. Draper had begun his career as a chemist with the Manhattan Project in Los Alamos in 1946-47, but soon realized his calling was international affairs, not science.

49 Only in force: This is according to an Israeli politician who asked not to be identified by name, but many other sources say the same (for example, Sachar, p. 172)

49 Hopeless: Sharon, p. 434-35

49-50 Formula, shat: Draper 4-25-93. Draper was deputy assistant secretary of state in the Bureau for Near Eastern Affairs responsible for the Israel-Lebanon-Syria geographic area. Habib had met with Sharon at least once before, on May 12, 1980, when Sharon was agriculture minister and Habib was in the region to try to mediate disputes between Arabs and Israelis over water rights ("U.S. envoy Habib relaying Yarmuk water 'bargaining,'" *Jerusalem Post* 5-13-80).

50 Map, his analysis: Brown cable Tel Aviv 18681, 051155Z Dec 81; Habib interview with Tueni; Draper 4-25-93; Sharon, p. 429, 434-35. Like other Arab states, Lebanon had since 1949 been technically still at war with Israel. Sharon's point about Lebanon associating with the free world was meant to contrast with Syria's association with the Soviet Union and

thus to resonate with Haig's Cold Warrior view of the Middle East.

50 Adhering, violating: Lewis ADST oral history; Habib interview with Tueni; Habib cable Jerusalem 01781, 082022Z Jun 82, par. 7-8

50 Fast move: Sharon, p. 435

50 Quite clear, own opinion: Draper 4-25-93; Schiff & Ya'ari, p. 66. Calling this just his own opinion was true, if disingenuous (Lewis 4-10-94): A defense minister's opinion of what should be done tends to soon become official policy. It is normal for countries to have contingency plans for military operations (Howell 9-6-93), and the Israeli Defense Forces had been developing such a plan for Lebanon since before Sharon became defense minister ("Begin's Rhetoric and Sharon's Tactics," *Foreign Affairs*, Fall 1982, p. 73-74).

50-51 Instructed his chief: Brown cable Tel Aviv 18681, 051155Z Dec 81, par. 9

51 Twentieth century: Schiff & Ya'ari, p. 66. This is the earliest published account of what Habib said. Other accounts attribute different words to him, but all accounts are consistent that he expressed astonishment, alarm about the dire consequences of such an ill-advised move, and strong opposition (Brown cable Tel Aviv 18681, 051155Z Dec 81; Draper 4-25-93, 4-13-93, and 12-22-94; Habib interviews with Mulcahy and Tueni; Lewis 4-10-94; Lewis ADST oral history; Teicher, p. 193; Seale, p. 375; Howell 9-6-93; Hill 6-15-93; "Minutes of Sharon-Habib Meeting," TA241034 Tel Aviv DAVAR in Hebrew 24 May 82, pp. 1,2, in *Foreign Broadcast Information Service Daily Reports, Middle East & Africa*, 1982, 05/28, p. 14; "Sharon Reportedly Outlined Lebanon War Plan in 1981" and "U.S. Backs Lewis Version," *New York Times*, 5-26-85). Draper (4-25-93) says Sharon "did not think the Syrians would intervene. He thought they would just retreat. He told us he thought the chance of all-out war with Syria was tiny. That was a point where Phil strongly disagreed. But what he said was so staggering that it's not something you might discuss the pros and cons with because it might suggest that there *are* pros."

51 Lewis, denied: "Envoy Says Sharon Outlined Invasion Plan to U.S. in 1981," *Washington Post*, 5-24-85; "Sharon Reportedly Outlined Lebanon War Plan in 1981" and "U.S. Backs Lewis Version," *New York Times*, 5-26-85; "Sharon Reacts to Lewis' Disclosures on Lebanon War," TA230904 Tel Aviv Yedi'ot

Aharonot in Hebrew 23 May 85, pp. 1, 14, and "Sharon Explains Contacts With U.S. on Lebanon, TA240745 Jerusalem Government Press Office in English 23 May 85, both in *Foreign Broadcast Information Service Daily Reports, Middle East & Africa*, 1982, 05/23-24, p. 11. Draper too was amazed: "I mean, telling us their secret plans so openly. Jesus, it was remarkable. Foreign governments don't tell you in advance what they're going to do militarily" (Draper 4-25-93). Sharon's denials focused mostly on whether he had revealed details, not on whether he had revealed the grand sweep of his plan. Habib backed up Lewis' account (*Foreign Broadcast Information Service Daily Reports*, May 23 and 24, 1985), which was consistent with his own account and with Draper's.

51 Trap Palestinian: Habib interview with Tueni

51 Arrogant, disdain, anti-American, oppose anything: Draper 4-25-93 and 12-18-94

51-52 Drip method, nuclear: Schiff & Ya'ari, p. 65; Lewis in Quandt, p. 230-31; Seale, p. 370; Petran, p. 262. Sharon explicitly told Habib in the meeting that, if something happened, he did not want the US taken by surprise (Brown cable Tel Aviv 18681, 051155Z Dec 81, par. 9).

52 Become a party: Draper 4-25-93

52 Alarm, Sinai: Draper 1-13-02; Veliotes 4-20-93; Veliotes ADST oral history. The declassified cable that reports on Habib's meeting with Sharon (Brown cable Tel Aviv 18681, 051155Z Dec 81) is silent about the most important parts of the meeting. "We sanitized the cable of the most sensitive parts," says Draper (1-13-02), choosing to report them instead orally by secure phone and in person when they returned to Washington. Haig (5-11-94) later would not remember ever having heard about this meeting from Habib.

52 Feeble: Schiff, "The Green Light," *Foreign Policy*, #50, Spring 1983. Schiff writes that "the American nay was so feeble that the Israelis regarded it merely as a diplomatic maneuver designed to exonerate the United States should the military operation go sour." *Feeble* is not a word one would expect to hear applied to anything Habib said. His colleagues agree that it was not Habib's communication that Schiff was referring to. "Phil wasn't *in* the later meetings where this 'feeble' response came out," says Draper (4-25-93).

52 Mostly out: Veliotes 5-6-93

52-53 Scout out, your business, Chamoun: Sharon, p. 437-43; Schiff & Ya'ari, p. 48-51; also Schiff, "The Green Light," *Foreign Policy,* #50, Spring 1983; Randal, p. 246-47. Chamoun was also the president who invited American troops into Lebanon in 1957.

53 Consul general: Veliotes ADST oral history

53 Bashir told: Dillon ADST oral history

53 UN: Draper 4-25-93

53 Journals: Jansen, p. 1

53 25,000: Jansen, p. 1; Schiff, "The Green Light," *Foreign Policy,* #50, Spring 1983; Habib interview with Tueni

53 Chancellor: Schiff, "The Green Light," *Foreign Policy,* #50, Spring 1983

53 Pretext: The word *pretext* is often used in the context of Sharon's lead-up to the invasion (e.g., Veliotes 4-29-93; Yaacobi 2-14-95; Schiff, "The Green Light," *Foreign Policy,* #50, Spring 1983). As Israeli Foreign Ministry Director General David Kimche puts it, Israel was "on a course for war; it required only some inflammatory act by the PLO to light the fuse" (Kimche, p. 144-45, cited in Parker, p. 176).

53 Single incident: Habib interview with Dusclaud. Habib said, "Matter of fact, there was practically no evidence of any hostile action from Lebanese territory directly into Israel from that point [July '81] on. Israelis don't admit that, but it's true. We kept track in those days" (Habib interview with Mulcahy). Yaacobi (2-14-95) agrees that the border had been quiet since the ceasefire. On the quiet of the border since the July 24 ceasefire, see also Benziman, p. 268-69, and Bavly and Salpeter, p. 234 (quoted in Davis, p. 3). Habib did agree that the ceasefire applied to attacks on Israel that originated in Lebanon but were carried out across the Jordan-Israel border (Habib cable Jerusalem 01781, 082022Z Jun 82, par. 8). There had been one such instance: A squad of guerrillas went from Lebanon into Jordan and crossed from there into Israel to attempt an attack (Habib interview with Tueni).

53 I said no: Habib interview with Tueni

54 Cannot afford, no one agreement: Habib cable Jerusalem 01781, 082022Z Jun 82, par. 7-8; Lewis ADST oral history

54 With the situation: Sharon, p. 450. Israel

by now had withdrawn from the Sinai, as scheduled, in April.

54 I'd kick: Haig 5-11-94

54 Feel inclined: The one quoted is Defense Secretary Caspar Weinberger (10-7-93), who, it should be noted, is himself extremely critical of Israel. But virtually all State Department people interviewed on the subject offer essentially the same assessment of Haig's position.

54 Presidential ambitions: Veliotes ADST oral history

54 Indians: Haig 5-11-94

54-55 Content of Haig-Sharon meeting: Memorandum of Conversation, "The Secretary's Meeting with Israeli Defense Minister Sharon," 5-28-82, S/S number 8215555, P900060-0673 and P900060-0674. Substantial portions of the declassified record of the discussion are excised. The memo sometimes uses quotation marks but usually does not. The quotes here are what the document says, which may or may not be the speakers' actual words. Punctuation altered for clarity.

55 Loudly: Teicher, p. 195

55 Did not apply: Sharon, p. 335

56 Audience, privately: Haig, *Caveat,* p. 335; Haig 5-11-94; Draper 4-25-93

56 Right to tell: Haig, *Caveat,* p. 335

56 Conceded the point: Schiff & Ya'ari, p. 73; Teicher, p. 195. As Haig put it on another occasion, "How do we think, as Americans, we can be allies with anyone if we tell them they don't have the right to defend themselves?" (Haig 5-11-94).

56 Thought he did: Habib interview with Tueni; Shultz 7-25-94

56 Your opposition: Draper 4-25-93

56 Bully: E.g., Draper 4-25-93; Lewis 4-10-94; Hill 7-16-94; another State Department official who asked not to be identified by name.

56 Utterly opposed: Draper 4-25-93; Dillon ADST oral history. See p. 99-100 for Habib's wording of what he considered an appropriate warning to Begin. A week and a half before Sharon met with Haig, Ambassador Lewis sent State a stark warning about what Sharon needed to hear: "All senior U.S. officials whom he sees in Washington should talk turkey to Sharon about the dangerous situation in Leba-

non. To slide over it would be to give him a dangerous signal and reinforce his conviction that whatever Israel ultimately decides it must do about the PLO in Lebanon can be done without long-lasting damage to U.S.-Israeli relations. . . . We are skating on extremely thin ice at this moment with respect to Lebanon. Although there is not a strong majority yet in the Cabinet, much less in the country at large, to support Sharon's determination to deal the PLO in Lebanon a devastating blow, regardless of the international diplomatic consequences, there is a growing sense of inevitability here that it is only a matter of time. One major successful terrorist act which produces several dead could tip the balance . . . . For this reason, it is extremely important that Sharon hear clearly from top U.S. officials what kind of complications would inevitably result for Israel if a major operation were launched using American supplied weapons. He has a considerable capacity to minimize these complications and to assert to his colleagues that the U.S. reaction will be merely verbal and short-lived. If in fact our reaction would be different, Sharon should know it well in advance, as should Begin. We run grave risks of misleading the Israelis and producing even more complications for both our countries if they believe a major military move into Lebanon would have no direct consequences past U.N. condemnations or other symbolic or verbal sanctions. . . . Don't allow Sharon to leave Washington with any illusion about the degree to which a major military move into Lebanon would affect the course of U.S.-Israeli relations, if indeed it would have those consequences" (Lewis cable Tel Aviv 07285 May 14, 1982, quoted in State 133828, 172000Z May 82).

56 Clearly agreed: When interviewed for this book, Haig said (5-11-94), "How do we think, as Americans, we can be allies with anyone if we tell them they don't have the right to defend themselves? My God! Of course the Israelis had a right to go in and defend themselves. And we had no right to tell them they didn't if they were attacked from sanctuary, and they were." The chapter "The Other General" discusses Haig's agreement with Sharon about other issues, including the applicability of the July 24 ceasefire to attacks against Jews in Europe.

Sharon may or may not have sensed Haig's excitement with the invasion plans. But Veliotes says he and Draper did when they met with him later that night. A "rather enthusiastic" Haig still had a large map of Lebanon on an easel by his desk. With an air of what Veliotes calls "excitable belligerency," Haig showed them Sharon's ambitious plan, including linking Bashir's Christian militia in the middle of Lebanon with a proxy Christian militia that Israel sponsored in the south. Draper blurted out, "For Christ's sake, Mr. Secretary, there are a million and a half Muslims between them, and at least a million of them are Shi'a!" Haig seemed surprised. Veliotes said, "If [Israel's] plan is to do all of this, that means war with Syria, and God knows the carnage. You will have a Middle East policy in tatters." He and Draper also recommended sending a follow-up message (Veliotes 4-29-93; Veliotes ADST oral history). Shi'a are followers of the smaller of the two main branches of Islam, with adherents concentrated in Iran and Lebanon. This meeting was only a few months after the end of the Teheran hostage crisis, in which militant Shi'a in Iran had held American diplomats hostage for over a year. The Shi'a of Lebanon had so far been not been active in opposing Israel, but an invasion through their ranks would certainly alienate and possibly radicalize them (Dillon 2-27-02).

56 Went home confident: Habib heard from an Israeli whom he considered very authoritative that Sharon "went away with the idea that he had the green light to go ahead with this campaign" (interview with Tueni).

56 Job done: Gabriel, p. 14, 82

56 OK from us: Habib interview with Tueni. Several others also urged Haig to send a follow-up letter. As Haig puts it (5-11-94), "The guys in the bureau's pants started to get wet. They came rushing in and said, 'Hey, this guy's dangerous! You better get another message out to him.'" Though he did send the letter, he brushed off their concerns since they had heard only what was said in the big meeting, not what he considered the real one, the private one.

56 Letter: Haig letter to Begin 5-28-82, "Dear Mr. Prime Minister," 8215157. The understated letter urges "complete restraint," but reiterates "how deeply we understand the very real threat of violence Israel faces. As Minister Sharon said, no one has the right to tell Israel what decision it should take in the defense of its people. We are only expressing our belief that nations facing threats, including the U.S. and Israel, should carefully weigh the consequences of how such challenges are handled."

56 Approval: Sharon, p. 451. Schiff writes that

"For Sharon's plan to succeed, however, Israel needed an assurance from the United States that it would not obstruct Israeli moves into Lebanon" ("The Green Light," *Foreign Policy,* #50, Spring 1983). Howard Teicher, who represented the National Security Council in the meeting, writes (p. 195), "considering the glint in Sharon's eye and the forceful, overbearing way he clutched his briefing papers and pounded the conference table that day, I believe that Sharon would have found a way to interpret Haig's comments about the nice weather in Washington as encouragement of an Israeli invasion of Lebanon."

57 Disproportionate: Yaacobi 2-14-95

57 Hunting license: Veliotes 4-29-93. Schiff writes that "the import of Haig's response for Sharon was that the United States did not oppose a limited military operation provided there was sufficient reason for one. From Sharon's point of view the American had provided a green light. The halfhearted, feeble warnings subsequently voiced by Haig were irrelevant" ("The Green Light," *Foreign Policy,* #50, Spring 1983).

57 Professionalism: Habib interview with the author, *The Stanford Magazine,* Spring 1984

57 Wildly in love, respected: Veliotes 4-29-93. Veliotes (ADST oral history) adds that Reagan "in his first year and a half in office, was most proud of Phil Habib's peace missions."

57 Habib's attitude: This source, one of Habib's colleagues, asked not to be identified by name.

57 Aimed at the heart: Howell 9-6-93. In fact, they were surface-to-air missiles designed to shoot down jet planes flying overhead. Even if one missed and fell to earth, it lacked the range to land in Israel.

57-58 Soviets: Dillon ADST oral history. As the ambassador to Lebanon and thus the diplomat working in the PLO's home base, Dillon considered such notions ludicrous.

58 Read few papers, entertained: Draper ADST oral history

58 Talking points: Lewis ADST oral history; Salem, p. 25

58 Couldn't remember: Habib interview with Stuart Eizenstat, 5-13-92, p. 41. Reagan was the best friend Israel ever had in the White House. He had what Dillon (ADST oral his-

tory) calls "an emotional pro-Israeli bias. He had a romanticized Hollywood view of brave, little Israel." Draper (ADST oral history) says he was a genuinely nice man, whose benign, forgiving nature led Israel's leaders to think they could take the US for granted.

58 Educate him: Veliotes 4-29-93

58 Habib earned: Veliotes 4-29-93

58 That crowd: Veliotes 4-29-93

58 His turf: Reagan, p. 270

58 Baker, Bush, Clark: Haig 5-11-94

58 Do him in, suicidal: Veliotes 4-29-93; Reagan, p. 361; Haig 5-11-94. Haig blamed them for allowing Israel to invade Lebanon, by ignoring his prior warnings. He says he sent a memo to Reagan two months prior to the invasion warning that a war was imminent and suggesting steps to prevent it. But, he says, "that memo never even *got* to the president! It sat on Bill Clark's desk!" (Haig 5-11-94).

58-59 Isolated, stupid: Haig 5-11-94. Haig adds, "Now, I'm sure there were exceptions" to Reagan's lack of engagement, "like when he went into Grenada." One writer says, "This chaotic situation [as described by Haig in his resignation letter] in foreign policy affairs during the Reagan Administration reflected the poor leadership of the president, the lack of cohesiveness inside the Administration, and the unsteadiness of purpose in adopting one clearcut line of foreign policy. Instead, a mixture of policies and personalities clashes [sic] among the decision-makers laid bare the management problem of the Administration" (Korbani, p. 191).

59 Sanitize: Habib interview with Parker, which is the basis of Parker, p. 181

59 Broader issues: The US had recently decided to try to breathe fresh life into a series of talks on Palestinian autonomy, with the aim of reaching an outcome within sixty days. This plan was revealed during the Ditchley conference, perhaps by Habib himself in the "candid analysis" he gave the conference (Patrick Seale, "The Search for an Arab-Israeli Settlement," reporting the conference held at Ditchley Park, 4-6 June 1982; Ditchley Conference Report No. 7/1982, p. 1).

Habib also hoped to establish a contact group (representatives of several interested and influential countries) and eventually an international conference at which the Lebanese factions could work out their differences and thus stabilize Lebanon (Eagleburger cable State 155256, 070141Z Jun 82, p. 3).

59 Four vacations, Greek islands: Habib interview with Mulcahy; Marjorie Habib 2-27-93; Phyllis Habib 7-7-97. He got a month of leave every year and never took it.

59 Get after something, have to leave: Habib interviews with Mulcahy and Parker. Though Argov lived, the bullet lodged in his spine and he was badly disabled for life. He was shot by the Abu Nidal terrorist organization, an independent and virulently anti-PLO group. Abu Nidal was in fact under a death sentence by the PLO for having assassinated moderate Palestinians (Dillon ADST oral history; Draper 5-4-93; Yaacobi 2-14-95). Though Begin and his Cabinet knew that the culprit was Abu Nidal, it made no difference to Begin. "They're all PLO," he said. "Abu Nidal, Abu Smidal. We have to strike at the PLO" (Schiff & Ya'ari, p. 98).

59 Israeli response: Gabriel, p. 25, 82; Cannon, p. 200; Gowers, p. 201

59 Palestinian response: Gabriel, p. 59; Seale, p. 377, 379. The PLO's response was a colossal blunder, since it gave Israel the final straw it needed to launch its invasion.

4 Playing on Two Ropes

60 Lost causes: Barron letter to author 5-4-94. Barron was administrative officer in the Beirut embassy.

60 Relations: Veliotes 4-29-93

60 My subordinate: Haig 5-11-94

60 Haig not invited: Howell 9-6-93; Haig, p.337.

60 Reagan's instructions: Habib interviews with Parker and Tueni. Habib would later describe them as "general guidelines."

60 Habib meeting with Haig: Haig 5-11-94; Haig, p. 337.

60 Different instructions: Habib interview with Parker

61 Motions: Howell 9-6-93. Haig (p. 337)

writes that "I asked Habib to go immediately to Begin and urge an immediate end of hostilities before the conflict widened."

61 Welcomed: Randal, p. 289; Parker, p. 178; Norton, p. 84; Draper 4-13-93; Howell 9-6-93

61 Inner circle, others overjoyed: Draper 4-25-93. Draper mentions NSC staff member Howard Teicher specifically as one of these. Haig himself wrote to Reagan on the sixth day of the invasion that the US should "seize the initiative quickly" to capitalize on the occasion (Haig memo to The President, "A Forward U.S. Strategy in Wake of Israel's Offensive," 6-12-82).

61 Having warned: Eagleburger 7-3-93

61 Considered the invasion: Habib interviews with Parker and Dusclaud

61 Habib-Begin meeting: Habib cable Jerusalem 01745, 072224Z Jun 82, par. 2. In most of Begin's other statements, he said 40 kilometers. "In his presentation," Habib wrote, "Begin stated Israel's firm commitment not repeat not to remain in Lebanon" (Habib cable Jerusalem 01743, 071925Z June 82, par. 2). A week later Begin was still telling Habib that, once a multinational force took control of a 40-kilometer zone to keep terrorists out, "we will be out of Lebanon completely." The Israelis considered defining the zone as 43 to 48 kilometers, but decided to stick with 40 (Habib cable Jerusalem 01903 of June 13, 1982, repeated in State 163551, 142321Z Jun 82, par. 6).

61 Artillery range: Habib cable Jerusalem 01745, 072224Z Jun 82, par. 6

61 Didn't believe: Habib interview with Parker

61 More grandiose scheme: Habib cable Jerusalem 01785, 082248Z Jun 82, par. 2 and 3. Habib's suspicion about an Israeli-Phalange linkup was strengthened the next day when he met with Begin and asked him directly whether Israel's current military moves were a prelude to such a linkup. Begin was "somewhat coy" and evaded the question, leaving Habib and Amb. Sam Lewis with the "distinct impression" that they were (Lewis cable Tel Aviv 08563, 091533Z Jun 82, par. 8 and 11). Despite his skepticism that the IDF would stop at any 40- or 43-kilometer limit, he set about trying to get a ceasefire anyway (Hopkins, p. 7 and 63, citing a 3-12-92 interview with Habib). Nathaniel Howell, who accompanied Habib

for the first week or so of the war, says that in the early days he and Habib really did think they were dealing with Israeli ambitions for a 40-kilometer security zone (Howell 10-23-96).

62 Few days of quiet: Crocker 4-25-94

62 Genuinely believed: Kadishai 6-29-95

62 By tomorrow: Habib cable Jerusalem 01743, 071925Z Jun 82. Begin and Sharon were "supremely overconfident" of the IDF's ability to root out the PLO within days without triggering a wider conflict with Syria (Lewis in Quandt, p. 242; see also Schiff & Ya'ari, p. 103-6). Sharon told the cabinet the operation should take 12 to 24 hours (Schiff & Ya'ari, p. 105-6).

62 Sharon told Knesset: Yaacobi 2-14-95. Again on August 4, Begin predicted "a historic period of peace, of 40 years or 50 years" once the PLO left Lebanon ("Israelis push toward guerrilla strongholds," *St. Petersburg Times* based on *New York Times* and *Washington Post* wire reports, 8-5-82). Four days later he said in a speech, "Because the other Arab countries are completely incapable of attacking the State of Israel, there is reason to expect that we are facing a historic period of peace. It is obviously impossible to set a date. It may well be that 'The land shall be still for 40 years.' Perhaps less; perhaps more. But from the facts before us, it is clear that, with the end of the fighting in Lebanon, we have ahead of us many years of establishing peace treaties and peaceful relations with the various Arab countries" (Begin speech "The Wars of No Alternative and Operation Peace for Galilee," delivered at the National Defense College in Israel 8-8-82, in Laqueur and Rubin, p. 655).

62 Achieved: Schiff & Ya'ari, p. 187

62 Too massive: Dillon ADST oral history

62 Terrible terrain: Dillon 5-9-94

62 Without a fight: Dillon 5-9-94

62 Any illusions: Lewis 4-10-94

62 Phyllis: Marjorie Habib 2-27-93; Phyllis Habib 7-7-97; Grove 6-12-94. Despite his instructions, Phyllis did not stay at the hotel the whole time. She spent part of her two weeks at Consul General Grove's residence.

62 Dillon and embassy, lie: Dillon ADST oral history. Dillon 5-9-94; "The 'Beirut Summer,'" by Dundas McCullough, *State,* 12-82, p. 6-7

62-63 Intermingled: Habib cable Jerusalem

01745, 072224Z Jun 82, par. 6. Israelis viewed PLO artillery as shooting at Israeli villages from "under Syrian umbrella" (Habib cable Jerusalem 01782, 082059Z Jun 82, par. 6).

63 Overriding priority: Habib cable Jerusalem 01785, 082248Z Jun 82, par. 2

63 Escalate: Haig memo to The President, "Lebanon: Critical Moment at Hand," 6-9-82, 8216678, warning that, unless the Israelis pulled back to within their declared 40-kilometer zone, "there is a strong likelihood of a Syrian-Israeli war"; Draper ADST oral history

63 Not want a fight: Howell 10-11-93; Howell 9-6-93; Seale, p. 378-79; Begin and Sharon told Habib at their first meeting with him after the invasion that they "wanted to avoid any battle with Syria" (Habib cable Jerusalem 01745, 072224Z Jun 82, par. 6). Israeli Labor Party leaders told Habib June 7 that Israel "had sought to inform the Syrians in every possible way that it desired no clash with Syrian forces" (Habib cable Jerusalem 01782, 082059Z Jun 82, par. 5).

63 Far more equipment: Seale, p. 379-80

63 Confronting the Syrians: At their first meeting after the invasion began Sharon told Habib his troops were trying to avoid any battle with Syria, but that "there had been a very dangerous development": Syria was taking advantage of Israeli caution to move new forces and missiles into Lebanon and had shelled Israeli troops, inflicting casualties and "complicat[ing] the IDF's mission" (Habib cable Jerusalem 01745, 072224Z Jun 82, par. 6 and 8).

63 Provoke: Draper ADST oral history

63 Mobilize: Howell 10-11-93

63 Cut off: Gabriel, p. 64-66. Sharon, in a meeting with Habib June 7, accused the Syrians of attacking the IDF (Habib cable Jerusalem 01745, 072224Z Jun 82, par. 6 and 8).

63 Red Line: Cobban, p. 39. The Red Line agreement was an informal division of Lebanon brokered by Henry Kissinger in 1976. Under the agreement, Syria tolerated Israel's presence in certain areas while Israel tolerated Syria's presence in other areas (Seale, p. 378). Syrian president Assad now concluded that Syria was Sharon's real target (Seale, p. 380).

63 Race: Former Lebanese Prime Minister Sa'ab Salaam would later say "Sharon is winning the race against a political settlement"

(Habib cable Beirut 05089, 040531Z Aug 82, par. 9).

63 War plan: A major strategic premise of Israel is a fast war doctrine, to achieve its objectives before the US intervenes to force a halt to the fighting (Gabriel, p. 14; Yaacobi 2-14-95; Draper 4-13-93).

63 Bogged down: Schiff & Ya'ari, p. 109-160, particularly 137, 159-60

63 Operating assumption: Haig cable (no number) from Windsor to Habib, 6-9-82; Haig memo to The President, "Lebanon: Critical Moment at Hand," 6-9-82, 8216678; Lewis cable Tel Aviv 08563, 091533Z Jun 82, par. 4-5; State cable 159059 from NEA to Haig, par. 6; Habib cable Jerusalem 01871, 121152Z Jun 82, par. 3D and E. Other options for a security force in southern Lebanon included involving the Lebanese Armed Forces in it (Haig memo to The President, "A Forward U.S. Strategy in Wake of Israel's Offensive," 6-12-82, p. 2). When Habib first pointed out to Begin that the IDF was considerably past 40 kilometers already, Begin said those were just "'tactical' positions. Begin stated strongly that it is not an Israeli objective to press military operations with the goal of doing away with the PLO entirely" (Habib cable Jerusalem 01781, 082022Z Jun 82, par. 10; Habib cable Jerusalem 01785, 082248Z Jun 82, par. 6).

63-64 Sleep, feisty, glee: Howell 9-6-93. At Habib and Sharon's first meeting after the invasion, the first words out of Sharon's mouth were a pointed reminder that he had just recently emphasized in Washington that he didn't want the US to be caught by surprise (Habib cable Jerusalem 01745, 072224Z Jun 82, par. 6).

64 No wider war: Gabriel, p. 67, citing *Newsview,* July 20, 1983, p. 19.

64 Asked Habib to go: Haig memo to The President, "Lebanon: Critical Moment at Hand," 6-9-82, 8216678; Seale, p. 381. In his memo, Haig told Reagan that "the Syrians are very unlikely to agree" to Begin's terms as long as Israeli troops kept attacking well beyond Begin's 40-kilometer zone. Seale and Schiff & Ya'ari (p. 168) both describe this message as an ultimatum, but Draper says, "Phil would never deliver an ultimatum on behalf of the Israelis or anybody else." In Draper's view, Habib was simply bringing, in good faith, a reiteration of the Israeli position on the missiles that everyone had known for over a year

(Draper 4-25-93). Assad apparently did not view it as any more of an ultimatum than he viewed other messages from Begin (Paganelli 11-2-96). Hopkins, p. 6, and Sharon, p. 465, give differing texts of Begin's message to Assad.

Sharon claimed that Syria introduced six additional SA-6 missile batteries between June 7 and 9 (Lewis cable Tel Aviv 08505, 090841Z Jun 82, par. 3); Assad told Habib that he had added no new missile batteries in the Bekaa, only shifted existing ones around (Habib cable Damascus 04030, 092111Z Jun 82, par. 1).

64 Leaks: Hill 7-9-94; Habib cable Damascus 04013, 091207Z Jun 82, par. 3 and 4. Lewis conveyed to Begin Habib's message that Israeli leaks like this virtually guaranteed Habib's failure. But Lewis said "this will not be the first or the last time that Israeli leaks complicate your missions. I have long since run out of arguments to forestall them" (Lewis cable to Habib, State 158952, 092310Z Jun 82, par. 3-4).

64 Night owl: Howell 9-6-93

64 His disposal: Paganelli 11-2-96

64 Attack while Habib waits: Seale, p. 381-82; Schiff & Ya'ari, p. 167-68; Gabriel, p. 67, 97. Nathaniel Howell, who was the only person traveling with Habib in the first few days of the war, points out that the missiles were positioned "pretty well far up the Bekaa" nowhere close to the Israeli border. Despite Reagan's uninformed statement that the missiles were pointed at the heart of Israel, they were defensive missiles. "They couldn't hit Israel and they couldn't threaten Israel," says Howell. "What they did threaten was Israel's ability to fly at will over the Bekaa Valley. So those missiles were a red herring all along. . . . Among the professionals dealing with this there was some understanding of why the Syrians had moved the missiles in and a feeling that the Israelis had really provoked them to do it" (Howell 9-6-93).

65 Careful not to strike: Gabriel, p. 92. The only explanation Gabriel offers is that "the political situation changed" on the ninth and "Begin finally authorized" Sharon to launch a preemptive strike (p. 97). Sharon's version is that, as soon as Habib received the message from Begin on June 8, the US embassy in Damascus forwarded it to Assad. Meanwhile, Assad was introducing new missiles into the Bekaa to supplement the ones he already had there. Begin demanded, through US ambassador Lewis, that Assad remove those new missiles

by 5 A.M. the next day, June 8. Assad failed to comply. While the Israeli Cabinet pondered what to do, and while Habib coincidentally was waiting to see Assad, Israeli intelligence notified Sharon that more missiles were on their way to Lebanon. The Cabinet thus decided to take them out (Sharon, p. 465-66).

Sharon did tell Begin on the morning of June 9 that the Syrians had moved six additional surface-to-air missile (SAM) batteries into Lebanon (Lewis cable Tel Aviv 08505, 090841Z Jun 82, par. 3). But Habib cabled Washington that "Assad told me last night that he had not [repeat] not sent additional SAM batteries into the Bekaa but had rotated units [that were already] there for tactical reasons." Begin's request that Habib discuss with Assad the question of "additional SAMs" was "misleading," Habib said, because the supposedly new units at issue were not in the Bekaa Valley but "located on the border. It is simply not reasonable," Habib wrote, "to expect the Syrians not to augment their air defense, particularly within their own territory, and use them in certain circumstances under conditions that approximate war. . . . [The Israelis] really wanted to bomb them out and did not even give me a chance to get Assad to move back to June 5 deployment, despite [the] fact that I had been tasked by them to raise the issue" (Habib cable Damascus 04056, 100943Z Jun 82).

Robert Paganelli, the American ambassador in Damascus at the time, also disputes Sharon's crucial point about his embassy forwarding Begin's message to Assad on June 8: "No, that's wrong. Phil carried that message. We never in any of the time that I worked with Phil, when he had a message to deliver, we would *never* preempt that message. Never" (Paganelli 11-2-96).

65 Begin extremely eager: Sicherman 8-4-98. Lewis cabled Habib in Damascus on June 9 that "Begin has telephoned several times during the day today (Wednesday, June 9) to ask whether I had any word about your movements or meetings. He is obviously extremely eager to know whether anything helpful occurred. When I spoke to him about 3 P.M. local this afternoon, we had just gotten the first word of the firing of the SAM-6 missiles, the Israeli attack on those missiles, and the ensuing air battle" (Lewis cable to Habib, State 158952, 092310Z Jun 82, par. 2-3).

65 Biggest: Seale, p. 381-82; Schiff & Ya'ari, p. 167; Gabriel, p. 67, 97. Israel shot down

twenty-nine Syrian MiGs that afternoon. Schiff & Ya'ari point out that Syria's loss of pilots was even greater than its loss of equipment.

65 Knew nothing: Habib cable Damascus 04039, 100047Z, par. 3. Howell also confirms that Habib did not know about the missiles having been hit when he walked into the first meeting with Assad (Howell 10-23-96).

65 Afternoon: Schiff & Ya'ari, p. 169

65 Listening to the roar: Howell 10-11-93. Paganelli (11-2-96) says the Syrian military bases were far away from town, but Howell distinctly remembers the sounds of the jets.

65 No hint: Draper 4-25-93; Howell 9-6-93; Sicherman 8-4-98

65 No worse: Paganelli 11-2-96

65 Deceived: Paganelli 11-2-96

65 Ceasefire for 6 A.M.: Eagleburger cable to ambassadors, State 158441, 091807Z Jun 82

65 Called foreign ministry: Habib cable Damascus 04039, 100047Z Jun 82, par. 3. Howell (10-23-96) and Paganelli (11-2-96) both confirm that Habib did not know about the missiles having been hit when he walked into the first meeting with Assad.

65 Wild goose chase: Habib cable Damascus 04030, 092111Z Jun 82, par. 1

65 Turning point: Gabriel, p. 97. Gabriel, who wrote his book with the cooperation of the IDF, says the dogfights were no accident. Rather, "A second part of [Israel's] strategy was to draw Syrian aircraft into battle and destroy as many as possible in order to establish air superiority over the entire Lebanese battle zone" (p. 97).

65 Crippled: Gabriel, p. 100. Assad told Habib that he would replace whatever equipment the Israelis destroyed (Habib cable Damascus 04030, 092111Z Jun 82, par. 2).

65 Humiliate: Habib cable Damascus 04030, 092111Z Jun 82, par. 5; see also Seale, p. 382

65 False sense of security: Howell 9-6-93

65 Feint: Seale, p. 381

66 Feet taken out: Draper 4-25-93

66 Two ropes: Howell 9-6-93. A newsletter that got hold of Habib's cables reported that Habib believed he was "set-up" by the Israelis (*Middle East Policy Survey*, June 18, 1982, No.

58, p. 1, "War in Lebanon"). Habib complained about the leak of his cables, but did not dispute the accuracy of the report (Hill 7-9-94).

66 More tense: Howell 10-23-96; Habib cable Damascus 04039, 100047Z Jun 82, par. 2

66 Atmosphere: Paganelli 11-2-96

66 Habib meeting with Assad: Habib cable Damascus 04039, 100047Z Jun 82, par. 6-12. In fact, Habib had "tried strenuously" that very morning to extract from Begin a promise to pull back to 40 kilometers; Begin not only refused, but confided to him that pulling back would contradict the Israeli strategy of keeping a certain amount of pressure on the Syrians to "persuade them" to move the PLO north. Indeed, Begin had emphasized, forcing Syria to move the PLO north was the "only purpose" behind Israel's operations north of the 40-kilometer line (Lewis cable Tel Aviv 08563, 091533Z Jun 82, par. 2 and 4-7). Begin said the IDF's strategy was to encircle the Syrians and the PLO much as it had encircled the Egyptian Third Army on the east bank of the Suez Canal in the 1973 war. He pointed out that in 1973 the IDF had not fired on that army, but that keeping it encircled facilitated the subsequent negotiations. Likewise, he said he had ordered the IDF not to attack the Syrians (par. 4 and 6).

One of the two cables Habib was handed during this meeting (Eagleburger cable to Habib and Paganelli, State 158653, 092031Z Jun 82, par. 2) contained talking points for Habib to make to Assad and reinforced the US position "that Israeli forces must be withdrawn from Lebanon." The other (Draper cable to Habib, State 158702, 092056Z Jun 82) authorized Habib to make clear to Assad that the US did not view the ceasefire as "the end of the game" and to leave Assad with the "clear implication that other steps will follow the ceasefire" (par. 2). Draper was sending this cable in his capacity as deputy assistant secretary for Near Eastern affairs; within days he would take over for Howell travelling with Habib.

66 Not divert: Habib cable Damascus 04056, 100943Z Jun 82, par. 2, 6

67 Sharon fights on: Sharon, p. 467-68; see also Gabriel, p. 104. It had been three days since Sharon had told the Israeli Cabinet that the IDF had "achieved almost all our objectives!" within the first twenty-four hours (Schiff & Ya'ari, p. 187). Begin's reply to Reagan's letter was, in Lewis' description, "vintage Begin, an extravagantly polite and legalistic way of rejecting the president's simple proposal and restating Begin's previous conditions" (Lewis cable Jerusalem 01809, 100509Z Jun 82, par. 5).

67 Pissed, double-crossed: Draper 4-25-93

67 Achieved objectives: Sharon, p. 467-68; see also Gabriel, p. 104

67 Worst fear: Habib cable Jerusalem 01785, 082248Z Jun 82, par. 2, 7

67 Meat grinder: Habib cable Damascus 04082, 101739Z Jun 82, par. 3. Habib had written two days earlier, "I do not believe the Syrians can in any way accept . . . the virtual loss of their dominant position in Lebanese affairs" as a result of Israeli action. "I believe they might just make a major fight now rather than swallow this humiliation, even at the cost of a military defeat" (Habib cable Jerusalem 01785, 082248Z Jun 82, par. 7).

67-68 Habib meeting with Assad: Habib cable 6-11-82. Assad typically had visitors meet first with his foreign minister, then repeat their message to him later. Habib knew that Assad had played the same game with Kissinger and Vance. This practice is one reason Habib had to wait to see him on June 9. Having been burned by that experience, Habib took steps to prevent an encore. He sent word via a Syrian intermediary, "This is ridiculous. I don't want to go and sit for two hours and tell [Foreign Minister] Khaddam everything I have to say and then have to go repeat it to Assad" (Habib interview with Parker).

68 Attitude: Draper 12-22-94 and 4-13-93; Draper ADST oral history; Howell 9-6-93

68 Welcome: Habib cable 6-11-82. The American ambassador in Damascus would say on July 16 that the "Syrians would welcome a Habib visit for . . . any . . . purpose" (Paganelli cable Damascus 05050, 160720Z Jul 82).

68 Begin would announce: Haig cable Bonn, Secto 08064, 110102Z Jun 82, par. 2

68 Would have preferred: Habib cable Damascus 04097, 110702Z Jun 82, par. 7

68 Ceasefire at noon: Cable 111738Z June 82, RUEKJCS/1022. The PLO rejected the ceasefire. Assad's biographer says that, on the strength of Habib's words the night before, Assad had already agreed to pull back his own troops and to move the PLO fighters northward (Seale, p. 384). Howell, who was in the meeting with

Habib and Assad, says flatly, "He did not agree to pull them back" (Howell 9-6-93).

68 Assumption: Paganelli 11-2-96

68 Unilateral ceasefire: An incorrect story has it that the Israelis decided on their ceasefire while Habib was flying from Damascus to Israel and that Habib knew nothing about it until he arrived in Jerusalem (Hopkins, p. 9, quoting his interview with Paganelli 1-11-92). The story cannot be correct because Habib's cable commenting on "the ceasefire which they intend to declare unilaterally" was sent from Damascus at 9 A.M. local time. Another report is that the Israelis learned of Habib and Assad's understanding during the night of June 10-11, perhaps by monitoring the less-than-secure line Habib used to report back to Washington. The communication facility at the US embassy in Damascus had broken down, and Habib was forced to fall back on a voice line (Seale, p. 384). When Habib heard of Israel's unilateral ceasefire, he said he didn't think Assad would agree to it unless it carried some provision for beginning an Israeli withdrawal—which it of course did not (Habib cable Damascus 04097, 110702Z Jun 82, par. 8). See Sharon, p. 469.

68 Didn't mean a thing: Quoted in Seale, p. 385, from Seale's interview with Habib 7-25-87. Sharon's explanation in his memoirs (Sharon, p. 470-71) is that the PLO south and west of Beirut kept shooting, so Begin ordered the IDF to strike back at them.

69 Hell of a fight: Habib interview with Tueni

69 Clobbered: Habib interview with Parker

69 Line of defense: Howell 10-23-96; Paganelli 11-2-96

69 Cleaners: Veliotes 4-29-93

69 Deceived and betrayed him: Seale, p. 407. The American ambassador in Damascus talked with the Syrian deputy foreign minister June 26 about a report that Assad believed Habib had deceived him in their June 9-10 discussions. He argued that Habib had not misled Assad, but that his discussions had been overtaken by developments on the ground (Paganelli cable Damascus 04565, 261130Z Jun 82).

69 Breaking a promise: Draper ADST oral history; Draper 4-13-93. Why would Assad blame Habib instead of Sharon? Paganelli, the American ambassador to Syria, says this was a case of Assad shooting the messenger (Paganelli 11-2-96).

69 Rage: Draper 4-25-93

69 My word: Quoted by a State Department official who asked not to be identified by name.

69 Really shouted: Draper 4-25-93

69-70 Habib exchange with Begin and Sharon: Habib recounted this exchange several times, with some variations each time. So did Draper and Howell, who were both in the meeting with him. This version is based primarily on Habib's account in his interview with Parker, with additional material from Draper's accounts (Draper 12-22-94 and 4-13-93) and Howell's account (Howell 9-6-93). Habib also told the story in interviews with Hopkins 3-12-92 (Hopkins p. 9-10) and Tueni 6-28-87. Habib repeatedly complained about Begin's "mind-boggling definition—foreign to any rational definition of a cease-fire" (Habib cable Beirut 04240, 162045Z Jun 82, par. 2). The letter was of course not written by the president himself, but by an official in the State Department. It got the usual approvals, including a "No objection" stamp from the NSC (State 158645 TOSEC 080359, 092024Z).

Habib reported on a June 13 meeting in which he and Begin argued about whether "in place" is intrinsic to the concept of a ceasefire. This may have been the same meeting described in the text, though it may also have been a later one in which they went at it again. In that meeting, Habib told Begin he "found it hard to believe that Israel would deal this way with the appeal of the president. Clearly, the president had proposed a ceasefire in place. Begin repeated that *that would be true* if it had been negotiated into an agreement. As it is, it is a unilateral undertaking" [italics added]. Lewis reminded Begin in this meeting that, when he had first presented Reagan's message to Begin, he had "made it clear that the cease-fire was in place" (Habib cable Jerusalem 01903 of 6-13-82, repeated in State 163551, 142321Z Jun 82, par. 15-23; Habib cable Beirut 04240, 162045Z Jun 82, par. 2).

The Israelis had continued moving not only on the Syrians, but also on the PLO in the Beirut area. Their rationale there was that their unilateral ceasefire applied only to Syria, not to the PLO (Habib cable Beirut 04240, 162045Z Jun 82, par. 2). In his memoirs, Sharon goes out of his way to emphasize that this ceasefire had been *unilateral*, that Israel declared it because the army "had achieved the war's objectives in full," and that, as Begin put it, "Israel wasn't negotiating with anyone" (Sharon, p. 468-69). It is therefore unclear why, in justifying his troop movements during the ceasefire, he and Begin felt the need to cite Reagan's message at all.

Begin apparently had no qualms about his and his army's conduct. The same day, June 11, he told the Cabinet that the operation in Lebanon so far "has been one of the greatest actions, and not only of our nation in its thirty-four years of independence, but throughout the history of our people" (Sharon, p. 474). At about the same time, though, the CIA was calling the invasion "a grave mistake" and saying that Israel had "over estimated the ease with which it could achieve its military objectives." Israeli losses, the CIA reported, had been "considerable," "much higher than Israeli media sources have admitted." There had been "large numbers" of helicopter Medi-Vac flights out of southern Lebanon, and Haifa Hospital was reportedly full (CIA cable 250164, 12 June 82).

70 Carrying water: Howell 9-6-93

70 Snookered: A colleague of Habib's who asked not to be identified by name

70 Wariness: Hopkins, p. 10, citing his interview with Habib 3-12-92

70 All ceasefires specified: Draper 12-22-94; Habib interview with Tueni

70 Moonbeams: Howell 9-6-93

70 Would not go past: Howell 10-11-93. Sharon's forces had blown past that point days ago. *The Middle East Journal,* Autumn 1982, vol. 36, no. 4, "Chronology April 16, 1982-July 15, 1982," p. 566, cites a *New York Times* report that an Israeli Army spokesman said on June 10 that all opposing forces had been cleared from a 25-mile-wide zone (approximately 43 kilometers) north of Israel.

70 Control of suburbs: Kahan Commission report, p. 7

70 Surrounded: Beirut had plenty of PLO fighters in it when the invasion began, but their numbers swelled as fighters deployed in the south and east fled into the city to escape the Israeli northward advance. There they could hide out and defy the Israelis, confident that the Israelis would not come into the city to get them (Draper ADST oral history; Dillon ADST oral history). Syrian numbers per Paganelli 11-2-96. Quarter mile per Associated Press story "Habib makes peace in his ancestral land," in *Clearwater Sun,* 8-21-82.

70 Looking for general: Sharon, p. 472-83

70-71 Tamerlane: Gowers, p. 205. See also Schiff & Ya'ari, p. 196.

71 Now under siege: Dillon 11-5-96. Beirut had previously come under siege by the Crusaders, by Saladin in the twelfth century, and by the Anglo-Turkish fleet in 1840 (Fisk, p. 278).

71 Focus shifted: Israeli and Syrian forces did continue to skirmish in various places now and then, but these became peripheral to the main event in Beirut.

71 No getting around the fact: Schiff & Ya'ari, p. 181. The same point is made by Draper ADST oral history and "Ministers: Sharon strung us along," *The Jerusalem Post,* 6-13-82.

72 Cornered Palestinians: Habib cable for the President from Beirut 04247, 6-17-82, par. 4

72 Standard estimation tables: Smith 11-25-96; Smith email to the author 7-12-01; Mead email to the author 7-15-01 confirms Smith's numbers. Smith adds that "Israel's air superiority might have lessened the cost, but such an attack would most likely have drawn Syria, Egypt, and others into the fray, which would certainly have changed the equation." Mead adds that, to the small nation of Israel, 2,000 dead would be the equivalent of 35,000 deaths to America. The casualty tables they refer to are based on military experience stretching all the way back to the Peloponnesian War. The Israelis would no doubt have consulted comparable tables of their own in planning their attack.

72 Loose cannon: Sharon later said that he had decided in January 1982 that he wanted to avoid entering Beirut because it is the capital. "I solemnly affirm that I never wanted to enter Beirut unless it was absolutely indispensable. And believe me, had I been convinced that we had to enter Beirut, nobody in the world would have stopped me. Democracy or not, I would have entered even if my government didn't like. I mean, I would have persuaded them. . . . Militarily speaking, we could get in any moment. Just in case it would become necessary, all was arranged to get in" ("Sharon: 'I Wanted Them Out of Beirut; I Got What I Wanted,'" *The Washington Post,* 8-29-82).

72 Exterminate: Quoted by a senior Labor party member of the Knesset at the time, who asked not to be quoted by name. That source emphasizes that "exterminate" was Sharon's word, but notes that Sharon meant to destroy the PLO

as an organization, not to kill each person who was a member of the PLO.

72 Wipe out: According to one of Habib's colleagues who asked not to be identified

72 Get the PLO: Habib interview with Parker. Hopkins, p. 12, citing his 3-12-92 interview with Habib, says, "Sharon was hell-bent on getting what he wanted, which was the wholesale destruction of the PLO in Lebanon; he was going to stop at nothing less." Habib said on June 17, "Sharon knows he has the PLO on the ropes," Habib said, "but he prefers to have someone else finish them off. I doubt that he would want to risk the Israeli casualties involved in house-to-house fighting. But I cannot rule it out. He may try to use the Phalange for this, but that will be just as bloody" (Habib cable for the President from Beirut 04247, 6-17-82, par. 4). Habib repeatedly insisted that, whatever else might happen, the Israelis must not be allowed to enter West Beirut.

One of Habib's colleagues, who asked not to be identified by name, says, "Paint the picture we faced at the time: You're not sure who's really in control of the Israeli army. Every time you're told what their position is, they're actually 10 miles or 20 miles or 50 miles further than you think. You know that the leader of this enterprise, Arik Sharon, has talked about the Palestinians as being like insects and like a disease that has to be cut out. The Israelis seem very, very close to going into Beirut, where you would have *massive* destruction, *massive* casualties—on both sides." Begin had referred to Palestinian terrorists as "animals on two legs" and Gen. Raful Eitan would later describe West Bank Palestinians as "drugged cockroaches" (*The Times*, 4-15-83, cited in Fisk, p. 399; Sachar, p. 194)—an ironic choice of words, since Anne Frank had written with disgust in her diary of German plans to "cleanse" Utrecht of Jews "as though Jews were cockroaches" (Fisk, p. 399).

72 Storm into Beirut: Shultz 9-16-93

72 Major bloodletting: Weinberger 10-7-93

72 Fight to the last man: Seale, p. 386

72 Spark an all-out war: In the judgment of the American ambassador to Syria, Robert Paganelli, 11-2-96. That's what Habib feared most (Tueni 11-15-95): "Once you get into national wars," he said, "you get into danger of major conflagration. Then you're talking big stuff" (Habib interview with the author, *The Stanford Magazine,* Spring 1984).

72 Broader consequences: Draper ADST oral history; Dillon 5-9-94

72-73 American-made: Draper 4-13-93; also Draper ADST oral history

73 Green light: Draper ADST oral history. For example, Arafat said that "the U.S. will pay a high price in the near future for its collaboration with Israel." Eighteen West Bank labor unions and student organizations denounced "American imperialist collaboration with Israeli policies" in Lebanon, and a Palestinian politician reportedly criticized "American-Israeli conspiracy in the massacre being implemented against the Palestinians in Lebanon" (Palestinian newspapers *Ashaab* and *Al Fajr,* 6-28-82, summarized and quoted in Grove cable Jerusalem 02057, 281105Z Jun 82, par. 3-4). The pro-Jordanian newspaper *Al Quds* titled one of its lead editorials "The Futility of Habib's Mission," in which it concluded that the United States is unfit to play the role of mediator since "American and Israeli aims are identical" (6-28-82, summarized and quoted in Grove cable Jerusalem 02057, 281105Z Jun 82, par. 4). The Soviets also accused the US of, at least, advance knowledge of the invasion and, at worst, complicity in it (Reagan, p. 422).

73 Quixote, shill: "Israeli attacks into Beirut will make the U.S. appear to have been acting as an accomplice in a pattern of Israeli deception, i.e., declare a ceasefire and then move ahead to take more territory. This can utterly destroy our credibility in future efforts to help meet Israel's security objectives" (Assistant Secretary of State memo to the Secretary, 6-15-82, 8216710).

73 Anti-American violence: Hill 6-15-93. Hill hastens to point out that academics frequently predicted upheavals in the Arab world in response to Israeli actions, but that the Arab states have really never cared enough about the Palestinians to react that way.

73 Fanatics: Draper ADST oral history. Hill says Draper felt even more strongly about this than Habib: "Draper was just really wild about this. He just believed that if the Israelis went into an Arab capital and the US was seen as allowing this to happen, it would be such an affront to Arab pride that God knows what would happen *all over* the Arab world. It could be just upheaval and embassies in flames and everything." Hill was skeptical about that prospect (Hill 7-19-95). A coalition of Syrian parties appealed to Arab masses on June 19 to hit and

destroy American interests in the region *(Journal of Palestine Studies,* Summer/Fall 1982, "Chronology of the Israeli Invasion of Lebanon June-August 1982," p. 148).

73 Soviet Union intervening: Draper (2-24-02) says, "We were concerned about a US-Soviet clash. We couldn't rule out the possibility that the Soviets might come to Syria's aid." The Soviets "indicated they might provide air defense help in the event of Israeli attacks on Syrian positions in the Bekaa Valley. The Soviets have suggested that they might become more directly involved in supporting Syrian forces if Israel attacked inside Syria" (Eagleburger cable State 155256, 070141Z Jun 82, p. 3, p. 6).

73 Draw in the US: Draper ADST oral history. To many, the prospect was very real: The Arab-Israeli wars of 1967 and 1973 had brought the U.S. and the USSR very close to an all-out confrontation over the Middle East. US ambassador to Syria Paganelli disagreed, considering it unlikely the Soviets would really intervene (Paganelli 11-2-96).

73 Secretly flown: Seale, p. 383

73 Brezhnev: Teicher p. 200-202. Teicher says this letter arrived from Brezhnev early in the second week of the war. Haig, p. 339, says it was June 9. As it turned out, Brezhnev's messages to the US were hollow. In his last months of life, he was too feeble and too distracted by his own crises in Afghanistan and Poland to really want a superpower confrontation (Seale, p. 395). But at the time, his threats had to be taken seriously.

73 Averting these disasters: As Schiff & Ya'ari (p. 201) put it, the Israelis had "two choices: to let Philip Habib negotiate a withdrawal of the Palestinian forces or to force their way into West Beirut and clean it out themselves."

5 We Corner Them, You Kill Them

74 Murdering: Dillon 11-16-96

74 Deputy: Prior to the invasion, Nathaniel Howell and Draper had taken turns accompanying Habib in the Middle East. While one was in the region, the other served as Habib's main contact in the State Department. At the moment the invasion began, Howell happened to be in England with Habib, so he went with him to the region. But he had a new job waiting for him in Washington. So by June 13 or so, Howell had returned to Washington and Draper took his place. Draper would remain with Habib for the remainder of the mission. With Howell no longer in his old job, Charlie Hill became Habib's main contact in the department. Date of the events described here is per Paganelli cable Damascus 04206, 141618Z Jun 82, par. 2 and 11; and Lewis cable Tel Aviv 141629Z, 141611Z Jun 82, par. 2.

74 Airport closed: Habib interview with the author, *The Stanford Magazine,* Spring 1984

74 We'll drive: Draper 4-13-93 and 5-4-93. "I couldn't talk Phil into using a helicopter," Draper says (4-13-93). Dillon (11-5-96) thinks a direct helicopter flight from Damascus to Beirut would not have been standard procedure anyway, but Habib could have flown around to the port of Junieh just north of Beirut. Col. Charles Smith (11-25-96) points out that the closure of the Beirut airport was the main reason the Marines would later fly Habib in helicopters. Just a few days earlier, while still in Washington, Draper had taken the unusual step of advising Habib in a cable that, if he went from Damascus to Beirut, "take care of your personal safety" (Draper cable to Habib, State 158702, 092056Z Jun 82 [6-9-82], par. 2).

74 Notoriously bad: Dillon 11-5-96

74 5,000 feet: Dillon note to author commenting on a draft of this chapter; Paganelli 11-2-96 thought the road went to 10,000 feet.

74 Bombardment: Habib interview with the author, *The Stanford Magazine,* Spring 1984

74 Hated helicopters: Bider 4-24-93. Habib's aversion to helicopters may suggest not only why Habib gave a different explanation, but why he became touchy in giving it:

> Interviewer: You mentioned a drive from Damascus to Beirut.
> Habib: Yeah, over the mountain.
> Interviewer: What was happening?
> Habib: The airport was closed!
> Interviewer: No, I mean—
> Habib: I had to get there! I was in the process of trying to persuade people to stop killing each other, and in order

to do that I had to talk to them! And in order to talk to them, I had to get to where they were. And in order to get to where they were, I had to physically move myself from one capital to another (Habib interview with the author, a differently edited version of which appeared in *The Stanford Magazine,* Spring 1984).

74 Back roads: Draper 4-13-93; Paganelli 11-2-96.

74-75 Drive to Beirut: Story drawn primarily from Draper 4-13-93. Some details from Draper 9-19-97, Dillon 11-5-96, and Habib interview with Parker. Quotes from Habib are from Habib interview with the author. Draper notes "We had to pay for all kinds of damages later on" for the other cars they smashed along the way. When they finally arrived at Ambassador Robert Dillon's residence in a suburb of Beirut, Habib and Draper were making edgy jokes about how terrible the roads were and how lucky they were not to have pitched over a cliff (Dillon 11-5-96). But Draper would later say, "I'll never forget that horrendous ride." Habib would later say, "That's just dramatic stuff. Doesn't count."

75 Barely controlled: Weinberger 10-27-93. The press of 1982 often talked about "the 1975-76 civil war" (e.g., "Israelis Say They Have Achieved the 'Primary Objective' of Invasion," *New York Times,* 8-22-82), but the civil war had not really ended (Dillon note to author, 11-29-82). It continued until 1990 ("Crushing Lebanon's Dream," *Time,* May 6, 1996).

75 Capital in flames: Pakradouni, p. 240

75 Deal cooperatively: His nominal official purpose was to discuss with them how the US could help strengthen the central Lebanese government so it could extend its control over all of Lebanon, to be followed by a withdrawal of all foreign forces from Lebanon (Paganelli cable Damascus 04206, 141618Z Jun 82, par. 3).

76 Coexisting: Habib cable Damascus 04097, 110702 Z Jun 82, par. 5

76 Alliance of convenience: There was nothing new about this. It had long been American policy to promote reconciliation among the Lebanese factions (Dillon ADST oral history; Veliotes cable 6-11-82, "Possible Habib Travel to Lebanon," sec. C). But the policy hadn't accomplished much. What was new was a special envoy on the scene with a rare passion for getting Lebanon's house in order and a national crisis that he hoped might prompt them to bounce off the bottom of their fortunes and start working their way back up. The US policy goal was to have a revivified central Lebanese government extend its authority over all Lebanese territory (Veliotes cable State 163040, 140045Z Jun 82). Habib, the State Department, and Lebanese officials also hoped—despite the overwhelming odds against it—to bring about a "national unity cabinet" to facilitate national reconciliation. Habib's argument to the other factional leaders was that, the more they cooperated with Bashir, the less Bashir would be hostage to his Israeli allies. They would then have a better chance of national unity around an independent Lebanese leader (Tueni 11-15-95). He also believed that, if they presented a united front in cooperation with him, the PLO would not be able to play them off one another (Hopkins, p. 18, based on his 10-29-91 interview with Draper).

76 Six years: *The Jerusalem Post,* "Rival factions meet in Beirut to attempt Lebanese solution," 6-21-82

76 Clout, fond: Dillon 11-5-96 and 11-16-96; Crocker 4-28-94

76 Assassinate: Dillon 11-5-96. Draper 5-4-93 points out that Walid's home village was surrounded by Israelis and Syrians at the time and suggests that Walid may have been in danger; Dillon 11-5-96 says he was not.

76 Assurances: Draper 12-22-94

76 Fetch Walid: Dillon 11-5-96; Crocker 4-29-98. There may have been an additional dimension to Habib's reasons for wanting Walid at the meeting. Draper (5-4-93) says that when Habib arrived in Beirut June 13, Walid was in a tight spot. He had decided not to fight the advancing Israelis, and his mountain village of Mukhtara was surrounded by Israelis on one side and by Syrians on the other. Claiming neutrality behind Israeli lines could look a lot like collaboration with the Israelis, and that could hurt Walid's potential as a force for national reconciliation (Crocker 4-28-94 and Dillon 11-5-96). So Habib dispatched Crocker to Walid's castle with a warm personal letter saying, in effect, "Dear Brother Walid, we need to see you in Beirut—immediately." Had Walid come on his own, Draper says, he would certainly have been killed (Draper 5-4-93, 12-22-94, and 9-19-97).

76 Coached, arrogant: Draper 12-22-94 and 9-19-97

76 Invited: Schiff & Ya'ari, pp. 11-44; Sachar, p. 173. Sharon, of course, did not *need* an invitation from Bashir or anyone else.

76 Stay around Beirut: Grove cable Jerusalem 01863 of June 11, 1982 (repeated as State 16650, 170133Z Jun 82, par. 5-6)

76 Accusations, murderous, insult, stomped: Draper 12-22-94 and 9-19-97. Press reports of the meeting said the group discussed issues, adjourned, and agreed to meet again within forty-eight hours. "Committee sources said President Sarkis was relieved that there was no confrontation between" Bashir and Walid. The prime minister was quoted saying, "The mere fact that the meeting was held brings optimism and augers well. It reflects the determination of the Lebanese to save Lebanon, starting by relieving it of Israeli occupation . . ." ("Rival factions meet in Beirut to attempt Lebanese solution," *The Jerusalem Post,* 6-21-82). Walid would later describe the National Salvation Council as "a committee for burying the dead, its task was to make the Palestinians leave Beirut and not to condemn the Israeli invasion." He bowed out of it because "I wouldn't be the one to put the coup de grace on the Palestinians" (Foreign Broadcast Information Service, MEA, January 5, 1983, pp. G6 and G8).

77 Trundle: Dillon 11-5-96 and 11-16-96; Crocker 4-29-98. It's unclear exactly when this meeting happened. Most indications are that it was the group's first meeting when Habib first arrived in Beirut, but Walid did not actually resign from the National Salvation Committee until June 25, so it could conceivably have been as late as that date. (NEA Veliotes memo to Bremer 8217953, "Recorded Radio Report from Habib, 1800, June 25, 1982,—Late Afternoon Meeting with Sarkis," 6-25-82). Hopkins, p. 26, gives Habib's version of the story, that Walid was nearly assassinated after the meeting. In addition to Crocker's role, Habib said he had Lebanese intelligence chief Jonny Abdu send some of his men along to escort the car. Walid asked for Habib's help getting home not only out of fear of assassination by Bashir's thugs, but also because the trip would take him across Phalange lines, Syrian lines, and Israeli lines. Crocker says the assassination attempt on Walid came a few months later. Walid Jumblatt told Habib, apparently on June 29, that Bashir had given him an ultima-

tum to relinquish his armory and his house at Mukhtara by 4 P.M. that day (Haig cable State 180288, 292004Z Jun 82, par. 5).

The first time the author met Habib, in December 1983, he noticed various strings of worry beads on the coffee tables in Habib's living room. Habib picked up one string and said, "Yeah, this one was given to me by Walid Jumblatt. He and I disagreed about a lot of things, but I bailed his ass out of some tight corners."

77 Sharon and Bashir's understanding: Sharon's own way of putting it was that "the main effort in the city should be carried out by Lebanese forces with the IDF playing only a supporting role" (Sharon, p. 487). Also Kahan Commission Report, p. 8; Sachar, p. 184; Khalidi, p. 172. "Lebanese Forces" was another name for Bashir's militia.

77 Finish them off: Habib cable Beirut 04247, 171230Z Jun 82, par. 4. He added, "He may try to use the Phalange for this, but that will be just as bloody."

77 Do something: Sachar, p. 181

77 Cajoled and threatened: Schiff & Ya'ari, p. 107, 196-201; Seale, p. 286-87

77 Advice to Bashir: Quote compiled from both Dillon's and Habib's accounts (Dillon 11-5-96; Habib interview with Parker, in which Habib draws the connection between his advice and Bashir's refusal); see also Seale, p. 288-89 and NEA Veliotes memo to Bremer 8217986, 6-26-82, "Recorded Radio Report from Habib, Evening Meeting with Bashir Gemayel, June 26," par. 8. This advice was right in line with US policy toward Lebanon (Dillon ADST oral history).

77 Two choices: Schiff & Ya'ari, p. 196-201; see also Seale, p. 387

77 Improvisation: "Sharon: 'I Wanted Them Out of Beirut; I Got What I Wanted,'" *The Washington Post,* 8-29-82, p. A18

78 Sharon's war: This is more or less the theme of Schiff & Ya'ari's whole book (e.g., p. 301-8). Draper described Israel's invasion of Lebanon as one of "the most colossal blunders in its history" (Draper ADST oral history).

78 Can't really rely: This is Paganelli's (11-2-96) quote of what Habib had said to him.

78 Rogue, vastly exceeded: "Court rules in libel case: Sharon misled Begin," *Jerusalem Post,*

11-5-97; "Sharon deceived Begin on Lebanon, judge rules; throws out libel suit against Ha'aretz," *Ha'aretz,* 11-5-97. Tel Aviv District Court judge Moshe Talgam ruled November 4, 1997, that Begin knew "that Sharon had not dealt with him honestly, and had taken advantage of his trust . . . . While Sharon received [the Cabinet's] approval to launch a limited operation 'Peace for Galilee,' he estimated and knew that in fact he was embarking on a far greater plan known as Pine Tree. He had tried in the past, and failed, to receive approval for his plan, yet still proceeded to prepare for its implementation. The green light given by the prime minister and the government to commence with Peace for Galilee cannot, therefore, be interpreted as a conscious consent for the Lebanon war" ("Begin knew Sharon deceived him," *Ha'aretz,* 11-5-97).

That ruling against Sharon came in a libel case he filed against the Israeli newspaper *Ha'aretz* over an article written by Uzi Benziman. In his book about Sharon, Benziman wrote that Sharon, with his war in Lebanon, "proved that one man alone could drag the country into events which would change its future" (Benziman, p. 266).

By the time of the invasion, writes Rabinovich (p. 128), "Sharon had come to dominate, nearly to monopolize, Israel's defense (and, to a large extent, its foreign) policy." Lewis writes that "Operation Peace for Galilee looked more and more like Sharon's personal grand concept for driving the PLO from Lebanese soil" (in Quandt, *Middle East,* p. 238). *Newsweek* wrote that Sharon's "many critics now accuse him of turning the Lebanese war into a personal crusade against the PLO" ("Who's in Charge Here?" 8-23-82). Israeli opponents of the war called it "Arik's war" (Schiff & Ya'ari, p. 216, 251).

Sharon denies everything said here. "This is not my war, Sharon's war . . . . This is Israel's war" ("Sharon: 'I Wanted Them Out of Beirut; I Got What I Wanted,'" *The Washington Post,* 8-29-82). "I never misled Menachem Begin. I never lied to Menachem Begin" (Reuters Information Service story 4-2-96). "Not one single decision during the war was taken without Begin's knowledge and approval, and in many cases at his own initiative. Moreover, each and every one of these decisions was brought to the cabinet and duly ratified" ("I'll fight for 20 years—Sharon," *Jerusalem Post,* 11-5-97).

78 Reconfigure: This is according to a Labor party member of the Knesset at the time, who

asked not to be identified by name, but many other sources say the same. Sharon's obsession is one of the major themes of Schiff & Ya'ari's book. Mikdadi, p. 70, quotes Jacobo Timerman saying "This is General Sharon's personal war, first step towards total expulsion of the Palestinians and the installation of puppet governments in Lebanon and Jordan." Friedman (p. 131) is one writer who agrees that this was not Sharon's war. See also, for example, Parker p. 167-69 and 176 on Sharon's and Begin's miscalculations.

Creating facts on the ground was Sharon's specialty (McFarlane, p. 187): For example, when relegated to the hapless job of agriculture minister in an earlier administration, he pushed the policy of expanding Israeli settlements in the occupied territories (Sharon, p. 355-72). Those settlements would become the thorniest issue in later attempts to make peace between the Israelis and Palestinians.

The Israeli defense ministry had sketched out a contingency plan for a major operation in Lebanon well before Sharon arrived as defense minister. Such plans are not unusual in military circles anywhere. But it took Sharon's vision and persistence to blow the dust off of an academic contingency plan and elaborate it into an urgent mission.

78 Sharon's plan: This is according to a Labor party member of the Knesset at the time, who asked not to be identified by name, but many other sources say the same (see, for example, Sachar, p. 172). This Israeli describes Sharon's vision as his "masterplan"; Lewis describes it as Sharon's "grandiose scheme" (Lewis unpublished ms., p. 14); Schiff & Ya'ari describe it as Sharon's "grand design" (p. 44 and 230); Friedman (p. 145) calls it "a strategic design" and "his grand designs"; Ball calls it a "geopolitical scheme" and "spacious" "apocalyptic vision" (p. 27-28); Sachar refers to "this master plan," "his grand strategy" (p. 172), and "an audacious scheme" (p. 184); an Israeli academic writing in *The Jerusalem Post* (6-27-82) says "Ariel Sharon, after all, has never sought to keep secret his grand strategy" (cited in Jansen, p. 122). Sharon believed, in Friedman's words (p. 144-45), "that this military strength could, in an almost mechanical fashion, solve a whole knot of complex, deeply rooted political problems." Also Ball p. 27-28.

78 Bashir, controlled by Israel: Habib cable Damascus 04082, 101739Z Jun 82, par. 7. Habib said "the Israelis are going to stay in here [Lebanon] and . . . put Bashir in under

their guns" ("Transcription of Recorded Radio Conversation between Amb. Habib—Charlie Hill, July 9, 1982—1030 hours," p. 2). "It's the Sharon plan all the way," Habib said. "They're going to put Bashir in power; meanwhile they are going to control the whole country" (NEA Veliotes memo to S/S Bremer, 8219693, "Telcon with Habib July 10," p. 3).

Lebanon would then have, Habib wrote, "something like a quisling government in power" (Habib cable Damascus 04082, 101739Z Jun 82, par. 7). A quisling is a person who betrays his/her own country by aiding an invading enemy, often serving later in a puppet government *(The Random House Dictionary of the English Language,* second ed.). Habib believed such an arrangement "will never be acceptable to the Arab countries in the region and will merely increase the area of confrontation. . . . I believe that any collusion with Israel for the political restructuring that they seem to intend . . . is unacceptable." He had an indication that Haig might be coming to Israel and that Israeli ideas for restructuring Lebanon politically might be on the agenda. "For the secretary to engage in this kind of discussion with the Israelis at this time, which [a cable the American embassy in Tel Aviv] suggests the Israelis intend, would be unseemly to say the least. If it were to include the dismembering of Lebanon in addition, we would have violated every precept and every statement of policy which has guided our attitude toward Lebanon for many years. The fact that some Lebanese may be willing to play this game should not convince us that it is in our overall interest" (Damascus 04082, par. 7).

Veliotes said July 11, "Everything points to their literally settling in, dictating the next government, bullying, and with guns trying to create what they consider to be the millennium" (NEA Veliotes memo to S/S Bremer, 8219695, "Telecon between Phil Habib and Charlie Hill, 12:30 P.M., July 11, 1982," p. 2; punctuation altered for clarity).

78 West Bank, Gaza, Jordan: Sachar, p. 172; Friedman, p. 144; and a Labor party member of the Knesset at the time, who asked not to be identified by name. Jordan's King Hussein considered his country Israel's "next target" (Habib cable London 16170, 261738Z Jul 82, par. 8). Sharon has frequently said that there is an obvious solution to the Palestinian quest for a homeland. For example, "Jordan, I mean Transjordan, is the only solution. . . . Believe me, it's the perfect solution. . . . Some [Palestinian refugees] could stay where they are,

some could transfer themselves to Transjordan. . . . What counts for me is that a Palestine already exists, a Palestinian state already exists, so there is no need to create another one." ("Sharon: 'I Wanted Them Out . . . ,'" *Washington Post,* 8-29-82). Habib paraphrased Sharon telling him that, "Palestinians should be given political expression in that part of former Palestine where they already are a majority, namely in Jordan. Why keep the king there, he added rhetorically, and let an entire nation (unnamed) suffer because of one selfish man. I told him to forget it" (Habib cable Beirut 04461, 051600Z Jul 82, par. 8).

Sharon denied having ambitions vis a vis Lebanon beyond expelling the PLO and the Syrians from it. When journalist Oriana Fallaci asked him about ambitions to install Bashir as a puppet to give Israel a "colony de facto" in Lebanon, Sharon replied, "I have never heard such a slander! Such a lie! Such an insult! You are slandering me, you are insulting me!" He also denied his preference for force: "We sincerely prefer a peaceful solution. Why should war be always the way to settle things?" ("Sharon: 'I Wanted Them Out...,'" *Washington Post,* 8-29-82, p. A19)

78 Sharon expected: According to an Israeli politician who asked not to be identified by name.

78 Rid of Begin: "A Defiant No to Reagan," *Time,* 9-20-82, p. 27. Sharon didn't mind talking publicly about his ambitions. For example, he told the Paris daily *Le Matin* (7-2-82) that "as prime minister he would give King Hussein 24 hours to leave Amman" (cited in Jansen, p. 122). He was often greeted in oriental neighborhoods of Israel as "Arik, King of Israel" (Sachar, p. 171). IDF soldiers devoted to him called him "king of Israel" and "King Arik" ("Sharon: 'I Wanted Them Out...,'" *Washington Post,* 8-29-83). Also "For Likud Party, Sharon Is the 'King of Israel,'" *The New York Times,* 2-7-01. Begin too was sometimes hailed as "King of Israel" ("A Flame Burnt Out," *The New York Times,* 8-31-83).

78 Rob him: Hopkins, p. 12. Shultz told Reagan August 12 that the "pattern of Israeli behavior raises questions once again about whether [the Israelis] really want a negotiated settlement— or at least whether Sharon does" ("Talking Points for use with The President," 10:00 A.M. 8/12/82, 8224185, p. 2).

78 Intervene: Yaacobi 2-14-95. Gabriel, p. 14, 16. Draper adds that it certainly looked to him

and Habib at the time that Sharon was deliberately trying to scuttle any progress they might make (Draper 12-18-94). Sharon's approach throughout most of the war was, in the words of one American official who asked not to be identified by name, to "stall us, lie to us if necessary, do whatever he had to do until the facts on the ground brought about the inevitable."

78 Means of delay: Sharon, p. 485. An American official said toward the end of the war, "Sharon has tried to sabotage Habib all along" ("Who's in Charge Here?" *Newsweek,* 8-23-82, p. 19).

79 Against the man: "Mixed reaction in Jerusalem," *The Jerusalem Post,* 8-8-82

79 Hated: Marjorie Habib 2-19-95

79 Cold-bloodedly: Habib interview with Parker

79 Bowl you over: This official asked not to be identified by name. Sehulster says, "Yes, he would bump into people. His girth is such that it's kind of hard to walk in a group without it. He's overwhelmed with himself" (Sehulster 7-12-94).

79 Arik gets: Newman and Rogan, p. 152

79 Squire: Lewis ADST oral history

79 Never to trust: Draper 10-25-98

79 Biggest liar: Paganelli 11-2-96. These are Paganelli's words reporting what Habib had said to him.

79 Worth nothing: Seale, p. 392

79-80 Baabda, tanks: Hill 7-9-94; State Department report "Discussions with Israelis on tanks in Baabda," 890326, 6980; State cable 163040, 140045Z Jun 82, par. 6

80 Ballistic, prisoner: Howell 10-11-93 and 9-6-93

80 Significance: This message was given to the State Department through the Israeli ambassador in Washington, reporting a phone conversation he had just had with Begin after Haig told him that, if Israel wanted Begin's scheduled meetings in the US to go ahead as planned, the tanks around the presidential palace had to go (State Department report "Discussions with Israelis on tanks in Baabda," 890326, 6980; State cable 163040, 140045Z Jun 82, par. 6).

80 Already in Ba'abda: Schiff & Ya'ari p. 193,

italics added

80 Sharon on phone: Undated State Department report "Discussions with Israelis on tanks in Baabda," 890326, 6980, section headed "June 14 (10:34Z)"; State cable 163040, 140045Z Jun 82, par. 11. Israeli Foreign Ministry official David Kimche relayed to Lewis at 5:50 P.M. June 14 Sharon's word that he would personally attend to the matter of the tanks (Lewis cable Tel Aviv 08846, 141611Z Jun 82, par. 4). At 6:20 Sharon called Lewis directly to assure him that he was "giving orders immediately to have them moved" (Lewis cable Tel Aviv 08880 141731Z Jun 82, par. 2-3). Habib had talked with Sharon about the tanks around lunchtime that day ("Discussions with Israelis on tanks in Baabda," 890326, 6980, section headed "June 14 (10:34Z)").

80 Around Dillon's residence, cabbage patch: Lewis cable Tel Aviv 08880, 141731Z Jun 82, par. 2-3; undated State Department report "Discussions with Israelis on tanks in Baabda," 890326, 6980; Haig memo to the President 8217048, 6-17-82; Habib cable Beirut 04247, 171230Z Jun 82, par. 3

80 Observation post: The Lebanese, of course, refused. Habib was outraged by "this gross insensitivity": "Sharon had promised us on Tuesday night that he would reduce the IDF presence from around the Baabda area in the vicinity of the palace. It is shocking and almost unbelievable that the Israelis could now make such an approach. Ask the Israelis whether they are trying to destroy the Lebanese government?" (Message from Habib party in State cable 175122, 240945Z Jun 82, par. 3). Israeli soldiers also asked Dillon to use his residence. He too refused (Dillon 11-5-96).

80 July 5: Habib cable Beirut 04461, 051600Z Jul 82, par. 11. An IDF jeep had been parked right in front of the American ambassador's residence too. "It's indecent!" Habib said. "I waved them out of the way" (Hill 7-10-94).

80 July 8: NEA Veliotes memo to S/S Bremer, 9219393 [*sic,* should be 8219393], 7-9-82, "Recorded Radio Conversation with Amb. Habib [*sic,* actually Draper], July 8, 1928 [*sic,* should be 1982], at 1430 hours," p. 1-2. Sharon may have outsmarted himself by positioning tanks around the palace. It helped defeat one of his own purposes in the war: evicting Syrian forces from Beirut. Habib believed that, if President Sarkis asked Assad to get his troops out of Beirut, Assad would do it. But when

Sarkis did talk to Assad about it, Assad dismissed the idea, replying that Sarkis "might no longer be considered a free agent [to make that request], as his country and *even the area of his presidency* were under foreign occupation" by the Israelis. By the same token, though, Paganelli reminded the Syrians that the same could be said of PLO and Syrian military presence in Lebanon (Habib 7-2-82 cable Beirut 4415, quoted in State 184218, 021729Z Jul 82, par. 15; italics added; this quote is Habib's paraphrase of Sarkis' account of the discussion, not necessarily Assad's words; Paganelli cable Damascus 04934, 101438Z Jul 82, par. 16-17).

81 Begin weeps: Draper 9-19-97

81 How many Arabs: Draper 4-13-93

81 Lost sleep: Draper 4-25-93

81 Agony: Draper 4-25-93 and 9-19-97

82 Fancy himself: This is according to Sam Lewis (4-10-94), who as US ambassador to Israel for eight years knew Begin better than did any other American. He adds that, prior to Begin's re-election in 1981, Begin was "somewhat in awe of generals," but with his re-election "Begin now felt confident of his military judgments as well as his political mastery. Unfortunately . . . [he also] largely put aside doubts, moderate advice, and much sense of proportion" (Lewis in Quandt, *Middle East*, p. 232).

82 Man of dreams: This Israeli politician asked not to be identified by name. This politician points out that, even after thirty years as a member of the Knesset's Foreign Affairs and Security Committee, Begin would ask questions that revealed a remarkable degree of detached unrealism. "I was every time again and again shocked by his questions," says this politician. Schiff & Ya'ari describe Begin as "naive about military matters" (p. 112). David Ben Gurion described Begin as "a romantic fool, essentially a windbag full of rhetoric and metaphors" (quoted in "Begin's Rhetoric and Sharon's Tactics," *Foreign Affairs*, Fall 1982, p. 68). Lewis points out that, even when Begin assigned himself the additional job of defense minister during his first term as prime minister, he spent only one day a week at the Defense Ministry and relied heavily on a very able military secretary (Lewis 4-10-94).

Friedman sees Begin's fascination with military strength in psychological terms: "He lived for the chance to correct the indignities that he and his forefathers had suffered for cen-turies. Begin loved the idea of Jewish power, Jewish generals, Jewish tanks, Jewish pride. They were his pornography. He needed a war to satisfy his deep longing for dignity and to cure all his traumas about Jewish impotence. . . . What made Begin even more dangerous was that his fantasies about power were combined with a self-perception of being a victim. Someone who sees himself as a victim will almost never morally evaluate himself or put limits on his own actions. Why should he? He is the victim" (Friedman, p. 143-44).

82 No longer first class: Maj. Gen. Uri Simhoni, in Strober & Strober, p. 206

82 Military background: Schiff & Ya'ari, p. 38-39, 113; Jansen, p. 12

82 Forbidden, sole source: Lewis 4-10-94

82 Sold Begin: According to a leading Israeli politician who asked not to be identified by name

82 Strung along: "Ministers: Sharon strung us along," *Jerusalem Post*, 6-13-82, cited in Jansen, p. 12. On June 15, 1982, Lewis described "Sharon's technique" as "following his own timetable and leading his colleagues along subsequently to endorse it" (Lewis 6-15-82 cable quoted in Haig cable 051526, 170048Z Jun 82, par. 4).

82 Eleventh hour: Schiff & Ya'ari, p. 115. Sharon took the same approach with the Cabinet, getting them to approve one move at a time (Jansen, p. 12).

82 Vote: Yaacobi 2-14-95. The closest thing to a Knesset vote on the war was a no-confidence vote on Begin during the war. He survived.

82 Discussion of objectives: "Ministers: Sharon strung us along," *Jerusalem Post*, 6-13-82, cited in Jansen, p. 12. Though this particular article appeared early in the war, the same lack of discussion of objectives prevailed throughout the war.

82 Pit bulls: Bider 4-24-93

82 Hold my own: According to one of Habib's colleagues, who asked not to be identified by name.

82 Alley fighter: Lewis unpublished manuscript about Habib, April 22, 1985

83 Almost every time: Lewis 4-10-94

83 Blamed: Habib reported that "Sharon said

that the July [1981] cease fire, in which, as he put it, the killing of Jews elsewhere in the world was not considered a ceasefire violation, had become intolerable to the point that it had contributed to the recent Israeli action" (Habib cable Jerusalem 01745, par. 6, 072224Z Jun 82). Sharon wrote in his memoirs that "the reality of why we were involved in this war [was] the years of horrific terrorism from Lebanon, the attempted destruction of the Israeli north, the massive PLO buildup of Katyusha rockets and artillery, [and] the utter failure of the American negotiators," i.e., Philip Habib (Sharon, p. 482).

83 Enemy: Lewis cable Tel' Aviv 11097, 221519Z Jul 82, par. 3

83 Heart: Schiff & Ya'ari, p. 220-21; Hill undated letter to author received 6-13-97

83 Do the opposite: Hill 6-15-93

83 Ridiculed, lecturing, give response to Begin: Lewis 4-10-94; Howell 9-6-93

83 Crap: Lewis 4-10-94

83 Nasty to Morrie: Lewis 4-10-94

83 Falling asleep, guts: Draper 12-18-94. Draper took Sharon's words to indicate he wanted him dead. He adds, "I think he disliked Phil too, but he really had a real dislike for me. I never knew why. I think he thought I was a typical WASP and was anti-Semitic into the bargain and anti-Israeli."

6 The Other General

84 Every step: Veliotes 5-6-93

84 Fascination: Draper ADST oral history. Veliotes says Haig had "a romantic view" of the IDF that "sort of mesmerized" him (Veliotes 4-29-93).

84 Bombing in Vietnam: Haig 5-11-94

84 Soviets: Haig 5-11-94. Draper says Haig rejected the prevailing State Department view that the Palestinian issue was the hub of the Middle East; the real problem, as Haig saw it, was Soviet efforts to expand into the region (Draper ADST oral history).

84-85 Oversimplification, strategic consensus: According to a colleague of Habib's who asked not to be identified by name; "Transcript of Radio Conversation Between Lawrence Eagleburger, Ambassador Habib, and Charles Hill, July 18, 1444-1516 EDT," 8220873, p. 18. Habib would later say, "There is no place for the USSR in a peace process in the Near East because, unlike us, the Soviets are not sincerely in favor of peace." But neither did he see much advantage or relevance to Haig's idea of a stragegic cooperation. "I have never believed in the interest of this idea, and I don't think that anyone in the Near East has any interest in it whatsoever. This proposal is a mistake. It has prevented [people] from considering the [really] important problem: that of peace between Israel and the Arab states. At the time, I gave my honest opinion to General Haig, by reminding him that the real question consists in resolving the inter-regional conflicts" (Habib interview with Michel Dusclaud, translated by Susan Bree, p. 9 of translation). Habib also said, "AI is too caught up with strategic consensus," Haig's concept for regional opposition to the Soviets (Hill 7-16-94). While Syria was certainly a client of the Soviets, Veliotes (ADST oral history) says, "You've got to make some pretty insane conceptual leaps to consider Assad a Communist or an agent of the Soviet Union—he was his own son of a bitch. That was tough enough." The strategic consensus outlook, he says, led to proposals of "legitimized idiocy."

85 Habib's view of US-Israel relations: According to a colleague of Habib's who asked not to be identified by name. Haig's perception of Habib's views: "Phil never liked the Israelis. I mean, you gotta know that. He had an Arabist view, but not as bad as some of the guys over in the State Department" (Haig 5-11-94). Habib's closer colleagues scoff at that assessment.

85 Couldn't afford: Haig 5-11-94

85 Habib watch assaults: Habib interview with Parker 5-9-90

85 Haig on Israeli bombing: Haig 5-11-94. Haig believed that most of the destruction in Beirut came from car bombs and other terrorism from the prior seven years of civil war, not from Israeli attacks in 1982. An official in the Near Eastern Affairs bureau who asked not to be identified by name says that, while earlier car bombs and terrorism certainly did account for some of the damage, Haig is "just totally

full of shit about that. I was there in September 1982. You've got buildings flattened, buildings with major pock marks in them—those aren't from car bombs. That's artillery. That's aerial bombs."

85 Border quiet: Habib interview with Tueni, p. 48. Habib notes "there was only one suspicious day when they had come out of Lebanon, gone around through Jordan, come across the river, and were caught." On the quiet of the border since Habib's 1981 ceasefire, Sam Lewis, the U.S. ambassador to Israel, writes that "along the border, the cease-fire held in large measure for the next eleven months" (in Quandt, *Middle East,* p. 237). See also Benziman, p. 268-69, and Bavly & Salpeter, p. 234 (quoted in Davis, p. 3).

85 Border active: Haig 5-11-94. The point is not who was right and who was wrong, but that they disagreed.

85-86 Habib on 1981 deal: Though Habib rejected the idea that the 1981 arrangement applied to any attack on Jews anywhere in the world, he did speak of "my formulation that it also applied to attacks mounted through third countries" (Habib cable Jerusalem 01781, 6-8-82, par. 8).

86 Haig on 1981 deal: Haig 5-11-94

86 Top priority: Hill 7-9-94

86 Lawyering us: Hill 7-9-94

86 Committed to stopping: Eagleburger 7-3-93

86 Press on: Haig memo to The President, "A Forward U.S. Strategy in Wake of Israel's Offensive," 6-12-82. Veliotes says, "Haig's basic orientation was the Israelis should finish the job on the PLO and Beirut; Phil's strong belief was the PLO should be evacuated and we should seek to address the Palestinian problem through the peace process. And Haig disagreed with that" (5-6-93).

86 Exactly the opposite: Hill 6-15-93. Hill was director of the Office for Israel and Arab-Israeli Affairs. With Draper, who was deputy assistant secretary of state for Near Eastern Affairs, in the region with Habib, Hill filled in as acting deputy assistant secretary during the summer of 1982.

86 Military instincts: Hill 3-27-93; Eagleburger 7-3-93. Once they had the PLO by the throat, Haig reasoned, that would be the time to stop,

because they would then have maximum leverage for a negotiated settlement (Hill 3-27-93).

86 Bay of Pigs: Hill 7-6-95. The reference is to a US-backed operation in April 1961 in which 1,500 CIA-trained Cuban exiles invaded Cuba at the Bay of Pigs in an unsuccessful attempt to overthrow its leader, Fidel Castro. Haig apparently felt that the US had failed to follow through in supporting the invaders so they could win. Like Sharon, Haig considered this invasion the prime opportunity to get rid of the PLO once and for all; stopping the war prematurely would only ensure that the PLO problem would fester and flare up again a year or two later (Haig 5-11-94).

86 Should not intervene: Eagleburger holds out for a more subtle view, that Haig was prepared to let Habib do what he could do as long as that didn't mean getting too tough on the Israelis. Haig would have been happy for Habib to find a way to stop the fighting without forcing the Israelis back out of Lebanon. That matter of how tough to be with the Israelis was, in Eagleburger's view, where Haig and Habib diverged (Eagleburger 7-3-93).

86 Imaginary line: Hill 7-19-95. Even as Habib was trying to persuade the Israelis to withdraw at least to the 40-kilometer zone that they had initially declared (Habib cable Jerusalem 01871, 121152Z Jun 82, par. 3B), Haig was writing to Reagan that "We must not, however, be compulsive about pressing Israel to move back to any line as it is even conceivable that the Lebanese government may want the Israeli presence in advanced positions—at least for a short time—as leverage for Syrian withdrawal" (Haig memo to the President, "A Forward U.S. Strategy in Wake of Israel's Offensive," 6-12-82, p. 2). In the same memo (p. 1), Haig warns against "the development of heavy pressure to press only for Israeli withdrawal, a situation which would threaten to isolate us with Israel and to create a policy vacuum to be exploited by the radical Arabs and the Soviets." Haig wanted instead to capitalize on the invasion to accomplish various policy objectives in the region.

86 Renegade, nuts: Hill 3-27-93; Haig memo to The President, "A Forward U.S. Strategy in Wake of Israel's Offensive," 6-12-82, p. 2. Hill adds that "Haig wanted the Israelis to drive so far north that the PLO and Syria would have to negotiate. If the IDF were stopped halfway, world opinion would just turn toward forcing

them out with no quid pro quo" by the PLO or Syrians (note from Hill on manuscript of this chapter).

86-87 You're wrong: "Being Patient Brings Habib Final Victory," *The New York Times,* 8-22-82. Punctuation altered for clarity.

87 Begin visit to Washington: Veliotes, Association for Diplomatic Studies oral history, p. 204-5. By this time, says Veliotes, Haig "clearly was supportive of their finishing the PLO in Lebanon" (Veliotes 4-29-93). Haig said that if he were president he would tell the Israelis to go ahead (Hill 7-6-95). In later years, Haig would say the US had made a big mistake by not letting the Israelis finish off the PLO, according to a State Department official who asked not to be identified by name.

87 Privately, instructions: Sharon, p. 487

87 Subtlety, take Lebanon, mirrors: Haig 5-11-94

87 Haig on simultaneous withdrawal: Haig (5-11-94) says, "We had one set of objectives, and that was to get a successful three-party agreement to withdraw."

87 Too tall an order, linkage: Paganelli cable Damascus 04206, 141618Z Jun 82, par. 5-6. The Syrians' rationale was that their presence and the Israelis' presence in Lebanon must not be equated because Syrian troops had been invited in as peacekeepers by the Lebanese government and sent in by the Arab League, whereas the Israelis had entered Lebanon as aggressors (par. 5, 10). Syrian troops had long since ceased serving any bona fide peacekeeping role, but they stuck with their argument. A year later their position was unchanged.

As Habib saw it, simultaneous three-way withdrawal was impossible because, regardless of what the Palestinians thought of it, the Israelis and the Syrians would never buy it. He saw zero chance that the Israelis would withdraw until after the PLO was gone, and zero chance that the Syrians would withdraw until after the Israelis were gone. The Syrians insisted that they had entered Lebanon at the request of the Lebanese government and the Arab League and that their presence there was thus legitimate. The Israelis, by contrast, had invaded. For Syria to agree to leave Lebanon in the context of a simultaneous Israeli withdrawal would, Syria believed, be to put its presence and Israel's presence on an equal footing. Such an agreement would repudiate the legitimacy of Syria's own presence there and, in effect,

capitulate to Israel. Habib felt the Syrians would never agree to that humiliation in order to spare themselves another humiliation. The Israelis (and Habib and the rest of Washington) felt that whatever legitimacy may have attached to the Syrian's original entry into Lebanon in 1976 had long since passed and that they had now become an occupying army. Though Habib agreed with that position, he considered it academic, since he saw no chance that Syria would ever acknowledge it, much less withdraw on Israeli or American terms. This Syrian view remained a central issue after the siege (see chapters 16 and 17).

Habib felt that simultaneous withdrawal of all three foreign forces "was a huge cake, and you had to eat it bite by bite" (Smith 6-21-94). The first bite was to defuse the most volatile situation by getting the PLO and the three Syrian brigades out of the city of Beirut peacefully. The second bite would be to get the rest of the Syrian forces and the Israelis out of Lebanon altogether. The third bite would be to enable the Lebanese army to take control of Beirut and then expand their control to the rest of the country (Smith 6-14-94). Sharon reports Habib telling him that, because of Syria's security interests in Lebanon, "The withdrawal of external forces cannot be symmetric" (Sharon p. 478).

On July 10, Israeli general Avraham Tamir confirmed to Habib Israel's intention "that Israeli forces would not withdraw one inch and there would be no disengagement anywhere until all Syrian and PLO elements had left Lebanon." Habib deferred arguing about it at the time but told Tamir that that notion was "unrealistic" and that "if he thought that all foreign forces were going to leave before the Israelis move one inch from their present position, he would soon discover otherwise" (Habib cable Beirut 04561, 101755Z Jul 82).

87 Gunpowder: Howell 10-11-93

88 Hostility: Weinberger 10-7-93

88 Megalomaniac: Lewis 4-10-94

88 MEPS article: "War in Lebanon," *Middle East Policy Survey,* June 18, 1982, No. 58, p. 1

88 Quotes my cables: Hill 7-9-94

88 Somebody could die: Sicherman 8-4-98

88-89 Conversation with Eagleburger: Hill 7-9-94. Hill (7-12-95) explains how *MEPS* probably got the information: Some officials would tell reporters what they had been reading in the cables, often for no purpose except to show off that they were important inside people in the know. The editor of *MEPS* declined to tell the author who leaked the cables or even to confirm that the cables were leaked. But Sicherman (8-4-98), who was Haig's special assistant, speculates that the material might have been leaked by an enemy of Haig's. Making it seem like a leak by Haig would make Haig look bad.

89 Suffer together: Haig cable to Habib, State 170177, 192358Z Jun 82, par. 2-4

89 Brilliant job: Hill 7-6-95

89 Dark side: Hill 7-9-94. He said this to Reagan a week earlier, June 15.

89 Openly decided: Veliotes 4-29-93 and 5-6-93. Weinberger hints at the same thing: "Phil gave very good, wise briefings, and the president was impressed with him and benefited greatly from his briefings. There were times when probably some of the State Department masters of Habib were not happy that he spoke so frankly. I think there probably were attempts made to keep him out of direct contact with the president" (Weinberger 10-7-93).

89 Declared war: Veliotes, ADST oral history, p. 203. Grunwald, p. 533-34, says, "Apart from any policy differences [with the White House], Haig was near paranoid about attacks on his authority. Behind his forced composure, one could sense the steam rising. He repeatedly complained that 'guerrillas' in the White House were out to get him."

89 Serving Begin: Hill 7-9-94

89 Wanted instructions: Habib cable Jerusalem 01871, 6-12-82, par. 2 and 3

89 Obey: Hill 3-27-93; Grove 6-4-94

90 Variously: Habib wrote that Israeli actions made it "increasingly impossible to salvage anything out of my instructions and the basic goals contained therein" (Habib cable Beirut 04200, 6-15-82, par. 4).

90 Choose: Hopkins, p. 40, based on his 3-12-92 interview with Habib. As Lewis says, "He followed the president's guidance" (Lewis 4-10-94).

90 Ultimately: "Concluding Remarks" by Habib in Staar, p. 283-84

90 Nightmare: Haig 5-11-94

90 Set up: Howell 9-96-93

90 Undermined: Gowers, p. 210

90 Five minutes: Haig 5-11-94. Haig adds, "But Phil never would double-cross his secretary of state. That's not in Phil's makeup."

90 Little guidance: Hill 6-15-93

90 Go forward: Hill 6-15-93

90 Messenger boys: Draper 12-18-94. That is not to say he did not transmit Israeli demands to other parties at all. He did. But he tended to bring them up as though they were his own ideas or otherwise make them more palatable. He said, "I do not present conditions as Israeli demands for the sake of necessary ambiguity" (Veliotes memo to the Secretary, 8217557, 6-23-82, Report From Habib/Draper for your 0930 Secure Telcon with Habib).

90 Maximum concessions: Haig cable Bonn, Secto 08064, 110102Z Jun 82, par. 3

90 Stand by idly: Habib cable Damascus 04097, 110702Z Jun 82, par. 2 and 8. Reagan asked Habib whether this might be a propitious time, while Syria was bloodied, to strike a deal on the Golan Heights, which had been a bone of contention ever since Israel had captured them from Syria in the 1967 war. "There is no way we can use this war now to make movement in that direction," Habib wrote, "despite the lessons the Syrians have learned. The Syrians will not negotiate with the Israelis while the Israelis are in Lebanon. They may not negotiate afterward either, but there are other ways and other days to deal with that problem" (Habib cable for the President from Beirut 04247, 6-17-82, par. 4).

90 Same answer: State Dept. transcript of Habib tacsat call, "Secure Voice Conversation of June 25, 1982, 0550," 8217642, p. 6

90 Best you can: Draper ADST oral history

91 Conjure: Grove 6-12-94

91 Reasonable objective: Habib cable Damascus 04097, 110702Z Jun 82, par. 5

91 Vacuum: Lewis 4-10-94

91 Wrote own instructions: Grove 6-12-94; Lewis 4-10-94. One mark of an outstanding diplomat, says Hill, is the ability to "answer your own question," i.e., to propose a solution to the problem you are reporting. Habib always did, and his proposal was usually ap-

proved. In that sense, Habib wrote his own instructions (Hill 3-27-93).

91 Accepted Phil's views: Draper 4-13-93. As Hopkins puts it, "whatever Habib did, essentially, became US policy" (Hopkins, p. 3).

91 Rarely overruled: Hill 3-27-93. Habib had "almost a carte blanche" from the president, says Lewis, yet he continually kept Washington informed of what he was doing and what he planned to do next and gave them time to disagree if they wanted to. They rarely did (Lewis 4-10-94).

92 Local scenery: "Radio Telecon Eagleburger/ Habib, 1545 June 29, 1982," NEA Veliotes memo to S/S Bremer, 8218313, 6-29-82, "Department Response to Lebanese Questions Concerning the 9 Points"

92 Never disregard: This source, a State Department official involved in giving Habib his instructions, asked not to be identified by name.

92 Clarified: Hill 6-15-93

92 Dumb: Grove 6-12-94

92 Rant: This source, a State Department official involved in giving Habib his instructions, asked not to be identified by name.

92 Meet with Sharon: "Radio Telecon Draper/ Hill, 0130 June 28, 1982," NEA Hill memo to Bremer, 8218166, 6-29-82

92 Bulldozing tactics: "Message from Habib 0500 June 29: Day's Activities, June 29," NEA Veliotes memo to S/S Bremer, 8218168, 6-29-82

92 Details, crazy: This official in the Near Eastern Affairs bureau asked not to be identified by name. Habib's ploy with written instructions was, according to this source, "a classic technique."

92-93 Guy on the ground: Habib interview with the author, *The Stanford Magazine,* Spring 1984

93 Just smile: Hill 6-15-93

93 Immensely creative: Grove 6-12-94

93 Anything that interfered: Grove 6-4-94

93 Rebuilding: So did the Israelis (Grove cable Jerusalem 01863 of 6-11-82, repeated as State 16650, 170133Z Jun 82, for example). The difference was that Habib wanted a Lebanese

central government strong enough to stand on its own two feet in the community of nations. Begin and Sharon wanted a Lebanese government strong enough to run the country but weak enough to be controlled by Israel.

Driven largely by Habib (Sicherman 8-4-98), America's policy goals in this crisis were to strengthen the Lebanese government, dramatically reduce Syrian presence in Lebanon, end the Palestinian state-within-a-state, end the southern Lebanon enclave of Maj. Haddad (an ally of the Israelis who controlled parts of southern Lebanon on their behalf), strengthen peacekeeping operations in southern Lebanon, and eliminate the Green Line barrier separating East Beirut from West Beirut (Habib cable Beirut 04233, 161325Z Jun 82; Haig cable to Habib, State 166582, 170207Z Jun 82).

Habib later said his four goals were to get external forces out of Lebanon, establish Lebanese sovereignty, strengthen the Lebanese government, and ensure that Lebanon would no longer be used as a base for hostile action against Israel (Habib interview with Mulcahy tape 2). These goals, along with the goal of reconciling Lebanese factions, were US policy. They were not merely Habib's own idiosyncratic goals (Draper 12-18-94; Dillon ADST oral history), but the policy was "driven very much by Phil," says Haig's special assistant (Sicherman 8-4-98). US policy was to try to "help the central government in Lebanon to consolidate its control and thereby diminish the threat" to Israel from Lebanon-based Palestinian terrorism (cable STATE 155256 TOSEC 080198, for the Secretary from Eagleburger, June 7, 1982, p. 2-3).

It certainly is not normally an American diplomat's job to bolster a foreign government. But this was no normal situation. For one thing, the Lebanese have long looked to outsiders to solve their problems for them (Dillon ADST oral history). Second, the anarchy in Lebanon had repercussions throughout the region and, by allowing the PLO and Syrian troops to occupy Israel's northern neighbor, threatened America's ally Israel. Habib and the Israelis both recognized the need for a viable Lebanese government and the probability that the next president of Lebanon would be Bashir Gemayel. The difference was Begin and Sharon wanted to install Bashir as a puppet who would sign a peace treaty with them, while Habib wanted Bashir to be independent so he could unite Lebanon in a pluralistic nation. Third, since Habib was of Lebanese descent himself, the Lebanese considered him almost one of their own and looked up to him more than to most foreigners.

93-94 Sovereign control: This was important to Habib for several reasons. First, it was right. Lebanon's suffering would not end until a strong central government prevailed over the anarchy that had ravaged the country for seven years. Second, it was US policy. Third, Israel's security required a stable, sovereign Lebanon next door that could and would prevent terrorists on its soil from attacking Israel. Habib's approach put him on a collision course with the Israelis on this political front as well as on the military front, since Begin and Sharon's objective was to install a puppet to control Lebanon on their behalf. Habib was determined that Lebanon regain its full sovereignty as an independent nation. In this effort, Habib had a staunch ally in Morris Draper, who as head of State's Lebanon affairs office had long repeated American insistence on Lebanon's independence, sovereignty, and territorial integrity (Hill note to the author 4-8-98 commenting on a draft of this chapter).

94 Quixotic, tide turn: Habib's ego was certainly also a factor: Who better than he to make it happen? He had a sense that this was his moment, that this mission was what he had been born to and what his whole life had prepared him for. He believed firmly that any problem created by human beings can be solved by human beings. And he loved solving problems—the thornier, the better.

94 Structure: Draper 5-4-93

94 Coached: An important part of Habib's negotiations in Beirut around June 23-25 consisted of coaching the National Salvation Council and Lebanese officials on how to assert governmental authority over Palestinians and everyone else residing in Lebanon. The reason was that an agreement specifying the future role of Palestinians in Lebanon would be an intrinsic part of the terms under which the PLO would leave Lebanon and the Israelis would end their invasion.

Habib knew perfectly well that the Lebanese government had "no clout with Arafat" (NEA Hill memo to Bremer 8217615, 6-23-82 "Radio Telecon Secretary Haig/Ambassador Habib—0950, June 23, 1982," p. 2). Nonetheless, he urged them to start behaving as if they did. He insisted that the Lebanese decide for themselves answers to basic questions about the government's relations with Palestinians once this invasion was over, and then tell the

PLO what the new terms were going to be. "I stressed that while the PLO could 'propose', the Lebanese government should 'demand'. It was their country and their sovereignty which we were talking about." The basic questions he wanted them to decide included such issues as whether Palestinians would be permitted to remain in Lebanon as peaceful, law-abiding citizens subject to government authority. Would Palestinians be allowed to maintain a military force not subject to the government's authority? What would be the nature of a PLO (as opposed to general Palestinian) presence in Lebanon, if any?

Habib pushed the Lebanese to answer each question in the direction of asserting Lebanese government sovereignty over all people on Lebanese soil. The National Salvation Council was then supposed to meet with the PLO to work out an agreement about such matters, all within the context of an agreement that the PLO leaders would leave Lebanon, Palestinian fighters would disarm, and the Lebanese Armed Forces would take control of West Beirut (Veliotes memo to the Secretary, 8217557, 6-23-82, "Report From Habib/Draper for your 0930 Secure Telcon for your "; Hill memo to Bremer 8217614, 6-23-82, "Radio Telecon Draper/Hill—0800, June 23"; "Response to Phil Habib, 1000 June 24," attachment to NEA Veliotes memo to Bremer 8217677, 6-24-82, "Response to Phil Habib").

94 Believed in: Sicherman 8-4-98

94 Consensus: Habib 6-15-82 cable Beirut 4214 repeated in State 166572, 170133Z Jun 82, par. 2E

94 Proposal: Hill 7-9-94; Veliotes cable to Habib, State 166587, 170239Z Jun 82, par. 2

94 Enormity: On July 10, Israeli Gen. Avraham Tamir told Habib what the IDF intended, "and I tell you, it's exactly what we feared all along," Habib said. ". . . It's the Sharon plan all the way. You know, they're going to put Bashir in power; meanwhile they are going to control the whole country" (NEA Veliotes memo to S/S Bremer, 8219693, "Telcon with Habib July 10, 1982 - 1058," p. 2-3; punctuation altered for clarity). Bashir's brother Amin Gemayel would later use the term "Israel's . . . puppet" himself (Habib cable Beirut 06791, 030900Z Oct 82, par. 2).

94 Satrapy: Hill 7-9-94. A satrapy is a state controlled by a foreign ruler.

94-95 Chevy Chase Circle: Habib cable Beirut

04200, 6-15-82. He said that, on his way back from lunch in Beirut the same day, he had driven through a convoy of Israeli trucks "moving into the heart of Beirut" (Hill 7-9-94).

95 Sneaking forward: Sharon, p. 475-76

95 Incomprehensible, reworded: Habib 6-17-82 cable Beirut 4255 quoted in State 167752 TOSEC 090014, 172116Z Jun 82, par. 3, 6

95 Spelling an end: Hill 7-9-94

95 Destroying it: Hill 7-9-94

95-96 June 22 proposal, frantic, breakthrough day: Hill 7-9-94; Frank, p. 8-9; Brown 6-21-82 cable Tel Aviv 09329, repeated in State 173001, 222242Z Jun 82, par. 3. Dillon had evacuated dependents of embassy personnel on June 6 and 7.

96 Sharon on his way: Veliotes memo 8217487 to the Secretary, 6-22-82

96 Meeting with Sharon: Radio Telecon from Habib 2130, 6-22-82; Veliotes memo to the Secretary 8217487, 6-22-82; Hill 7-9-94; Tanter, p. 138-39

96 Bush, Weinberger, why budge: Habib 6-18-82 cable to Murphy from Beirut 4267 repeated in State 169293 TOSEC 090039, 181749Z Jun 82, par. 4; Teicher, p. 206; Haig, p. 343; Hill 7-9-94. Some accounts mention only Weinberger, not Bush, talking with the Saudis; others mention only Bush. Habib sent word to the PLO "that there was nothing in the vice president's talks in Saudi Arabia that should give the PLO hope that there is another way out except through the offer" that he and the Lebanese government were making (Habib cable 4267, par. 4).

Habib muttered that it might take 48 hours just to persuade Arafat to agree to the 48 hours (Hill 7-9-94). Lewis (oral history, summer 1982 portion, p. 6) mentions only Weinberger and says, "In retrospect, if we in fact conveyed the wrong signal, either intentionally or inadvertently, that may have been one of the major causes for Beirut's great damage and suffering. Had the PLO not thought that we would come to their rescue at the last second, they might well have fled Beirut shortly after the Israeli invasion, thereby sparing Beirut and its inhabitants from a few weeks of hell."

The PLO came to believe "that Israel was incapable of storming Beirut, or unwilling to suffer the casualties involved, or otherwise prevented from doing so by domestic or external restraints." On June 20 Arafat proclaimed that "no one will accept to lay down his arms. . . . I am here and I am staying here" (Khalidi, p. 86). Even Druze leader Walid Jumblatt, who was quite sympathetic to the PLO, said "Arafat is trying to gain time, hoping for a miracle in the Arab world, but I don't believe it will happen" (Mikdadi, p. 51).

96 Joke: Mikdadi, p. 57-58

97 Winds: Bill Brown, the number two official in the US embassy in Tel Aviv, wrote on June 21 that "The PLO, however, is probably on the edge of on the one hand moving toward greater immediate flexibility, while on the other becoming crazed with fear, deciding that there is no other way out and resorting to suicidal military measures" (Brown 6-21-82 cable Tel Aviv 09329, repeated in State 173001, 222242Z Jun 82, par. 3).

97 Competing, stock: Veliotes 4-29-93

97 Work things out: Draper 4-13-93; Haig, p. 310-11, 342

97 Mustn't happen again: Haig, p. 311; Cannon, p. 201-2. Haig emphasizes that Reagan gave no indication that he disagreed with the content of the instructions to Habib.

97 Accused Clark, Reagan decided: Cannon, p. 204

97 Cheering: Howell 9-6-93. Veliotes reportedly ran down the hall of the State Department saying, "Don't anyone dare cheer. Keep at work" (Charles Stuart Kennedy in Viets oral history, p. 33).

97 Champagne: Viets oral history, p. 33

97 Dancing: The report was in Randal, p. 251. "No, no, no. That's bullshit," says Draper (12-18-94).

97 Days numbered: Habib interview with Parker, p. 5

98 Guessed Shultz, more balanced: Dillon 11-5-96. "Relieved" is the word Draper and Lewis use to describe Habib's reaction (Draper 12-18-94 and Lewis 4-10-94). One of Habib's colleagues, who asked not to be identified by name, distinctly recalls being surprised and put off by "the vehemence of Phil's remarks" about how happy he was that Haig was leaving. But Dillon, in whose home Habib was when he got the news, says that, unlike the others in the residence, Habib did not pause to criticize Haig. "I think this was part of his idea of being

professional," he says. "The rest of us would make very critical remarks, but Phil never did that. From his point of view, he thought of the rest of us as kids: 'That's the way kids act, but I, Phil Habib, don't act like that.'"

98 Sick few days: Letter from Veliotes in Cairo to Habib, April 4, 1983. Haig took refuge at the Greenbriar resort in West Virginia (Cannon, p. 397) mostly as a means of escaping the press.

98 Begged: Haig 5-11-94

98 Master of ceremonies: Eagleburger 7-3-93. State's number two person, Walter Stoessel, officially became acting secretary, but had little to contribute.

98 Complicating Habib's problems: Lewis 4-10-94; Hill 7-9-94; Schiff & Ya'ari, p. 206

98 Threats: Habib interview with the author, *The Stanford Magazine,* Spring 1984

98 Authority to penetrate: Schiff & Ya'ari, p. 206. The Cabinet declined (*Journal of Palestine Studies,* Summer/Fall 1982, "Chronology of the Israeli Invasion of Lebanon June-August 1982," p. 145).

98-100 Habib's recommendation: NEA Veliotes memo to Bremer 8217987, 6-27-82, "Recorded Radio Report from Habib, 0430 A.M., June 27, 1982." Italics are not in the State Department's transcription of Habib's tacsat dictation but are added according to the recollection of Charlie Hill (who took the call from Habib) of what Habib emphasized in his dictation (Hill 7-9-94). The same day, the Grand Mufti (the Sunni Muslim spiritual leader of Lebanon) phoned Habib and explained that "Islamic thought in Lebanon holds the United States accountable for what has already happened." Two days earlier the Grand Mufti had told Habib that continued Israeli attacks on Lebanon would transform Muslim opinion in that country, which was basically favorable to the United States, into hostility against the US (NEA Veliotes memo to S/S Bremer 8218010, 6-27-82, "Radio Message from Amb. Habib, 6/27/82, 11:30 A.M.: Appeal from Grand Mufti"). There was precedent that Habib hoped to draw on. When Israel had invaded Lebanon in the 1978 Operation Litani, President Carter decisively stepped in and threatened to cut off aid to Israel unless they left Lebanon. The threat worked, though Israel left a residual military presence north of their border (Veliotes ADST oral history, p. 199).

100 Will not withdraw: Hill 7-9-94. In addition to shooting, the Israelis were dropping leaflets on the city as part of a psychological warfare campaign telling people to leave town (Bavly, p. 102). It was working: People were leaving the city in droves. Habib thought "A degree of panic now in Beirut is good. But this must not lead to action."

100 Take orders, I accept: Hill 7-9-94; also Shultz, p. 14. Reagan by this point had bought Haig's argument that it was premature to make threats. On June 25, Haig was convinced that he had assurances from Israel not to enter West Beirut. But, just to make sure, Haig did tell the Israeli ambassador that morning that if they did go in, the US would cut off all military and economic assistance—precisely the threat he wouldn't hear of from Habib the same day. At the same time, Haig encouraged Israel to play a bluffing game to frighten the PLO into making the necessary concessions. The IDF did shelling, then declared a ceasefire, then followed up with radio broadcasts—all of which, Haig believed, were part of a bluff. Haig said, "If we can get the PLO finished, it will all be worth it." But nobody told Habib any of this. Convinced that the IDF's moves were real preparations for a brutal assault, Habib demanded that Reagan phone Begin immediately to say that the U.S. would apply strict sanctions if the IDF went into West Beirut. There was no time for a letter; it had to be by phone. He insisted that State pass his demand on to the White House (Hill 7-9-94).

100 Wazzan conveys symbolic force: Habib unnumbered cable to Secstate, "Meeting with President Sarkis, et al, June 28, 1982," 6-28-82, par. 3 and 6; "Radio Transmission from Habib—0700 EDT June 28," 8218031, 6-28-82; unnumbered State Dept. paper "Habib Report from Beirut 0630, June 28"; Hill 7-9-94. Of course, Jordan and Egypt, unlike Lebanon, also had governments strong enough to exert strict control over symbolic PLO forces on their territory.

The PLO also argued that, in accordance with the Arab League and the Rabat Conference, they had a right to have a political presence in any Arab capital, including Beirut ("Radio Transmission from Habib—0700 EDT June 28," 8218031, 6-28-82, par. 3).

101 Too serious: Habib unnumbered cable to Secstate, "Meeting with President Sarkis, et al, June 28, 1982," 6-28-82, par. 6

101 Game is up: NEA Veliotes memo to S/S

Bremer, 8218052, 6-28-82, "Message from Habib—Summary Review of Situation as of Monday Morning, June 28," par. 3

101 Middle of nowhere: Hill 7-9-94. Habib said he would push for 500, but could live with 1,000. The Lebanese government was willing to accept a "symbolic presence." Bashir, however, was not.

101 Last ditch: "Radio Transmission from Habib—0700 EDT June 28," 8218031, 6-28-82, p. 1. Hill 7-7-98 says no one in the loop at the State Department had any interest in the face-saving rationale, despite Habib's lectures to them about the importance among Arabs of saving face.

101 Opening he needed: NEA Veliotes memo to S/S Bremer, 8218052, 6-28-82, "Message from Habib—Summary Review of Situation as of Monday Morning, June 28," par. 3; "Message from Habib 0500 June 29: Day's Activities, June 29"; NEA Veliotes memo to S/S Bremer, 8218168, 6-29-82, p. 1. Haig received a clandestine message the same day from the Israeli intelligence agency Mossad that "Habib is getting a deliberately inaccurate reading out of his meetings with Lebanese and that information is being distorted to imply [the] impression of progress but there is actually nothing but stalling" ("Radio Telecon Draper/Hill, 0130 June 28, 1982," NEA Hill memo to Bremer, 8218166, 6-29-82; Hill 7-9-94). Habib realized that was a possibility, so he wrote, "In the course of [detailed] discussions, we will be able to determine whether the proposals have a truly valid basis or whether the [government of Lebanon] is being strung along by the PLO" ("Message from Habib 0500 June 29: Day's Activities, June 29," NEA Veliotes memo to S/S Bremer, 8218168, 6-29-82, p. 1). At his next meeting with Wazzan he pressed him on whether the proposals were truly valid and on the importance of speed. He reminded Wazzan "I would not be strung along. . . . There is no possibility of [the proposal] being acceptable if the PLO strings us along or seeks to get out of this" ("Radio Telecon Habib/Hill 0745, June 29, 1982," Memorandum for the Record, 8218324, 6-29-82). Habib figured that the Mossad's source was Bashir Gemayel, who opposed the PLO's proposal to leave behind a symbolic armed presence. Habib's response: "I'm tired of Israeli sniping. The Israelis want to accept what Bashir says rather than what I report. So what?" (Hill 7-9-94).

101 Ultimatum, flip-flop: Hill 7-9-94 and 7-7-

98. A likely factor in Haig's decision was the Mossad message he received the same day saying that Habib was being deceived about progress.

101 Haig issued: Haig cable to Habib, "Guidance for Habib from the Secretary," State 180100, 6-29-82. Specifically, the nine points were:

1 Ceasefire in place

2 All PLO leaders to leave Lebanon under assurances of safe passage

3 All PLO fighters in Beirut are to leave Lebanon under assurances of safe passage without heavy weapons (individual weapons will be permitted).

4 There will be no redeployment of any armed PLO fighters from Beirut to other locations in Lebanon.

5 A PLO political presence in Lebanon is acceptable, but preferably not in Beirut.

6 A readjustment of IDF lines will take place after an agreement is reached and as implementation is well underway.

7 The LAF will take control of all Beirut.

8 Other armed elements in West Beirut will turn over their arms to the LAF. The Syrian ADF force and associated units will return to Syria.

9 Related to the above, but not linked to West Beirut issue, it is a matter of policy that in the final arrangements there will be no foreign military presence in Lebanon: PLO, Syrian or Israeli.

101 No redeployment: Haig cable to Habib, "Guidance for Habib from the Secretary," State 180100, 6-29-82

101 Stunk, will not go: Hill 7-9-94. Eagleburger denied it was an ultimatum. Seeming uncomfortable with his role as middleman conveying the nine points to Habib, in the end Eagleburger said, "It is an instruction. I have saluted. I don't disagree" (Hill 7-9-94). Perhaps not surprisingly, the Israelis found Haig's nine points "not very different from our own positions," says Sharon. They rejected only point 5, which would allow the PLO to maintain some political presence in Lebanon (Sharon, p. 482).

101 Mistake: Hill 7-9-94

101 Equivalent: Memorandum for the Record, 8218312, 6-29-82, "Informal Lebanese Response to Habib's Presentation of the 9 Points"; Hill 7-9-94

101 Trying to do something: Hill 7-9-94; "Radio Telecon Eagleburger/Habib, 1545 June 29, 1982"; NEA Veliotes memo to S/S Bremer, 8218313, 6-29-82, "Department Response to Lebanese Questions Concerning the 9 Points"

102 Frightening: Hill 7-9-94

102 Didn't ignore: Memorandum for the Record, 8218312, 6-29-82, "Informal Lebanese Response to Habib's Presentation of the 9 Points"; Radio Telecon Eagleburger/Habib, 1545 June 29, 1982, NEA Veliotes memo to S/S Bremer, 8218313, 6-29-82, "Department Response to Lebanese Questions Concerning the 9 Points"; Hill 7-9-94

102 Remarkably like: Hill 7-9-94

102 Stupid, brooding: Hill 7-9-94. Haig, meanwhile, was incorrectly reporting to Reagan that "as a result of Habib's efforts, the Lebanese are now completely with us and realize that the nine points represent the only realistic course to follow" (Haig memo to the President, 8218424, 6-30-82, "Lebanon Crisis: Status Report as of Mid-day June 30," p. 2). One can only speculate about the basis of his inaccurate report.

102-3 Burying us, three weeks: Memorandum for the Record, 8218312, 6-29-82, "Informal Lebanese Response to Habib's Presentation of the 9 Points"

103 Never mentioned, on track: Hill 7-9-94; Hill 7-12-95

103 Shinola, declined: Shultz, p. 14; Haig, p. 350-51; Haig 5-11-94

7 Fight the Fire Anyway

T104 Tough, driven: Randal, *Tragedy,* p. 232-33

104 Impossible: Habib interview with the author, *The Stanford Magazine,* Spring 1984

104 Never doubted: Hill 6-15-93 and 3-27-93; Habib interview with Parker 5-9-90, p. 25; Grove 6-12-94; also according to a Near Eastern Affairs bureau official who asked not to be identified by name. Many of his colleagues agreed that Habib was the only one who could succeed (for example, Grove 6-12-94; Hill 7-19-95). Some disagreed (Crocker 4-25-94; Eagleburger 7-3-93).

104 Authority derives: "Oakley's Gambit," *Time,* 10-18-93

104-5 Most players: Habib interview with the author 12-20-83; also Draper ADST oral history and Grove 6-12-94

105 Knew their ambitions: Grove 6-12-94

105 Care greatly: According to a colleague who asked not to be identified by name

105 Legend, best: Lewis unpublished ms., p. 3; Doug Waller 6-30-98; Grove 6-12-94

105 Unique crisis: Dillon 5-9-94

105 Totally unconventional: Tueni 11-15-95

105 Knack: Dean 5-12-94

105 Resiliency: According to a State Department colleague who asked not to be identified by name

105 Clout: Habib interview with the author, *The Stanford Magazine,* Spring 1984

105 Trying to solve: Hill 7-12-95

105 Lie for country: Habib interview with Kreisler, page 2 of 6. His own view was that "the best diplomat is the one who most accurately and honestly presents the policies of his government" (from an undated draft of Habib's speech to the South Korean National Defense College in one of his personal scrapbooks about his time as ambassador to South Korea 1971-74).

105 No flies: Habib interview with the author, *The Stanford Magazine,* Spring 1984

105-6 Lost the whole show: Grove 6-4-94 and Grove letter to author 6-8-97. There is a certain difference of opinion about the extent to which Habib toned down his ways when dealing with foreign counterparts. Some say simply that he was the same no matter who he was talking with. Others say he toned down the profanity and theatrics with foreigners. Dillon (11-5-96) is critical that Habib was not nearly as tough with the Israelis as he was with

Americans.

106 Foolishness: Grove 6-12-94

106 Didn't hesitate: Sometimes that was genuine, sometimes it was a ploy. A US Marine lieutenant colonel, who knows something about such matters, says that even when intimidation was just a tactic, "he was *good* at it. He was a forceful man. Very forceful" (Smith 6-14-94).

106 Toe-to-toe: This diplomat asked not to be identified by name

106 Eyeballs, hands: Bider 5-23-93. For example, after a particularly exasperating tacsat call to the State Department, Habib slammed down the receiver, turned to a Lebanese official who happened to be nearby, and said, "This is Washington for you. The guys there only believe what they read in the telex. Who the hell invented the written word? Was it you, the Phoenicians?" (Salem, p. 37).

106-7 Challenge or ridicule: Veliotes 5-6-93. Veliotes adds that, while Habib didn't hesitate to ridicule your point of view, he would never ridicule you as a person. Dillon points out, "Phil was quite capable of letting you believe what you wanted to believe. He wouldn't lie, but he wouldn't correct you. This is not unusual among diplomats" (Dillon 11-16-96).

107 Defend your opinion: Bider 5-23-93

107 Overwhelm them: Kreczko 5-11-94

107 Always appear in control: Crocker 4-28-94

107 Heart problem: Sicherman 7-4-98

108 Don't waste your time: Tueni 11-15-95

108 Negotiation without compromise: "Peace Envoy's Postscript," Habib as told to Larry Engelmann, *Vietnam* magazine, April 1993; "Habib habits: Facts, humor, pressure, honesty," *The Spokesman-Review/Seattle Chronicle,* April 25, 1987, report on a speech by Habib at the University of Idaho; also Habib's speech "Diplomacy and the Search for Peace in the Middle East," p. 6-7

108 That's a joke: Kreczko 5-11-94

108 Blame: Habib testimony to US Senate Committee on Foreign Relations, "Briefing on Central American Peace Initiative," June 16, 1987, p. 26

108 Hour ago: Bider 4-26-93

108 Little point of agreement: Tueni 11-15-95

108 No particular method: Hopkins, p. 36, citing Sam Lewis

108 Scorn: Habib interview with Parker 5-9-90, p. 24

108 Leave your books: Tueni 11-15-95

108 Definition of success: Cyrus Vance 2-14-94

108-9 Least bad solution: Dean 5-12-94

109 Two kinds of conflicts: Dusclaud 4-19-95, citing a speech by Habib at the University of Bordeaux in November 1991

109 Not always necessary: Habib interview with Dusclaud

109 Habib's rule, moral story: Grove 6-4-94 and letter to author 6-8-97; also Dillon 11-5-96. Habib made this point often, usually with a self-satisfied chuckle. Dillon is critical of Habib about this view: "That's partly right, but it's not always right. It seemed to me that he was too quick to take the soldiers seriously. I could never quite engender the same respect for men with guns—including our own—that Phil seemed to have."

109 Show more anger: Bider 4-24-93; Howell 9-6-93

109 Tell genuine anger: Bider 4-26-93; Lee 10-2-94; Tueni 11-15-95; Hill 7-12-95

110 Every Habib sentence: Hill 7-7-98

110 Master of tirade: Hill writing in "Philip Habib: A Remembrance," *Foreign Service Journal,* July 1992, p. 12

110 Shitty way to deal: According to a diplomat who asked not to be identified by name

110 Yelling from other room: Crocker 4-25-94

110 Histrionics: Draper 12-18-94

110 Uncontrollable way: Shultz 7-25-94

110-11 Use theatrics: This source asked not to be identified by name.

111 Being impossible, bully me: Habib interview with the author, *The Stanford Magazine,* Spring 1984

111 Threats: Habib interview with the author, *The Stanford Magazine,* Spring 1984

111 Anger no act: Lee 10-2-94; Crocker 4-25-

94; Hill 6-15-93

111 Anger tended to be: Howell 9-6-93; Bider 5-23-93 and 4-26-93

111 Classic definition: Barron letter to author 5-4-94; quote is from Caskie Stinnett, in *Simpson's Contemporary Quotations*, p. 216 (Humor and Wit)

111 Rare gift: Hill note to author on manuscript of chapter 12

111-12 Syrian announcement: NEA Veliotes memo to S/S Bremer, 8219690, 7-10-82, "Telecon with Habib July 10, 1982 0700," p. 3-4; punctuation altered for clarity, characteristic profanity added to bowdlerized transcript

112 Beat up on: Sehulster 6-23-94; and an official who asked not to be identified by name

112 Morrie Goddammit: Crocker 4-25-94. Crocker adds, "It was a Mutt & Jeff routine." In fact, according to a diplomat who asked not to be identified by name, their radio call signs were Dagwood (Draper) and Mr. Bumstead (Habib). In the comic strip "Blondie," Dagwood was forever being yelled at and kicked in the pants by his boss, Mr. Bumstead.

112 Shooting off mouth, magazine: Hill 7-12-95; Hopkins, p. 29

112 Screaming moral outrage: Hill 3-27-93

112 Cared too much: Shultz 7-25-94

112 He was Lebanese: Haig 5-11-94

112-13 Extraordinarily emotional: Lewis 4-10-94

113 I must say, cucumber: "Radio communication between Habib and Veliotes, July 7/82, A.M.," 8218994, p. 5. Punctuation altered from State Department transcript for clarity. A few days earlier Habib sent a cable arguing that Israeli military moves were counterproductive and that he considered Israeli cutoffs of water and power "unbelievable in the 20th century, inhumane, and unnecessary in the present circumstances." He concluded by saying, "In making these points, I assure readers of this message that I am not 'panicking.' However I am frustrated by my inability to see Wazzan [due to Israeli fighting] about the results of his crucial meeting last night with the PLO" (Habib 7-4-82 cable Beirut 4439, quoted in State 186503, 061812Z Jul 82, par 5-7).

113 Overly committed: Veliotes 5-6-93

113 Pissed as shit: State Department official who asked not to be identified by name

113 Weren't exposed: Sehulster 6-23-94. Another Marine who worked with Habib in Beirut, Col. Robert Johnston, in fact, viewed him as "a pretty damn composed individual. He knew what he wanted, and at the drop of a hat he could give you a shopping list. He could cuss at the Israelis, and he did that quite often, but basically he had a calm demeanor. You never felt like he in any way had lost his control of the situation" (Johnston 12-4-96).

113 The tough guys: Hill 7-19-95, 7-9-94. Dillon comments that, "the tough guys in the Department—the ones who would say 'if you want to make an omelet, you gotta break some eggs,' or 'let the peasants die to achieve our noble goals'—were by and large people who had no real experience with violence or combat. One thing I admired about Phil was that this tough-talking guy from Brooklyn wasn't like that. It really pained him to see the suffering" (Dillon 12-31-97).

113-14 Eagleburger: Hill 7-19-95. The description of Eagleburger as "one of the tough guys" is Hill's. Hill says Eagleburger was being "a smartass" in his remark about Sedan and the Somme. "Ardennes" refers to the Battle of the Bulge, a bloody battle in December 1944 as the World War II Allies were retaking Europe. "Saint-Lô" refers to a July 1944 Allied assault in which 2,500 planes dropped some 4,000 tons of bombs on a fourteen-square mile area around the northern French town of Saint-Lô. This key part of Gen. Omar Bradley's Operation Cobra, seven weeks after D-Day, helped clear the way for an Allied advance toward Paris. Sedan was the site of the climactic battle of the Franco-Prussian War in 1870, in which the French were routed and Emperor Napoleon III was captured. The Battle of the Somme, France, was one of the bloodiest battles in history, claiming over a million lives in 1916.

114 Study in personal contrasts: Crocker 4-25-94

114 Posturing, parties might buy: Habib interview with the author, in *The Stanford Magazine,* Spring 1984

114 Firefighter: Hill 7-12-95

114 Keep on trying: Lee 10-2-94

115 Always hope: Bider 4-26-93

115 We can't do this: Barrett 5-9-94

115 I never saw: Crocker 4-25-94. Crocker also says Habib sometimes seemed nervous, but Pascoe says "Worried, yes; nervous, no" (Pascoe 6-4-94).

115 Beliefs sustained: Crocker 4-25-94

115 Get to work: Habib interview with the author, *The Stanford Magazine,* Spring 1984

115 Common ground: Crocker 4-25-94

115 Logical line: Habib interview with Dusclaud

115 Being retired: Dean 5-12-94

115 Dueling brains: Bider 4-24-93

115 Loved challenges: Bider 5-23-93

115 He did it to right: Dean 5-12-94

115 Jazzy: Habib interview with the author, *The Stanford Magazine,* Spring 1984

115 Loved the drama: Daniel O'Donohue writing in "Philip Habib: A Remembrance," *Foreign Service Journal,* July 1992, p. 13

116 Hardest negotiations: Quoted by Hill 7-12-95

116 Roundabout diplomacy: The State Department did two slightly different transcripts of this tacsat call; the quote uses elements of both (NEA Veliotes memo to S/S Bremer, 8219690, 7-10-82, "Telecon with Habib July 10, 1982 0700," p. 4; NEA Veliotes memo to S/S Bremer, 8219694, "Telecon between Phil Habib and Charlie Hill, Saturday, July 10 11:00 A.M.")

116 Some special envoys: Parker, p. 209, quotes David Newsom's intriguing discussion of this phenomenon, from *Middle East Journal,* Summer 1981.

116 Taking the ambassador: Habib interview with Parker 5-9-90, p. 25

116 Before I'd go: Habib interview with the author, *The Stanford Magazine,* Spring 1984

116 Involve the local ambassador: Hopkins, p. 39-43; Habib interview with the author, in *The Stanford Magazine,* Spring 1984. The ambassadors in the region consistently commend Habib for this practice while criticizing his successors for arrogantly failing to do so (Hopkins, p. 39-45; Paganelli 11-2-96; Dillon 5-9-94). Hill adds that Habib's practice of involving the local ambassador and staff rooted his negotiations in the local process of diplo-

macy (Hill note on manuscript of chapter 12).

116-17 Cooks, maids: Gaucher 5-15-94

117 Jonny Abdu: Sehulster 6-23-94; Crocker 4-25-94; Gaucher 5-15-94

117 Numbing torrent: Lee 10-2-94; Bider 5-23-93

117 I don't carry: Kreczko 10-6-93. Kreczko was not with Habib in the summer of 1982, but in the fall and winter of 1982-83.

117 Painting themselves blue: "Middle East ripe for new peace talks, says former presidential envoy Habib," *Campus Report* (a publication of Stanford University), February 20, 1985

117 My parents' home: "An old pro wins a new peace," *Washington Post* story in *St. Petersburg Times,* 8-21-82; "The Habib Diplomatic Style: Unorthodox but Effective," *Latin America Daily Post,* 8-26-82

117 Red-white-and-blue: Bider 4-26-93

117 FSOs are trained: Howell 10-11-93. By the time Habib got to the Middle East, State had dropped that practice. Besides, he was retired. Ironically, recent presidents have increased the frequency of sending political appointees to the homelands of their forebears (according to a source who asked not to be identified by name).

117-18 Cozy up: Howell 9-6-93 and 10-11-93

118 My first cousin: Dean 5-12-94. This was in fact true—except that his father's real name was Jamous. John Gunther Dean was ambassador to Lebanon when Habib began his 1981 mission.

118 Uncle: Bavley, p. 104

118 One conversation: Crocker 4-25-94

118 Massive attempt: Dillon ADST oral history

118 Folk hero: Hill 7-17-93. *Effendi* is an Arabic term of respect, comparable to *sir* in English.

118 Bill: Grove letter to author 6-8-97, speaking specifically of a waiter in the Philadelphia restaurant in Jerusalem.

118 Not God, swept: Dillon 11-16-96 and 5-9-94. Ghassan Tueni, the Lebanese ambassador to the UN, said, "To us in the little old country, Philip Habib was yet another prophet, but one who was physically bringing back peace

from the America of which his people dreamt for generations past. . . . He was our giant" (eulogy at Habib's memorial service, June 10, 1992, Washington).

118-19 Suddenly realized: Hill letter to the author received 6-13-97

119 Inaccessible: Dillon 11-16-96

119 One of the boys: Tueni 11-15-95. Among the Lebanese, it was crucial to view the interlocutor as being of their same universe, competent, and a representative of a party with clout (Crocker 4-28-94).

119 Role of mentor: Hill 7-17-93; Lewis 4-10-94

119 Bashir, advice: Seale, p. 388

119 Avuncular: Tueni 11-15-95

119 Could they really trust: Lewis 4-10-94

119 Arab leaders: Hill 7-17-93

119 Rug merchant: Paganelli 11-2-96

120 Sympathetic, mistaken: Draper 4-13-93

120 Sister disparaged: Marjorie Habib 4-19-95

120 Phil never liked: Haig 5-11-94

120 Much more sympathetic: Lewis 4-10-94. Habib believed that "Although the right to [Palestinian] self-determination as a concept is undeniable, the exercise of self-determination through an independent Palestinian state is not practical at this time." He also accepted as a given America's "unshakable commitment to the existence and security of the State of Israel" (Habib speech "Diplomacy and the Search for Peace in the Middle East," April 29, 1985). He privately acknowledged to Assad Syria's legitimate security interests in Lebanon (Hopkins, p. 63).

120 Pro-Arab: Eagleburger 7-3-93. Eagleburger readily describes himself as strongly pro-Israel. Haig (5-11-94) considered Habib an "Arabist." Hill (7-19-95) argues that there is no way Habib could be considered an Arabist, since he spent most of his career as a Far East expert.

120 Any American: Kreczko 5-11-94

120 Clearly understood: This source asked not to be identified by name.

120 Internationally disliked: Davis, p. 68, based on Bavly and Salpeter, p. 75. The Ameri-

can public, like Habib, remained committed to Israel generally while becoming increasingly critical of Begin *(International Herald Tribune,* 7-22-82; cited in Jansen, p. 84).

120 Begin's excesses: Randal, *Tragedy,* p. 286. Goldwater, a US senator from Arizona, was a leading conservative and the Republican candidate for president in 1964.

120 A lot of right: Hill 6-15-93

120 Pox: This source asked not to be identified by name.

121 Balanced view: Eagleburger 7-3-93. But, he adds, they "would view him as being pro-Arab on occasion."

121 Self-righteous: Dillon ADST oral history

121 Enemy: Eagleburger 7-3-93

121 Product of Brooklyn: Such as Barrett 5-9-94; Crocker 4-25-94; Kreczko 5-11-94

121 Stereotypical: Pascoe 6-4-94; Draper ADST oral history; Haig 5-11-94; Marjorie Habib 2-27-93; Tueni 11-15-95; Dillon 11-5-96

121 Shrug: Lee 10-2-94. *Malesh* is an Arabic word roughly translated "What the hell. Never mind. It doesn't matter" (Lee and "Saving the Children," *The Stanford Magazine,* Winter 1987, p. 62).

121 Lebanese food: For example, Dillon 5-9-94; Crocker 4-25-94; Lee 10-2-94

121 Bazaar: Draper ADST oral history

121 Shrewd bargaining sense: Grove 6-4-94

121 Price of a rug: Dean 5-12-94

121 Jewish haberdasher: Tueni 11-15-95

122 Only diplomat: Hill 3-27-93. Hill adds that he felt that other Americans—who want to get to the point and get every item clearly understood and nailed down—could never understand how things got done in the Middle East.

122 Middle Eastern feel: Draper ADST oral history

122 Kissed: Draper 4-13-93; Green 7-10-93

122 Touch: Crocker 4-28-94

122 Brother, food: Draper 4-13-93

122 In Jerusalem, in Beirut: Gaucher 5-15-94

122 Whipped cream: Eagleburger 7-3-93

122 Thirty-five subparagraphs: Hill 3-27-93

122 He could recall: Bider 4-24-93

122-23 Lawyer's discussion: Lewis 8-11-82 cable Tel Aviv 12220, quoted in State 226747, 130526Z Aug 82, par. 1, 7

123 Courtly, dour: Veliotes 5-6-93. Begin was also extremely tenacious. Lewis, who knew Begin better than any other American diplomat, describes one letter from Begin to Reagan as "vintage Begin, an extravagantly polite and legalistic way of rejecting the president's simple proposal and restating Begin's previous conditions" (Lewis cable Jerusalem 01809, 6-10-82, par. 5).

123 Dare to tease: Draper ADST oral history; "Habib habits: Facts, humor, pressure, honesty," *The Spokesman-Review/Seattle Chronicle,* April 25, 1987, report on a speech by Habib at the University of Idaho

123 Poker: Habib in informal talk to Jewish Community Federation at Silverado, January 21 or 22, 1984; Marjorie Habib 2-27-93. He was much more relaxed with Lebanese officials and Director General of the Israeli Foreign Ministry David Kimche (Kreczko 10-6-93; Veliotes 5-6-93).

123 Arabs tended: Hill 6-15-93. As Howell points out, there is not a clean division between Israeli and Arab negotiating styles. The Egyptians, for example, could be every bit as punctilious as the Israelis. And Assad was more explicit than other Arabs. He was relaxed, congenial, and joking until he realized he'd been had on June 11. Howell also points out the drawbacks to both the legalistic and the lax styles: "Arabs sometimes reach agreements that aren't agreements. It sounds good and everybody leaves happy, but they haven't achieved anything. The Israelis, on the other hand, at least when they're in that kind of legalistic mode, never get to an agreement because you can never clear up all the little nit-picks" (Howell 9-6-93).

123 Talk around: Habib interview with Parker 5-9-90, p. 22

123 Traditional Middle Eastern way, if you tried: Hill 6-15-93

123 Shrug shoulders: Hill 3-27-93. This may help explain why Assad mistakenly thought he had an understanding with Habib over a

ceasefire on June 11, discussed in chapter 4.

123 Take the eyebrow: Howell 9-6-93

124 Always insisted: Crocker 4-25-94. This was to avoid confusion or deliberate distortion. Habib and Draper sent their messages to the PLO in a form they called "non-papers": written in the third person to maintain a certain distance and typed on plain white paper to avoid looking like official US policy statements (Hopkins, p. 20). Crocker says Habib's messages to Arafat were often neatly typed in English; Arafat's messages to him would come back handwritten in Arabic.

124 Yank him back: "A Sterling Achievement," *Time,* 8-30-82, p. 26

124 Sum up: Howell 9-6-93

124 Diplomat's job: Dillon 11-16-96

124 Just outstanding: Shultz 7-25-94

124 Slightly exaggerating: Dillon 5-9-94

124 Tell Reagan: Barrett 5-9-94

124 Every right: Hill 7-12-95

124-25 In my opinion: Hopkins, p. 35, based on his interview with Veliotes 2-7-92

125 No one way: Habib interview with the author 12-20-83, p. 20 (not included in *Stanford Magazine* edited version)

125 Own interest: According to a diplomat who asked not to be identified by name

125 Bashir: Seale, p. 388-89. Seale says, "Bashir often came to Habib for advice, developing a dependence on the older, wiser man whom he sometimes addressed as *Ammo* (uncle)." For another example, in trying to persuade Sharon to stop bombing Beirut, Habib would point out how the press was portraying the destruction and misery he was causing. "What the hell is the world seeing you for, Arik?" (Draper 4-13-93)

125 Re-equipping: Habib 7-24-92 cable Jidda 5532, quoted in State 206640 TOSEC 110050, 250019Z Jul 82, par. 6B (punctuation altered for clarity)

125 Essentially the same: Grove 6-4-94; Kreczko 10-6-93; Veliotes 5-6-93

125 Ladies: Lee 10-2-94

125 Bunch of crap, joke: Kreczko 10-6-93

125 Rarely raised: Lewis 4-10-94

125-26 Wicked, firm: Marjorie Habib 3-26-94; Veliotes 5-6-93; Draper 4-13-93

126 High commissioner: Lewis 4-10-94

126 Curse: Draper 4-13-93

126 Baton: Barron letter to author 5-4-94

126 Naked lady dance: Habib interview with the author, *The Stanford Magazine,* Spring 1984

126 Interesting person: Shultz 7-25-94

126 Enjoy being around: Kreczko 10-6-93. Despite their substantive differences, many Israelis liked Habib and enjoyed his sense of humor (Bavly and Salpeter, p. 104).

126 Say or do next: Mead 6-5-94

126 Serendipitously, 1980 assignment: Grove 6-12-94 and 6-4-94

8 The Plan

127 Call spirits: Act III, scene I, 52. Associated with this context by *The New York Times.*

127 No precedent: Habib cable Beirut 05901, 011245Z Sep 82, par. 4; Shultz 9-16-93; Hill 7-17-93

127 Somehow extract: Hopkins, p. 15-17, citing his 3-12-92 interview with Habib. It wasn't just the PLO that Habib needed to get out: A top-flight unit of 3,500 Syrians and a Palestinian faction under Syrian command were also trapped in West Beirut (Draper 5-4-93).

127 Buffer force: Habib cable Jerusalem 01903 of June 13, 1982, repeated in State 163551, 142321Z Jun 82, par. 4, 6, 7. Begin told Habib he would be "delighted" if such a buffer force could be established so Israeli troops could get home "in weeks." Once the ostensibly modest invasion turned into a massive siege of Beirut, the idea of a multinational buffer force in southern Lebanon became irrelevant.

127 Own evacuation: USMC 2, Tel Aviv Is 08807, 13 June 1982; Cable RUEKJCS/8807, 132226Z Jun 82. Habib had been all for it, since that would spare the civilians of Beirut needless suffering. But Sharon and Menachem Begin at first forbade evacuation since, in their minds, evacuation was escape. They had not

come this far to let the PLO now slip through their fingers, regroup, and roar back with a vengeance a year later. Sharon and Begin soon changed their minds, however. Driving the PLO out of Lebanon to somewhere else, they decided, would be OK after all (Radio Telecon from Habib 2130, June 22, 1982).

128 Interested in listening: Habib cable to Secstate also for action, 6-28-82, "Meeting with President Sarkis, et al, June 28, 1982," p. 4

128 Deal with stupidity: Hill 7-9-94

128 Afraid to propose: Transcript "Recorded radio conversation between Mr. Eagleburger and Amb. Habib, July 7/82, 0900 hours" 8219191, p. 3-4; Hill 7-12-95. As Draper told the Syrian foreign minister July 10, the basis of US policy in Lebanon was not what the Israelis wanted, but "what would ensure a stable and secure Lebanon and prevent future Israeli military actions against Lebanon" (Paganelli cable Damascus 04934, 101438Z Jul 82, par. 12).

128-29 PLO could "propose": Veliotes memo to the Secretary, 8217557, 6-23-82, Report From Habib/Draper for your 0930 Secure Telcon with Habib, p. 1-2. At first the PLO thought this was as ridiculous as everyone else did. They couldn't be bothered to take the Lebanese government seriously enough to talk to them, much less take orders from them. As Sharon tightened the noose around West Beirut, though, that quickly changed.

Habib insisted that this be a deal between the PLO and the government of Lebanon. After the first week of the invasion, he spent most of his time in Beirut, meeting with the Lebanese president, prime minister, foreign minister, and other top officials, talking over possible scenarios and terms under which the PLO might leave.

A major reason Lebanese sovereignty was so important (and precarious) was that the modern state of Lebanon had been carved out of the traditional land of Syria. The Syrians had never fully accepted that division, and Assad still regarded Lebanon as part of greater Syria. He enjoyed pointing out to Habib that Habib's father, who had emigrated from "Lebanon" to America around 1900, would have carried a Syrian passport. That was true. In registering for college in 1938, Habib had listed his ethnic background as "Syrian-American."

129 A package: For example, "Radio Communication between C. Hill - Habib, 7/6/82,

0715" 8218995, 7-6-82, p. 3; also Habib cable Beirut 04461, 7-5-82, par. 4; Habib cable Beirut 4415, quoted in State 184218, 021729Z Jul 82, par 10. He told Washington the same thing. After receiving "a crashingly dumb idea" from the State Department, Draper called to say "it would be helpful if Washington did less creative thinking about ideas which make no sense on the ground in Beirut and spent more time consulting with Beirut and working on [the] agreed upon scenario" ("0350 Draper-Peters secure Telcon," undated, but hand notations imply 7-5-82).

129 Wedge: In the early days of the war, before the siege of Beirut set in for the long haul, the idea was that a military force would go into southern Lebanon as a buffer between Israel's northern border and PLO rockets.

129 Simply agree with Habib: Habib interview with the author, *The Stanford Magazine,* Spring 1984. Habib reported on June 28 that "it is unlikely that the PLO will put anything down in writing, again, for face-saving reasons" (summary of Habib tacsat call "Radio Transmission from Habib—0700 EDT June 28," 8218031, 6-28-82).

129 Mammoth operation: Nobody, including the PLO, knew how many PLO fighters were in Beirut. So nobody knew how many would need to be evacuated. Estimates ranged from 3,000 to 10,000. "I don't know how many we are going to end up with," Habib said. "We don't really know. It may be up to 10,000. Remember, some of them are going to have their families. We may run up to 15,000-20,000 people. We ain't going to take them out in a god damned airplane. We'll take them out by boat" (NEA Veliotes memo to S/S Bremer, 8218794, "TelCon Habib and Charles Hill/Adm. Howe, 12:07 P.M., July 3, 1982," p. 6).

129 Other powerful fears: Sharon agreed with Habib about this, writing that "the PLO's incentives to stay were far greater than their incentives to leave" (Sharon, p. 482). In Sharon's analysis, that meant he had to give them more incentive to leave by sending in more artillery and bombs. In Habib's analysis, such a "bludgeon approach" was no more likely to work in the future than it had so far (NEA Veliotes memo to Bremer 8217985, 6-26-82, "Recorded Radio Report from Habib, Late Evening Meeting with Sarkis, June 26").

130 Budget, Abu: "West Beirut Bids Farewell to P.L.O.," *The New York Times,* 8-22-82

130 Fat city: Hill 7-12-95

130 Last ditch: "Radio Transmission from Habib—0700 EDT June 28," 8218031, 6-28-82; Hill 7-9-94. That was one of Habib's greatest concerns, and he considered it a very real possibility. At one point he shouted to Washington, "The Palestinians are talking frantically now. They're really going wild. They're prepared to go down fighting" (Hill 7-9-94). The PLO's need to save face is why Habib considered it sabotage to his diplomacy for the Israelis to leak stories to the press: Any time the PLO gave him a concession and the Israelis leaked word to the press, it made the PLO look weak; the PLO would then promptly deny and backpedal on the concession, setting back Habib's efforts farther than they had been before the concession (Hill 7-10-94).

130 Rather die: Friedman, p. 147

130 Khadaffi, Mubarak: Hill 7-16-94

130 Come get us: This is the analysis of an American diplomat involved in the crisis who asked not to be identified by name. See also Lewis ADST oral history. Draper adds that Habib "had a lot of evidence" that the 3,500 elite Syrian troops trapped in West Beirut "were going to fight to the last man" (Draper 5-4-93), and Assad's biographer says in so many words that those were indeed their orders (Seale, p. 386).

130 Never surrender: Hill 7-9-94. Pakradouni writes that "never in [Arafat's] worst moments of melancholy did he imagine that he would be led to leave Beirut under conditions dictated by Philip Habib" (Pakradouni, p. 255).

130 Heads above ground: Hill 7-19-95. This fear of being massacred grew larger and larger over time, says an NEA official who asked not to be identified by name. A top official in the US embassy in Tel Aviv wrote on June 21 that "it was crucial that the PLO perceive us to be in a position to influence Israel [to hold fire] so as to overcome PLO paranoic fears, e.g. that should they allow the LAF to deploy, disarm and seek safe conduct they would not be butchered in a subsequent betrayal" (Brown 6-21-82 cable Tel Aviv 09329, repeated in State 173001, 222242Z Jun 82, par. 3).

130 Trucks, port: Draper 4-13-93

130 Sink the ships: The source, a State Department official involved with the crisis, asked not to be identified by name. That source said,

"they were scared shitless that as soon as they started boarding boats, Israeli planes would come over and sink the boats." The PLO had good reason to worry that the IDF would sink their ships. Bashir Gemayel himself had warned of that as early as June 26 (Hill 6-26-95).

130 Women and children: The Phalanges were Bashir Gemayel's Maronite Christian militia, also known as the Kataeb and the Lebanese Forces. Bashir had invited Sharon to invade Lebanon, and Sharon had coordinated his plans in advance with Bashir and his Phalange commanders. The PLO had good reason to fear for the safety of the Palestinian civilians they would leave behind. Six years earlier the Phalange and its allies had carried out a horrible massacre of Palestinians at the Tel El-Zaatar refugee camp in East Beirut. Since the Israelis had taken over southern Lebanon, the PLO had heard many reports of severe harassment of Palestinians in that region (Cobban in McDermott, p. 215).

131 Hoping for a miracle: Lewis ADST oral history; Hill 7-19-95 and 7-12-95; Lewis 4-10-94; Mikdadi, p. 51; Khalidi, p. 85-86, 88, 113, 115.

131 Guerrillas win: Kissinger quoted in Averell Harriman's Memo of Conversation with Under Secretary Elliot Richardson, Jan 22, 1969, National Archives, Harriman papers

131 Token force: Habib cable Beirut 04461, 051600Z Jul 82, par. 10; transcript "Recorded radio conversation between Mr. Eagleburger and Amb. Habib, July 7/82, 0900 hours" 8219191, p. 2-3

131 Political office: Habib cable Beirut 04460, 051345Z Jul 82, par. 9

132 Consistent, inconsistent: Hill 7-10-94; Begin said that any residual PLO presence would turn back into a full-blown armed presence.

132 Habib keeps telling: Transcript "Recorded radio conversation between Mr. Eagleburger and Amb. Habib, July 7/82, 0900 hours" 8219191, p. 1. State was at that moment busy drafting a message from Reagan to Begin, so Habib told State to emphasize in it that Habib's advocacy for a token force and political office "is the position of the United States, goddam it. It is not just me throwing out things [and] negotiating from my head" (p. 5; punctuation altered from the original for clarity). Coincidentally, at about the same time Begin was

saying that, the PLO gave up its demand for a token force (transcript "Recorded radio conversation between Mr. Eagleburger and Amb. Habib, July 7/82, 0900 hours" 8219191, p. 2). Instead, they just wanted their fighters outside of Beirut to be able to stay in Lebanon for an agreed-upon time.

132 Ship to come in: NEA Veliotes memo to Bremer 8217985, 6-26-82, "Recorded Radio Report from Habib, Late Evening Meeting with Sarkis, June 26," par. 4

132 Terms in writing: "Radio Transmission from Habib—0700 EDT June 28," 8218031, 6-28-82, p. 1; Habib interview with the author, *The Stanford Magazine,* Spring 1984

132 Greek ships: According to an NEA official who asked not to be identified by name

132 How else: Habib interview with Parker. The Lebanese government and the Palestinians also insisted on a military buffer because they were afraid of the Israelis (Draper 5-4-93). Haig disagreed with Habib that there was any need for a buffer: "Bullshit. Whether Phil said that or not, whether he was in his dotage or whether he had a good dinner or a bad dinner or an extra Martini, I can't answer. But let me tell you, there never had to be a buffer. Because they weren't engaged! There *was* no engagement" (Haig 5-11-94). As early as June 30 there was discussion in Washington about providing US Navy air and sea escorts for the evacuation ships. The Lebanese and PLO both liked the idea (Haig memo to the President, 8218424, 6-30-82, "Lebanon Crisis: Status Report as of Mid-day June 30"; Radio Transmission, Habib to Hill 0800 July 1, 1982, 8218541).

132 Gucci boots: Mead 6-5-94

132 Absolutely neutral: Dillon ADST oral history

132 Any buffer force at all: Draper 5-4-93. This was despite their having themselves proposed, back in the days when Begin was talking about 40 kilometer, a neutral buffer force for southern Lebanon to separate the PLO from the Israeli border (Habib cable Jerusalem 01781, 082059Z Jun 82, par. 6; Habib cable Jerusalem 01782, 082059Z Jun 82, par. 2; Habib cable Jerusalem 01871, 121152Z Jun 82, par. 3D and E; Haig cable [no number] from Windsor to Habib 6-9-82; Habib cable Jerusalem 01903 of 6-13-82, repeated in State 163551, 142321Z Jun 82, par. 4).

132-33 Reason to worry: Shultz memo to The President, "West Beirut Situation Looking Better," 8-6-82, 8223489, p. 2

133 Screen: Sharon, p. 488-89. The Israelis did not want any military force separating them from the PLO in Beirut because that would mean a relaxation of IDF pressure, and they believed that sustained IDF pressure was the only way to get them to leave. Once the PLO had a protective screen, Israel argued, they would refuse to budge (Shultz memo to The President, "West Beirut Situation Looking Better," 8-6-82, 8223489, p. 2). Lebanese President Sarkis shared that concern (Hill 7-10-94).

133 Red Cross: 6-27-82 Israeli Cabinet communiqué reported in Brown cable Tel Aviv 09703, 271402Z Jun 82

133 It should be the IDF, no way: Johnston 12-4-96

133 Phalange: The PLO did not trust the Phalange any more than they trusted the Israelis, and neither the PLO nor the Lebanese government believed that the Lebanese Armed Forces had the *capability* to protect them ("Recorded Radio Report from Habib, 0730 hours, July 2, 1982," NEA Veliotes memo to S/S Bremer, 8218691, 7-2-82, p. 2)

133 Liaison group: NEA Veliotes memo to S/S Bremer, 8219392, 7-8-82, "Recorded Radio Conversation with Amb. Habib, July 8, 1982, at 1230 hours", p. 2

133 Last busful: Sharon, p. 491-92; Shultz, p. 63. Sharon clung to this demand for weeks, with Habib batting it down over and over and over (Draper 5-4-93). It would turn out to be one of the plan's last stumbling blocks.

133 Trickle in: Lewis cable Tel Aviv 12139, 101505Z Aug 82, par. 11D

133 Habib wanted UN: Habib 6-18-82 cable Beirut 4261, repeated in State 169037 TOSEC 090033, 181403Z Jun 82 [6-18-82], par. 3. If the peacekeepers were a UN force, Habib wanted it to have a strong new mandate with a more sizeable armed force than UNIFIL had (Draper 5-4-93; Habib interview with Tueni; Habib interview with Parker). UNIFIL's mandate was due to expire August 19, 1982, anyway (Howe and Veliotes memo to The Secretary, 8-9-82, 8223857, p. 3, D+3).

133 Invented peacekeeping: Hill 7-17-93

133 Begin absolutely refused: Habib interview with Parker; Habib interview with Tueni; "U.N. Image Of Futility," *The New York Times,* 8-25-82

133 Insisted it be called: Habib cable Jerusalem 01903 of June 13, 1982, repeated in State 163551, 142321Z Jun 82, par. 5. American defense intelligence reported that the French also preferred the term "multinational," because it implied independence for the French unit and highly visible French national identity (DIA cable 200300Z Aug 82, par. 3).

133 Pathological: Draper 5-4-93. Dillon (ADST oral history) adds that "It's an article of faith in Israel that the UN is no good."

133 Biased: Draper ADST oral history; Hill note to the author received 9-15-98 on manuscript of this chapter; Kadishai 6-19-95. In 1956 UN forces pulled out of the Sinai when Egyptian President Nasser was about to start the 1956 war with Israel. See Stein and Lewis, p. 8, for the evolution of "Israel's growing conviction that the UN organization was largely hostile to it."

133 No diplomatic relations: Yaacobi 2-14-95. Begin had never forgiven the UN for pulling its peacekeeping troops out of the Sinai at Egyptian president Gamal Abdel Nasser's demand in 1967, a move that helped bring on the 1967 war (Shultz, p. 46). And the UN had gone through "an anti-Israel phase" in the late 1970s, only a few years earlier (Draper ADST oral history).

133 Hostile: Lewis cable Tel Aviv 12139, 101505Z Aug 82, par. 11A

133 All wanted: Radio Transmission, Habib to Hill 0800 July 1, 1982, 8218541; "Recorded Radio Report from Habib, 0730 hours, July 2, 1982," NEA Veliotes memo to S/S Bremer, 8218691, 7-2-82, p. 2; Draper ADST oral history; Draper 4-13-93; Shultz, p. 45-46

133 Include Americans: Paganelli cable Damascus 04934, 101438Z Jul 82, par. 4; Lewis interview with Israeli TV show "Moked," May 22, 1985, transcript p. 8; "Israel Pledges to Keep Cease-fire in Beirut," *Washington Post* 6-21-82, summarized in State cable 171362, 211630Z Jun 82; Friedman, p. 190

133 Arafat's reasons: Draper 4-13-93. Another US official adds that "the PLO felt that, if we weren't there, all the assurances in the world weren't worth the paper they were written on." This official asked not to be identified by name.

133-34 Earliest hours: Department of State cable STATE 155256 TOSEC 080198, for the Secretary from Eagleburger, June 7, 1982, p. 1, 5, 7. Though the concept was quite unclear at the time, Eagleburger thought the US might send troops to join the UN force (UNIFIL) already stationed in southern Lebanon, for "a strengthened strategic buffer on Israel's northern border." The Israelis scorned UNIFIL for its failure to keep the PLO in line in southern Lebanon, and the Arabs criticized UNIFIL for failing to even slow down the Israeli invasion. The State Department was thus thinking about expanding UNIFIL and its mandate while also "giving much thought to a possible non-UN international force" to replace UNIFIL (Draper memo to the Secretary 6-7-82, X26610, par. 3). The possibility of American troops going into southern Lebanon had come up at an Israeli Cabinet meeting even before the invasion began (Schiff & Ya'ari, p. 106).

134 If they were replaced: Habib cable Jerusalem 01781, 082059Z Jun 82, par. 6. Begin described this as his government's preference of three scenarios under which the IDF might withdraw. The Israeli Labor Party preferred an international force, not US forces (Habib cable Jerusalem 01782, 082059Z Jun 82, par. 2 and 9). Haig instructed Habib to remain completely noncommittal about "Begin's request for U.S. forces, . . . noting only that of course it has been passed to me and to president" (Haig unnumbered cable Windsor to Habib 6-9-82). On June 13, the Israeli Cabinet called for a multinational force, including an American contingent, to control the 40 kilometer buffer zone "so as to allow Israel's withdrawal" (Habib cable Jerusalem 01903 of June 13, 1982, repeated in State 163551, 142321Z Jun 82, par. 4). On June 15 American reporters were already asking the president's spokesman about use of US troops in "an occupation army in Lebanon" (transcript of Larry Speakes press conference 6-15-82 in Cross cable State 165239, 160128Z Jun 82, p. 3).

134 My idea: "Recorded Radio Report from Habib, 0730 hours, July 2, 1982," NEA Veliotes memo to S/S Bremer, 8218691, 7-2-82, p. 3

134 No other possibility: Draper 4-13-93, 9-19-97. As it turned out, Soviet participation never became an issue.

134 All agreed, clincher: Stoessel memo to the President, 8218744, 7-2-82, "Habib Mission: An International Force for Beirut." Habib "very, very reluctantly" resigned himself to the need

for Americans (Draper 5-4-93; Draper ADST oral history). American Defense Secretary Weinberger saw no reason to send in US troops. The Defense Department argued that alternate sources of troops—Tunisia, Egypt, India, Indonesia, Norway, anybody—should be urgently explored.

134 Commit US Marines: A Marine landing team was in the Mediterranean all the time anyway (Dillon 5-9-94), so they would be near at hand. A mere 800 of those Marines would come ashore: The rest—including infantry, armor, artillery, and an airborne detachment—would be close at hand as quick backup in case anything went wrong (Sehulster note to author 10-28-98).

134 Fifty/fifty: NEA Veliotes memo to S/S Bremer, 8218794, "TelCon Habib and Charles Hill/Adm. Howe, 12:07 P.M., July 3, 1982," p. 3. The Greeks and Italians volunteered to join too, and in time the Italians became the third contingent (Draper 9-19-97).

134 Arrogant: Draper 5-4-93

134 Ease the process: NEA Veliotes memo to S/S Bremer, 9218993, 7-7-82, "Recorded Radio Conversation with Amb. Habib, July 7, 1982, at 1420 hours," p. 6

134 Do our share: NEA Veliotes memo to S/S Bremer, 8218794, "TelCon Habib and Charles Hill/Adm. Howe, 12:07 P.M., July 3, 1982," p. 6

134-35 UN blessing, begged, recruit: "Transcribed radio conversation between Amb. Habib and C. Hill, July 9/82, 1440 hours," p. 1-2; Sehulster note to author 10-28-98. Habib told the French ambassador in Lebanon he didn't want any arrangement that required UN action (transcript, p. 2).

135 Discreetly shopping: NEA Veliotes memo to S/S Bremer, 9219393 [sic, should be 8219393], 7-9-82, "Recorded Radio Conversation with Amb. Habib [sic, actually Draper], July 8, 1928 [sic], at 1430 hours," p. 3. State sounded out US ambassadors in various countries about whether their hosts might be willing to join in, as a contingency in case the French dropped out. Ireland, Belgium, Norway all looked unlikely. Italy seemed the most promising backup.

135 Sacrilegious, edge us out: NEA Veliotes memo to S/S Bremer, 8219666, 7-10-82, "Radio Report from Ambassador Habib, 1030 EDT, July 9, 1982," p. 1-2

135 Arafat declared: "Radio Communication between C. Hill - Habib, 7/6/82, 0715" 8218995, 7-6-82, p. 2; Hammel, p. 15

135 Begin responded: "Radio Communication between C. Hill - Habib, 7/6/82, 0715" 8218995, 7-6-82, p. 2. At first, Lewis reported, the Israelis were "unhappy" about having the French in the MNF "but not deeply" (Hill 7-10-94). France did a lot of business with the Arab world and had never been pro-Israeli (Haig 5-11-94). More to the point, France openly supported the PLO, and the Israelis were suspicious of what French presence in the MNF mix might mean (Yaacobi 2-14-95).

135 Told his intermediary: Adapted from "Radio Communication between C. Hill - Habib, 7/6/82, 0715" 8218995, 7-6-82, p. 2

135 Backed down: "Jesus, if we hadn't had the French," says Draper, "it would have really been a debacle" (Draper 12-18-94). The Israelis had agreed to French participation July 7. Habib said, "They have given their agreement whether they say so or not" (NEA Veliotes memo to S/S Bremer, 9218993, 7-7-82, "Recorded Radio Conversation with Amb. Habib, July 7, 1982, at 1420 hours," p. 6).

135 French first: One of Habib's Marine liaisons says the French wanted to be afforded the courtesy of being the first to enter because of their historic connection with Lebanon (Smith 6-14-94)

135 Marines first: A good diplomat, like a good lawyer, can argue either side of an issue. And once Habib had resigned himself to the need for Americans, he advocated a strong American role. One of Habib's colleagues, who asked not to be identified by name, recalls that Habib "didn't fully trust the French. He thought they might screw it up with the Israelis, giving them the rationale for going in on the PLO."

135 Would not hear of: Draper 12-18-94

135 Mortifying: Draper 12-22-94. For example, Habib sent word to Shultz that "We will have to work on Israel, the PLO—and DoD—to get agreement to a compromise" about who enters when (NEA Veliotes memo to The Secretary, 8-3-82, 8223048, "Phil Habib's Views at End of Day August 3"). DoD is the Department of Defense.

135 Cowards: Draper 5-4-93

135 Horizon: Sehulster 6-23-94

135 250,000 men: Barrett 5-9-94

136 EUCOM: Sehulster note to author 10-28-98. American military brass in Europe had responsibility for the Middle East as well.

136 Take over, 90,000: Draper 5-4-93. Hill explains why such high numbers of troops were getting proposed in Washington: The Pentagon did not want to be involved at all, so they proposed such a ridiculously enlarged plan and such huge numbers of troops as to guarantee that the White House would reject it. The entire matter could then go away. Hill was in a meeting at which Weinberger and the Joint Chiefs staff "presented a plan to have the US seal the borders of Lebanon with troops ringing the entire country—after Shultz had achieved a lasting ceasefire, of course" (Hill note to the author received 9-15-98 on manuscript of this chapter).

136 Sarkis: Hill 7-10-94

136 Optimum number: Barrett 5-9-94

136 Logistical headaches: Gaucher 5-15-94. This is the same reason the US didn't want more than three countries contributing forces to the MNF (Howe memo to Eagleburger, "Your August 5 Meeting with the French . . . ," 8-5-82, 8223374, p. 1).

136 In the end: Frank, p. 12; Habib interview with Tueni; Frank, p. 162. In early August the French suggested sending 2,000 to 3,000 men as their own contingent. Habib didn't want more than about 2,000 total (Howe memo to Eagleburger, "Your August 5 Meeting with the French . . . ," 8-5-82, 8223374, p. 2).

136 Felt about right: Sehulster 7-12-94

136 Heavy weapons: NEA Veliotes memo to S/S Bremer, 8218052, 6-28-82, "Message from Habib—Summary Review of Situation as of Monday Morning, June 28"; Habib cable to Secstate also for action, 6-28-82, "Meeting with President Sarkis, et al, June 28, 1982," p. 2-3. Radio Transmission, Habib to Hill 0800 July 1, 1982, 8218541, p. 1; "Recorded Radio Report from Habib, 0730 hours, July 2, 1982," NEA Veliotes memo to S/S Bremer, 8218691, 7-2-82, p. 4. What Habib and his colleagues meant by "heavy weapons" was primarily crew-served weapons, i.e., machine guns, mortars, and rockets. Though the Israelis often talked about PLO artillery, Dillon says that no PLO artillery was ever found (Dillon letter to the author 9-11-98).

136 Not particularly supportive: Weinberger 10-27-93.

136 Deliberately dragging: Sehulster 6-23-94. In early August, for example, Adm. Jonathan Howe tried to get Pentagon agreement on a simple draft Aide Memoire that Habib needed in order to negotiate a legal underpinning with the Lebanese for deploying American forces in their country. "Phil wanted this on Tuesday," Howe wrote on a Thursday, "and we have worked it on an urgent basis, but due to Weinberger's and the Chairman's personal interest in this, Pentagon clearance has been agonizingly slow" (Howe memo to Eagleburger, "Lebanon Checklist," 8-5-82, 8223325, p. 2).

137 Port area: Draper 5-4-93; Shultz, p. 77, 80

137 Pussies: Sehulster note to author 10-28-98

137 Totally overwhelm, stand around: Hill 7-17-93. Habib's top Marine liaison agrees, adding that this attitude represented "a dramatic philosophical change in U.S. military policy and planning" (Sehulster note to author 10-28-98).

137 Wrong message, nuances: Shultz, p. 77; Shultz 7-25-94

137 Assurances: NEA Veliotes memo to S/S Bremer, 8218794, "TelCon Habib and Charles Hill/Adm. Howe, 12:07 p.m., July 3, 1982," p. 7; "Radio Communication between C. Hill - Habib, 7/6/82, 0715" 8218995, 7-6-82, p. 5-6. Punctuation altered from the State Department's transcript for clarity. In this discussion, Habib used the term *Kataeb* instead of *Phalange*. The two terms are, for all practical purposes, synonyms; *Phalange* used in the text for consistency. The Phalange also tried to veto the plan for the PLO to leave behind a token force. They eventually cooperated.

137 Gradually turn over, remain a deterrent: Hill 7-17-93. The sooner the LAF could take over, the better. But Habib had no illusions: The Lebanese Armed Forces was a joke. Their principal activity consisted of collecting their pay. They were terrified to come out of their barracks. How could Habib possibly predict when they would be ready to step up to the plate and take over the MNF's positions?

137-38 Worries, sufficient protection: "Recorded Radio Report from Habib, 0730 hours, July 2, 1982," NEA Veliotes memo to S/S Bremer, 8218691, 7-2-82, p. 4; Hill 7-19-95. The PLO had good reason to fear Bashir's mi-

litia, the Phalange: He avidly hated the Palestinians. Bashir told Habib that, when Lebanon let a small number of PLO into the country, "nobody could take care of them, nobody could go where they were, nobody could order them around, they became an independent little 'nit' and then a 'nit' grew into a bunch of lice" ("Recorded Radio Report from Habib, 0730 hours, July 2, 1982," NEA Veliotes memo to S/S Bremer, 8218691, 7-2-82, p. 3-4).

138 Limited time: "Recorded Radio Report from Habib, 0730 hours, July 2, 1982," NEA Veliotes memo to S/S Bremer, 8218691, 7-2-82, p. 4

138 Bide their time: Shultz 9-16-93

138 Reluctantly agreed: There are different accounts of how long Habib wanted them there. He told his Marine liaisons, "You're going to be in 30 days, but you might be in here longer than that" (Mead 6-5-94). Hill says Habib and his colleagues thought "it would take months at least" (Hill 7-17-93). Draper says "Phil and I didn't want the Marines to stay a lengthy period—contrary to a lot of the myths. But we felt that, all things considered, they ought to stay about 30 days to take care of the political problems" (Draper 12-18-94). The Marines on the ground didn't care. Col. Mead, the Marine who would lead them ashore, says, "To us, what the hell, we're just going to do what we're told. Marines, we don't want to be on the goddam ships anyway. We'll be ashore and it'll be wonderful" (Mead 6-5-94).

138 Dump the bastards: NEA Veliotes memo to S/S Bremer, 8218794, "TelCon Habib and Charles Hill/Adm. Howe, 12:07 P.M., July 3, 1982," p. 2

138 Most intractable: Draper 5-4-93

138 If we don't: NEA Veliotes memo to S/S Bremer, 8218794, "TelCon Habib and Charles Hill/Adm. Howe, 12:07 P.M., July 3, 1982," p. 4

138 Lack of destinations: Sharon knew quite well about the lack of destinations (Sharon, p. 488), but apparently did not take the logical next step of considering how the PLO could possibly relocate *from* Beirut if they had nowhere to relocate *to*.

138-39 Move Palestinians to north: Draper ADST oral history; Draper 4-13-93; Draper 5-4-93

139 Best candidate: Stoessel memo to the Presi-

dent, 8218744, 7-2-82, "Habib Mission: An International Force for Beirut," p. 1; Draper ADST oral history; Draper 5-4-93

139 PLO had proposed: Memorandum for the Record, 8218323, 6-28-82, "Radio Telecon Habib/Hill, 1030 June 28, 1982," par. 2

139 Temporary asylum: Habib cable to Cairo, "Egyptian position," 6-28-82, par. 2. This offer was within the concept of establishing a Palestinian government in exile.

139 Mubarak's ticket: NEA Veliotes memo to S/S Bremer, 8218794, "TelCon Habib and Charles Hill/Adm. Howe, 12:07 P.M., July 3, 1982." Egypt was an outcast in the Arab world at the time for having signed a peace treaty with Israel in 1978. When a colleague raised various potential problems with sending them to Egypt, Habib brushed him off: "Stop worrying every problem to death. Let the PLO and Egypt sort it out. We don't care. They should get the PLO to accept a deal that saves their ass" (Hill 7-9-94).

139 Sympathy, jeopardize: Lewis ADST oral history. Mubarak might be willing to take some fighters, but certainly not let Egypt become the new PLO headquarters (Draper ADST oral history; Draper 5-4-93).

139 Could not receive Arafat: Sicherman 8-4-98

139 Initial destination: Stoessel memo to the President, 8220115, 7-13-82, "Habib Mission: Letter to King Fahd," attached talking points

139 Game is up: Hill 7-9-94

139 Diddled: Draper 4-13-93. An Arab League meeting in Saudi Arabia in early July produced nothing but "pap," Habib said. The Lebanese took its message as, in Habib's interpretation, "OK, Lebanese, it is all on your shoulders. We won't help you by saying anything strong but, of course, if you manage to pull it off, we would be happy" ("Recorded Radio Report from Habib, 0730 hours, July 2, 1982," NEA Veliotes memo to S/S Bremer, 8218691, 7-2-82; punctuation modified here from the State Department's transcript for clarity). Sermons in West Bank mosques June 25 called on Arab kings and presidents to "bury themselves in the sand" because of their "shameful silence" about the "war of extermination against the Palestinians in Lebanon" (*Ashaab* newspaper 6-28-82, summarized and quoted in Grove cable Jerusalem 02057, 281105Z Jun 82, par. 5D).

139 Speculated: Hill 7-10-94

139 The Palestinian cause: "Making Sense of the Middle East," *The Stanford Magazine,* Summer 1986, p. 23

139-40 Saudis and Syrians explained: Shultz, p. 50-51. Taking the PLO was not the only thing Habib needed the Arabs to do. Trapped in Beirut along with the PLO were a couple of thousand elite Syrian troops. The Syrians had been invited into Lebanon as peacekeepers in 1976 by the Lebanese government and blessed by the Arab League. And the Syrians had no intention of leaving—even under Israeli guns—unless that invitation and blessing were formally revoked. They had not been much interested in hearing from Philip Habib since the rolling ceasefire fiasco of June 11. So he needed the Saudis, who had special clout with their Arab brethren, to persuade the Syrians to take their troops out of Beirut when the PLO came out. Lebanese president Sarkis had tried. He told the Syrians he was going to issue an order for them to get out. But Assad replied that, since Sarkis was surrounded by Israeli troops, his orders were not freely given, therefore the Syrians need pay no attention. "Now, that just doesn't go," Habib said. "It just isn't acceptable and the Saudis have to make that clear [to Syria]. I don't give a shit how much [the US] has to impress that on [the Saudis], . . . that's their part of the job, being that they have backed away from getting really involved in the Palestinian problem" ("Recorded Radio Report from Habib, 0730 hours, July 2, 1982," NEA Veliotes memo to S/S Bremer, 8218691, 7-2-82 [punctuation modified here from the State Department's transcript for clarity]; Habib 7-2-82 cable Beirut 4415, quoted in State 184218, 021729Z Jul 82, par. 15).

140 Real reason: Draper 4-13-93; Gabriel, p. 31-33

140 Ruin: Friedman, p. 16; Gabriel, p. 33-34

140 Helped spark: Korbani, p. 77-78; Salem, p. 60

140 Afraid to take: Draper 5-4-93

140 Internal opposition: Hill 7-12-95; Gabriel, p. 33

140 Mafia: Draper 4-13-93

140 Great shock: Hill 7-12-95. Dillon points out that the situation was a perfect illustration of the Palestinian problem: They had no place to go (Dillon ADST oral history). Despite all

the Arab doors closing in their faces, Habib did not take the refusals at face value. For example, when he and the Lebanese officials heard on July 10 that Syria had decided not to take any PLO fighters, "we sat around and moaned about that a while. I told them I did not accept that [Syria's] statement was a rejection; that I knew the Syrians. . . . I said, 'Look, all I read into that announcement is that the Syrians want the PLO to ask them to come. And then Assad will say yes.'" He was sure that "in the end they would accept them and then presumably disperse them around a little bit if they didn't want them all." So he told his intermediary to go back to Arafat "and *act as if* we had the Syrians" (NEA Veliotes memo to S/S Bremer, 8219690, 7-10-82, "Telecon with Habib July 10, 1982 0700," p. 1-2; punctuation altered for clarity).

He was wrong. He concluded three days later that Syria really did mean no. Syria's rationale was that accepting thousands of Palestinian fighters would (1) simply transfer the Palestinian problem geographically from one location to another, (2) mean accepting the principle of suspending the Palestinians' right to resolve their problem, and (3) mean rewarding Israel for its aggression (Paganelli cable Damascus 04934, 101438Z Jul 82, par. 25, 27, 29, 30; Hill 7-10-94).

140 Carry on: Hill 7-10-94. Oddly enough, the Israelis agreed with the PLO on this point: Begin and Sharon specifically wanted them, Draper said, "in a rejectionist state . . . within easy striking distance of Israeli power," because they would have "far fewer compunctions" about launching a retaliatory strike against them in a state hostile to Israel than in a moderate state like Egypt. Syria was fine with Begin and Sharon—in fact, they proposed Syria June 27—because they knew Assad would keep the PLO under strict control. Egypt would be OK as long as Mubarak didn't allow them to set up a government-in-exile there (NEA Veliotes memo to S/S Bremer, 8218795, 7-4-82, "Recorded Radio Report from Habib, July 3, 1982," p. 1; Habib cable Beirut 04461, 7-5-82, par. 6; text of June 27 Israeli Cabinet communiqué, in Brown cable Tel Aviv 09703, 271402Z Jun 82). But ultimately, the Israelis had surprisingly little to say about where the PLO should and should not go. Begin considered the destinations "somebody else's problem," US ambassador to Israel Sam Lewis reported. Begin's attitude was "Just get out of Lebanon and leave no seed" (Hill 7-10-94).

140 Motive, declined: Draper ADST oral history; Draper 5-4-93; Draper 4-13-93; Hill 7-16-94; State Department paper "Habib Report from Beirut 0630, June 28," par. 1. The PLO and Syria had engaged in brutal fighting in 1975-76 as part of the Lebanese civil war ("Agreement on Lebanese peace plan reported near," *New York Times* article in *St. Petersburg Times*, 8-12-82). Perhaps a contributing factor to the PLO's refusal to go to Syria, at least as of June 28, was that that destination had been proposed by Israel (State Department paper "Radio Transmission from Habib—0700 EDT June 28, 8218031, 6-28-82).

140 Cannon fodder: Draper 5-4-93

140 Screw around: Hill 7-16-94

141 Pessimist: Habib interview with Kreisler

9 The Darkest Days

142 Terrible: Habib interview with Mulcahy

142 PLO had agreed: Habib cable Beirut 4415, quoted in State 184218, 021729Z Jul 82. They agreed in principle to the substance of US terms, conditional on the presence of an international force in Beirut to oversee the evacuation.

142 Can't go on: Quote adapted from Habib's report of what he had said, in "Recorded Radio Report from Habib, 0730 hours, July 2, 1982," NEA Veliotes memo to S/S Bremer, 8218691, 7-2-82, p. 2 and 5

142 Important night: Hill 7-10-94. Former prime minister Sa'eb Salaam was going with Wazzan to see Arafat.

142 Next few days: "Recorded Radio Report from Habib, 0730 hours, July 2, 1982," NEA Veliotes memo to S/S Bremer, 8218691, 7-2-82, p. 5; Shultz, p. 46

142 Firefight: Shultz, p. 46

142 Hysterical: Shultz, p. 46-47

143 Only portals: "Israeli tanks rumble into western Beirut," *Washington Post* article in *St. Petersburg Times*, 8-4-82

143 Took over checkpoints: NEA Veliotes memo to S/S Bremer, 8218796, 7-4-82, "Recorded Radio Report from Habib, July 4, 1982"; Habib cable Beirut 04460, 7-5-82; Hill 7-19-

95, 7-10-94. The IDF also took over the road that Wazzan would have to travel to meet with Habib. The road led to the suburb of Baabda, where the presidential palace was, and to the adjacent suburb of Yarze, where Habib was headquartered. Habib held most of his meetings with Lebanese officials at the palace.

143 Carrying the paper, indignity: Hill 7-19-96; Draper 4-13-93. Beyond the indignity was the physical impossibility of getting from point A to point B and doing meaningful diplomacy with shells exploding outside the door. Wazzan had resigned June 25 in part because Sharon's attacks had prevented him from negotiating (NEA Veliotes memo to Bremer 8217953, "Recorded Radio Report from Habib, 1800, June 25, 1982—Late Afternoon Meeting with Sarkis," 6-25-82).

143 Standstill: "Transcript of Habib/Peters Conversation of July 6, 1982, 0531"; "Radio communication between Habib and Veliotes, July 6/82, A.M.," 8218994. Ironically, the *Financial Times* speculated that the Israeli Cabinet might decide at the next day's meeting "that it can no longer wait for the diplomats to try to reach a negotiated settlement and may order the army to move into the city to crush the Palestinian guerrillas and destroy their headquarters" (*Financial Times,* July 3, 1982).

143 Couldn't negotiate: Transcript "recorded radio conversation between Mr. Eagleburger and Amb. Habib, July 7/82, 0900 hours" 8219191, p. 1 and 3; Habib interview with Tueni. The telephones in Beirut worked most of the time, but they were notoriously unreliable.

143 Leverage: Draper 12-18-94. It wasn't just that Wazzan objected to the indignity to himself of passing through an Israeli checkpoint. He stopped working also to protest Israel's refusal to let any ordinary Lebanese pass through ("Radio communication between Habib and Veliotes, July 6/82, A.M.," 8218994, p. 4).

143 Misunderstood, inexperienced: Hill 7-19-95. A few weeks later, US congressman Paul McCloskey made precisely this mistake. After meeting with Arafat, McCloskey announced that he had obtained Arafat's agreement (on the back of an envelope) to recognize Israel. The PLO promptly denied having agreed to any such thing (Bavly, p. 107-8).

143 Eyes: Howell 10-11-93

143-44 Abandon their strongholds, hours:

Gowers, p. 207-8; Cobban in McDermott, p. 213

144-45 Meeting with Sharon July 5: Habib cable Beirut 04461, 7-5-82, par. 3-4, 8, 15-16; Habib cable Beirut 04460, 7-5-82. The passage quotes Habib's account of what he and Sharon said, not necessarily their actual words. Jordan quote adapted from Habib's account of what Sharon said. This meeting happened on a Monday. Though Habib had still not seen the paper, Wazzan had presumably by now read it to him over the phone. Privately, Habib knew there was a lot of what Draper (12-18-94) calls "play acting" going on: Arafat had agreed to leave, but didn't say when or to where, which Habib took to mean that "Arafat wants to string things out" (Hill 7-10-94). Indeed, Arafat's letter was "deliberately vague," says Khalidi (p. 115). Arafat was hoping to deflate Sharon's pressure until Habib could come up with destinations—by which time maybe Arafat could get a better deal or worm out of this one altogether (Gowers, p. 208-9).

145 Despite instructions: Hill 7-10-94

145 Galerie Samaan: "Transcript of Habib/Peters Conversation of July 6, 1982, 0531"

145 Technical difficulties: Hill 7-10-94

145 I don't know: "Transcript of Habib/Peters Conversation of July 6, 1982, 0531." Punctuation revised from the State Department's transcript for clarity.

145-46 Begin's orders, hurry: "Radio Communication between C. Hill - Habib, 7/6/82, 0715" 8218995, 7-6-82, p. 1 and 5; Hill 7-10-94. Italics added and punctuation altered from the State Department's transcript for clarity. The Israelis repeatedly imposed deadlines on Habib. For example, when the Lebanese government asked in mid-June for a forty-eight-hour ceasefire during which they would negotiate with the PLO, the Israelis treated that as a forty-eight-hour deadline by which time a political settlement had to be reached. The Israeli Cabinet on June 27 "gave the Habib mission a few more days to work out a political solution" but made it clear that time was limited (Lewis cable Tel Aviv 09770, 281704Z Jun 82, par 2).

146 Two possibilities: Hill 7-10-94

146 Landing craft: Hill 7-10-94; NEA Veliotes memo to S/S Bremer, 8218795, 7-4-82, "Recorded Radio Report from Habib [sic, actually Draper], July 3, 1982," p. 4

146 Hold our fire: Transcript "Recorded radio conversation between Mr. Eagleburger and Amb. Habib, July 7/82, 0900 hours" 8219191, p. 1

146 Joke: Hill 7-10-94

146 We don't work: Transcript "Recorded radio conversation between Mr. Eagleburger and Amb. Habib, July 7/82, 0900 hours" 8219191, p. 5. Tel Aviv radio reported July 9 that Begin denied setting any deadline for negotiations (Stoessel cable State 190043, 091424Z Jul 82, par 2).

147-48 Reagan letter to Begin: Source asked not to be identified by name.

148 Chastened, already ordered: Per Hill 7-10-94. Reagan's message carried extra punch because 100,000 Israelis had just turned out in Tel Aviv July 3 to demonstrate against the war. The Israeli public as a whole still supported the war, but in a nation as small and as supportive of its army as Israel, this was a resounding vote of no-confidence in Sharon's war. The *Financial Times* reported that the majority of protests against the war were coming from soldiers returning from the battlefield (*Financial Times,* July 3, 1982).

148 Five days, satisfied: Quotes adapted from Habib's summary of the conversation in NEA Veliotes memo to S/S Bremer, 8219392, 7-8-82, "Recorded Radio Conversation with Amb. Habib, July 8, 1982, at 1230 hours" (Hill 7-10-94). The transcript says "Morris," doubtless an editorial change by the transcriber, since everyone always called Draper Morrie (according to an NEA official who asked not to be identified by name).

148-49 Checkpoint Draper: Draper 12-18-94, 4-13-93, 9-19-97; NEA Veliotes memo to S/S Bremer, 9219393 [*sic,* should be 8219393], 7-9-82, "Recorded Radio Conversation with Amb. Habib [*sic,* actually Draper], July 8, 1928 [*sic*], at 1430 hours"; Stoessel cable State 190043, 091424Z Jul 82, par. 1-2. Draper also got Sharon to remove a tank and two big guns from the edge of the presidential palace on the road Wazzan would have to take to the palace to meet with Habib. Lebanese soldiers then lined the road to the palace.

149 Indispensable: Draper 12-18-94

149 Strongest reed: NEA Veliotes memo to Bremer 8217985, 6-26-82, "Recorded Radio Report from Habib, Late Evening Meeting with

Sarkis, June 26." During the war, Draper described Wazzan as a "weak interlocutor" (Hill 7-21-94). Hill says Wazzan "never seemed to me to be effective" (Hill 7-12-95).

149 Straight dope: Draper 12-18-94. Journalists covering the war believed that, had Habib been able to talk to the PLO directly, he "would have been much more persuasive than the Moslem Lebanese intermediaries in making clear to the PLO that there was no alternative but to leave. The Lebanese, and especially Prime Minister Shafik al-Wazzan, were believed to fear the PLO chieftains; they seemed to prefer to water down some of the facts, never fully spelling out the options as clearly as Habib would have presented them. They allowed the leaders of the PLO to harbor their illusions too long" (Bavly & Salpeter, p. 105-6). Sometimes Wazzan apparently overcompensated. For example, on July 28 he met with Arafat and presented Habib's positions *too* forcefully: Arafat responded that Habib was giving him an "ultimatum" and demanding "unconditional surrender" (Hill 7-16-94).

149 Had resigned: NEA Veliotes memo to Bremer 8217953, "Recorded Radio Report from Habib, 1800, June 25, 1982—Late Afternoon Meeting with Sarkis," 6-25-82, par. 3

149 Forget about me: Barrett 5-9-94. This may have been on August 12 (Habib cable Beirut 05338, 121420Z Aug 82, par. 8). Habib couldn't blame him too much: On July 28 Habib himself considered threatening to stop working unless the Israelis restored electricity (Hill 7-16-94).

149 In tears, calm him: Draper 12-18-94

149 Get to work: Habib interview with the author, *The Stanford Magazine,* Spring 1984

149 Couldn't fire: Draper 12-18-94. Nor was Habib relieved when Wazzan resigned, since that meant discontinuity.

149 Adequately forthright: Habib cable Beirut 94744, 200805Z Jul 82 [7-20-82], par. 4. In the copy of this cable declassified and provided to the author by the State Department, Abdu's name is whited out each time it appears. But there is no question that the person is Abdu. In interviews conducted long before the declassified cable was received, Hill (7-16-94 and 7-12-95) discusses Habib's dissatisfaction with his intermediaries and identifies Abdu as the one he preferred. Also, everything Habib says about this person in this cable is consistent with

other things he had said about Abdu. At the end of July, Habib tried to replace Wazzan as his intermediary to Arafat with Abdu (Hill 7-16-94 and 7-12-95). Rather than simply drop Wazzan, the idea was that Wazzan would then supervise two Lebanese generals who would handle the daily routine technical talks with the PLO. Whereas Wazzan would refuse to negotiate because of Israeli attacks, Hill says, "Abdu, with shells falling all around him, would just go do the job. So he was our kind of guy" (Hill 7-12-95).

150 Patience thin, Wazzan suggested: Hill 7-10-94. On at least one occasion former Lebanese prime minister Sa'eb Salaam stood at Habib's side talking on the phone with Arafat (Brown 6-21-82 cable Tel Aviv 09329, repeated in State 173001, 222242Z Jun 82, par. 3).

150 Bunche: Stein/Lewis, p. 5-6. This approach was dubbed "proximity talks" or the "Rhodes model" for the island where the talks were held.

150 Habib endorsed: Hill 7-10-94

150 Maronite fanatics: Draper 5-4-93

150 Track Habib: Draper 5-4-93. The IDF put tremendous energy into trying to locate and kill Arafat, often bombing buildings moments after he had left.

150 Proud, sabotaged: Draper ADST oral history

150 One minute: Hill 7-16-94. Habib did get Washington's approval in principle to have proximity talks with the PLO. On July 9, Hill told Habib that Acting Secretary of State Walt Stoessel and Undersecretary Larry Eagleburger had discussed the idea of proximity talks and "no one raised any policy objection to this. . . . If you would come back and say that you want to do that, the answer would be 'sure, go ahead'" ("Transcription of Recorded Radio Conversation between Amb. Habib—Charlie Hill, July 9, 1982—1030 hours," p. 3). When Habib told Wazzan that he had US permission for proximity talks, the prime minister joked dryly, "You Americans will go into the dining room, the Palestinians will go into the living room, and we Lebanese will go into the outhouse" (Draper ADST oral history, Draper 5-4-93).

151 Kissinger has confirmed: Kissinger 5-19-94; Dillon ADST oral history; Draper ADST oral history. Here is the pertinent passage from the author's interview with Kissinger.

Author: "Ambassador Dillon says that, when you first said the United States would not talk to the PLO, you never meant for that to be an ironclad rule, that you meant only that the US would not negotiate with the PLO behind Israel's back. What is the case?"

Kissinger: "I think Ambassador Dillon was essentially right in saying that."

Author: "So you did not mean for that to be an ironclad rule."

Kissinger: "I felt that we would not talk openly with the PLO but we would keep open channels of some kind."

Ambassador Alfred Atherton also heard Kissinger personally confirm "that the US commitment (to Israel re the PLO) always was meant to reserve the right to have contacts" ("Memorandum of Conversation: Subject: Middle East Developments," 4-25-83, 8312692, p. 25). Sam Lewis objects that "Henry is rewriting history. He *did* make a commitment in the 1975 Memorandum of Understanding with Israel agreed upon in connection with Sinai II withdrawal not to *negotiate* with the PLO. Period. But he never intended it to preclude *contacts*" (Lewis note on manuscript of this chapter).

151 Supporters, like hawks: Dillon ADST oral history. Draper (ADST oral history) says, "Kissinger had always left a little wiggle room. Carter sent word that there was to be no room."

151 Legislation: Lewis note on manuscript of this chapter

151 Special authorization: Dean 5-12-94

151 Plenty of dealings: Draper says, "There is a long history of communications with the PLO for security reasons, primarily in connection with our people in Beirut. We had established a security channel and kept it open" (Draper ADST oral history). Also Hill 7-17-93.

151 Dean and Dillon contacts: Dillon ADST oral history; Dean 5-12-94; Draper ADST oral history. Dillon adds that he also had indirect ways of communicating with the PLO. It was impossible for anyone in Lebanon *not* to talk to Palestinians, and many of those Palestinians had excellent contacts with the PLO.

151 Rewarding: Dean 5-12-94

151 Meloy, hostage, evacuation, damn glad: Dean 5-12-94; Draper ADST oral history; Dillon 10-13-98 note to author; Dillon ADST

oral history; Howell 10-11-93. Dillon adds that the PLO provided security for the 1976 evacuation. The Druze also offered protection, which the US also accepted. The chancery was located on the border between a PLO-controlled area and a Druze-controlled area. In 1979 Draper was a deputy assistant secretary in the Bureau of Near Eastern Affairs. The US was, of course, trying to get all of the hostages released from the US embassy in Teheran, but the Iranians agreed to release only the women and the blacks. They kept the white male diplomats hostage for well over a year. Habash's group represented the extreme leftist wing of the Popular Front for the Liberation of Palestine (PFLP). Howell adds that, when he was stationed in Beirut in the mid-1970s, "the only order that was in West Beirut was provided by Palestine Armed Struggle Command, which is the PLO's military police." Even *The New York Times* says that "in the chaos of west Beirut, Fatah, the main [branch of the PLO], often proved the most responsible force in operation, protecting, among other things, the American Embassy, and quelling gun battles between groups struggling for territory" ("West Beirut Bids Farewell to P.L.O.," 8-23-82).

151 Alternatives: Marjorie Habib

152 Washington permission: In March 1982 NEA had considered starting direct talks with the PLO if Israel invaded Lebanon (Hill 7-9-94). On June 24 Haig and Assistant Secretary Veliotes discussed threatening Israel, "If you shell Beirut, we will talk to the PLO" (Hill 7-9-94). Eagleburger proposed direct talks as an option July 6 (Hill 7-10-94). The Reagan letter of July 7, quoted in text, threatened direct talks (Hill 7-20-94).

152 Chose neither: Habib did benefit from the quiet US-PLO cooperation, though. The PLO sent out word that he and Draper were not to be killed (Draper 5-4-93).

152 Ready access: Draper ADST oral history

152 Never allowed: Habib interview with Tueni; Mikdadi, p. 64. IDF officers once came to Yarze to call on Dillon; he refused to see them. "I was later told that that was very impolite of me," Dillon says. "It wasn't; I was accredited to Lebanon and I didn't have any business receiving the officers of an invading army. What they clearly expected to do was to use my house as sort of a headquarters, which I of course refused" (Dillon ADST oral history).

152-53 Secret meetings with Sharon: Draper

12-18-94, 9-19-97, and 4-13-93; Habib interview with Tueni; Howell 10-11-93

153 Lob shells, strange: Draper 12-18-94; Hill 7-21-94 and 8-8-95

153 Unreasonable, scorching: Hill 7-10-94

153-54 Out of control, disrupt: Hill 7-10-94

154 July 11, calm: Hill 7-10-94

154 Not good enough: Hill 7-10-94

154 High and dry: Crocker 4-25-94

10 A Concise Formula for Hell

155 Modern war: Habib interview with the author

155 Caves: Smith 6-14-94; Weinberger 10-7-93

155 Provisions: Draper 9-19-97 and 5-4-93; Hill 6-15-93; Barrett 5-9-94; Jansen, p. 44. "The PLO has enormous stores of food, water, and other required provisions," Habib told Sharon July 5. "They have generators of their own and could last under the siege. In short, the PLO is not hurting, but others are" (Habib cable Beirut 04461, 051600Z Jul 82, par. 3; Habib cable Beirut 04460, 051345Z Jul 82).

155 Not cushy: Crocker 4-25-94.

155 Arafat's bunker: Smith 6-21-94. Lt. Col. Smith, one of Habib's Marine liaisons, was given a tour of Arafat's bunker by the Lebanese Forces after the siege ended.

155 Urban warfare: Smith 11-25-96

155 Starve them out: Smith 6-21-94

155 Unless PLO convinced: Sharon, p. 482

156 Punishing: Hill 7-10-94; also Habib cable Beirut 04461, 051600Z Jul 82, par. 3; Habib cable Beirut 04460, 051345Z Jul 82.

156 Israeli troops: Jansen, p. 56-60; Habib reported the water wheel incident to Washington (Hill 7-16-94). At a meeting with Begin July 4, Israeli opposition leader, military hero, and future prime minister Yitzhak Rabin endorsed Sharon's plan to shut off West Beirut's water. Though Rabin did not support the war, he

hoped that this measure would help end it faster. He later regretted his decision (Gilbert, p. 507).

156 When Habib would protest: Crocker 4-25-94

156 Restoring, tightened: Hill 7-16-94

156 Begin ordered: NEA Veliotes memo to The Secretary, 8-2-82, 8223177; Hill 7-21-94

156 Assholes: "Recorded Radio Report from Habib, 0730 hours, July 2, 1982," NEA Veliotes memo to S/S Bremer, 8218691, 7-2-82, p. 5. The transcript omits the expletive; Hill (7-7-98) provided it. The State Department had heard, presumably from the Israelis, that the water was under the control of Israel's ally the Phalange, not the Israelis themselves. Nonsense, said Habib. "Did you hear what I said? I said that anybody who said [the water is controlled by] the Phalange are full of shit. Bashir, himself, has told me he has nothing to do with it. It is completely an Israeli operation, cutting off water and electricity" ("Radio communication between Habib and Veliotes, July 6/82, A.M.," 8218994, p. 4; the State Department transcript deleted the expletive).

156 Without water, cholera: Jansen, p. 56-60; Mikdadi, p. 49, 99, 101, 107. UNICEF worried about the potential for plague from rats, typhoid, and cholera (Mackey, p. 179). When Sharon did turn the water back on, it might just run down the street, since so many water pipes had been blown up (Mikdadi, p. 111).

156 Disease: Hill 7-21-94

156 Without electricity, fuel, supplies: Mikdadi, p. 106, 89, 51; Jansen, p. 57; Hopkins, p. 46-47

157 One-day supply: Hill 7-10-94

157 Same time, fruits, banks: Mikdadi, p. 44, 49, 59; Jansen, p. 114; also Parker, p. 177

157 Black market, hashish, bribes, meat, price: Draper 12-18-94; Mikdadi, p. 99, 51, 119, 73; Jansen, p. 57-59; Draper 9-19-97 says the IDF allowed smuggling in exchange for money. Mikdadi says 25 pounds equaled about $6.

157 No less reprehensible: Habib would not have used these words, but the conclusion is inescapable from all the things he did say about the conduct of the war.

157 Steal milk powder: "Sharon: 'I Wanted Them Out of Beirut; I Got What I Wanted,'"

The Washington Post, 8-29-82

157 Most positive: Habib cable Jerusalem 01903 of June 13, 1982, repeated in State 163551, 142321Z Jun 82, par. 25

157 Preventing UN agencies: *Sunday Times* of London, 6-20-82, cited in Jansen, p. 35-36. "It is utterly appalling," the paper wrote, "that the Israeli victors should obstruct these humanitarian non-political operations." On July 6 Israel's ally the Phalange helped maintain the blockade of West Beirut by turning back a Red Cross convoy at the port (Stoessel cable State 186129 TOSEC 100100, 060031Z Jul 82, par. 3).

157 Obstructing deliveries: *The Observer,* July 4, cited in Jansen, p. 37

157 Hospitals, doctors, four trucks: Jansen, p. 37, 52-53; Mikdadi, p. 100; Hill 7-16-94

157 Unbelievably serious: Hill 7-21-94. Draper suggested having Red Cross convoys bring in the medicines. Habib had said on July 7 that the Israelis at last seemed willing to let medicine and other essential supplies in (NEA Veliotes memo to S/S Bremer, 9218993, 7-7-82, "Recorded Radio Conversation with Amb. Habib, July 7, 1982, at 1420 hours"); if so, they later changed their minds. On August 11 Sharon made a point of informing Habib that, "as a demonstration of Israel's flexibility," the IDF had just allowed the Red Cross to bring food and other supplies into West Beirut, even though "it goes to the terrorists." Habib was not much impressed with what he considered Sharon's token magnanimity (Lewis 8-11-82 cable Tel Aviv 12220, quoted in State 226747, 130526Z Aug 82, par. 12).

158 Collateral damage: "Sharon: 'I Wanted Them Out of Beirut; I Got What I Wanted,'" *The Washington Post,* 8-29-82; "Begin Is Optimistic All Foreign Units Will Quit Lebanon," *The New York Times,* 8-29-82. There is little question that the PLO did indeed put guns and ammunition in civilian areas, though Khalidi, p. 133-35, argues that that claim is "a gross canard."

158 Comparable civilian sites: Jansen, p. 9; Dillon 5-9-94; Dillon ADST oral history. During an Israeli artillery and tank barrage July 9, Habib said, "A lot of these gun positions are around here [i.e., the American ambassador's residence in Yarze]. So this big argument that 'you put your guns up against . . . civilians': these guns are up against—close—to the Presi-

dential Palace, the Ministry of Defense and us" (NEA Veliotes memo to S/S Bremer, 8219664, 7-10-82, "Radio Report from Ambassador Habib, 1240 EDT, July 9, 1982," p. 1; punctuation altered for clarity).

158 Necessary evil, blowers, generators, food: Draper 4-25-93; Lewis 8-11-82 cable Tel Aviv 12220, quoted in State 226747, 130526Z Aug 82, par. 12; Hill 7-16-94 and 7-21-94

158 Wasn't as bad, phony, diesel: Hill 7-16-94

158 Burgundy's: "Radio communication between Habib and Veliotes, July 6/82, A.M.," 8218994, p. 4.

158 Suffered enough: According to an Israeli official who asked not to be identified by name; also Lewis ADST oral history and Rabinovich, p. 141. At a meeting July 10, Habib wrote, the head of Israeli military intelligence, Yehoshua Segui, "added the gruesome note that the Israeli cutting off of water and electricity may not have affected the PLO directly, but that its impact on the other citizens in Beirut was a very successful form of pressure on the PLO" (Habib cable Beirut 04561, 101755Z Jul 82, par. 8). Habib disputed this point every time it was made.

158 Only through: Hill 7-16-94

158 Blow them out: "Radio communication between Habib and Veliotes, July 6/82, A.M.," 8218994, p. 1-2. Punctuation altered from State Department transcript for clarity.

158 Common destiny: Khalidi, p. 131-33; Mikdadi, p. 132

158 Arafat's head: Kemal Salibi, quoted by Friedman, p. 153

158 Don't care: "Radio communication between Habib and Veliotes, July 6/82, A.M.," 8218994, p. 1-2. Punctuation altered from State Department transcript for clarity.

158 Time from main task: Shultz 9-16-93; Shultz, p. 56. Shultz summed up the problem to the Israeli ambassador to Washington: "If Israeli actions force Habib to focus on water and power or on repeatedly renegotiating broken cease-fires, then he can't get to the real negotiations to get the PLO to leave. We face a cycle of self-denying factors" (Shultz, p. 65).

159 Mayor: Draper 9-19-97; Hill 7-16-94

159 Diverted: Hill 7-16-94

159 Syrians: Hopkins, p. 46-47, citing his interview with Paganelli 1-11-92

159 Discredits, stop working: Hill 7-16-94 and 7-21-94. "Adjustments to IDF lines" was his working euphemism for getting the Israelis to pull back at least a little from Beirut. Even his own State Department was getting bored with his continual harping about the blockade. Hill muttered, "There has to be *some* pressure, for God's sake" (Hill 7-16-94).

159 Duels: Dillon (ADST oral history) says, "Occasionally, the newspapers reported rocket and artillery 'duels.' Rocket and artillery 'duels' consisted of Israeli rounds—a lot of 155 millimeters which are large shells—going into the city and every once in a while some Palestinian popping out of a hole with a hand launcher, firing a rocket."

159 4 to 1: Sachar, p. 177. Four to one is conservative: Sharon's own estimate of the number of PLO in Beirut was 8,000, making it more like ten to one (Lewis 8-11-82 cable Tel Aviv 12220, quoted in State 226747, 130526Z Aug 82, par. 11). An unknown number of additional PLO fighters were still scattered elsewhere around Lebanon. Not all of Sharon's 80,000 were involved in the siege of Beirut.

159 Outgunned: Crocker 4-25-94

159 Small arms, World War One: Gabriel, p. 51; Draper ADST oral history; Smith 6-14-94 and 11-25-96; Mead 6-5-94 and 11-25-96. Habib's top military adviser, Col. Jim Sehulster, says, "They had a lot of material, but some of it was in really dismal condition. I don't recall any of the stuff that I saw being modern or very well maintained at all. The question is not so much How much is there? as What it is? They didn't have a lot of heavy weapons or anti-tank weapons" (Sehulster 7-12-94).

159 Expertise: Gabriel, p. 50-51. Colonel Mead laughs that the PLO had air-to-ground munitions, even though they lacked aircraft to shoot them from (Mead 11-25-96).

159 Unused: While the war was still going on, a cache of 25,000 AK-47s was found, still in cases (Hill 7-10-94).

159-60 Revealing locations: This analysis is by a colleague of Habib's who asked not to be identified by name.

160 Lanyard: Crocker 4-25-94. He adds that "sitting down in West Beirut was like sitting on the inside of a barrel trying to shoot out.

The Israelis did take casualties, of course, but I think that was more luck [on the part of the Palestinians] than real design."

160 Indiscriminately: Gaucher 5-15-94. *Indiscriminate* is Habib's word (Memcon Draper [Habib]/State June 25, 6:59 A.M., 8217804; Habib cable Beirut 05338, 121420Z Aug 82, par. 10). On July 9, for example, Habib said "I think it is inhumane myself because I don't think they are shooting at any particular target. I just think they are dropping [shells] in. This is the general view of the military people around here who watch this thing by the hour" (NEA Veliotes memo to S/S Bremer, 8219664, 7-10-82, "Radio Report from Ambassador Habib, 1240 EDT, July 9, 1982," p. 2; punctuation altered for clarity). The highest ranking military person with Habib, Marine Col. Jim Sehulster, says Israeli fire tended to be "indiscriminate, as far as I'm concerned" (Sehulster 7-12-94). Khalidi, p. 133, attributes the indiscriminate hits to the great expense of pinpoint munitions. Smart bombs were a novelty in 1982 (Hill 7-12-95); most bombs were rather inaccurate, indiscriminate, general-area weapons (Sehulster 11-24-96).

160 3,000 feet: Hill 7-21-94

160 Never be persuaded: Crocker 4-25-94

160 Artillery shells: "In Balance With This Life, This Death," *Harper's Magazine*, 11-99, from Anthony Loyd, *My War Gone By, I Miss It So*

160 Cluster bombs: Draper ADST oral history; Jansen, p. 32-34; Fisk, p. 277-78. An Israeli said "The experts admit this bomb is made by satan. The area of killing of the bomb is very large. No less is its wounding area. Watching it in operation is like watching a rain of terror. Small fatal grenades that create a horrific mushroom of death" (quoted in Jansen, p. 35). The US suspended shipments of cluster bombs to Israel in July (Jansen, p. 86; Lewis ADST oral history).

160 Phosphorous: White phosphorous rounds were identified by the American defense attaché in Beirut (LWG Welch memo to Bremer, "Message from Habib: Artillery Barrages in Beirut," 6-25-82, 8217839). Seale, p. 388; Jansen, p. 32.

160 Hit everything: Fisk, p. 316-17

160 8,000 rounds: Dillon ADST oral history

160 Engineering professor: Sami al-Banna, "The Defense of Beirut," *Arab Studies Quarterly,* vol. 15, No. 2 (Spring 1983), p. 108, cited in Hopkins, p. 13. Banna expressed his estimate in metric units: several million kilograms of high explosives going into West Beirut, an area of less than 15 square kilometers, during the siege. "Conservatively speaking," he wrote, "this amounted to . . . 2,500 kg. [of high explosives] per sq. km. per day." A kilometer is about two-thirds of a mile; a kilogram is about 2.2 pounds. Conversion by Mike Boykin.

160-61 Stunned: Viets ADST oral history. Begin had apparently long forgotten his first meeting with Habib after the invasion started, at which Begin had expressed to Habib "concern for not bombing urban areas" (Habib cable Jerusalem 01744, June 7, 1982, par. 7). In their second meeting, Habib asked whether it was necessary to continue bombing Beirut in light of Begin's claim that the IDF had already achieved its objectives everywhere except in the southern Bekaa. Begin was quite defensive, arguing that he had not bombed Beirut but only the PLO headquarters there. Saying he recognized Begin's strong objections to civilian casualties, Habib asked him to consider ending air strikes that, whatever their target, inevitably caused heavy civilian casualties (Habib cable Jerusalem 01781, 6-8-82, par. 5).

161 Dark, lit up: Lee 10-2-94; Mikdadi, p. 91. West Beirut was predominantly Muslim, but not exclusively. Some Christians and many foreigners lived there. The American University of Beirut and the American chancellery (the building that houses the embassy) were both located in West Beirut (Dillon ADST oral history).

161 Jets, sonic booms: Bavly, p. 102; Fisk, p. 279. The flares may have served as decoys to fool heat-seeking anti-aircraft missiles that the PLO might shoot ("In Lebanon, it's easier to see the losers than the winners," *St. Petersburg Times*, 8-12-82). As far as Habib was concerned, though, there was no reason for the flares but to intimidate the population (Hill 7-9-94). Along the coast south of Beirut, some buildings were damaged, others totally destroyed. Hardly any were untouched. A former prime minister had machine gun bullet holes through his dining room walls (NEA Veliotes memo to Bremer 821819, 6-27-82, "Radio Report from Beirut Political Section, 6/27/82, 12:45 p.m.: Visit to Salim Al-Hoss").

161 Coffins: Mikdadi, p. 109.

161 East Beirut, suburbs: Mikdadi, p. 121; Dillon ADST oral history; Mead 6-5-94

161 Seven years: Crocker 4-25-94. One ironic benefit of the Lebanese civil war having gone on for seven years before the Israeli invasion was that some number of the people of West Beirut had generators or pumps or wells, which helped the city get through the siege (Crocker 4-25-94; Draper 12-18-94).

161 We get bombed, Skyhawk, gauge: Mikdadi, p. 95, 114, 125

161 Intense: Sehulster 7-12-94

161-62 More controlled, pain: Mikdadi, p. 73, 122

162 Leaflets, population: Dillon ADST oral history; Dillon note to the author 10-13-98. Dillon emphasizes that figures such as these are only estimates, since no accurate counts were possible. People had been leaving West Beirut over recent months; during the siege some temporarily left East Beirut too. The French ambassador in Beirut estimated that the non-Palestinian population of West Beirut dropped to 300,000 July 17 from his estimate of 500,000 a week earlier (Habib cable Beirut 04703, 171445Z Jul 82, par. 4A).

162 Stayed: Habib cable Beirut 04703, 171445Z Jul 82, par. 4A; NEA Veliotes memo to S/S Bremer 8218010, 6-27-82, "Radio Message from Amb. Habib, 6/27/82, 11:30 A.M.: Appeal from Grand Mufti"; NEA Veliotes memo to Bremer 8218018, 6-27-82, "Radio Message from Habib June 27, 1:10 P.M.: Flight From West Beirut"; Bavly, p. 109; Mikdadi, p. 47, 52, 56-58, 69; Jansen, p. 60-63

162 Twelve ceasefires: Habib interview with Mulcahy. See also Fisk, p. 228-29. Habib always said twelve ceasefires; press reports in 1982 usually said eleven. "Hell, I had ceasefire after ceasefire," Habib said. "Beirut was totally raped, being shelled constantly right over my head. And I was spending most of the time in Beirut trying to get the goddam ceasefire, which would last a few hours and then be broken" (Habib interview with Parker, p. 6-8). Habib later said these ceasefires did not hold "because they were improperly agreed upon or violated [without] compunction" (testimony to the Senate Committee on Foreign Relations' Subcommittee on Western Hemisphere and Peace Corps Affairs, "Briefing on Central American Peace Initiative," 6-16-87, p. 47-48; the transcript has Habib saying "with compunction"—surely a typographical error or verbal slip, given

everything else Habib is known to have said about the Israeli ceasefire violations).

162 Israeli action: "Radio Communication between C. Hill - Habib, 7/6/82, 0715" 8218995, 7-6-82, p. 1. Punctuation altered from the State Department's transcript for clarity.

162 Every time: Dillon 5-9-94. Lewis (ADST oral history) is even more specific: "Sharon became the focus of our frustration and anger because we held him accountable for all the cease fire break-downs, for the shelling of Beirut, the misinformation, the alleged double-dealings, etc." In any war, the stronger force rarely has as much incentive as the weaker force to maintain ceasefires. They'd rather win their victory and then dictate the terms of surrender (Dillon 5-9-94 and Dillon ADST oral history).

162 Responded: Stoessel cable, State 228797, 142019Z Aug 82, par. 5. Israel's policy was, as Begin put it, "If the others break the ceasefire, we shall react with severity" (Transcript "recorded radio conversation between Mr. Eagleburger and Amb. Habib, July 7/82, 0900 hours" 8219191, p. 1).

162 Crazies: Habib cable Beirut 05338, 121420Z Aug 82, par. 10; Letter to Prime Minister Begin from Secretary Shultz, State 213728, 310424Z Jul 82, par. 4

162 Now-famous: Habib 7-4-82 cable Beirut 4439, quoted in State 186503, 061812Z Jul 82, par 2-3 (italics added and punctuation altered for clarity). He used as an example the situation he faced on July 6: "I've been screaming for three weeks now about the importance of cease-fire *in place*. You want to know why they got into a fire fight the day before yesterday—which set everything back another two days [for a total of] four days?" Because, he said, "Israeli forces crept forward and quite naturally encountered resistance from the Palestinians" (cable Beirut 4439; "Radio Communication between C. Hill - Habib, 7/6/82, 0715" 8218995, 7-6-82, p. 1; italics added and punctuation altered from the State Department's transcript for clarity).

162 Hit me first: This State Department official asked not to be identified by name.

162-63 At 4:45: Mikdadi, p. 98

163 Disingenuous, bullet: Jansen, p. 10, citing an article by Hirsh Goodman in *The Jerusalem Post* 6-28-82

163 Fathom: Habib cable Beirut 05338, 121420Z Aug 82, par. 10

163 June 21, July 11, July 29: Hill 7-9-94, 7-10-94, 7-16-94. Habib's top Marine liaison says, "They were killing flies with sledgehammers. Massive retaliation of all types of ordnance for a single rifle shot" (Sehulster 7-12-94).

163 Hysterical: Shultz, p. 59; Hill 7-21-94; "Sharon: 'I Wanted Them Out of Beirut; I Got What I Wanted,'" *Washington Post,* 8-29-82

163-64 10:30: Lee 10-2-94

164 His angles: NEA Veliotes memo to S/S Bremer, 8219664, 7-10-82, "Radio Report from Ambassador Habib, 1240 EDT, July 9, 1982," p. 1

June 28 ceasefire: Hill 7-16-94. The IDF headquarters at Beirut was at Beit Meri, very close to Habib's headquarters at Yarze.

164 Quiet, peaceful: Mikdadi, p. 49-50

164 Pattern: Hill 7-16-94. This was the view also of a leading Israeli Labor Party politician who asked not to be identified by name. Draper 12-18-94 says it certainly looked to him and Habib at the time that Sharon was deliberately trying to scuttle any progress they might make. A writer observed that "There was one thing that was predictable, however: that whenever it looked as though a solution were near, the planes would return and the gunners would resume their 'political bombardment'" (Jansen, p. 62; see also p. 45).

By the same token, Habib also said, "When we make progress here, the Arabs backslide on taking" PLO evacuees (Hill 7-21-94). Shultz sent word to Begin that "radical diehard [Palestinian] elements—which are probably communist inspired—are attempting at virtually every moment when progress appears possible to destroy our efforts by violating the ceasefire through attacks against Israeli forces. It is vital that these radical elements be denied their objectives. To play their game by retaliating in a disproportionate fashion that results in a breakdown of the negotiations is to work against our own interests" (Letter to Prime Minister Begin from Secretary Shultz, State 213728, 310424Z Jul 82, par. 4 talking points).

164-65 Not pushing: Sharon, p. 482-83

165 Repeatedly pushed: For example, Habib 7-2-82 cable Beirut 4415, quoted in State 184218, 021729Z Jul 82. The meeting recounted in that cable concludes with Habib telling the Lebanese officials that "we both [have] to go our separate ways and do the serious jobs that [are] at hand and that time [is] pressing. . . . If we don't hurry, I had better leave," apparently meaning that otherwise the Israelis would soon destroy the city around him (par. 16-17).

165 Vitally important: "Radio Telecon Habib/Hill 0745, June 29, 1982," Memorandum for the Record, 8218324, 6-29-82

165 June 28, July 2, July 19, July 30, August 9: Hill 7-9-94, 7-10-94, 7-16-94; NEA Veliotes memo to S/S Bremer, "Recorded Radio Conversation with Amb. Habib, July 30, 1082, A.M.," 8222642, "Radio Conversation between Amb. Habib and Peter Dodd (LWG)"; Habib cable Beirut 05232, 090940Z Aug 82, par. 2; Habib cable Beirut 05240, 091220Z Aug 82, par. 2

165-66 Defiant, pound them: Lewis 4-10-94; Lewis ADST oral history; Hill 7-16-94 and 7-16-94; Rabinovich, p. 140-41. Israel's experience with Sadat was that he often broke deadlocks by giving in to what the Israelis wanted (Draper ADST oral history). "The Israeli lesson was not that Sadat was a great man, but that if you hit the Arabs long and hard enough, they would eventually cave in" (Dillon ADST oral history).

166 Might as well stay: Stoessel cable, State 228797, 142019Z Aug 82, par. 6. Though the words were spoken in this context by Stoessel, it was Habib's thinking that Stoessel was reflecting.

166 Hell-bent: Hopkins, p. 12. Hopkins does not use quote marks around these words, but does attribute them to his interview with Habib 3-12-92.

166 Some degree of force: Shultz 9-16-93

166 Motivating: "I recognize the value of 'Israeli pressure' on the Palestinians," Habib wrote (Habib 7-4-82 cable Beirut 4439, quoted in State 186503, 061812Z Jul 82, par. 5)

166 Such pressure, not opposed: Hill 7-9-94

166 Erroneously, frankly: "Transcript of Radio Conversation Between Lawrence Eagleburger, Ambassador Habib, and Charles Hill, July 18, 1444-1516 EDT," 8220873, p. 10. Charlie Hill, who was in the meeting with Shultz and Arens, said the story was "made out of whole cloth" (p. 12). Habib heartily wanted Shultz to say

that sort of thing to the Israelis; what he didn't want was for the PLO to know about it.

166 Holding out longer: Khalidi, p. 148, cites a calculation that, if the truces during the 1948-49 conflict are factored in, this war was the longest of all Arab-Israeli wars. At seventy days, it approached the durations of the 1948, 1956, 1967, and 1973 wars combined. "We taught the Arabs how to fight," Arafat boasted. "We held off the Israelis longer than any Arab army in history" ("In Lebanon, it's easier to see the losers than the winners," *St. Petersburg Times,* 8-12-82). A *New York Times* reporter wrote from Israel, "Actually some military people [here] offer grudging admiration for the fighting ability of the guerrillas in west Beirut" ("West Beirut Siege Is Affecting Israelis' Self-Image," 8-23-82).

166 Atom bomb: Hart, p. 456-57

167 Increased unwillingness: Khalidi, p. 173

167 Spotlight: *U.S. News & World Report* ("End of The Road For PLO?" 8-23-82) quoted a long-time observer in Beirut as saying that "The PLO's stand already is giving birth to exactly what the Israelis did not want—a new upswing in Palestinian nationalism."

167 Standstill: Hill 6-15-93

167 Boom-boom: "Recorded Radio Report from Habib, 0730 hours, July 2, 1982," NEA Veliotes memo to S/S Bremer, 8218691, 7-2-82, p. 2

167 Break off negotiations: Barrett 5-9-94

167 Spectre of force: According to a State Department official who asked not to be identified by name

167 Redefine: Hopkins, p. 55

167 New lease: "Radio communication between Habib and Veliotes, July 6/82, A.M.," 8218994. Punctuation modified from the State Department's transcript for clarity. On July 13 he wrote that "the PLO leaders must realize that they cannot operate freely while surrounded by the IDF. Even if Israel does not resort to the military option right away, the PLO leaders probably recognize that the Israelis will be able to continue a long siege of Beirut. . . . The PLO seems to think that Arab pressure on the U.S. may still save them from destruction" (Habib cable Beirut 04611 to SecState, 132115Z Jul 82, par. 3E).

167 Belief persisted: Khalidi, p. 86. A well-placed Palestinian, Khalidi writes that, after hearing "repeated unfulfilled threats to attack Beirut," the PLO developed "a clear belief" that Israel was either unwilling or incapable of storming Beirut.

167 Surrounding the city: Habib 7-4-82 cable Beirut 4439, quoted in State 186503, 061812Z Jul 82, par 5; Hill 6-15-93

168 This will keep: Habib cable for the President from Beirut 04247, 6-17-82, par. 3

168 All believed: Haig 5-11-94; Shultz 9-16-93 and 7-25-94; Eagleburger 7-3-93; Draper 12-22-94; Hill 6-15-93, 7-16-94, and 7-10-94. On a 1-to-10 scale, where 1 is stubborn unwillingness to see force used, Eagleburger ranks Habib as a 3 and ranks himself as a 7 or 8.

168 Dampen the effect: Hill 3-27-93

168 Threaten to cut off: Hill 3-27-93 and 6-15-93

168 Litani: Howell 9-6-93; "Mortal Friends," *Time,* 8-16-82, p. 13

168 Defensive use: Hill 7-21-94. Sharon has always insisted that "The Lebanon War, like all of Israel's wars, had been a defensive struggle. Like the Sinai campaign of 1956 and the Six Day War in 1967, it had taken the form of a pre-emptive strike" (Sharon, p. 494).

168 No US administration: Hill 3-27-93. Shultz says Habib "became quite extreme at one point, I think: that we should threaten to withdraw our military support from Israel, in some fashion. He knew that we wouldn't, but [thought] we should" (Shultz 7-25-94). One argument in Washington against taking dramatic steps to force the Israelis to stop or to prevent them from entering West Beirut to dig out the PLO, was that doing so might have encouraged the PLO to stall (Hill 7-19-95). Another argument was that, if the Israelis *did* respond to Habib's calls for less pressure, then it would seem like confirmation of many Arabs' belief that the US controlled the Israelis, turning them off and on like a faucet. In the longer term, says Eagleburger, "to force them out with their tail between their legs could be very dangerous. The danger is that it would encourage Israel's enemies to take advantage of that, not to be more reasonable" (Eagleburger 7-3-93).

168 Finding: Howell 9-6-93

168 Suspending deliveries: Lewis ADST oral

history; Jansen, p. 86, says this was mid-July.

168-69 Abundantly clear: Habib cable Jerusalem 01744, June 7, 1982. Begin sent Shultz a message that "sanctions will never change our decisions" (Shultz, p. 68). American sanctions could even help Begin domestically, by making him a martyr and enabling him to change the subject of domestic debate from the war to the cutoff (according to a diplomat who asked not to be identified by name). When Begin became angry with the US, says Lewis, "he would take some action that he knew would make us very angry, to demonstrate to us in unmistakable terms that we weren't able to push him around." For example, he might proceed with a few more settlements on the West Bank. In December 1981 the US suspended an agreement that Begin wanted; he reacted by annexing the Golan Heights (Lewis 4-10-94; Lewis ADST oral history). Begin's view did not change over the course of the war. An Israeli official said on August 6 that sanctions would "have a contrary effect and America will lose all of its leverage. What Israel will do is unpredictable but it could make Beirut look like peanuts" ("Beirut: Fighting—and talks—go on," St. Petersburg Times, 8-7-82).

169 Facts on the ground: McFarlane, p. 187

169 Everything he needed: Hill 3-27-93

169 Come this far: Habib cable Beirut 04640, 141457Z Jul 82, par. 5C

169 Won't go along: Hill 7-21-94. Frustration—the need to do something, anything, to show US outrage—was also a reason, according to an NEA official who asked not to be identified by name.

169 Nazi genocide: "Arafat in Greece in Snub to Arabs," The New York Times, 9-2-82. The Greek prime minister, Andreas Papandreou, was an avid supporter of the PLO.

169 Survivors: Mikdadi, p. 66

169 White hats, see you for: Draper 4-13-93

169 Most humane: "Israelis Seeking to Win Battle of the Headlines," The New York Times, 8-21-82. An Israeli pilot, speaking after the siege, insisted that bombing targets had been precisely selected, through aerial photography or intelligence or both. "There were mistakes, maybe one or two, but . . . we aimed at no civilian targets. We went where the P.L.O. took their guns, and they sat behind the civilians' backs. . . . We did not do area bombing but

rather precision dive bombing" ("Israeli Pilot Tells of Great Effort to Spare Civilians," The New York Times, 8-25-82). For details of the Israeli version, see Gabriel, p. 159-62.

170 Purity of arms: "West Beirut Siege is Affecting Israelis' Self-Image," The New York Times, 8-23-82

170 American public: International Herald Tribune, 7-22-82; cited in Jansen, p. 84. A Newsweek poll released August 8 found that 60 percent of Americans surveyed disapprove of Israel's thrust into Lebanon, and that 43 percent favored suspending or cutting military aid to Israel ("Lebanon talks stall over PLO withdrawal process," Los Angeles Times article in St. Petersburg Times, 8-9-82).

170 Washington's sympathy: Lewis ADST oral history. This deterioration began when Begin suddenly decided to annex the Golan Heights in December 1981, says Lewis.

170 Relations: Yaacobi 2-14-95. Even so, this decline was relative to America's traditionally exceptionally supportive approach to Israel (Beinin 10-30-93; Viets ADST oral history). American ambassadors in the region, other than Lewis in Tel Aviv, felt Washington was still too pro-Israel (Dillon ADST oral history).

170 Unity: Habib cable Jerusalem 01745, June 7, 1982, par. 5

170 National sense: Grove 6-4-94 and 6-12-94

170 Always agreed: As Gabriel puts it, "The IDF is virtually at the center of Israeli society" (Gabriel, p. 10).

170 Poll ratings: "Begin's Popularity is Rising," The New York Times, 8-28-82; Time, 8-23-82, p. 31

170 Academics: "Academics blast 'unjust war, mass slaughter,'" The Jerusalem Post, 6-13-82

170 20,000: "West Beirut Siege Is Affecting Israelis' Self-Image," The New York Times, 8-23-82. Hundreds of Israelis demonstrated at the Knesset June 27 to demand Sharon's resignation and an immediate end to the war (reported in most Israeli newspapers 6-28-82, summarized and quoted in Grove cable Jerusalem 02057, 281105Z Jun 82, par. 5).

170 July 3: Sachar, p. 193; Bavly, p. 103. Though a majority of Israelis supported the war while it was going on, in later years nine out of ten Israelis would say they had opposed the

invasion from the start (Friedman, p. 130). Israelis would overwhelmingly come to view the
war as a catastrophe (Beinin 10-30-93).

170 Disenchantment: The *Financial Times* (July
3, 1982) reported that "the majority of the protests against the war had been coming from
soldiers returning from the battlefield who have
expressed strong reservations about the scope
and aims of the invasion of Lebanon."

170 Mindlessly: Sachar, p. 192

170 Pilots, paratroop: Gabriel, p. 162, 185.
Gabriel points out that this would be equivalent to almost 11,000 American soldiers in the
Vietnam war openly signing a petition against
that war.

170 Officers: Sachar, p. 193; Bavly, p. 103;
Gabriel, p. 185. IDF officers blamed Sharon
directly for policies that led to the needless
deaths of their colleagues (Fisk, p. 298).

170 Entebbe, tank soldier: Jansen, p. 124, 126,
quoting *Al-Hamishmar*, July 2, 1982

170-71 Geva: Schiff & Ya'ari, p. 214-16;
Sachar, p. 192-94; Davis 103; Gabriel 184-86.
Rather than abandon his brigade, Geva offered
to remain with them as an ordinary tank of-
ficer, but he was fired instead (Schiff & Ya'ari,
p. 216). Sharon blamed Geva for boosting the
PLO's morale and thus prolonging the war
(Sharon, p. 489; "Sharon: 'I Wanted Them Out
of Beirut; I Got What I Wanted,'" *Washington
Post,* 8-29-82).

171 Abba Eban: Sachar, p. 194, quoting an
article in the newspaper *Ma'ariv.*

171 Seemed to be calling: Crocker 4-25-94,
who was political officer in Beirut

11 Suspicions and Lies

172 Are there moments: Tueni eulogy at
Habib's memorial service, 6-10-92, Washington. Tueni was Lebanese ambassador to the UN
during the siege.

172 Jordanian: "Habib the Peacemaker,"
Newsweek, 8-30-82

172 Voice: Khalidi, p. 107-9,114,132-
33,136,138-39,161

172 Assad: Habib interview with Dusclaud,
who is quoting an interview Assad gave to the
newspaper *Le Monde.* This was not a new criticism from Assad. On December 1, 1981, his
foreign minister told Habib that, by having just
signed a Memorandum of Understanding with
Israel on military matters, "you have become
a direct party in this conflict" ("Habib Returns
to Syria and Is Rebuffed on a U.S. Peace Role,"
Los Angeles Times, 12-2-81).

172 Representative: "Withdrawal Leaves Many
Questions," *The New York Times,* 8-22-82

172 Mouthpiece: Khalidi, p. 114

172-73 Difficult to believe: Paganelli cable
Damascus 04216, 151108Z Jun 82, par. 2-3, 5

173 Arafat's proposal: Hill 7-10-94. A top PLO
official made a point of sending word to Washington and to Habib July 2 that he had no confidence in Habib. Habib sent word back that
"my confidence in him is also limited but that
I have certain objectives which required the
cooperation of many people" (Habib cable
Beirut 4415, quoted in State 184218, 021729Z
Jul 82, par. 6-7).

173 Lever: Khalidi, p. 172. Pakradouni, an aide
to Bashir Gemayel, mistakenly believed that
during the war Habib was "indirectly influencing military operations. Each time that the
Palestinians posed conditions that were unacceptable to Washington, Habib suggested to
his government that Ariel Sharon be given free
rein. For this diplomat also believed in the
use of force" (Pakradouni, p. 256).

173 Could force: Habib cable Beirut 04611,
132115Z Jul 82, par. 3; "Talking Points for use
with The President," 10:00 A.M. 8/12/82,
8224185, p. 2; Hill 7-21-94 and 7-16-94. Even
the French and Italians, America's partners in
forming the MNF, had the same belief (Hill 7-
21-94). The Arabs were not the only ones to
view Habib as part of a charade. *The Wall
Street Journal* simplified Habib's diplomatic
effort to a "good cop, bad cop" technique. In
the *Journal's* analysis, Habib was the good cop;
the Israeli army was the bad cop. "Mr. Habib
is saying, in effect, that if the PLO won't make
a deal now, it will have to reckon with the
frightening bad cop in a few days or hours. To
be convincing, this approach requires that the
good cop *seem to have* enormous difficulty
restraining the bad cop from pummeling the
suspect" ("U.S. Diplomat in Delicate Negotiations To Determine PLO's Future in Lebanon,"
Wall Street Journal, 6-24-82; italics added).

173 Presiding: These are Draper's words (Hill 7-16-94). The rampant breakdown in confidence that characterized July 1982 extended also to Habib's dealings with Lebanese officials. "I am not going to fool around with these people," he said of the Lebanese July 7, "because I don't trust any of them" ("Recorded radio conversation between Mr. Eagleburger and Amb. Habib," July 8/82, 0900 hrs, 8219191, p. 3). The problem in their case wasn't dishonesty or lack of good intentions. It was timidity and lack of clout (Draper 4-13-93). Time and again Habib leaned on them to rise to the occasion, decide what they wanted, make demands, issue deadlines, assert themselves, start acting like leaders of a sovereign state. But they just couldn't or wouldn't. "They are beginning to wonder if they can trust me," he said, "because I am always so hard [on them] . . . . I keep trying to get them to tell me what they want, but they won't tell me because they are afraid to ask for anything. Then they would be accused of kicking the PLO out. They can't afford that" ("Recorded radio conversation between Mr. Eagleburger and Amb. Habib," July 8/82, 0900 hrs, 8219191, p. 3-4) Their fear was that other Arabs, who gave the Palestinians lip service as long as they resided somewhere else, would criticize them.

173 Biased: Draper 4-25-93. Lewis 4-10-94 says Habib's Lebanese background, which had not been a big issue earlier, came to have an effect on Israel's trust in him. Hill points out that it has long been standard procedure for both Israelis and Palestinians to undermine and attack the negotiator. Even in the late 1990s both the Palestinians and Israelis would occasionally declare that special envoy Dennis Ross no longer had their confidence (Hill 7-19-95 and 10-1-98 note to the author). But the attacks on Habib seemed particularly strong, and this time the stakes were higher than in routine negotiations.

173 These guys, bullshitted: Hill 7-9-94; "Radio Telecon Draper/Hill, 0130 June 28, 1982," NEA Hill memo to Bremer, 8218166, 6-29-82; Hill 7-9-94. Habib realized that was a possibility, so he wrote, "In the course of [detailed] discussions, we will be able to determine whether the proposals have a truly valid basis or whether the [government of Lebanon] is being strung along by the PLO ("Message from Habib 0500 June 29: Day's Activities, June 29," NEA Veliotes memo to S/S Bremer, 8218168, 6-29-82, p. 1). Habib figured that the Mossad's source was Bashir Gemayel. His response: "I'm

tired of Israeli sniping. The Israelis want to accept what Bashir says rather than what I report. So what?" (Hill 7-9-94).

173 By July 6: Hill 7-10-94. The specific unacceptable result Sharon was thinking of in this context was letting the PLO leave behind a token force and an office in Lebanon, which Habib had resumed advocating.

173 Cabinet, falls: Hill 7-10-94

173 Brilliant: "Habib Still Plays For Time," *Newsweek,* 6-1-81

173 Well known: Draper ADST oral history

173-74 July 11 ceasefire: Hill 7-10-94

174 Worst: Shultz, p. 49. The Israelis reportedly announced July 18 that there was nothing to be gained from the Habib mission and suggested he go home (Mikdadi, p. 74).

174 Characteristic of enemies: Lewis ADST oral history. On August 7 Undersecretary Eagleburger, widely considered very pro-Israel (Eagleburger 7-3-93), said that Washington is "greatly concerned that Israel has some insane paranoia that we're conspiring to save the PLO. Some people here believe Israel does not want a diplomatic settlement" (Hill 7-21-94).

174-75 Palaver, friend, Phil is suspected: Hill 7-16-94; Lewis cable Tel Aviv 11097, 221519Z Jul 82, par. 4-7. Palaver is aimless talk, chitchat. Habib had been in Beirut the whole time since June 14. The text of Habib's recommendation to Reagan is in chapter 6, quoting NEA Veliotes memo to Bremer 8217987, 6-27-82, "Recorded Radio Report from Habib, 0430 A.M., June 27, 1982." One service Begin mentioned specifically was having just sent Reagan a twenty-page document detailing the PLO's connections to the USSR and to terrorist groups around the world.

175 Rarely complained: Hill 6-15-93; Sehulster 7-12-94

175 Class by themselves: Draper 5-4-93; also Shultz 7-25-94

175 Face value: Howell 9-6-93

175 Israel would assure: According to an American diplomat who asked not to be identified by name and who adds that Sharon's approach throughout most of the war was to "stall us, lie to us if necessary, do whatever he had to do until the facts on the ground brought about the inevitable."

Notes to 11: Suspicions and Lies

One of Habib's colleagues who had been involved in the Israel-Egypt peace treaty talks in 1979 says he found the Israelis then to be tough negotiators, but honest. They might decline to answer a question, but never gave false answers. In 1982, though, "We found that they were *way* over that line," he says. "They'd tell us things that were just flat untrue, about where they were positioned, what they were doing, what their intentions were. We'd say, 'The Palestinians say Israelis are active in this area,' and they'd say, 'Absolutely not true, never happened' or 'We were never anywhere near there.' And we *knew* that they had been where they were alleged to be. We started making rounds on our own: The defense attaché and in some cases Morrie or I would go out in a car and go out and have a look and, sure enough, they would be *exactly* where they were alleged to be and *exactly* where they insisted they weren't." This wasn't just Sharon, but "the range of guys we were dealing with." This official asked not to be identified by name.

Lewis, from his vantage point in the US embassy in Tel Aviv, was skeptical that Habib's reports of IDF locations and movements around Beirut were more accurate than Sharon's. He believed that Habib was relying on information from the Palestinians and Lebanese, neither of whom were neutral observers (Lewis ADST oral history). Habib did have high confidence in Lebanese intelligence chief Jonny Abdu, but his own location high in the hills overlooking Beirut afforded him a panoramic eyewitness view of much of what was going on ("An old pro wins a new peace," *Washington Post* story in *St. Petersburg Times*, 8-21-82).

175 Pattern of false: Habib interview with Parker

175 Disaster: Hill 7-10-94

175 Capacity, trust: Hill 7-21-94

175 Biggest liar: Paganelli 11-2-96

175 Some emphasize: Haig 5-11-94; Hill 6-15-93; Lewis 4-10-94; Lewis in Quandt, *Middle East*, p. 239

175-76 Being lied to: Veliotes 4-29-93. The Israeli ambassador in Washington at the time was Moshe Arens.

176 Flat-out lies: Draper 9-19-97

176 Steadily lost: Lewis unpublished sample chapter manuscript dated 4-22-85, p. 17

176 Feeding Begin: Lewis in Quandt, *Middle East*, p. 239

176 Foreboding, scheme: Habib cable Jerusalem 01785, 082248Z Jun 82, par. 7. Sharon had two plans for operations in Lebanon, one grand and one modest. The Cabinet had only approved the modest one. "Sharon's grandiose scheme," Habib wrote, was to put Israeli forces alongside Bashir's east of Beirut to force Syrian withdrawal from the Beirut area and "redraw the political map of Lebanon once and for all" (par. 3). Habib wrote that he suspected Bashir Gemayel shared Begin's growing ambitions.

176 Never confined: Habib cable Beirut 04640, 141457Z Jul 82, par. 4 and 5D. Habib went on to say, "To do this they want to end Palestinian military presence in Lebanon: end the presence of the PLO political and institutional framework in Lebanon; and, set back for as long as possible an integrated Palestinian movement widely recognized as the sole representative of the Palestinian people" (par. 5D).

Haig (5-11-94) suspects that Sharon just "had it in his craw to get up there [to Beirut] and clean the PLO and Syrians out" and thus exceeded his authority. Indeed, Chief of Staff Rafel Eitan would later say he had never been told to stop at any limit like 40 kilometers (Bavly, p. 165). Veliotes (4-29-93) has no doubt that pushing back the PLO was just a pretext, that Beirut was the objective all along. Lewis (4-10-94) says that he believes Begin's original assurance that the invasion would only go 40 kilometers was "a lot of double-talk."

176 June 13 meeting: Habib cable Jerusalem 01903 of June 13, 1982, repeated in State 163551, 142321Z Jun 82, par. 19

176 Years later, court: This is according to Ze'ev Begin's deposition in Sharon's lawsuit against an Israeli newspaper, reported in "Begin knew Sharon deceived him" and "Sharon deceived Begin on Lebanon, judge rules; throws out libel suit against Ha'aretz," *Ha'aretz*, 11-5-97.

177 July 2: Habib 7-2-82 cable Beirut 4415, quoted in State 184218, 021729Z Jul 82, par. 10

177 These leaks: Hill 7-10-94. In this episode, the Israelis leaked word not only of the PLO's agreement to leave, but of America's and France's commitment of troops to the MNF. Reagan had not yet consulted with Congress, who was on recess for the Fourth of July. Mem-

bers of Congress were upset that a foreign government knew about his decision before they did, and some tried to invoke the War Powers Act to prevent him from sending troops (Teicher, p. 208).

177 This can't string out: Hill 7-10-94. Sources cited in the articles were Reagan's California White House and the Israelis.

177 Political capital, only alternative: Lewis cable Tel Aviv 09770, 281704Z Jun 82, par. 7-8. Lewis warned in this cable that "If the diplomatic process does not yield significant results rather soon, we believe he [Begin] would ultimately recommend to the Cabinet to go into West Beirut militarily in some form or other despite the human costs, domestic opposition to such a move and the anticipated very sharp reaction from the United States" (par. 8).

177-78 Cruel dilemma: Hill 7-10-94. The Likud was Begin's political party. Lewis reported on July 14 that even Sharon, "sensitized to his political future, would like to see Habib succeed" (Hill 7-10-94). This was a momentary lapse on Sharon's part. Hill later wrote that the siege of Beirut "drove each of them [Habib and Sharon] to polar opposites—far beyond the balanced statecraft that each was normally capable of. This brought them into a symbiotic relationship that could have been productive but increasingly became detrimental. Phil needed Arik's pressure to get the PLO to go. Arik needed Phil to get them out. But Arik put too *much* pressure on, and Phil complained about it instead of using it" (Hill note to author received 11-30-98).

NEA prepared talking points July 18 for Shultz to use with Reagan that said in part that Begin "now seems to realize the quandary Israel is in. If they assault West Beirut, the probable damage to our relationship would cause him serious domestic problems. If they don't and Habib's negotiations drag on without success, Begin will pay a heavy domestic price for launching a major operation with heavy Israeli casualties without accomplishing the ultimate objective" ("Talking Points for Use With the President," 7/18/82, 8220840).

178 Frustration: "Talking Points for Use With the President," 7/18/82, 8220840. Only five days later, Habib and Sharon got into yet another shouting match. Sharon told him all about the Cabinet's resentment of Habib. But he invited Habib to come to Jerusalem and added, "We won't embarrass you while you're there" (Hill 7-16-94).

178 More to their liking: Shultz 9-16-93; Hill 7-12-95. A June 28 cable Sam Lewis is telling in this regard for its glaring omission of any mention of Phil Habib: "There is clear apprehension [in the Israeli Cabinet] over what the U.S. position will be regarding IDF entry into West Beirut in light of Secretary Haig's sudden resignation. Israelis will scrutinize every word from Washington for hints in this particularly crucial time. Any statement, positive or negative, regarding possible Israeli military action will be analyzed carefully and, with the right combination of events, could tip the balance" (Lewis cable Tel Aviv 09770, 281704Z Jun 82, par 6; punctuation altered for clarity). Habib's awareness that Israel was listening much more to Washington than to him is the reason he never stopped trying to imbue Washington with his views.

At one point, Sharon even tried to literally go to Washington over Habib's head. On August 9 he asked for meetings with Shultz and Reagan. "He's coming to say I've been duped," Habib told State when he heard about Sharon's request. "He'll come with intelligence that this is a plot, that the PLO doesn't intend to leave. The Israelis can't accept the idea that we won't permit the military option." Shultz politely declined to let Sharon do an end run around Habib, and the trip was aborted (Shultz, p. 65-66; Hill 7-21-94).

One of Habib's colleagues who asked not to be identified by name says, "Phil did tell the Israelis to stop shooting. In fact, he did it so often and with such force that the Israelis (remember, 'the Israelis' at this time was Sharon and only him) basically blew him off. What Phil needed was the same message with the same force from Reagan, Haig, and later Shultz."

178 Phil could talk: Shultz 9-16-93. The Israeli preference for hearing from Washington may have been stronger in this case, but it was not unique to Habib. For example, during the October 1998 Wye River, Maryland, talks between the Israelis and the Palestinians that the Clinton administration moderated, *The New York Times* quoted an official describing President Clinton's involvement as "a drug for leaders who have built up a tolerance for lower-ranking officials like the special envoy, Dennis B. Ross, or even [Secretary of State Madeleine] Albright. 'Why give concessions to Ross when Albright is there?' the official asked. 'And why give concessions to Albright when Clinton is there?'" ("Clinton Keeps Up Hope of Success in Mideast Talks," *The New*

Notes to 11: Suspicions and Lies

York Times, 10-20-98).

Hill says that, while a message from high State Department officials may suffice for some countries and some problems, "when it comes to Israel and the US, that is never sufficient. It must be from the president" (Hill 7-12-95). Lewis adds that "Any [Israeli] government has to be able to demonstrate to the electorate that it can get along with the United States even though at times it may have to be very confrontational. There is a political price to be paid by Prime Ministers who get into public fights with the U.S. Presidents" (Lewis ADST oral history).

178 Circuitous: Draper 12-18-94; Lewis ADST oral history. Logistics were another reason for this circuitous process. Begin would sometimes argue with a message, sometimes comply. But even the compliance was always short-lived: Begin would agree to a ceasefire conditioned on a stern warning that it must be absolute and mutual, the IDF would advance under cover of the ceasefire, somebody would take a shot at them, Israel would declare that the other side had broken the ceasefire, and the IDF would unleash a round of massive retaliation.

178 Solve the problem: Hill 7-12-95. Hill points out that "Washington" here refers to the elected and appointed leaders, not the career diplomats, who knew better. American ambassadors in the region were "rewarded if you were able to adduce evidence that the Washington policies were correct" (Dillon ADST oral history). Habib was constantly and loudly saying the policies—insofar as they varied from what he wanted—were wrong.

178 Insert themselves: Hill 7-12-95; Draper 12-18-94; Holbrooke, p. 301. For one thing, presidents are too busy dealing with every issue under the sun. For another, they rely on experts, such as the regional bureaus in the State Department, to handle foreign crises up to and including writing any statements the president does make on the crisis. Finally, too much involvement by a president dulls the impact of any given intervention. Memorable instances of high-profile personal presidential involvement in a foreign crisis, such as Jimmy Carter's mediation between Anwar Sadat and Menachem Begin at Camp David in 1978 or Bill Clinton's mediation between Benjamin Netanyahu and Yasir Arafat at Wye Plantation in 1998, are notable precisely because they are so unusual.

179 Wouldn't stop: Hill 7-12-95

179 Anything that keeps: Hill 7-10-94

179 Bureaucratic sniping: Hill 7-12-95

179-80 Pressler, Bechtel: *The Washington Post,* 7-25-82; Associated Press story carried in the *St. Petersburg* (Florida) *Times,* 7-26-82. Shultz, Secretary of Defense Caspar Weinberger, CIA Director William Casey, and a number of other officials in the Reagan administration also had connections with Bechtel.

180 Editorial writers: For example, the *St. Petersburg* (Florida) *Times,* 7-28-82

180 Candidate: George Sheldon, Floridian candidate for Congress, in the *St. Petersburg* (Florida) *Times,* 7-27-82

180 Understanding with George, $7,500: Habib interview with Mulcahy; AP, 7-26-82; Habib's 1982 datebooks; Habib's 1982 tax papers. Habib said, "My job was to be available when they wanted to sit down and talk about things." Shultz says, "He came and talked about what actually took place and how it took place and what the problems were and what were the peculiarities" of whichever countries they wanted to know about (Shultz 9-16-93).

180 George Will: *Newsweek* 8-2-82. *Newsweek's* cover date is nearly a week later than its actual appearance on newsstands.

180 Joseph Kraft: "Recall Habib?" *San Francisco Chronicle,* 7-28-82

180-81 France, broker, advocate, bonus: Khalidi, p. 123-26, 135-47, 153, 163; Hill 7-9-94. France's partner in this hope was the PLO. Among the reasons France thought it should have a more prominent role was its longstanding relationship with Lebanon. The League of Nations had given France a mandate over the territory now called Lebanon after World War One, and it was the French who in 1920 made Lebanon a state separate from Syria (Dunnigan & Bay, p. 36). Fourteen years later, French president Jacques Chirac became the first head of state to address the Palestinian legislative council, a step *The New York Times* described as "widely viewed as an attempt to increase France's role in Middle Eastern politics by presenting himself as an active advocate of Arab interests" ("Chirac Gets Warm Welcome On a Visit to the Palestinians," 10-24-96). Chirac's step prompted *The New York Times'* columnist A.M. Rosenthal to write that "France watches the U.S. on center stage in the Mideast. That burns Mr. Chirac's presidential stomach. . . . Lebanon [is] a country for which French bureaucrats never tire of announcing their love" ("The Chirac Caper," 10-25-96). The Egyptians, the Saudis, and the Jordanians were also pressing for a political bonus ("Transcript of Radio Conversation Between Lawrence Eagleburger, Ambassador Habib, and Charles Hill, July 18, 1444-1516 EDT," 8220873, p. 7-8).

181 All the world's problems: Hill 7-10-94. Habib wouldn't even let himself get sucked into a discussion with an Israeli general about Israel's plans for after the evacuation. "You've got a completely unreasonable position," he told the general, "but I'm not going to argue with you now. When the time comes, when we get through these first days, then we'll have something to say. . . . I have other ideas, but there is no point in discussing them. We've got to get these people out, then we'll talk about the next stage." Larry Eagleburger did, however, quickly follow up with the Israeli ambassador in Washington (NEA Veliotes memo to S/S Bremer, 8219693, "Telcon with Habib July 10, 1982 - 1058," p. 2-3; NEA Veliotes memo to S/S Bremer, 8219695, "Telecon between Phil Habib and Charlie Hill, 12:30 P.M., July 11, 1982," p. 2).

181 Probably never: Habib cable Beirut 04658, 151445Z Jul 82, par. 4

181 Resented: Eagleburger 7-3-93

181 Advising PLO, intoxication, alternative, trap: Khalidi, p. 11-13, 86, 136-38, 143, 145-47. As for a plan for getting the PLO out of Beirut, the French advocated what Habib called the PLO's "standard line": The UN would send in a buffer force, the IDF would pull back 5 kilometers, the PLO would reoccupy the camps on the outskirts of town, and the PLO would leave by road. On July 10 the Israelis asked Habib about that plan, and he told them, "That's the official PLO position, but it is not the position which I am negotiating. . . [That plan is] irrelevant, that's no longer under discussion" (NEA Veliotes memo to S/S Bremer, 8219664, 7-10-82, "Radio Report from Ambassador Habib, 1240 EDT, July 9, 1982," p. 2; NEA Veliotes memo to S/S Bremer, 8219693, "Telcon with Habib July 10, 1982 - 1058," p. 5).

181 Limited extent: Khalidi, p. 11-13, 122-26, 135-47; Habib cable Beirut 04561, 101755Z Jul 82, par. 6. Washington too used France to a limited extent.

181 Sucking up, Liechtenstein: Hill 7-9-94. The matter he was referring to was a French-sponsored resolution in the UN Security Council calling for the withdrawal of Israeli forces from the Beirut area. The US vetoed the resolution, saying it failed to call for disarmament of the PLO or for restoration of the authority of the Lebanese government throughout the country (State 181755, 302122Z Jun 82, p. 2-3).

181 Sceptical: Salem, p. 36. More generally, Khalidi writes of "the stubborn resistance of the U.S. to any scheme which did not give it a central role" (p. 169).

182 Divided: Evron, p. 148

182 Mendacious: "Mixed reaction in Jerusalem," The Jerusalem Post, 8-8-82. Begin's compliment for Habib's efforts and comment about his prospects were contained in a letter from Begin to Reagan, which he discussed with the Cabinet in this meeting.

182 Fraud and deception: "Who's in Charge Here?" Newsweek, 8-23-82

182 Trickery, reneging: "Habib accused of conniving to save bulk of PLO forces," "Mixed Reaction in Jerusalem," and "Disconcerting attack," Jerusalem Post 8-8-82. Though these articles identified their source(s) only as "authoritative Israeli circles" and circles "known to be close to the defence minister," Shultz believed "Sharon has launched a media campaign aimed at discrediting Phil and undercutting his mission" (Shultz memorandum for the president, "Status Report on Lebanon," 8-9-82, 0223742). The Washington Post described the sources as two close advisers to Sharon. It reported that "Sharon has been waging an increasingly open campaign against" Habib's plan. "Israeli sources say he personally has supervised a campaign of leaks in the Israeli press designed to discredit Habib's proposals even before they were formally presented to Jerusalem" ("Sharon campaigning against Habib ideas," Washington Post article in Spokesman Review, 8-9-82).

Draper says there is no merit whatsoever to the charge that Habib was reneging on an agreement with Begin not to bring any MNF troops into Beirut until after the PLO had left. Deliberately or not, the source(s) were distorting the fact that Habib had given in to Weinberger's refusal to allow American troops to enter Beirut until after the evacuation was well under way. He had never wavered from his plan to have somebody's troops enter at the beginning. Knowing that the PLO would never leave without MNF protection, he had consistently rejected Sharon's demand that the MNF not enter until after the evacuation was over (Hill 7-21-94).

Gen. Tamir had criticized Habib a week earlier as working for a political outcome favorable to the Palestinians. He was told in reply that in Beirut Habib was criticized as being pro-Israeli (Dillon cable Beirut 05026, 010355Z Aug 82).

182 Editorial: "Disconcerting attack," *The Jerusalem Post,* 8-8-82

182 French had warned: Khalidi, p. 147

182 Desperate: Hill 7-21-94. Shultz considered Sharon the originator of "a media campaign aimed at discrediting Phil and undercutting his mission" (Shultz memo to The President, 8-9-82, 8223742).

183 Legendary: Crocker 4-25-94

183 Obviously, pretext, Algeria, convinced: Hill 7-10-94. See also Rabinovich, p. 141.

183 Getting nowhere: Hill 7-10-94

183 Pressure the Arabs: "Transcript of Radio Conversation Between Lawrence Eagleburger, Ambassador Habib, and Charles Hill, July 18, 1444-1516 EDT," 8220873, p. 9-10; Hill 7-10-94 and 7-16-94. The foreign ministers of Syria and Saudi Arabia were about to meet with officials in Washington to discuss the Arabs' responsibilities in the crisis. Another option State considered was letting Sharon "tear it up for a while to get the PLO back in line" at the risk of Habib resigning (Hill 7-10-94).

183 Pressure Israel, protest, wash hands: Hill 7-10-94. As early as June 14 the State Department was considering bringing Habib home "for consultations"—a traditional form of diplomatic protest—but NEA felt it was too early to decide on that (State cable 163040, 6-14-82, par. 3).

183 Kissinger: "Transcript of Radio Conversation Between Lawrence Eagleburger, Ambassador Habib, and Charles Hill, July 18, 1444-1516 EDT," 8220873, p. 16-17 (punctuation altered for clarity); Shultz, p. 50. "Well, frankly," Habib said, "I think the only special peace negotiator I would sort of go for at this point is Henry. If you could persuade him, I think it would be a damn good idea, and you can tell George that I think so. Henry's the only one with the kind of clout that could deal with

the total comprehensive peace package."

183 July 6: Hill 7-10-94

183 July 28: Hill 7-16-94

184 My staying: "Transcript of Radio Conversation Between Lawrence Eagleburger, Ambassador Habib, and Charles Hill, July 18, 1444-1516 EDT," 8220873, p. 9-10

184 Succeed or fail: Hill 7-10-94

12 Life in the Pressure Cooker

185 Terrible heart condition: Paganelli 11-2-96

185 Nobody knew: Habib interview with the author 1-10-84, not included in the edited version that appeared in *The Stanford Magazine,* Spring 1984

185-86 Helicopters in Vietnam: Draper 4-13-93; Conroy 5-27-93; Hill note commenting on manuscript of this chapter 6-97

186 Top treatment: Letter from George Kerlek Jr. to author, 10-13-94

186 Huey description: Draper 4-13-93; Bider 4-24-93; Geske 6-5-94; Hill note on the manuscript of this chapter 6-97

186 Habib on helos, backup, flight surgeon: Letter from George Kerlek Jr. to author, 10-13-94

187 Eulogy: Francis Meloy and Robert Waring were killed June 16, 1976, along with embassy employee Zohair Moghrabi. Habib delivered his eulogy for them at the National Cathedral June 21, 1976 (Department of State press release No. 313 June 21, 1976).

187 RPG: Dillon ADST oral history; McCullough, *State,* Dec. 1982, p. 5. Rightly or wrongly, the ambassador at the time, John Gunther Dean, believed the Phalange (a.k.a. the Lebanese Forces) had tried to kill him, and he personally blamed their leader, Bashir Gemayel. Dean was shot at several times (Dillon ADST oral history).

187 French ambassador: Dillon ADST oral history. The gunmen were part of the PLA, the Palestinian Liberation Army.

187 Pistol, sniping: Dillon ADST oral history; Dillon 5-9-94; Crocker 4-25-94

187 Nearly every: Crocker and Dillon in Dammarel, p. 51-52

187 Ride of your life: Crocker 4-25-94

187 Booby traps: Gaucher 5-15-94

187 Nasty: Dillon ADST oral history

187 Any gang: Lee 10-2-94

187 Greatest danger: Barrett 5-9-94; Draper 5-4-93

187 Constant fire: Draper 4-13-93; Associated Press story "Habib makes peace in his ancestral land," in *Clearwater Sun*, 8-21-82

187-88 Convoy: Dillon ADST oral history; Sehulster 7-12-94

188 Delta Force: Sehulster 7-12-94. Delta Force personnel are assigned to protect US politicians abroad when in quasi-combat situations, where conventional State Department Diplomatic Security protection is not enough.

188 Lebanese guards: Dillon ADST oral history; Salem, p. 77. Habib and Dillon had the same security precautions, personnel, and equipment (Crocker 4-25-94). Much of this description of Habib's security is based on Dillon's description of his own security.

188 Kurdi: Dillon ADST oral history; Robert Dillon and Susan Dillon 5-9-94

188 The less time: Sehulster 7-12-94

188 Docility: Bider 4-24-93; Hill note on manuscript of this chapter 6-97

188-89 Drive time, raped: Sehulster 7-12-94

189 Habash: "A Sterling Achievement," *Time*, 8-30-82; "Habib the Peacemaker," *Newsweek*, 8-30-82, p. 41-42. Dillon (5-9-94) did not believe there were any serious efforts to kill Habib in particular.

189 Death threats, immune: Draper 5-4-93

189 Beirut proper: Dillon 5-9-94

189 Two shells: Robinson memo to S, D, P, S/S, NEA, LWG, S/S-O, 7-5-82, "Draper-Robinson radio-telecon"

189 Cairo veranda: Atherton 9-19-93

189 Closed the embassy: Apart from the danger of getting shot or blown up on the street,

there was the less likely danger of getting captured within a diplomatic sanctuary. Between 1971 and 1981, forty-three diplomatic facilities of various nationalities had been seized in at least twenty-seven countries; five more takeover attempts were unsuccessful. American embassies were one of the two favorite targets. Of those forty-eight episodes, more than half occurred in 1979 and 1980 (Jenkins, p. v). Note "Greatest danger" below explains why this was not a likely prospect in the case of Yarze. Technically, the State Department considered Dillon's decision not a closure of the embassy but a move from West Beirut to East Beirut, where his residence was located (Hill note on manuscript of this chapter 6-97).

189 Suburb: Associated Press story "Habib makes peace in his ancestral land," in *Clearwater Sun*, 8-21-82

189 Highway, entire city: Lee 10-2-94; Bavly and Salpeter, p. 103

189 Entertaining: Smith 6-21-94; Dillon article "Caught in the Crossfire," *Duke* magazine, May-June 1986, p. 6

189-90 Bazillion: Mead 6-5-94

190 By day, privilege: Dillon 5-9-94

190 Guest suite: Crocker 4-28-94; Dillon 5-9-94

190 Snoring, roommate: Dillon 5-9-94. Habib sometimes shared a room with a communicator (Lee 10-2-94). Of the civilians at Yarze, probably the only one with experience in this kind of thing was Draper. As a young FSO in Baghdad during the Iraqi revolution of 1958, he had spent more time than he cared to remember crowded with his colleagues into the besieged chancellery, eating out of cans and getting showers only rarely (Draper ADST oral history).

190 Gotta send a telegram: Pascoe 6-4-94

190 Crockers, not try to leave: Pascoe 6-4-94; Crocker 4-28-94

191 Any belligerent: Barrett 5-9-94. This was also the Marines' assessment (Smith 6-21-94; Sehulster 6-23-94).

191 Greatest danger, small caliber: Smith 6-21-94; Crocker 4-25-94; Draper 5-4-93. The residence had the traditional contingent of Marine guards as security to deter intruders, but intruders were not the danger. The residence was in an affluent Maronite neighbor-

hood: The Maronites were delighted to have the American ambassador's residence there (Dillon ADST oral history), and no Muslim would dare venture into such a hostile neighborhood even in normal times (Draper 5-4-93), much less at a time when the neighborhood was filled with Israelis and when Israeli fire had the Muslims trapped in West Beirut. An artillery shell is like an enormous bullet. When it lands, it explodes and shatters into a thousand small fragments that go ripping through the air at high speed. Those jagged scraps of flying metal can easily kill or maim. Before the invasion, Deputy Chief of Mission Robert Barrett was sitting in his fifth-floor downtown Beirut residence when a truckful of PLO drove by shooting nowhere in particular. A stray bullet hit the ceiling right above him (Mrs. Barrett 5-9-94).

191 Humor, several effects: Dillon ADST oral history; Dillon 5-9-94; "Radio Report from Amb. Habib 11:55 EDT - Israeli Firing on West Beirut," 8219017, 7-6-82. Sharon viewed the hill called Yarze (or Yarzah) as a strategic location because the Beirut-Damascus Highway ran on its slopes (Sharon, p. 439), so of course he would position guns there. It is interesting that, while the Israelis have always blamed terrorists for positioning their guns near civilian sites and thus disclaimed responsibility when Israeli fire hits those civilian sites (the Israeli destruction of a UN camp housing civilian refugees in Lebanon in April 1996 being a particularly notable case in point), Sharon in this case was doing very much the same thing as the terrorists that Israelis criticize.

191 Palestinian fire: Crocker 4-28-94 and 4-25-94

191 Shrapnel on shack, English: NEA Veliotes memo to S/S Bremer, 8219693, "Telcon with Habib July 10, 1082 - 1058, p. 3 and 7; punctuation altered for clarity; characteristic profanity added to State Department's bowdlerized transcript.

191 Breakfast, urgency: Habib interview with the author. Habib's favorite souvenir of Beirut would be a nasty-looking four-inch long piece of jagged shrapnel that he kept on a bookshelf in his study.

191 See the gun: Pascoe 6-4-94

191-92 Garage: Lee 10-2-94

192 Air conditioner, sauna: Bider 4-24-93; Dillon ADST oral history

192 Acoustics: Bavly and Salpeter, p. 103

192 Interpret the sounds, quiet night: Dillon ADST oral history

192 No special windows, face: Dillon 5-9-94; Dillon ADST oral history

192 Laundry room: Crocker 4-28-94; Sehulster 6-23-94; Lee 10-2-94

192-93 Outgoing, incoming: Crocker 4-28-94. At dinner, for example, Habib and his colleagues would hear firing, look at each other, and someone would say, "Outgoing." The others would nod in agreement and resume eating (Hill note on manuscript of this chapter 6-97).

193 I sleep well: Habib interview with the author

193 Description of artillery: Crocker 4-28-94; Pascoe 6-4-94; Draper 5-4-93

193 MiG shot down: Draper 12-18-94; Sehulster 6-23-94; Smith 6-14-94. The press reported a Syrian MiG getting shot down over Beirut on August 31 and said that was the first downing of a Syrian plane since June 24 ("Israelis Report Shooting Down Syrian Photo Jet," *The New York Times,* 9-1-82). But the details of that incident do not match the details of the incident Sehulster describes, which he is certain happened between August 6 and 21 (Sehulster 12-7-98). Smith recalls it as between August 21 and 25 (Smith 11-25-96).

193 Physical grind: Draper 4-13-93

194 Stamina: Bider 4-24-93

194 What better way: Habib interview with the author. A colleague later asked him whether he would do it again. "Oh, of course. Christ, it's fascinating. Who wouldn't? Why do you think I came back in '81 and '82? I knew it might be risky for my health, but it was really worth it. It was worth it to get back in the action again, the things that really count. That's what we [as FSOs] were supposed to do" (Habib interview with Mulcahy).

194 Rest, recharge: Dillon 5-9-94

194 Do the travelling, worried: Draper 12-22-94

194 Collapsing: Howell 10-11-93

194 Doctor: Draper 12-22-94 and Grove letter to the author 6-8-97. The same cardiologist treated Begin.

194 Overexcited: Schiff and Ya'ari, p. 220-21; also Hill note on manuscript of this chapter 6-97

194 Golf course, walked: Gaucher 5-15-94. A butterfly bomb is a booby-trap bomb that falls out when a cluster bomb opens. Wherever they land, they sit quietly until someone or something nudges them, then they explode. After the war, the Italian ambassador asked his golfing partner, Lt. Col. Gaucher, to get the butterfly bombs cleaned out of the trees at the golf course so they could play in safety. Gaucher brought in bomb disposal experts from the MNF to do it.

194 Boring: According to a colleague who asked not to be identified by name

195 Reaction to stress: Bider 4-23-93

195 Chef: Lee 10-2-94; Pascoe 6-4-94

195 Lebanese food, eloquent: Sehulster 6-23-94

195 Every morning: Gaucher 5-15-94

195 Set a plate, crème caramel: Robert and Susan Dillon 5-9-94. "My god, did he love pistachio nuts!" says Pascoe (6-4-94). "They would disappear. Literally disappear."

195 Four desserts: Kreczko 10-6-93. This happened after the war. The king remarked that no one else had ever done that.

195 Getting fat: Lee 10-2-94; Crocker 4-25-94; Bider 4-24-93. The cherries incident happened after the war. Howell considered it part of his job to keep Habib from eating too much, but he left the mission two weeks into the war.

196 Fullest: Bider 4-24-93

196 Coffee, tea: Habib interview with author. Habib was a connoisseur of fine wines, but he barely touched alcohol of any kind on the mission (Grove 6-4-94; Dillon 5-9-94). He would sometimes have a glass of wine on the Yarze veranda in the evenings (Lee 10-2-94). In Jerusalem he would occasionally have one shot of scotch with a lot of water (Grove 6-4-94).

196 During breakfast: Crocker 4-25-94. Habib loved this typical moment in an FSO's day, reading "the take," i.e., the day's cables (Hill note on manuscript of this chapter 6-97).

196 Blur: Lee 10-2-94; Pascoe 6-4-94

196 Palace: Draper 5-4-93

196 Tacsat: Hill 3-27-93; Hill note on manuscript of this chapter 6-97; and Hill in "50th Anniversary of the Executive Secretariat," a panel discussion for the Association for Diplomatic Studies' Foreign Affairs Oral History Program, 6-21-94, p. 13-14. Habib had his support team draft cables after the fact reporting what had happened, but they were more for the historical record than for conducting present business. The operations center in the State Department was a bedroom, about 8 x 10 with a hospital-style bed in it, normally used by FSOs doing twenty-four-hour duty, on the seventh floor, one flight up from Near Eastern Affairs and near the secretary's office (Hill 7-7-98).

196-97 Calls to Hill: Hill 7-19-95; Hill, "50th Anniversary," p. 13-14; Hopkins, p. 29; Lewis 4-10-94. Habib and Hill usually talked about four times a day. He sometimes talked to Undersecretary of State Lawrence Eagleburger, Assistant Secretary for NEA Nicholas Veliotes, NEA staffers Thomas Miller, David Welch, David Mack, and others. The State Department transcripts of these calls generally omit Habib's characteristic profanity. Hill was filling in for Assistant Secretary Draper while Draper traveled with Habib in the region. Hill had been director of the Office of Israeli and Arab-Israeli Affairs. Before the end of the summer, Hill changed jobs, becoming executive secretary of the department and executive assistant to Secretary Shultz (according to a staff member who asked not to be identified by name).

197 Swimming pool: Dillon 5-9-94

197 Silent movie, learned to expect: Grove 6-4-94. Habib's fellow American diplomats were nearly as tight lipped. "He gave us the word a long time ago," says one: "Keep your big mouths shut" ("A Cautious Habib works close to home," Clearwater Sun, 8-7-82). One book does say that Habib sometimes gave in-depth backgrounders to American reporters that were not for attribution. "They never let Habib down" (Bavly and Salpeter, p. 105). He had done many such backgrounders in Vietnam and Korea, but denied talking to the press in the Middle East (unrecorded comment to author 12-20-83).

197-98 Counterparts: They might leak like rusty buckets themselves, but at least Habib could know that he hadn't been the one to screw things up. The PLO and the Israelis both leaked whatever morsels—accurate or not—suited their purposes. That would usually send Habib into a steaming rage. In diplomacy, "The greater the distance maintained between participants and journalists, the less likely that individual participants will be tempted to disclose information prematurely, which can reduce flexibility among the negotiators" (Stein/Lewis, p. 19).

A possible origin of Habib's aversion to the press occurred while he was political counselor in the South Vietnam embassy in 1965. Henry Kissinger was in town as a consultant to assess the political situation for President Johnson. Kissinger made disparaging remarks about the South Vietnamese government during an off-the-record luncheon with reporters. The *Washington Post* reporter arrived late and did not realize that Kissinger's remarks were off the record, so he published them. The article outraged LBJ and nearly ended Kissinger's budding career as a consultant to the US government. As one of the people who had briefed Kissinger, Habib's name got dragged into the flap (Clifford, p. 429-32). The episode may have made a lasting impression on Habib about the unintended consequences of talking to the press. He did talk to the press, but usually off the record. He rarely said anything interesting on the record. Often he would listen to what a reporter was planning to report and give oblique indications of whether or not it was sound. If he liked and trusted a reporter, he might suggest where the reporter should hang out, without saying why; an important development would then happen there, and the reporter would be on the spot. On his post-retirement missions such as the Lebanon crisis, he basically didn't talk to reporters at all, other than banter and brief non-informative exchanges such as when Reagan would turn the microphone over to him.

198 Late afternoon: Crocker 4-25-94

198 Library, pool, book, nap: Crocker 4-28-94; Pascoe 6-4-94; Dillon 5-9-94; Lee 10-2-94

198 Lucky tie, stay at residence: Gaucher 5-15-94

198 Restaurants, tension: Lee 10-2-94

198 Security at restaurants: Bider 4-24-93; Gaucher 5-15-94. Bider was with Habib in Beirut after the war, but the security measures she describes applied during the war as well.

198 Headquarters: Whereas the US has only one embassy and ambassador in a country, it may have consulates in major cities other than the capital. Israelis considered Jerusalem the capital of Israel, but the US did not. So, while the Israelis had most of their government offices in Jerusalem, the US embassy was thirty miles northwest in Tel Aviv, and Jerusalem had only a US consulate (Lewis ADST oral history; Grove letter to author 6-8-97). Most of Habib's business was in Jerusalem, so he made the consul general's residence there his Israel headquarters. Lewis and Tel Aviv embassy staff would travel to Jerusalem to support him (Lewis note to author 1-15-00).

198-99 Residence description: Hill 7-17-93 and 3-27-93; Grove ADST oral history

199 Escape, Muhammad: Grove 6-4-94; Dillon 5-9-94; Hill 7-17-93 and 3-27-93. Mohammad and the other servants were all Palestinians from the nearby village of Batir.

199 Coming home, nap, take over: Grove 6-4-94

199-200 Garden: Susan Habib 3-93; Grove 6-4-94

200 Dealings, this way: Eagleburger, eulogy at Habib's memorial service, 6-10-92; Bider 4-23-93, 4-24-93, and 4-26-93

200 Turned Lebanese, welcomed: Hill 3-27-93. Hill had been on staff at the consulate general in Jerusalem in 1981 during Habib's mission that led to the July 24, 1981, ceasefire. It may seem odd that Habib felt the tug of his ancestry more at the consul general's residence in Jerusalem than he did at Yarze. Here's a possible reason. Though Yarze overlooked the capital of Lebanon, it was a noisy crucible teeming with Americans obsessed with the siege next door. It ill-afforded him the luxury of nostalgia. Nearly all of the Arabs he encountered in Yarze and Beirut were politicians, generals, and other leaders—i.e., ones he could not afford to let down his professional guard with. The Jerusalem consulate, by contrast, was basically an office going about its routine business in a peaceful city. The office and residence were in the same building. The building and grounds were suffused with the quiet ambiance of ancient Arab culture. The Arabs he encountered there were servants with no involvement in his mission.

201 Mark, slept only: Grove 6-4-94. Habib was the same way with many middle-ranking and junior FSOs. The more he kidded them, the more he liked them (according to an FSO who asked not to be identified by name).

201 Mind busy: Bider 4-24-93; Grove 6-4-94

201 Worst thing: This source, one of Habib's colleagues, asked not to be identified by name

201-2 Relaxing, Scrabble: Grove 6-4-94; letter from Martha Hayward to Brandon Grove 5-20-94. This particular Scrabble game happened in February 1983. In Scrabble, each player has up to seven wooden tiles, each of which has a letter on it. The players take turns placing one or more letters at a time on the playing board to form words.

202 Glass: Grove 6-4-94. The Roman glass was made on the coast of what is now Israel and Lebanon, about 50 miles from the consulate. Today, if you walk on the beach north of Tel Aviv, you can see tiny bits of light green-blue Roman glass, rounded into pebbles by the force of the sea (Hill note on manuscript of this chapter 6-97).

202 Local, junk, accredited, office, family time: Grove 6-4-94; Bider 4-26-93; Lewis note to author 1-15-00

203 Junior staff, stand up to him: Grove 6-4-94; Kreczko 10-6-93; Bider 4-23-93

204 Stellar performance: Grove 6-4-94; Bider 5-23-93; Howell 10-11-93

204 Devoted: Grove 6-4-94; Howell 10-11-93. Over a decade later, Grove would say, "To this day I hear from people in the State Department who look back with great professional satisfaction and nostalgia to what he taught them" (Grove 6-4-94).

204 Guiltily: Grove in *Foreign Service Journal,* May 1994

204 Wanted to conceal: Grove 6-12-94

13 The Marines

205 He needed: Mead 6-5-94

205 Handful: As early as July 3, the day Reagan approved American participation in the MNF, Habib asked that French-speaking Marine liaison officers be identified and placed on standby to come meet with him. "But I don't [want] them to come until I know that we have something. That may be tomorrow, it may be the next day" (Johnston 12-4-96; NEA Veliotes memo to S/S Bremer, 8218794, "TelCon Habib

and Charles Hill/Adm. Howe, 12:07 P.M., July 3, 1982," p. 4). Habib specified that he wanted Marine officers who spoke French because French would be the first or second language of most of the participants in these meetings. Though the liaisons had been chosen in early July, one flare-up or another made it pointless for them to come ashore.

205 *USS Guam:* Smith 6-21-94; Mead 6-5-94. Commodore Richard White and Adm. William Rowden of the Sixth Fleet were also present.

205 Maronite: The Palestinians hated the Maronites even more than they did the Israelis. A chant heard in the streets of West Beirut during the siege was "Even Sharon, but not Maron"—i.e., the Maronites (Mikdadi, p. 84).

206 Buffer: Smith 11-25-96. Sharon's original plan called for the Lebanese Christian forces, the Phalange, to enter West Beirut and kill the PLO once the IDF had the city surrounded. Though Sharon was disappointed that the Phalange had so far basically sat out the war, the PLO feared that the Phalange would strike at the first opportunity. The two had, after all, been regularly killing each other in the civil war that had raged from 1976 until interrupted by Sharon's invasion.

206 Sandwich: Mead 6-5-94; Sehulster 6-23-94

206 Marine responses to Habib: Mead 6-5-94; Smith 6-14-94 and 6-21-94. Disarming the Palestinians had been a goal of Habib, Washington, and Lebanese leaders since the early days of the invasion (Habib cable Beirut 04233, 161325Z Jun 82, par. 1C and 3F; NEA Veliotes memo to Bremer 8217953, "Recorded Radio Report from Habib, 1800, June 25, 1982—Late Afternoon Meeting with Sarkis," 6-25-82, p. 2). In fact, the goal of disarming them was a given even before the idea of an evacuation emerged (Hill 7-9-94). It was always assumed that disarming them would be one of the MNF's basic jobs.

206-7 Attitude, guys from Brooklyn: Mead 6-5-94

207 Always outnumbered: Draper ADST oral history. *Peacekeepers* is an unfortunate term that inevitably raises platitudinous objections that there is no peace to keep. *Calming forces* would be a much more apt term.

207 Impossibilities, consent: Smith 6-21-94

207 Marines chosen: Johnston and Smith were

aboard a ship in the Mediterranean; Sehulster and Gaucher were working in Germany awaiting the call to go to the region and didn't actually go until August 6 (Sehulster letter to the author 1-12-97). After early consultations with Habib ashore, Johnston would need to be on ship to make preparations for the Marines to land, so he would be relieved ashore by Smith.

207 Matter of days: Hill 7-21-94

207 August 7: Johnston 12-4-96

207 General outline: Johnston cable, USMC 2 07 Aug 2030Z, to Cmdr. White and Col. Mead

207-8 Textbook: Johnston 12-4-96

208 Ongoing obstacle: Hill 7-21-94

208 Ridiculous: Draper 5-4-93

208 Matter of command, overall commander: Johnston 12-4-96; Lewis cable Tel Aviv 12139, 101505Z Aug 82, par. 5

208 Dirty work, dollies: Johnston 12-4-96. During this first meeting ashore Habib also emphasized how important it was to give the LAF a role suitable to the army of a sovereign country.

208 Good spirits, close out: Johnston cable USMC 2 07 Aug 2030Z, to Cmdr. White and Col. Mead; Hill 7-21-94

209 Helicopters and Israeli jets: Account compiled from Sehulster 7-12-94 and 11-24-96; Draper 4-25-93; Gaucher 5-15-94; Geske 6-5-94; Johnston 12-4-96; Kerlek 12-8-96; Frank p. 11; and Johnston (CTF Six Zero) cable LIAA00144 to COMSIXTHFLT 111011Z Aug 82. Kerlek was the pilot of the lead Huey; Sehulster, Johnston, and Gaucher were on board; Geske was in charge of the Hueys. Geske says the Marine helicopters that flew Habib typically flew in pairs 100 feet apart. Sehulster says the jets came within 20 or 30 feet; other estimates by people not in the helicopters at the time range up to 200 feet. Even 200 feet is extremely close for a jet to pass by a helicopter. The Pentagon and State Department were anxious to keep the Marine liaisons' meeting with Habib secret (Howe memo to Eagleburger, "Lebanon Checklist," 8-5-82, 8223325, p. 1). So the liaisons had been instructed to keep a low profile, making day trips ashore in civilian clothes to meet with Habib and spending nights on ship (Johnston 12-4-96).

209 Reported the incident: Kerlek 12-8-96

209-10 Intention to issue orders: Sehulster 11-24-96. In the words of Johnston's official cable, the Marines requested authority to scramble an armed fighter escort to "take harassing action" at the first hint of any encore (Johnston [CTF Six Zero] cable LIAA00084, 071835Z Aug 82). This was the Marines' closest and most dangerous encounter with the IAF, but not their first. Johnston's report on the incident mentioned without elaboration that "Previous flights to and from Junieh had been intercepted by what were believed to be Israeli aircraft" (cable LIAA00144).

210 Should a hostile act: Cable LIAA00112 from COMSIXTHFLT 090951Z Aug 92.

210 Protested, apologized: Shultz, p. 63-64. Israeli officials told an American diplomat in Tel Aviv that the helicopters were buzzed because they had not coordinated their flight with the IDF. They said it was not harassment and was no problem. Begin told Habib that the Israelis were suspicious because the French had said they would be in touch with the IDF and had not been. The Americans rejected such explanations, pointing out that they were not trying to keep the French from talking to the IDF and that the French had nothing to talk about with the IDF yet since they had not yet met with Habib's MNF planning team (Hill 7-10-94 and 7-21-94). NEA suspected the incidents described here stem from "Sharon's entirely mistaken suspicion that we were transporting French military personnel as part of a French attempt to enter Beirut before an agreement is reached. We have told the Israelis that this is utter nonsense" (Evening Reading Item "Israelis Harass U.S. Helicopter," 8-8-82).

210-11 Detainment incident: Account compiled primarily from Sehulster 11-24-96; also from Sehulster 7-12-94; Gaucher 5-15-94; Johnston 12-4-96; Frank, p. 11; cable LIAA00102 from COMSIXTHFLT and USCINCEUR to the Joint Chiefs of Staff 081315Z Aug 82; Kerlak 12-8-96; Shultz memorandum for the president, "Status Report on Lebanon," 8-9-82, 0223742. Johnston's version is quite different from Sehulster's and Gaucher's: He says he never felt captured or threatened, that the Israelis never surrounded the Americans, and that Col. Yahya just insisted on giving them an unwanted escort to Yarze. Johnston considered this just "a little bit of arrogance by the Israelis." He agrees that the IAF was monitoring their ship and their helicopter flights (Johnston 12-4-96).

211 Unglued: Sehulster 7-12-94

211 Phone: Gaucher 5-15-94. The general was Amir Drori (Sharon, p. 503).

211 Power play, sandbox: Sehulster 7-12-94; Johnston 12-4-96. Washington strongly protested this helicopter incident too. Begin sent his personal apologies (Shultz memo to The President, 8-9-82, 8223742).

211 Stay ashore: Johnston 12-4-96

211 As though nothing: Sehulster 11-24-96. He did, however, forbid the Marines to have any direct dealings with the Israelis. They would, of course, have to have some dealings, but those must always be in their capacity as members of Habib's political/military committee for the multinational force, not as US Marines. The IDF was anxious to have highly visible meetings with the American military, but Habib was determined to avoid any appearance of the Americans being in cahoots with the Israelis in their war (Johnston 12-4-96).

Sharon had repeatedly said he wanted an IDF representative to be a member of the MNF planning group. Habib had repeatedly refused (Hill 7-21-94). As late as August 18, the Israelis were still demanding to know why they were not included as members of the MNF (Johnston 12-4-96). The Israelis were pointedly not invited (Sehulster 7-12-94; Smith 6-21-94), but Habib would send representatives of the committee to brief the IDF every morning on how the plan was evolving. Because of the buzzing and detainment incidents, though, Habib specifically instructed them to drag their feet at every opportunity about giving the IDF any information that might provide better insight into what the MNF was doing (Sehulster 7-12-94; Smith 6-21-94). While these Americans would meet with the Israelis, some of the Lebanese army officers in the meetings served as liaisons with the PLO.

211-12 Habib's helicopter: Entire story Draper 4-25-93 and 9-19-97. Date and time per Beirut 05272, 101300Z Aug 82 and Beirut 05282, 101515Z Aug 82. Draper says Habib never even reported the incident to Washington, but an official of the Near East Asia bureau recalls having heard about it at the time. Habib confided the story to his University of Idaho classmates at a 1985 reunion, quoting himself telling the Israelis, "Get the hell out of here! That's for me!" (Easterbrook 2-21-94). The Beirut embassy had sent word to the Tel Aviv embassy to notify the Israelis of Habib's flight plans in advance (Beirut 05272, 101300Z Aug 82). Schiff and Ya'ari tell an abbreviated version of the story on p. 223-24. In their version, Sharon ordered his troops to Junieh to prevent American helicopters from landing French troops on the beach. IDF jeeps scurried around the tarmac to keep this helicopter from landing. Draper arrived (their version does not place Habib himself at the scene) and screeched "That's Habib's helicopter!" The IDF troops were gone a few hours later. Schiff and Ya'ari give August 8 as the date of the incident. The declassified documents give no indication of any Habib trip to Israel between July 28 and August 10.

212 Surrendering, shelter: Smith 11-25-96, 6-14-94, and 6-21-94

212 Land mines: Sehulster 6-23-94. The LAF had virtually no mine-clearing capability (Johnston cable, USMC 2, Beirut 5311, 11 Aug). The French did send some of their soldiers out with the LAF to clear land mines and booby traps. After three or four of them got blown up, they backed out (Sehulster 6-23-94). Habib knew quite well from personal experience how dangerous mine clearing was, having been required during his WWII service to probe for mines by poking bayonets in the ground (Draper 9-19-97).

212 Buffer along Green Line: Sehulster 6-23-94

213 Signal: Sehulster 11-23-96

213 Bone of contention: Sehulster 6-23-94. As the guy on the ground who had actually looked at the places Habib had in mind for the Marines to go, Sehulster found himself in the awkward position of having to tell his superiors that Habib's idea was "far less dangerous" than they thought, while telling Habib that it was more dangerous than *he* thought. Though Sehulster did not support Habib's idea, his superiors accused him of being too close to the situation and too sympathetic to Habib (Sehulster 6-23-94).

213 Veto: Sehulster 6-23-94. The decision was made by the US Commander in Chief in Europe, almost certainly with the approval of the Joint Chiefs of Staff (Sehulster letter to the author 1-12-97).

213 Let it drop: Mead 11-25-96

213 Grasp: Smith 6-14-94; Johnston 12-4-96. Both Smith and Johnston talk about some of

Habib's utterly unworkable military ideas, and in the next breath say things like "he had a good sense for what was in the art of the doable from a military standpoint" (Johnston 12-4-96). They apparently reconcile the two themes by Habib's willingness to listen to their comebacks, learn quickly from their feedback, and revise his ideas accordingly.

213 Personal level: Sehulster 7-12-94. This contrasts markedly with his treatment of fellow Foreign Service Officers, to whom he rarely expressed appreciation.

213 Fairly gush: Smith 6-9-94, 6-14-94, and 6-21-94; Mead 6-5-94; Johnston 12-4-96; Sehulster 7-12-94

213-14 Kept apprised, Pentagon, freewheeling: Mead 6-5-94

214 Unprecedented: Shultz 9-16-93

214 Nobody knew: Mead 11-25-96

214 Left it to Mead: Mead 1-19-97; Sehulster letter to the author 1-12-97. Sehulster adds, "We, of course, always advised our seniors of such decisions. I do not know of any being overturned."

214 Tactical command: Smith 6-14-94 and 6-21-94

214-15 Issuing directions, responsible guys: Johnston 12-4-96; NEA Veliotes memo to S/S Bremer, 8218794, "TelCon Habib and Charles Hill/Adm. Howe, 12:07 P.M., July 3, 1982," p. 4

215 Full authority: Sehulster 6-23-94; Smith 6-14-94

215 Why can't you, LAF: Sehulster 6-23-94; Johnston 12-4-96. The Lebanese Armed Forces were capable of little more than getting out of bed in the morning. But, this being their own country, Habib had bent over backwards to involve them. He asked the LAF to come up with a plan for going into West Beirut in advance of the MNF. But the LAF generals were extremely cautious and loathe to commit themselves to anything that might upset the Israelis, the Syrians, or anyone else.

215 Driven: Smith 6-21-94; Johnston 12-4-96

215 Stay until they did, mahogany: Smith 6-14-94 and 6-21-94

215 Sit at the middle: Sehulster 6-23-94

215-16 Map on floor: Sehulster 6-23-94 and

11-23-96. This happened August 11 when Habib returned from Israel with Cabinet acceptance in principle of the plan. His helicopter touched down in Junieh at 4:15 P.M., and he started the meeting as soon as he drove back to Yarze.

216 Three words: Tueni 11-15-95. Draper says, "He did not speak Arabic, but many of the phrases were familiar to him from his childhood, especially the curse words" (Draper ADST oral history). Howell says "As far as I know, he didn't speak any of the language. He may have known a few words, but I never saw him use the language" (Howell 10-11-93).

216 Holy Ghost: Mead 6-5-94. The nickname is based on Acts, chapter 2, in the Bible. That chapter recounts the Holy Spirit (or Holy Ghost) filling Jesus' apostles and suddenly enabling them to speak in languages they did not previously know.

216 Routinely: Smith 6-21-94 and 6-14-94

216 Italian: Sehulster 6-23-94; Mead 6-5-94. They were almost certainly mistaken.

216 Political officer: Crocker 4-25-94. Habib says "Arabic was probably my first language, because my parents did not speak English to one another. I spoke sort of a simple Arabic, colloquial Arabic as a child" (Habib interview with Tueni). Dillon says Habib's Arabic was better than people give him credit for (Dillon 12-31-97).

216 Positive impact: Sehulster 6-23-94

216 Swore beautifully: Mead 6-5-94

216 Lapsed into French: Smith 6-21-94; Johnston 12-4-96. When Habib had first asked the US military to send liaisons, he specified that he wanted ones fluent in French (Smith 6-21-94).

216-17 French volunteered: Sehulster 6-23-94 and 11-23-96; Draper 12-22-93

217 French do everything, agenda, envy, excuse: Sehulster 11-23-96; Gaucher 5-15-94

217 Liked Henry: Dillon 11-5-96 and 11-24-96; Sehulster 6-23-94 and 11-23-96

217 Mistress: Dillon 11-16-96

217 How many girls: Gaucher 5-15-94

218 Weird, unthinkable, *fini,* race: Sehulster 6-23-94 and 11-24-96; Gaucher 5-15-94

218 Dinner party: Sehulster 6-23-94, 6-23-96, and 6-24-96

218 Worried: Pascoe 6-4-94

218-19 Stress: Sehulster 6-23-94; Barrett 5-9-94; Lee 10-2-94; Pascoe 6-4-94

219 Heart pill, bedroom: Sehulster 6-23-94

219 Always worried: Mead 6-5-94

14 The Endgame

220 Sharon is winning: Habib cable Beirut 05089, 040531Z Aug 82, par. 4-9. Salaam was a former prime minister of Lebanon.

220 Single Arab country: Habib did briefly explore the idea of moving the PLO to an enclave in northern Lebanon, but the Lebanese government shot down that idea (Draper note on draft of this chapter)

220 Not now active: Habib cable Beirut 04703, 171445Z Jul 82, par. 4

220 Two options: Habib cable Beirut 04656, 151445Z Jul 82, par. 3

220 My horse, then they'll know: "Transcript of Radio Conversation Between Lawrence Eagleburger, Ambassador Habib, and Charles Hill, July 18, 1444-1516 EDT," 8220873, p. 5 and 16. The foreign ministers of Syria and Saudi Arabia were due in Washington within days. The visit tied in well with Habib's decision to travel, since the American gameplan was to impress upon the two foreign ministers that, as Eagleburger put it, "we have done our damnedest and have been more concerned about the lives of the PLO than the Arabs seem to have been and we have not succeeded, and it is now their problem" (p. 14).

221 New wave: Seale, p. 388, 390; Bavly, p. 107

221 Learned not to assume: On July 7 he reported that he had heard on good authority that "The Palestinians are ready to give me everything I want. . . . [But] you know me: I've been through so many of these things, something's liable to happen by tomorrow" (transcript "Ambassador Habib and Charlie Hill," July 7, 1982, 1420).

221 July 1: On July 1 Habib said, "They should not go to Syria. For one thing, if a Jew gets killed in Europe, the Israelis would bomb the PLO in Damascus. And if they were in Syria they would simply infiltrate back into Lebanon in two weeks" (radio transmission, Habib to Hill 0800 July 1, 1982, 8218541).

221 Meeting with Assad: Seale, p. 390. See chapter 4 for the story of the June 11 ceasefire. Assad never wavered from his insistence that Habib misled him in their discussion just before that fateful event. Habib and other American diplomats repeatedly insisted that Assad had read into Habib's words assurances that Habib did not make.

221 The sooner: Seale, p. 390

221-22 Reiterated: Habib 7-24-92 cable Jidda 5532, quoted in State 206640 TOSEC 110050, 250019Z Jul 82, par. 4-5. Habib did go out of his way to emphasize that a prisoner exchange proposal he was bringing from Begin was not his own and that he was acting "only as a messenger" on that subject (Habib cable Damascus 15216, 231829Z Jul 82, par. 2). Habib also took up with Assad the matter of getting Syrian troops out of West Beirut along with the PLO. Assad replied that, since they were there as (the dominant) part of the Arab Defense Forces sent to Lebanon years earlier by the Arab League, the Lebanese government should talk to the Arab League about it. Habib said that for the time being he just needed them out of Beirut; going to somewhere else in Lebanon would help end the siege of Beirut without compromising their Arab League mandate. He did suggest to Assad a face-saving way to bring them home, though: that "practically speaking they needed to return to Syria for re-equipping" (par. 6B).

222 Urged the king: Habib 7-24-92 cable Jidda 5532, quoted in State 206640 TOSEC 110050, 250019Z Jul 82, par. 2, 5

222 Saudis paid, back door: Barrett 5-9-94; Draper 4-13-93. Shultz (7-25-94) says he does not know whether in the end the Saudis paid Syria to take evacuees. In any case, it probably wouldn't matter whether the Saudis gave any Arab state money directly to take evacuees: The Arabs all understood that, if they did what pleased the Saudis today, the Saudis would be more forthcoming when their brethren needed money for something else tomorrow (Draper 9-19-97).

222 Accept 5,000: Hill 7-16-94

222 US recognition: Hill 7-16-94. Draper's recollection differs. While a number of Arab states clearly insisted on a political bonus for the PLO, Draper recalls that Mubarak himself at most just implied that the US should move toward some kind of recognition. Even then, Draper says, Mubarak would not have accepted the PLO in strength (Draper note on draft of this chapter). Whatever Mubarak's own feelings about the PLO, he had a constituency to consider. Support for the PLO was strong among the Egyptian public, and Mubarak had been president for less than a year. Winning points for the PLO would enhance his political standing. Moreover, his consistent criticism of the Israeli invasion went a long way toward redeeming Egypt in the eyes of other Arabs in the wake of the Egyptian-Israeli peace treaty of 1979 *(Time*, 8-23-82, p. 31).

222 Gesture: "Transcript of Radio Conversation Between Lawrence Eagleburger, Ambassador Habib, and Charles Hill, July 18, 1444-1516 EDT," 8220873, p. 7-8. Mubarak had said earlier, "Don't come to me with the request to take them unless you have something to say to me about the [long-term] peace process." Habib said that, with Shultz replacing Haig, "there's a chance to have a peace process again." He urged the State Department to reinvigorate the stalled peace process. As a gesture toward the broader peace process, Habib no doubt made the same point to Mubarak that Reagan had made a few days earlier to the foreign ministers of Saudi Arabia and Syria, that "the US recognizes that the real issue is not West Beirut or Lebanon but the Palestinian issue. We intend to work hard and creatively to solve it" ("Talking Points for Use with the President," July 20, 1982, 8221006, p. 4).

222 Jump the traces: Hill 7-16-94. Habib's opposition to US recognition of the PLO in this context only seems to contradict his willingness to negotiate the particulars of departure directly with Arafat. His view was that, if Washington chose to recognize the PLO after due deliberation in the normal course of events, fine. But he was unwilling to have the US rushed and blackmailed into granting recognition in the heat of this crisis. In the context of US-PLO contacts in Lebanon on security issues (see chapter 9), he was willing to talk directly with Arafat to bring this immediate crisis to an end. But he was unwilling to have the US manipulated into broad concessions. Shultz, heavily influenced by Habib's input, told Reagan that "we must take care not to be

stampeded into" granting "some political concessions or recognition to the PLO to compensate for their military defeat. . . . We should be careful not to play our Palestinian card over a tactical issue like the West Beirut crisis alone. We should husband such a tool until the opportunity is clear to use it to influence the peace process" ("Talking Points for Use With the President," July 20, 1982, 8221006, p. 5).

222 Intact, quid pro quo: Hill 7-16-94. Mubarak didn't believe Habib that the PLO didn't want any quid pro quo, because at this point he had not heard that from Arafat. Even after he later did hear it from Arafat, though, Mubarak wouldn't budge. He agreed only to take members of the PLO's Ayn Jallut Brigade, which had been trained and equipped in Egypt (Hill 7-16-94; Habib interview with Tueni; Draper note on draft of this chapter).

Habib no doubt also used the argument that the Arabs' failure to accept PLO evacuees delegitimized the PLO as a representative of the Palestinian people. This was a point that Shultz, drawing heavily on Habib's input, made to the foreign ministers of Syria and Saudi Arabia July 19 ("Talking Points for Use with the President," July 20, 1982, 8221006, p. 2) and that the State Department conveyed to Reagan (Stoessel memo to the President, 8220115, 7-13-82, "Habib Mission: Letter to King Fahd" page "The President: Talking Points for Use With Foreign Ministers Saud and Khaddam"; "Talking Points for Use With the President," 7/18/82, 8220840, p. 3).

By August 6 the PLO sent word to Habib that they had told the Egyptians that they did not wish to link their withdrawal from Beirut to their longer-term political claims (Habib cable Beirut 05165, 061510Z Aug 82, par. 5).

222 Same argument: Hill 7-16-94. Back on July 3, King Hussein had told US ambassador Richard Viets that he would urge Mubarak to accept PLO evacuees only on the condition that the US agree to drop the Camp David Accords and pursue a peace initiative centered on UN Resolution 242. The feeling was that Mubarak would be politically destroyed by taking them unless the US gave him some such political protection (Hill 7-10-94).

222 Despaired: Draper ADST oral history

223 Somebody has to, your decision: Habib cable London 16134, 261551Z Jul 82; Habib cable London 16170, 261738Z Jul 82; Djerejian 2-18-97. The "your decision . . ." quote is put in the first person based nearly

word for word on Habib's account in the third person (London 16170, par. 5).

223 My responsibility: Habib cable London 16170, 261738Z Jul 82, par. 5-6. The king was offering to take Palestinians born in Jordan or who had Jordanian citizenship. He had obviously given this all a good bit of thought in advance. For example, when Habib asked how he would prefer that they travel from Beirut to Jordan, he replied firmly and without hesitation, "By land, direct and unimpeded through Syria."

223 Conditions, screen: Habib interview with Tueni; Djerejian 2-18-97; Habib cable London 16170, 261738Z Jul 82, par. 2, 5-7; "265 Palestinians Arrive in Jordan," *The New York Times* 8-23-82

223 Elated: Habib cable London 16170, 261738Z Jul 82. A further reason Habib was pleased was that he knew Jordan would put its PLO contingent under military discipline (Hill 7-16-94; Habib interview with Tueni).

223 Statesmanlike: Habib cable London 16134, 261551Z Jul 82, par. 2

223 Next target: Habib cable London 16170, 261738Z Jul 82, par. 8. Jordan's population is mostly Palestinian. After Habib left, the king told the US ambassador to Jordan, Richard Viets, that it was imperative for the US to link a resolution of the Lebanon problem with a comprehensive regional peace initiative (Hill 7-16-94). This would be one of the origins of the September 1 Reagan plan (see chapter 16).

223 Confident: Hill 7-16-94

223 Impossible conditions: Hill note on a draft of this chapter. The moderate Lebanese newspaper *An-Nahar* reported that "Habib did not succeed in his tour of the capitals of the Arab states, in spite of the words he heard in these capitals about their readiness to receive the Palestinian fighters, because the conditions which were imposed have undermined the idea from its basis" (reported in Reid cable Beirut 05079, 031100Z Aug 82).

224 Sarkis: Pakradouni, p. 255-56. A few days later after a similar conversation about a different topic, Sarkis said, "The other day I was mistaken in telling you that you needed two years to understand Lebanon. You need at least another twelve!"

224 Message to Begin: NEA Veliotes memo to S/S Bremer, "Recorded Radio Conversation

with Amb. Habib, July 30, 1082, A.M.," 8222642, "Radio Conversation between Amb. Habib and Peter Dodd (LWG)," p. 1-3. Shultz followed up with a message of his own to Begin emphasizing that the next few days would spell success or failure. He acknowledged that Palestinian "radical diehard elements" were trying to scuttle Habib's efforts by violating each ceasefire, and he exhorted Begin not to play into their hands by retaliating disproportionately (Letter to Prime Minister Begin from Secretary Shultz, State 213728, 310424Z Jul 82, par. 4).

224 Hit back: Brown cable Tel Aviv 11591, 301724Z Jul 82, par. 2, 5

224 Wazzan threatened: Hill 7-16-94

224-25 Proximity talks, hit the ceiling, could push: Hill 7-16-94 and 7-21-94; Shultz, p. 52-53. Habib wanted David Kimche on hand to represent Israel.

225 Habib tried, handshakes, 300 yards: Shultz, p. 52-53; Hill 7-16-94 and 7-21-94; Begin gave his specification of 300 yards to Draper.

225 50,000: "Fiercest attacks yet strike Beirut," *The New York Times* article in *St. Petersburg Times,* 8-2-82, citing state-run Beirut radio

225 Pretext, charade: Hill 7-21-94

225 Phony ceasefire: Hill 7-21-94. Habib said that Sharon's August 1 operation was intended for the express purpose of taking over the Beirut airport, which was just south of several major Palestinian camps, after the Israelis heard that Habib was thinking of using it for the MNF. And they did. The operation followed close on the heels of a letter from Shultz calling for restraint. "The IDF have grossly violated Shultz' letter," Habib said. "It's a direct rejection. They have taught Shultz a lesson to show him who's boss."

226 Actually entered, Normandy: Hill 7-21-94; Khalidi, p. 96

226 Route suggested: "Israeli tanks rumble into western Beirut," *The Washington Post* article in *St. Petersburg Times,* 8-4-82; "Israeli armor pushes into west Beirut," *The New York Times* article in *Clearwater Sun,* 8-4-82; "Israelis push toward guerrilla strongholds," *St. Petersburg Times* based on *The New York Times* and *The Washington Post* wire reports, 8-5-82. *The New York Times* reported them about 500 yards into the port area.

226 Waiting for Habib: "Again, Begin ignores Reagan," *St. Petersburg Times,* 8-5-82

226 Ashamed, overtaken: Hill 7-21-94

226 Martyrdom: "Israelis push toward guerrilla strongholds," *St. Petersburg Times* article based on *The New York Times* and *The Washington Post* wire stories, 8-5-82

226 Pursue the plan: Hill 7-21-94. The IDF's August 4 entry into West Beirut cost it 83 casualties, 19 killed and 64 wounded. This may have given Sharon a taste of what to expect if he did launch an all-out ground assault ("In Lebanon, it's easier to see the losers than the winners," *St. Petersburg Times,* 8-12-82). They quickly pulled back out.

226 I called Sharon: Fisk, p. 316. A woman who was on the ground in West Beirut during this attack wrote "Dresden, Nuremberg and Berlin together can't compare with what we went through yesterday," August 4 (Mikdadi, p. 106).

226-27 Tacsat, out the window: Account compiled from Habib's own telling of it in his interviews with Parker, p. 12, and with Tueni, p. 58; Hill's account in "Philip Habib: A Remembrance" in *Foreign Service Journal,* July 1992, p. 12; Hill note on draft of this chapter; Shultz, p. 58-59; Dillon ADST oral history; Salem, p. 36-37. The "listen carefully" quote is from Salem. I have altered his punctuation for emphasis and have corrected one error. Salem, who was with Habib at the time, has Habib saying, "Tell *Reagan* someone there is lying to him." But what Habib actually said is "Tell *Begin* someone there is lying to him," according to Charlie Hill, the person to whom Habib was talking (Hill note to author 1-20-99). Since the names *Reagan* and *Begin* sound alike, and since Salem mistakenly thought Habib was talking to the White House, his error is understandable, but I have corrected it here. After this remarkable exchange, Habib sent State a written account of Sharon's latest onslaught and added,

> Thus the ninth ceasefire before Beirut is broken. There is no question that this is deliberate on the part of the Israelis. We should no longer accept the hypocrisy of statements about the PLO firing first. The amount of devastation being wrought, on top of the immense amount already inflicted on the Beirut area, is so great as to be hard to imagine at a distance.
> All this comes on top of the cutoff

of essential services and the blockade of West Beirut. No one, from President Sarkis to Prime Minister Wazzan on down believes the United States cannot stop what is going on. Therefore, they associate us with Israeli actions. I have this minute received a telephone call from the Prime Minister pleading with me to do something to stop the bombardment. He still has some faith that I can change things. Why, I do not know—except that these people still believe they can touch the conscience of the United States.

> There is no way that Israeli use of American arms in Beirut these days can be characterized as defensive. It is offensive in every meaning of the word—military and moral. . . . The time has come for us to put a stop to it—whatever pressure is necessary. . . .

> It is quite possible the Israelis will now bring to a halt their latest escalation, and mouth the false explanation of responding to PLO fire while pledging to restore the ceasefire. They may even try to convince us that it is necessary to aid the negotiating effort. . . . They should be told that if they continue to disregard our views, we will take the drastic action the law allows" (Habib cable Beirut 05089, 040531Z Aug 82, par. 4-9).

It was not unusual for Israelis to argue that their attacks helped Habib's negotiations by motivating the PLO to talk seriously. One Israeli writer put it this way: "The fierce attacks, particularly those on August 4 and 12, . . . served to persuade the PLO that a full-blown Israeli attack was imminent, which enabled Habib to negotiate an agreement for the PLO's evacuation" (Rabinovich, p. 143). Indeed, David Kimche had warned Draper a few days earlier that Israel was compelled to step up the military pressure, since there were no alternatives (Draper note on draft of this chapter). Habib rejected that line of thinking.

Sharon ridiculed this episode. "Come by helicopter and see for yourself that we don't have any artillery near the embassy," he fumed to Brown. "How does [he] know who is shooting? Do Israeli mortars have a special sound? If one of my officers stuck a phone out the window to report to me like that, I'd fire him in thirty seconds for not going out and checking on his own!" (Schiff & Ya'ari, p. 222; also Fisk, p. 316) Habib thought it was "about as authentic a report as you could make. There was no doubt they [the Israelis] were misleading"

(Habib interview with Parker). His colleagues think Sharon's objection is absurd. The first thing anybody living in a war zone learns, they point out, is how to tell incoming fire from outgoing fire. The only possible source of outgoing fire from the vicinity of Habib's headquarters was the IDF, who controlled that whole area. No one else but the IDF *had* tanks and artillery up there. Habib and his colleagues could *see* the guns blazing and could see where the shells landed in West Beirut (Hill 6-15-93; Crocker 4-28-94).

This episode was widely reported at the time, often inaccurately portraying Ambassador Dillon as the one who held out the receiver (Dillon ADST oral history). Schiff & Ya'ari's account (p. 222) reflects that inaccuracy. The confusion may be due to the Israelis relying on a first-person account in a cable Beirut signed by Dillon. In fact, *all* cables are signed by the ambassador, no matter who writes them. Sharon's denial of having artillery "near the embassy" would be true in the sense that the building (called the chancellery) normally housing the embassy was well inside West Beirut, and he did not have artillery at that location. But that would be irrelevant hairsplitting about terminology, not a candid response to the substance of Habib's report: Habib was calling from Dillon's residence in Yarze, which had been the temporary embassy since Dillon closed the chancellery six weeks earlier, and Sharon most certainly had artillery and tanks in the vicinity of Yarze.

This was not the only time Habib held the tacsat out the window for Washington to hear the shooting. What was different this time was that the prime minister was simultaneously denying that the shooting was happening (Hill 7-19-95). This was also not the first time such a thing had happened in a war: In World War Two, "J. Edgar Hoover, in New York City for the weekend, took a telephone call from his Honolulu agent-in-charge, who was seeing Zeros bombing. 'You can hear the bombs yourself! Listen!' He held the telephone out his office window while Hoover sat in New York listening" (David Brinkley, *Washington Goes to War*).

227 Manhunt: Sachar, p. 185

227 Berlin: Shultz, p. 54

227 Obsession: Sehulster 7-12-94; also Dillon ADST oral history; Draper 12-18-94; Hill 7-19-95; Sachar, p. 185. Sharon confirmed August 14 that "we have an interest in hitting the headquarters of the terrorists and the com-

manders of the terrorists" ("Habib brings new peace proposals to Israel," *St. Petersburg Times,* 8-15-82).

227-28 August 6 smart bomb: Mikdadi, p. 107-8; Hill 7-21-94 and 7-12-95; Khalidi, p. 97; "Beirut: Fighting—and talks—go on," *St. Petersburg Times,* 8-7-82. Reports of the number of stories in the building vary.

228 Confronted Sharon, I wouldn't tell: Hill 7-21-94. Hill adds that use of a smart bomb made this particular attack a "deliberate use of professional military force against innocent unarmed civilians."

228 Safire: *The New York Times* column in *Clearwater Sun,* 8-7-82

228 Homestretch: Hill 7-21-94

228-29 Elements: Habib cable Beirut 05165, 061510Z Aug 82, par. 4

229 Surely not reject: Lewis cable Tel Aviv 12017, 071532Z Aug 82

229 Lewis urgently warned: Hill 7-10-94; Lewis cable Tel Aviv 12017, 071532Z Aug 82, par. 6

229 Compromise: Habib preferred to have the Americans come in first or simultaneously with the French. But the French wanted to come in first, Weinberger did not want Americans in at the beginning, and the Israelis did not want Americans on the front line. So Habib gave in.

229 Paranoia: Hill 7-21-94

229 Convinced: Lewis cable Tel Aviv 12017, 071532Z Aug 82, par. 2-5; Sharon, p. 491-92; Habib cable Beirut 05338, 121420Z Aug 82, par. 7, 11. Begin told the Cabinet August 1 that if the MNF comes in and separates the PLO from the IDF, "the criminals will never leave Beirut" (Sharon, p. 488-89).

229 Fail-safe: Lewis cable Tel Aviv 12139, 101505Z Aug 82, par. 7

229 MNF's mandate: Hill 7-21-94. The "mandate will terminate" part was explicit in Habib's plan, but the "turn around and go home" part was implicit since, if the MNF's mandate terminated, they certainly were not going to hang around Beirut. But Habib hadn't spelled that out in so many words. So Begin wanted to add the language "MNF units will leave Beirut" (Lewis cable Tel Aviv 12139, 101505Z Aug 82, par. 11C). In the end, the wording used was: "In the event that the departure from Lebanon of the PLO personnel referred to above does

not take place in accord with the agreed and predetermined schedule, the mandate of the MNF will terminate immediately and all MNF personnel will leave Lebanon forthwith" ("Lebanon: Plan for the PLO Evacuation From West Beirut," *Current Policy* No. 415, August 1982, p. 8, par. 8).

Also implicit in this stipulation was that, once the MNF arrived, it would not be in the PLO's interest for them to leave: If they left, it would be virtually impossible to ever get them back. The PLO, having squandered their one chance to save their necks, would then be left to the tender mercies of Ariel Sharon (Lewis cable Tel Aviv 12139, 101505Z Aug 82, par. 11C).

The Joint Chiefs of Staff instructed the American commander-in-chief in Europe (USCINCEUR), who would have overall responsibility for the Marines participating in the MNF, on August 12 that "You will withdraw on order if the PLO members (civilian and military) do not withdraw as agreed" (JCS cable for Gen. Rogers 111500Z Aug 82, par. 1). The USCINCEUR specified on August 14 that "any PLO noncooperation with preestablished schedule terminates U.S. involvement" (USMC 2, USCINCEUR 141013Z Aug 82).

229 No contingent: Shultz letter to Begin, 8-7-82, 92224503, p. 3. In the same letter Shultz added that "There is no doubt Mr. Prime Minister that the PLO, for several weeks during this negotiation, sought every means to delay the talks and to avoid a decision to depart. It is now clear, however, that they have made that decision. Ambassador Habib is at present engaged in most urgent and intensive discussions on the operational details of the time and modalities of departure. The period during which many of us shared an understandable concern that the PLO wished to delay and divert the negotiations now belongs to the past. We are in a new phase. The momentum is with our side. The PLO have crossed the Rubicon and have accepted the necessity of departure; they no longer have the strength, the will, or the support to do otherwise. Indeed, their primary consideration now is for safety—both for the combatants who will depart and for those non-combatants who remain behind. The United States has pledged itself to do all it can to ensure that the PLO has a safe passage out of Beirut; the presence of the multinational force will be an important symbol of that assurance" (p. 2).

229-30 Too far along, plan won't start, the facts:

Hill 7-21-94; Shultz, p. 64. Habib's allusion to Egypt and Syria referred to their delays in agreeing to receive PLO evacuees. The same IDF firing that Habib referred to also troubled Col. Johnston, who cabled his superiors, "Clear that cooperation of Israelis essential for any plan to work. Heavy bombardment of West Beirut presently underway . . . should suggest how accommodating they now appear" (Johnston cable 5219, 08 1630Z Aug 82). Habib sent a follow-up message to Begin via Lewis making the same points while emphasizing that it was not just the PLO who wanted the French MNF contingent in on D-Day: So did the Lebanese government (Lewis cable Tel Aviv 12139, 101505Z Aug 82, par. 6-7; Habib cable Beirut 05338, 121420Z Aug 82, par. 7). But Begin was unmoved. And while on the subject, he asked, "Why the French?" The French government, he said, was "bitterly hostile" to the Israeli government and to Jews. Israel should never have consented to French participation in the MNF at all, he said. But he stopped short of now vetoing them altogether (Lewis cable Tel Aviv 12139, 101505Z Aug 82, par. 5, 11B).

This meeting occurred a few hours after Habib read the *Jerusalem Post* article in which Sharon or his associates had anonymously denounced Habib's plan as a "fraud" and a "piece of trickery" ("Habib accused of conniving to save bulk of PLO forces," *Jerusalem Post* 8-8-82). In the meeting with Sharon, Habib said nothing about the article. He stuck to the business at hand (Hill 7-21-94). That article is discussed in chapter 11.

230 Map, not possible: Lewis 8-11-82 cable Tel Aviv 12220, quoted in State 226747, 130526Z Aug 82, par. 2, 4; Habib cable Beirut 05367, 131337Z Aug 82, par. 2

230 Not convinced, mathematician: Lewis 8-11-82 cable Tel Aviv 12220, quoted in State 226747, 130526Z Aug 82, par. 4; Habib cable Beirut 05338, 121420Z Aug 82, par. 5-7, 11. The "mathematician" quote is adapted from Lewis' account.

230 Wazzan wanted the French: Habib cable Beirut 05338, 121420Z Aug 82, par. 4-7. Wazzan quotes adapted from Habib's account of what he said. Rather than let the deal unravel over the issue of when the French could enter Beirut, Habib in desperation proposed to Washington a contingency fallback idea: Sending 60-75 unarmed French, Italian, and American civilians in on D-Day as monitors (Habib cable Beirut 05367, 131337Z Aug 82, par. 2-3; NEA Veliotes memo to The Secretary,

"Habib Fallback," August 13, 1982, 8224301). State thought the idea stunk. Too dangerous. Congress would revolt. But, equally stuck, Shultz gamely offered to talk to Weinberger and Reagan about sending in a handful of armed Marines on D-Day instead, a prospect that Begin had already rejected (Secretary cable to Habib, 8-13-82, 82038301221; Habib cable Beirut 05338, 121420Z Aug 82, par. 5, 7).

231 Israeli press: Grove 6-4-94. Lewis says that by late July Begin "began to realize that Sharon was misleading him and carrying out operations without his approval" (Lewis 4-10-94). The tacsat incident gave him something solid to base that feeling on.

231 Praised: *Jerusalem Post,* 8-8-82. In the same breath, Begin added that Habib's prospects for success were not bright and never had been.

231 Fraud and deception: "Who's in Charge Here?" *Newsweek,* 8-23-82, p. 19; Evron, p. 148, 159 note 1. The next day Begin criticized "certain Christian circles in Lebanon" for dismissing Habib's plan as a fraud, "an oblique reference which fooled no one that he was directing his ire at Sharon," writes Lewis (cable Tel Aviv 12068, 091436Z Aug 82, par. 2-3).

231 Assumption, clean out: Shultz, p. 65; "Begin turns optimistic about PLO withdrawal," *The New York Times* article in *Clearwater Sun,* 8-9-82

231 Leg injury, annoyance, let them take: Lewis cable Tel Aviv 12139, 101505Z Aug 82, par. 1-4, 10; Shultz, p. 66. Begin first said, "we'll discuss it in the Cabinet," but then went ahead and made the decision himself. The strains between Begin and Sharon were evident to Habib and Draper. When they heard on August 9 that Sharon had invited himself to Washington to try to go over Habib's head, Draper speculated that Begin might be "setting up Sharon for a giant pratfall" (Hill 7-21-94).

231 We accept, wrap up: Lewis cable Tel Aviv 12139, 101505Z Aug 82, par. 1-4, 11; Shultz, p. 67. Begin ended the meeting by asking Lewis to send word to Habib that, if he accepted Begin's changes, "he had a deal." If not, Habib should come to Jerusalem to discuss things in person. As always, Begin had a few quibbles about language: He wanted the words "Palestinian" and "died" replaced throughout with "PLO" and "killed," and wanted Habib's term for departure day, "D-Day," replaced with "E-Day" for *evacuation.* Begin didn't want the plan

to carry any echoes of World War Two's D-Day, a prelude to VE (Victory in Europe) day. He felt the term D-Day in Habib's plan implied that a PLO "V" day would follow (par. 4; "Habib brings new peace proposals to Israel," *St. Petersburg Times,* 8-15-82). More substantively, he still objected to any MNF contingent, especially the French, arriving at the beginning of the evacuation.

231 Sharon has prepared: Hill 7-21-94

231 Sabotage: "Sharon campaigning against Habib ideas," by William Claiborne, *The Washington Post* article syndicated in *Spokesman Review,* 8-9-82

231-32 Nose, frightened: Shultz, p. 68; Lewis 4-10-94

232 Argue Begin: Hill 7-21-94

232 Pleading: Hill 7-21-94; Shultz, p. 67

232 Virtually apologized, technical realization: Lewis 8-11-82 cable Tel Aviv 12220, quoted in State 226747, 130526Z Aug 82, par. 1, 5-6. The same day, August 11, the Israeli Cabinet approved the Habib plan in principle (Schiff & Ya'ari, p. 225).

232 Pressure on Tunisia: Dillon ADST oral history; Draper note on draft of this chapter. The other Arab states also pressured Tunisia, in the spirit of *You take them so we don't have to.* The destination of the PLO headquarters was a crucial issue. Even the Arabs who were willing to take some fighters were adamant that they would not host a PLO headquarters. Besides all the annoying political activity a headquarters would entail, it would also be likely to draw an Israeli attack someday. Who needed that? (Habib cable to Secstate also for action, 6-28-82, "Meeting with President Sarkis, et al, June 28, 1982," par. 13; Hill 7-12-95; Radio Transmission, Habib to Hill 0800 July 1, 1982, 8218541). Some people proposed Greece for the headquarters, but Habib rejected that (Draper note on draft of this chapter).

Syria had offered to accept the leaders and headquarters, but the leaders adamantly refused to go to Syria. One reason was their certainty that Assad would put them under strict control. Another was Arafat's preference to live in a moderate Arab state where he would have better access to Western media. And the US, fearing that Assad would use them to start a new conflict, didn't want them there (Paganelli cable Damascus 04934, 101438Z Jul 82, par. 19, 29; Dillon letter to author 9-11-98; Draper

Notes to 14: The Endgame

ADST oral history; Draper 5-4-93; Draper 4-13-93; Hill 7-16-94). Some Arab nations were reportedly afraid that Assad would use the PLO to subvert them ("Agreement on Lebanese peace plan reported near," *The New York Times* article in *St. Petersburg Times,* 8-12-82).

So Habib had to find someplace else for the headquarters. He had met with Lebanese leaders on July 1 and heard of Foreign Minister Butros' suggestion that Arafat and the other PLO leaders go to Tunis (Radio Transmission, Habib to Hill 0800 July 1, 1982, 8218541; Hill 7-10-94; Draper note on draft of this chapter). That would put their headquarters in the same city as the Arab League headquarters, which would be politically prestigious for them. Tunis would also offer them, as Draper said, "the easy living that they all seem to prefer." The idea stayed in play for the next several weeks, as did many others, but never really got much serious consideration one way or another. In the end, though, that idea turned out to be the breakthrough in Habib's quest for destinations (NEA Veliotes memo to S/S Bremer, 8218795, 7-4-82, "Recorded Radio Report from Habib [*sic,* actually Draper], July 3, 1982," p. 3; Hill 7-12-95). The headquarters of the Arab League had been moved from Cairo to Tunis in 1979 after Egypt became an outcast among Arabs for signing a peace treaty with Israel.

232 Advantage of distance: Gowers, p. 212; Dillon 5-9-94

232 Arab credentials: Draper 9-19-97

232 Tunisians gave in: Dillon 5-9-94 and Barrett 5-9-94; Shultz, p. 67-68; Draper note on draft of this chapter. Dillon and Barrett say the Tunisians agreed only to take the headquarters and high command. Tunisia wound up taking 1,000 people (Hill 7-23-98). They did, however, arrange to put the PLO out on an isolated cape well away from the center of Tunis and had them pay their own way (Draper 9-19-97).

232 Became much easier: Dillon 5-9-94; "Mideast talks down to details," *Clearwater Sun,* 8-11-82

232 Yemen, confirmed: "PLO's evacuation a danger to its hosts," *Clearwater Sun,* 8-13-82. Assad's biographer explains that "By 10 August, it was clear to Asad that, whether he liked it or not, the Palestinians would soon be forced out of Beirut. . . . [He then] changed his mind and agreed to give refuge in Syria to the bulk of the Beirut evacuees. No doubt he hoped to

regain some control over 'Arafat's men who blamed Asad for abandoning them and who now in adversity seemed more independent than ever" (Seale, p. 391). Sudan had offered to take the PLO as early as July 27, but Habib was tepid about the offer. He wanted to keep it as a contingency while continuing to focus his energy on the countries with strong, stable governments that he considered most suitable, primarily Egypt (Hill 7-16-94).

233 Standing idly by, Saudi pressures: Barrett 5-9-94; "The End Game in Beirut," *Newsweek,* 8-23-82, p. 20; Herzog, p. 352. Habib would have had an even harder time persuading Arab countries to accept PLO evacuees had he not been able to say that the US was committing ground troops to the effort (Smith 6-14-94).

233 Deeper level: Draper 4-13-93. Saudi Arabia in particular helped break the deadlock. It was out of the question that the Saudis take any Palestinians themselves—in fact, the Saudis tried to prevent their next-door neighbors the Yemenis from taking any lest they sneak across the border. The Saudis were probably responsible for the Syrians taking as many Palestinians as they did (Barrett and Dillon 5-9-94).

233 Egypt: "Withdrawal Leaves Many Questions," *The New York Times,* 8-22-82

233 At Yarze briefing: Johnston 12-4-96

233 Most awesome: Shultz, p. 71; Mikdadi, p. 121; Schiff & Ya'ari cite unofficial statistics of 300 dead (p. 225). Col. Johnston, one of Habib's Marine liaisons, cited a report of 180,000 shells but adds, "My God, regardless of the numbers, it was unbelievable, the number of air strikes and the artillery rounds that were fired in on West Beirut" (Johnston 12-4-96). A photographer who spent most of the day at the American University Hospital in West Beirut reported that while "dozens and dozens" of civilian casualties, including many burned by phosphorous bombs, had been brought in, only one PLO fighter, whose leg had been hurt in a car accident, was brought in ("Israel rips Beirut; Reagan outraged," *Los Angeles Times* article in *St. Petersburg Times,* 8-13-82).

233 Smashing Beirut: "The End Game in Beirut," *Newsweek,* 8-23-82, p. 17

233 Bombing Berlin: Johnston 12-4-96. *Blitzkrieg* is Johnston's word.

233-34 Wazzan: Habib cable Beirut 05338, 121420Z Aug 82, par. 5-6; Hill 7-21-94. Tense of Wazzan quote adapted from Habib's account of what he said. The American government was not doing what was necessary to stop the Israelis, Wazzan said. Maybe Habib was doing his job, but Washington was not. "We had placed our total reliance on the US government to put an end to this crisis," Wazzan said, "and still we are being bombed. Maybe we should transfer our reliance to the United Nations" (Habib cable Beirut 05338, 121420Z Aug 82, par. 4; quote put in first person from Habib's account).

Habib had asked the PLO to leave, and they had agreed. He had asked the Arabs to take them in, and they had agreed. He had asked Menachem Begin to accept his plan and to exercise restraint so that negotiations could proceed, and Begin had agreed. But still Sharon sent wave after wave of bombers over Beirut. How could Philip Habib—how could the United States—be taken seriously as good-faith negotiators? And where was Ronald Reagan to back up Habib? "Continuing silence from Washington," Dillon wrote, "will re-enforce the growing conviction here and elsewhere that we are colluding in this massive blitz carried out after the PLO has already agreed to what we have asked." Wazzan publicly blamed the US (Dillon cable Beirut 05339, 121439Z Aug 82, par. 3-5; Stoessel cable, State 228797, 142019Z Aug 82, par. 4).

234 Fire his defense minister: Hill 7-21-94

234 Progressively destroyed, Mother Teresa: Shultz, p. 70

234 Recommend: Habib interview with Mulcahy; also Habib interview with Parker; Hopkins, p. 57-58, quoting his 1-3-92 interview with Lewis. Reagan was getting the same message from others too, including NSC adviser Bill Clark and Michael Deaver, who threatened to resign unless Reagan told Begin to stop (Cannon, p. 401).

234 Appalled, already ordered: Lewis 4-10-94; Shultz, p. 70; Schiff & Ya'ari, p. 226; Lewis quoted in Hopkins, p. 57; Lewis ADST oral history; "Excerpts From Interview With Begin," *The New York Times,* 8-29-82. Reagan tried twice to reach Begin. The first time, at 10 A.M. Washington time, Begin was in a Cabinet meeting and declined to take the call. Fifteen minutes later the US received word that Begin had ordered the bombing halted. Reagan did not finally get through to Begin until 10:45 A.M.

Though at the time the White House played the story as though Begin halted the bombing in response to Reagan's tough phone call, the Israelis (Hill 7-23-94) and Lewis have always hastened to point out that the order had already been issued by the time Reagan got through. Both may be right. Though Begin declined to take Reagan's first phone call, he would surely have been notified that Reagan was on the line and would surely have figured out why. Word of Reagan's first, unsuccessful call may well have helped prompt Begin—who did not want to look as though he had bowed to US pressure—to get the order issued before Reagan could call back.

Schiff & Ya'ari reported that Reagan threatened in this phone call to pull Habib out and discontinue American mediation efforts. The Israeli press did report at the time that Lewis had made such a threat to Begin, but Lewis says he did not. He just said that Washington was furious and that Habib couldn't do his job if the firing didn't stop (Hill 7-21-94). Other press reports said the threat was in "private messages" between Washington and the Israelis (e.g., "U.S.-Israel relations mendable," AP article in *Clearwater Sun,* 8-14-82).

234 Straw: Lewis quoted in Hopkins, p. 57

234 Furious: Lewis 4-10-94

234 Looking as if: Shultz, p. 72, citing the analysis of the US embassy in Tel Aviv

234 Known nothing, might fire: Shultz, p. 71; Lewis' 1-3-92 interview with Hopkins, quoted in Hopkins, p. 57; Lewis ADST oral history. Despite the Cabinet's overwhelming disapproval of what he had already done, Sharon pressed to escalate the fighting even more. Begin reportedly replied, "Let me remind you as I reminded your predecessor Ezer Weizman [who had been fired in a policy dispute with Begin] that you are representing the government when you talk to the army and not the other way around" ("Israel rips Beirut; Reagan outraged," *Los Angeles Times* article in *St. Petersburg Times,* 8-13-82). Sharon later insisted that the bombings of August 12 "were not a personal initiative of Arik Sharon. They were decided and approved by the government" ("Sharon: 'I Wanted Them Out of Beirut; I Got What I Wanted,'" *The Washington Post,* 8-29-82).

234 Cabinet: Schiff & Ya'ari, p. 226-27; *Time* 8-23-82, p. 29; Evron, p. 149; Lewis 4-10-94. In *Newsweek's* account of the meeting, Begin

told Sharon, "Once and for all I want to make clear who is running this government" ("Who's in Charge Here?" 8-23-82, p. 18). After the meeting, Sharon said he had been trying to defend the lives of IDF soldiers but that the other Cabinet ministers were competing with each other to claim a share of credit for a negotiated settlement ("Israel rips Beirut; Reagan outraged," *Los Angeles Times* article in *St. Petersburg Times,* 8-13-82).

234 Hardly anyone: For example, Schiff & Ya'ari, p. 225; Seale, p. 388; Shultz, p. 69; even Gabriel, p. 157-58

234-35 Because Arafat: "Sharon: 'I Wanted Them Out of Beirut; I Got What I Wanted,'" *The Washington Post* 8-29-82. In his memoirs, Sharon says simply "I had done what I believed was necessary to bring about a conclusion to this siege" (Sharon, p. 492-93). What finally broke the impasse, Sharon says, happened on the night of August 12: "Philip Habib finally used the kind of whip he had had available to him for weeks. He issued an ultimatum to the PLO. The cease-fire that had been called at the end of the day would last only forty-eight hours, he told them. What might happen afterward was anybody's guess. They would have to agree to leave now, without any buffer zones and without the multinational force to protect them. When Habib said this, Arafat knew that the end had come. . . . He would get out, he decided that night" (p. 492).

Habib would dispute Sharon's account. First, there is no way Habib could have given Arafat any such message about forgoing MNF protection. He was not talking to Arafat directly, and his intermediary to Arafat, Prime Minister Wazzan, declined to even *ask* the PLO about such a thing since *he himself and his own army* insisted that the French come in (Habib cable Beirut 05338, 121420Z Aug 82, par. 7; Hill 7-21-94). Indeed, Habib reported on August 13 that the PLO would clearly "continue to insist that there be a French unit of 350 men present on D-Day." Though he began brainstorming contingency plans in case Israeli intransigence prevailed, Habib himself most certainly had not given up on having a French MNF contingent on the ground on D-Day (Habib cable Beirut 05367, 131337Z Aug 82, par. 2).

Second, there is no hint in Habib's communications with the State Department on August 12, 13, or 14 that the PLO had just made any major new decisions. As far as he was concerned, the PLO had already firmly and sincerely decided to leave well before August 12

(for example, Shultz letter to Begin, 8-7-82, 92224503, p. 2).

Third, the only available record of Habib talking at this point about a ceasefire lasting forty-eight hours is his report that Wazzan demanded on August 12 that Israel stop shooting for forty-eight hours so he could finish ironing out the details, or else he would stop working at all (Habib cable Beirut 05338, 121420Z Aug 82, par. 2, 8).

Fourth, August 12 would hardly have been the first time Habib might have sent word to the PLO that "what might happen [after a ceasefire] was anybody's guess." As *The New York Times* says, "Habib always made plain to the Palestinians that he might not be able to restrain the Israelis next time" ("Being Patient Brings Habib Final Victory," 8-22-82).

Habib's only available explanation for the August 12 assault was that Sharon "was determined to prove something" (Habib interview with Parker).

235 Saguy: Hill 7-21-94. The IDF announced that their relentless attack of August 12 was in retaliation for Palestinian shelling the night before. The PLO had indeed done some shelling that night, Dillon reported—*after* three hours of Israeli air raids. "All of this is an old story" by now, wrote Dillon. Israel may be correct that the PLO consistently shoots first; "we are not in a position to judge. [But] it is clear that Palestinian fire is not destroying Beirut. What the Israelis are doing is" (Dillon cable Beirut 05339, 121439Z Aug 82, par. 3-4).

235 Satisfied, Shamir: "In Lebanon, it's easier to see the losers than the winners," *St. Petersburg Times,* 8-12-82

235 Finally dropped: Shultz memo to the President, August 16, 1982, "Habib Mission: Close to Final Agreement," 82038400007, p. 1; Hill 7-10-94; "Israel offers concessions on plan for PLO evacuation," AP and UPI reports in *St. Petersburg Times,* 8-16-82. In announcing the Cabinet's August 15 decision to allow the French in on the first day, Israeli radio gave as the reason a French promise to withdraw its force if the guerrillas tried to back out and use the French forces as a screen. This was the same promise Habib and Shultz had already made multiple times, but Israel considered this French commitment "more specific than a general commitment in the Habib text, which Israel considered sufficient for Italy and the U.S. but not hard enough to remove distrust here of French sympathy for the PLO" ("Israel offers

concessions on plan for PLO evacuation," AP and UPI reports in *St. Petersburg Times,* 8-16-82; "Cabinet okays Habib schedule for PLO exit," *The Jerusalem Post,* 8-20-82).

235 Names, ringers: Lewis 8-11-82 cable Tel Aviv 12220, quoted in State 226747, 130526Z Aug 82, par. 9; Shultz memo to the President, August 16, 1982, "Habib Mission: Close to Final Agreement," 82038400007, p. 1; Sharon, p. 494-95

235 Punctilious: Habib letter to PLO "U.S. Requirement for Information," August 11, 1982, in Yuzo 149-50, par. 4; Schneider cable State 232640, 190049Z Aug 82; Djerejian cable Amman 06953, 191126Z Aug 82. Habib thought Jordan "may be too strict on processing" (Hill 7-21-94).

235 Too disorganized: Djerejian 2-18-97. Draper also reported that the PLO was also afraid to give lists of names (Hill 7-21-94). The press said they refused (e.g., "Habib brings new peace proposals to Israel," *St. Petersburg Times,* 8-15-82).

235 Gave up: Shultz memo to the President, August 16, 1982, "Habib Mission: Close to Final Agreement," 82038400007, p. 1; Lewis ADST oral history says the Cabinet withdrew Sharon's demand for lists of names August 14.

235-36 Djerejian: Djerejian 2-18-97

236 Foregone: Shultz, p. 72

236 Twenty million: Hill 7-23-94, Shultz, p. 73

236 Announce, premature: NEA Veliotes memo to the Secretary, August 19, 1982, "U.S. Reaction to Approval of Habib Plan," 8224890, handwritten note at top signed "Nick." Two days before the Israelis signed off, Shultz was advising Reagan to wait until Habib and Lewis gave the "all clear" (Shultz memo to the President, August 17, 1982, "Habib Mission: Focus on Prisoners," 8224657).

236 Only candidate: Habib interview with Parker, p. 10; "More P.L.O. Forces Leave West Beirut Despite a Problem," *The New York Times,* 8-23-82; "What Next for Arafat and the PLO?" *U.S. News & World Report,* 8-30-82. The election was originally scheduled for August 19, but was postponed to August 23.

236-37 Quorum, one government, had it out: "Recorded Radio Conversation with Amb. Habib August 19, 1982 at 1400 hours," NEA

Veliotes memo to S/S Bremer, 8-19-82, 8225401, p. 1-3; Hill 7-23-94; Shultz, p. 75-76. The Syrians, Habib said, were "threatening in a most crude way members of the Parliament not to come" (p. 2). Bashir's faction owned part of the port (Draper 12-22-94). Punctuation altered and italics added for clarity. There is no available record of exactly what Habib actually said to Bashir August 19; parts of this argument are inferred from what Habib told Hill he was *going to say* to Bashir as soon as he finished talking to Hill ("Recorded Radio Conversation with Amb. Habib August 19, 1982 at 1400 hours," NEA Veliotes memo to S/S Bremer, 8-19-82, 8225401).

237 Dreamed up: Draper 12-22-94; Hill 7-23-94; "Recorded Radio Conversation with Amb. Habib August 19, 1982 at 1400 hours," NEA Veliotes memo to S/S Bremer, 8-19-82, 8225401, p. 4; Shultz, p. 76). Habib had also arranged pressure on Bashir from the Israelis. Draper emphasizes that the real audience for this show was Bashir's men, because "he didn't have complete control of all those nuts. This was designed in part to *get* control." It was designed also "to make good the US pledge that the Palestinian evacuees would not be attacked that that the stay-behinds and families would be safe," Draper says. "This was one of Phil's most clever ploys, in my opinion, but it was also strictly sincere in its overall objective" (Draper note on draft of this chapter).

237-38 Now you know: "Recorded Radio Conversation with Amb. Habib August 19, 1982 at 1400 hours," NEA Veliotes memo to S/S Bremer, 8-19-82, 8225401, p. 4. Punctuation altered for clarity.

238 Announced the deal: "Presidential Statement on the Occasion of Agreement on Plan for Resolution of West Beirut Crisis," 82038600305; Hill 7-23-94; Hill cable State 234464, 201710Z Aug 82, par. 2; "Reagan Orders Marines to Beirut To Oversee Withdrawal by P.L.O.," *The New York Times,* 8-21-82

238 Resolution: H. Con. Res. 397; State 234810, 202127Z Aug 82

238 Nobel: Percy letter in State 235111, 210017Z Aug 82; excerpts in "Habib Is Nominated For Nobel Peace Prize," *The New York Times,* 8-21-82. Habib was again nominated for the Nobel Peace Prize in January 1983 by Chief Justice Warren Burger and by the majority and minority leaders of the US Senate and

the minority leader of the House. The dates on those letters say January 1982, but Tom Miller, a protégé of Habib's who spearheaded the nomination effort and wrote both letters, says the date should be January 1983 (Burger letter January 15, 1982, to Norwegian Nobel Peace Prize Committee; Baker, Byrd, and Michel letter January 26, 1982, to Norwegian Nobel Peace Prize Committee; email to the author from Tom Miller 11-11-01).

238 One last demand: Cobban in McDermott, p. 214

238 Bashir's assurances: Hill 7-21-94

238 American assurances: For example, Habib's 8-4-82 letter to the PLO, par. 10 and 13 point 8, in Yuzo, p. 147-48; Habib's 8-6-82 letter to the PLO, par. 6, in Yuzo, p. 148-49; and Paganelli cable Damascus 04934, 101438Z Jul 82, par. 9

239 Signed off on rules: Crocker 4-25-94

239 United States will provide: Excerpt from the final text of Habib's plan, "Lebanon: Plan for the PLO Evacuation from West Beirut," *Current Policy* No. 415, August 1982, p. 8, par. 4. Here is an excerpt of the letter drafted by Draper and signed by Habib August 19 to make American assurances official:

> On the basis of [assurances from the Government of Israel], the United States Government is confident that the Government of Israel will not interfere with the implementation of the plan for the departure from Lebanon of the PLO leadership, offices and combatants in Beirut in a manner which will
> (A) assure the safety of such departing personnel;
> (B) assure the safety of other persons in the area [i.e., Palestinian civilians]; and
> (C) further the restoration of the sovereignty and authority of the Government of Lebanon over the Beirut area.
>   I would also like to assure you that the United States Government fully recognizes the importance of these assurances from the Government of Israel and that my government will do its utmost to ensure that the assurances are scrupulously observed.

(Habib letter to His Excellency Shafiq Al Wazzan, President of the Council of Ministers, Republic of Lebanon, August 19, 1982; provided by Milton Viorst of *The Washington Post*; printed in Yuzo, p. 154; Draper note on draft

of this chapter.) The letter was addressed to Wazzan even though its intended audience was the PLO. A variation on these words was included in the final wording of Habib's departure plan. In that plan, Habib also reiterated that "the United States will provide its guarantees on the basis of assurances received from the Government of Israel and from the leadership of certain Lebanese groups with which it has been in touch" (US Department of State *Current Policy No. 415*, "Lebanon: Plan for the PLO Evacuation from West Beirut," August 1982, p. 9). Draper (12-22-94) says that "certain Lebanese groups" is a euphemism for the Christians, specifically Bashir Gemayel.

239 I'm your protection: Barrett 5-9-94

239-40 Bashir and Wazzan meetings in library: Dillon ADST oral history; Dillon 10-30-98 and 5-9-94. Dillon hastens to add that he did *not* interpret Bashir's wry smile to mean *I'll lie today and butcher them tomorrow*. Though Dillon doesn't remember the exact date of the phone call, he says it was just before the evacuation began.

This phone call could be interpreted as yet another in Arafat's long string of evasions and vacillations about whether the PLO would leave. It can also be read as a powerful indictment of the common practice of righteously refusing to talk to one's adversary. Arafat had conveyed to Habib multiple times over the past seven weeks his willingness to quit Beirut: Habib had taken those offers seriously, Sharon had dismissed each as a lie. Sharon firmly believed that Arafat would make a genuine decision to leave only after Sharon pounded him to within an inch of his life. Sharon believed Arafat finally made that decision only on the night of August 12, after IDF bombing had reached its horrific crescendo (Sharon, p. 492-93). Yet here was Arafat at least a week later—at least a week after the bombs stopped—still indecisive, but nudged over the edge in short order by Habib's and Wazzan's arguments.

Though Habib had avoided negotiating over the telephone before, this was not really a negotiation as much as a reiteration of things everyone already knew. And at the eleventh hour and fifty-ninth minute, there was no time for the usual routine of Wazzan shuttling back and forth between Habib and Arafat carrying written messages.

240 Captured, remains, too late: Shultz memo to the President, August 17, 1982, "Habib Mission: Focus on Prisoners," 8224657, p. 1; Habib letter to PLO "U.S. Requirement for In-

formation," August 11, 1982, in Yuzo, p. 149-50; Johnston cable Beirut 5529, 191655Z Aug 82, par. 2A; "PLO, Lebanon make new demands," *Clearwater Sun,* 8-15-82; "Habib brings new peace proposals to Israel," *St. Petersburg Times,* 8-15-82. One of the captives was a pilot shot down on the first day of the invasion; the other had been taken from his observation post August 16 ("P.L.O., Set to Pull Out, Frees 2 Israelis," *The New York Times,* 8-21-82). Some press reports incorrectly said that all nine of the soldiers were killed in 1978. The Israelis were willing to consider trading the 300-or-so Syrian POWs they held for the one pilot Syria held (Shultz, p. 73). Begin originally said he would withhold final acceptance of the Habib plan until the pilot and the remains were returned; on August 15 he went ahead and accepted the plan but said it could not be implemented until they were returned.

240 US was concerned: Habib 8-18-82 cable Beirut 5490, quoted in State 233655, 192321Z Aug 82. The letter was addressed to Wazzan, but its audience was the PLO. Within a week, Israel started releasing "sizable" numbers of the 7,000 Palestinian and other detainees it had held in southern Lebanon since the invasion began. The Israelis declined to specify a reason for the release, saying the timing of the release was "a pure coincidence" ("Israelis Say Some Seized in Lebanon Are Being Freed," *The New York Times,* 8-26-82). A State Department official said four months later that the prisoners discussed in Habib's letter got little attention at the department. He could not cite any specific American intercession on their behalf ("America's Broken Pledge to the PLO," *The Washington Post,* 12-19-82).

240 Bodies on Shabbat: Hill 7-23-94; Draper 4-13-93; Draper note on draft of this chapter; "For 2 Israelis, Ordeal Ends Amid Smiles," *The New York Times,* 8-21-82. Jewish law prohibits touching the dead on the Sabbath ("P.L.O., Set to Pull Out, Frees 2 Israelis," *The New York Times,* 8-21-82). The two captives were released around 5:15 P.M.

241 Breakthrough: Sharon, p. 492-93; *Commentary,* "Lebanon, The Case for the War," 10-82; Hill 7-12-95; Dillon 5-9-94; Schiff and Ya'ari, p. 224; Seale, p. 391; Bavly & Salpeter, p. 108-9; Cobban in McDermott, p. 214-16. See note "Because Arafat" above for a quote of and remarks about Sharon's explanation of what finally broke the impasse.

15 Sail Away

242 Heavy superstructure: "P.L.O. Starts One-Way Trip Out of West Beirut," *The New York Times,* 8-22-82

242 French arrive: "P.L.O. Troops Begin Pullout in Beirut; French Enter City," *The New York Times,* 8-22-82; "French Paratroopers Land at Beirut Port—City is Reviving," *The New York k Times,* 8-21-82; Sehulster 12-10-01; Fisk, p. 336; "P.L.O., Set to Pull Out, Frees 2 Israelis, *The New York Times,* 8-21-82. The plan for the LAF to secure the port prior to the arrival of the French was decided on August 17 (Johnston cable Beirut 5462, 171550Z Aug 82, par. 1A). A few days later, *The New York Times* reported that the Israelis were displeased about "the tardy arrival of the Lebanese the first day—they were said to have overslept" ("Israelis Complain That Guerrillas Are Being Allowed to Violate Pact," *The New York Times,* 8-24-82).

242 Tenuous: Johnston 12-4-96

242 Amphitheater: Johnston cable Beirut 5462, 171550Z Aug 82

243 Could snipe: According to a source who asked not to be identified by name

243 Barged, fingers: Habib interview with Tueni

243 Spiffed up: Schiff & Ya'ari, p. 227; "P.L.O. Troops Begin Pullout in Beirut; French Enter City," *The New York Times,* 8-22-82

243 PLO looks like: Hill 7-23-94. Among the criticisms of the IDF often voiced by American Marines working with Habib is that the IDF soldiers were unkempt (e.g., Johnston 12-4-96; Mead 6-5-94).

243 As they rode: "P.L.O. Troops Begin Pullout in Beirut; French Enter City," *The New York Times,* 8-22-82

243 Noise, bullets: "More P.L.O. Forces Leave West Beirut Despite a Problem," *The New York Times,* 8-23-82; "West Beirut Bids Farewell to P.L.O.," *The New York Times,* 8-23-82. These casualty figures are just for the first day of the evacuation.

243 Today 397: Habib cable Beirut 05921, 012000Z Sep 82; "P.L.O., Set to Pull Out, Frees 2 Israelis," *The New York Times,* 8-21-82; "P.L.O. Troops Begin Pullout in Beirut; French Enter City," *The New York Times,* 8-22-82; Fisk, p. 334

243 Obstructing: Shultz, p. 78

243 PLO has lost: "P.L.O. Troops Begin Pull-out in Beirut; French Enter City," *The New York Times,* 8-22-82

243-44 Gift: "Sharon: 'I Wanted Them Out of Beirut; I Got What I Wanted,'" *The Washington Post,* 8-29-82

244 Spokesman: "P.L.O. Troops Begin Pullout in Beirut; French Enter City," *The New York Times,* 8-22-82

244 Expulsion medal: Schiff & Ya'ari, p. 227. Sharon's first association with yellow was the yellow stars that the Nazis forced Jews to wear.

244 Pretty good: Draper 5-4-93

244 Jeeps, no more vehicles: Gaucher 5-15-94; Lewis' 8-22-82 cable Tel Aviv 12774, quoted in State 237229, 240516Z Aug 82; "More P.L.O. Forces Leave West Beirut Despite a Problem," *The New York Times,* 8-23-82. Gaucher recalled 10-12 jeeps, Lewis' cable said 13, and news reports at the time said 20 or 21. Lewis' cable doesn't say whether the French found any weapons. Schiff & Ya'ari (p. 228) say that French troops had removed RPGs hidden inside the jeeps. Habib's call sign corrected per an FSO at Yarze who asked not to be identified by name.

244 Begin was furious: Shultz, p. 78; Hill 7-23-94

244 New era: Lewis 8-22-82 cable Tel Aviv 12774, quoted in State 237229, 240516Z Aug 82

244-45 Dot and comma, simple solution: Habib cable Beirut 05599, 221055Z Aug 82, par. 2-5; Lewis 8-22-82 cable Tel Aviv 12774, quoted in State 237229, 240516Z Aug 82; Hill 7-23-94. An Israeli official said, "Maybe a jeep is not a weapon. But they've also been taking RPG rocket launchers, and perhaps they will try for a Sagger [missile] and then they have a real weapon, perhaps to be followed by a cannon and a tank" ("Israelis Complain That Guerrillas Are Being Allowed to Violate Pact," *The New York Times,* 8-24-82). He was willing to bar jeeps from future voyages, but was not willing to disrupt momentum by unloading these.

245 Matter of face: Lewis 8-22-82 cable Tel Aviv 12774, quoted in State 237229, 240516Z Aug 82; Hill 7-23-94

245 Tell Israel, there's no way, would be es-

corting: Shultz, p. 78-79; Hill 7-23-94; Lewis ADST oral history

245 We thought: Lewis ADST oral history

245 9 P.M., a year later: Shultz, p. 79; a diplomat who asked not to be identified by name; "Lebanon Assembly Elects a Rightist to the Presidency," *The New York Times,* 8-24-82; "Israelis Complain That Guerrillas Are Being Allowed to Violate Pact," *The New York Times,* 8-24-82. Habib's plan called for all movements to occur during daylight hours. The jeeps continued to collect dust in a warehouse for many years longer.

246 I want escorts: Johnston 12-4-96; Johnston cable Beirut 5560, 201640Z Aug 82, par. 5; a diplomat who asked not to be identified by name. A French gunboat had escorted the first ship out on August 21 ("P.L.O. Troops Begin Pullout in Beirut; French Enter City," *The New York Times,* 8-22-82). This actually was not the first time the subject had come up. When told August 10 that the US might provide Navy escorts for evacuation ships, Begin responded, "Against whom? Us?" But he did not object (Lewis cable Tel Aviv 12139, 101505Z Aug 82, par. 6). The American military was alerted to prepare for the *contingency* of escorting ships (USCINCEUR cable to JCS, 141013Z Aug 82, par. B2C2A), but as of August 21 the Secretary of Defense was still saying that it would provide escorts "if asked to do so" (SECDEF cable 210006Z Aug 82, A49).

246 Eyeball distance, very presence: Johnston 12-17-98. The Israeli gunboats were a couple of miles offshore, but Johnston says, "two miles doesn't look like much at sea."

246 Sharon instructed: Schiff in McDermott & Skjelsbaek, p. 200

246 I want two: Smith 6-14-94 and 11-25-96; Johnston 12-17-98. Habib quote compiled from Smith's two tellings of the same episode. As a precaution against the Israelis sinking the evacuation ships, Habib had arranged to have five Greek soldiers aboard each voyage (according to an official involved who asked not to be identified by name). Mead (11-25-96) says that what Habib requested was "precisely the right thing to do" in the situation. The PLO was not the only one thinking about Israeli strikes on evacuees. *The New York Times* quoted an Israeli woman saying, "We should shoot down their planes when they leave Cyprus" ("West Beirut Siege Is Affecting Israelis' Self-Image," 8-23-82).

246 Asked Begin to withdraw, macho: Lewis ADST oral history

247 Brief statement, almost caused: Lewis ADST oral history

247 Crew-served: Dillon letter to the author 9-11-98

247 One individual: "Lebanon: Plan for the PLO Evacuation From West Beirut," *Current Policy* No. 415, August 1982, par. 17, p. 9. Among the many reasons for not letting the PLO take more weaponry was that the ship captains were nervous about having weapons aboard their ships.

247 Captains: According to a participant who asked not to be identified by name

247 RPGs, objected: Habib interview with Tueni; Smith 6-14-94. "What the hell do you mean, 'Not an individual weapon,'" said PLO negotiator Abu Walid. "That's how they're armed: A man carries either an automatic rifle or he carries an RPG" (interview with Tueni).

247 Might consider: Habib cable Beirut 05703, 251845Z Aug 82, par. 4

247 Authorized twelve: Hill 7-23-94.

247-48 *Alkyon* and RPGs: Johnston 12-4-96 and 12-17-98; Hill 7-23-94; Frank, p. 18. Kabuki is a highly stylized ancient Japanese theatrical form. Johnston may have taken someone else aboard with him. Whatever procedures may have been in place before, once the 800 US Marines landed on August 25, no RPGs were allowed on any ship. Each evacuee was checked to make sure he carried no unauthorized weapons. When one PLO fighter on August 25 refused to give up his RPG, Lebanese soldiers simply blocked his access to the ship until he gave it up (Hammel, p. 23-24).

The Israelis complained also that the PLO was not turning its heavy weapons over to the LAF as Habib's plan required. They were right. The PLO instead did exactly what the Lebanese government had always feared: They gave most of the weapons that they couldn't sell or carry out to leftist Muslim guerrillas of West Beirut with whom they had previously fought side by side ("New Withdrawal Goes Without a Hitch," *The New York Times*, 8-26-82; "Israeli Worry: Arms Given to Leftists," *The New York Times*, 8-31-82; DIA Washington DC//JSI-5A// memo to USCINCEUR VIAHINGEN GE 202204Z Aug 82, par. 2D). The Israelis complained that the PLO had not turned over any

heavy weapons to the LAF. Draper reminded them that "the LAF didn't really want the heavy weapons," but he and Habib then leaned on Lebanese officials to get moving on it (Habib cable Beirut 5687, 260712Z Aug 82, par. 6; Habib cable Beirut 5703, 260715Z Aug 82, par 6). A convoy of Syrian civilian trucks was due in to pick up the first batch of overland evacuees, and Sharon tried to use the lack of arms surrenders "as an excuse" to keep that convoy out. Habib got Sharon to OK the convoy in exchange for Habib's promise to work hard on the matter. Habib had the French check the incoming trucks to assuage Israeli concerns that the trucks might be bringing in weapons (Habib cable Beirut 5721, 280925Z Aug 82, par. 4, 6; Habib cable Beirut 05703, 251845Z Aug 82, par. 4, 6).

248 Trojan horse: Lewis 4-10-94

248 Scheming to leave: Lewis 8-22-82 cable Tel Aviv 12774, quoted in State 237229, 240516Z Aug 82, par. 5; "Israelis Complain That Guerrillas Are Being Allowed to Violate Pact," *The New York Times*, 8-24-82. Though the Israelis had withdrawn their demand for identities in mid-August, they resurrected the demand once the evacuation began (Shultz memo to the President, August 16, 1982, "Habib Mission: Close to Final Agreement," 82038400007, p. 1; Lewis ADST oral history, says the Cabinet withdrew Sharon's demand for lists of names August 14).

248 Processing of evacuees, tables: Johnston 12-17-98; Frank, p. 17; Hammel, p. 24

248 Poor verification, best: Hill 7-23-94; "Israelis Complain That Guerrillas Are Being Allowed to Violate Pact," *The New York Times*, 8-24-82

248 Madhouse: Habib interview with Tueni; "P.L.O. Starts One-Way Trip Out of West Beirut," *The New York Times*, 8-22-82; "Israel Pledges to Take Steps For a General Mideast Peace," *The New York Times*, 8-23-82). Most PLO fighters had a nom de guerre beginning with "Abu," which is Arabic for "father of" ("To Fend Off Cabin Fever, Long Walks [at the Mall]," *The New York Times*, 10-23-98). Arafat, for instance, was known as Abu Ammar (e.g., Fisk, p. 330).

248 Definitions: Habib cable Beirut 05921, 012000Z Sep 82. The Israelis claimed that some women and children were going out disguised as men "to confuse the numbers" ("Israelis Complain That Guerrillas Are Being Al-

lowed to Violate Pact," *The New York Times,* 8-24-82).

248 Pakistanis: Gaucher 5-15-94; note to author by Dillon 1-25-99; diplomat who asked not to be identified by name; Fisk, p. 295, says the PLO had its share of Third World military trainees.

248 Legionnaires: Dillon ADST oral history

249 Become part: Mikdadi, p. 74. Examples of Habib's involvement are discussions he had with Bashir and with Sa'eb Salaam July 30 about the Muslims' vehement objections to Bashir's candidacy (Habib cable Beirut 04979, 301430Z Jul 82).

249 Energy, opening bells: He had proposed to President Sarkis that he stay on for an extra year, until after things settled down, but Sarkis was too sick and exhausted (Dean 5-12-94). The election was a longstanding concern of Habib's and everyone else's. It figured strongly in some of his discussions in 1981. A few days before the invasion began, Habib had dinner in New York with his friend Ghassan Tueni, the Lebanese ambassador to the UN, for the express purpose of picking Tueni's brain about who the next president of Lebanon might be. "I detected then that he was not as anti-Bashir Gemayel as I thought he would be," says Tueni, who describes himself as having been "violently against Bashir" (Tueni 11-15-95). Dillon (11-5-96) perceived that, once the evacuation had moved from concept to reality, Habib was even more interested in the election than in the hour-by-hour operations of the evacuation.

249 If anyone, all of Lebanon: Dillon 11-16-96 and 11-5-96, ADST oral history; Draper 12-22-94. Though, as events turned out, there was no opportunity to really test the authenticity of the changes of heart that Habib and Dillon saw in Bashir, the few indications that there are do tend to support it. Bashir certainly had disappointed the Israelis throughout the siege by refusing to do what they expected of him. And when Begin pressed him in early September to quickly sign a peace treaty with Israel, Bashir refused (e.g., Schiff & Ya'ari, p. 233-36). After the election, Bashir's statements were conciliatory ("New Withdrawal Goes Without a Hitch," *The New York Times,* 8-26-82). Habib and Sarkis arranged for him to meet with Sa'ab Salaam and other Muslim leaders and he "more or less made his peace" with them, says Ghassan Tueni (11-15-95). Lewis says that by September 14 Bashir "had begun a healing

process to bring all the various factions together and had by this time managed to gather considerable popular support from both the Muslims and the Christians" (Lewis ADST oral history).

249 Worsen: Habib cable Beirut 04979, 301430Z Jul 82; Mikdadi, p. 74; "Christians Clash With Syrian Units on Lebanese Road," *The New York Times,* 8-25-82

249 Anathema: Tueni 11-15-95. One reason suggested for the timing of Sharon's invasion of Lebanon is that "the deed had to be done before Lebanon's presidential elections," i.e., to ensure that Bashir won (Seale, p. 374, 385). Indeed, clearing the way for that election was prominent in Sharon's first conversation with Habib about it, December 5, 1981 (Brown cable Tel Aviv 18681, 051155 Dec 81).

Thinking that Saudi views would carry weight with Lebanese Muslims, Habib arranged for Bashir to fly secretly to Saudi Arabia to try to enlist their support (or at least quiet their opposition). Habib's argument was that, while Bashir certainly had been in cahoots with the Israelis lately, he had been in cahoots earlier with the Syrians and was now ready to be his own man (Tueni 11-15-95) This support was important, says one Lebanese official, "because the fact that Phil Habib was behind this carried credibility with those who knew Phil, and particularly Arabs." The Saudis warned Bashir to keep his distance from the Israelis, but agreed to mute their opposition (Tueni 11-15-95; Fisk, p. 279; Bavly, p. 101; Pakradouni, p. 247). Bashir made this trip to Saudi Arabia at the beginning of July. Bashir and the Syrians had been allies in 1975-76 but then Bashir found it more expedient to ally himself with the Israelis ("Victor in Lebanon Assailed in Syria," *The New York Times,* 8-24-82).

249 Don't do that: "Election Under the Gun," *Time,* 9-6-82, p. 32

249 Walid, going to win: Crocker 4-28-94

249 Would have taken: Tueni 11-15-95. Partition of Lebanon was always a fear for Habib and many others. There wasn't a lot holding Lebanon together in the first place. The fear was that the Christians and the Muslims would secede from one another so each could have their own country without having to suffer the other.

249 Notable: "Lebanon Assembly Elects a Rightist to the Presidency," *The New York Times,* 8-24-82

249 Contingency fund, paying off: This is all according to Hill 7-16-94, who adds that "clandestine US support for factions or parties that were pro-West or pro-democracy" was not unusual: "that's how stuff got done. It wasn't just America. This is the way votes get cast in OAU [Organization of African Unity] sessions. People get paid off." But in this case there came a point when "no amount of money was going to change those people" because the threats and killings trumped money.

249 Had plenty: Tueni 11-15-95; Dillon 11-5-96.

250 Serious doubt: Draper 12-18-94. Draper adds that, if the election were held, the most likely outcome was impasse. Washington expected that, as president, Bashir would "give priority to asking the Syrians to leave the Bekaa Valley," something Assad would be loathe to do ("Washington Hails Lebanon Outcome," *The New York Times,* 8-24-82).

250 Dillon swung: Draper 12-18-94. Dillon (11-5-96) says that Americans let anti-Bashir Christians know that the US liked Bashir "in a very subtle way, so that it was deniable." Tueni disagrees with Draper's version, saying, "This is not how Lebanese elections happen. That's not true. There are always a few stray hats, one or two members of parliament willing to spend some money to make sure that they're on board. But I don't think that money is what got Bashir elected. He was elected because of the Israeli presence and massive Israeli pressure. This is like getting elected during the German occupation: You didn't have to buy French members of parliament" (Tueni 11-15-95).

250 Hatfields: Hill 7-23-94. Shi'a and Sunni are the two main branches of Islam.

250 Deputy shot: Both incidents occurred in Syrian-controlled areas and, Habib said, "there can be little doubt over who is responsible" for them. He arranged for both Washington and the Saudis to emphasize to Assad that "this kind of blatant political violence" was intolerable (Habib 8-22-82 cable Beirut 5602, quoted in State 236805, 232242Z Aug 82). The deputy shot in the back said, the day after Habib sent his cable, that his attackers were two of Bashir's Phalange thugs who had come to his home to demand that he vote for Bashir ("Victor in Lebanon Assailed in Syria," *The New York Times,* 8-24-82). Washington expected that, as president, Bashir would "give priority to asking the Syrians to leave the Bekaa Valley," something

Assad would be loathe to do ("Washington Hails Lebanon Outcome," *The New York Times,* 8-24-82).

250 Escorts: Schiff & Ya'ari, p. 233

250 Seventeen homes: This was in the first two and a half days after the election ("New Withdrawal Goes Without a Hitch," *The New York Times,* 8-26-82); "Lebanon Assembly Elects a Rightist to the Presidency," *The New York Times,* 8-24-82; "Christians Clash With Syrian Units on Lebanese Road," *The New York Times,* 8-25-82).

250 Delighted: Smith 6-21-94. Seale writes that, after winning, Bashir paid a courtesy call first on outgoing president Sarkis and then on Habib, "who he knew had softened Muslim opposition to him and saved him from total dependence on Israel" (Seale, p. 389).

250 Celebrations, wanging away: Smith 6-21-94. One person who was not celebrating was Druze leader Walid Jumblatt. He had always feared that Bashir would have him killed. After the election, Habib arranged for Ryan Crocker to drive Walid through Israeli lines, Bashir's lines, and Syrian lines to safety. He then slipped out of the country and flew to Paris (Crocker 4-28-94; Tueni 11-15-95).

250 Unit refused: The Palestinian unit in question, the PLA, considered the LAF too pro-Christian and feared that, if they turned their positions over to the LAF, the LAF would then allow in one of their Christian enemies, the Kataeb (i.e., Phalange) militia (Shultz, p. 80).

251 Needed more soldiers: Habib cable Beirut 5723, 271246Z Aug 82, par. 7. Habib's plan originally called for the US Marines and the rest of the MNF to land "approximately" August 26-28. The Israelis wanted to keep them out as long as possible, but Habib decided he needed more bodies by August 25. "Israel will object to our coming in before 50 percent are gone," Habib said, "but you can't *get* 50 percent out without the MNF in here" (Hill 7-23-94).

251 Sehulster driving, tacsat, pushing the button: Sehulster 6-23-94 and 11-24-96; Hill 7-23-94. Habib had been unavailable when Sehulster got back from his tour, so Draper had already reported Sehulster's observations to Washington before Habib learned of them. Habib thought that Shultz, after seeing the report, would go along with his request (letter from Sehulster to the author 1-12-97). In the

end, the French and the LAF deployed along the Green Line.

251 Can't just sit, galled: Shultz, p. 80-81; Sehulster 6-23-94; Hill 7-23-94. The Marines on the ground agreed with Habib, says Mead, and shared his embarrassment at being restricted to the port while the French and Italians were out around town (Mead 6-5-94). But it was not their decision to make. Mead said that "I had received only three orders during the whole operation. [They] were to go in, to stay off the Green Line, and to come out!" (Frank, p. 21).

251-52 I won't accept: Hill 7-23-94; Shultz, p. 80-81

252 Livid, furor: Shultz, p. 81. Sharon finally approved deployment of the French at the checkpoints along the Green Line August 25 (Hill 7-23-94).

252 Get the president: Hill 7-23-94. Sharon eventually agreed to allow the French to join the LAF along the Green Line (Habib cable Beirut 5723, 271246Z Aug 82, par. 3-4).

252 Disclose the locations: "Lebanon: Plan for the PLO Evacuation From West Beirut," Current Policy No. 415, August 1982, par. 19, p. 9

252-53 Gotta find out, drive a car: Smith 6-14-94 and 6-21-94; Draper 9-19-97. Smith's only real scare was when he heard an oddly familiar sound approaching from another street and looked up to see a World War Two Russian T34 tank, controlled by one of the city's militias, clanking around the corner toward him. Only in Beirut.

253 Waiting to greet marines: Sehulster 7-12-94; an FSO at Yarze who asked not to be identified by name. Sehulster vaguely recalls that that the reason for holding Habib back was the Marines' need to keep the actual landing simple, and Habib's security entourage was a complication they could do without. The FSO vaguely recalls that the reason was that the first Marines ashore would be the grunts, and that there wouldn't be any commander ashore at first to greet Habib.

253-54 Habib at port: Sehulster 7-12-94; Mead 11-25-96; Mead 6-5-94

254 Three tanks, allow to stay: Mead 6-5-94 and 12-6-98; Draper 5-4-93; Johnston 12-4-96 and 12-17-98; Sehulster 12-7-98; Habib interview with Tueni. "Menacing" is Sehulster's

word. Mead, the Marine commander on the ground, says the corporal acted on his own but had Mead's full support. Quite apart from whatever threat the tanks posed to the ships and evacuees—and recollections vary on whether they posed a threat—Mead felt that their presence around the Marines compromised the neutrality that was the Marines' only real weapon. "The port was ours," he says. "They were supposed to have been the hell out of there. Then they were abrasive as normal. So from the first day, we said, 'Wrong-o. You're not going to do that to the United States Marines, because here's what you agreed to. Your word is no good, but with us it better be good.'" Everyone who tells this story has a different recollection of how it ended. The ending written is based mostly on Johnston's account. Habib had by this time returned to Yarze, so his talks with the Israelis were not in person.

254 Cabbage: Mead 6-5-94

254 IDF gagged: Lewis ADST oral history

254 Incandescent: This diplomat asked not to be identified by name

255 Hand grenades: Johnston 12-17-98

255 Instructed the Marines: Frank, p. 17

255 Johnston-PLO meetings: Johnston 12-17-98. Johnston was later a general.

255 Showmanship, Fiats: Johnston 12-4-96; Smith 6-14-94; Habib interview with Tueni

255 His feelings: Draper 5-4-93. A week before the evacuation began, the American military expected about 7,000 combatants to be evacuated (USCINCEUR cable to JCS, 141013Z Aug 82, par. B2). About double that number went out.

255 Nearly every day: Mead 6-5-94

255-56 Fielding problems: Draper 5-4-93

256 Taxi driver: "Israelis Watching on TV Wonder if It Is All Over," *The New York Times,* 8-22-82; Draper 4-13-93 and 5-4-93. There are enough differences between Draper's account and the *Times'* account that they could possibly be describing two separate incidents.

256 Amal itself captured: Habib cable Beirut 05918, 011630Z Sep 82. Habib encouraged Berri to tell his followers that, with Lebanon now turning a new page in its history, the time for revenge and retribution was over. He sent

word to the Israelis to keep sightseers and journalists out of West Beirut. He declined to tell
anybody who his source was for the information about the fate of the eighteen men.

256 Details, brave: Sources who asked not to
be identified by name. Many ship owners declined before one in Cyprus agreed to charter
his old ships, which one participant describes
as "rust buckets," for a hefty price.

256 Anxiety: This source asked not to be identified by name.

256 Over their shoulders: Smith 6-14-94;
Draper 5-4-93; and another colleague of
Habib's who asked not to be identified by
name. The operation's better ships were available because late August was toward the end
of the Mediterranean cruising season, and the
war in Lebanon had cut into their business by
scaring off would-be tourists. The Saudis paid
for the ships and the other costs of the evacuation.

256 Two-thirds, mattresses: A colleague of
Habib's who asked not to be identified by name

256-57 Workhorse, Sudan: Habib cable Beirut
[no number available], 261905Z Aug 82

257 Standby: Habib cable Beirut 5766,
280817Z Aug 82; an official who asked not to
be identified by name

257 Certified: Habib cable Beirut 5845,
301938Z Aug 82, par. 6

257 Equipped: Yuzo, p. 159

257 Flora, compromise: Draper 5-4-93; Habib
cable Beirut 5721, 280925Z Aug 82, par. 8;
Habib cable Beirut 5687, 260712Z Aug 82,
par. 6; Habib cable Beirut 05703, 251845Z
Aug 82, par. 6; Habib cable Beirut 05922,
012010Z Sep 82, par. 3; Habib 8-23-82 cable
Beirut 5647, quoted in State 236898, 232316Z
Aug 82; Habib cable Beirut 5877, 021006Z
Sep 82

257 Radiated, whoops: Crocker 4-28-94

257 Phone Marge: "A quiet Belmont man is
the hero in Beirut," Peninsula Times Tribune,
8-28-82; Marjorie Habib 11-18-98

257 All business: Hill 7-19-95

257-58 Looked awful, twenty-two-hour, hides:
This source asked not to be identified by name;
Hill 7-23-94

258 Special treatment, Arab solution, re-equip:

Hill 7-21-94; Lewis cable Tel Aviv 12139,
101505Z Aug 82, par. 1-4, 10; Shultz memo
to the President, August 16, 1982, "Habib Mission: Close to Final Agreement,"
82038400007, p. 1; Habib 7-24-92 cable Jidda
5532, quoted in State 206640 TOSEC 110050,
250019Z Jul 82. Officially, the Syrian troops
were in Lebanon not as the Syrian army per
se, but as the Arab Defense Forces, i.e., the
Arab League's designated military presence in
Lebanon.

258 Burdensome: Habib cable Beirut 5766,
280817Z Aug 82 (par. 5).

258 Idiot lecture: This FSO asked not to be
identified by name; Schiff and Ya'ari, p. 109-
160, particularly 137, 159-60

259 First convoy: The first convoy was supposed to have left a few days earlier, but fighting along that highway forced Habib to put
several batches of Syria-bound evacuees on
ships instead. This meant that a lot of evacuees were arriving in an entirely different part
of the country from where the Syrians had been
set up to receive them. Habib worried whether
Syria would continue to accept more shiploads.
But things had settled down enough by the 27th
to start the trucks rolling ("Israelis Say Some
Seized in Lebanon Are Being Freed" and "600
Guerrillas in Al Fatah Force Reach Syrian Port,"
The New York Times, 8-26-82; Habib cable
Beirut 5766, 280817Z Aug 82). There were
conflicting accounts of who was fighting whom
along the route: The Israelis and Phalange each
said the other was fighting the Syrians. Sea
voyages were simpler and quicker. Doing more
sea voyages enabled Habib to finish the evacuation two days ahead of schedule.

259 Gunner: An observer who asked not to be
identified by name; Sehulster letter to author
1-22-99

259 Thumbing: Transcript "Recorded radio
conversation between Mr. Eagleburger and
Amb. Habib, July 7/82, 0900 hours" 8218991,
p. 5. At the time of this discussion, it was un-
decided whether the PLO would be leaving
by land or by sea. So the discussion was
couched in terms of what would happen if the
PLO (and, by implication, other evacuees) went
out by land.

259 Kimche: NEA Veliotes memo to S/S Bremer,
9218993, 7-7-82, "Recorded Radio Conversation with Amb. Habib, July 7, 1982, at 1420
hours," p. 3. At a meeting Habib had with
Kimche and Sharon the next day, that assur-

ance was reiterated (Hill 7-10-94).

259 Became part: "Lebanon: Plan for the PLO Evacuation From West Beirut," *Current Policy No. 415*, August 1982, par. 16, p. 9

259 Finger, squad car: Hill 7-23-94; Shultz, p. 82; Habib interview with Tueni; "Syrian-Led Force Quits West Beirut" and "First Guerrilla Land Convoy Welcomed Warmly in Syria," *The New York Times*, 8-28-82. *The Times* reports that at least one group of IDF soldiers along the route did move out of sight as the convoy went by, though some took off their uniforms and changed into slacks and sports shirts to stand at the roadside and watch. The Israelis brought militia leader Major Sa'ad Haddad, who had acted as the Israelis' surrogate in southern Lebanon for six years, up to Beirut to watch on August 30. He stood at Hazmiye Circle giving each group of passing Syrians the finger (Fisk, p. 349; *Time*, 9-6-82, p. 32). The records and memories are unclear on whether the flags were out on just one occasion or two and whether it was during the first convoy and/ or second.

259-60 Flags, tank battalion, deliberate, absolutely refusing: Hill 7-23-94; Lee 10-2-94; Smith 6-14-94; Sehulster 12-7-98; Seale, p. 389, citing his interview with Habib 9-27-86; Habib interview with Tueni. Sharon's rationale, Habib inferred, was that he was not going to have his troops hide, and that he wanted his troops to see their enemy in person. Habib's plan originally called for the IDF to "vacate" the route when the convoys passed, but he reluctantly agreed to change the wording to "clear" the route on condition that the Israelis honor Kimche's agreement that the IDF be "out of sight" along the road (Lewis cable Tel Aviv 12139, 101505Z Aug 82, par. 3). This change was Lewis' recommendation.

On August 18 Habib's MNF liaisons met with their IDF liaison officers to go over various particulars, including that the IDF would be "out of sight" (Johnston cable Beirut 5485, 181530Z Aug 82, par. 1). Draper reported on August 26, the day before the first convoy moved, that "we now had an absolute commitment from the Israelis that when the convoys leave Beirut there will be . . . no Israelis in view from the road" (Habib cable Beirut 5712, 261531Z Aug 82, par. 4). An IDF spokesman reiterated the same day, August 26, that the evacuees would not be able to see Israelis along the way. Habib reportedly conveyed to Lebanese leaders the same day Sharon's further assurances that there would be no

Phalangists along the highway ("Overland Pullout of P.L.O. Is Scheduled to Start Today," *The New York Times*, 8-27-82).

Though the IDF presence along the route clearly violated the spirit of Habib's understanding with the Israelis, it may have capitalized on a loophole in the letter of the final text of the plan, which talks about *PLO* (not PLA or Syrian) overland convoys: "In those instances when convoys of departing PLO personnel pass through positions of the Israeli Defense Forces, whether in the Beirut area or elsewhere in Lebanon, the Israeli Defense Forces will clear the route for the temporary period in which the convoy is running" ("Lebanon: Plan for the PLO Evacuation From West Beirut," *Current Policy No. 415*, August 1982, par. 16, p. 9).

260 Confronting commanders, lightened: Smith 6-14-94; Hill 7-23-94. Palestinian and Syrian evacuees did have to drive by some flags and IDF soldiers. Some evacuees made obscene gestures at them, others smiled and waved, some Israelis waved back (Fisk, p. 347).

260 Galerie Samaan: Gaucher 5-15-94

260 At this stage: Sehulster 12-7-98

260-61 Mossad, Drori: Sehulster 7-12-94 and 12-7-98. A few days earlier, Drori had told Habib and Draper he was concerned that the PLO intended to give the Syrians a lot of its vehicles and heavy equipment to take out and hold for them to reclaim later. Draper reminded Drori of "Sharon's view that PLO equipment was better out of Beirut by whatever means than to remain behind." Drori "reluctantly accepted" that answer at the time, Habib wrote (Habib cable Beirut 5687, 260712Z Aug 82, par. 6). Sehulster adds that it's one thing to sort out a problem like this at the staging area, but once an evacuation actually begins, any interruption is a major *dis*ruption that can easily be the end of it. He doesn't remember whether any vehicles were ever actually pulled out or not. Habib had never seen any reason to thank people for doing their jobs.

261 Sent word, stuck with: Hill 7-23-94; Shultz, p. 81; Yuzo, p. 159-60. American defense intelligence said that "Arafat has demonstrated the ability to maintain internal discipline and to move quickly and ruthlessly against those who act against his wishes." They also believed that, if Arafat were assassinated, the evacuation would probably collapse (DIA Washington DC//JSI-5A// memo to USCINCEUR VAIHINGEN GE 202204Z Aug 82, par. 2B and 3).

261 Expulsion going: "The Marines Have Landed," *Time,* 9-6-82

261 Responsible, watch over: Hill 7-23-94; Habib interview with Tueni. Arafat's ship was not the first to travel with Greek troops aboard. They went along on earlier voyages as well (according to an FSO who asked not to be identified by name).

261-62 I won't change, Arafat's jeeps: Shultz, p. 82; Hill 7-23-94 and 7-19-95

262 Instructions: Mead 6-5-94

262 Wazzan, tricolor: Johnston 12-17-98; Habib cable Beirut 05884, 010743Z Sep 82; Fisk, p. 347-48; "P.L.O. Leader Is Mobbed By Well-Wishers at Port," *The New York Times,* 8-31-82; Randal, p. 271; Salem, p. 62

262 Habib resented: Gaucher 5-15-94. Henry had made a similarly effusive display of greeting Sharon a week or two earlier (Johnston 12-4-96 and 12-17-98).

262 Obviously: Habib cable Beirut 05884, 010743Z Sep 82

263 Checkpoint 54: Johnston 12-17-98; Frank, p. 18; Habib cable Beirut 05884, 010743Z Sep 82; Mead letter to author 1-19-99. Why were so few Marines assigned to such a crucial and potentially volatile task as receiving Arafat? Understated strength was part of the Marines' whole psychology strategy on this mission: A large force at the gate might have been interpreted as a sign that the Marines were intimidated and might have inspired the crowd to respond aggressively. Besides, the dozen could load their weapons in a flash and had plenty of big sticks close at hand if needed (Sehulster letter to author 1-22-99; Johnston 12-17-98). Mead adds that Checkpoint 54 was by design quite narrow and therefore did not require more than a dozen Marines to staff it.

263 Lost somewhere, led Arafat's limo: Fisk, p. 347-48; Johnston 12-17-98; Frank, p. 18; "P.L.O. Leader Is Mobbed By Well-Wishers at Port," *The New York Times,* 8-31-82. Henry told Johnston that Draper had agreed to their being there. Johnston got Draper on the walkie-talkie, saying he knew nothing about any such agreement and that the excessive number of French forces were creating a problem (Frank, p. 18). A series of empty large steel cargo boxes lined the route that Arafat would travel from Checkpoint 54 to the ship. Though the Marines had no idea who had put those boxes

there or why, the boxes had the value of blocking the line of fire that any sniper outside of the port would have. But when Johnston and Mead reconnoitered the route at 4 A.M. in advance of Arafat's arrival, they discovered that some of the boxes had been removed, opening up a superb line of fire. The Marines immediately closed those gaps (Mead letter to author 1-19-99; Johnston 12-17-98).

263 Brook no stunts: Johnston 12-17-98

263 Crosshairs: Gilbert, p. 508. Sharon would later say he regretted not killing Arafat at this moment ("Sharon is Sorry Israel Didn't Kill Arafat in the 80's," *The New York Times,* 2-1-02). Johnston (12-17-98) says, "Had they chosen to pick off Arafat then, it would not have played well with their US allies, if you want to say we were allies in any sense of the word. It would not have been a smart move while Arafat was within our control to have some Israeli knock him off."

263 *Mediterranean Sun:* Habib cable Beirut 05895, 011109Z Sep 82

263 Statistics: Habib cable Beirut 05921, 012000Z Sep 82. Technically, the Syrians were considered Arab Defense Forces.

263 Half-again more: Draper 5-4-93. Sharon had said only a few days earlier that "the PLO terrorists were ten thousand only, with the Syrians included" ("Sharon: 'I Wanted Them Out of Beirut; I Got What I Wanted,'" *The Washington Post,* 8-29-82), yet Habib had evacuated a total of 14,738 Palestinian and Syrian fighters (Habib cable Beirut 05921, 012000Z Sep 82). A week before the evacuation began, the American military expected about 7,000 combatants to be evacuated (USCINCEUR cable to JCS, 141013Z Aug 82,par. B2). The Israelis didn't think he would get more than 12,000 evacuated all told (Draper 5-4-93).

264 Tens of thousands: Habib interview with the author in *The Stanford Magazine,* Spring 1984

264 Not my baby: NEA Veliotes memo to S/S Bremer, 8219693, "Telcon with Habib July 10, 1082 - 1058, p. 5; Hill 7-21-94; Rabb cable Rome 20143, 031740Z Sep 82, par. 15. There are conflicting indications in the record and conflicting recollections among Habib's colleagues about what role, if any, he expected to have after the evacuation was complete. His only firm plans were some naps, some golf, and attending Bashir's inauguration. Draper

would take his place at least for a while. Being retired, he was working for the government on this mission without pay in part because he was just delighted to be active and in part because accepting pay from the State Department might have affected his medical disability pension. The State Department did reimburse him $7,186 in expenses for 1982 (Marjorie Habib 2-27-93; Habib's 1982 tax papers).

264 Heading now: Smith 6-21-94. Smith bowdlerized his account, quoting Habib saying "blanking business."

264 Came swarming, dinner and dancing: Draper 5-4-93; Pascoe 6-4-94

265 Walked lighter: Grove 6-4-94

265 Order of Cedars: Dillon 11-16-96 and 5-9-94; Pakradouni, p. 255; Parker 11-3-96; Habib interview with the author 12-21-83 transcript p. 61. Parker, for one, had received the medal when he ended his term as US ambassador to Lebanon in 1978, and Dillon would receive it when his term ended in 1983. Pakradouni quotes Sarkis' view of Habib's plan, but does not specify when Sarkis articulated it.

16 Foreigners in Combat Boots

266 Phil pulled off: Shultz 9-16-93

266 Miracles in the Middle East: Draper 12-22-94

266 Thirty days: Draper 5-4-93; Mead 6-5-94. The Lebanese wanted them to stay longer; Washington wanted them out sooner. Habib resisted both tugs (Draper 12-2-94; Draper 5-4-93; Mead 6-5-94; Hill 7-23-94). The final plan called for the MNF to depart Beirut "not later than 30 days after arrival" (US Department of State *Current Policy* No. 415, August 1982, "Lebanon: Plan for the PLO Evacuaton from West Beirut," p. 7).

266 Nervous: Eagleburger 7-3-93; Mead 6-5-94

266 Habib furious: Mead 6-5-94. Habib had said in a 1976 speech that, when the American military was necessary in hot spots to reduce tensions, "We should be careful not to increase the chance of war by a premature

withdrawal" (*Charleston* [South Carolina] *News & Courier,* 1-31-76).

266 Mead to Weinberger: Mead 6-5-94

267 Backed off and bowed: Dillon 11-5-96

267 Between September 21 and 26: US Department of State *Current Policy* No. 415, August 1982, "Lebanon: Plan for the PLO Evacuation from West Beirut," p. 10

267 September 10: Hill 7-23-94. Shultz and the French foreign minister reached this agreement on August 29.

267 Resigned himself: Hill 7-23-94. There is a suggestion that Habib may have gone with September 10 just to keep the Defense Department from picking an even earlier date. Once resigned to a September 10 pullout, Habib expressed it as a recommendation (Draper cable Beirut 5959, 031735Z Sep 82; Rome 20044, 031041Z Sep 82; Veliotes memo to Eagleburger, September 3, 1982, 85D251 7516), which Draper calls a tactical move (Draper 12-18-94 and 12-22-94). Draper and Lt. Col. Sehulster observed in early September that the city showed promising signs of returning to normal (Beirut 6021, 041217Z Sep 82; Beirut 5989, 031250Z Sep 82), which suggested that maybe September 10 might not be premature after all. Draper adds that he was instructed by Eagleburger to tell the French and Italians that all three contingents of the MNF would be moving out on the seventeenth day. The French ambassador was upset (note on draft of this chapter).

267 Draper point man: State Department press briefing 9-20-82 (State 265136, 210529Z Sep 82)

267 Bashir's assassination: Dillon ADST oral history; Schiff and Ya'ari, p. 247; Friedman, p. 157-59. No one knows for sure on whose behalf the assassin acted. Though everyone was suspected—even the Israelis and Bashir's own people—the strongest evidence points to Syria (Draper 5-4-93; Dillon ADST oral history).

267 Draper meeting with Begin: Tel Aviv 13875, 151634Z Sep 82; Draper 12-18-94; Draper notes on draft of this chapter. The quotes are not necessarily of the actual words spoken, but of the cable's account of what was said. George Shultz, like Draper, was prepared to accept the possibility that "some limited moves by the IDF could well have been constructive for the security situation" (State

260100, 160304Z Sep 82, par. 5), the key word being *limited*. The US had first raised inquiries about Israel's moves through the Foreign Ministry prior to Draper's meeting with Begin.

267-68 Draper arrival in Beirut: Draper cable Beirut 06289, 152105Z Sep 82; Draper ADST oral history; Draper 5-4-93 and 12-18-94. The Kahan Commission reports fire coming from Sabra and Shatila as the IDF advanced on them, but apparently most of the shooting that Draper observed was by the IDF. Sharon phoned Begin from near the camps around 10 A.M. and told him there was "no resistance in Beirut." He and his top aides drafted an announcement that "the entry of the I.D.F. forces was executed without resistance" (Kahan, p. 9).

268 Begin lied: Draper 12-18-94, also 5-4-93; Draper ADST oral history; Draper cable Beirut 6289, 152105Z Sep 82. Lewis told the acting director general of the Israeli foreign ministry the same day that "the scope of the IDF action in Beirut today seems inconsistent with the limited objectives described by the prime minister to Ambassador Draper this morning. We noted that this may seem to Washington as deliberate deception by the government of Israel" (Tel Aviv 13886, 151951Z Sep 82). The Kahan Commission is silent about a dawn Begin-Draper meeting on September 15, but says (p. 10) they met at 11:30 A.M. and that at that meeting Begin told Draper the IDF had entered Beirut earlier that morning. Either the Kahan Commission had the meeting time wrong or perhaps Begin's 11:30 statement was actually to Ambassador Lewis or some other American official, since Draper was already in Beirut by then.

268 Draper, Lewis, Sharon meeting: Tel Aviv 13962, 162033Z Sep 82; Schiff & Ya'ari, p. 259; also Beirut 06289, 152105Z Sep 82, par. 4. Lewis (ADST oral history) says in this meeting Sharon was furious that Bashir's death had ruined his plans and was bitter, disdainful, and condescending to Draper.

268 2,500 terrorists: Tel Aviv 13962, 162033Z Sep 82, par. 7-13, 16; Sharon, p. 500; Lewis ADST oral history; Pintak, p. 78. Israeli intelligence had reported in August that the PLO was planning to leave behind thousands of fighters (Lewis 8-22-82 cable Tel Aviv 12774, quoted in State 237229, 240516Z Aug 82, par. 5; Sharon, p. 494-95; "Israelis Complain That Guerrillas Are Being Allowed to Violate Pact," *The New York Times*, 8-24-82); it now believed they had in fact done so. Technically, Sabra

was a neighborhood, in the center of which was a refugee camp called Shatila (Dillon ADST oral history). But they are both generally referred to as camps. Even the term *camp* is somewhat misleading, since these were not collections of tents but built-up residential neighborhoods.

268 Surrounded: Tel Aviv 13962, 162033Z Sep 82, par. 8; Kahan, p. 10-11, 23

268 Argument about stay-behinds: Tel Aviv 03962, 162139Z Sep 82

268 Handful of guerrillas: Draper ADST oral history. Sachar, p. 189, attributes the Israeli estimate of stay-behinds to their count of vehicles in the convoys evacuating Beirut in August. The Israelis were certainly correct about the vast amounts of weaponry the PLO had left behind.

268-69 Division of responsibility: This is all discussed in chapter 5. As applied to this immediate context, see Sharon, p. 501-2, and Kahan, p. 8, 14, 27.

269 LAF's problem: Tel Aviv 03962, 162139Z Sep 82

269 Little confidence: Tel Aviv 03962, 162139Z Sep 82, par. 7, 13

269 Inviting LAF to clean out: Draper cable Beirut 6441, 210620Z Sep 82, par. 2-3; Kahan, p. 17; Shultz, p. 105; Sharon, p. 505; Schiff & Ya'ari, p. 257, 269

269 Hobeika: Dillon ADST oral history; Kahan, p. 5, 8; Petran, p. 284; Gilmour, p. 174. The 1976 massacre at Tel Za'atar was in retribution for a Palestinan massacre of Christians at Damour eight months earlier. The Kahan Commission reports Begin telling Draper that the Phalange commander "is a good man and we trust him not to cause any clashes" (p. 10).

269 Specially trained: Kahan, p. 11; Schiff & Ya'ari, p. 259

269 Pregnant women: Fisk, p. 359

269 *Terrorist* and *Palestinian:* Friedman, p. 163

269 Pure intention: Kahan, p. 22. Begin also drafted a Cabinet statement that the IDF had taken control of West Beirut "in order to forestall the danger of violence, bloodshed and chaos" (Kahan, p. 14). The IDF's own wording was "to prevent possible grave occurrences and to ensure quiet" (Kahan, p. 9). The Cabinet's statement goes on to blame the move on some

2,000 stay-behind terrorists. A reporter later said that "Draper has been accused by unnamed officials in Israel of holding back the Israelis from the camps, thus preventing them from carrying out some protective function and thus making the United States responsible in some way for what happened" (question in State Department briefing 9-20-82, State 265136, 210529Z Sep 82).

269 Sharon professed: Sharon, p. 500-1. This may well have been another occasion when Begin and Sharon were pursuing different agendas. According to the American record of Draper's September 15 meeting with Begin (Tel Aviv 13875, 151634Z Sep 82), the two discussed many issues but Begin expressed no concern at all about stay-behind terrorists in West Beirut. Indeed, he said "the two key issues remaining now that the PLO has been evacuated from West Beirut" were getting the PLO out of the *rest* of Lebanon and getting the Syrians out (par. 5). Sharon's memoirs are silent about how the IDF's entry into West Beirut violated the Habib agreement; they talk only about how the PLO had violated the agreement.

269 Violation of agreement: Draper cable Beirut 6289, 152105Z Sep 82; Draper ADST oral history; Jansen, p. 95-96, 137; Sachar, p. 192

270 Eitan quote: Schiff & Ya'ari, p. 259-60; Tel Aviv 13962, 162033Z Sep 82, par. 13-14; also Kahan, p. 14. It wasn't that the Phalange blamed the PLO for killing Bashir. There was no more reason to suspect the PLO than any other group. They blamed the Palestinians for ruining Lebanon long before Bashir got killed. His death was just a pretext for doing what they had long been itching to do.

270 Killings in camps: Schiff & Ya'ari, 258-82; Fisk, p. 357-72; Beirut 06353, 181201Z Sep 82; Draper cable Beirut 06369, 181652Z Sep 82; Kahan, p. 12-23; Friedman, p. 159-66; Seale, p. 392; Randal, p. 15-16

270 Whole idea: Sharon, p. 500-5

270 2,000-plus stay-behind terrorists: Tel Aviv 13962, 162033Z Sep 82, par. 7-8 (in par. 13 Eitan raises the number to 5,000; in par. 15 Draper notes that "by Mossad's own admission there were no significant third echelon PLO leaders left behind, as had been anticipated"); the Americans considered those numbers "highly inflated" (Pintak, p. 78); Schiff & Ya'ari, p. 259; Kahan, p. 7; Sharon, 494. See

Fisk, pp. 359-70, particularly 369, on the IDF's conviction that terrorists were in the camps. Sharon (p. 504, 507) emphasizes that the IDF had instructed the Phalangists that "the mission was only against [the terrorists]. Civilian residents, they were specifically instructed, were not to be harmed." Khalidi writes that "it requires an assumption of gross incompetence on the part of Israeli military intelligence to believe that the IDF did not know that there were no P.L.O. fighters there. In fact, as is acknowledged by most sources, there were none" (p. 179). Habib said Sharon "had a pretty broad definition of fighting men, including the political cadre" (Khalidi, p. 172). There were reports that another of Israel's allies, Major Sa'ad Haddad, also participated in the massacre. The Kahan Commission concluded that those reports were false (Kahan, p. 24).

270 Found rather few: Dillon ADST oral history; also Draper ADST oral history. This is not to say there were none. There had been gunfire coming from the camps earlier, and Kahan (p. 12) reports some shooting at the Phalangists once they entered. Schiff & Ya'ari (p. 257) cite IDF soldiers on the scene as having "estimated that a few dozen Palestinian fighters were probably involved in the exchanges of fire, and that there may have been up to 200 armed men in the camps." Kahan, p. 11, says that at the time the Phalangists entered the camps, "there were armed terrorist forces in the camps. We cannot establish the extent of these forces" but believes they were stay-behinds.

270 No terrorists: Schiff & Ya'ari, p. 262; Kahan, p. 13, quotes slightly different wording

270 Whoever they did find: Randal, p. 15-16; Fisk, p. 359. Sharon, p. 508, cites Phalangist reports that "they were facing stiff resistance and had suffered casualties" in what Sharon assumed was "a street battle with the PLO." But the IDF intelligence officer on the scene reported a few hours after the operation began, "The impression is that fighting is not too serious. [The Phalangists] have casualties, as you know—two wounded, one in the leg and one in the hand" (Kahan, p. 13).

270 Hardly any resistance: The Phalange claimed casualties of only two dead and 40 wounded (Schiff & Ya'ari, p. 272). They claimed hundreds of terrorists killed, but the evidence did not back up their claim that those people killed were terrorists in any meaningful sense of the word.

270 Clear indications: Kahan, p. 12-17. Israeli

journalist Ze'ev Schiff received a tip from a source in the IDF General Staff at 7:50 A.M. Friday that there was a slaughter in the camps (Kahan, p. 16; Schiff & Ya'ari, p. 266-69), but was unable to get far in rousting Israeli officials to confirm it or do anything about it. Ryan Crocker, the American embassy's political officer, was one of the first non-participants in the camps as the massacre was winding down. He says (4-28-94) "I find it very hard to believe the Israelis didn't know pretty damn well what was going on."

270 Kill the terrorists: Shultz, p. 105; Sharon, p. 505. Sharon and Habib and Draper all agreed that the LAF should be the ones to go into the camps. But whereas Draper and Habib viewed any LAF presence in the camps as a calming police presence, Sharon wanted them in there to kill terrorists for him (Tel Aviv 03962, 162139Z Sep 82, par. 2).

270 LAF again refused: Draper cable Beirut 6441, 210620Z Sep 82, par. 2-3; Kahan, p. 17; Shultz, p. 105; Sharon, p. 505; Schiff & Ya'ari, p. 257, 269. Drori even tried to persuade the LAF general that he could get permission from Draper to enter the camps (Kahan, p. 17). Gen. Eitan told Draper on Thursday, "I know [Gen. Hamdan, the LAF's operations chief] better than you; I know that the Lebanese Armed Forces are not capable of doing the job" of cleaning out the camps; Sharon then elaborated that "the Lebanese Army never entered a single building unless we held their hand" (Tel Aviv 03962, 162139Z Sep 82, par. 13, 17).

270 Halted the operation: Schiff & Ya'ari, p. 261-82; Sharon, p. 505; Kahan, p. 19. Gen. Drori met with Hobeika and others at 4:30 P.M. Friday and told them the Phalangists had until 5 o'clock the next morning to leave the camps (Schiff & Ya'ari, pp. 271-72). The last of them did not actually leave until 8 A.M. (Kahan, p. 20).

270-71 Estimates: Schiff & Ya'ari, p. 282; Dillon ADST oral history; Kahan, p. 21. The IDF estimated 700-800. The PLO estimated 3,500. Dillon's estimate is 1,500. The Phalangists, anxious to hide evidence, used a bulldozer to dig pits to dump the bodies in and carted other bodies away in trucks (Kahan, p. 21)

271 Went too far: Sharon, p. 505-8. Sharon explicitly accepted the inevitability that civilians would die as unfortunate collateral casualties (p. 505). There were just too many of them.

271 No disorder: Dillon ADST oral history. Draper and Shultz made the same point (Draper cable Beirut 06289, 152105Z Sep 82, par. 4; State 260100, 160304Z Sep 82, par. 3).

271 You must stop: Schiff & Ya'ari, p. 276; Draper ADST oral history; Gilmour, p. 175; American representatives had made several phone calls to the Israeli Foreign Ministry Friday evening complaining about the presence of Phalangists in the camps and warning of the consequences (Kahan, p. 20), but until Saturday morning there were few hard facts available to them or anyone else about exactly what was going on in the camps.

271 Terrace: Fisk, p. 372

271 Devastated: According to Habib's friends ("Reagan's Remarkable Mideast Man," *San Francisco Chronicle*, 2-22-83)

271 Signed this paper: Fisk, p. 372. Nonetheless, Habib always maintained that the extent of his commitments had been exaggerated by the PLO (Lewis ADST oral history).

271 Given assurances, deceived: Habib cable Amman 08129, 281006Z Sep 82, par. 8. Though Habib's assurances had consisted mostly of reporting the assurances he had received from Begin and Bashir, he had indeed gone further, using the words *US guarantees,* and even going so far as to say "*I* am your protection!" (Barrett 5-9-94). The text of Habib's letter about guarantees of safety for Palestinian civilians left behind is in the endnotes for chapter 14, "The Endgame."
  The following is part of a working paper that Habib sent to the PLO on August 3, 1982: "Regarding U.S. Government guarantees as regards security for the departing Palestinian forces *along with the security of the camps.* Comment: We [the U.S.] will provide these guarantees" (cited in Davis R. Robinson memo to The Deputy Secretary, "U.S. Responsibilities Concerning the Protection of Civilians in the Beirut Area," Oct. 18, 1982, attached to memo from NEA Veliotes to The Deputy Secretary, Oct. 22, 1982, 85D251 7517, p. 10; emphasis and bracketed clarification added by author of this memo).

271 Killer: Seale, p. 392, citing his September 27, 1984, interview with Habib. George Shultz said, "The brutal fact is, we are partially responsible. We took the Israelis and the Lebanese at their word" (Shultz, p. 105).
  Sharon felt no such responsibility. Ironically, though he never tired of chiding Philip

Habib for naïveté, Sharon would claim naïveté of his own to defend his use of the Phalange. Though Sharon knew that "in past years both Palestinians and Arab Christians had committed far more terrible slaughters on each other," he claimed "there had not, however, been any real anxiety that [the Phalangists] would act improperly" after the IDF "explicitly told [them] to avoid harming civilians" (Sharon, p. 507-10) The Kahan Commission, the Israeli panel appointed to investigate the massacre, found it "impossible to justify the Minister of Defense's disregard of the danger of a massacre" (Kahan, p. 32). It dismissed "the routine warnings that I.D.F. commanders issued to the Phalangists" not to harm civilians as "the same kind as were routinely issued to I.D.F. troops" and found those instructions "could not have had any concrete effect" (Kahan, p. 33).

Though his own military intelligence branch regarded the Phalange as "unreliable" (Kahan, p. 7), Sharon claims to have believed that the caliber of men he was sending into the camps could be trusted to follow IDF instructions to "be careful in their identification of the PLO terrorists" as they selected whom to shoot (Sharon, p. 504, 507-8; Kahan, p. 11, 13; also Schiff & Ya'ari, p. 257).

Though Begin believed that "after the assassination of Bashir, their beloved leader, the Phalangists would take revenge on the Muslims" (Kahan, p. 22), Sharon claims "the simple fact was that no one had foreseen the danger" (Sharon, p. 516, 507; Kahan, p. 27, 32). Begin's preceding sentence was that he had told the Chief of Staff "that we must seize positions precisely to protect the Muslims from the vengeance of the Phalangists." In his memoirs, Sharon explains his lack of concern on the fact that everyone knew Bashir had not been killed by a Palestinian. Therefore, he reasoned, the Phalange should have no reason to wreak revenge on Palestinians and "no one had batted an eye at the idea of sending in the Phalangists" (p. 507; see also Kahan, p. 22 and 27). But it was not at all certain in the hours and days following the assassination whom the bomber was working for. Indeed, it is still not. Two and a half weeks after the bombing, Habib speculated that the PLO or someone else might have been behind it (Rome 22562, 051748Z Oct 82, par. 7).

Regardless of who thought who had killed Bashir, the Phalange had wanted revenge against Palestinians for various wrongs for years before Bashir was assassinated. Khalidi writes that "the barbarities against the camp popula-

tion" were what "virtually everyone in Lebanon fully expected if Israel's Phalangist allies were allowed to have their way. . . . No Israeli official who had had anything to do with the Phalangists could possibly have had any illusions as to what they would do if introduced into a Palestinian refugee camp; moreover, the historical record was full of bloody examples" (p. 176, 178). Fisk quotes an IDF colonel having said earlier "our problem is going to be stopping the Phalange going in to west Beirut and settling old scores" (p. 354). Of the IDF's instructions to the Phalange to conduct themselves honorably in the camps, Schiff & Ya'ari write (p. 257) that "such repeated warnings would seem to indicate, especially in light of the Phalange's known record of atrocities, that the senior military men in the field were wary of their intentions from the start." Other than having authorized the Phalange's operation and getting confirmation that it had begun, Ariel Sharon is conspicuously absent from accounts of the IDF's dealings with the Phalange just before and during the massacre. While it was proceding, Sharon kept himself busy far away in Israel (Sharon, p. 504-6).

For various views of Habib's share of the responsibility, see Randal, p. 275-77; Beinin 10-30-93; "Open Letter Addressed by Hizb Allah to the Downtrodden in Lebanon and in the World," Appendix B in Norton, p. 171; Pintak, p. 80.

272 Send back MNF: Shultz, p. 109; Shultz 7-25-94

272 Presence: Jidda 07234, 291755Z Sep 82, par. 4. This was the way Habib articulated the MNF's mission to King Fahd. See Shultz, p. 109, for the way he articulated it right after Reagan and Shultz made the decision.

272 Indignant: Draper 4-25-93

272 Sovereignty, regional peace: Letter from the Secretary to Syrian Foreign Minister Khaddam, State 262428, 172025Z Sep 82; Habib/Draper cable Damascus 07144, 031038Z Oct 82, par. 2; Habib cable Damascus 07155, 031914Z Oct 82, par. 6

272-73 Same time, two-stage, negotiating purposes: Damascus 07136, 022222Z Oct 82, par. 18-19; Habib/Draper cable Beirut 6769, 012050Z Oct 82, par. 7; Habib cable Damascus 07144, 031038Z Oct 82, par. 3-4, 6. Whatever the particulars, Habib said, "withdrawal must be achieved without preconditions as to who goes first" (Damascus 07136, par. 7-8). The Syrians, Habib noted, were even more mistrustful than ever of the Israelis "because the Israelis violated their understandings with us, invaded West Beirut, and created conditions which led to the massacre" (Damascus 07144, par. 6). Specifically, Habib envisioned the Syrians pulling back to the Bekaa Valley and the Israelis pulling back to within 40 kilometers of the Lebanese-Israeli border (Habib/Draper cable Beirut 6769, 012050Z Oct 82, par. 8). Habib's plan also called for international troops patrolling a 40-kilometer buffer zone along Lebanon's southern border (Damascus 07136, par. 10).

273 Syrians and Israelis gone: Habib of course wanted the PLO out of the rest of Lebanon too. But since he was not allowed to negotiate with them anyway, he left the PLO for the Lebanese government to worry about while he focused his energies on getting the Syrians and Israelis out. Every indication was that they would cooperate (e.g., Habib cable Jerusalem 00469, 091821Z Feb 83, par. 11; undated Dam memo to The President, "Lebanon Negotiations: Next Steps," 85D251 7517, apparently early January 1983, p. 2).

273 Drive home the urgency, constant series: Damascus 07136, 022222Z Oct 82, par. 6. He also worried that "the longer the forces are where they are, the greater the chances of an incident which could set back the whole process" (Habib cable Damascus 07144, 031038Z Oct 82, par. 8). Indeed, on the same day he was writing that cable, an ambush killed six Israeli soldiers and wounded 22, prompting Begin to threaten a strong retaliation (Draper cable Jerusalem 03039, 052253Z Oct 82, par. 6).

273 Informal understandings: Habib interviews with Parker and Mulcahy; cable Rome 22562, 051748Z Oct 82, par. 5; Draper 4-25-93 and 5-4-93; Kreczko 10-6-93; Seale, p. 404. Informal understandings are appropriate in the Middle East, says Veliotes, because they let "you deal with constructive hypocrisy: People deny things but they go ahead and do them" (Veliotes 4-29-93).

273-74 Technicalities of transportation: Habib cable Damascus 07155, 031914Z Oct 82, par. 5, 10; Habib/Draper cable Damascus 07153, 031537Z Oct 82, par. 10

274 So little influence: Paganelli cable Damascus 07045, 281049Z Sep 82, par. 5

274 What to expect: Paganelli cable Damascus 06917, 221636Z Sep 82

274 Assad's position, one day after: Habib interviews with Parker and Dusclaud; Habib cable Damascus 07155, 031914Z Oct 82; Habib cable Damascus 07135, 022121Z Oct 82, par. 5; Damascus 07136, 022222Z Oct 82, par. 6; Salem, p. 65-66, 71, 76; Secto 13032, 011822Z Oct 82, par. 6. Habib had two meetings with Assad's acting foreign minister Farouk Shar'a before meeting with Assad. Since Shar'a was only articulating Assad's position and reporting Habib's words back to Assad, I group what was said in the three meetings all together here for the sake of simplicity and clarity only. This summary of Assad's position includes points made earlier by Shar'a, not all of which were repeated by Assad in his meeting with Habib. Habib said that, when he presented to Assad US goals including a Lebanon free of all external forces, Assad "told me that they corresponded exactly with the wishes of Syria and that he didn't want to maintain armed troops in Lebanon—troops which are not necessary to the defense of his interests" (also Habib cable Damascus 07135, 022121Z Oct 82, par. 4). Shar'a said that massacres could be prevented by forming a national unity government in Lebanon and disarming the militias (Secto 13032, 011822Z Oct 82).

274-75 Habib response to Syrians: Damascus 07135, 022121Z Oct 82, par. 6-9; Damascus 07136, 022222Z Oct 82, par. 7; Habib/Draper cable Damascus 07153, 031537Z Oct 82, par. 3-10. This meeting—actually a pair of meetings in the same day—happened during Habib's swing around the region on his return for Amin's inauguration. On the day Habib was in town, Assad was on vacation and his foreign minister was in Washington (Secto 13032, 011822Z Oct 82, par. 8). So he met with the acting foreign minister and others.

275 Full justification: Habib interview with Parker; also Habib interview with Mulcahy; Salem, p. 72-73

275 Political futures: Habib cable Rome 27001, 021716Z Dec 82, par. 4

275 Second Arab country: Kadashai 6-19-95

275 Lose its historical ties: Salem, p. 50. Lebanese foreign minister Elie Salem writes further that "we could not, on our own, normalize relations with Israel. Lebanon was not Egypt. . . . To us the question of normalizing relations was an existential one; it threatened our national unity, our relations with our Arab breth-

ren, and ultimately our existence" (Salem, p. 50). Also Habib cable Jerusalem 00672, 271554Z Feb 83, par. 15.

275 Satrapy: Hill 7-9-94. Others used the term *North Bank* to refer to Israel's designs on Lebanon (e.g., Shultz, p. 200, 219).

276 Treaty written in August: Kadashai 6-19-95. Kadashai, Begin's secretary, stated bluntly in the interview that the treaty was written by the time Bashir was elected (August 23), but later in the interview backpedalled from that assertion.

276 Begin-Bashir meeting: Schiff & Ya'ari, p. 234-35; Randal, p. 10-11; Petran, p. 283. Randal says Begin demanded the treaty by October 23, one month after Bashir's inauguration; Schiff & Ya'ari say the date he demanded was December 31.

276 Israeli preconditions: Draper cable Jerusalem 03039, 052253Z Oct 82. Habib believed that, once the Syrians agreed to leave, the Palestinians in northern Lebanon would not want to stay without Syrian protection (Habib cable Jerusalem 00469, 091821Z Feb 83, par. 11; Habib cable Beirut 01647, 121732Z Feb 83, par. 2, 17; undated Dam memo to The President, "Lebanon Negotiations: Next Steps," 85D251 7517, apparently early January 1983, p. 2).

276 PLO leave only with Syrians: Habib cable Beirut 01647, 121732Z Feb 83, par. 17. Habib said, "Once you get the major forces out, the others can't survive. They survive under the umbrella of others" (Habib testimony, "Review of Adequacy . . . ," p. 360).

276 Linchpin: Riyadh 00251, 231306Z Jan 83, par. 5. He said, "The concept was that if we would get Israeli agreement to withdraw, then the Syrians would agree" (Habib testimony, "Review of Adequacy . . . ," p. 353).

276 Springboard: Crocker 4-25-94

277 Just blew up: Draper 9-19-97, 4-25-93, and 4-13-93. The quote is a compilation from these three accounts of the incident. In some accounts, Draper recalls it as happening the day after the massacre; in others, the day after Bashir was killed.

277 Feces at airport: Smith 6-14-94; Gaucher 5-15-94; Sehulster 7-12-94; Mead 6-5-94. Beirut resident Jean Said Makdisi (p. 190) describes feces as the IDF's "trademark . . . a ghastly joke, symbol of an overriding con-

tempt" that they left behind "wherever they had been." She writes that, when the Israelis left any area in Lebanon, returning residents routinely found feces on furniture and school desks and clothes, in books and bathtubs and washing machines. Petran, p. 19, says the IDF had a practice of leaving heaps of their excrement in Palestinian cultural and other institutions, homes, and offices. Mead and Smith interpreted the piles of feces as just a sign of abysmal basic soldiering: using their own sleeping quarters as a latrine. They say that minimal standards of basic soldiering would dictate having an outdoor latrine within the secured perimeter so soldiers could use it safely. As Smith and Mead read the evidence, though, the Israelis did not patrol their perimeter at night. Instead, they just locked themselves inside. With no extended protection, they didn't want to expose themselves to danger by going out to use an open-air latrine. So they just did their business inside their quarters. Mead says his patrols later encountered the same conditions often when coming upon quarters elsewhere that IDF soldiers had just left.

277 Bomblets: Smith 6-14-94. He adds that the IDF had left bomblets scattered into the suburbs of Sabra and Shatila and the refugee areas north of the airport. Another Marine described the US sector of responsibility as "inundated with unexploded ordnance" (cable BLT Two Slant Eight 050900Z Nov 82). The first Marine killed in Beirut died while clearing bomblets at the airport.

277 Arens proposal: State 281604, 061654Z Oct 82, par. 2

277 Replaced the word: Parker, p. 184; State 021684, 250655Z Jan 83, par. 20, quoting Jerusalem 00250 of 1-23-83; NEA/ARN memo "Evening Reading item: Israel-Lebanon Talks Open," 12-28-82, 85D251 7517; NEA/ARN memo "Lebanon Negotiations," 12-28-82, 85D251 7517

277 Requisite nods: Draper cable Jerusalem 03039, 052253Z Oct 82, par. 9

278 Butt out: Kreczko 10-6-93; Habib/Draper cable Beirut 09489 171752Z Dec 82, par. 10; Draper cable Beirut 09657, 230020Z Dec 82, par. 2-4; Habib cable Tel Aviv 01043, 211628Z Jan 83, par. 17; Salem, p. 49

278 More likely, strengthen his hand: Salem, p. 37; Parker, p. 183

278 Just stalling: Salem, p. 37; Kreczko 10-6-

93; Draper 4-25-93; Habib cable Rabat 08980, 011418Z Dec 82. On February 3, 1983, the US still saw Israel, and specifically Sharon, as delaying as a way of letting the September 1 plan die of neglect (Dam memo to The President, "Lebanon Negotiations: Next Steps," 2-3-83).

278 Had it with the stalling, I do not believe: Habib cable Rome 27001, 021716Z Dec 82, par. 6E, 9

278 Habib's lunch with Reagan, intransigence: Reagan, p. 439-40. Sharon emphasized that the PLO would have to be completely gone from Lebanon before the IDF would move one yard (Habib cable Jerusalem 03845, 190953Z Dec 82, par. 14).

278 Letter from Reagan: *St. Petersburg* (Florida) *Times,* 12-19-82; last page of Habib's 1982 address book

279 Nicknames: "Who Lost Lebanon?" *Los Angeles Times,* 3-11-84

279 Description of Amin: Crocker 4-28-94; Dillon ADST oral history. Crocker's criticism of Amin's entourage does not apply to his actual top officials, such as foreign minister Elie Salem, upon whom Habib bestowed his ultimate compliment of "professional."

279 Plan that would accommodate, Habib envisioned: Habib cable Rome 27001, 021716Z Dec 82, par. 8; Acting Secretary Dam memo to the President, "Withdrawal of External Forces from Lebanon," 85D251 7517, 12-8-82. The words *price* and *peace treaty in all but name* are from Draper mission (Ross) cable Beirut 09083, 071709Z Dec 82, par. 12. Habib was not the sole author of the plan he had in his pocket. Major contributors included Draper, Ned Walker (special assistant to Deputy Secretary Kenneth Dam), and legal adviser Alan Kreczko. Shultz of course signed off on it (Krezcko 10-6-93).

279 Comparable to the Beirut evacuation: Veliotes memo to Acting Secretary Dam, 12-10-82, "Your Meeting and Luncheon with Foreign Minister Elie Salem of Lebanon, 11:00 A.M., Tuesday, December 14," section 2

279-81 Account of Jerusalem meeting, number one rule, blindsided, amateurs, pigeon: Jerusalem 03815, 162257Z Dec 82; Habib interviews with Mulcahy and Parker; Kreczko 10-6-93; Draper 4-25-93; Parker, p. 259-60, note 11; Salem, p. 41-42; Habib interview with

the author, *The Stanford Magazine,* Spring 1984; Habib interview with Donald Stokes, Stanford University News Service, 2-8-79. The deal was a complete surprise to Habib, but less so to Draper. Some months earlier, Amin had told Draper he wanted a representative of his own to talk to the Israelis. "So I said sure, go ahead," says Draper. "But I didn't know he'd send some dummy there to talk to the Israelis and let them walk all over him." While Draper knew that secret talks were going on—he had in fact helped arrange the earliest talks—he did not know they had produced an agreement (Draper 4-25-93; Tueni 11-15-95). Draper, who knew Marun, describes him as "incredibly naïve" about diplomacy and says he would walk alone into meetings "with twenty or thirty Israelis all shouting at him and telling him what to do. The Israelis felt they had an absolute doormat, which they did" (Draper 4-25-93).

281 Laughing: Draper 4-25-93. Kreczko (10-6-93) adds, "They just loved one-upping Phil." *The Jerusalem Post* (12-20-82) reported that Sharon's disclosure of his "framework agreement" set off a "sense of near-jubilation that has pervaded official Jerusalem. . . . In the initial flush of triumph in Sharon's circles over the framework agreement there was some crowing over the Americans having been 'taken by surprise.'" Draper suspects that Sharon's tactic of surprise was payback for the US having surprised Israel with Reagan's September 1 peace initiative (Draper 4-25-93).

281 Give Habib a copy: Jerusalem 03815, 162257Z Dec 82, par. 11

281 Wormed: Habib interview with Parker

281 Resembled Habib's plan: Jerusalem 03815, 162257Z Dec 82, par. 12; Habib stressed that the paper was "not bad" (Habib/Draper cable Beirut 09489 171752Z Dec 82, par. 18).

281 Because of the way, fait accompli: Draper 4-25-93; Paganelli 11-2-96. Shultz often said that, while the US favored peace treaties between Israel and all of its Arab neighbors including Lebanon, a "peace treaty at gunpoint is no peace treaty" (e.g., Secto 13032, 011822Z Oct 82, par. 7). That this agreement had been imposed at gunpoint is indicated by the presence of Israeli troops occupying much of Lebanon and surrounding Beirut and by the fact that the deal had been negotiated not by Israel's diplomats or foreign minister but by its defense minister.

281 Diplomacy is a process: Habib interview

with the author, *The Stanford Magazine,* Spring 1984; Habib White House press conference 12-9-82

281 Forfeited: Parker, p. 185

281-82 Choppering: Habib interview with Parker; Parker, p. 184

282 Habib encounter with Amin: Habib interview with Parker; Parker, p. 185; Habib's interview with Mulcahy; Krezcko 10-6-93; Habib/Draper cable Beirut 09489 171752Z Dec 82. Amin had told Draper on October 8 that he wanted "everything that Lebanon does to fit within a US-designed package plan" (Draper cable Beirut 07040, 081745Z Oct 82, par. 2A). Draper accompanied Habib into the meeting with Amin "since I had okayed secret talks when Amin approached me. I had to go in with Phil to make sure Amin told the truth" (Draper note on draft of this chapter).

The Israelis leaked word of the paper right after their meeting with Habib. He wrote that "Israeli leaks are causing great difficulties" in Beirut (Habib cable Beirut 09455, 171515Z Dec 82). The paper had in fact been signed by Marun, but not by Amin (Tueni 11-15-95).

282-83 Salem's part in meeting: Salem, p. 41-43. On October 8 Amin confided to Draper that he had two representatives (not including Marun) meeting secretly with the Israelis to discuss the future of Lebanese-Israeli relations. He asked Draper "to be discreet" about those talks since his new foreign minister, Salem, "will know something about that channel but not all" (Draper cable Beirut 07040, 081745Z Oct 82, par. 2B-C).

283 Issue a communiqué: Tueni 11-15-95. Sharon's fellow Cabinet members were irritated with the publicity he gave to his Beirut talks. An editorial in the Israeli newspaper *Ha'aretz* criticized Sharon's "theatrics" and advised him "to wait with the toasts until Beirut and Jerusalem start telling the same thing" (USIS/Tel Aviv 18681, 191128Z Dec 82).

283 Not want US involved: Habib/Draper cable Beirut 09489 171752Z Dec 82, par.10

283 Communiqué, Sharon's threats: Tueni 11-15-95. Salem, p. 44, describes some of Sharon's specific threats to keep the Lebanese from backing out of the deal and summarizes, "Sharon's threats against us were continuous. He would often send messages indicating that if the president did not comply with his demand, then Israel would make sure that his

authority would not extend beyond the gardens of the presidential palace." Amin had said in the meeting that the real negotiations would have to involve the US as a full partner (Beirut 09489, 171752Z Dec 82, par. 9). Despite his anger over the secret agreement, Habib emphasized repeatedly both to the Israelis and to Amin that he had "no problem with a working paper as such, particularly if it helped get negotiations started" (Habib/Draper cable Beirut 09489, 171752Z Dec 82, par.14; Habib/Draper cable Jerusalem 03815, 162257Z Dec 82).

283 Fully agreed document: Habib cable Jerusalem 03845, 190953Z Dec 82, par. 3; Habib cable Jerusalem 03849, 191946Z Dec 82, par. 3

283 Go ahead and sign: Habib cable Jerusalem 03845, 190953Z Dec 82, par. 15. Right after Habib flew home, Sharon met with Amin's no-longer-secret envoy and insisted that, as a precondition of starting formal negotiations, he sign a document labeled "Agreement" specifying that the secret paper "determines the basic elements and guidelines for the negotiations." Draper reported that Sharon added a "not-too-veiled threat that Israel could not predict what would happen" in various Lebanese hotspots "if the agreement were not signed allowing negotiations to proceed. The Israelis were also clearly trying to keep the U.S. completely out of the act" (Draper cable Beirut 09657, 230020Z Dec 82, par. 2-4).

283-84 Informal understandings, ghost: Veliotes 4-29-93; Parker, p. 205

284 Changed everything: Habib interview with Parker

284 Stuck with it: Kreczko 10-6-93

284 Basis: Habib letter to Reagan, Jerusalem 03839, 182146Z Dec 82. Leaping to the front of the parade, Habib treated Sharon's secret paper as a major step forward and repeatedly urged Begin to keep up the momentum by getting the formal talks started within a few days and finished within one week (Habib cable Jerusalem 03845, 190953Z Dec 82; Habib cable Jerusalem 03849, 191946Z Dec 82).

17 Baking Stones

285 No force: Draper cable Beirut 00859, 242116Z Jan 83, par. 8. Gen. Tamir was speaking specifically on the subject of the security zone Israel demanded in southern Lebanon.

285 Omit mention: NEA/ARN memo "Evening Reading item: Israel-Lebanon Talks Open," 12-28-82, 85D251 7517; NEA/ARN memo "Lebanon Negotiations," 12-28-82, 85D251 7517

285 Resist concessions: Parker, p. 180-81; Habib interview with Parker

285 Shield: Habib cable Jerusalem 00996, quoted in State 076524, 211634Z Mar 83, par. 14. The context of this particular quote is a specific aspect of the negotiations, but aptly summarizes their feelings.

285 Avoided them: Parker, p. 185

285-86 Leapfrogging: Habib cable Jerusalem 00124, 131632Z Jan 83; Shultz memo to the President, "Lebanon: How to Force the Pace," 1-7-83. Habib spun it all much more diplomatically than this, of course, but this was the upshot. The plan Habib carried in January differed from the one he had carried in December, in that it incorporated some noncontroversial points from Sharon's secret paper. Baking stones is what Arabs call going through the motions of an exercise you know to be doomed (Randal, *Tragedy*, p. 294).

286 Overt talks would endorse: Habib cable Jerusalem 0159, 170853Z Jan 83, par. 8

286 First session: Habib cable Jerusalem 0159, 170853Z Jan 83

286 Against expanded American role: Habib cable Jerusalem 00124, 131632Z Jan 83, par. 17; Habib cable Jerusalem 0159, 170853Z Jan 83, par. 19; Habib cable Tel Aviv 01043, 211328Z Jan 83

286 Habib's draft proposal: Habib cable Jerusalem 00193, 181730Z Jan 83; Habib cable Jerusalem 00214, 191914Z Jan 83, par. 6; Habib cable Tel Aviv 01054, 211826Z Jan 83

286 Israel's minimum: Habib cable Jerusalem 00227, 201701Z Jan 83, par. 3

286 Canada: Habib cable Jerusalem 00214, 191914Z Jan 83, par. 7

286 Israel's draft: Habib cable Jerusalem 00194, 181755Z Jan 83

286 Kitchen sink: Habib cable Jerusalem 00191, 181610Z Jan 83, par. 10

286-87 Habib's criticisms and Israel's replies: Habib cable Jerusalem 00191, 181610Z Jan 83; Habib cable Jerusalem 00194, 181755Z Jan 83, par. 2-4; Habib cable Jerusalem 00227, 201701Z Jan 83; Habib cable Tel Aviv 01054, 211826Z Jan 83; Pendleton memorandum for the record, "January 18 Habib Discussions with Israelis on Lebanon," 1-18-83; Habib cable Jerusalem 00202, 191410Z Jan 83; Habib cable Jerusalem 00214, 191914Z Jan 83; Habib interview with Mulcahy. This account of the argument summarizes what was said in a number of Habib's meetings with Shamir and Begin, and his reports to Washington. The Lebanese, Saudis, and Egyptians all underlined Habib's arguments when he met with them January 21-22 (Draper cable Beirut 00789, 221445Z Jan 83; Riyadh 00251, 231306Z Jan 83; Cairo 02044, 221829Z Jan 83). The Saudis—America's best Arab ally for protecting Lebanon's sovereignty—had already begun a temporary ban on imports from Lebanon, since Israeli goods might be mixed in (Habib cable Jerusalem 00191, 181610Z Jan 83, par. 7; Veliotes cable State 059864 TOSEC 020026, 041548Z Mar 83, par. 6). Saudi King Fahd warned Habib personally that if Lebanon agreed to normal movement of people and goods with Israel, the Arabs would boycott Lebanon (Riyadh 00251, 231306Z Jan 83, par. 2, 10; State 021684, 250655Z Jan 83, par. 11, quoting Jerusalem 00250 of 1-23-83).

287 Meeting with Begin: Habib cable Tel Aviv 01054, 211826Z Jan 83; untitled declassified document 85D251 7517, 1-9-82, which bears hand notations that Habib was authorized to use the quote "at his discretion with Begin" and did so 1-21-83.

287 Mission is complete: State 021684, 250655Z Jan 83, par. 15, 20, 22, quoting Jerusalem 00250 of 1-23-83. Habib replied that he had fulfilled only the first step of his mission.

287 Did not plan, gravitas: Hill 7-19-95

287 Best guy: Shultz 7-25-94

288 Double-crossed: Lewis 4-10-94; Draper 5-4-93

288 Biased, non-objective: Lewis 4-10-9

288 Syria denounced: Habib/Draper cable Damascus 07153, 031537Z Oct 82, par. 3

288 Attacking mediator: Hill 7-19-95

288 Hate me: Bider 4-24-93

288 Arab in disguise: Draper 4-25-93

288 Rug merchant: Paganelli 11-2-96

288 Professional rudder: Lewis in Quandt, p. 242-43. The Israeli government saw the US as "too solicitous of Lebanon" (Schneider memo to S/S Charles Hill, "Phil Habib's Recommendation that the Secretary Visit Beirut before Israel," 4-21-83).

288 Draper and Shultz agree: Draper 12-22-94; Shultz 7-25-94

289 Only game: Veliotes 5-6-93; also Lewis quoted in Parker, p. 198; Draper note to author received 8-11-01

289 Never actively opposed: Shultz 7-25-94

289 Genuinely believe: Habib interview with Mulcahy; Habib interview with Parker; Tueni 11-15-95; Paganelli 11-2-96; Kreczko 10-6-93; Draper 5-4-93; Veliotes 4-29-93 and 5-6-93; Weinberger 10-27-93. Of Habib's colleagues interviewed for this book, nearly all agree that he just went along with the negotiations as a good soldier because it was Shultz' policy and the only game in town. Shultz (7-25-94) perceived Habib to be fully on board. Charlie Hill's perception was that Habib did become an enthusiastic believer in this negotiation "because as it emerged, it really was potentially a treaty of peace like the Israel-Egypt treaty. It really would have gotten the Israelis out of Lebanon" (Hill 7-17-93). Ghassan Tueni (11-15-95), the coordinator of the Lebanese negotiating effort who became a close friend of Habib's, says bluntly, "He was just being a good soldier. He never thought it was going to go through."

289 Disastrous situation: Pagenelli 11-2-96; Veliotes 4-29-93. Alan Kreczko (5-11-94) says, "He was too much of a professional to have allowed his skepticism about the venture to affect his willingness to implement it when it was US policy."

289 Boss: Paganelli 11-2-96; Habib interview with the author, *The Stanford Magazine,* Spring 1984

289 Shifted his tack: Habib cable Beirut 01647, 121732Z Feb 83, par. 2-6; Habib cable Jerusalem 00544, 151817Z Feb 83, par. 4; Habib cable Jerusalem 00543, 151755Z Feb 83, par. 17; Schneider memo to The Secretary, "Lebanon Negotiations," 2-18-83; undated memo

"The Middle East: Status Report," from the 2-24 to 3-2 time frame

289 No coincidence: Schneider memo to The Deputy Secretary, "Your White House Briefing on the Middle East, Friday, February 25 at 10:00 A.M.," 2-24-83, p. 5; Schneider memo to The Secretary, "Lebanon Negotiations," 2-18-83. The cause and effect was not certain, but there was no mistaking the sudden thawing as soon as Sharon resigned. Another factor may have been positive Israeli responses to noises from Washington about wanting better relations.

289-90 Kahan Commission report: Kahan, p. 32, 33, 49. Sharon chalked up his dismissal to being a scapegoat for "what Christian Arabs had done to Moslem Arabs" (Sharon, p. 519, 521-24).

290 Glimmers of moderation: for example, Habib cable Jerusalem 00543, 151755Z Feb 83; Draper cable Jerusalem 00620, 221814Z Feb 83; Schneider memo to The Deputy Secretary, "Your White House Briefing on the Middle East, Friday, February 25 at 10:00 A.M.," 2-24-83, p. 4; Habib and Draper cable Jerusalem 00590, 181800Z Feb 83; Schneider memo to The Secretary, "Lebanon Negotiations," 2-18-83

290 Never brightened: The window of flexibility began closing February 28, when Shamir resumed the hard line with Habib (Habib cable Jerusalem 00696, 281641Z Feb 83; Draper cable Beirut 03753, 061607Z Apr 83, par. 5).

290 Neutrality: Mead 6-5-94

290 Bless: Draper cable Beirut 06532, 231950Z Sep 82, par. 8

290 Better they liked it: Draper (5-4-93) says the Marines were under Pentagon orders not to enter into an active liaison arrangement with the Israelis because that would suggest that they were cooperating with them. On January 6, 8, and 10, Israeli forces tried to enter US positions and set up direct conferences between themselves and the Marines, but were escorted out with advice to make such requests through diplomatic channels (Frank, p. 44).

290 Date of first IDF intrusion: Frank, p. 44; Long Commission, p. 30

290 Continuous: Mead 6-5-94

290 Israeli sense of humor: Dillon ADST oral history. Sehulster (7-12-94) adds, "Yes, there was taunting all the time by them. Just arro-

gance and belligerence." A Marine commander complained to Gen. Drori about "the danger of locking and loading weapons in confrontation with US Marines, as IDF members had done on at least one occasion" (Beirut 01077, 281636Z Jan 83, par. 11).

290 Reconnaissance by fire: Beirut 01077, 281636Z Jan 83, par. 10-11; Frank, p. 44. Dillon ADST oral history refers to "the Israeli fondness for clearing the roads with machine guns."

290 Stray IDF rounds: Long Commission, p. 30

290-91 Johnson pistol episode: Frank, p. 45-46; Long Commission, p. 30; Dillon ADST oral history; Lewis ADST oral history; "A Marine, Pistol Drawn, Stops 3 Israeli Tanks," *The New York Times,* 2-3-83. Dillon says this IDF officer was "assigned to deliberately provoke the Marines." The Israelis circulated the story that Johnson was drunk, but he was a teetotaler (Frank, p. 46; Dillon ADST oral history).

291 Patrol intrusions: Mead 6-5-94

291 Next patrol: Mead 6-5-94

292 Mead-Lifkin, uniforms: Mead 6-5-94; Habib/Draper cable Jerusalem 01052, 231857Z Mar 83; Pendleton memo to Veliotes, "IDF-Marine Liaison: Arens call to Eagleburger," 3-31-83; Habib cable Beirut 03414, 282110Z Mar 83; Habib/Draper cable Tel Aviv 04363, 310920Z Mar 83; Howe memo to The Secretary, "Update on the Status of Relations Between the Marines and IDF in Beirut," 3-31-83; Draper 5-4-93. Arens, dissatisfied with what he had got from Mead and Habib, went over Habib's head to Undersecretary of State Larry Eagleburger.

292 The average Marine: Mead 6-5-94. Sehulster (7-12-94) says the IDF was "the best *in the area,* but I think any good European military could kick their pants off." Mead rotated out of Lebanon on May 29, 1983 (Frank, p. 67). Dillon adds that the IDF "greatly overestimated their own virtues as fighters; after all they had won easy wars against inferior opponents. So they came to believe their own propaganda" (Dillon ADST oral history).

292-93 Never gone to bed: Paganelli 11-2-96

293 Shopping: Bider 4-24-93

293-94 Ross on runway: Ross letter to the author 7-30-93 and Bider 5-23-93. Ross was late because he had gotten stuck in traffic.

294 Respected and loved: Ross letter to the author 7-30-93. Ross later served as US ambassador to Syria.

294 No thank yous: Dillon 5-9-94

294 Rudest: Sue Dillon 5-9-94. Mrs. Dillon had been evacuated right after the invasion began in June, but returned in September.

294 Slump incident: Sehulster 7-12-94

294-95 Pass out incident: Mead 6-5-94

295 Eventually kill him: Habib's cardiologist says (Cheitlin 3-10-01) that what he was experiencing in both of these incidents is probably ventricular tachycardia, an episode in which the heart starts beating so fast that it empties. With no more blood coming out, blood pressure drops, and the person faints. Usually the episode soon stops by itself and the person comes to. If the episode continues for long, though, the person dies. Habib never reported either of these incidents to Dr. Cheitlin. Ventricular tachycardia is one kind of arrhythmia. Habib would eventually die from a different kind of arrhythmia.

295 Bider on food, weight: Bider 4-23-93 and 4-24-93

295 Four seats, rest: Bider 4-24-93

295 Sleep, itch: Bider 4-23-93

295-96 Virtually a prisoner, grim: Bider 4-24-93

296 Habib in car: Salem, p. 77

296 Armored personnel carrier: Draper 9-19-97

296-97 Public recognition, my name is Shultz, testimonial dinner: Bider 4-24-93 and 4-26-93; Kim 9-21-93. Habib usually travelled under the alias P. Harris. For variety, Habib, a mediocre golfer, sometimes travelled under the name Jack Palmer, an ironic combination of Jack Nicklas and Arnold Palmer (State 343274, 100143Z Dec 82; TWA ticket stub in Habib's home office).

297 Quibbling: Parker, p. 179

297 Contentiousness was deliberate: Veliotes memo "Lebanon: How to Force the Pace," 1-5-83, p. 2. Begin was more amenable to fast progress (Shultz memo to The President, "Lebanon: How to Force the Pace,"

1-7-83, p. 1; Habib cable Jerusalem 00124, 131632Z Jan 83, par. 2).

297 Life-and-death, retaliation, smuggling: Habib/Draper cable Jerusalem 00697, 281721Z Feb 83, par. 4; Habib cable Jerusalem 00672, 271554Z Feb 83, par. 15; Draper cable Jerusalem 00620, 221814Z Feb 83, par. 2, 6; Tel Aviv 02862, 011834Z Mar 83, par. 10

298 Israelis went along: Draper cable Jerusalem 00620, 221814Z Feb 83, par. 2, 6; Habib cable Jerusalem 00543, 15175Z Feb 83, par. 13, 19

298 Admirer: Hill 7-17-93; Begin's longtime friend and aide Yehiel Kadishai agrees (6-19-95)

298 Military Committee: Habib and Draper cable Jerusalem 01398, 221258Z Apr 83. Draper drily suggested they not "fall on a sword" about the name. The name that eventually stuck was "Security Arrangements Committee" (Jerusalem 01782, 092147Z May 83, par. 16; Article 8, par. 1a of final agreement). The other three issues were integration of Sa'd Haddad's forces into a territorial brigade, whether the IDF would have the right to enter Lebanese waters in "hot pursuit" of terrorists, and the number of military supervisory teams there would be.

298 Pickles: Parker, p. 185. Draper says pickles were just used as an example for trade generally.

298 Unreasonable, overkill: Habib cable Tel Aviv 05212, 191145Z Apr 83; Habib cable Beirut 5001, 210900Z Apr 83

298 Don't mean Haddad: Memorandum of Conversation, "Middle East Developments" (Shultz' Cairo meeting with regional ambassadors), 4-25-83, 8312692, p. 13

298-99 Security issue, Haddad: Veliotes memo to The Secretary, "Ideas for Handling the Haddad Problem," 3-29-83; Habib cable Beirut 03210, 231052Z Mar 83; Habib cable Jerusalem 01062, 241012Z Mar 83; Cluverius memo to Veliotes, "Phil Habib's Plans," 3-24-83; Habib and Draper cable Beirut 03426, 291214Z Mar 83; Habib cable Jerusalem 01121, 301215Z Mar 83; Habib/Draper cable Tel Aviv 04377, 311150Z Mar 83; Draper cable Jerusalem 0177, 011659Z Apr 83; Draper cable Beirut 03584, 011516Z Apr 83, par. 12; Habib cable Beirut 04003, 131029Z Apr 83; Habib cable Beirut 04007, 131129Z Apr 83; Habib

cable Beirut 04022, 132000Z Apr 83; Habib cable Beirut 04061, 141021Z Apr 83; NEA memo "Status of the Lebanon Negotiations," 4-14-83; Habib cable Jerusalem 01336, 151916Z Apr 83; Lewis cable Tel Aviv 05196, 171701Z Apr 83.

Haddad had a sister in Australia. The Lebanese and Americans suspected that the Haddad issue was bogus—hadn't the Israelis learned from Bashir's assassination not to pin their hopes on a single man?—so they could later compromise down to what they really wanted in the first place, free run of south Lebanon themselves. The Americans and Lebanese wanted a UN force and possibly an expanded MNF to patrol the security zone along with the LAF. The Israelis said that a solution to the Haddad problem—even if his role lasted only for a few months—would make agreement on the remaining differences "easy." Shamir was "dug in" on Haddad because, as Draper reported Kimche telling him, Shamir had "very serious political problems within the cabinet and was not about to go out on a limb for security arrangements that were less than perfect."

For their part, the Israelis threatened that, if the impasse continued, they might unilaterally pull back to southern Lebanon. The Lebanese and Americans hotly opposed this. First, they believed that, if the IDF did that, they would settle in there indefinitely. Second, Habib's leverage to get the Syrians and PLO out would then vanish, so they would never leave, and Lebanon would be partitioned into an Israeli zone and a Syrian zone. Habib said the US and Lebanon could accept a partial withdrawal only as step one of an agreed staged complete withdrawal by all foreign forces (Abington memo to Schneider, "Sam Lewis' Views on Where the Lebanese Negotiations Stand," 3-25-83; Habib/Draper cable Tel Aviv 04377, 311150Z Mar 83, par. 5, 21; Beirut 03349, 261832Z Mar 83, par. 15).

299 Hair down: Draper cable Jerusalem 01177, 011659Z Apr 83. This passage quotes Draper's account of what Kimche said, not necessarily the words Kimche himself said.

299-300 Amin blasts Habib: Salem, p. 48, 73-74; Habib cable Beirut 04166, 161148Z Apr 83; Habib cable Jerusalem 01336, 151916Z Apr 83. Amin had complained to Habib the day before that "if the U.S.—with all its power—could not get Israel to withdraw from Lebanon on reasonable terms, then the end of the negotiating process was at hand" (Habib cable Beirut 04061, 141021Z Apr 83, par. 9). On this day he said that, if the US was not going to stand up for Lebanon's interests, then "something else" would be looked at (Beirut 04166, par. 7). For Israelis accusing Habib of favoring Lebanon, see, for example, Beirut 03349, 261832Z Mar 83, par. 10; and Schneider memo to S/S Charles Hill, "Phil Habib's Recommendation that the Secretary Visit Beirut before Israel," 4-21-83.

300 60 percent: State 194811, 131243Z July 83, par. 10, quoting Tel Aviv 09222

300 Easily crush: Though no one knows for certain, many informed observers including Draper believe that Bashir's assassin was working for Syria (Draper 5-4-93; Schiff & Ya'ari, p. 247; Friedman, p. 158). But outright assassination was only one of many means Assad had to work his will in Lebanon.

300 90 percent: State 194811, 131243Z July 83, par. 18, quoting Tel Aviv 09222

300 Satisfied Assad: Salem, p. 55

300 Only sensible approach: Shultz 7-25-9; Lewis quoted in Parker, p. 198. One of Habib's colleagues who asked not to be identified by name points out that Middle Eastern leaders regularly say "I won't go along" and that, if diplomats gave up every time a Middle Eastern leader said that, nothing would ever get done.

300 Lever: Habib interview with Parker; Shultz 7-25-9 said much the same thing. In November 1982, Syrian vice president Khaddam met with Draper and Deputy Secretary Kenneth Dam in Washington and, Draper writes, "promised cooperation with the US negotiating effort, which at that time was still to be similar to the PLO evacuation agreement in its simplicity (until the Israelis got even more stubborn)" (Draper note to author received 8-11-01).

301 Astonished: Draper note to author received 8-17-01

301 Exponentially harder: According to an American official who asked not to be identified by name

301 Arafat: Habib cable Beirut 01647, 121732Z Feb 83, par. 17

301 Unless we're involved: Paganelli 11-2-96

301 Discuss directly, not arrogate: Draper cable Beirut 00747, 211336Z Jan 83, par. 6; Dam-

ascus 00843, 021534Z Feb 83, par. 10; also Habib cable for Damascus Rugh, Jerusalem 03840, 190538Z Dec 82; Habib interview with Parker. Habib saw the US role as that of "an intermediary, particularly between the Lebanese and Israelis," but not between the Syrians and anybody (Damascus 07136, 022222Z Oct 82, par. 16).

301 Reject anything: Kreczko 10-6-93. Moreover, Habib wrote on January 19, "We could anticipate that the Syrians would always be opposed to what was agreed [between Lebanon and Israel]. The trick was to arrive at a situation where sufficient pressure were placed on the Syrians so that they had no alternative to withdrawal" (Habib cable Jerusalem 00202, 191410Z Jan 83, par. 9).

301 Horrible truth: Hill 7-17-93

301 Not negotiating with Syrians: Habib interview with Mulcahy; Veliotes 6-3-01. Veliotes adds that "The Israelis resisted mightily the involvement of Syria."

301 Let the Lebanese: Habib also thought Assad would put greater credence in what the Lebanese said they could accept if he heard it from them directly (Habib interview with Parker).

301 Separate negotiations: Acting Secretary Dam memo to the President, "Withdrawal of External Forces from Lebanon," 85D251 7517, 12-8-82; Veliotes memo to Acting Secretary Dam, 12-10-82, "Your Meeting and Luncheon with Foreign Minister Elie Salem of Lebanon, 11:00 A.M., Tuesday, December 14," section 2; Reagan letter to Mubarak, State 343116 TOSEC 170107, 100012Z Dec 82; Veliotes memo to Acting Secretary Dam, 12-10-82, section V, p. 6; Salem 69; Kreczko 10-6-93. Draper asked Amin in December 1982 to send an emissary to Syria regularly. He did but, Draper says, the person Amin chose "was a disaster. Assad despised him" (Draper note to author received 8-11-01).

301 Lying in the weeds: Habib cable Jerusalem 00543, 151755Z Feb 83, par. 7. Another reason the Lebanese decided not to press for meaningful negotiations with Assad until there was progress with Israel, the Lebanese foreign minister writes, was that "we were dealing with Lebanese territory only, and we felt that to involve Syria was to complicate an already complex question" (Salem, p. 55). In mid-April the Lebanese said they intended to talk at a high level with the Syrians "as soon as we were close

to reaching an agreement in order to verify that the Syrians and the PLO would leave. The Lebanese did not believe the Syrians would engage in detailed negotiations" until the Israelis were at least committed to leaving (Habib cable Beirut 04007, 131129Z Apr 83, par. 24).

301-2 Sabotage, interfere: Habib cable Jerusalem 00606, 221033Z Feb 83, par. 2; Habib cable Jerusalem 00673, 271737Z Feb 83, par. 4; State 075834, 190031Z Mar 83. Nonetheless, Habib continued to press the Lebanese to stay in touch with Syria (Kreczko 10-6-93).

302 Sent a letter: Habib cable Beirut 01647, 121732Z Feb 93, par. 16. This was not the first compelling indication from Assad. About January 21 both Amin and Saudi King Fahd assured Habib that Assad was coming to accept the principle of simultaneous withdrawal (State 021684, 250655Z Jan 83, par. 11-12, quoting Jerusalem 00250 of 1-23-83). Habib told Begin January 23 that, based on what King Fahd had told him the day before, "I was now 90 percent sure that Syria had accepted" simultaneous withdrawal (par. 11). By early February the Saudis had conveyed "flat statements from the Syrians . . . which amount to an unequivocal assurance that Syria will withdraw simultaneously with Israel" (Habib cable Jerusalem 00469, 091821Z Feb 83; Paris 04631, 071231Z Feb 83, par. 5).

302 "We will withdraw": Salem, p. 71, also p. 65-66; Habib cable London 05972, 192138Z March 83, par. 3, 9-10.

302 Free of concessions: Salem, p. 71

302 Palace meeting: Salem, p. 75; Draper 5-4-93; Habib testimony, "Review of Adequacy . . . ," p. 358. Draper recalls hearing that there was a fire at the embassy and that only later did he and Habib learn it had in fact been a bomb. Salem, who was also in the meeting with Habib and Draper, recalls that the first news was in fact of a car bomb.

303 Returns to Yarze: Draper 5-4-93. Any visit by a VIP to a disaster scene, such as Shultz' visit to the embassy six days later, complicates matters (Dammarell, p. 65, 120).

303 Most massive car bomb: Long Commission, p. 30; Crocker 4-25-94. Bombs in parked cars were nothing new, and the embassy had precautions in place against parked cars. But kamikaze drivers were a novelty that the embassy was ill-prepared for (Dillon ADST oral history). This was the first violent indication

that America was wearing out its welcome in Lebanon and that Habib's efforts were becoming counterproductive (Long Commission, p. 47; Lewis ADST oral history; Kreczko 5-11-64).

303 Description of embassy bombing scene: Draper 5-4-93; Dillon ADST oral history; Dillon, "Caught in the Crossfire," *Duke* magazine, May-June 1986; Pintak, p. 103-04

303 63 killed: Seale, p. 406

303 Bloodiest: Wright, p. 16

303 Hezbollah: Dillon ADST oral history; Draper 5-4-93; Dillon in Dammarell, p. 54-56; Pintak, p. 103-4. An American official who asked not to be identified by name confides that Syrian intelligence had "culpability."

303 Lookout: Diane Dillard in Dammarell, p. 150; Beth Samuel in Dammarell, p. 226-27

303 Protection: Dillon ADST oral history; Dillon in Dammarell, p. 55. The building was right on the border between an area controlled by Walid Jumblatt's Druze and an area controlled by the PLO.

303 Visit the embassy: *The New York Times,* 4-20-83

303 First American inside: Crocker 4-28-94; Dillon ADST oral history

303-4 Crocker-Habib encounter: Crocker 4-28-94; Dillon letter to the author 5-17-01

304 Get the talks finished: Habib cable Jerusalem 00469, 091821Z Feb 83, par. 4-6; Salem, p. 73

304 Price too high: Shultz 7-25-94

304 Death warrant: Shultz, p. 212-13. That applied on both the national scale and the personal: The Lebanese negotiators were increasingly afraid they might be assassinated if they reached an agreement with Israel (Shultz, p. 209).

304-5 Slice the issues, inevitably spark, escalate: Kreczko 10-6-93; Habib cable Tel Aviv 05212, 191145Z Apr 83; NEA Veliotes cable 04/09/83, 85D251 7519, par. 4; Habib cable Beirut 5001, 210900Z Apr 83; Memorandum of Conversation, "Middle East Developments" (Shultz' Cairo meeting with regional ambassadors), 4-25-83, 8312692, p. 27.

305 Injected: NEA Veliotes cable 04/09/83 ext. 21018, 85D251 7519; Dam cable 4/20/83 X29588, 85D251 7519

305 Last concession: Shultz memo to The President, "The Middle East: Lebanon, the Peace Process and U.S.-Israel Relations," 3-3-83; 85D251 7517.

305 Final agreement to Secretary: Undated, unsigned memo "Issue: How, not if, we seek to resolve Lebanon in the near future," 85D251 7519, p. 2; the memo's internal content, along with indications from Draper cable Jerusalem 01177, 011659Z Apr 83, strongly suggest that the memo was written April 1 or just before. The memo concludes that, while the risks of failure were obvious if Shultz got directly involved, "we are damned if we do and more damned if we don't."

305 Reasons Shultz came: Shultz 7-25-94. Neither he nor Al Haig had visited this important region in well over a year.

305 Accept or reject: Shultz, p. 215, italics his. Shultz had planned all along to stay about ten days (Veliotes memo 4/20/83 X29588, Eyes only for Habib from Dam, 85D251 7519, par. 5) and planned to use a scheduled May 9 Organization for Economic Cooperation and Development meeting in Paris as a deadline (Shultz, p. 198; Memorandum of Conversation, "Middle East Developments" [Shultz' Cairo meeting with regional ambassadors], 4-25-83, 8312692, p. 3). The final Shultz draft dropped Haddad.

305 Worth the paper: Habib interview with Mulcahy. Kreczko (10-6-93) recalls Habib believing at the time that there was no chance of convincing Assad to withdraw under the circumstances. Draper says that in the days before the agreement was signed, "Phil told me privately and repeatedly we should give up ('scrap') the draft final version and start all over again" (Draper note to author received 8-11-01).

306 Side letter, veto: Shultz, p. 221; Veliotes 6-3-01; Kreczko 10-6-93; Salem, p. 92-93; Draper cable Tel Aviv 06574, 151841Z May 83, par. 4. At least as early as April 14 the Israelis had raised the stipulation that the agreement's provision about Israeli withdrawal should be conditioned upon the withdrawal of all foreign forces. Habib suggested putting it "elsewhere in the package of documents" rather than in the main text (Habib cable Beirut 04097, 141525Z Apr 83, par. 6C). But the Lebanese rejected that condition, on the grounds that they had no control over what the Syrians and PLO did and that Lebanon's agreement with Israel was an entirely separate matter. "We

never considered the agreement to be conditioned on" that stipulation, Salem writes (p. 92-93). Habib had counseled the Lebanese that "Lebanon had to decide its own limits, and could not grant Syria a veto over its negotiating positions" (Habib and Draper cable Beirut 03426, 291214Z Mar 83, par. 11).

306 Tactical: Salem, p. 99

306 Most hostile: "Damascus Rejects Appeal by Reagan to Leave Lebanon," *The New York Times*, 5-19-83

306 Run out my string: Habib interview with the author, *The Stanford Magazine*, Spring 1984. In his interview with Dusclaud as well (p. 4) Habib portrayed his offer of resignation as immediate after Assad rejected him. He may not in fact have offered it until some time later.

306 Going to fly, one-sided: Crocker 4-28-94

306 Without access: Lebanese foreign minister Elie Salem writes that, by the end of June, Amin at least once refused to see Habib (Salem, p. 105). Draper's recollection differs from Salem's: "I don't believe this. I was there in Beirut when Phil was there" (Draper note to author received 8-17-01).

306-7 McFarlane's trip, Habib's and Shultz' resignations: Shultz 7-25-94; Shultz, p. 312-13; Teicher, p. 232-33; Cannon, p. 416-17. This quotes Shultz' interview with the author. Shultz gives a more detailed and somewhat reworded account of his proffered resignation in his book. This is the probable sequence of events. The exact chronology is impossible to piece together, since different participants have different recollections of dates, and the declassified documents released to the author by the government are silent about these events. It is conceivable, though extremely unlikely, that Habib had not yet learned of McFarlane's trip by the time he resigned and that the timing was a coincidence. Clark insisted that Shultz not only did know in advance about McFarlane's trip, but had in fact proposed it (Cannon, p. 417). It seems unlikely Shultz would forget something like that.

307 Charade: Veliotes 4-29-93. In public, Habib always duly supported the agreement and argued the case for it. The consensus of his colleagues is that in private he never had much more than a grim hope that maybe it just might work.

307 I failed: Salem, p. 187

308 Opposed to any agreement: Memorandum of Conversation, "Middle East Developments" (Shultz' Cairo meeting with regional ambassadors), 4-25-83, 8312692, p. 9

308 Garden trail: Habib interview with Parker. Most of Habib's colleagues, including Shultz and Draper and Dillon, agree. The notable dissenter was Bob Paganelli, the US ambassador to Syria and thus the one who knew Assad best, who says, "The Syrians would have found a way. Through the whole period they had capabilities to scuttle any agreement that they considered a direct threat to their security" (Paganelli 11-2-96).

308 Die of neglect: The Americans certainly believed that was their purpose in stalling before the formal negotiations began. The Lebanese believed it during the negotiations (Haddad, p. 90; Habib and Draper cable Beirut 03426, 291214Z Mar 83, par. 3). Habib told Amin March 26 he doubted that the Israelis were "delaying the Lebanese negotiations simply to keep [King] Hussein out of the peace process"—a choice of words that leaves a lot unspoken (Beirut 03349, 261832Z Mar 83, par. 11). Ghassan Tueni, the coordinator of Lebanon's negotiating effort, says, "I don't think the Israelis wanted the May 17 agreement. They wanted the signature; they didn't want it applied. They knew all along it couldn't be implemented" (11-15-95). A hundred days into the negotiations and over seven months after Reagan proposed the September 1 plan, Jordan's King Hussein, the pivotal figure on whom the whole plan depended, announced that he would not play the role that it envisioned for him (Teicher, p. 225). With his departure from the game, the long-moribund plan was finally dead.

308 Prerogatives: Yaacobi (2-14-95) says that some key people in the Israeli Defense Ministry and intelligence actually preferred that the Syrians stay in Lebanon, because at least the Syrians were a disciplined army that obeyed orders, unlike the ragtag bands of terrorists who would fill the vacuum if they left.

308 Overplay their hand: Kreczko 10-6-93

308 Better agreement, proud: Habib interview with Parker. Among the "silly things" Habib may have had in mind was Sharon's January 28 proposal to have Israeli military bases in Lebanon and the Lebanese army "under Israeli control" (State 027307, 291938Z Jan 83, par. 13).

308 A lot of pressure: Habib interview with Parker

308-9 Successes and failures, speculation: Habib interview with Parker. The US policy objectives he was following had been the same all along:
1. Withdrawal of all foreign forces, period
2. Arrangements to assure the security of Israel's northern border
3. Restoration of a stable government in Lebanon
4. Extension of Lebanese sovereignty throughout its territory
5. Arrangements to assure the security of all residents in Lebanon, including the Palestinians.

18 Denouement

310 Pessimists: Quoted in Arias, p. 74

310 Civil war worse: Crocker 4-25-94

310 Unilateral withdrawal: Veliotes 5-6-93; Shultz, p. 221-23; Veliotes 5-6-93

310 Marines at airport: With the IDF withdrawal from the Shouf, the Marines' reason for being at the airport no longer applied. The airport was just *west* of Sidon Road, a major highway. Lt. Col. Charlie Smith, who scouted out potential locations for the Marines in mid-August before they came back, had wanted the higher ground on a ridge overlooking that highway to the *east*. But the IDF insisted on continuing to use the highway to supply its troops in the Beirut area. Draper did not want Marines perched above the highway, because the Lebanese Muslims would object that they were protecting the IDF convoys. So Draper told Smith the Marines would have to set up at the airport instead (Smith 6-14-94 and 6-21-94; Draper 5-4-93; Frank, p. 24-26). Frank, p. 25-26, incorrectly identifies Habib as the one who told Smith that (Smith 6-21-94).

310 Training LAF: Habib cable London 05972, 192138Z Mar 83, par. 9

310-11 Partisan prop, McFarlane, participants: Cannon, p. 418-22; Long, p. 31-32, 40-42, 46, 60; "Who Lost Lebanon?" *Los Angeles Times,* 3-11-84. Smith (6-14-94) says that the main value the Lebanese factions saw in the MNF II was protection from the Israelis. Once the IDF had pulled out of the Beirut area, the local factions had no further use for the MNF.

To a limited extent, the Marines had become targets early in 1983. But as Habib put it in mid-April, "the Lebanese knew very well that we would not engage in a combat role in Lebanon" (Habib cable Beirut 04022, 132000Z Apr 83, par. 15). That changed during McFarlane's time. "Up until [July] there was no basic problem," Habib later said. ". . . But the circumstances changed so that the nature of the security threat changes" (Habib testimony, "Review of Adequacy . . . ," p. 357).

Habib, Draper, and Dillon are scathing in their denunciations of McFarlane's approach to the mission. He declined to even be briefed by Habib because he did not want to be "contaminated" by Habib's thinking (Draper 5-4-93; Dillon in Dillon/Barrett 5-9-94). McFarlane's decision to call in American strikes at Suq-al-Gharb was "a disastrous mistake," decided by "a real imbecile" (Draper 5-4-93). Dillon describes McFarlane and his staff as self-important, secretive, and ignorant "NSC sons of bitches" who "believed they had a duty to somehow restore the use of military force as an American policy option. . . . McFarlane and company were constantly coming up with schemes that would have required naval gunfire or forays from ships anchored off the coast. [The military] mainly resisted these ideas. . . . The Marine officers on the ground, although aggressive young men the way Marines must be, were really fairly apprehensive about American involvement which would have forced them to take up arms on one side or another. Therefore the Marine officers were in increasing opposition to Bud McFarlane and his team" (Dillon ADST oral history; Dillon 5-9-94). McFarlane in his memoirs is equally critical of Habib's work.

311 Truck bombs: Long, p. 32-33; Frank, p. 94. The IDF's partial withdrawal concentrated Israeli troops in southern Lebanon, whose population is predominantly Shi'a Muslim. This move radicalized the Shi'a there. The spiritual heart of the Shi'a sect of Islam is Iran. The truck bomber was an Iranian ("Making Sense of the Middle East," The Stanford Magazine, Spring 1986, p. 28-31; Veliotes 6-5-93; Draper 5-4-93).

311 Anger at McFarlane, my watch: Bider 4-26-93; Dusclaud 4-19-95; Habib interview with Parker, p. 25. Technically, it didn't happen on McFarlane's watch either. Six days before the bombing, Reagan appointed him head of the National Security Agency.

311 Thoroughly planned: Sachar, p. 173; and one of Habib's colleagues who asked not to be identified by name

311 Also the most: Khalidi, p. 148; Jansen, p. 13; Habib interview with Dusclaud, p. 3. The 1948-49 war would be considered longer if the number of truce days were added to the number of combat days (Khalidi, p. 148). In the immediate aftermath of the siege, Sharon and Begin pronounced the effort a great victory and an unqualified success. ("Sharon: 'I Wanted Them Out of Beirut; I Got What I Wanted,'" The Washington Post, 8-29-82; Sachar, p. 192; Lewis OH8/11; Jansen, p. 91). But that coat of paint didn't last long. Sharon later publicly blamed Habib, Veliotes, Draper, and Lewis as the architects of the defeat in Lebanon (Lewis OH 10/81).

311 Most colossal blunders: Draper OH2. In "The Commando," The New Yorker, 4-17-00, Connie Bruck writes that the invasion was "made for all the wrong reasons, and a quagmire from which they cannot escape. [Sharon's] aim was, among other things, to drive the P.L.O. out of Lebanon, neutralize Syria, and (with the P.L.O. routed) force the Palestinians in the West Bank and Gaza to forgo their struggle for independence and accept Israeli rule. On every count, it failed."

311 This tragedy: "The Commando," The New Yorker, 4-17-00

311 Israel's Vietnam: For example, "The Commando," The New Yorker, 4-17-00

311 PLO's career: One could argue that this ceased to be the case in the second intifada, which began in October 2000, but other anti-Israel players were much more prominent in that violence. The name PLO was rarely heard anymore.

311 Alternatives: Marjorie Habib on multiple occasions

311-12 Hezbollah: Shimon Shapira, "The Origins of Hizballah," The Jerusalem Quarterly, no. 46, spring 1988, p. 121-23; Yaacobi 2-14-95; "Courage Under Fire," Time, 6-5-00. Hezbollah's longer-range goal was to establish in Lebanon an Islamic movement loyal to Iran's Ayatollah Khomeini that would overthrow the Lebanese government and replace it with an Islamic regime on the Iranian model (Shapira, p. 122).

312 Average of 25: CBS Evening News, 1-1-

99. Twenty-one died in southern Lebanon in 1998 ("Israel Mourns More War Dead in Lebanon," *The New York Times,* 2-24-99).

312 Mini-invasion: "Israeli Aircraft Strike Guerrillas in Beirut Suburbs," *The New York Times,* 4-12-96; "Ending the Pain," *Time,* 5-6-96; "Beirut Staggers As Israel's Raids Enter Sixth Day," *The New York Times,* 4-17-96. This was not Israel's first serious attack in Lebanon ("Israeli Jets, in Answer to Attacks, Bomb Guerrilla Bases in Lebanon," 7-26-93).

312 Replaced: Yaacobi 2-14-95. It might be more accurate to say that the war in Lebanon replaced one terrorist threat with two, since Hamas also rose to fill part of the void left by the weakening of the PLO. But Hamas' rise was not directly attributable to the war in Lebanon.

312 Political factor, idea: Yaacobi 2-14-95

312 Puppet state: "Israel Mourns More War Dead in Lebanon," *The New York Times,* 2-24-99. This defense minister was Moshe Arens, who had been Israel's ambassador to the US during the siege.

312 Epitaph: Ze'ev Manowitz, writing in *Ha'aretz* in early August 1982, quoted in Sachar, p. 194-95; see also "After a General Tells of Killing P.O.W.'s in 1956, Israelis Argue Over Ethics of War," *The New York Times,* 8-21-95

312 Security zone: "Courage Under Fire," *Time,* 6-5-00; "Israel Quitting Lebanon After 22 Years," *The New York Times,* 5-24-00 (the 22 years counts back to Israel's 1978 invasion, Operation Litani); "Barak Declares End to 'Tragedy' as Last Troops Leave Lebanon," *The New York Times,* 5-24-00; "The Commando," *The New Yorker,* 4-17-00. The 1,550 figure is *Time's; The New York Times'* "Barak Declares..." article says more than 900 since 1978.

313 Estimates: Jansen, p. 38; Dillon OH2; Seale, p. 388; Mikdadi, p. 137, 140. An independent Lebanese newspaper, *An Nahar,* published by Habib's friend Ghassan Tueni, determined that there were 17,825 dead and 30,103 wounded, not counting Israelis ("Lebanese Paper Puts Toll at 17,825 Killed," *The New York Times,* 9-2-82).

313 Killed more than 650: This number is mentioned in an Israeli judge's ruling quoted in "Begin knew Sharon deceived him," *Ha'aretz,* 11-5-97; another article, "Court rules in libel case: Sharon misled Begin," *The Jerusalem Post,* 11-5-97, says over 600. The IDF earlier said they had 368 dead and 2,902 wounded (Gabriel, p. 235); Fisk (p. 298) and Schiff & Ya'ari (p. 301) both say over 500 Israelis died.

313 Begin: Kadishai 6-19-95; "Mr. Begin's Legacy," by Anthony Lewis, *The New York Times,* 9-1-83; "Israel Loses Its Nerve," by Joseph Kraft, *The Washington Post,* 9-1-83. Begin's friend and longtime aide Yehiel Kadishai points out that Begin had said some years earlier that he would retire from politics at age seventy, and that he turned seventy twelve days before announcing his resignation, which took effect September 15.

314 Sharon deceived Begin: "Begin knew Sharon deceived him," *Ha'aretz,* 11-5-97; "Court rules in libel case: Sharon misled Begin," *The Jerusalem Post,* 11-5-97

314 Temple Mount, *Intifada:* "Sharon Touches a Nerve, and Jerusalem Explodes," *The New York Times,* 9-29-00; "Cease-Fire Doesn't Quell Holy Land Violence," Associated press, 10-1-00; "As Arabs and Israelis Fight On, Albright Seeks Talks" and "At Arms Again, Suddenly," *The New York Times,* 10-3-00; "The Great Unraveling: End of Oslo Era, With a Bang," *The New York Times,* 10-26-00; "Arafat's Gift," *The New Yorker,* 1-29-01, p. 54; National Public Radio's "Morning Edition," 10-6-01

314 Sharon's path to prime minister: "Sharon Easily Ousts Barak to Become Israel's Premier; Calls for a Reconciliation," *The New York Times,* 2-7-01; "As Israelis Vote, Dreams of Peace Seem to Be Fading," *The New York Times,* 2-6-01; "Out of exile Once Again, Sharon is Focus of Israel," *The New York Times,* 1-24-01; "Desert Hawk," *Vanity Fair,* January 2002

315 Arrest, liquidate: "Playing Into Sharon's Hands," *The New York Times,* 1-25-02; "Sharon is Sorry Israel Didn't Kill Arafat in the 80's," *The New York Times,* 2-1-02

315 Carson: "The Tonight Show," March 13, 1986, per a note in one of Habib's scrapbooks

315 December 1983 journalist: Habib interview with the author 12-21-83

316 Depressed: Cheitlin 3-26-93

316 Shifting gears: Shultz 7-25-94; Shultz, p. 627. His wife Marjorie was very protective of

him. Whenever the phone would ring, she would race him for it so that, if someone was calling to ask him to make a trip somewhere, she could say, "He's not here." Phil grumbled to a friend that he had to get more phones around the house, including one in the bathroom, so he could get it before Marge did (Dusclaud 4-19-95; Dusclaud interview with Yves LeGouar 8-95). Whenever he would go to Washington, he would have her drive him to the San Francisco airport. He would never take a cab, she says, "because that would cost the taxpayers money! One time I couldn't get out of a bridge game to take him. He was furious at me for making him take a taxi!" (Marjorie Habib 3-26-94).

316 Heroes: Bush letter to the author 7-1-93; also Bush note to Marjorie Habib 5-27-92

316 Seldom ask: Habib letter to Wyn Hall, 8-14-89

316 Discarded, moped: Cheitlin 3-26-93

316 Redeeming: Habib letter to Wyn Hall, 8-14-89

316-17 Heart: Cheitlin 3-26-93 and 3-10-01

317 Itchy feet: Habib letter to Walter Orebaugh, 5-18-92

317 Drove, suspected: Dusclaud interview with Yves LeGouar 8-95, translated by Alice Eddé; Dusclaud 4-19-95

317-18 Habib's death: Dusclaud interview with Yves LeGouar 8-95; Cheitlin 3-26-93 and 3-10-01. Some press reports inaccurately said he had died after visiting several wine cellars in Burgundy. In fact, he died just before his winetasting would have begun.

318 Military cemetery: Marjorie Habib 5-18-97 and 8-19-01

318 Some lifetimes: "Personalities," The Washington Post, 3-1-80

Appendices

Appendix A:
The Greatest Career

330-31 Letter to Holbrooke: Letter provided by Holbrooke; also published in "A 25-year-old letter from Phil Habib, and its relevance today," State, 8-94, p. 16-17. I have altered the punctuation for clarity. Holbrooke did take the Peace Corps job, but went on to become assistant secretary of state for European affairs, the central figure in pushing through the 1995 Dayton Accords that ended the war in Bosnia, and ambassador to the UN.

Appendix B:
Basis for Mistrust

322 June 6-8: Bavly, p. 165

322 June 13: Habib cable from Jerusalem 01903 of June 13, 1982, repeated in State 163551, 142321Z Jun 82, par. 25; Sunday Times of London, 6-20-82; cited in Jansen, p. 35-36. "It is utterly appalling," the paper wrote, "that the Israeli victors should obstruct these humanitarian non-political operations." On July 6 Israel's ally the Phalange helped maintain the blockade of West Beirut by turning back a Red Cross convoy at the port (Stoessel cable State 186129 TOSEC 100100, 060031Z Jul 82, par. 3).

322 June 14-July 5: Discussed in chapter 5

322 June 15: Lewis 6-15-82 cable quoted in Haig cable 051526, 170048Z Jun 82, par. 3-4; Paganelli cable from Damascus 04216, 151108Z Jun 82 [6-15-82]

323 July 5: "Radio Communication between C. Hill - Habib, 7/6/82, 0715" 8218995, 7-6-82, p. 1 and 5

323 July 30: Hill 7-16-94

323 Aug 1: Hill 7-21-94

323 Aug 2: NEA Veliotes memo to The Secretary, 8-2-82, 8223177; Hill 7-21-94

323 Intermediary pass: Habib cable from Beirut 05338, 121420Z Aug 82, par. 7; Habib cable from Beirut 5321, quoted in State 226706, 130147Z Aug 82, par. 1-3; Hill 7-21-94

Appendix C:
Habib's Last Two Missions

324 Darnedest: unidentified friend of Habib's quoted in "Habib Finds Himself in a Hot Seat," The New York Times, 7-17-86

324 Clout: Bosworth cable from Manila 05382, 170956Z Feb 86, par. 8; *The Washington Post,* editorial 2-14-86. America's history of having ruled the Philippines from 1898 to 1946 ("Aquino Warns Reagan: Don't Plot With Marcos," *The Washington Post,* 2-13-86), its two decades of support for Marcos, and its hordes of journalists covering the story put America squarely in the middle of the crisis. Habib would later hear over and over from the Filipinos he talked with that they were counting on the US to push Marcos out.

324 Crook, no flies: Helble 2-28-94; Karnow, *Image,* p. 417; "Reagan's Double Take," *Newsweek,* 2-24-86; Shultz, p. 628. Buss (5-10-93) says that as assistant secretary Habib found Marcos so distasteful that he tended to skip the Philippines on his tours of Asia to minimize his dealings with him. William Bundy (1-29-94) says "Phil trusted Marcos as far as he could throw him. He considered him selfish, a schemer, a slippery character."

324 Botched: For all his concern about not repeating the mistakes the US had made in the shah affair, Reagan botched this one in a different way. In the same February 11 news conference in which he announced Habib's mission, he also said that there may have been fraud "on both sides" ("President to Send an Envoy to Seek Views of Filipinos, *The New York Times,* 2-12-86). Those three simple words, for which there was no evidence, deeply insulted Aquino and her followers. The gaffe also made her suspicious of Reagan's motives in sending Habib, and her spokesman said he was not sure whether she would even agree to meet with him. She said that Habib would "no doubt" be welcome in Manila, but "I must confess to some alarm, however, that his last task for the president was trying to negotiate an end to Lebanon's civil war. I hope neither Mr. Reagan nor Mr. Marcos is expecting to see our beloved country go the same way" ("Aquino Warns Reagan: Don't Plot With Marcos," *The Washington Post,* 2-13-86; "Habib Arrives in the Philippines; Aquino Camp Suspicious on Goal," *The New York Times,* 2-16-86). Reagan did back away from the blooper on February 15.

A backdrop to the story was that the US had long maintained two critical military bases in the Philippines, for which the US paid the Philippines a handsome rent. In the years preceding the election, the bases had become increasingly controversial among Filipinos. Marcos had always supported the bases. Some in the US administration feared that, if Marcos were gone, his successor would force the US to abandon the bases. Marcos threatened to abrogate the treaty allowing the bases if the US cut its support of his regime to pressure him to relinquish office *(Manila Times,* 2-19-86).

325 Messy, good sport: Lugar 5-9-94

325 Misinterpreted mission: For example, "Public relations, Reagan Style," *Philippine Daily Inquirer,* 2-19-86; "Habib Arrives in the Philippines; Aquino Camp Suspicious on Goal," *The New York Times,* 2-16-86; *The Washington Post* editorial 2-13-86. Aquino said she was relieved to hear from Habib personally that he had no instruction to urge her to join hands with Marcos (Bosworth cable from Manila 05558, 181204Z Feb 86, par. 2).

325 Personally: Reagan had already heard the first-hand report of a US congressional delegation of election observers headed by Sen. Richard Lugar, but even that wasn't enough to persuade him.

325 Declared winner: "Habib Arrives in the Philippines; Aquino Camp Suspicious on Goal," *The New York Times,* 2-16-86

325 Speculation: For example, "A Mission in Manila for Habib," *The New York Times,* 2-12-86; "Lugar Says Vote Fraud Could Halt Manila Aid," *The Washington Post,* 2-13-86; "Habib Arrives in the Philippines; Aquino Camp Suspicious on Goal," *The New York Times,* 2-16-86; "Marcos Named Winner Of Philippine Election," *The Washington Post,* 2-16-86; "Reagan Didn't Order Habib to Tell Marcos To Do Something," *Manila Bulletin,* 2-20-86. Bosworth cable from Manila 05297, 141329 Z Feb 86, par. 9, reports that some Aquino supporters thought Habib "was coming simply to provide President Reagan with a basis for whitewashing the election."

325 What lay ahead: For example, Bosworth cable from Manila 06168, 211333Z Feb 86, par. 5

325 Sugar magnate: Bosworth cable from Manila 06164, 211258Z Feb 86; see also Shultz, p. 630-31. The quote is the cable's summary of what the businessman said, not necessarily his own exact words. Habib met with this man the day before his second meeting with Marcos.

326 Horrible, dump him: Shultz, p. 633

326 Meetings with Marcos: Bosworth cable

459

from Manila 06183, 211434Z Feb 86; Bosworth cable from Manila 0693, 221354Z Feb 86. Habib later told his wife that his most important source of information had been Cardinal Jaime Sin (Marjorie Habib 9-26-98). Unfortunately, the declassified cable reporting their meeting (Bosworth cable from Manila 05559, 181209Z Feb 86) has nearly everything Sin said blocked out.

326 Dominant view: Shultz, p. 630

326 Meeting with Reagan: Shultz, p. 635-36; Karnow, *Image,* p. 420. Shultz places the argument with Don Regan after Habib's dramatic concluding statement; Karnow, who interviewed Habib for his account, places it before. Reagan authorized two messages to Marcos: The first, urging restraint, was immediate; the second, about a peaceful transition, came a few hours later. In deference to the president's sensibilities, Shultz always emphasized giving Marcos an honorable out and asylum in the United States.

327 Dignified transition: Shultz, p. 632

327 Authenticity, Laxalt, exile: "My Conversations With Ferdinand Marcos: A Lesson in Personal Diplomacy," by Senator Paul Laxalt, *Policy Review,* no. 37, Summer 1986, p. 4-5; Shultz, p. 614-15, 637-38; Karnow, *Image,* p. 421; Larranger 4-18-94.

327 Crisis was over: Miscellaneous information about the Marcos episode is drawn from Shultz, p. 610-42; Karnow, *Image,* p. 417-21; Reagan, p. 362-67; Lugar, p. 152-59; Buss, p. 32-41; Lugar 5-9-94; Sigur OH, p. 49-50; and Bosworth cables from Manila such as 05772, 191455Z Feb 86; 04999, 130909Z Feb 86; 05083, 131156Z Feb 86; 05297, 141329 Z Feb 86; 05558, 181204Z Feb 86; 05467, 180839Z Feb 86; 05737, 190955Z Feb 86; 05930, 201230Z Feb 86; 06163, 211235Z Feb 86; 06187, 220425Z Feb 86; "President to Send an Envoy to Seek Views of Filipinos, *The New York Times,* 2-12-86; "President Sending Habib to Manila To Assess Situation," *The Washington Post,* 2-12-86; "Lugar Says Vote Fraud Could Halt Manila Aid," *The Washington Post,* 2-13-86; "Habib Arrives in the Philippines; Aquino Camp Suspicious on Goal" and "Marcos Declared Victor, but Aquino Says He Lost," *The New York Times,* 2-16-86.

327 Completed Manila mission: After Marcos left, Habib returned to Manila to meet again with Aquino and see how the US could help her new government (Habib cable from Ma-

nila 06640, 271426Z Feb 86; Bosworth cable from Manila 06826, 011322Z Feb 86; etc.).

328 Core Four: This term is used routinely in the cables reporting Habib's meetings. However, Oscar Arias points out that the idea of four democracies against Nicaragua was purely an American notion (email to the author 8-6-01).

328 100,000 killed, refugees: LaFeber, p. 345. He says 100,000-200,000 killed. The guerrillas in El Salvador, Habib said, "are supplied spiritually and materially from the Sandinistas" (Habib testimony, "Recent Events . . . ," p. 20).

328 Nicaragua Decade, subject of more: "The United States and the Nicaraguan Revolution," The National Security Archives, Digital National Security Archive online at http://192.195.245.32/niessayx.htm. "Nicaragua Decade" also cited there.

328 Beachhead, threat: Reagan address to the nation, 3-16-01 *(Administration of Ronald Reagan, 1986/Mar 16,* p. 371. Bruce Cameron of the Center for Democracy in the Americas wrote in July 1986 that "Habib had great credibility among House moderates . . . . by mid-June he had . . . made the term 'good-faith diplomatic effort,' and its exhaustion, more meaningful" (Cameron memo to Spitz Channell, "Why the President Won on Contra Aid," 7-2-86).

328 Moral, eschatological: "Full-Court Press," *Time,* 3-17-86; Elizabeth Drew's "Letter From Washington," *The New Yorker,* 7-7-86

328 Moral equivalent: "The United States and the Nicaraguan Revolution," The National Security Archives, Digital National Security Archive online at http://192.195.245.32/niessayx.htm, citing a March 1985 Reagan speech.

329 Ammunition, Coca-Cola: LaFeber, p. 339; Gutman, p. 341. Contra leader Adolfo Calero's former business in Managua, Nicaragua, had been managing Coca-Cola's franchise there. Habib's more diplomatic way of putting it was that, "From all I heard from our own people closest to the conflict, however, we should be under no illusion that within a foreseeable time frame the Contras can march into Managua after success on the battlefield" (Habib memo to The Secretary, "Contadora," 4-29-86, 8613556, p. 6; repeated as State 134039 TOSEC 820168, 300125Z Apr 86). After five years of effort, they held no territory in Nicara-

gua (Elizabeth Drew, "Letter From Washington," *The New Yorker,* 7-7-86). McFarlane was at this point Reagan's national security adviser.

329 No effort: Shultz, p. 951

329 Aura: Shultz, p. 951

329 Whole point: Kornbluh 5-12-94

329 Asking for tools: "Reagan Appoints Habib as Envoy to Central America," *The New York Times,* 3-8-86; Gutman, p. 323. Habib's appointment came at the end of a week in which four out of five congressional panels had voted against Reagan's funding request. In his Message to the Congress on Aid to the *Contras,* 3-19-86, Reagan said, "If the Congress approves my request [for another $100 million for the Contras] I will send my special envoy on an urgent mission to the capitals of the Contadora and Support Group nations" (*Administration of Ronald Reagan, 1986/Mar 19,* p. 391).

329 Uninterested, telling stories, rehearsing: Cheitlin 3-26-93. "Totally uninterested" is Cheitlin's wording of what Habib had told him.

330 Typical days: Habib's 1986 datebook

330 Plane incident: Hamilton 10-10-93; Habib 1986 datebook. The actual pilots on this flight could not be found to interview, but airline pilot Dave Forsyth explains that some planes fly this high for fuel economy. Airplanes in flight are pumped up like a balloon, and standard procedure for an actual or potential loss of pressure is to dive to altitudes low enough that air pressure outside equals air pressure inside: probably around 14,000 feet. Pilots would do this in fear of possible structural failure of the plane. The shaking would have resulted from the speed brakes: flaps on the wings that stand up to create sudden drag and force a dive. Forsyth says the plane would probably have dropped at a rate of 4,000 to 6,000 feet per minute, which would take 5-7 minutes (Forsyth 7-18-01 and 7-26-01 email to the author).

330-31 Plausible: "Habib Finds Himself in a Hot Seat," *The New York Times,* 7-17-86. Elizabeth Drew quoted an unnamed administration official admitting that Habib's mission was largely "for show," but that Habib had taken it seriously ("Letter From Washington," *The New Yorker,* 7-7-86).

331 Sabotaged: Shultz, p. 952. Kornbluh 5-12-94 says, "Habib was set up and cynically used. His personal credibility gained points with Congress to assure that the diplomatic track was serious and thus get Contra aid. Yet Ollie North and Elliott Abrams promptly started undercutting him to make sure he accomplished nothing. When he came close, they sabotaged diplomacy."

331 Prominent hardliners: Other prominent hardliners were Caspar Weinberger, CIA director William Casey, UN ambassador Jeanne Kirkpatrick, White House communications director Patrick Buchanan, National Security Advisers Bud McFarlane and John Poindexter and Frank Carlucci, Oliver North, and various conservative members of Congress.

331 Day one, theological: Hamilton, 10-10-93; also Wisner 6-12-94

331 Grousing: Hamilton, 10-10-93

331 Letter controversy: Hamilton 10-10-93; Habib memo to The Secretary, "Contadora," 4-29-86, 8613556, p. 4; Gutman, p. 330; Elizabeth Drew's "Letter From Washington," *The New Yorker,* 7-7-86; "President rejects Kemp request to fire envoy Habib," *The Washington Times,* 5-23-86; "Behind Habib's mission," *The Washington Times,* 5-15-86; "Contra-Indicated," *The National Review,* 6-20-86; "Habib Finds Himself in a Hot Seat," *The New York Times,* 7-17-86; William Safire's column "They Were Expendable," *The New York Times,* 5-26-86. Hamilton adds that the letter "was more a statement of political reality than a policy statement." Several Latin American governments were pushing the US to cease support for the Contras *prior* to signature (Habib memo, "Contadora," p. 4).

332 Should fund: For example, Habib memo to The Secretary, "Contadora," 4-29-86, 8613556, p. 2, 6

332 Indispensable element: Habib memo to The Secretary, "Contadora: Visit to Costa Rica, El Salvador and Guatemala," 6-4-86, p. 3; italics added; Hamilton 10-10-93. He said, "the thrust is to get to the table. . . . I happen to believe that it is possible for the diplomatic track to make substantial progress if we can get [the Sandinistas] to the table." He hastened to point out that "when I talk about pressure, I don't just simply mean the contras. I think the contras are one form of pressure. Another form of pressure is the attitudes and views expressed by the other Central American democracies. A third form of pressure is the internal disarray, the economic shambles, and the dissatisfaction that is now right visible in the Nicaraguan structure itself" (Habib testimony, "Recent

Events . . . ," p. 21, 26).

332 Purpose of Contras: Habib testimony, "Recent Events..." 7-9-87, p. 26. Habib said the bottom line of his instructions were the words Shultz had used with him: "Make sure . . . that all of us can live with the proposals; don't go for any phony proposals" (p. 18).

332 Means to end: Hamilton 10-10-93; Habib cable State 035102, 010229Z May 86, par. 3. Habib wrote bluntly, "In my view, the only solution to the problem in Central America is a diplomatic and peaceful one" (Habib letter to Betty Estersohn, 3-17-87, in his home files).

332 Would not approve: AP story "Reagan names Habib special envoy to Central America," *St. Petersburg Times,* 8-8-86

332 Symbol: Gutman, p. 353. Many Democrats in Congress "regarded Habib as one of the administration's few sincere advocates of a diplomatic solution in Nicaragua" (*Newsweek,* 8-24-87, p. 25).

332 Arias' campaign: Arias 6-24-95; Habib cable from Mexico 09107, 281816Z Apr 86, par. 16. After meeting Arias for the first time, Habib wrote that he "has the potential to develop into our strongest asset. Despite his opposition to our Contra policy, and in part owing to it, he speaks with the moral authority of an independent actor. He is an ideological democrat who I think is dead serious about pursuing a Latin American collective effort to pressure the Sandinistas on democratization" (Habib memo to The Secretary, "Contadora," 4-29-86, 8613556, p. 3).

332 Signaled, prestige: Arias 6-24-95. When Habib and Arias first met on April 26, 1986, Arias said that Habib's visit "had given the Latin Americans security that the U.S. was supporting their efforts to find a peaceful solution" (Habib cable from Mexico 09107, 281816Z Apr 86, par. 7).

333 Military issues, outsiders: Arias 6-24-96; Habib memo to The Secretary, "Contadora," 4-29-86, 8613556, p. 4-5. Mexico's partners in pushing Contadora were Venezuela, Colombia, and Panama, none of which were considered "Central American." The Sandinistas in particular would have none of it. The Central Americans certainly were participants in the Contadora process, but, Oscar Arias (6-24-95) says, "Central Americans didn't want to be preached at by Panama and Mexico. So what we needed was an indigenous peace plan."

333 Beach: Arias 6-24-95

333 Committed, declined, Pope: Arias 6-24-95

333 Plan called for: LaFeber, p. 342; Hamilton 10-10-93

333 Honduras and El Salvador reservations: Habib memo to The Secretary, "Status of the Diplomatic Track in Central America," 4-1-87, p. 1. President Duarte of El Salvador considered the proposals "defective and incapable of implementation" at this point (cable State 129588, 300136Z Apr 87, par. 2).

333 Encyclopedia: Arias 6-24-95

333 Humored: LaFeber, p. 343

333 Discredit: For example, Thomas F. Gibson, special assistant to the president, director of public affairs, sent out a letter on White House stationery to newspaper editors across the country on June 2, 1986, saying in part "Either Arias is hopelessly naïve or his critics are right. As a president limited to one term in office, Arias is strutting around as the champion of peace to maximize his moment in the sun." When a member of Congress read that to Habib during a hearing and asked Habib why the White House would put out such a letter, Habib replied, "I think that is an unfair comment, and I don't give a damn who put it out. . . . I have now been dealing with the man since before he was elected. I do not question his dedication to democracy" (Habib testimony, "Recent Events . . . ," p. 24-25).

333 Strengthen: Habib testimony, "Recent Events . . . ," 7-9-87, p. 6-8, 17, 24; Habib testimony, "Briefing on Central American Peace Initiative," 6-16-87, p. 4-9, 42-45, 64. In his June 16 Senate testimony Habib said, "my instructions [from Shultz] were to get the agreement approved" (p. 60).

333 Exception was Habib: Arias 6-24-95. Washington variously suspected Arias was a dreamer, a dupe out to save the Sandinistas, or a communist himself. The Sandinistas mistrusted him because they thought he was a tool of the American State Department. The Contras hated him because he had thrown them out of Costa Rica (Arias 10-1-95). Arias made clear his opposition to the Sandinistas at his first meeting with Habib (Habib cable from Mexico 09107, 281816Z Apr 86).

334 Lots of loopholes: Habib enumerated his reservations about the plan in Habib memo to

462

Notes to Appendix C: Habib's Last Two Missions

The Secretary, "The Negotiating Track in Central America: Esquipulas and Beyond," 5-28-87, p. 2-4. Understanding Arias' reasons for resisting changes to the text of the plan, Habib tried to get him to tighten the definitions without major changes to the text itself (cable San Salvador 07510, 092355Z Jun 87, par. 5).

334 Cosmetic: Habib memo to The Secretary, "The Diplomatic Track and the Guatemala Summit," 6-15-87, p. 4; also cable Tegucigalpa 10051, 122208Z Jun 87, par. 10. Habib said they would "do just enough to make the situation fuzzy."

334 Teeth: Arias 6-24-95

334 Pillow: Quote compiled from Arias 6-24-95 and 10-1-95

334 Simultaneity: Arias 6-24-95; Arias email to the author 8-6-01; Habib testimony, "Briefing on Central American Peace Initiative," 6-16-87, p. 42-45; Shultz, p. 960; Gutman, p. 349. The plan did not call for elections to occur simultaneously with the other steps, saying instead that elections would occur on schedule as already specified in each country's own constitution (Arias email to the author 8-6-01). As early as June 1986 Habib had said he was working "to keep the attention of the democracies focussed on essentials: comprehensiveness, verification, and simultaneity" (Habib memo to The Secretary, "Contadora: Visit to Costa Rica, El Salvador and Guatemala," 6-4-86, p. 3).

334 My ambassador: Arias 6-24-95

334 Dominated: LaFeber, p. 367

334 Fire Habib: cable San Salvador 07510, 092355Z Jun 87, par. 5

335 Core Four split: Habib memo to The Secretary, "Status of the Diplomatic Track in Central America," 4-1-87, p. 1, 4; cable State 101700, 042023Z Apr 87, par 2; cable from Tegucigalpa 06981, 281832Z Apr 87, par. 2; Habib memo to The Secretary, "Assessment of the Negotiating Track: My April 27-28 Trip to Central America," 4-29-87; cable State 129588, 300136Z Apr 87, par. 2; Habib memo to The Secretary, "The Diplomatic Track and the Guatemala Summit," 6-15-87, p. 1; etc. By June 1987 Habib said he had impressed upon Arias "that his proposals may turn out to be a disaster if the democracies are not substantially united" (cable San Salvador 07510, 092355Z Jun 87, par. 23). The presidents of El

Salvador and Honduras were heavily dependent on the US, and Habib felt observers would assume that the US, whose president clearly was committed to another course, had pressured them to vote against the plan and thus sink it. Honduras took a position of "active neutrality" (Habib memo to The Secretary, "The Negotiating Track in Central America: Esquipulas and Beyond," 5-28-87, p. 1). By June 11 both Honduras and El Salvador indicated that, if the other three signed the plan, they would be inclined to go along (cable Tegucigalpa 09917, 111858Z June 87, par. 9).

335 Accept changes: Cable Tegucigalpa 10051, 122208Z Jun 87, par. 8-10. Arias said if he tried to negotiate all the changes the other three democracies wanted, "it would take another four years"). Habib's main complaint about the plan was not its substance but that the presidents had not conferred more about it (Habib testimony, "Recent Events..." 7-9-87, throughout; Habib testimony, "Briefing on Central American Peace Initiative," 6-16-87, p. 74 and throughout). Arias (6-24-95 and email to the author 8-6-01) felt they had conferred plenty, by phone.

335 Crazy: Shultz, p. 956; also Habib testimony, "Recent Events . . . ," 7-9-87, p. 10; Habib testimony, "Briefing on Central American Peace Initiative," 6-16-87, p. 4-9, 15. Arias recognized that the ceasefire provision of his first draft was weak. Since Costa Rica had no army, he had no experience with ceasefires, so he expected El Salvador and his other neighbors to develop that aspect of the plan.

335 Weak agreement: Habib 6-16-86 speech to the World Affairs Council of Northern California, reported in "Habib: U.S. aid is necessary in Nicaragua," *Peninsula Times Tribune*, 6-17-86

335 Little else: Habib memo to The Secretary, "The Diplomatic Track and the Guatemala Summit," 6-15-87, p. 6

335 Personally visited, revised: Arias email to the author 8-6-01; Julie Whitman email to the author 8-7-01. Whitman is a colleague of Arias' at the Arias Foundation for Peace and Human Progress. Arias felt he and his colleagues had consulted plenty over the course of "many, many telephone conversations with all four" in the months since he had announced his plan.

336 Cowboys, his crowd: According to a State Department official who asked not to be identified by name. There has never been any sug-

463

gestion that Habib was involved or even knew about the Iran-Contra affair activities until the rest of the world did. Indeed, Peter Kornbluh of the National Security Archives says, "Abrams would have made sure Habib did not know about the diversion" (Kornbluh 5-12-94).

336 Determined: Cable State 102852, 031330Z Apr 86, par. 6

336 Make peace: Cheitlin's 3-26-93 quote of what Habib had told him. Besides being his cardiologist, Cheitlin was also his friend. When Reagan and Arias met on June 17, 1987, Reagan said his plan was unacceptable because it would require the US to stop funding the Contras (Chicago Tribune, 6-19-87).

336 Football player: Marjorie Habib 6-20-95, 2-19-95, 8-19-01. Kemp had entered politics after retiring from a career as a football player.

336 Not altogether stupid: Habib testimony, "Briefing on Central American Peace Initiative," 6-16-87, p. 76 (punctuation altered for clarity)

336 Shultz' testimony: "An Edge of Anger," Time, 8-3-87; Shultz, p. 908-23

336-37 Resignation letter: Unsigned draft letter dated July 24, 1987, in Habib's scrapbook #3. On June 16, he mentioned in passing that he had been "dreaming of going back to California by this fall" (Habib testimony, "Briefing on Central American Peace Initiative," 6-16-87, p. 73). He had inquired about getting access to classified records of his various missions, apparently in anticipation of writing his memoirs (Frank Machak letter, July 17, 1987). He never got any records and never got very far toward writing memoirs.

337 Aftermath of agreement on Arias plan: Drawn primarily from Gutman, p. 349-57, who had interviewed Habib; also Shultz, p. 959-69; LaFeber, p. 342-45; Habib letter to "Dear George" dated August 12, 1987, in Habib's scrapbook #3; "More to Habib mission than buying time, votes," Houston Chronicle, 3-13-86. Arias (6-24-95) says the hardliners' opposition to his plan had the unintended effect of helping get it adopted: "When the Sandinistas realized that this was not a US peace plan, that I was not being a puppet of Washington, and that the US was not supporting the plan, then they supported it." During his sixteen-month mission, Habib never dealt directly with the Sandinistas, but his predecessor had had nine rounds of meetings with them (Habib testi-

mony, "Recent Events . . . " 7-9-87, p. 10; Bider memo to Mr. Dugstad, May 12, 1987; Reagan radio address 3-15-86). The quote of how Carlucci framed the question is LaFeber's quote of special lobbyist for Contra aid Tom Loeffler's account of how the NSC framed the question, not necessarily Carlucci's own words. Habib noted in a House hearing on July 9 that "there are some Members of these august bodies who have called on the President to fire me" (Habib testimony, "Recent Events . . . ," p. 25). Habib had said on May 28 that, if the five presidents agreed to a plan that included revisions the US required, "our stated conditions for talking with the Sandinistas will have been met" (Habib memo to The Secretary, "The Negotiating Track in Central America: Esquipulas and Beyond," 5-28-87, p. 4). Six months after Habib's resignation, Oscar Arias visited him at his home in California. He told Arias he had asked Reagan to support the Arias peace plan and resigned when Reagan refused (Arias 6-24-95). One of Elliott Abrams' top aides told reporters that, when the Nobel Peace Prize was given to Arias, "All of us . . . reacted with disgust, unbridled disgust" (LaFeber, p. 343-44).

338 Forced out: Shultz, p. 961. Even Abrams was the third person in his job since Reagan took office: "Anyone who seemed too keen on negotiations departed for one stated reason or another" (Elizabeth Drew, "Letter From Washington," The New Yorker, 7-7-86).

338 Elections and aftermath: LaFeber, p. 351-53; "The United States and the Nicaraguan Revolution," The National Security Archives, Digital National Security Archive online at http://192.195.245.32/niessayx.htm.

Miscellaneous information about Habib's Central America mission from Dunnigan & Bay, p. 205-24; Arias 6-24-95 and 10-1-95; Arias emails to the author 8-6-01 and 8-9-01; Shultz 7-25-94; Shultz, p. 950-69; Hamilton 10-8-93 and 10-10-93.

Sources and Bibliography

This book is based almost entirely on primary sources: declassified government documents and interviews and oral histories with participants in the events described. As this book goes to press I am arranging to place copies of the documents and other source materials at the Hoover Institution Archives at Stanford University, the Lauinger Library at Georgetown University, and the National Security Archives. Most of my interviews will also be included in the Association for Diplomatic Studies and Training's Oral History Program at Lauinger Library, Georgetown University.

When working from declassified documents, I occasionally adapt a quote from the written record. For example, Habib might say in a cable "I told Sharon I could not accept that." I might then quote Habib telling Sharon, "I cannot accept that." Likewise, I sometimes alter punctuation for the sake of clarity. Such adaptations are infrequent, do not change the meaning, and are acknowledged in the endnotes.

Many of my sources are transcribed records of oral conversations. I treat oral sources a little differently from written sources. People do not use capitalization or punctuation when they speak, and the various transcribers use a wide variety of conventions about things like capitalization and punctuation. So I sometimes adapt such things for the sake of clarity and consistency. State Department transcripts of Habib's conversations often bowdlerize his characteristic profanity, according to Charlie Hill, the official to whom he was usually talking. Based on Hill's guidance, I often put the profanity back in.

A given source would often talk about a particular point or tell a story more than once. In such cases, I often use the common journalistic practice of taking parts from one telling and parts from another by that source and weaving them together into a single cohesive quote. That is for a single source. Often I have several sources for a particular incident, and those sources often give multiple and varying accounts. For example, Habib told the story of his June 12, 1982, confrontation with Menachem Begin several times, and a little differently each time. Morris Draper and Nathaniel Howell also have their accounts of that confrontation. In such cases, I analyze all of the accounts, distill from them my own account of what happened, and use the endnotes to explain any notable wrinkles.

How and when to use quotation marks is a judgment call, so let me spell out the practice I have tried to follow. Virtually every thought and piece of information in this book is based on material from some source. I generally put sources' words in quotation marks. But there comes a point at which quotation marks would so pepper the text as to do more harm than good by becoming obtrusive. The problem would be compounded by having to include the name and further identification of each source—often two or three for a single sentence—even when the name of the source is irrelevant to the point at hand.

So my practice is to use quotation marks when the source's words are particularly colorful or eloquent or otherwise distinctive, when they express a strong opinion, or when they say something that clearly needs to be associated with them rather than with me. I do not use quotation marks, however, when picking up more pedestrian information: "Phil didn't talk to the press," for example, may be verbatim what some source said, but in my judgment does not warrant quotation marks because it is just a plain vanilla piece of information. Whether quotation marks are used or not, I carefully identify each source in the endnotes.

In all of these judgment calls, my guide has been clarity for the general reader. Scholars and other serious readers should treat the endnotes as an intrinsic part of the text, since that is where I present explanations and elaboration and subplots, detail the sources, and note any significant disagreements among sources.

The manuscript has been reviewed for accuracy by several of my principal sources.

INTERVIEWS

This list includes everyone I interviewed for the book except for some who asked not to be identified by name. I have placed most of these interviews in the Association for Diplomatic Studies and Training's Oral History Program at Lauinger Library, Georgetown University.

Arias Sánchez, Oscar	Buss, Claude
Armacost, Michael	Cheitlin, Melvin
Ashley, Fred	Colby, William
Atherton, Alfred (Roy)	Conroy, Raymond
Ball, George	Crocker, Ryan
Barrett, Robert	Dean, John Gunther
Beinin, Joel	Dillon, Robert
Beyda, Joe	Djerejian, Edward
Bider, Lori	Draper, Morris
Boschwitz, Rudolph	Duly, Gilda
Boulos, Al	Dusclaud, Michel
Brown, Fred Z.	Eagleburger, Lawrence
Bundy, William	Easterbrook, Paul
Burns, John	Eilts, Herman

Gaucher, Edward
Geske, Graydon
Grazi, Jack
Green, Marshall
Grove, Brandon
Habib, Alice
Habib, Marjorie
Habib, Philip
Habib, Phyllis
Haig, Alexander
Hall, Winifred
Hamilton, John
Helble, John
Hendee, John
Hill, Charles
Holbrooke, Richard
Howell, Nathaniel
Jabara, Evelyn
Jabara, Raymond
Jacobs, Joseph
Johnston, Robert
Jungel, Paul
Kadishai, Yehiel
Katzenbach, Nicholas
Kerlek, George
Kim, Eva
Kirby, William
Kissinger, Henry
Kliewer, Betty
Kliewer, Robert
Kreczko, Alan
Kuehner, Roy
Lake, Anthony
Lantos, Tom
Lee, Faith
Lewis, Samuel
Lugar, Richard
Marbach, Marty
Matthews, John
McArthur, George
McManaway, Clay
McNaughton, Finley

Mead, James
Michaels, Susan Habib
Miller, Robert
Miller, Thomas J.
Moore, Elaine Habib
Murphy, Elva
Negroponte, John
O'Donohue, Daniel
Orebaugh, Walter
Owen, Robert
Paganelli, Robert
Parker, Richard
Pascoe, Dorothy
Pell, Claiborne
Rockefeller, David
Rosenthal, James
Rusk, Dean
Santé, Henry
Saunders, Harold
Sehulster, James
Shepard, William
Shultz, George
Sicherman, Harvey
Slusher, Edward
Smith, Charles
Solarz, Stephen
Spiridon, George
Sullivan, William
Tarnoff, Peter
Toomey, Isabelle Spiridon
Tueni, Ghassan
Vance, Amy
Vance, Cyrus
Veliotes, Nicholas
Ward, Robert
Weinberger, Caspar
Weyand, Frederick
Wharton, David
Whitehouse, Charles
Wisner, Frank
Yaacobi, Gad
Zorthian, Barry

ORAL HISTORIES

From the Association for Diplomatic Studies and Training's Foreign Affairs Oral History Program, housed at the Lauinger Library, Georgetown University

Brown, Dean
Brown, Frederick Z.
Burke, John
Cumming, Isabel
Dillard, Dianne
Dillon, Robert
Draper, Morris
Du Vivier, Paul
Eilts, Hermann
Fairbanks, Richard
Green, Marshall
Grove, Brandon
Habib, Philip C.
Hummel, Arthur
Keeley, R.

Koren, H.
Lacey, J.
Lehmann, Wolf
Levine, Robert Don
Lewis, Samuel
McDonald, D.
Miller, Robert
Pike, Douglas
Ryan, Robert
Sigur, Gaston
Sisco, Joseph
Sober, Sidney
Underhill, Frank
Veliotes, Nicholas
Vest, George S.

From the Lyndon Baines Johnson Library

Bruce, K.E. David. AC 73-39
Bundy, William P. AC 74-187
Dillon, D. Douglas. AC 74-12
Harriman, W. Averell.
Katzenbach, Nicholas D. AC 78-24
Rusk, Dean. I through IV, AC 74-245
Vance, Cyrus R.
Zorthian, Barry. AC 79-45; AC 82-37; AC 84-63; AC 84-64, 84-65

PHILIP HABIB INTERVIEWS

With John Boykin, 12-20-83 and 1-10-84. An edited version appeared in
    The Stanford Magazine, Spring 1984.
With Michel Dusclaud, published in French in *Politique Internationale,*
    no. 28, *édition d'été* 1985; translated for the author by Susan Bree
With Stuart E. Eizenstat, 5-13-92
With Harry Kreisler, 5-14-82, Conversations with History, Institute of
    International Studies, University of California, Berkeley. "The Work
    of Diplomacy: Conversation with Philip Habib."
With Edward Mulcahy, 5-25-84 and 5-29-84 for the Association for

Diplomatic Studies and Training's Foreign Affairs Oral History
Program, housed at the Lauinger Library, Georgetown University
With Richard Parker, 5-9-90, for Parker's book *The Politics of Miscalculation in the Middle East.* Parker had been ambassador to Lebanon.
With Ghassan Tueni, 6-28-87. This interview was intended to be the
basis of Habib's memoirs. The idea was that his good friend Tueni,
publisher of *An-Nahar* newspaper in Beirut and Lebanon's former
ambassador to the UN, would publish the memoirs. Nothing came of
the project after this interview.

GOVERNMENT DOCUMENTS

Hundreds of cables and other individual documents too numerous to cite
individually here, declassified by the State Department, National
Security Council, FBI, and other agencies. Each is cited in the notes
by city of origin, number, and date/time. Most cables cited use
military time, with a 24-hour clock, so 21 means 9 P.M. Z stands for
"Zulu," shorthand for Greenwich Mean Time. Example: 062147Z
Jul 82 means July 6, 1982, at 9:47 P.M. GMT. As this book goes to
press, I am arranging to place copies of the documents at the Hoover
Institution Archives at Stanford University, the Lauinger Library at
Georgetown University, and the National Security Archives.
American Foreign Policy; Current Documents. 1982. Chapter 11,
Document 391, "Plan for the Departure of the PLO from Beirut."
US Department of State.
Briefing on Central American Peace Initiative, Stenographic Transcript
of Hearings Before the Committee on Foreign Relations, Subcom-
mittee on Westrn Hemisphere and Peace Corps Affairs, United States
Senate, June 16, 1987. Washington, DC: Anderson Reporting.
Provided by The National Archives, Records of the U.S. Senate,
Record Group 46.
Recent Events Concerning the Arias Peace Proposal, Hearing and
Markup Before the Committee on Foreign Affairs and its Subcom-
mittee on Western Hemisphere Affairs, House of Representatives,
One Hundredth Congress, First Session on H. Con. Res. 146, July 9,
15, and 28, 1987
*Review of Adequacy of Security Arrangements for Marines in Lebanon
and Plans for Improving That Security,* Hearings Before the Commit-
tee on Armed Services and the Investigations Subcommittee of the
Committee on Armed Services, House of Representatives, Ninety-
Eighth Congress, First Session, November 1, 2, 12, 18; December 8,
9, 14, 15, 1983

BOOKS

Though my text is based mostly on primary sources, I do draw on many of these books. All were helpful in the course of my research, whether I quote from them or not.

Abramson, Rudy. *Spanning the Century: The Life of W. Averell Harriman 1891-1986.* New York: William Morrow and Company, 1992.

Ambrose, Stephen E. *Nixon: The Education of a Politician, 1913-1962.* New York: Simon and Schuster, 1987.

Arias Sánchez, Oscar. *Horizons of Peace.* San Jose, Costa Rica: Fundación Arias para la Paz y el Progreso Humano (Arias Foundation for Peace and Progress of Humanity), 1994.

Attwood, William. *The Reds and the Blacks: A Personal Adventure.* New York: Harper & Row, 1967.

Ball, George W. *Error and Betrayal in Lebanon: An Analysis of Israel's Invasion of Lebanon and the Implications for U.S.-Israeli Relations.* Washington: Foundation for Middle East Peace, 1984.

Ball, George W. *The Past Has Another Pattern: Memoirs.* New York: W.W. Norton, 1982.

Ball, George W., and Douglas B. Ball. *The Passionate Attachment: America's Involvement with Israel, 1947 to the Present.* New York: W.W. Norton, 1992.

Barakat, Halim. *Toward a Viable Lebanon.* Washington, DC: Center for Contemporary Arab Studies, Georgetown University.

Bavly, Dan, and Eliahu Salpeter. *Fire in Beirut: Israel's War in Lebanon with the PLO.* Briarcliff Manor, NY: Stein & Day Publishers, 1984.

Benziman, Uzi. *Sharon: An Israeli Caesar.* New York: Adama Books, 1985.

Boettcher, Robert, with Gordon L. Freedman. *Gifts of Deceit: Sun Myung Moon, Tongsun Park, and the Korean Scandal.* New York: Holt, Rinehart, and Winston, 1980.

Brinkley, Douglas. *Dean Acheson: The Cold War Years 1953-71.* New Haven and London: Yale University Press, 1992.

Bundy, William. *A Tangled Web: The Making of Foreign Policy in the Nixon Presidency.* New York: Hill & Wang, a division of Farrar, Straus & Giroux, 1998.

Bush, George, with Victor Gold. *Looking Forward: An Autobiography.* New York: Doubleday, 1987.

Buss, Claude A. *Cory Aquino and the People of the Philippines.* Stanford, California: The Portable Stanford, 1987.

Buss, Claude A. *The United States and the Republic of Korea: Background for Policy.* Stanford, California: Hoover Press, 1982.

Cannon, Lou. *President Reagan: The Role of a Lifetime.* New York: Simon & Schuster, 1991.

Clifford, Clark, with Richard Holbrooke. *Counsel to the President: A Memoir.* New York: Doubleday, 1991.

Clifton, Tony, and Catherine Leroy. *God Cried.* London: Quartet Books Ltd., 1983

Cobban, Helena. *The Superpowers and the Syrian-Israeli Conflict: Beyond Crisis Management?* New York: Praeger, Center for Strategic and International Studies, 1991.

Cronkite, Walter. *A Reporter's Life.* New York: Alfred A. Knopf, 1996.

Davis, M. Thomas. *40 Km Into Lebanon: Israel's 1982 Invasion.* Washington, DC: National Defense University Press, a National Security Affairs Monograph, 1987.

Diem, Bui, with David Chanoff. *In the Jaws of History.* Boston: Houghton Mifflin, 1987.

Drysdale, Alasdair, and Raymond A. Hinnebusch. *Syria and the Middle East Peace Process.* New York: Council on Foreign Relations, 1991.

Dunnigan, James F., and Austin Bay. *A Quick & Dirty Guide to War.* New York: William Morrow and Co., 1985, 1986.

Eisenhower, Julie Nixon. *Pat Nixon: The Untold Story.* New York: Simon and Schuster, 1986.

Evron, Yair. *War and Intervention in Lebanon: The Israeli-Syrian Deterrence Dialogue.* Baltimore: The Johns Hopkins University Press, 1987.

Fisk, Robert. *Pity the Nation: The Abduction of Lebanon.* New York: Atheneum, 1990.

Friedman, Thomas L. *From Beirut to Jerusalem.* New York: Doubleday, 1989.

Gabriel, Richard A. *Operation Peace for Galilee: The Israeli-PLO War in Lebanon.* New York: Hill and Wang, 1984.

Gibbons, William Conrad. *The U.S. Government and the Vietnam War: Executive and Legislative Roles and Relationships, Part III: January-July 1965.* Princeton, NJ: Princeton University Press, 1989.

Gilbert, Martin. *Israel: A History.* New York: William Morrow and Company, 1998.

Gilmour, David. *Lebanon: The Fractured Country.* Oxford: Martin Robertson, 1983.

Glueck, Grace, and Paul Gardner. *Brooklyn: People and Places, Past and Present.* New York: Harry N. Abrams, 1991.

Gordon, David C. *The Republic of Lebanon: Nation in Jeopardy.* Boulder, CO: The Westview Press, 1983.

Gowers, Andrew, and Tony Walker. *Behind the Myth: Yasser Arafat and the Palestinian Revolution.* Brooklyn: Olive Branch Press, 1992.

Grant, Zalin. *Facing the Phoenix.* New York and London: W.W. Norton & Company, 1991.

Grunwald, Henry. *One Man's America.* New York: Doubleday, 1997

Gutman, Roy. *Banana Diplomacy: The Making of American Policy in Nicaragua 1981-1987.* New York: Simon and Schuster, 1988

Haig, Alexander M., Jr. *Caveat: Realism, Reagan, and Foreign Policy.* New York: Macmillan, 1984.

Hammel, Eric M. *The Root: The Marines in Beirut, August 1982- February 1984.* New York: Harcourt Brace Jovanovich, 1985.

Hart, Alan. *Arafat: Terrorist or Peacemaker.* London: Sidgewick & Jackson, 1984.

Hatch, Alden. *The Lodges of Massachusetts.* New York: Hawthorn Books, Inc., 1973.

Henry, Paul-Marc. *Les Jardiniers de L'Enfer [The Gardeners of Hell].* Olivier Orban, 1984 (no place).

Herring, George C., ed. *The Secret Diplomacy of the Vietnam War: The Negotiating Volumes of the Pentagon Papers.* Austin, Texas: University of Texas Press, 1983.

Herzog, Chaim. *The Arab-Israeli Wars.*

Hickey, Gerald Cannon. *Free in the Forest: Ethnohistory of the Vietnamese Central Highlands 1954-1976.* New Haven and London: Yale University Press, 1982.

Holbrooke, Richard. *To End a War.* New York: Random House, 1998.

Hosmer, Stephen T., Konrad Kenne, Brian M. Jenkins. *The Fall of South Vietnam: Statements by Vietnamese Military and Civilian Leaders.* New York: Crane, Russak & Co., 1980.

International Commission, The. *Israel in Lebanon: The Report of the International Commission to enquire into reported violations of International Law by Israel during its invasion of the Lebanon.* London: The Ithaca Press, 1983.

Isaacson, Walter. *Kissinger: A Biography.* New York: Simon & Schuster, 1992.

Isaacson, Walter, and Evan Thomas. *The Wise Men: Six Friends and the World They Made.* New York: Simon and Schuster, 1986.

Israeli, Raphael, ed. *PLO in Lebanon: Selected Documents.* London: Weidenfeld and Nicolson,1983.

Jacobs, Joseph J. *The Anatomy of an Entrepreneur: Family, Culture, and Ethics.* San Francisco: ICS Press, 1991.

Jansen, Michael. *The Battle of Beirut: Why Israel Invaded Lebanon.* Boston: South End Press, 1982.

Jenkins, Brian M. *Embassies Under Siege: A Review of 48 Embassy Takeovers, 1971-1980.* Santa Monica, California: The Rand Corporation, 1981.

Johnson, Lyndon Baines. *The Vantage Point: Perspectives of the Presidency 1963-1969.* New York: Holt, Rinehart and Winston, 1971.

Jones, Howard. *The Course of American Diplomacy: From the Revolution to the Present.* New York: Franklin Watts, Inc., 1985.

Kalb, Marvin, and Elie Abel. *Roots of Involvement: The U.S. in Asia 1784-1971.* New York: W.W. Norton and Co., 1971.

Kalb, Marvin, and Bernard Kalb. *Kissinger.* Boston: Little, Brown and Company, 1974.

Karnow, Stanley. *In Our Image: America's Empire in the Philippines.* New York: Random House, 1989.

Karnow, Stanley. *Vietnam: A History.* New York: Penguin Books, 1983.

Khalidi, Rashid. *Under Siege: PLO Decisionmaking During the 1982 War.* New York: Columbia University Press, 1986.

Kissinger, Henry. *White House Years.* Boston: Little, Brown and Co., 1979.

Kissinger, Henry. *Years of Upheaval.* Boston: Little, Brown and Co., 1982.

Komisar, Lucy. *Corazon Aquino: The Story of a Revolution.* New York: George Braziller, 1987.

LaFeber, Walter. *Inevitable Revolutions: The United States in Central America.* Second ed. New York: W.W. Norton and Co., 1993.

Laqueur, Walter, and Barry Rubin, eds. *The Israel-Arab Reader: A Documentary History of the Middle East Conflict.* Revised and updated ed. New York: Penguin Books, 1991.

Lodge, Henry Cabot. *The Storm Has Many Eyes: A Personal Narrative.* New York: W.W. Norton & Co., 1973.

Lugar, Richard G. *Letters to the Next President.* New York: Simon and Schuster, 1988

Mack, Dayton, and Charles Stuart Kennedy. *American Ambassadors in a Troubled World: Interviews with Senior Diplomats.* Westport, CT: Greenwood Press, 1992.

Mackey, Sandra. *Lebanon: Death of a Nation.* New York: Anchor Books, 1989.

Makdisi, Jean Said. *Beirut Fragments: A War Memoir.* New York: Persea Books, 1990.

Maoz, Moshe, and Avnery Yaniv, eds. *Syria Under Assad.* New York:

St. Martin's Press, 1986.

Massoulie, Francois. *Middle East Conflicts*. Brooklyn: Interlink Books, Interlink Illustrated Histories series, 1999.

McDermott, Anthony, and Kjell Skjelsbaek, eds. *The Multinational Force in Beirut 1982-1984*. Miami: Florida International University Press, 1991.

McDowall, David. *Lebanon: A Conflict of Minorities*. Report No. 61. Minority Rights Group.

McFarlane, Robert C. *Special Trust*. New York: Cadell & Davies, 1994.

Mikdadi, Lina. *Surviving the Siege of Beirut: A Personal Account*. London: Onyx Press, 1983.

Mosher, Frederick C. Introduction to John E. Harr, *The Anatomy of the Foreign Service—a Statistical Profile*. Carnegie Endowment for International Peace, Foreign Affairs Personnel Study No. 4, 1965.

Newman, Barbara, with Barbara Rogan. *The Covenant: Love and Death in Beirut*. New York: Crown Publishers, 1989.

New York Times, The. *The Pentagon Papers*. New York: Bantam Books, 1971.

Nixon, Richard. *RN: The Memoirs of Richard Nixon*. New York: Grosset & Dunlap, 1978.

Norton, Augustus Richard. *Amal and the Shi'a: Struggle for the Soul of Lebanon*. Austin, Texas: University of Texas Press, 1987.

Oberdorfer, Don. *Tet! The Story of a Battle and its Historic Aftermath*. Garden City, New York: Doubleday and Co., 1971.

Orfalea, Gregory. *Before the Flames: A Quest for the History of Arab Americans*. Austin, Texas: University of Texas Press, 1988.

Pakradouni, Karim. *La Paix Manquée: Le Mandat d'Elias Sarkis (1976-1982)*. [No city] Editions FMA, second ed., 1984.

Parker, Richard B. *The Politics of Miscalculation in the Middle East*. Indianapolis: Indiana University Press, 1993.

Petran, Tabitha. *The Struggle Over Lebanon*. New York: Monthly Review Press, 1987.

Pilger, John. *The Last Day: America's Final Hours in Vietnam*. New York: Vintage Books, 1975.

Pintak, Larry. *Beirut Outtakes: A TV Correspondent's Portrait of America's Encounter with Terror*. Lexington, Mass.: D.C. Heath & Co., Lexington Books, 1988.

Pratt, Julius W., Vincent P. DeSantis, Joseph M. Siracusa. *A History of United States Foreign Policy*. Englewood Cliffs, New Jersey: Prentice Hall, 1980.

Quandt, William B. *Camp David: Peacemaking and Politics*. Washington, DC: The Brookings Institution, 1986.

Quandt, William B., ed. *The Middle East: Ten Years After Camp David.* Washington, DC: The Brookings Institution, 1988.

Rabinovich, Itamar. *The War for Lebanon, 1970-1985.* Revised Edition. Ithaca, New York: Cornell University Press, 1984, 1985.

Radvány, János. *Delusion and Reality: Gambits, Hoaxes, and Diplomatic One-Upsmanship in Vietnam.* South Bend, Indiana: Gateway Editions, Ltd., 1978.

Randal, Jonathan C. *Going All the Way: Christian Warlords, Israeli Adventurers, and the War in Lebanon.* New York: The Viking Press, 1983. Re-issued in revised and up-dated edition as *The Tragedy of Lebanon: Christian Warlords, Israeli Adventurers and American Bunglers.* London: Thke Hogarth Press, 1990.

Reagan, Ronald. *An American Life.* New York: Simon & Schuster, 1990.

Rusk, Dean, as told to Richard Rusk, edited by Daniel S. Papp. *As I Saw It.* New York: W.W. Norton, 1990.

Sachar, Howard M. *A History of Israel, Vol. II: From the Aftermath of the Yom Kippur War.* New York: Oxford University Press, 1987.

Salem, Elie. *Violence and Diplomacy in Lebanon: The Troubled Years, 1982-1988.* London: I.B. Tauris Publishers; New York: St. Martin's Press, 1995.

Schiff, Ze'ev, and Ehud Ya'ari. *Israel's Lebanon War.* New York: Simon & Schuster, 1984.

Schoenbaum, David. *The United States and the State of Israel.* New York and Oxford: Oxford University Press.

Schoenbaum, Thomas J. *Waging Peace & War: Dean Rusk in the Truman, Kennedy & Johnson Years.* New York: Simon and Schuster, 1988.

Seale, Patrick. *Asad: The Struggle for the Middle East.* Berkeley, California: University of California Press, 1988.

Shamir, Yitzhak. *Summing Up: An Autobiography.* Boston: Little, Brown, 1994.

Sharon, Ariel, with David Chanoff. *Warrior: An Autobiography.* New York: Simon and Schuster, 1989.

Sheehan, Neil. *A Bright and Shining Lie: John Paul Vann and America in Vietnam.* New York: Random House, 1988.

Shultz, George. *Turmoil and Triumph: My Years as Secretary of State.* New York: Charles Scribner's Sons, 1993.

Silver, Eric. *Begin: The Haunted Prophet.* New York: Random House, 1984.

Simpson, James B., ed. *Simpson's Contemporary Quotations: The Most Notable Quotes Since 1950.* Boston: Houghton Mifflin, 1988.

Snepp, Frank. *Decent Interval: An Insider's Account of Saigon's Inde-cent End Told by the CIA's Chief Strategy Analyst in Vietnam.* New York: Vintage Books, 1978.

Staar, Richard F., ed. *Public Diplomacy: USA Versus USSR.* Stanford, California: Hoover Institution Press, 1986.

Stein, Kenneth W., and Samuel W. Lewis, with Sheryl J. Brown. *Making Peace Among Arabs and Israelis.* Washington, DC: United States Institute of Peace, 1991.

Strober, Deborah Hart, and Gerald S. Strober. *Reagan: The Man and His Presidency.* Boston: Houghton Mifflin Co., 1998

Strober, Gerald S., and Deborah Hart Strober. *Nixon: An Oral History of His Presidency.* New York: HarperCollins, 1994.

Tanter, Raymond. *Who's at the Helm? Lessons of Lebanon.* Boulder, San Francisco, Oxford: Westview Press, 1990.

Teicher, Howard, and Gayle Radley Teicher. *Twin Pillars to Desert Storm: America's Flawed Vision in the Middle East from Nixon to Bush.* New York: William Morrow and Co., 1993.

Thalken, Thomas T., ed. *The Problems of Lasting Peace Revisited: A Scholarly Conference.* West Branch, Iowa: Herbert Hoover Presi-dential Library Assoc., Inc., 1986.

Tillman, Seth P. *The United States in the Middle East: Interests and Obstacles.*

Timerman, Jacobo. *The Longest War: Israel in Lebanon.* New York: Alfred A. Knopf, 1982.

UN Yearbook 1982.

Vance, Cyrus. *Hard Choices: Critical Years in America's Foreign Policy.* New York: Simon and Schuster, 1983.

Warshaw, Mal. *Tradition: Orthodox Jewish Life in America.* New York: Schocken Books, 1976.

Weinberger, Caspar. *Fighting for Peace: Seven Critical Years in the Pentagon.* New York: Warner Books, 1990.

Westmoreland, William. *A Soldier Reports.* Garden City, New York: Doubleday & Co., 1976.

Willensky, Elliot. *When Brooklyn Was the World: 1920-1957.* New York: Harmony Books, 1986.

Wright, Robin. *Sacred Rage: The Crusade of Modern Islam.* New York: Simon & Schuster, 1985.

Yaniv, Avner. *Dilemmas of Security: Politics, Strategy, and the Israeli Experience in Lebanon.* New York: Oxford University Press, 1987.

Young, Ronald J. *Missed Opportunities for Peace: U.S. Middle East Policy 1981-86.* Philadelphia: American Friends Service Commit-tee, 1987.

Yuzo, Itagaki, Oda Makoto, and Shiboh Mitsukazu, eds. *The Israeli Invasion of Lebanon, 1982: Inquiry by the International People's Tribunal, Tokyo.* Tokyo: Sanyusha, 1983.

Zamir, Meir. *The Formation of Modern Lebanon.* Ithaca, New York: Cornell University Press, 1985.

THESES AND DISSERTATIONS

Beck, William Granville. *U.S. Foreign Policy in Lebanon Under the Reagan Administration 1981-1989.* George Washington University, Department of Political Science, 1989.

Dammarell, Anne. *Hidden Fears, Helpful Memories: Aftermath of the 1983 Bombing of the United States Embassy in Beirut.* Georgetown University, School for Summer and Continuing Education, 1994.

Hopkins, Kevin. *Philip C. Habib: Presidential Emissary to the Middle East. PLO Withdrawal Negotiations: Beirut, Summer 1982.* Georgetown Unversity, Institute for the Study of Diplomacy, 1992.

Korbani, Agnes Gerges. *Presidential Working-System Style, Cognition, and Foreign Policy: A Comparative Study of U.S. Decisions to Intervene Militarily in Lebanon in 1958 and 1982.* Northwestern University, Field of Political Science, 1989.

BOOKLETS

Al-Qazzaz, Ayad. *Transnational Links Between the Arab Community in the U.S. and the Arab World.* Sacramento, California: California State University.

Azar, Edward E., Harold H. Saunders, and I. William Zartman. *Mediation in Middle East Conflicts.* Maxwell Summer Lecture Series 1986. Syracuse University: Maxwell School of Citizenship and Public Affairs, 1987.

Habib, Philip. "Diplomacy and the Search for Peace in the Middle East," the Fifth Samuel D. Berger Memorial Lecture, April 29, 1985. Occasional Paper, Institute for the Study of Diplomacy, School of Foreign Service, Georgetown University, 1985.

Herz, Martin F., ed. *Contacts with the Opposition: A Symposium.* Washington, DC: Georgetown University Institute for the Study of Diplomacy, n.d.

Hewett, Robert B., conference rapporteur. *Future Economic and Security Cooperation in the Pacific Region.* Honolulu: Pacific Forum, 1979

NEWSPAPERS, MAGAZINES, JOURNALS
Foreign Affairs, The New York Times, The New Yorker, Newsweek, State, Time, The Washington Post

Of special note
Philip Habib's friend and early colleague Gilda Duly collected six albums full of wire service stories about him over the years, mostly from various Florida newspapers, and sent them to Marjorie Habib.

Boykin, John. "Philip Habib: Whatever It Takes," *The Stanford Magazine,* Spring 1984.

Collins, Carole. "Chronology of the Israeli Invasion of Lebanon June-August 1982," Journal of Palestine Studies, Summer/Fall 1982, vol. XI no. 4/vol. XII no. 1, issue 44/45. ["JPS Chronology" in my chronology]

Habib, Philip (as told by, to Larry Engelmann). "Peace Envoy's Post-script," *Vietnam Magazine,* April 1993.

Habib interview with Michel Dusclaud, *Politique Internationale,* number 28, *édition d'été* 1985

SPECIAL COLLECTIONS
Habib, Philip, private collection of scrapbooks, memorabilia, books, and other materials in his home office, which Marjorie Habib kindly made freely available to me

Haldeman, H.R., meeting notes in National Archives, Nixon Presidential Materials

Harriman, Averell, papers in Library of Congress, Manuscript Division

Nixon Presidential Materials, National Archives

POW-MIA Files, National Archives, Nixon Presidential Materials

UNPUBLISHED MANUSCRIPTS
Bundy, William P., on events of 1968 about Vietnam. At the Lyndon Baines Johnson Library

Lewis, Samuel, untitled, about Habib's Middle East work

Index

*Note: Some names come up so often in the text that indexing each appearance would not be helpful. This index therefore does not list passing references to key players or instances when frequently cited sources are quoted. Only particularly notable mentions of those players are given here. Those players are identified by **bold type**. This index also does not cover endnotes.*

Index

480